Capstone Simulation for Coding

Capstone Simulation for Coding

Stacey Mosay, RHIA, CCS-P, CPC-H

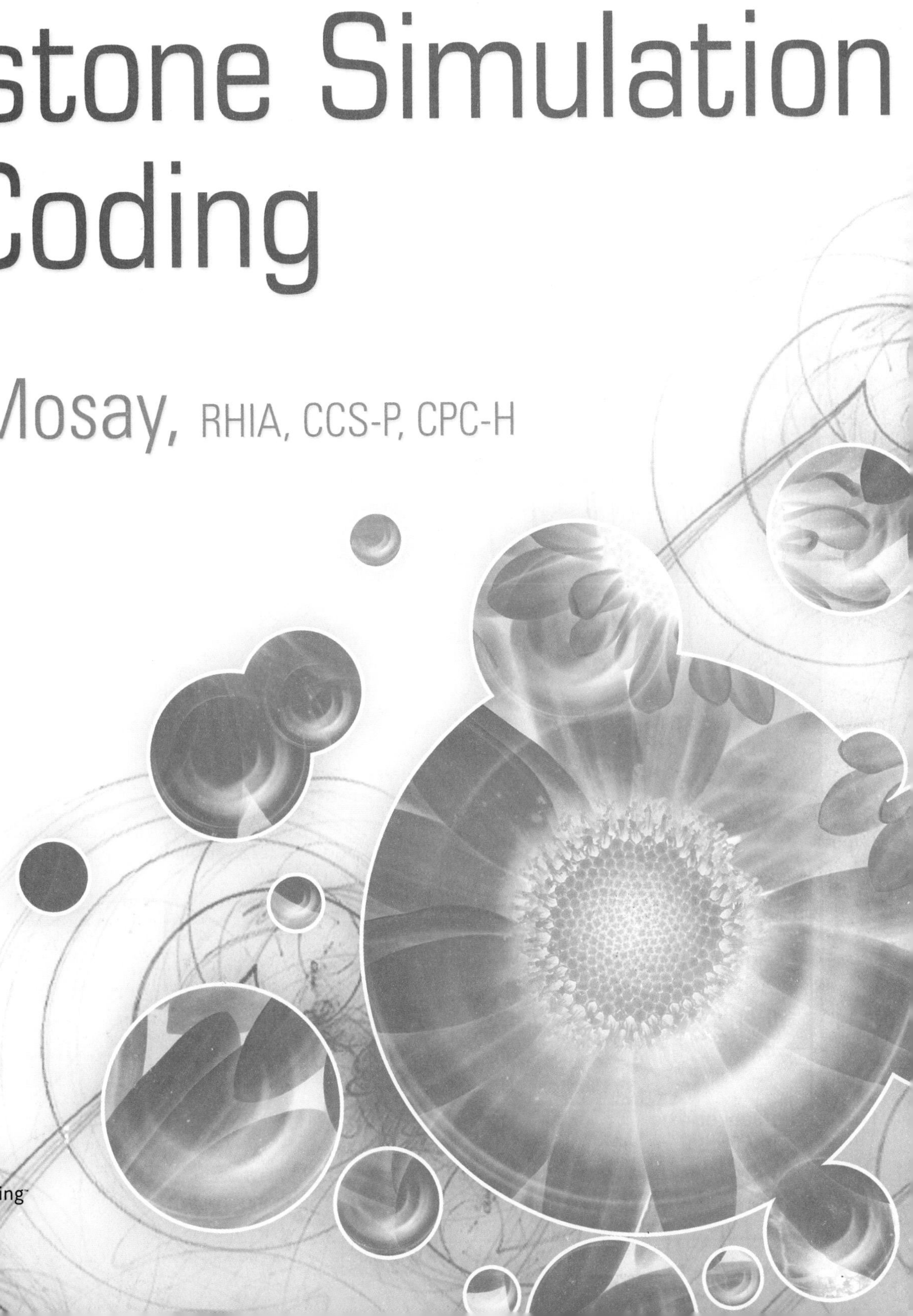

DELMAR
CENGAGE Learning™

Capstone Simulation for Coding
Stacey Mosay

Vice President, Career and Professional Editorial: Dave Garza

Director of Learning Solutions: Matthew Kane

Senior Acquisitions Editor: Rhonda Dearborn

Managing Editor: Marah Bellegarde

Product Manager: Jadin Babin-Kavanaugh

Editorial Assistant: Lauren Whalen

Vice President, Career and Professional Marketing: Jennifer Baker

Marketing Director: Wendy Mapstone

Senior Marketing Manager: Nancy Bradshaw

Marketing Coordinator: Erica Ropitzky

Production Director: Carolyn Miller

Production Manager: Andrew Crouth

Content Project Manager: Allyson Bozeth

Senior Art Director: Jack Pendleton

Technology Project Manager: Erin Zeggert

Compositor: PreMediaGlobal

For product information and technology assistance, contact us at
Cengage Learning Customer & Sales Support, 1-800-354-9706
For permission to use material from this text or product,
submit all requests online at **www.cengage.com/permissions.**
Further permissions questions can be e-mailed to
permissionrequest@cengage.com

Library of Congress Control Number: 2010931609

ISBN-13: 978-1-4180-5346-8

ISBN-10: 1-4180-5346-5

Delmar
5 Maxwell Drive
Clifton Park, NY 12065-2919
USA

Cengage Learning is a leading provider of customized learning solutions with office locations around the globe, including Singapore, the United Kingdom, Australia, Mexico, Brazil, and Japan. Locate your local office at:
international.cengage.com/region

Cengage Learning products are represented in Canada by Nelson Education, Ltd.

To learn more about Delmar, visit **www.cengage.com/delmar**

Purchase any of our products at your local college store or at our preferred online store **www.cengagebrain.com**

Printed in the United States of America
1 2 3 4 5 6 7 12 11 10

Table of Contents

Preface

Introduction

The health care industry is multifaceted and ever changing and requires professionals with qualifications to wade through the complex and stringent regulations and requirements of coding and insurance processing so that the physician can be properly reimbursed for services. Computers and the Internet have opened up the way that physicians and their staffs conduct business, communicate, and train. Software is used to compile and maintain medical records, schedule appointments, process insurance claims, audit coding trends, analyze practice patterns, and assist with compliance efforts to name a few. Today, virtually every aspect of daily operations is computerized. Offices can communicate with insurance carriers and hospitals via email and fax. Websites are useful tools to access for changes and updates to insurance programs, reimbursement schedules, training of staff, and so on. Some practices even communicate with their patients via email and have the capability for patients to complete their health history and even schedule appointments from their websites to expedite office visits.

Administrative duties in medical offices are computer-based. Students who enter a medical career are required to master computer skills regardless of program type (e.g., medical coding, medical assisting, nursing). Practice management software utilized by physician offices is the most common software type students are exposed to. Every health care organization manages computerized patient, financial, and operational data. In addition to computer skills, students must have a general knowledge of medical insurance and coding as these have a direct impact on reimbursement. Managed care affects when, where, and how often patients are seen and what treatments are necessary. Many plans require preauthorization, referrals, and utilization review protocols that staff are required to comply with. Patients are more confused about their insurance coverage and financial responsibilities than ever before. Explanation about their benefits and statements received from insurance carriers and providers is often necessary. Insurance carrier plans and guidelines vary across the country, necessitating the skill of an individual versed in medical and insurance terminology along with a medical background to decipher and implement. All of this requires coders and billers to be well trained and involved in the communication with and education of staff and patients.

Educators are constantly challenged to provide ways to provide well-rounded educations that encompass coding, billing, practice management software usage, and internship. The *Capstone Simulation for Coding* is designed to be used as an enhancement to traditional and online didactic instruction. It allows the student the opportunity to apply theory learned in the classroom setting to real-life scenarios and tasks typically performed by a medical coder and billing specialist. This book is intended to be used as an exercise book rather than an instructional text. Moreover it is not tailored toward any specific insurance type.

The simulation provides a two week life-like experience as a coder and biller. One week is spent in a medical practice performing front and back office duties. The second week is spent working for a remote coding company coding for a multi-specialty ambulatory surgery center (ASC). This is an excellent way to develop skills and provides the student with experience in the day-to-day operations of a medical practice and the revenue cycle without the demands of placing students in clinical internship sites. At the end of this course, the student can use the exercises completed and the operative reports coded to build a profile for prospective employers to demonstrate mastery of these competencies. This book reviews the fundamentals of health insurance, documentation, coding guidelines, and the revenue cycle and applies these concepts to practice management software.

The book sequentially discusses each aspect of a patient encounter and proceeds through claims submission and account maintenance. Assignments and exercises allow students to participate in each step of the revenue cycle process. Students will reinforce essential skills such as patient registration, appointment scheduling, coding for physician medical and surgical services, searching reference sources for correct coding and reporting, inputting charges, posting payments, claims denial management, printing insurance claims, submitting electronic claims, patient billing, and analyzing reports.

Organization of the Coding Simulation Package

Included in the portfolio package for *Capstone Coding Simulation* are the following items:

- *Capstone Coding Simulation* textbook with CD of additional documents and files
- 10 manila file folders
- MOSS 2.0 software
- User access card for 59-day trial of EncoderPro.com—Expert software

Organization of the Textbook

Capstone Coding Simulation is divided into five parts. Part I, Orientation and Introduction, covers general flow of information in a medical office, computer usage, medical insurance, and HIPAA guidelines. This information is necessary as an overview because students will come from varying programs and backgrounds and it cannot be assumed that they have received prior instruction or mastered this knowledge previously. Part II, Computer and Coding Orientation, teaches students how to use MOSS, input data, schedule appointments, make transactions, generate claims, and run reports. Coding from documentation and coding guidelines are also discussed. Part III, Office Internship, allows students to apply their knowledge and perform specific jobs of the coder and biller in the medical office using MOSS. Students are classified as a new hire at Douglasville Medicine Associates and will participate in orientation, obtain a job description, and receive a policy and procedure manual before they begin working. Part IV, Remote Coding Internship, walks the students through the daily tasks of a coder and biller at Surgical Coding Solutions, a third-party contracted billing service. Students will read and interpret medical documentation and assign codes for the medical and surgical services rendered by their client providers. Part V, the Appendices, includes all the source documents needed to complete the assignments and exercises located in Parts II–IV. These forms include routers, fee schedules, patient records, payment advices, and polices and procedures.

The appendices and the CD both contain key items for successful completion of the simulation. Appendices A–F are located in the back of the book. Throughout the text, specific appendices and forms are referenced in order to direct the student to locate the documents necessary to complete assignments and jobs in chapters 3–9.

The CD-ROM included with the textbook contains documents and forms that are needed for various activities. The documents can be printed and completed by hand, or completed electronically and emailed. The CD-ROM contains the following files for Douglasville Medicine Associates (DMA):

- **Deposit Ticket.** Needed to complete jobs in chapters 6 and 7.
- **DMA letterhead.** This is used in chapters 6–8 to draft letters to patients and providers.
- **DMA Payer Contracts and Medicare Fee Schedule.** Utilized in chapter 6 of this text.
- **DMA Payment Plan-Payment Agreement.** Required for work in chapter 6 of this text.
- **DMA Procedure Fee Schedule.** This is required for work done in chapters 3 and 6 of this text.
- **Great West Application for Initial Credentialing/Appointment.** Required for a job in chapter 3 of this text.
- **Meadway Coding Capture form.** This is used in chapter 9 of this text.
- **Medicare Secondary Payer questionnaire.** Referenced in chapter 3 of this text.

A glossary is located in the back of the text for reference.

Chapter Format

Parts I and II are instructional chapters and provide the student with detailed narrative supported by figures, tables, and MOSS screen shots. Parts III and IV are hands-on simulation chapters where the work is completed and specific jobs are carried out for the two weeks of internship. With the exception of chapters 6–8 that lack key terms, all chapters begin with the following items:

- **Objectives** describe key concepts and skills that will be attained by studying the material and performing the exercises.
- **Key Terms** and abbreviations are listed in alphabetical order at the start of each chapter. These are printed in bold-faced type and defined the first or second time they are introduced in the text.
- **Background Basics** feature itemizes basic knowledge or skill sets that the student should possess in order to successfully complete the chapter.
- **Competency Checklist** explains how the chapter information relates to the job of a coder or biller and the ability of the student to competently perform the job upon completion.
- **Real-World Application** exercises pose realistic situations in the workplace for students to ponder and discuss with the group.

Each chapter includes chapter review exercises and practice activities to test your understanding while allowing you to apply practical knowledge using the enclosed software and the Internet for research.

Chapters 6–9 contain jobs Sample jobs mimic those encountered in the daily job description of a coder and medical office employee to include making transactions in MOSS (scheduling and registering patients, entering charges, and submitting claims); researching payer policy on the Internet; drafting communication to patients, providers, and insurance carriers; as well as coding for visits and auditing medical record documentation for reported services and a claim form.

Goals and Objectives of the Capstone Simulation Course

The content and activities chosen for this textbook simulation are based upon expectations and requirements of coders and billers in medical practices. In the real world, experienced staff is highly desirable; the goal of this simulation is to help students learn as if they were actually employed by the practice and obtain some practical experience. After completing the *Capstone Coding Simulation,* students will be able to:

1. Create and maintain patient medical records.
2. Schedule patients using learned reasoning for the most appropriate appointment time based upon scheduling policies and availability.
3. Assign CPT, ICD-9, and HCPCS codes to office visits and surgeries, applying and mastering all applicable coding guidelines.
4. Create and submit accurate and complete insurance claim forms for private, commercial, and government payers for reimbursement.
5. Use the Internet to research coding and billing questions, insurance carrier policies, and medical and surgical protocol, and obtain authorizations and insurance coverage and benefits.
6. Register patients by checking them in and out of the computer system and accurately completing paperwork.
7. Input charges and post payments received in the computer.
8. Assign codes for professional services for multiple specialties by interpreting medical documentation.
9. Discuss the revenue cycle by identifying each step in the process and the responsibilities of the coder and biller.

10. Create insurance claims for primary and secondary insurances and submit for claims processing.
11. Interpret Explanation of Benefits from carriers and post appropriate payments and adjustments according to carrier contract.
12. Demonstrate the ability to produce and analyze reports necessary to meet operational needs of the clinic.
13. Role-play difficult telephone and office situations with patients, physicians, and insurance carriers.
14. Query physicians for clarification of diagnosis or procedure when necessary.
15. Appeal insurance denials following carrier-specific processes in addition to using prescribed denial management.
16. Perform pre-bill reviews of claims by auditing documentation and applying coding and carrier specific guidelines for claim submission.
17. Credential a provider with an insurance carrier.
18. Use encoder software to assist in code assignment.
19. Be able to utilize front office software.

Supplements for the Instructor

There is an Instructor's Manual available that includes full answer keys and screen shot solutions to all of the exercises and jobs in *Capstone Simulation for Coding*. The Instructor's Manual is posted online, and the ISBN is 1-4180-5346-5. Contact your Delmar sales representative to gain access.

About the Author

Stacey Mosay has over 18 years experience in health information management as a Director of Medical Records for a multi-hospital health system and Business Office Manager and coder for an ambulatory surgery center. Ms. Mosay owns her own consulting company entitled Private Practice Solutions where she provides operational analysis of physician practices, coding and billing education, medical record audits, coding and billing, revenue cycle management, and temporary staffing. She served five years as the Medical Record Coder Program Coordinator and instructor for the academic Coding Certificate program in the Division of Allied Health at Trident Technical College. She is a graduate of the Medical University of South Carolina with a B.S. in Health Information Management. She served as chairman of the AHIMA CCA test construction committee from 2006 to 2007. She is a registered member of the American Health Information Management Association and the American Academy of Professional Coders. She is the former President of the Low Country Coders Association and a member of the Palmetto Coder Association, and AHIMA's Assembly of Education. She is a member of the Round Table Group of expert witnesses. Stacey also serves as a coding and billing textbook auditor/reviewer and author for Delmar Cengage Learning and McGraw-Hill Publishing.

Reviewers

The author and publisher would like to thank the following reviewers for their contributions to this product.

Cherika de Jesus, CMA
Medical Assistant Coordinator
Minnesota School of Business
Plymouth, MN

Alice Macomber, RN, RMA, AHI, CPI, RPT, BXO
Medical Assisting Program Coordinator/Extern Coordinator
Keiser University, Port Saint Lucie Campus
Port Saint Lucie, FL

Pat G. Moeck, PhD, MBA, BA, CMA (AAMA)
Director, Medical Assisting Program
El Centro College
Dallas, TX

June M. Petillo, MBA, RMC
Instructor, Medical Assisting Program
Manchester Community College & Capitol Community College
Manchester and Hartford, CT

Tiffany Rosta, CMA
Medical Instructor
Kaplan Career Institute, ICM Campus
Pittsburgh, PA

Gladine Q. Stapleton, CPC
Program Director, Insurance Coding and Billing Specialist Program
Concorde Career College
San Diego, CA

Gayla Taylor
Instructor
PCI Health Training Center
Dallas, TX

Thomas J. Wesley, AAS, BS
Medical Assistant Instructor
Minnesota School for Business
Shakopee, MN

Tina M. Williams, MSHSA, CPC
President, San Francisco Medical Coding Institute
Faculty, Heald College
San Francisco, CA

Technical Reviewer

Cecile Favreau, MBA, CPC
Adjunct Faculty
Salter College
West Boylston, MA

Acknowledgments

To my husband Ted for his patience, endless support, and boundless belief in me, and to my children Zachary, Jeremy, and Abbey for their understanding for why I "worked all the time" and for cheering me on as I continue my pursuit in writing and teaching.

To Roberta Classen and Daphne Neris for their expertise with E/M guidelines and tools and being my sounding board for ideas and concepts used to challenge the students.

To Robinlee Hackney Speakmon for encouraging me to be creative and inspiring me to share my passion for what I do.

To my former students for helping me grow and develop my talent as a teacher. Without you, I wouldn't have had the vision for this project.

How to Use the Medical Office Simulation 2.0 (MOSS) Software

Delmar Cengage Learning's Medical Office Simulation Software (MOSS) is provided in this package. MOSS is generic medical office software designed for student practice. It provides a realistic look and feel, as well as functionality similar to name-brand practice management systems on the market today. MOSS enables students to perform activities like appointment setting, claims submissions, and patient billing as if they were in a clinic setting. As a result, students who complete *Capstone Simulation for Coding* should be able to quickly adapt to and use other practice management software in the real world with minimal training. For more information getting started with MOSS, see Appendix F of this textbook.

Log-In Procedure for MOSS Network Version

Step 1. Start Medical Office Simulation Software by following your instructor's directions. (Hint: Click on Start, then Programs, then click on the software title to open. If a desktop icon is available, you can also open the software by double clicking on it.)

Step 2. A logon dialog box will open. The login level should be set to Student. If it is not, use the drop-down menu to select Student (see Figure 1).

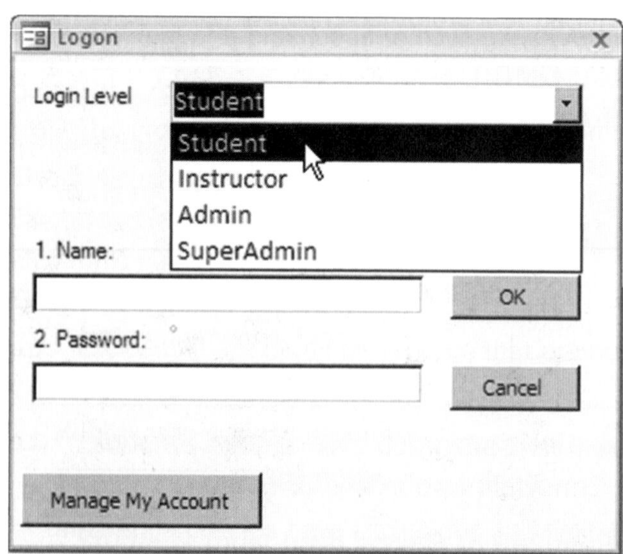

Figure 1

Step 3. Your instructor will provide you with your logon name and password. Using this information, enter the logon name in Field 1 and the password in Field 2 of the logon dialog box. (Hint: Note that logon names and passwords are case sensitive, so pay special attention to using capital and lower case letters where needed.) Then, click on the *Manage My Account* button. (See Figure 2).

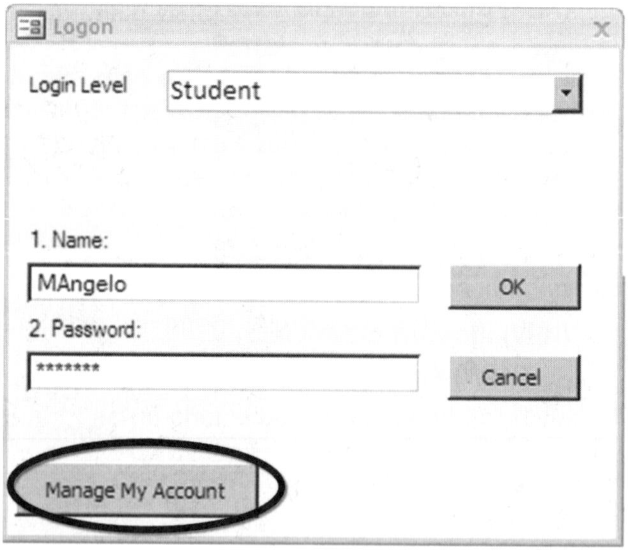

Figure 2

Step 4. Move your cursor into the Password field and delete the existing password. Enter a new password of your choice, making sure that it is at least five characters in length. (Hint: Choose a password that is easy to remember, yet not something obvious that many people may know about you, such as a birth date.)

Step 5. Re-type the new password in Field 3 to confirm it. Then, click *Save Record* (see Figure 3). Note: if there is a typing error, a prompt will alert you to re-enter the password correctly.

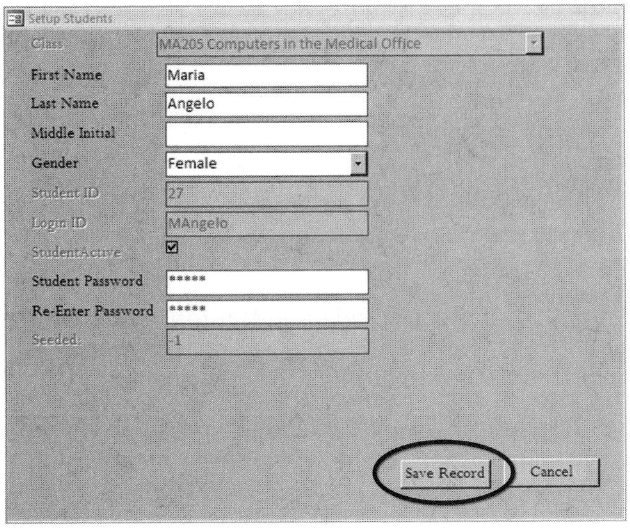

Setup Students
Class MA205 Computers in the Medical Office
First Name Maria
Last Name Angelo
Middle Initial
Gender Female
Student ID 27
Login ID MAngelo
StudentActive ☑
Student Password *****
Re-Enter Password *****
Seeded: -1
Save Record Cancel

Figure 3

Step 6. The original logon dialog box should now be displayed on your screen. Move your cursor into Field 2, Password, and type the new password you just created. Click the *OK* button to enter the program. (See Figure 4).

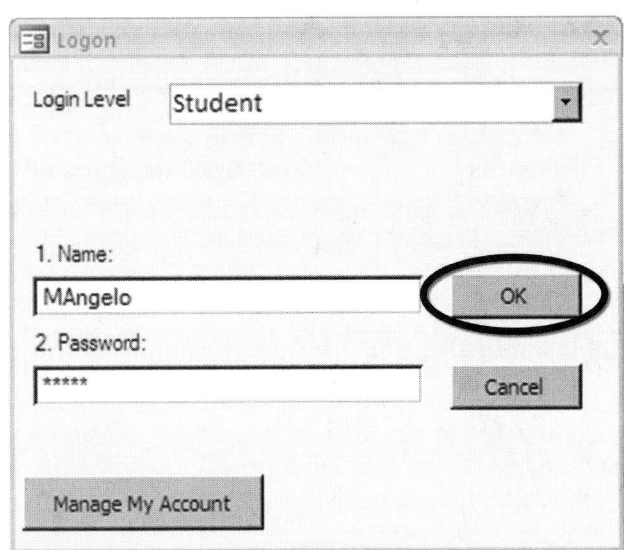

Figure 4

Step 7. When logging in to MOSS Network in the future, you will simply enter your logon name and password and then click the *OK* button. (Hint: You will select *Manage My Account* to change your password or other information; you will choose *OK* to directly log into the program.)

How to Use the EncoderPro.com 59-Day Free Trial

With the purchase of this textbook you receive 59-day access to EncoderPro.com—Expert, the powerful online medical coding solution from Ingenix®. With EncoderPro.com, you can simultaneously search across all three code sets.

How to Access the 59-Day Trial

Information on how to access your 59-day trial of EncoderPro.com is included on the printed card bound into this textbook. Your unique user access code is printed on the card. Be sure to check with your instructor before beginning your trial period because it will expire 59 days after your initial login.

Features and Benefits of *EncoderPro.com*

EncoderPro.com is the essential code lookup software for CPT®, ICD-9-CM, and HCPCS code sets from Ingenix®. It gives users fast searching capabilities across all code sets. EncoderPro can greatly reduce the time it takes to build or review a claim, and helps improve overall coding accuracy.

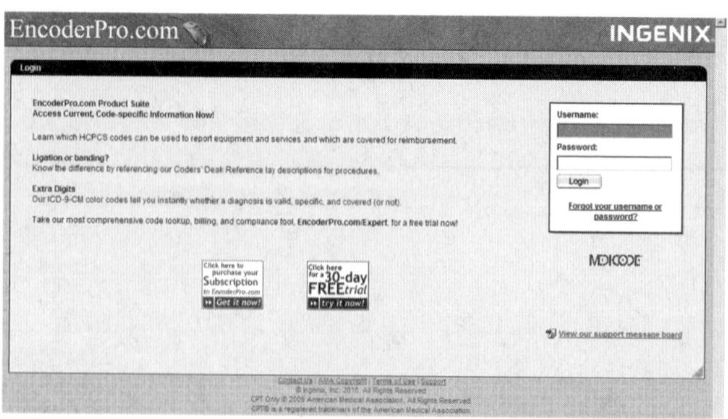

During your free trial period to *EncoderPro.com—Expert*, the following tools will be available to you:

- **Powerful Ingenix CodeLogic™ search engine**. Search all three code sets simultaneously using lay terms, acronyms, abbreviations, and even misspelled words.
- **Lay descriptions for thousands of CPT® codes.** Enhance your understanding of procedures with easy-to-understand descriptions.
- **Color-coded edits.** Understand whether a code carries an age or sex edit, is covered by Medicare, or contains bundled procedures.
- **ICD-10 Mapping Tool**. Crosswalk from ICD-9-CM codes to the appropriate ICD-10 code quickly and easily.
- **Great value.** Get the content from over 20 code and reference books in one powerful solution.

For more information about *EncoderPro.com*, or to become a subscriber beyond the free trial, email us at **esales@cengage.com**.

PART I

ORIENTATION AND INTRODUCTION

CHAPTER 1

Orientation to Douglasville Medicine Associates

Learning Objectives

When finished with this chapter, the student will be able to:

1. Describe the organizational structure and staff of Douglasville Medicine Associates.
2. Explain the objectives and purpose of the simulation.
3. Discuss the importance of orientation in a new job and compliance with organizational policies and procedures.
4. Identify coding and billing competencies and characteristics of such staff.
5. Recognize job duties of a coder/biller at Douglasville Medicine Associates.
6. Discuss the purposes of the HIPAA law and the importance of adhering to it.
7. Describe the purpose of a health care compliance plan.
8. Define and recognize differences between fraud and abuse.
9. List attributes needed to achieve effective communication.

Key Terms

Abuse
American Recovery and Reinvestment Act (ARRA)
Breach
Business associates
Code Set
Communication
Compliance
Covered Entity
Family Practice (FP)
Fraud
General Practitioner (GP)
Health Insurance Portability and Accountability Act of 1996 (HIPAA)
Health Information Technology for Economic and Clinical Health Act (HITECH)
HIPAA Privacy Rule
Independent Practice Association (IPA)
Minimum Necessary Standard
National Provider Identifier
Protected Health Information (PHI)
Physician self-referral

Background Basics

- Students should have had some prior instruction on the Health Insurance Portability and Accountability Act of 1996 (HIPAA).
- Students should have a general understanding of the job tasks of a coder/biller.

Competency Checklist

- Coders and billers must be able to identify potential abusive and fraudulent billing patterns within their own practices.
- Coders and billers must have expert knowledge in the HIPAA mandated code sets to report diagnoses, procedures, and supplies to insurance carriers for reimbursement.
- All office staff, to comply with federal law, must complete HIPAA training.
- Office staff must understand the HIPAA rule and feel confident about when and how information can be released.

Purpose of the Course

This simulation will provide the student with a realistic experience that emulates the day-to-day tasks and activities of a coder/biller in a medical office setting. It parallels an externship by providing the student with life-like scenarios, documentation, and tangible activities without requiring the student to report to a classroom or clinical site. This simulation is not meant to replace the externship but merely provide a means to further prepare students before entering the work force. This course can prepare students by providing a review of important coding and billing concepts and exposing them to situations and tasks that will be encountered on the job. Students will apply knowledge learned throughout their program to real-life scenarios to practice their skills in coding and performing medical office tasks. Students will have the opportunity to:

- Create medical records
- Read clinical documentation
- Code, abstract, and bill office encounters
- Assign ICD-9, CPT-4, and HCPCS codes to office visits and surgical operative reports
- Create insurance claims
- Perform financial counseling
- Post insurance and patient payments
- Read and interpret the CMS Physician Fee Schedule
- Prepare daily bank deposits
- Draft correspondence to medical staff, the office manager, patients, and insurance carriers
- Research carrier coverage policies
- Research Correct Coding Initiate (CCI) edits, National Coverage Determinations (NCDs), and Local Coverage Determinations (LCDs)
- Generate reports and analyze data
- Interpret Explanation of Benefits (EOBs) and perform contractual adjustments
- Generate patient statements
- Credential a provider
- Apply knowledge of HIPAA to patient encounters and requests
- Utilize source references and society websites

Staff Welcome

DOUGLASVILLE MEDICINE ASSOCIATES

5076 BRAND BLVD, SUITE 401 • DOUGLASVILLE, NY 01234 • (123)456-7890

Welcome to our practice! We are glad you joined our team. The physicians in this practice make every effort to get to know you and want to make you feel like a valuable team member. Your role in this organization is a very important one. It is crucial that our office has a qualified coding/billing specialist. This position is key in the financial success of our business not to mention adherence to regulatory and compliance requirements. This position may be referred to by many names: Medical Billing Specialist, Insurance Billing Specialist, Reimbursement Specialist, Coder, Accounts Receivable Representative, etc. Regardless of title, your ongoing education is essential and you must be able to multi-task. Performing this job efficiently and accurately requires varied technical and problem solving skills along with impeccable organization. Your function here at Douglasville Medicine Associates is to enter charge information, code for services performed, submit electronic and paper insurance claims, research insurance denials, follow-up on unpaid insurance claims, post insurance and patient payments, and perform patient collections. Your job description is located in chapter one of this manual.

We are a busy practice seeing patients with private, commercial, managed care, and government-sponsored insurance. We participate with all carriers except Cigna and Tricare. Managed care patients that participate with Great West Network can see Drs. Heath, Schwartz, Murray, Mendenhall and Alberta Lynn our PA only at this time. Dr. Sally Kemper is new to the practice and must be credentialed with them first. This will be a job for you to do over the next week. At the back of this manual you will find copies of our contracts and fee schedules in Appendices B and D.

These contracts and fee schedules will assist you in ensuring that the practice has been paid correctly according to negotiated schedule.

Your first priority is to read your job description, the policy and procedure manual, and familiarize yourself with our medical record forms and physician fee schedules. You will next need an orientation to our practice management system, MOSS whereby you will conduct your day to day activities of entering charges and releasing claims, posting payments, and generating patient statements. MOSS software training is carried out in chapter 4 of this manual. The Insurance supervisor, Lindsay Morgan, will assist you with your orientation. She is your immediate supervisor and will participate in your training and will direct your work flow. Should you have any documentation questions or compliance concerns, please address these with Lindsay Morgan your supervisor or April Kennedy, the office manager. She will then address these with our group at our monthly partnership meetings.

Warm Regards,

Sarah Mendenhall
Sarah Mendenhall, M.D.
Family Practitioner

D. J. Schwartz
D. J. Schwartz, M.D.
Family Practitioner

Alberta E. Lynn
Alberta E. Lynn, P.A.C.

L.D. Heath
L. D. Heath, M.D.
Family Practitioner

Lance Murray, MD
Lance Murray, MD
General Practitioner

Sally Kemper
Sally Kemper, M.D.
General Practitioner

Introduction

This section of the chapter will introduce the student to the practice. The student will learn the general organization of the practice along with HIPAA privacy and security rules and practice policies and procedures. This chapter will explain the role of the coder/biller and responsibilities at the practice, which include coding, billing, posting payments, account follow-up, collections, insurance precertification, patient scheduling, registration, and credentialing. In chapters 3 and 4, precertification, scheduling, and registration are discussed. In many offices the coder will also perform these functions if not daily, then from time to time, and it is advantageous that the coder understand each of these processes and how they are ultimately tied to coding and reimbursement.

Orientation

All new employees of our clinic participate in a two-hour orientation to the company's mission, policies, procedures, HIPAA requirements, work flow, expectations, customer service, and specific job duties. It is important that each employee undergo this training to get acquainted with the clinic's operations. We strongly feel that this one-on-one time adds to employee satisfaction and retention. This is the time for the employee to get to know supervisory staff and an opportunity for supervisory staff to assess skill level and baseline learning opportunities of the new employee.

Douglasville Medicine Associates (DMA) is a clinic located in Douglasville, New York. We are part of an **independent practice association (IPA)** made up of 45 doctors in our area. An IPA is an organization of physicians who have joined together for purposes of contracting with insurance companies and to share in administrative expenses. In addition to our physician practices we have a state-of-the-art diagnostic imaging center. Our clinic is unique in that we own a CT scanner and ultrasound machine. Services currently available include: multi-slice CT, echocardiography, 2D color ultrasound, and bone densitometry.

Our physicians specialize in family practice and internal medicine. Doctors L.D. Heath, D.J. Schwartz, and Sarah Mendenhall are family practitioners. **Family practice (FP)** strives to provide comprehensive health care for individuals and families. As defined by the American Academy of Family Physicians, "The scope of family practice encompasses all ages, both sexes, each organ system, and every disease entity." The family practice physician is the first point of contact with health care concerns and he/she will then direct the patient to necessary specialists, as needed. Drs. Sally Kemper and Lance Murray are general practitioners and are Fellows, American Academy of Family Physicians. **General practitioners (GP)** are also referred to as family physicians, and they treat acute and chronic illnesses, provide preventive care, perform minor office surgeries, and conduct health education for all ages. Many GPs treat infants in lieu of a pediatrician and deliver babies. Our GPs do not deliver babies. The clinic also employs a physician assistant (PA.C) named Alberta Lynn. She helps with overflow and screening patients for the physicians.

At DMA, we strive to be a patient care team working in tandem to achieve our mission. We make every effort to treat staff and patients with courtesy and due diligence. We want our staff and patients to experience a pleasant and nurturing atmosphere while in the clinic. Excellent customer service is proven to attract and retain patients as well as high quality staff, and that is our goal.

Mission

Caring for all people with compassion, integrity, and excellence.

Values

Douglasville Medicine Associates' values form the foundation of the ethical standards provided by its partnership as a guide to carrying out its mission. These values are:

Integrity: We strive to be honest and forthright, upholding the highest ethical standards.

Compassion: We care about the sick, injured, pregnant, and those for whom medical care is out of reach or unaffordable.

Respect: We recognize the worth, quality, diversity, and importance of our staff and co-workers and of those we serve.

Quality: We work together to deliver excellent care to our patients and maintain accurate health information. We seek to hire well-trained staff and be efficient and cost effective in all we do.

Organizational Structure and Staff

DMA employs 18 staff members at this location. Each physician has a dedicated medical assistant who travels to the various locations when his/her physician is at that site. The business office consists of six people. The organizational chart (Figure 1.1) illustrates the reporting structure.

Coder Competencies

In this simulation, you are the coder and biller at DMA. You are responsible for many tasks and from time to time will assist the front desk staff in scheduling, financial counseling, registration, and so on. Depending on the size of the practice, the coder and biller may be two different individuals or be one in the same. This section lists the tasks of a coder/biller and the skill set required for completing these tasks. Specific jobs associated with these tasks are assigned in chapters 6–9.

Coder Job Description

Job Title: Coder/Biller

Department/Area: Insurance Department

Reporting Structure: This position reports to the Insurance Supervisor

Education Requirements: Must be a high school graduate. Associate's degree in Health Information Management, Business, or Accounting preferred. Must be certified with one of the following certifications: CCA, CPC, CPC-A, CPC-H, CCS-P, CCS.

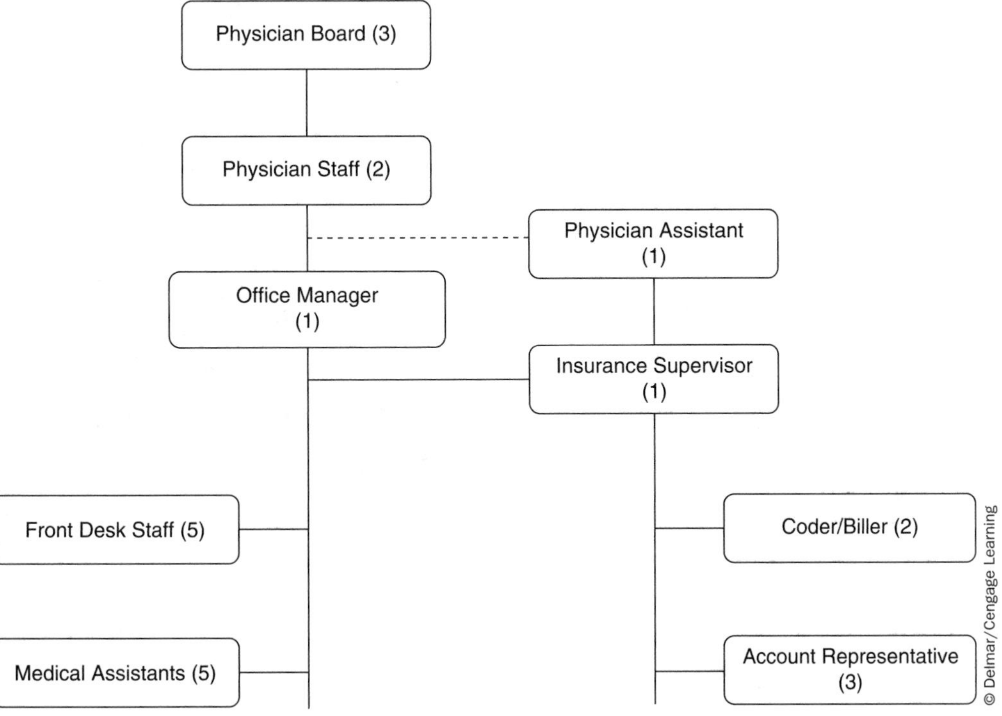

Figure 1.1 Organizational Chart

Job Duties:

1. Enter medical and surgical charges for services performed by our providers in the office or offsite at the hospital.
2. Use ICD-9, HCPCS, and CPT-4 coding methodologies to code from operative reports, medical records, superbills/routers, and pathology reports. At times, the router will not have a box provided for every service rendered or available diagnosis. In these cases, the physician writes by hand the diagnosis or procedure description, and the coder must code from this documentation written on the superbill. The coder will always append applicable modifiers.
3. Research Local Coverage Determinations (LCD), National Coverage Determinations (NCD), and insurance carrier coding reporting requirements and policies.
4. Check codes against the CCI for potential unbundling of services provided to Medicare and commercial patients.
5. Track global periods and determine when it is appropriate to submit charges for services not related to the procedure performed or when the global period expires.
6. Release claims from MOSS daily.
7. Correct any rejections from the clearinghouse and resubmit electronically through MOSS.
8. Maintain current codes in the MOSS system and update routers at least annually according to ICD-9, CPT-4, and HCPCS code changes.
9. Appeal any inappropriately denied insurance claims within one week of receiving the denial.
10. Post all insurance and patient payments to MOSS.
11. Prepare the daily deposit.
12. Generate patient statements every 30 days.
13. Perform patient collections for balances greater than 120 days.
14. Execute insurance claims follow-up on a revolving 15-day cycle for all claims 15 days and older.

Basic Skill Requirements

Candidate must possess one year of coding/billing experience. Candidates seeking employment as a coder/biller must exhibit the following:

- Strong foundation in medical terminology
- Basic knowledge of anatomy and physiology
- Knowledge of diagnosis and procedure coding conventions and rules
- Critical reading and comprehension skills
- Sufficient math skills to maintain patient financial records
- Excellent oral and written communication skills
- Ability to enter financial and demographic data into a patient database
- Ability to access information through the Internet
- Strong sense of ethics
- Attention to detail
- Knowledge of health insurance contractual language

Individuals seeking the position of coder or biller must exhibit the following skills and competencies:

1. Analyze health records to ensure that documentation supports the patient's diagnosis and procedures, clinical findings, and supplies consumed.

2. Request patient-specific documentation from other sources (e.g., outside labs, physician offices, hospitals, etc.).
3. Apply clinical vocabularies and terminologies used in the clinic's medical records and MOSS practice management system.
4. Evaluate the accuracy and completeness of the patient record as defined by external regulations and standards.
5. Report compliance findings according to clinic policy.
6. Use electronic encoder applications to support coding.
7. Assign primary and secondary diagnoses codes, including complications and comorbidities using ICD-9-CM *Official Coding Guidelines*.
8. Assign primary and secondary procedure(s) using CPT coding guidelines.
9. Assign appropriate HCPCS codes for services and supplies.
10. Identify discrepancies between coded data and supporting documentation.
11. Consult reference materials to facilitate code assignment such as the *Coders Desk Reference Procedures, Coders Desk Reference Diagnoses,* Medicare CCI Edits, Medicare LCD, carrier websites, anatomy and physiology textbooks, cross coders, and so on.
12. Comply with the National Correct Coding Initiative (NCCI) for all Medicare patient claims by applying bundling and unbundling guidelines.
13. Corroborate with the National and Local Coverage Determinations (NCD/LCD) for medical necessity.
14. Apply clinic policies and procedures for access and disclosure of personal health information.
15. Apply ethical standards of practice by complying with AHIMA's Code of Ethics and AAPC's Code of Conduct.
16. Recognize and report privacy or compliance issues/problems to the office manager.
17. Justify assigned Evaluation and Management codes based on health record documentation using the E/M guidelines.
18. Validate the accuracy of the required data elements on the claim form.
19. Conduct coding and billing audits for compliance and trending.
20. Determine educational needs for physicians and staff on reimbursement and documentation rules and regulations related to coding.
21. Evaluate payer remittance or payment (EOB or ERA) reports for accuracy of payment, reason for denials, and carrier adjustments.
22. Apply global surgical package guidelines to surgical procedures.
23. Interpret health record documentation to identify diagnoses and procedures for code assignment.
24. Process claim denials and/or appeals by using ERISA guidelines.
25. Differentiate and assign codes for the professional versus technical component, when applicable.
26. Append appropriate modifiers to procedure codes when required.
27. Consult with physicians or other health care providers when additional information is needed for coding and/or to clarify conflicting or ambiguous information.

HIPAA and Patient Confidentiality

Clinic medical records, whether hard copy or electronic, are legal documents. Patients have the right to information located in these medical records. They also have authority to control how the information housed in these records is used and who it is released to—in most cases. Any information needed for use to treat them medically or for the clinic to conduct normal day-to-day business transactions is excluded.

Health care workers in all capacities should know what information and under what circumstances medical record information can be released and why. The medical record department of organizations is no longer the only department faced with requests for information from patients, family members, and outside agencies. Employees of the clinic are charged with safeguarding privacy and confidentiality of patient information. Any unauthorized release of protected information aside from that needed to medically treat an individual or to conduct the course of normal business is a violation of the law.

The **Health Insurance Portability and Accountability Act (HIPAA)** of 1996, Public Law 104-191, was enacted to protect health information, enforce security of health records, provide standards for electronic transmission of health information, uncover fraud and abuse, and provide continuous coverage of health insurance to employees and their families when they change or lose jobs. A goal of this law is to improve the efficiency and effectiveness of the health care system and simplify the way we collect and report data about services provided and charges for such. There are three parts to the law:

1. HIPAA Privacy Rule
2. HIPAA Security Rule
3. Administrative Simplification of HIPAA Electronic Transaction and Code Sets

HIPAA Privacy

The government published a final regulation in the form of the Privacy Rule in December 2000, which became effective on April 14, 2001. This Rule set national standards for the protection of health information, as applied to three types of entities: health plans (e.g., Cigna), health care clearinghouses (e.g., Web MD, McKesson, Companion), and health care providers (e.g., hospitals, physicians) who conduct health care transactions such as billing, enrollment, and eligibility verification electronically. The Office for Civil Rights is the oversight agency for the privacy standards.

A **covered entity** is one or more of these types of entities, according to the Administrative Simplification regulations. Our clinic is a covered entity because we are a health care provider. We must comply with HIPAA because we employ more than ten full-time employees. **Business associates** are also bound by the HIPAA law. Business associates perform functions on behalf of a covered entity such as a billing company, a transcription company, a copying service, an attorney, a consultant, or a marketing firm such as Gallop Poll that conducts patient satisfaction surveys. This is a new provision under the **Health Information Technology for Economic and Clinical Health Act (HITECH)**. This act was passed as part of the **American Recovery and Reinvestment Act (ARRA)** of 2009, signed into law by President Bush. ARRA establishes the first federal requirements on health data breach reporting and notification. This act modifies the HIPAA privacy and security regulations and was designed to facilitate the widespread adoption of electronic technology used to exchange medical information. The ARRA includes the statutory authorization of the Office of the National Coordinator for Health Information Technology (ONC). This office was created by President Bush in 2004 and falls under the Department of Health and Human Services (DHHS). It is charged to develop a national health information technology infrastructure. HITECH is considered to be a framework or a health information technology (HIT) infrastructure to protect electronic medical records. Business associates, since this enactment, are required to fully comply with HIPAA or face civil and criminal penalties for not having a designated security officer; not having written policies addressing electronic protected information that they create, store, or transmit; and not conducting employee training on information security.

HIPAA Security

The security portion of the HIPAA law was released on February 20, 2003. The Centers for Medicare and Medicaid Services (CMS) is the oversight agency for HIPAA Security. Security entails controlling access to information with physical safeguards (e.g., locks, fire protection, alarms, shredding, and visitor access to restricted areas of the clinic) and electronic/technical safeguards (e.g., software, passwords, encryption, user rights, screen savers, time outs, and audit trails). Proper disposal of paper and faxed information in designated PHI containers with locked lids is enforced. Paper is not reused. All paper with potential PHI is placed in these bins and shredded weekly.

Under ARRA, the secretary of DHHS is required to issue annual guidance on the most effective and appropriate safeguards for implementing security requirements. This secretary is also required to report to Congress on breaches, compliance, and the overall impact of ARRA on the health care industry.

Administrative Simplification

Administrative simplification provisions required the government to create national standards for electronic health care transactions. As part of the administrative simplification portion of the rule, HIPAA identifies and mandates the use of code sets used to collect and submit medical data to payers. **Code sets** are the codes used to identify specific diagnoses and clinical procedures on claims and encounter forms. There are three sets approved, which all insurance carriers must acknowledge: HCPCS, CPT-4, ICD-9-CM (to be replaced with ICD-10 in October 2013).

Nature of Privacy Practice

The **HIPAA Privacy Rule** is the first federal privacy standard to protect patients' health information and physical medical records. This Rule provides patients access to their medical records and gives them more control over how their medical information is used. The Rule limits the ways in which hospitals, physicians, pharmacies, insurance carriers, and other covered entities use a patient's personal health information. It protects patient information whether it is in paper or electronic format or spoken word. Employees must take extra measures to not hold conversations in front of other staff or visitors, which could jeopardize the patient confidentiality.

For the average health care provider or insurance carrier, the Privacy Rule requires the following elements:

- Notifying patients about their privacy rights and how their information can be used
- Adopting and implementing privacy procedures for its practice, hospital, or plan
- Training employees so that they understand the privacy procedures
- Designating an individual to be responsible for seeing that the privacy procedures are adopted and followed
- Securing patient records containing individually identifiable health information so that they are not readily available to those who do not need them

In actuality, in most physician practices, three or four of these five elements were already being carried out prior to implementation of the Privacy Rule. Covered entities of all types and sizes are required to comply with the Privacy Rule. To ease the burden of complying with these requirements, the Privacy Rule gives some flexibility for providers and plans and allows them to create their own privacy procedures, tailored to fit their size and needs.

Protected Health Information

HIPAA has very specific rules for how and when a patient's **protected health information (PHI)** is used and released. PHI is defined as individually identifiable health information that is collected, transmitted, or housed in paper form or electronically such as on CD-ROM, over the Internet, or via modem. These data elements are specific to a particular patient and no one else. Only staff with a legitimate need to know will have access to PHI. The following elements are considered PHI when released in conjunction with a diagnosis or procedure:

- Photographs, fingerprints, footprints, or voice recordings
- Name
- Address
- Phone number
- Birth date
- Social Security number

- Medical record number
- Account number
- Certificate or license number
- Health plan beneficiary ID number
- Driver's license number

Releases without patient consent should be limited to those who need them to provide medical treatment, payers to obtain payment for services, research, and for every day business to support the clinic's operations. If information is not being used for treatment, payment, or operations (TPO), including mandatory reporting to state and federal agencies, then use is not allowed without consent. Providers are required by law to submit statistics to the state regarding certain injuries and illness. In addition to specific illnesses, providers are also required to report instances of abuse (child, spousal, or elderly), gunshot wounds, rape, and unexpected deaths such as SIDS. In these events, patient consent is not needed.

A patient must consent to or authorize the release of any other information for any other purpose. When information is released, it must be kept to the minimum necessary to meet the needs of the requester. The **minimum necessary standard** expects reasonable efforts to limit PHI to the least amount of information necessary to accomplish the intended purpose of the use, disclosure, or request. The covered entity retains the right to make its own minimum necessary determination for disclosures to which the minimum necessary standard applies. Employees should ask themselves, "Do I need to know this in order to do my job?" If the answer is "no," then the minimum necessary standard is not being applied. For example, if a request is made for a progress note from February 18, 2002, that is all that should be provided. It is inappropriate to release all progress notes because that is not what was requested.

A covered entity is required to maintain a list of each time a patient's information was disclosed. An individual has a right to obtain an accounting of disclosures from their paper or electronic record. Currently under the HIPAA law, providers and covered entities must provide patients with a record, or accounting of disclosures, for each time PHI was released for reasons other than patient treatment, payment, or health care operations. Now under the HITECH Act, entities that maintain PHI in electronic format must track all disclosures—even if they were necessary for treatment, payment, or health care operations—and provide this accounting to a patient upon request going back as far as three years of disclosures. With this change from the initial requirement of HIPAA, providers and facilities will see an exponential increase in tracking of and accounting for these disclosures. This additional accounting provision becomes effective January 1, 2014 if an electronic record was purchased on or before January 1, 2009. If an electronic health record (EHR) was acquired after January 1, 2009, this requirement is effective January 1, 2011. As a result of HITECH patients are now able to obtain electronic PHI in an electronic format rather than the previous paper copy method. The ARRA also requires that covered entities account for the disclosures of their business associates or require them to make their own accounting.

Breach Notification

A **breach** occurs when protected information is released, without consent, to unauthorized entities or if security of patient records is compromised and accessed by unauthorized entities. For example, this can occur when records are improperly disposed of or when a computer system is "hacked" and information is then obtained. Currently 40 states have breach notification laws. The HITECH Act requires that patients be notified of any unauthorized acquisition, access, use, or disclosure of their unsecured protected health information that compromises the privacy or security of such information, with some exceptions for unintentional or inadvertent use or disclosure by employees or authorized individuals within the "same facility." The HITECH Act specifies the timeliness of such notifications ("without unreasonable delay and in no case later than 60 calendar days after discovery of the breach") and describes the information that must appear in the notification to affected patients. Written notice is required for patient medical information breaches.

For electronic medical information breaches, HITECH now requires that if a breach involves 500 or more people in a particular state, the covered entity must also notify prominent media outlets in the area where these individuals reside. They must also notify the DHHS so that a notice can be posted on its website. For breaches that involve fewer than 500 patients, the DHHS still must be notified by submitting a log of all the breaches. If a state's breach notification law is more stringent than the requirements of the HITECH Act, the state's law will continue to apply. HITECH also applies to vendors of personal health records (PHR) such as Google and business associates. The Federal Trade Commission has been solicited to enforce these rules for vendors such as this. Business associates must notify covered entities of any data breaches they encounter.

Consequences

The secretary of the DHHS is responsible for performing periodic audits to ensure that entities are in compliance with HIPAA regulations. Our clinic is committed to securing and protecting patient privacy. There is no exception that each staff member be trained on the Privacy and Security Rules and their application. Employees must report any breach or suspected breach to the office manager. If you fail to follow our policies, you will put our organization in jeopardy and as well as yourself. DMA will impose disciplinary actions, including termination, on employees who breach patient confidentiality. Patients and employees may file complaints about violations to the rules to the provider or health plan or directly to the Department of Health and Human Services Office for Civil Rights (OCR).

Aside from notifying patients and regulatory agencies of a breach or violation, there are stiff civil and/or criminal penalties for breaching privacy or security of PHI. ARRA explains that individuals, not just covered entities, are subject to penalties. If a patient is made aware of a breach, they can file a civil suit with fines up to $100 for each violation of the rules *per person* up to a limit of $25,000. Criminal penalties for wrongful disclosure of PHI or lack of safeguards involve fines and prison time. Unintentional disclosure can impose bring a fine of up to $50,000 and/or one year in prison. Disclosure with intent to sell or use the information warrants fines as high as $250,000 per fine or a prison sentence of 10 years.

The HITECH Act imposes a four-tiered penalty system for privacy violations as illustrated in Table 1-1. What is different about this new change under ARRA and HITECH is that patients whose PHI was

Table 1-1 HITECH Penalty Tier

Penalty Tier	Scenario	Minimum Penalty	Maximum Penalty
A	Entity did not know a violation occurred. Unintentional breach caused by lack of knowledge or carelessness. Exercised reasonable diligence and would not have known of violation. Ex. Keying error or selecting wrong name to mail PHI to.	$100 for each violation	UP Up to $25,000 for each violation, not to exceed $50,000 per calendar year
B	Deliberate unauthorized access to PHI without a disclosure. Violation due to reasonable cause but not willful neglect by the covered entity. Ex. Staff accessing a celebrity's PHI.	$1,000 for each violation	Not to exceed $100,000 per calendar year
C	Deliberate unauthorized disclosure or tampering with data for personal gain. Violation due to willful neglect. Covered entity took corrective action. Ex. Employee views a neighbor's PHI and discloses it to other neighbors.	$10,000 for each violation	Not to exceed $250,00 per calendar year
D	Deliberate unauthorized disclosure of PHI for malice or personal gain. Violation due to willful neglect that has not been corrected within 30 days of the first day the entity knew or should have known a violation occurred. Ex. Identity theft, opening credit accounts with a patient's information.	$50,000 for each violation	Not to exceed $1,500,000 per calendar year

breached can share in the remuneration of the penalty or settlement. The HHS Secretary will base the amount of the penalty on:

- The nature and extent of the violation
- The nature and extent of the harm resulting from such violation

Discussion

What penalty tier do you think the following violation would fall under? A billing company is contracted by individual physicians and large physician groups such as emergency room (ER) physicians and radiologists to submit the physicians' professional claim to the insurance company for payment and to perform patient collections. As a courtesy to their patients, the billing company allows online payments at the billing company's website or by sending in a payment coupon with a check or credit card number. A patient calls the billing manager and states that she believes her credit card number has been compromised and she suspects someone at the company has used her credit card to purchase apparel as well as other items online. The patient explains that she lives in North Carolina and the purchases were made online and shipped to an address in Michigan, where the billing company is located. The billing manager researches the address and finds that it matches a customer service representative's home address.

Patient Bill of Rights

Patients are assumed certain rights with respect to their care, handling of their PHI, disclosure of fees and financial terms and conditions, and safety.

Notice of Privacy Practice

HIPAA requires that offices provide all patients with a notice of privacy practices the first time the patient receives services with the practice. It must be displayed in a prominent location in the clinic. At our office it is currently displayed in the waiting room near the sign-in window and is also displayed at the registration desk. The patients are provided a booklet size copy upon check-in. This notice outlines the office's policy for use and disclosure of PHI. It also describes when and how PHI is used, when additional consent for other information is required, and the effort this office makes to release the minimum necessary information. It also explains the process for channeling patient complaints. A sample notice is available at the Department of Health and Human Services Office of Civil Rights website http://www.hhs.gov. Select Policy and Regulations. Scroll down under Laws and Regulations and choose Office of Civil Rights. Look for Resources for Consumers, Providers, and Advocates and click on Privacy of Health Information for Consumers. Select Fact Sheet: Privacy and Your Health Information. You can view our privacy notice in MOSS by selecting the Patient Registration button. Select any patient name and then choose the HIPAA tab. Click on the Privacy Notice button.

In addition to the requirement to notify patients in the Notice of Privacy Practices about how their information is used, a consent form must be obtained for the clinic to use and disclose information according to HIPAA (Figure 1.2). A signed consent must be filed in the patient's medical record for purposes of treatment, payment, and operations of the clinic.

Authorization to Release Medical Information

Information found in medical records (hard copy or electronic) and/or that which is orally communicated is confidential. The challenge of responding to requests for information typically rests on the front desk staff. Any other request for use or disclosure must be accompanied by a signed authorization from the patient allowing for this release to take place. It is required by law, standards, and professional ethics that all health care employees heed this practice. Physicians, by virtue of the Hippocratic Oath, have

CONSENT FOR THE USE OR DISCLOSURE OF PROTECTED HEALTH INFORMATION (PHI)

CONSENT TO THE USE AND DISCLOSURE OF HEALTH INFORMATION FOR TREATMENT, PAYMENT, OR CLINIC OPERATIONS

I understand as part of my treatment and services that Douglasville Medicine Associates creates and maintains medical records describing my personal and family health history, conditions, examinations, testing, diagnoses, treatment, discussions with my doctors, test results, and recommendations for future care. I understand this information acts as:

- A tool for planning my care and carrying out treatment
- A written communication among all providers participating in my care
- A means to document services provided, supplies used, and items provided to me to properly bill my insurance company
- A resource to assess safety, consumption, quality of care, and competence of providers participating in my care.

I have been provided with a copy of the clinic's Notice of Privacy Practices. I have read the notice prior to signing this consent. I understand that the clinic reserves the right to change this notice and its practices and if I request they will mail me a copy or provide one to me at my next visit. I understand that I have the right to object to the use of my health information in marketing material. I understand that I have the right to restrict how my health information may be used or disclosed to carry out treatment, payment, and operations. I also recognize that the clinic is not required to agree to the restrictions I have requested. I realize that I can revoke this consent in writing and recognize that this will not apply to information released prior to my revocation.

I am requesting the following restrictions to the disclosure or use of my personal health information. ☐ None

______________________________ ____________________
Signature of Patient or Legal Representative Witness

____
Date

Figure 1.2 Consent for Use and Disclosure of PHI

historically been responsible for keeping patients' medical information confidential. The following list provides some of the standards, ethics, and laws that bind us:

- Physicians' Patient Records Act (44-115-40)
- Medicare Conditions of Participation (COP) (42 CFR 405-1026)
- American Medical Association (AMA) Code of Ethics (Standard IV)
- AHIMA code of Ethics (Appendix D)
- Patients' Bill of Rights
- HIPAA

Authorization is not required to release medical information to our state's Department of Health and Environmental Control (DHEC) in specified circumstances that affect the wellness of the population. Providers are required to report to the state when patients acquire certain communicable diseases, are victim of abuse, or are assaulted by gunshot. They do not need permission from the patient to release this information. Each state has specific mandates for reporting. When deciding your response to a request for information, the most important elements to consider are the identity and authority of any party making the request, the nature of the record, and the information contained. The records that are considered most sensitive are those concerning psychiatric history and treatment, AIDS/HIV, drug and/or alcohol abuse, adoptions, genetic testing, and treatment of minors for certain conditions. When you are referencing laws that apply to the release of medical information, the strictest law always applies.

Consent/Authorization to Release Information

A separate consent to release medical information is required for all records requests except for treatment, payment, or clinic operations or when a subpoena or court order is issued. Under the HITECH Act, patients now have a right to restrict disclosure of PHI related to treatments or services for which the patient paid out of pocket and which did not get filed on a claim to the insurance company. Previously, HIPAA allowed covered entities to decline a patient's request to limit or restrict disclosure of PHI related to self-pay services. This is a challenge to providers and facilities to discriminate between self-pay visits and information generated during those visits from charges submitted to an insurance company.

A signed written authorization from the patient must contain the following to be valid:

- It must be signed and dated within 90 days by the patient or legal representative. The signature is checked with records to verify that it matches.
- Name and address of requesting body along with the name of the individual that is to receive the information. A new authorization should be obtained for each requestor.
- Statement that the authorization can be revoked at any time by the patient.
- Statement of the extent or purpose of the request.
- Indication of exactly what they are requesting copies of (e.g., operative report, entire record).
- Identifying information describing the patient must be present to verify correct patient (e.g., date of birth, Social Security number).

Health information cannot be released over the phone without a written signed consent unless it is a bona fide medical emergency. Information should not be faxed without proper consent for release along with a statement that the patient is aware that the medical information is going to be faxed (Figure 1.3). If a patient presents to the office to examine their medical record or to pick up a copy, a valid driver's license must be shown before records are provided.

The HIPAA training requirement for DMA employees is satisfied by providing each new employee with a copy of our privacy policies and documenting that new members have reviewed the policies.

Electronic Health Care Transactions and Code Sets

HIPAA Electronic Health care Transactions and Code Sets (TCS) standardize the way that physicians and health plans exchange electronic data. Standards exist for the following HIPAA transactions:

- Insurance referral authorization inquiry/response
- Insurance claim status inquiry/response
- Health care payment and remittance advice
- Eligibility for a health plan inquiry/response
- Coordination of benefits

AUTHORIZATION TO RELEASE MEDICAL RECORD INFORMATION

Date: ______________

I, ___________________________, authorize Douglasville Medicine Associates to release the following information from my medical record. I reserve the right to revoke this authorization in writing at any time. I understand that the clinic will charge for administrative fees and copying expenses for requests that are not sent directly to a physician or medical facility for continuation of my care. I acknowledge that the clinic cannot protect against redisclosure by the recipient requester and that this information may no longer be protected by law. This authorization expires 90 days from the date of my signature.

☐ Entire Medical Record for all dates of service
☐ Operative note from DOS:___________
☐ Radiology reports from DOS:___________
☐ Consultation from DOS:______________
☐ Other- Specify:_____________________________________
☐ Progress notes from these dates:________
☐ History and Physical DOS:_______________
☐ X-ray Films from DOS:_________________
☐ Laboratory Reports from DOS:___________

Send this information to the requester below for the purpose of

____.

Name of Requestor:____________________________

Address:_____________________________________

Fax number:__________________________________ Phone number:____________________

____

Signature of Patient or Legal Representative

____

DOB

____

SSN

Figure 1.3 Authorization to Release Medical Records

Each of these transactions is carried out daily by an employee in our practice. These are further explained in chapters 2 and 3 of this module.

Standard Code Sets

Medical code sets are used in transactions to identify what procedures, services, diagnoses, and supplies pertain to a patient encounter. The codes are maintained by professional societies and public health organizations. The Secretary of Health and Human Services has adopted the following code sets as the standard medical data code sets:

1. ***International Classification of Diseases, 9th Edition, Clinical Modification, (ICD-9-CM), Volumes 1 and 2*** (including The Official ICD-9-CM Guidelines for Coding and Reporting), as updated and distributed by HHS, for the following conditions:
    1. Diseases
    2. Injuries

3. Impairments
4. Other health health-related problems and their manifestations
5. Causes of injury, disease, impairment, or other health-related problems

Effective October 1, 2013, ICD-9 will no longer be a valid HIPAA approved code set. It is being replaced with ICD-10.

2. The Centers for Medicare & Medicaid Services' Health care Common Procedure Coding System (HCPCS), as updated and distributed by CMS, for all other substances, equipment, supplies, or other items used in health care services. These items include, but are not limited to, the following:
   1. Medical supplies
   2. Orthotic and prosthetic devices
   3. Durable medical equipment
3. ***Current Procedural Terminology,*** as updated and distributed by the American Medical Association, for physician services and other health health-related services. These services include, but are not limited to, the following:
   1. Physician services
   2. Physical and occupational therapy services
   3. Radiological procedures
   4. Clinical laboratory tests
   5. Other medical diagnostic procedures
   6. Therapeutic surgical services

HIPAA National Identifiers

Identifiers are unique numbers of predetermined length used in electronic transactions that link an individual or entity to a transaction.

Employer Identification Number (EIN)

Employer Identification Numbers are issued by the IRS. They act in the same fashion as a Social Security number for a company or employer when they enroll or disenroll employees in a health plan or make premium payments to the plan for the employee. The EIN number is essentially the tax ID number of the business. DMA's EIN number is 045093221. This number is needed when filing insurance claims and performing follow-up for outstanding insurance claims.

National Provider Identifier (NPI)

The **National Provider Identifier** is a ten-digit number assigned to each health care provider and is the standard for identifying them to payers when filing claims. It is assigned by the government to all health care providers who will submit claims to insurance carriers or transmit health information electronically. This number is unique to the provider, is recognized by all payers, and will never change. Facilities such as pharmacies, hospitals, and clinics must also have an NPI number. Our group NPI number is 7189396873. Each of the physicians is required to have their own individual NPI number as well.

Compliance

Compliance with HIPAA and coding guidelines is not an option. DMA takes pride in our HIPAA compliance program to ensure all staff members comply with HIPAA law. This is one component of the clinic's overall compliance program. **Compliance** is a means of adhering to state and federal laws and requirements. Compliance programs consist of checks and balance to "self audit" and "self monitor" the practice in preventing fraudulent or abusive erroneous conduct or careless behavior while providing high-quality, cost-effective health care services. Having a program in place demonstrates the effort made by the provider to understand and adhere to federal regulations. A compliance plan or program is a route for identifying, correcting, and preventing illegal practices. The program is a written document that outlines the steps needed to (1) audit and monitor compliance with government regulations, (2) establish consistent policies and procedures (3) provide for ongoing staff education and communication about coding and regulatory changes, and (4) respond to and correct errors. The goal of the program is to promote ethical conduct and establish a culture of compliance throughout the organization. It should prevent waste, fraud, and abuse; promote adherence to HIPAA and ARRA; and promote accurate and consistent coding and reporting practices. The components of the program that directly relate to coding and billing will be discussed in this simulation. The Centers for Medicare & Medicaid Services (CMS) regulates policies and procedures with respect to Medicare and Medicaid beneficiaries. Medicare is taking action to combat fraud and abuse of the system in key areas of coding and billing.

One of CMS's missions is to prevent fraudulent and abusive coding and billing practices. CMS uses a number of resources to identify coding/billing patterns and problems. According to Medicare, **fraud** is purposely billing Medicare for services that were never provided or received and/or intentionally deceiving or misrepresenting the intentional deception or misrepresentation that could result in unauthorized benefit. Categories of fraud include: misrepresented diagnosis, billing for services not rendered, and waiving patient deductibles and co-pays. To commit fraud there has to be "intent" such as deliberately falsifying information or knowingly submitting a claim that is false. Participating in schemes that involve collusion between patient and provider or between a provider and a supplier of equipment resulting in higher costs to the Medicare program are examples of intentional deception.

Abuse consists of practices that are inconsistent with sound fiscal, business, or medical practices and that result in unnecessary cost or in reimbursement for services that are not medically necessary or that fail to meet professionally recognized standards for health care. Abuse is a more frequent offense than fraud. It often happens due to lack of education and not from the intent to defraud.

Insurance carriers identify signs of fraud and abuse by looking at the following nonexclusive list:

Fraud

- Billing for services not provided, including charges for "no shows."
- Duplicate billing that is out of the norm for providers in a specialty or geographic area.
- Reports of solicitation or receiving kickbacks, that is, bribes for patient referrals.
- False representation of services rendered.
- Routine billing for noncovered services as covered services. Falsely billing for a more involved service than the routine limited service that was really provided and noncovered.
- Altering hard copy claims and medical records.
- Submitting claims for physician services for providers not yet credentialed with CMS under another physician's provider number.

Abuse

- Excessive charges for services.
- Billing Medicare patients at higher fee schedules than non-Medicare patients.
- Waiving co-pays and deductibles.
- Exceeding the maximum allowable actual charge (Medicare).

The compliance program is built into everyday operations of the clinic. Documentation of the services and care provided is the cornerstone of fraud investigations and the evidence of compliance.

April Kennedy, the office manager, is the compliance officer for DMA. She is responsible for the validity and maintenance of the compliance program. She is responsible for:

- Training all new staff as well as new physicians to the practice in all aspects of compliance with HIPAA, OSHA, coding, and billing. Every staff member must sign an employment agreement outlining the expectations of following our compliance program.
- Enforcing and monitoring adherence to clinic policies and procedures, and implementing changes as needed.
- Performing corrective action for noncompliance.

The Office of Inspector General (OIG) is charged with monitoring practice activity and adherence to many regulations and laws that affect physician practices. It is the "enforcer" of the law with respect to Medicare and the Department of Health and Human Services.

Employees in health care settings need to know how and when to report suspected fraud or abuse. If employees find themselves in a situation where they suspect fraudulent activity, before taking any action, there are several things to consider. Before reporting such accusations, employees need to collect information on the who, what, where, when, why, and how. They should do the research and document the situation clearly. They should be able to describe the exact fraudulent practice with details of the activity, trends, timing, and reference sources used to defend your position and to dispute why the activity is wrong. Provide names of individuals responsible and contact information. Identify payers affected by the fraudulent activity. Provide a financial estimate of the value of these violations. Before reporting any activity outside the practice, discuss this suspected violation with the practice manager.

Anti-Kickback Statute/Stark Law

Stark law governs physician self-referral for patients enrolled in a federally funded health plan. **Physician self-referral** is the practice of a physician referring a patient to a medical facility in which he/she or a member of the immediate family has a financial interest, be it ownership, investment, or a structured compensation arrangement. This is considered to be a conflict of interest, given the physician's position to financially benefit from the referral. There is potential that such arrangements may encourage over-utilization of services, in turn driving up health care costs. In addition, it is thought to be a restraint of trade in that this creates a captive referral system and limits competition by other providers. The intent of this law is to prevent health care providers from inappropriately profiting from referrals. The government regards any type of incentive for a referral as a potential violation of these laws because the opportunity to reap financial benefits may tempt providers to make referrals that are not medically necessary. Forms of incentive include free lunches, tickets to events, gift cards, and so on. When a provider routinely waives a patient's co-payment or deductible, the government views the situation as an inducement for the patient to choose the provider for reasons other than medical benefit. A clear Stark violation would be a physician referring patients for treatment to his or her spouse.

The Stark law prohibits referrals for the following specific designated health services:

- Clinical laboratory services
- Physical therapy
- Occupational therapy
- Radiology services, including magnetic resonance imaging, computerized axial tomography scans, and ultrasound services
- Radiation therapy services and supplies
- Durable medical equipment and supplies
- Parenteral and enteral nutrients, equipment, and supplies
- Prosthetics, orthotics, and prosthetic devices and supplies

- Home health services
- Outpatient prescription drugs
- Inpatient and outpatient hospital services

Violations of the anti-kickback statute are considered felonies, with criminal penalties of up to $25,000 in fines and five years in prison. In addition, civil penalties can involve up to $50,000 in fines and exclusion from federal program participation. As a civil statute, the Stark law does not subject violators to the threat of imprisonment. However, violations of the Stark law could result in denial of payment for the prohibited transaction; required refunding of payments; monetary penalties ranging from $15,000 to $100,000; and exclusion from federal program participation. Providers are required to reveal any financial interest in facilities outside of their respective practice that they refer patients to or for which they perform services. By informing the patient of such vested interests, patients can elect to change the location of the services being ordered by the physician. It is recommended that physicians with an ownership interest in certain imaging facilities, diagnostic labs, physical therapy practices, sleep labs, and surgery centers provide written notification at the time of referral, informing patients they could obtain these services from another health care provider or supplier and providing them with a list of others providers or suppliers in the area. We notify our patients that we own our equipment and give them an option to go to the local hospital or various imaging centers in the area before scheduling these services because DMA owns their own CT scanner and ultrasound machine.

Exceptions

To date, the HHS Office of Inspector General (OIG) has published 21 safe harbors that, in general, narrowly define exceptions to the statute. For example, routinely waiving co-payments and deductibles violates the statute and ordinarily results in a sanction; however, a safe harbor has been created wherein a provider granting such a waiver based on a patient's financial need would not be sanctioned.

DMA Compliance Plan

Staff is committed to ethical and legal business practices. Staff is committed to complying with federal and state statutes and regulations, payer policies, and official coding rules and guidelines. Staff will develop and maintain internal policies and procedures that are consistent with reimbursement regulations and official coding rules and guidelines. Staff value high quality health information, integrity, accuracy, consistency, and validity thereof. Staff respects the confidentiality of individually identifiable health information.

As part of our hiring process at DMA, licensed staff (RN, PA. C, MD, LPN, RNP) are investigated to see if they have been excluded from the Medicare or Medicaid programs. This is done by visiting the OIG website (http://www.oig.hhs.gov) and searching for List of Excluded Individuals and Entities. Employment is conditional upon verifying status of licensure and sanctions. The Department of Health and Human Services (DHHS) state websites also post this information. Each staff member must sign a code of conduct at the time of employment and annually thereafter. Coders will also sign a copy of AHIMA's Standards of Ethical Coding (Appendix D). A signed copy of this statement should be maintained in the employee file. Comprehensive policies and procedures on coding, documentation requirements, payer regulations, and contractual agreements for coding consulting and outsourcing, confidentiality, and record retention must be adhered to. All polices and procedures are kept in a simple to use format and given to all new coders upon hire. Staff is required to sign a statement that they have read and understand these policies. Polices are located in Appendix A of this manual.

Policies identify the approved coding resources to reference, steps taken to code from a health record, how to query physicians when there is more information needed, coding accuracy levels, and medical necessity to name a few.

DMA Policies Include:

- Scheduling
- Registration

- Coding and Billing
  - Waiving of co-pays
  - Coding Guidelines must be followed for ICD-9, CPT-4, and HCPCS code assignment
  - Billing for services not rendered will not occur
  - Upcoding
  - Unbundling
  - Billing for physician services provided by nonphysicians
  - Billing for noncovered services as if they were covered
  - Credit balances for patients and insurance carriers
  - Proper use of modifiers
  - Misrepresenting diagnoses to justify services
  - Obtaining Advanced Beneficiary Notices (ABN)
  - Proper linkage of diagnoses to procedures on the ANSI 837P
- Documentation
  - Record content necessary to complete claim form
  - Physician querying for additional information or clarification
- HIPAA Privacy
  - Education
  - Physical, administrative, and technical safeguards
  - Notice of Privacy Practices

Employees and physicians receive clarification on policies and procedures, elements of the compliance program, and answers to coding questions at the monthly board meeting. When a change is made to a policy, it is disseminated to all staff members in email form. It is also posted on the bulletin board in the break room. All documents containing regulatory information affecting coding are maintained with the coding policies. Any suspected compliance violation can be reported to the privacy officer by sending her an email, leaving her a voicemail, completing a written statement, or by anonymously completing a statement and placing it in the suggestion box.

Human Relations

In general, most employers have three major expectations of their employees:

- Dependability. He/she must be reliable, follow through with tasks, work with little supervision, and do a good job.
- Appearance. He/she is required to look, dress, and act professionally and exhibit a pleasant posture by smiling, using positive body language, and focusing their attention to the customer.
- Skills. He/she will have the necessary training, experience, and credentials to perform the best job possible. He/she will communicate clearly and use proper grammar and etiquette.

Customer service is a priority at DMA. We recognize that we have internal and external customers. Our internal customers are our co-workers, doctors, and support staff. Our external customers are our patients, insurance carriers, hospitals, referring physician practices, and vendors. We strive to treat all of our customers with respect, kindness, and compassion. Medical office staffs are in constant communication with patients, physicians, hospitals, co-workers, insurance companies and the like. Office staffs have the professional responsibility to communicate effectively in their daily interactions with patients and health care practitioners. We communicate by speaking, writing, gesturing, signaling, signing, touching, and drawing. **Communication** is the sharing of information and the manner in which we relate to others. Effective communication within the office is necessary for task completion and organization. People must work together effectively and efficiently as a team. The root of many office problems that result in employee turnover and poor patient retention falls back on the lack of effective communication. The emotions and feelings of employees, patients, and providers affect communication. Tone of voice, attitude, choice of words, and body posture all communicate a variety of messages—some intended and some unintended. Stressful situations tend to break down communication and bring out the worst communication styles in us.

DMA is consistently working on improving communication and teambuilding. We have a bulletin that is produced twice a month notifying staff of changes, updates, and fun things such as birthdays and staff accomplishments. We also pride ourselves in obtaining feedback from members of the team and in acquiring specific responses to performance surveys that are used in rating staff during their annual performance evaluations. This is an opportunity for staff that directly work together to offer feedback on a staff member's communication style, attitude, quality of work, and so on. Rather than being evaluated solely by your supervisor, other members of your team will have input, hopefully painting a full picture of your abilities and accomplishments.

All people have the capacity to provide outstanding customer service when they are skilled at what they do. We all have the ability to impress the customer and provide this exceptional service, but it hinges on two things: attitude and conviction. Outstanding service results when employees put their own needs and egos aside. This is a difficult thing to do for most of us. It is impossible for some of us. Customers and providers alike have a basic desire to feel respected. In the customer-provider relationship, the customer's needs must always come before our own to achieve genuine customer service. We have to make a conscious effort to connect with our customers. To do so, we need to be skillful at what we do and continually question and improve our interpersonal skills. John Rockefeller, Sr. said that "truly successful people are not those with the most brains or the most skill. The people who seem to be the happiest are usually those who have a way with people." When filling open positions, organizations seek those with the ability to get along with others and possess social skills, and they will often select these candidates over those with more knowledge or job skills. Staff must develop strong interpersonal skills to relate to physicians, patients, family members, co-workers, insurance carriers, attorneys, and other health care facility employees.

Most of us are not acutely aware of everything that we say or do, and just as important, what we don't say or do, and how this affects our interactions with others. It is up to the staff at DMA to help the physicians make our patients feel respected, comfortable, understood, and important. Behavior is reciprocal: when a staff member smiles, that smile encourages others to also smile. Likewise, when a staff member frowns or is agitated or angry, this behavior will generate the same type of response from the customer. When communicating with customers (patients, co-workers, physicians, etc.) employ the following elements to achieve effective oral and written communication:

1. Respect
2. Genuineness
3. Patience
4. Empathy
5. Honesty
6. Specificity instead of generalizations
7. Poise and self control
8. Timing that is appropriate for the communication
9. Assertiveness

Personality Types

Personality boils down to the ability to work and get along with other people. According to Ezinearticles.com and Associated Content the inability to get along with others and not being a team player are ranked in the top 10 reasons for employees losing their jobs. Offices typically have staff that displays seven negative personality or communication types. People may come across as being offensive; defensive; melancholic; a brown noser; an expert; a meddler; a gossip; or a critic. These are personality traits/behaviors that the ideal employee does not want to portray. The offenders are dominating, disagreeable, skeptical, and blame others when things go wrong. These individuals are typically labeled as "tough guys." The defenders are passive and do very little on their own initiative. They tend to seek approval from others, take the blame, and not offer suggestions. The melancholic exhibit the "I don't really care" attitude and don't take their jobs or responsibilities seriously. They don't take ownership of actions and situations. They do the minimum required and nothing more. They are often perceived as resistant and uninterested in what is going on in the office.

The "brown-noser" is the sweet talker of the office. They are reluctant to share views about any critical office issue. Instead, they compliment everyone and tell everyone that all is fine and that the office has no problems. They are more interested in maintaining or promoting their position than anything else. The experts usually irritate others because they have seen it and done it all and proclaim to be experts on any subject discussed at the office. They seem to be "in the know" and have an opinion on whatever is happening. They often criticize others. The meddler appears to be a "pryor" and annoys or provokes others. They ask many questions (both business and personal) and try to get all the facts concerning an issue even if it is not their issue to be concerned with. They tend to nit-pick small details and can't process the bigger picture. The gossip is more concerned with everyone else's business than the job at hand. They are counterproductive and tend to play coworkers against each other. The critic is a habitual complainer and tends to criticize others and to focus on themselves. When they speak they use the words "I" and "me" frequently.

What each of us needs to strive for is giving feedback to others in positive terms so that we influence their behavior in a positive rather than a negative way. A person's personality and their perception of themselves will influence how others communicate with them and provide feedback—both positive and negative—once we are aware of the concept that what we say and do or don't do will influence other's opinions and behavior. The key to getting along with all of these personalities is accepting people as they are and appreciating the skills and traits that set us apart.

Customer Service

It has been proven that quality service is what customers are seeking, and in our business, what patients are seeking. Quality service attracts new patients when happy patients share their experiences and refer others to the practice. Quality is not always quantitative and tangible. Patient perception of quality varies and is driven by what is important to each patient. Patients measure quality based on overall experience and exposure to the practice, including cleanliness of the office, friendliness of staff (how they are greeted in person and on the phone), ability to contact the office and get an appointment, staff and provider communication, time spent with the patient, respect and honesty, and explanation of financial obligations. Other physicians are more likely to refer patients to our practice when they hear about our excellent service and clinical care. Today's patients are likely to shop around and if they feel they are treated with respect, they will stay on as loyal patients. Patients are now demanding more from providers and staff, especially better communication. Quality service also helps to retain quality staff. Practices that focus on service and a positive environment nurture an environment where people want to work. It has also been proven that quality service and high customer satisfaction decrease malpractice suits. A Wake Forrest University School of Medicine study showed that if a patient felt that his doctor cared about him and was open and honest, he was less likely to sue. Patients often make a decision to sue based on how they feel about the practice and the service they receive.

Aside from the obvious reasons for providing high quality service and making a connection with our patients, this behavior is also credited for improving compliance or adherence to treatment regimens.

The patients bond with the staff and open up about themselves, their habits, and other things that may impact their well-being. This creates a medium for the patient to ask questions and be truthful about what is ailing them and obstacles to their treatment. Patients often judge a physician's clinical expertise by his/her bedside manner. Patients need to feel trust and a personal connection with their caregivers. Bedside manner begins when the patient first calls the office. A typical office visit is 15 minutes in length, so physicians and support staff need to be efficient with this time while also tending to the patient's needs and grooming the provider-patient relationship. Staff members should make a conscious effort to read the body language of our the patients, take time to listen to them and find out how they want us to help them, empathize with their feelings of anxiety or fear, and always use language that they can understand by first assessing their education level and then avoiding "medicalese" and using terms they are more likely to comprehend.

The physicians and staff at our clinic are expected to provide exceptional customer service and communicate in the most appropriate manner given the situation. We work as a team, realizing that all staff is important to the team and without a cohesive team, our practice will not prosper. We do not tolerate any of the negative behaviors discussed previously. Staff meets each morning for 15 minutes before patient appointments to discuss the day ahead and anticipate any circumstances that need special attention. Staff at DMA will demonstrate the following customer service skills:

- Greet our customers with a friendly smile and welcoming attitude.
- Address our patients and visitors formally with Mr., Ms., or Mrs.
- Answer the phone by the third ring and provide this greeting in a cheerful voice. "Good Morning, Douglasville Medicine Associates, this is __________."
- Provide eye contact when communicating face-to-face with customers.
- Introduce ourselves to new patients.
- Extend a helping hand when patients appear to need assistance whether it is with completing paperwork, getting up and down in chairs, directions, and so on. Patients are customers, and if they feel their needs are being met and they are treated fairly, they will choose our office again for future health care needs. Repeat patients mean money to the practice.
- Refrain from making negative faces or gestures, or discussing patients or coworkers in a negative manner.
- Avoid making mistakes by asking for clarification or explanation if staff does not understand directions given by physicians, vendors, or facilities.
- When providing directions, instructions, or information, seek acknowledgement that the customer understood by asking for confirmation.
- Never criticize co-workers or office policies or procedures. Instead, look for the positive in every situation. Offer to help by mentoring or provide a viable solution to a problem.
- Strive to do the best job possible and anticipate the needs of our customers.
- Use proper grammar and sentence structure when drafting written communication. When writing letters to patients, providers, or insurance carriers, always site official sources of information for reference to substantiate actions or requests.
- Avoid finger pointing when faced with a problem. Instead look for ways to solve problems and change processes rather than repeating the same process hoping for a different outcome.
- Act honestly. If you are presented with a question or situation for which you don't know the answer or don't know how to respond, seek help or research reliable sources before acting. Never alter documents or try to cover up mistakes.
- Commit to life-long learning. The health care industry is in a constant state of flux. Insurance and coding staff must stay abreast of changes and continue their education in this profession.

Real-World Application

For the following scenarios, create a response to the party involved, keeping in mind what you have learned about effective communication.

1. You are assisting a patient at the desk by reviewing the instructions that the physician has provided to him. During this time, the office phone is ringing and another patient comes up to the front desk. Your co-worker is sitting behind the computer checking her Facebook messages. She has not attempted to answer the phone or help the patient at the window. You begin to get angry. What would you say to your coworker?

2. One of the doctors in the group is habitually late seeing and treating his patients. He's late much of the time because he gets to the office late most mornings and wants to read the newspaper and drink his coffee first. He also entertains many personal calls during the day and gets behind schedule. You are at the receiving end when patients voice their anger and frustration for waiting so long and not getting enough time with the doctor when he finally does see them. What's the best course of communication here, and what would you say to the doctor?

3. Wanda comes to work and always seems to be the victim of something. She is constantly complaining about life and work and sees the glass as half empty. Today she was late to work because she had a flat tire and when she got to the office all she could do was ramble on about why these things keep happening to her. You have taken all the negativity you can tolerate and today you want to talk to her about her attitude. What would you say?

Policies and Procedures

Staff is required to read the policy and procedure manual located in Appendix A of this manual. This manual was developed to promote consistency in carrying out the business of the clinic. Everyone is expected to sign an acknowledgement at orientation that they were educated about the policies and procedures of the clinic and agree to abide by them. This acknowledgement is filed in the employees' files. The manual is available to employees for reference at any time during working hours. This will be a useful tool when completing exercises and jobs located in later chapters. Sign the Employee Manual Acknowledgement and the Employee Privacy Acknowledgement located in the appendix and turn it in to your instructor for your file.

Exercise 1.1 Your Turn to Try

One of the tasks of a coder/biller is to communicate with physicians and office personnel about coding guidelines and reimbursement trends. Lindsay Morgan, your supervisor, has asked you to speak at your staff meeting about recurring problems. In the following situations, compile a script to be used when speaking to the staff so that you can describe the issue and ramifications of such. Outline possible solutions to the problems, corrective actions to be taken, education needs, and so on. Site any official guidelines or policies researched as necessary to clarify or demonstrate your point. What staff is responsible for rectifying the situation? Could these situations have been avoided or prevented?

1. DMA does not participate with Cigna. Over the course of the last three months, 20 Cigna patients have been scheduled, seen, and treated. Eighteen of them resulted in insurance denials. Two of them had out of network benefits but they had not met their out-of-network deductible so no payment was made. No money other than a $15.00 co-pay was collected from each patient at the time of service.

____

____

____

2. The billing department has seen an increase in data entry errors in patient demographics and in charge entry. Staff are still keying in dashes (-) and punctuation even though they have been instructed not to do so. Also, numbers are being transposed when entering codes and insurance ID numbers. Units are also being overlooked and at times not counted correctly.

____

____

____

3. One of the physicians is famous for not completing his charts in a timely manner. He is a week behind in dictation. The coder has noticed that he routinely lists diagnoses from previous visits on the router and orders a chest x-ray on every new patient. She is holding his charges until she can compare the router with the notes for that day.

____

____

____

Review Questions

Fill in the Blank

1. What should you do in the following scenario? Your co-worker is on the phone with a provider discussing a patient's treatment and diagnosis. You inadvertently hear PHI because you are in the next cubicle. This is information you do not need to know to perform your job.

____

____

2. You are walking by the trash can in the nurse's area and notice call slips with the clinic's name and address and faxed test results. The names have been blacked out. Is there concern for privacy or security breach? ______________________________

3. Physicians or patients sometimes request corrections to claims for services or supplies provided or to change the date of service so that claims will be considered for payment by their carrier. All of these changes should always be verified by documentation in the medical record. If changes were made without collaborating documentation, this would be considered ______________________.

____

4. A document imaging company hired by DMA to purge files and scan them into optical imaging for future electronic records is considered a ______________________.

True/False

5. A privacy officer oversees activities that relate to the development, implementation, and maintenance of policies and procedures covering the privacy and security of health information.
   T or **F**

6. Abuse is intentional deception or misrepresentation that could result in unauthorized benefit.
   T or **F**

7. Medical records cannot be released under any circumstance without expressed consent from the patient.
   T or **F**

8. Under ARRA, business associates are now subject to only the HIPAA security regulations.
   T or **F**

9. According to ARCCA and HITECH, an outside billing company or coding company is considered a business associate.
   T or **F**

Multiple Choice

10. A general practitioner treats:
    a. Females with genital tract problems
    b. Adults
    c. General problems of the body
    d. Chronic diseases

11. Compliance programs are a means of:
    a. Documenting the services and care provided
    b. Responding to patient billing questions within 72 hours
    c. Preventing fraudulent or abusive erroneous conduct
    d. Disclosing PHI as directed by law

12. Which of the following is not considered PHI?
    a. State of residence
    b. Date of birth
    c. Diagnosis
    d. Sex

13. ARRA strengthens the HIPAA enforcement by:
    a. Allowing patients whose PHI was breached a share of the settlement
    b. Subjecting an individual, not just the covered entity, to penalties
    c. Increasing the penalties to as high a $1.5 million per year to enforcement agencies
    d. All of the above

Internet Exercise

1. Visit the Office of Inspector General website and read the *OIG Compliance Program for Individual and Small Group Physician Practices.* This was published in the *Federal Register* October 5, 2000 Vol. 65, No. 194. Read the guidelines and list the seven elements of a compliance program. http://oig.hhs.gov/.
   1. ______
   2. ______
   3. ______
   4. ______
   5. ______
   6. ______
   7. ______
2. Visit the Institute for Health care Research and Policy, Georgetown University. Search the Health Privacy Project and read the State of Health Privacy for New York. Click on State Law and search for New York. *http://www.healthprivacy.org/*. Answer the following questions:
   1. What are the fees for searching for and copying medical records? ______
   2. Under the Physicians' Patient Records Act, who owns the medical record? ______
   3. Can a physician withhold copies of records because the patient has an outstanding balance? ______
   4. If an insurance carrier is requesting copies of records, does the physician have to get a consent signed by the patient before releasing them? ______
3. HIPAA terms and definitions can be referenced and downloaded from the WEDI website at *http://www.wedi.org*. Search for the HIPAA Glossary. It is always a good idea to keep this handy when reading and learning about HIPAA.
4. States are required by law to submit statistics to the state regarding certain injuries and illness. Follow this link to see what conditions are reportable to the state of New York. Do a search for reportable diseases and conditions. Turn this in to your instructor.
   http://www.health.state.ny.us
5. As part of your orientation, go to the following website and complete the Fraud and Abuse course. At the home page, select *Outreach and Education.* Scroll to the bottom of the screen and select *Web Based Training Modules.* Select *Medicare Fraud and Abuse.* You will be required to register for a user name and password. Take the course and turn in your certificate of completion to your instructor to add to your employee file. http:cms.hhs.gov.
6. Search the Internet and determine if New York is a state that has a data breach law. List the 45 states that have enacted this law.

______

______

______

CHAPTER

2 Technology in Health Care

Learning Objectives

1. Discuss the impact of computers and information technology in health care offices.
2. Discuss the use of software programs in all steps of the revenue cycle.
3. Identify common software used in a medical office and what functions are performed while using it.
4. List several websites coders and billers should frequent to stay abreast of changes and seek advice from trusted sources.

Key Terms

Access controls
Adjudication
Audit trails
Autoposting
Back Up
Batch
Clearinghouse
Database
Edits
Electronic claim
Electronic Data Interchange (EDI)
Electronic Funds Transfer (EFT)
Electronic Medical Record (EMR)
Electronic Remittance Advice (ERA)
Encoder
Encryption
HIPAA Transaction and Code Sets Standards
Hypertext Markup Language (HTML)
Information Technology (IT)
LISTSERV
Local Area Network (LAN)
Personal digital assistants (PDAs)
Personal health record (PHR)
Portal
Provider Report Card
Real-time
Real-time Claims Submission
Scrubbing
Swipe Cards
Telemedicine
Virtual Private Network (VPN)
Wide Area Network (WAN)

Background Basics

- Students should have completed an introduction to computers course covering basic terminology and use of a Windows platform.
- Students must have access to the Internet and be capable of performing searches.
- Students need to possess basic typing skills with a typing speed of at least 25 words per minute (WPM).

Competency Check List

- Medical office staff is required to use the computer and associated software to perform most administrative functions.
- Insurance carriers require that medical offices check their websites regarding claims status, patient eligibility, benefits, and payer policy information before calling their customer service departments.
- HIPAA mandates that insurance claims be submitted electronically from the provider's practice management system.
- Insurance and billing staff is expected to understand the technological jargon used in the coding and processing of claims.
- Staff is required to correspond with patients, physician practices, insurance carriers, and regulatory agencies using email, word processing, and spreadsheets.

Introduction

Technology has impacted the way we do business today from banking, payroll, communicating with patients, tracking charges, and referencing resources. Medical office staff uses information technology (IT) in almost every administrative function from scheduling, verifying insurance coverage, entering charges, and billing. Clinical functions such as prescribing medications are also impacted by technology and influenced by outside agencies to adopt more and more electronic substitutions for manual work. As patient information becomes more available and accessible, this information becomes vulnerable to foul play. Lost data or killer viruses result from doing simple searches on the Internet and are not necessarily a deliberate intention. The portability of patient information is a wonderful benefit but many healthcare providers are having difficulties dealing with employees not protecting their devices. Staff often download inappropriate material along with recreational software onto their devices that can trigger a virus to spread throughout the organization. Unfortunately, advances in technology often come with a price.

As discussed in chapter 1, the ARRA has established monetary incentives for facilities and physicians to use HIT. A significant number of physicians may be eligible for funds to improve and maintain their HIT systems stemming from the ARRA. This law included approximately $49 billion in investments and incentives for providers who treat Medicare and Medicaid patients to adopt HIT and demonstrate meaningful use of the technology. The average eligible provider can receive up to $44,000 in incentives over a five year period beginning in 2011. Those providers that do not become meaningful users of an electronic medical record (EMR, EHR) will be penalized through reduced Medicare reimbursements. More and more people are going on line for health information. Patients are getting more involved in their care and often seek information from the Internet. Patients now have more choices in health care options such as flexible spending accounts and individual plans where patients have control of their health care spending by choosing their provider, how often they will use health care services, and how much they will pay for it. This phenomenon is called consumer driven healthcare whereby patients will visit sites, price shop, and read commentary when searching for a physician or hospital as well as researching treatment options and holistic approaches to achieve wellness. Cigna has launched an e-learning series accessible through iTunes, Facebook and www.itstimetofeelbetter.com. Cigna University, the educational division of Cigna, has introduced an interactive online program free to the public combining written material, music, and a game that makes it easier and fun to access and absorb healthcare information and assist consumers in making confident healthcare decisions.

Essential pieces of patients' health information like records from every doctor office visit, every lab test performed, every hospital admission, and every prescription refill is scattered across America in computers and filing cabinets. Proposals to overhaul the U.S. healthcare system include the need for a standard electronic database of medical records for all physicians that will expedite patient care, improve the quality of care, and reduce medical errors. **Information technology** is a term used to describe an assortment of mechanical and electronic devices that automate the way we store, retrieve, communicate, and manage information. This can range from computers to fax machines and multipurpose copy machines.

Computers have simplified and expedited the accounting, billing, and scheduling functions of medical practices. Practice management systems allow staff to abstract information from the patient registration form, router, and other documents and enter it into the computer. Office staff enters information regarding communications with patients and insurance carriers, patient demographics, charges, services, insurance carriers, diagnoses, provider numbers and addresses, and payments into the practice management system's **database**. A database is a collection of data or files stored in the computer. Once the information is saved in the system, it is accessed for reporting, querying, scheduling, and billing all by a few keystrokes. Once you learn one system, such as MOSS, you will be able to navigate through most other programs because they operate in a Windows environment and have similar features.

Technology in Health Care Administration

Hospitals and physician offices alike are gradually automating more and more functions because it is proven that an efficient revenue cycle is critical to ensuring timely and appropriate reimbursement for services. Many hospitals and physician practices utilize e-tools to perform multiple functions that make up the revenue cycle. Refer to Table 2-1 for a list of common e-components of the revenue cycle.

Innovation of wireless technology has exploded with cell phones the length of a cigarette pack and as thin as a matchbook with infrared, web surfing, and picture taking capabilities. Hand-held devices known as **personal digital assistants (PDAs)** are becoming widely used because many health care workers are required to travel to different office locations and are inundated with reports, calls, medical data, etc. It is a small portable computer that utilizes internet wireless access, Microsoft desktop applications, phone directory, and calendar. These are being used to assist physicians in diagnosing illnesses, determining treatment, prescribing medication, assessing drug interactions, calculating dosages, and assigning codes at the bedside, at home, or in remote locations. Some of these PDAs are linked to hundreds of references. Physicians can track their hospital visits and charges in these and send this information to the office via email or directly into their office computer system. Technology allows providers and staff to be mobile and work in various locations, speeds up health information retrieval, and improves productivity and efficiency. BlackBerry and iPhones are also being used to access the Internet, manage physician schedules, and participate in podcasts, along with a host of other tasks. Cell phones are being used to not only access information but to document information by dictating into a voice recording system or using the keypad to document notes on patient visits and then synchronizing it with the electronic medical record (EMR). The cell phone is also projected to be used by patients as well for documenting medical situations to discuss with their doctors, receiving text message reminders to take medications, and to receive documentation of their office or hospital visits.

Practices today have a main server that all computers within the **local area network (LAN)** are connected to. This network is also called an intranet, which is private internet that is accessible by staff only. At DMA, MOSS is loaded on our server and all computers are networked to it. All data is stored on this sever and a **back up** is automatically performed daily at 9:00 pm. Back up refers to making a copy of every file on the server and storing it in a separate file for use in the event of a disaster, file corruption, or accidental deletion of data.

Computerization and **wide area networks (WANs)** have enabled physicians to open multiple clinic locations in their area while using the same computer system and database. WAN networks as opposed to LAN link together computers across a large geographical area. It is essentially two or more LANs connected by telephone lines. The networks can be wireless using electromagnetic waves (radio and infrared) to transmit

Table 2-1 E-Components of the Revenue Cycle

Revenue Cycle Component	Associated Software or System
Pre-Patient Visit	
Scheduling	Practice management software
Appointment reminders	Outside vendor software or component of practice management software
Preregistration	Practice management software
Preauthorization	Carrier website
Insurance verification	Practice management software or carrier website
Referral creation	Practice management software
Point of Care	
Point of care collection of copay or coinsurance	Practice management software
Registration and Insurance card scanning	Practice management software
Instant Messaging to nurse or doctor	Practice management software
Charge capture	Practice management software, Electronic Superbill/Charge Master
Clinical documentation	Practice management software -EHR module
Ancillary order entry	Order entry into hospital system, fax order to Facility
E-prescribing	Practice management software, pharmacy website
Coding	Practice management software, encoder
Real-time claims submission	Practice management software, clearinghouse software
Post-Visit	
Document imaging (lab tests, etc. that come from other offices)	Practice management software, interface with hospital system
Billing (for carriers not on real-time claim submission)	Practice management software clearinghouse
Accounts receivable	Practice management software, clearinghouse
Collections	Practice management software, outside vendor
Denial management	Practice management software, denial management software
Recovery audits	Recovery audit tracker software

data through the air at a predefined frequency. **Virtual private networks (VPNs)** allow external users to log into an organization's intranet and work as if they were onsite. It uses public networks but have a private circuit overlay. It is common place for business associates or vendors such as transcription companies to use this capability to transcribe dictation and upload it into the organization's computer system. VPNs are secure portals and provide flexibility for staff to work off site. A **portal** is an access point or gateway to a network that requires a user name and password. Hospitals are providing physicians and their office staff access to their computer systems through a portal to obtain lab, x-ray, and path results along with insurance and patient demographic information on patients admitted or referred by their respective practice.

Some insurance carriers have issued subscribers swipe cards that can be scanned at an office or facility to obtain a patient's medical benefits and eligibility. **Swipe Cards** are plastic cards representative of an insurance card that has a small processor and memory system with a magnetic stripe similar to a credit card. Information can be written to and read from the card. Office staff swipes an insurance card containing a magnetic strip or keys in the patient's identification number from a traditional insurance card, and enters only a few key data requirements. The system contains software that performs transaction functions over the Internet. The caveat to this is that to access this information, the office must have a card reader. The swipe card is being heavily considered as part of the solution for medical identity theft discussed later in this chapter. www.healthit.hhs.gov is a fabulous site to bookmark and stay abreast of changes in IT.

e-Prescribing

The Department of Health and Human Services, along with many other organizations is supportive of the e-Prescription initiative enabling physicians to prescribe medications by communicating directly with the pharmacy without writing a paper prescription. E-prescribing is an electronic way to generate prescriptions by entering required data directly into e-prescribing software and a transmission network that links to participating pharmacies. The e-prescribing initiative is part of the Medicare Improvements for Patients and Providers Act of 2008 and is published in the April 2, 2008 Federal Register. There are three electronic tools for use with e-prescribing:

1. **Formulary and benefit transactions**: lets providers know which drugs are covered by Medicare prescription drug plan.
2. **Medication history transactions**: gives providers information about the medications the patient is taking including those prescribed by other providers and any potential drug interactions.
3. **Fill status notification**: providers are electronically notified if the patient has picked up the prescription, not picked up their prescription, and whether the prescription was partially filled. From any web-enabled device e-prescriptions are ordered and delivered to retail and mail-order pharmacies.

Providers must use a qualified e-prescribing system either through an electronic health record (EHR) or a stand alone system. These systems can generate a complete list of patient medications, provide information on lower-cost alternatives if available, benefits information, and generate system warnings alerting the provider to possible drug interactions. Patients should provide consent to use e-prescribing. With the patient consent, all prescriptions are checked for potentially harmful interactions with the prescriptions the patient is currently taking. This is said to reduce medication errors due to illegible handwriting and alerts that can pop up in the database about refills, patient medical history to screen for drug contraindications, and drug interactions.

CMS has implemented the Electronic Prescribing (e-Prescribing) Incentive program. The program will provide an eligible professional with an incentive payment if the professional meets the program requirements for being a successful e-prescriber, which involves the reporting of a quality measure related to the use of e-prescribing technology. The e-prescribing incentive percent amount begins at 2.0 percent and is gradually reduced to 0.5 percent in the year 2013. The reason for this is because beginning in 2012, Medicare providers will be subject to a payment differential if they do not adopt e-prescribing. If an eligible par or nor-par Medicare provider is not determined by CMS to be a "successful electronic prescriber," the provider's professional fee schedule payments will be reduced by 1.0 percent in 2012, by 1.5 percent in 2013, and by 2.0 percent in 2014 and each subsequent year. This is just one example

Discussion:

Do some additional research about e-prescribing and its benefits. Do you think that the adoption of e-prescribing will reduce the amount of prescription drug dependence where physicians "enable" patients? What about reducing staff drug abuse when nurses and medical assistants call in unauthorized prescriptions and refills for fictitious patients or themselves?

___

___

___

of how technology is being mandated by the government as well as an example of how technology can improve health care.

The e-prescribing reporting measures are distinct from the Physician Quality Reporting Initiative (PQRI) reporting measures. (PQRI is discussed in chapter 5 of this simulation.) If the provider participates in both e-prescribing and PQRI, he is eligible for two incentive payments.

Software

Software consists of programs that allow us to operate a computer and electronically store data. We commonly use software to process data when typing letters in word processing applications such as Microsoft Word or in spreadsheets such as Microsoft Excel. Software has automated many functions in the office such as inventory, payroll, registration, billing, and accounting. We no longer type letters on a typewriter and can mass mail a letter via email or use the mail merge features in Word and print labels for our envelopes all at the same time. Excel is widely used to track accounts receivable and to report collections and write-offs. Days of keeping ledger books manually are gone. Many practice management systems have the ability to generate reports and export them to Word, Excel, or email for distribution and manipulation. Reports are generated to track insurance denials, outstanding claims, and patient balances at the click of a button. Excel and as well as other software programs enable facilities and provider offices to track expenses and inventory, trend revenue, and communicate, whether it be internally or externally, much more efficiently.

Software allows physicians to make medical decisions even when they are away from the office by providing all information needed to their phones. Capabilities include quick access to real-time patient information, ability to communicate with a local hospital ER, and e-prescribing.

Encoder

Technology has enhanced the skills of coding staff with the development of **encoder** software. Encoders are tools to assist the coder in assigning the most accurate and specific codes possible, grouping hospital inpatient services into (DRGs) and outpatient services into APCs. It prompts the coder with questions about the diagnoses and procedures entered to logically walk them through code assignment. Coding guidelines are built into the logic to guide code assignment. This software does not do the coding for you, it merely guides code assignment. The software contains information needed in calculating anticipated payments to the facility and will check codes against claim edits and payer policies. The software also includes reference material such as a medical dictionary, *Merck Manual, Coding Clinic, CPT Assistant,* etc., all available at the fingertips, and replaces the need to purchase expensive reference materials. Encoders are valuable tools to use in coding, but they are not a replacement for the traditional code book nor do they replace coder skill and experience. Coders must understand the logic of both ICD-9 and CPT coding guidelines to correctly answer the questions prompted by the software. Encoders are necessary in the inpatient setting but not widely used in physician offices. Software is available to assist coders in quickly locating codes and checking Medicare payment policies with a host of other features. Coders can search for codes by entering key words that are used to locate a code in the index of the code book. Included in this book is a printed access card for a 59-day trial of Encoder Pro.com software. You will have the opportunity to use this software first hand later in this book.

Internet

Insurance companies and providers alike are capitalizing on technology. Many offices have websites with practice policies, descriptions of providers and services, along with the capability to schedule appointments or communicate with office staff. Offices are using patient email addresses to confirm appointments and send patient statements. Companies are "going green" and reducing the amount of paper used by eliminating paper EOBs, provider newsletters, and patient statements and replacing them with electronic versions.

The Internet has opened up a wealth of knowledge and an avenue of information sharing amongst the medical community as well as assist in meeting the clinical needs of many communities lacking in trained clinicians. Computers are being used to obtain authorizations for prescription medications whereby before, it was a time consuming process of phone calls, faxes and request forms. CVS Caremark, BlueCross BlueShield of Tennessee and Horizon Blue Cross Blue Shield of New Jersey allow access to instant prior authorization status for medications.

Technology is allowed patients to be monitored from a remote location which enables providers to identify patients' conditions before they become acute and in many cases, reduces the number of visits to the ER and rehospitalization. Physicians can outsource radiology services to remote radiologists by emailing or having these physicians remotely access the provider's computer system to read and interpret digital radiographic studies such as MRI, CT scan, and chest x-rays. The availability of this information on the Internet has a positive impact on meeting the educational needs of physicians as well as coders and billers. As mentioned earlier, patients are using the Internet to obtain medical information about illnesses and plausible treatments. In fact, this electronic information is in most cases cutting-edge because the Internet can be updated in real-time and has been shown to be more accurate than printed texts. With access to the Internet, staff can query sources with coding questions, payer policies, clinical research, legislation changes, and code changes. The Internet enables staff to network with other professionals in organized discussion groups. Organizations in multiple locations can conduct online meetings called web conferencing and provide training to their staff without leaving their offices.

Payers, particularly Medicare, send email updates to those who subscribe to listservs. **LISTSERV** is a mailing list system that allows individuals to subscribe to an electronic mailing list. Mailing lists are email-based discussion groups where members can post questions and pose answers to other subscriber questions. Blast emails are sent out to members when recent information is posted or news is released. You may notice that email messages and websites contain **hypertext markup language (HTML)** and if you try to copy and paste data from these sources into a word document, it will not format properly. This is because this content is written in a special computer language that uses custom codes called tags. This is necessary to display information on the Internet and for creating web pages. It is recommended that coders subscribe to their state Medicare carrier at a minimum. By doing so, this will keep them current in changes in coverage, payer policy, and requirements for coding and billing.

Exercise 2.0 Your Turn to Try

Ingenix is a widely recognized supplier of coding and billing resources. Its website also has a dedicated location entitled *Coding Circle* with interesting articles, industry updates, and practice coding scenarios. Visit this site at www.shopingenix.com and click on *Industry Resources* and then *Coding Circle*. Spend some time reviewing recent articles and products offered through Ingenix. Take the coding challenge and try your hand at many of the coding cases and see if you get the right answers. Present a case to your class and discuss the rationale for reaching the correct answer.

Carriers have taken strides to provide information on their websites to providers, staff, and patients on their websites. Information is geared to the audience. Providers can log in and check coverage policies, fee schedules, claims status, patient eligibility and benefits, and a host of other things.

CMS's website offers day-to-day operating instructions, policies, and procedures based on statutes and regulations, guidelines, models, and directives. All of their policies are located here. The most common and widely used CMS publications are listed in Table 2-2. CMS, through their Medicare Learning Network, has also developed an informative site with web-based training courses that can be taken free of charge. They also publish Medlearn Matters articles that are blasted out to members of the LISTSERV on a gambit of topics. These are also archived on the site. Because most carriers model themselves after Medicare's coverage and payment policies, it is important that all coders and billers familiarize themselves with this website.

Table 2-2 CMS Website

Feature	Topic/Use	URL and/or Site Directions
Internet Only Manual	Includes CMS's program issuances, policies and procedures based on statutes, regulations, guidelines, models, and directives used by CMS contractors and state survey agencies to administer the CMS programs.	http://www.cms.hhs.gov. Click on *Regulations and Guidance, Manuals,* and then *Internet Only Manual (IOM).*
Publication 100-03	National Coverage Determinations	
Publication 100-04	Medicare Claims Processing	
Publication 100-05	Medicare Secondary Payer Manual	
Publication 100-08	Program Integrity Manual	
Publication 100-09	Medicare Contractor Beneficiary and Provider Communications Manual	
Publication 100-14	ESRD Network Organizations Manual	
Publication 100-16	Medicare Managed Care Manual	
Publication 100-18	Medicare Prescription Drug Benefit Manual	
Local Coverage Determinations (LCD)	An LCD is a decision by a CMS carrier concerning whether to cover a particular service on a carrier-wide basis in accordance with Section 1862(a)(1)(A) of the Social Security Act. Language is specific to frequency, ICD-9 codes, and CPT codes as to whether services are reasonable and necessary.	http://www.cms.hhs.gov. Click on *Medicare, then Medicare Coverage Determination Process,* and then *Local Coverage Determinations.*
CMS Transmittals	Used to communicate new or changed policies and/or procedures being incorporated into a specific CMS program manual. The cover page summarizes the change for quick reading.	http://www.cms.hhs.gov. Click on Regulations and Guidance and then Transmittals.
Fee Schedule Updates	Fee schedules for various lines of business are available. Used to look up RVU and status indicators along with other elements to determine physician payment. Fee Schedule Lookup Tool.	http://www.cms.hhs.gov. Click on *Medicare* and then *Fee Schedules.*
Coding Updates	These files contain the Level II alphanumeric HCPCS procedure and modifier codes, their long and short descriptions, and applicable Medicare administrative, coverage, and pricing data. HCPCS quarterly updates are located here. View and print HCPCS file, ICD updates.	http://www.cms.hhs.gov. Click on *Medicare* and then under *Coding,* click on *HCPCS Release and Code Sets* or *ICD-9Update.*
Ambulatory Surgery Center (ASC) Information	Material is divided by provider type so that the ASC section has everything in one location related to payment, policy, coding, and enrollment.	http://www.cms.hhs.gov. Click on *Medicare* and under *Browse by Provider Type* click on *Ambulatory Surgical Centers (ASC) Center.*
Medicare Learning Network	The Medicare Learning Network is the official CMS provider education product line designed to promote national consistency of Medicare provider information and provide ready access to materials providing further explanation about CMS initiatives. The network publishes articles called Medlearn Matters, offers online courses, and offers a host of other mechanisms to deliver education.	http://www.cms.hhs.gov. Click on *Outreach and Education.*
Correct Coding Initiative	Used to check for column I codes, column II codes, mutually exclusive codes, and medically unlikely edits when submitting claims for Medicare patients.	http://www.cms.hhs.gov. Click on *Medicare* and then under *Coding,* click on *National Correct Coding Initiative Edit or Outpatient Code Editor,* depending on which type of claim is submitted.

Exercise 2.1 Your Turn to Try

Caitlin Barrymoore has an appointment tomorrow. You are working the front desk today and one of your tasks is to check benefits for patients on the schedule tomorrow. MOSS has a feature that allows staff to quickly check insurance benefits for select payers. Proceed through the following steps to check her insurance status before you leave for the day.

Step 1 From the main menu in MOSS, select *Online Eligibility.*

Step 2 Search for our patient, Caitlin Barrymoore.

Step 3 Select her name and click on the *Send to Payer* button.

Step 4 View the report. Is the patient eligible?

Step 5 Print out the report and turn it in to your instructor. This will be filed in her medical record.

The Internet has enabled patients as consumers to shop around for health care. Patients can read online reviews about physicians and facilities regarding customer service, cost of care, and complication rates. Patients are becoming more empowered to choose their health care providers particularly those with traditional commercial indemnity plan coverage and those with health care spending accounts and self-insured plans. The uninsured patient has a particular need to shop for the lowest health care treatment available and they can do so now by researching **provider report cards** online. Physician and hospital report cards are similar to ratings published by *Consumer Reports* for a particular product comparing various features of the product like cost, durability, and quality across many brands in an effort to educate the public about the strengths and weaknesses of each product, ultimately guiding the consumer in choosing a high quality product for the least cost: the same concept applies for providers. Providers of the same specialty are compared based on several factors such as infection rate, mortality and morbidity rates, patient satisfaction, cost of services, education, and practice patterns. Historically, providers are not effectively held accountable—by governments, consumers (the patients), or medical professional associations—for the quality of care they provide. One method of increasing provider accountability is making this information available to the general public, which ultimately affects the providers' pockets. The better a provider's score the more apt patients will choose them for health care needs. Likewise, the providers with the higher quality and satisfaction score have greater influence with insurance carriers when negotiating contracts. The Healthgrades.com website compares physicians in a particular area and publishes reliable ballpark figures of average "list" prices or submitted charged by providers and negotiated payment rates by insurers for over 50 different procedures. It also includes doctors' schooling and disciplinary action history as well as ratings of local hospital providing all of this information at the fingertips. Websites such as U.S. Department of Health and Human Services (http://www.hospitalcompare.hhs.gov) are publishing data about how hospitals measure up in providing quality health care for a prescribed set of medical conditions. This site is a collaborative effort between CMS and DHHS to publicly promote quality health care by informing patients of those facilities that score high and in these areas. Data is gathered from hospitals that voluntarily report information about these prescribed medical conditions as well as from patients who were treated at these hospitals.

Discussion:

How do you think coding is related to or has an effect on provider report cards?

Telehealth Services

The Internet has made it possible for rural and under served medical communities to communicate with healthcare professionals. Clinics in remote locations can now interact and consult with specialists via satellite or web cam. This concept is referred to as **telemedicine** or telehealth. Telemedicine is essentially the delivery of some form of health care information or service via telecommunication via phone or Internet. It can be as simple as a telephone call or email or a complex interaction via video teleconferencing. It may also mean the use of remote medical devices that track and transmit health data from patient to physician. It requires the presence of both parties at the same time and a communications link between them that allows a real-time interaction to take place. Remote monitoring solutions enable healthcare providers to identify patients' conditions before they become acute. This technology can reduce ER visits and rehospitalizations.

Video-conferencing equipment is one of the most common forms of technologies used. There are also high-tech devices which can be attached to computers or the video-conferencing equipment that relay information to the receiver for interpretation and feedback such as a tele-otoscope which allows a remote physician to 'see' inside a patient's ear. Specialists can receive ancillary tests results and EKG strips and well as high definition films such as CT scans and MRIs and provide treatment recommendations where otherwise patients would have to travel several hours to a metropolitan community to seek this care. Telehealth offers options to patients and allows them to discuss embarrassing issues such as erectile dysfunction or bladder incontinence with their provider where otherwise they would be reluctant to being face to face. Studies show that patients like having the capability to talk with their providers in this format because it eliminates unnecessary visits to the office or ER and reduces wait time in the office waiting room. They get their medical advise in writing so they can refer it later if need be. These studies have also showed that providers who communicate through email to their patients are more productive.

In 2008 codes were adopted for reporting telemedicine services and are specific to who provided the service—a physician or non-physician. While there are codes that exist for telemedicine, that doesn't mean the services are reimbursed. As of 2009, CMS only pays for patient evaluations that are done during face-to-face visits.

Submitting Telehealth Claims

CMS has very specific guidelines for reporting telehealth services. According to *Publication 100-04 Medicare Claims Processing Manual, Section 190*, claims for professional consultations, office visits, individual psychotherapy, and pharmacologic management provided via a telecommunications systems are submitted to the carrier with the appropriate CPT procedure code for covered professional telehealth services along with the GT or GQ modifier. The HCPCS book defines modifier GT as "via interactive video and video telecommunication systems" and GQ as "via asynchronous telecommunication system." These modifiers are to accompany codes that are considered to be telehealth services.

By coding and billing the GT or GQ modifier with a covered telehealth procedure code, the distant site physician/practitioner certifies that the beneficiary was present at an eligible originating site when the telehealth service was furnished. Physicians and practitioners at the distant site bill their local Medicare carrier for covered telehealth services, for example, "90862-GT." Physicians' and practitioners' offices serving as telehealth originating sites should bill their local Medicare carrier for the originating site facility fee with HCPCS code Q3014, *Telehealth originating site facility fee*. Covered telehealth services include CPT codes 99241–99275, 99201–99215, 90801, 90804–90809, 90862, and G0308-G0318. When furnished as telehealth services these codes are billed with either the "GT" or "GQ" modifier.

Electronic Data Interchange

Some of the changes with the way health care has adopted technology is being mandated by HIPAA and payer policies. With the implementation of the HIPAA law came **HIPAA Transaction and Code Sets Standards**. These standards were meant to streamline and improve the efficiency of health care electronic transactions. These standards were set to require electronic transmission of health data to be done in a standardized format recognizable by all payers. The official adoption of ICD-9, CPT, and HCPCS code sets for use in all health care transactions is part of this law. Insurance claims transmitted digitally over the Internet to a carrier or clearinghouse is called an **electronic claim**. Very few claims are printed hard copy these days. Secondary insurance claims, some Workers' Compensation, liability cases where a third party is responsible for the claim such as in personal injury, and the very small insurance plans are the only claims sent paper since the adoption of the electronic claim.

The exchange of health care and financial information electronically over the Internet or phone lines between insurance carriers, providers, and their financial institutions is called **electronic data interchange (EDI)**. Any patient or health-related information shared by EDI must conform to a certain format called ASC X12. This was determined as part of the HIPAA rule. Examples of format and their uses are in Table 2-3.

Insurance carriers are moving toward reducing the amount of paper required in the course of processing insurance claims and payments. Insurance carriers are requiring preauthorization to be done online now versus calling and speaking to an insurance representative. They are also requiring providers to submit claims electronically and receive payments electronically through EFT. This is an aftershock of HIPAA Administrative Simplification Act. There are a few exceptions to this rule, however. If a practice is small and has less than 10 full-time employees, it would qualify for exemption of this rule and can continue to send paper claims. Electronic claims are not required for filing claims to secondary insurance carriers.

Real-time Claims Submission and Adjudication

More and more emphasis is being placed on how quickly claims are filed and adjudicated. Some clearinghouses and payers now have the sophistication to not only allow staff to track the progress of a claim and to fix claim errors at the time of submission but to also automate patient eligibility and claim status with hundreds of payers in real-time. ***Real-time*** is a computer term that describes the time an application receives information and how quickly it responds. With real-time, the information is received and the application immediately responds without any time delay so as to appear instantaneous. If a vendor has the capability to communicate in real-time with a payer, the provider will know instantaneously if a claim is rejected by the payer, not just by a clearinghouse: this concept is referred to as **real-time claim submission**. Providers are increasingly concerned about the impact of consumer-directed health care plans and high-deductible health plans because these plans require patients to pay more out-of-pocket

Table 2-3 Examples of ASC X12 Transactions and Use

HIPAA EDI Transaction	Use
X12-270/271 Health Care Eligibility Benefit Inquiry and Response	Staff can inquire online and request copies of a patient's insurance eligibility and benefits to confirm coverage for a service.
X12-837P Health Care Claim or Encounter	This is the actual claim file sent to carriers with information about the provider, patient, diagnoses, procedures, and charges.
X12-276/277 Health Care Claim Status Request and Response	Providers will contact payers to determine status of unpaid claims.
X12-278 Health Care Services Review-Request for Review and Response	Some plans require approval to seek a specialist or to have certain services rendered. This is done electronically by entering required information online.
X12-835 Claims Payment and Remittance Advice	Electronic version of the traditional EOB, outlining charges received, allowed charges, reductions, payments, and patient responsibility. The payment is sent electronically to the provider's bank account via **electronic funds transfer (EFT)** as in a direct deposit. The **Electronic Remittance Advice (ERA)** is sent to the provider via a clearinghouse. The provider can also download these from payer websites.

than traditional indemnity plans. The practice's ability to collect timely payment from their patients with these plans is very difficult not only because of the high out-of-pocket but because many of these plans don't provide a quick and hassle-free way to check benefits, eligibility, and claims status. With real-time adjudication, the provider can bill for services and get a fully adjudicated response back from the carrier before the patient leaves the office. The provider can print out the response, showing the total charge submitted, allowable charges, and the patient's responsibility (coinsurance, deductible, and copayment). This capability will confirm for the providers the amount the patient should pay at the time of service. With instant patient eligibility and benefits inquiry, the office can obtain any patient financial responsibility upfront and attempt to collect on this prior to the visit or at the very least at the time of service. Blue Cross Blue Shield and United HealthCare are two large carriers with this functionality. Visit http://www.unitedhealthcareonline.com, read about their real-time adjudication method, and look at the accompanying flowchart to visualize this process.

Clearinghouse

The majority of providers are complying with the electronic billing mandate because claims are processed much faster than paper claims. In order to be HIPAA compliant with claims format and code, providers contract with a clearinghouse to transmit claims on their behalf. A **clearinghouse** is a business associate that is contracted by a provider to receive electronic insurance claim files from the provider. The clearinghouse receives the claims **batch**, which is made up of several claims released as a group and submitted as one file on a given day. It checks the claims for errors and omitted information and then forwards them to the insurance carrier by transmitting them electronically in the HIPAA-compliant format. The process of checking or auditing the claim against predefined items is called **scrubbing**. The software checks for completion of all mandatory fields on the claim form. It should catch data entry mistakes such as the sex of the patient not consistent with the procedure performed (prostate screening on a female patient) or missing subscriber date of birth and so on. If the clearinghouse software discovers an error or omission, it will generate an edit back to the provider for correction. The **edit** will describe to the provider what the error is so it can be corrected and resent. This process will continue until the claim is *clean* meaning without errors and will then be forwarded to the carrier.

Once the carrier forwards the claim to the carrier it goes through a series of steps to validate the claim and determine payment. This process is called **adjudication**. During this process the claim is screened against payer edits and the patient's health plan coverage benefits. It is determined whether the claim is a duplicate claim that has been submitted previously and if required information is present to process the claim. Once the claim is screened, one of four things will happen:

1. The claim will be rejected back to the clearinghouse because information is not complete or patient names do not match what is on file in the database.
2. Procedures or services submitted will be denied because they are a non-covered benefit. The carrier will not reimburse the provider for these services, but the provider can bill the patient.
3. Procedures or services that were not preauthorized are denied as unauthorized services. Managed care plans will compare procedures and the date that a service is performed for services that must be preauthorized. This means that the payer requires certain services or procedures to be authorized or approved by the payer prior to the patient receiving the treatment. If this is not done, the claim will be denied. In this case, the patient can't be billed for the service. These balances will be written off by the provider.
4. The carrier deems the claim to be processable and the claim is paid. Payment is mailed to the provider in the form of a check or via electronic funds transfer.

Electronic Remittance Advice (Era)

Electronic Remittance Advice (ERA) replaces the traditional hard copy Explanation of Benefits (EOB). These documents house the payment information from the carrier to the provider. It serves as a way of communicating with the provider about the charges submitted, what was paid, what was denied, if a patient's deductible has been satisfied, and how much the patient owes for a particular date of service. The ERA has all of the same data elements as the former EOB, including: patient name, account number, CPT codes, charges, allowed amount, deductible, coinsurance, payment amount, and nonallowed amounts. Medicare calls this ERA a Provider Remittance Notice (PRN) and the paper copy that is sent to the patient is called a Medicare Summary Notice (MSN). Business office staff is responsible for keying this information into the computer system and determining if payments are correct. This is discussed in chapters 3 and 4 in greater detail. Chapter 3 will explain how to read the ERA and how to post the payments in MOSS. With advances in computer software development and EDI, some systems are able to import ERA data directly into their systems and bypass human data entry. This process is called **autoposting**. With autoposting, payments are automatically posted into the respective patient accounts and adjustments are made based on what the ERA lists as the charge amount, allowed amount, and paid amount.

Exercise 2.2 Your Turn to Try

Visit the SolAce Electronic Medical Claims website at http://www.snapinhipaa.com. Under *Product Summary* watch the flash demo. It walks you through how a clearinghouse software product interfaces with practice management software. It walks the viewer through the entire process from entering the charges to receiving the electronic remittance.

Internet Websites For Coders And Billers

The Internet is a wonderful tool for coders and billers to use. Coders can run searches on a specific disease or surgical procedure they are not familiar with. Practices that belong to the American Medical Association or a specialty association such as the American Academy of Family Practice can access coding help lines sponsored by these organizations. The help lines allow members to submit questions and get advice on how to assign codes for particular conditions or services. They also have blogs for members to communicate with other members about coding, billing, insurance, and practice management. These sites are helpful to coder/biller working in a specific specialty. For example, if you were working for an orthopaedic practice, the American Academy of Orthopaedic Surgeons would be a site you would probably visit frequently. There are many other sites that are useful to all coders/billers regardless of specialty such as the CMS website. Table 2-4 illustrates organizations and websites that coders/billers can access to get updates on codes as well as a host of other things. This list is by no means an all inclusive list but merely a snapshot of the most commonly used sites. Some of these sites have the option to sign up for LISTSERVs while others must be checked periodically. It is a good idea to bookmark many of these for quick access.

The Internet can assist business office staff with locating patients who have moved and not updated their information with the office. It is commonplace to have patient statements and correspondence be returned with *Address Unknown, Forwarding Address Expired,* or *Return to Sender.* There are many websites available to search such as the *White Pages.com* by patient name, city, and state. It is noteworthy to mention here that most of these sites are not free and a fee must be paid to obtain the information once it is located.

Coders should be members of at least one of the following professional associations: American Academy of Professional Coders (AAPC) (http://www.aapc.com) and the American Health Information Management Association (AHIMA) (http://www.ahima.org). Members can access journals and publications not otherwise accessible.

Table 2-4 Useful Internet Sites to the Coder/Biller

Website Name	URL	Content/Use
American Medical Association (AMA)	http://www.ama-assn.org	CPT Errata, CPT changes, fee schedule changes and impact to practices, Category II and III releases
Centers for Medicare and Medicaid Services (CMS)	http://www.cms.hhs.gov	HCPCS code changes, HCPCS Errata, Medicare national policies, eligibility, claim status, fee schedules, Correct Coding Initiative (CCI) edits, links to other related sites, coordination of benefits, CLIA waived tests, HIPAA general information, education, Medicare Learning Network (MLN), E/M coding guidelines, and so much more.
National Center for Health Statistics (NCHS)	http://www.cdc.gov	ICD-9 coding guidelines, ICD-9 code changes
Office of the Inspector General (OIG)	http://www.oig.hhs.gov	Compliance, annual work plan, regulatory guidance, semi-annual report regarding coding errors. Staff can also check this site to see if providers or staff have been sanctioned from the Medicare program.
Federal Register	http://www.gpoaccess.gov	Updates in federal laws, Balanced Budget Act
MEDLINEplus	http://medlineplus.gov	National Institutes of Health provides a medical dictionary, information on more than 600+ diseases, and information on drugs.
Health HIPPO	http://hippo.findlaw.com	Provides policy and regulatory materials related to health care.
HIPAA Privacy Statements	http://aspe.hhs.gov	HIPAA tools and news releases
Gray's Anatomy Online	http://www.bartleby.com/107/	Coders can search by body part and view anatomical pictures and text
Coding and Reimbursement Net	http://www.codingandreimbursement.net	Networking tool, shared resources
RiteCode.com	http://www.ritecode.com	Free quizzes, free forms, coding links, coding tips, and lots more
Acronym Finder	http://www.acronymfinder.com	Easy search capability for medical abbreviations
JustCoding.com	http://www.justcoding.com	Coding advice, member Q&A, news releases, discussion groups, practice exam questions, coding and billing links
American Medical Billing Association	http://www.ambanet.net	Discounts on billing products, discussion forum, certification for billers, online classes, and resources for starting a medical billing company.
National Plan and Provider Enumeration System (NPPES)	https://nppes.cms.hhs.gov	This is a national provider identification number registry; staff can enter a referring physician's name and city and obtain his/her NPI number to complete the claim form instead of having to call the referring physician's office.
The Coding Institute	http://www.codinginstitute.com	Education opportunities, coding support, newswires, publications

Exercise 2.3 Your Turn to Try

1. The patient is 68-years-old and is being seen in the clinic today by Dr. Schwartz for the first time. The patient was seen three years ago by Dr. Mendenhall for a preventative Welcome to Medicare exam. She is here today for complaints of muscle and joint pain and overall fatigue. History and exam were comprehensive. Medical decision making was moderate. Which code is billed for this patient—99204 or 99214?

____

Visit the American Academy of Family Physicians website (www.aafp.org) and search the site for guidance. Select *Family Practice Management* and then *Coding Resources and Assistance.* Scan through the documents and open the *FPM Decision Tree for New vs Established Patients.*

2. You notice as you are coding and entering charges that Dr. Heath tends to bill more level 1 office visits than the other doctors. After checking into things, it turns out he downcodes E/M visits for his lower-income patients so they don't have to pay a higher coinsurance. Take some time to peruse the Academy's site again in search of advice or guidance in this situation. What is their recommendation?

____

____

Electronic Medical Records

The traditional medical record is recorded and stored in the paper form. Maintaining records can be an overwhelming task to manage since offices generate and receive so much paper coupled with transporting these records to multiple office locations. With this in mind, the shift is towards **electronic medical records** (EMR, EHR). The driving force behind EMRs is increasing the efficiency of health care delivery, which usually means saving/making money and improving patient care through enhanced communication of medical information between health care workers, facilities, patients, and third-party payers. Some believe that the EMR can do both reduce costs and improve quality of care. Most providers think that adopting the EMR will produce little savings and fear that they will be able to see fewer patients after implementation. The ARRA authorizes CMS to provide a reimbursement incentive for physicians and hospitals who are successful in becoming "meaningful users" of an electronic health record (EMR, EHR). These incentive payments begin in 2011 and gradually phase down. Starting in 2015, providers are expected to have adopted and be actively utilizing an EHR in compliance with the "meaningful use" definition or they will be subject to financial penalties under Medicare.

Wal-Mart is now offering EMR systems through Sam's Club stores. These packages cater to small physician practices. Sams' Club has teamed with Dell for the systems' computer hardware and eClinicalWorks for the EMR solution. Wal-Mart is currently using this software in its in-store healthcare clinics. With as techno savvy as other industries are, the healthcare community has been somewhat slow to embrace this technology with respect to record keeping. Concerns stem from workflow disruptions, implementation and maintenance costs, and time required to train staff on how to use it.

The health care arena is in a state of transition from paper health records and manual processes in data collection, claims submission, and practice management to a virtual office where many if not most functions will be automated in one degree or another. Legally there is some debate from state to state about whether or not the electronic record is considered a legal medical record. Currently as it stands, each state's definition of a legal medical record may differ. With respect to legal rights of electronic health records, further clarification is needed about who owns the information. Property rights in electronic form at the time of this writing have not been finalized.

In the medical profession, everything centralizes about electronic health and financial information flow, usage, and how we communicate this information. The information is liquid as it follows patients through care and treatment to claim submission and payment and beyond. This liquidity allows for many more uses of this data by providers, public health, insurance carriers, and health policy researchers. The government is moving towards a bill that will require all providers to adopt electronic record. The Health Information Technology for Economic and Clinical Health Act was introduced in 2009 as part of an economic stimulus package. It provides US with $20 billion for the creation of a national electronic health records system that would fundamentally improve the way in which health information is electronically accessed, stored, and shared.

There are many advantages to the EMR:

- Everyone can perform their work without having to wait for a record to arrive or be completed. This expedites the workflow and increases revenues since coding staff has immediate access to the information and business office staff can quickly generate a bill.
- EMR reduces expenses involving staff because they are no longer needed to retrieve and deliver the record to the appropriate location. About 50% of charts pulled are for nonpatient visits. These are records that are needed for correspondence requests, referrals, prescription refills, studies, etc.
- Physicians no longer have to delay seeing patients or see them without the assistance of the information in the medical record since they can log on to a computer and pull up the information they need.
- Security of an Electronic Record may be superior to the old fashioned paper version. EMR systems routinely require password protections, **audit trails** that allow managers to monitor what staff members viewed what and when, as well as **access controls** that limit employees to what they can view or edit. Access is given on an as needed basis for activities required to perform their specific jobs.
- Business office staff can email information directly from the medical record to the insurance company and public agencies when requests from insurance carriers are received.
- EMR is said to employ a more complete medical record. The physician has a complete record to review, making diagnosing easier. Templates are developed to prompt physicians' documentation where they can fill in the blanks. EMR and the Internet enable the physician or provider to be more thorough in their history taking. It also eliminates prescribing errors by alerting the physician of drug interactions or other risk factors in the patient's history.
- Communication is improved between all care takers: nurses, specialists, labs, pharmacist, and physicians with linked electronic records.

EMRs can be Internet-based where information is encrypted or the more traditional electronic record where patient information stays on a local server. **Encryption** is a method of converting plain text into cipher text, which is similar to a secret code. It cannot be deciphered without a key. This code is embedded into HTML and is a way of achieving security of electronic data sent over the Internet. To this point, many offices and hospitals have been reluctant to adopt electronic records primarily because of the cost outlay for hardware, software, training, and support along with the looming potential downtime if the system goes down or if there is a power outage.

EMRs must be equipped with an audit function to account for all disclosures of PHI as discussed in chapter 1. The system must be able to provide a user friendly report accounting for all information disclosed, to whom, and when. Patient's now have a right to receive a full accounting of PHI disclosures through the EMR through the HITECH Act.

What happens when the power goes out or there are problems with the server and the computers are non-functional? How does an office continue to operate without them? This is a day that everyone dreads and thankfully these days are few and far between. Baring any natural disasters or freak ice storms, computer networks are very reliable. Offices should either contract with a trained computer technician or have one on staff. If the system goes down, immediately contact your computer tech. Back-ups are performed every day in preparation for days such as these. At the end of each day, front office staff prints a schedule for the following day for each provider. If the system is down, at least the office knows which patients have appointments. Staff must rely on the patient's insurance card or notes in the paper record to determine how much to collect from them until the system is restored. Follow-up appointments can't be scheduled so as patients are checked out, a list is maintained with patient names and timeframes for the next appointment, and calls will be made as soon as the system is working. Messages must be taken by staff for patients calling to schedule an appointment for other than the current day, to be returned when the system is restored. Any urgent patient calls are referred to the emergency room. Routers will be completed by the provider and maintained in the billing department until the system is restored. Money collected from patients will be written on a balance sheet. Deposit slips will be completed and a copy will be kept with the balance sheet for posting when the system is operational. Billing cannot be performed until the system is back up and running. If the system is down for more than one day, front office staff will have to pull charts as patients arrive for appointments.

Computers are an invaluable asset to health care. However, computers do not replace people. Whether performing billing or coding functions, staff must be diligent when entering data. The computer can scrub against some predefined elements, but it can process only what is entered by us. The old saying goes "Garbage in is garbage out." It starts with us doing a thorough job of collecting accurate information from our patients and providers and is finished by staff entering this data without error. Computers can assist coding and billing staff by speeding up the process in which we do our jobs and enable us to stay current in our profession if staff is trained to use this tool to its fullest.

The American Medical Informatics Association (AMIA) is dedicated to promoting the effective organization, analysis, management, and use of information in health care in support of patient care, public health, teaching, research, administration, and related policy. They are a forerunner organization in the initiative of development and implementation of health information and communications technology and the adoption of the EMR. They play a pivotal role in the lobbying with Washington and have members sit on the Health Information Technology Policy Committee, a new advisory body to the U.S. Government Accountability Office (GAO) established by the American Recovery and Reinvestment Act. The committee will make recommendations on creating a policy framework for the development and adoption of a nationwide health information technology infrastructure, including standards for the exchange of patient medical information. They are a major contributor in aligning the health care workforce with technology through their assistance in educating and leading colleges in drafting program and certification competencies in an effort to grow competent health care workers able to work in this highly technical environment of health information technology. Visit their website and bookmark it to stay abreast of changes in health care technology and impact on how care is delivered and recorded in practices (www.amia.org). Their website includes an e-learning center offering a wide variety of educational workshops, some at no cost.

Personal Health Records (PHR)

The practice of e-medicine is shifting some of the responsibility of health record keeping to the patient from the provider. A **personal health record (PHR)** is an electronic health record that is initiated and maintained by an individual-the patient. E-medicine allows the patient to enter their own medical history and update their record as necessary and viewed by any as a way to reduce data entry errors. Who else would know more about your health, wellness, current prescriptions, and care received by any and all providers you have been treated by better than you? The PHR function is to consolidate a patient's medical information into one place with the anticipated goal of reducing medical errors, improving quality of care, and improving the validity of information available to care providers regardless of where the provider or patient is located.

Organizations such as the American Health Information Management Association (AHIMA) are marketing this concept to its membership to stimulate the mainstream public in creating and maintaining their own health record. AHIMA defines the personal health record (PHR) as "an electronic, lifelong resource of health information needed by individuals to make health decisions." Individuals own and manage the information in the PHR which comes from various healthcare providers as well as themselves. It is maintained in a secure environment online, with the individual determining rights of access. The PHR does not replace the legal record of any provider. User Centric, Inc (www.usercentric.com) has identified several guidelines to be considered in a working model for PHR interfaces and developing a more usable PHR. Through PHR technology, patients can receive test results from their physicians, manage insurance information and patient accounts, and get reminders about checkups or treatments to name a few.

There is discussion that new and evolving technologies will enable PHR to work with Next Generation 9-1-1, Public Safety Emergency Response Systems, General Motors' OnStar, Mercedes-Benz TeleAid, and BMW Assist to provide first responders with the individual's medical information to expedite medical treatment decisions and reduce morbidity and mortality.

Health plans are beginning to partner with software vendors to provide PHR to patients. Payers can automatically populate the PHR with demographic, financial, benefit, and medical procedure data. Patients can then add information if they choose to do so. CMS is providing a pilot program for beneficiaries whereby they can select one of the commercial PHR tools and Medicare will load up to two years of the patient's claims data in to their PHR. PHR software is available now for individuals to enter their personal information that can provide sophisticated features such as data encryption, data importation from healthcare facilities and provider offices, and data sharing with health care providers. Some PHR products allow the downloading of health records to a mass-storage device such as a CD-ROM, DVD, smart card, or USB flash drive; this way when you travel you can take a USB flash drive with all of our personal information in case of emergency!

Security of Electronic Records

Protecting electronic data from unauthorized access was thought to be easier than protecting the former traditional paper record but as healthcare providers have come to realize, it's not as easy as first thought. The magnitude and extent of information access and data breach is vastly larger than the paper record and carries a much greater risk of exposure and penalty. Devices used to access and record electronic PHI are mobile and at risk for loss or tampering. According to a survey conducted by Deloitte & Touche and the Ponemon Institute, 85% of privacy and security professionals reported a data breach: 66% of the respondents reported multiple data breaches. Laptops, Smartphones, and other mobile devices have become more than a convenience but rather a necessity in today's healthcare environment. Computer viruses also play a role in the risk of losing or altering information stored on these devices as well as the network it operates on. When the device is disconnected from the network and used remotely, it doesn't get important updates such as antivirus and antispyware programs and when the device is brought back onsite and reconnected with the network, the infected device can then attack the corporate network. All servers, desktops, laptops, and mobile devices should be scanned and updated with the most recent software patches as soon as they are available from the software developers. Some computers systems are equipped with **remote wipe** capability. This software enables systems to remotely wipe a device clean after a set number of failed attempts to log into the device in an effort to protect the data. This also allows the owner of the device to send a "kill" code to lost device making it inoperable.

Identity theft is on the rise and the healthcare arena is continually looking for ways to protect patient information for such theft. Identity Theft Red Flags Rule went into effect November 1, 2009. This rule specifically focuses on an organization's ability to prevent identity theft and medical identity theft by implementing a program designed to detect the warning signs or "red flags" of identity theft in their day-to-day operations. **Medical identity theft** happens when a person seeks health care using someone else's name or insurance information. The Federal Trade Commission estimates that 9 million Americans have their identities stolen each year with medical identity theft accounting for 4.5% of that. Victims of medical identity theft can find themselves faced with enormous medical bills or cancellation of their insurance coverage. Entities covered under this rule are those that offer credit or payment plans to patients. A creditor is broadly described as anyone who defers payment on a debt, or anyone who defers payment on goods or services. If a provider or facility offers payment plans then they fall under the category of creditor. This rule requires all creditors to implement a program to identify patterns, practices, and specific forms of activity (i.e red flags) that allude to the existence of identity theft. The rule lists an extensive number of flags to identify. Have you ever wondered why provider offices ask for photo ID? Now you do. The program is required to be reviewed annually. The Red Flag Rules compliment the HIPAA law in its goal to protect patient privacy and the security of their information. The Federal Trade Commission published a document entitled *Fighting Fraud With The Red Flags Rule: A How-To Guide for Business* to assist providers with implementing their own program.

Internet Exercise

1. Visit CMS's website (http://www.cms.hhs.gov) and take the following web-based courses: Understanding the Remittance Advice for Professional Providers and CMS Form 1500 (08/05). To locate the courses, select *Outreach and Education* and then *MLN Educational Web Guides*. Select *Web Based Training (WBT) Modules*. Select each course. Turn your certificate of completion in to your instructor.
2. Dr. Schwartz has been treating a patient for migraine headaches. He wants to begin injecting the patient's forehead and base of the skull with Botox. This has been proven to be effective in treating chronic migraine sufferers. The patient has Aetna insurance. The doctor has asked you to research this with their plan and see if this is a covered service or if this needs to be preauthorized. Go to the carrier website at www.aetna.com and search for the answer. Select *Clinical Policy Bulletins* to begin your search. ____________________
3. Dr. Heath provides 20 minutes of psychiatric counseling to a Medicare patient during an E/M visit. Patient is experiencing anxiety and depression. What is the patient's coinsurance percentage for this service? Go to the CMS website www.cms.hhs.gov or the local carrier for your state to investigate.
____
4. Dr. Schwartz provides an inpatient follow-up telehealth consult. How is this to be reported for this Medicare patient? The exam was not provided but an expanded interval history was performed and medical decision making of moderate complexity. Search CMS's Carrier Manual publication 100-04 chapter 12 to find this information. ____________________
5. Visit the Wireless Healthcare website at www.wirelesshealthcare.co.uk and read about how technology is being used in healthcare. Read the article 101 Things to do with a mobile phone in Healthcare. Discuss with your class the top five uses you thought are the most likely to be used or adopted and why. Which ones did you think are less likely to be used?
____
6. Visit Codapedia, the largest collaborative online encyclopedia for medical coding and reimbursement for physician services website at www.codapedia.com. Discuss with your class the usefulness of this website and choose a topic of interest and share it with your classmates.
____

7. Visit AskTheMedicalSpecialist.com and review the types of questions being asked of physicians online. How do you see this benefits patients? Do you think this will open discussions with the patient and their own physician? Do you think the answers being given to patient questions are thorough and providing sound advice? Do you think that some patients may use this type of service as a replacement for their own personal physician?

____

8. Search the Internet to determine if New York has guidance on the legal definition of a medical record and ownership rights of an electronic medical record. If so, please describe and provide the website used to gather your response.

____

____

____

9. Our office is interested in participating in the e-Prescribing Initiative. Search the CMS website for eligible codes for the e-prescribing initiative. Provide a list of these codes. For Medicare claims, what other codes must be reported in addition to one of these eligible e-prescribing codes? If our computer system cannot send e-prescriptions and is only capable of faxing them to the pharmacy, will our office qualify for an incentive? Go to cms.hhs.gov and select Medicare and the select E-Health and then E-Prescribing.

____

____

____

10. CPRS is the computerized patient record system for the Veteran's Administration. Visit the Veteran Administrations web page and read the instructions on how to access and use the VA Computerized Patient Record System (CPRS) Demonstration System. The demonstration system only contains mock patient names and data. It will enable students to get a taste of what an electronic health record system is like and how to navigate through the screens. In order to access the system you need to follow the instructions below.

Initial Setup

The VA Computerized Patient Record System (CPRS) component of the VistA® system requires Windows 98 or later, Internet Explorer 4.0 or later and at least 15 megabytes of free disk space.

Get started by downloading the VA_CPRS_Demo.msi installation file (5,110,795 bytes) to your PC. When prompted select, *Save* to download the application to your PC workstation. When the file has finished downloading, simply double-click on your local copy of the VA_CPRS_Demo.exe file to install the demo.

Once the executable software is installed, an icon will appear on your desktop labeled *VA CPRS Demo*. Double click that icon to connect to the VistA demo system the VA has web-enabled. It will automatically log you into the demo system, so no username or password is required.

Using the System

The VistA® demo system works much like any windows-based system. Figure 2.1 shows the main screen where all activity is generated. The *Patient List* table allows the user to search and list patients by category such as provider, clinic, or specialty. The *Patients (DEMO List)* allows the user to select a specific patient and is used when the user already knows the patient's name. By double clicking on the patient name, the user can then navigate through the various tabs at the bottom of the screen and view reports and images, appointments, etc.

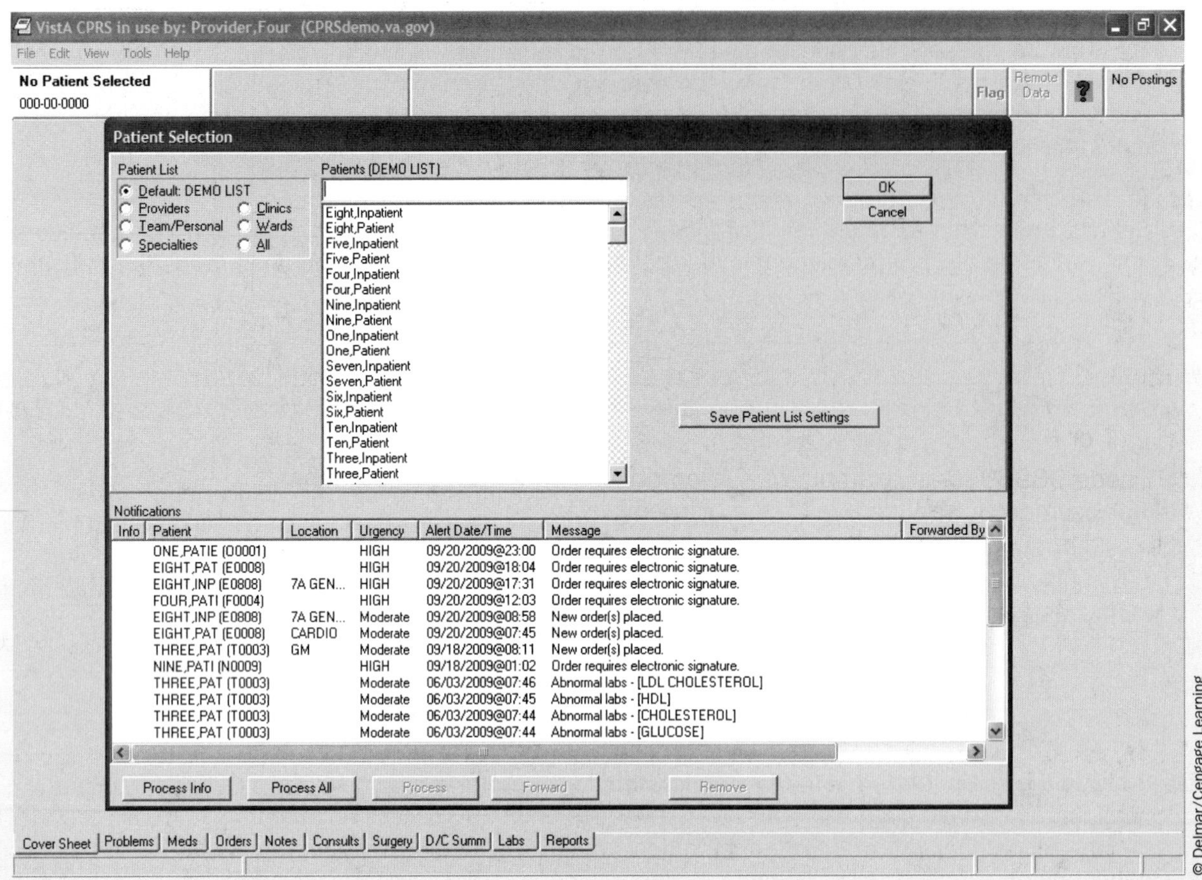

Figure 2.1 CPRS Demo Screen

Answer the following questions by navigating the VistA demo system. Explore the site and take time to read the visits and the progression of treatment. To navigate from one patient to the next, go to *File* and *Select New Patient*. Click on the tabs to access all the available documentation and electronically sign some orders. This is your time to pretend to be a doctor!

1. How many clinics are there?
2. How many providers are there?
3. The system has the ability to see appointments for each clinic for what time periods? How is this useful?
4. Find patient Bcma-Eightyfour-Patient. What Rm/bed are they in?
5. Double click the name to open this file. Is the patient male or female? Click on the orders. What meds is this patient getting and at what interval? Who is the attending physician? Read the inpatient health summary. The entry dated 3/31/2004, what type of report is this? What is the status of the patient's diabetes?
6. Select three, patient. How many signed notes are there? How many active problems does this patient have? Has this patient had previous surgery? If so, when and what procedure was performed?
7. Select ninety, patient. Read the D/C Summ. What was the date of admission? Why was the patient admitted? What procedures were performed at this admission? Why was the patient counseled for weight management?

Review Questions

True/False

1. Electronic Funds Transfer is the same thing as direct deposits to the provider.
   T or **F**
2. A batch refers to multiple claims sent in one transmission.
   T or **F**
3. System back-ups should be performed at a minimum of once per week.
   T or **F**
4. With the adoption of electronic claims filing, paper claims are not generated any longer.
   T or **F**
5. CPT code 98969 is an example of a telemedicine code that can be submitted to an insurance carrier for payment for online evaluation by a physician.
   T or **F**

Multiple Choice

1. A document sent to the provider outlining reimbursement is called a (an):
   a. X12-837P
   b. X12-835 Remittance Advice
   c. Explanation of Beneficiary
   d. Electronic Remittance Advisory
2. The American Medical Billing Association offers which billing certification exam?
   a. CMRS
   b. CCS
   c. CPC
   d. MCS-P
3. A ________________ is a third-party entity that receives transmitted claims, screens them, and forwards them to the correct payer for processing.
   a. Processing unit
   b. Billing company
   c. Practice management software vendor
   d. Clearinghouse
4. A device with a magnetic stripe containing a microchip is called a (an):
   a. Turn key
   b. Smart card
   c. Swipe card
   d. Flash strip
5. Conditions and rules that tell a carrier's system to pay, deny, or review an electronic claim are called:
   a. Guidelines
   b. Edits
   c. EDI
   d. Rejections

Fill in the Blanks

1. These codes are required when submitting claims to insurance carriers for payment.

   a. ____________________

   b. ____________________

   c. ____________________

2. List four uses a coder or biller would have for the Internet and why it is important in performing their job.

   1. ____________________

   2. ____________________

   3. ____________________

   4. ____________________

3. In order to receive incentives for implementing an EMR, physicians have to demonstrate meaningful use of the technology. Define meaningful use.

   ____

   ____

CHAPTER

3

Introduction to Medical Insurance and Revenue Cycle

Learning Outcomes:

After studying this chapter, the students will be able to:

1. Describe the responsibilities of the registration area and the billing department in the clinic.
2. Explain the flow of patient information at Douglasville Medicine Associates.
3. Discuss each step of the revenue cycle, from scheduling through collections.
4. Define common health insurance terminology.
5. Differentiate between various third-party payers and government-sponsored plans.
6. Calculate patient responsibilities such as co-pay, co-insurance, and deductible.
7. List the required patient information necessary for filing a claim form.
8. Accurately obtain Advance Beneficiary Notices from patients.
9. Read and interpret an explanation of benefits and carry out financial transactions based upon the carrier contract.
10. Use the Medicare Physician Fee Schedule (MPFS) as a reference for coding, billing, and processing payments.

Key Terms:

A/B MAC
Accounts Receivable
Advance Beneficiary Notice (ABN)
Adverse Benefit Determination
Balance Bill
Beneficiary
Billing Cycle
Birthday Rule
Carrier
Co-insurance
Content Reject
Contractual Adjustment
Coordination of Benefits (COB)
co-pay/co-payment
Coverage
Credentialing
Deductible
Dunning Message
Employee Retirement Income Security Act (ERISA)
Exclusions
Fee Schedule
Format Reject
Government Plans
Group Plan
Individual Plan
Limitations
Medicare Physician Fee Schedule (MPFS)
Medicare Secondary Payer
Medigap
National Provider Identification (NPI)
Nonparticipating
Participating
Premium
Provider
Self-funded Policy
Statement
Subscriber
Summary Plan Description (SPD)

Background Basics

- Students should have a general knowledge of the collection and flow of patient information in a physician practice.
- Students must have prior instruction on various insurance plans and mastery of basic insurance terms.
- Students should have familiarity with the CMS 1500 and how to populate correctly.
- Students should have a general understanding of the revenue cycle.

Competency Checklist

- Physician staff is required to collect fees from patients at the time of service and determine balances after insurance pays.
- Physician staff is responsible for determining and verifying accurate physician reimbursement from insurance companies.
- Business office staff references the Medicare Physician Fee Schedule regularly to determine coverage and allowed amounts and global periods for physician services.
- Office staff is expected to communicate with patients and insurance carriers regarding covered benefits, noncovered services, plan limitations, and patient responsibility.
- Appealing denied claims is essential for steady cash flow and a daily task of business office staff.
- Physician staff is often responsible for credentialing providers with insurance carriers.
- Business office staff is required to communicate with registration staff regarding insurance participation, denials, covered services, and collections.
- Billing and coding staff must be able to reference the Medicare Physician Fee Schedule (MPFS) to interrupt indicators, payment rates, and global days to properly submit claims for Medicare patients and work accounts receivable.

Introduction

Physician billing, otherwise known as Part B professional billing, encompasses many steps in a process of obtaining patient information, interpreting clinical documentation, and converting it into diagnosis and procedure codes. This process is complicated by deciphering payer rules and compliance regulations and transferring this onto a claim form for reimbursement. Required information is populated onto the claim form and sent to the insurance company for payment. All office staff plays a role in collecting patient and clinical information that impacts coded data and ultimately insurance processing and reimbursement. Everyone's job is important to this process—not just the coder's or biller's.

At DMA, all staff is cross-trained to schedule appointments, answer the phone, and register patients. Each day, you will participate in an array of activities. You will be required to research information on the Internet, answer patient questions, compile patient medical records, schedule patient appointments, interpret medical documentation, assign diagnosis and procedure codes for physician services, and conduct billing tasks such as printing claims, posting payments, claims follow-up, and transmitting electronic claims.

Each physician office has three main areas: front desk (front office), back office (insurance or billing department), and clinical (nurse station, exam rooms, and lab). The front and back office areas are the administrative areas. The front office area consists of the reception desk, medical record or filing room, and waiting room. These staff members have first contact with patients. Front office staff performs the following duties:

- Receive patient payments
- Register (check in) patients
- Answer phones
- Create and maintain patient medical records (i.e., charts)
- Schedule appointments
- Enter charges from router
- Verify insurance benefits
- Distribute mail

It is paramount that front office staff is adequately trained in HIPAA and the revenue cycle. They need to have a basic knowledge of contracts the office has with insurance carriers and what services are covered in their office. They are responsible for explaining to insured patients what services are not covered and securing payments for these services if the patient elects to proceed. They must understand how data obtained over the phone during appointment scheduling or during the registration process (patient check-in/check-out) impacts coding and billing. Errors made on the front end of this process directly affect accurate coding, claims submission, and reimbursement. There is a policy that should be adhered to for registering patients to ensure all paperwork is completed properly and co-pays and deductibles are collected at the time of service. Policies are located in Appendix A.

Back office staff consists of coders, billers, and accounts receivable staff. They are responsible for proper coding and modifier use, claims submission, claims follow-up, posting insurance payments, accounting transactions (refunds and adjustments), and collections. They must communicate with front office staff about changes to insurance contracts, noncovered services, insurance denials due to errors in check-in, missing charges, pricing changes, and discrepancies in a patient's primary or secondary insurance to name a few.

The *clinical* staff is comprised of nurses, medical assistants, and physicians who provided direct patient care. They also obtain records and test results from outside offices such as labs or hospitals for the physician to review before seeing his/her patient. They also take orders from the physician and if the provider office has access to the local hospital's network, they may enter these orders electronically into that order entry system. Clinical staff educates patients on treatment protocols and arranges for additional testing or referrals to see specialists. Their duties include taking patient calls about medications and triaging the urgency of a patient's condition and need for an appointment. Clinical staff often precert or draft the documentation necessary to obtain preauthorizations.

Flow of Patient Information

DMA does not have an electronic patient medical record at this time, so each day front desk staff pull patient charts according to the appointment schedule. Charts for established patients are pulled and organized according to appointment time. This is done either first thing in the morning or at the end of the day before. Staff creates charts for new patients as they check in. Registration paperwork, referrals, copies of reports brought with patients, and so on are filed in the charts. At registration (most often referred to as *check-in*), established patients should be asked if there are any changes to address, phone number, or insurance. It is imperative that insurance benefits are researched by either calling the carrier or querying online at the carrier website before services are rendered. The chart and router are placed in a bin labeled by doctor. The nurse calls the patient from the waiting room and he/she is taken to the appropriate examination area. The patient is then seen by the provider and receives services. The **provider** is the medical professional providing the care or service to the patient. Physicians, physician assistants (PA-C), nurse practitioners (RN-P), nurses, therapists, chiropractors, nutritionists, laboratories, and facilities are providers. Notice that medical assistants are not categorized as providers. Providers are those that have acquired a tax identification number (TIN) and a unique provider identification number from participating insurance carriers. Once the patient has been examined and released by the provider, the patient chart is placed in a bin in the back office for dictation and review by coding staff. The patient brings the router to the check-out desk. The check-out person enters charges into the computer and calculates co-pay, and co-insurance, credits and adjustments. At this time, patients pay their fees and schedule any necessary follow-up appointments. Billing staff matches up the router to the patient chart and code for services provided. Claims are generated and sent to the insurance carriers for payment.

Medical Records

Accurate and complete medical records are essential for optimal patient care and coding for reimbursement. Documentation for all services and treatments provided by our staff is housed in the patient's chart. Currently DMA uses paper records but is moving toward the adoption of a hybrid EMR. Communications between the patient and staff in addition to correspondence from insurance carriers are also filed in the chart. Copies of labs, x-rays, and reports from other sources such as the hospital, physician consultants, and referring physicians are also filed in the chart.

Building Patient Files

On the tab of each folder, the patient's account number is written at the top of the end tab with permanent black marker. The patient's name is written here, last name then first name. A sticker for the year the folder was created is placed on the bottom of the end tab. Each year the patient is seen, a new year tab is placed. Refer to Figure 3.1.

The left side of the chart is used for business office or administrative purposes. The patient's registration paperwork—including the HIPAA Privacy notice, Assignment of Benefits and Patient

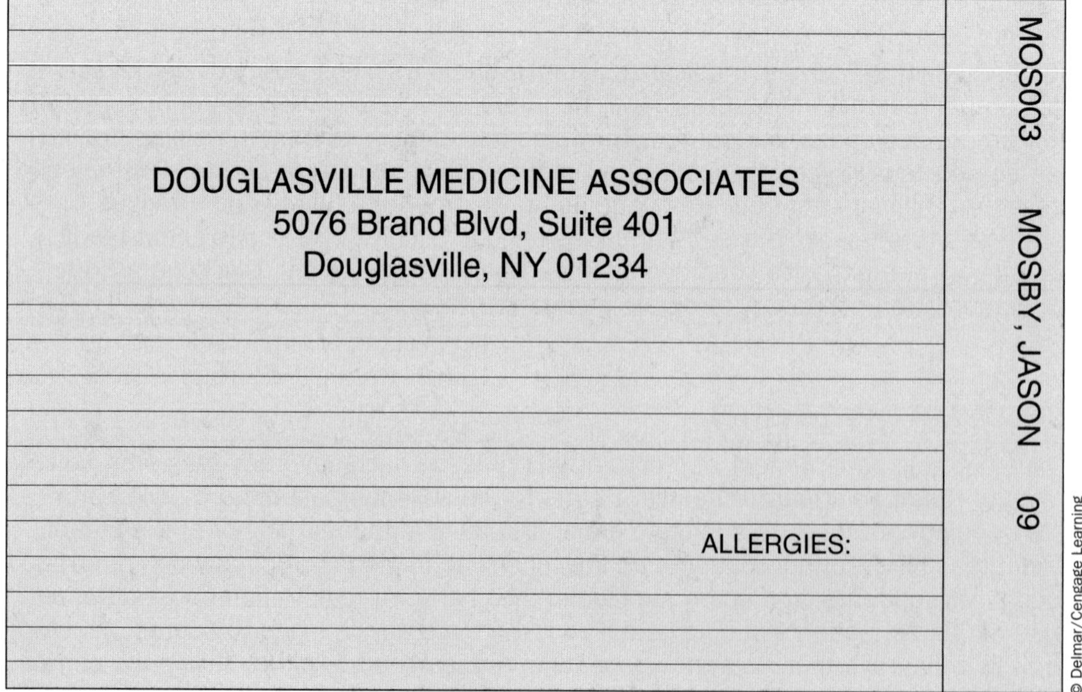

DOUGLASVILLE MEDICINE ASSOCIATES
5076 Brand Blvd, Suite 401
Douglasville, NY 01234
ALLERGIES:
MOS003 MOSBY, JASON 09
© Delmar/Cengage Learning

Figure 3.1 Sample Medical Record File Folder

Representation form, copies of insurance cards, driver's license, authorization for release of medical records, and correspondence from the insurance carriers—is filed here. Two dividers are located here entitled *Insurance* and *Correspondence.* The right side of the folder is used for clinical information such as progress notes, history and physical, labs, x-rays, immunization record, discharge summary, consults, copies of orders, medication record, and procedure notes. This side is divided by tabs for ease of finding specific information. These dividers are labeled: Lab, X-ray, History and Physical, Progress Notes, Orders, Procedure Notes, Consults, and Miscellaneous. The most recent visit or report is filed on top within each tab so that the provider can quickly refer to the most current data or results. Medical records are permanently filed in order by account number.

The providers complete the records as the patients are seen. Some of our providers like to dictate their progress and procedure notes. At a minimum, a brief note is written and the router is completed before the patient is released. Our transcription service provides 24-hour turnaround on our dictation. Three years of current records are kept on site. Each year, a year's worth or records are purged using the year label on the folder as a guide and scanned into our server in preparation for when we implement our electronic medical record.

Insurance Terminology Review

Medical insurance can be attained by an individual or by a group. Individual medical insurance is a contract between the patient and insurance company, also referred to as **carrier** or payer. The insurance company is also referred to as third-party payer, underwriter, and administrative agent. With group insurance, the contract is between the employer, employee, and insurance company. Each month, either the employer or patient pays a **premium** to secure insurance coverage for the following month. The premium can be compared to dues for a membership to a health club. The cost of the premium is determined by the carrier, cost saving provisions, types of coverage purchased, health factors, risk involved, and the law of averages. The payment of these dues allows the patient to receive discounts and access to services, but the plan may not cover the cost of these services in full. Coverage and benefits will vary among patients who have the same insurance carrier because of geographic location and contracts that are negotiated by employers. It cannot be assumed that because three patients have Cigna that all three patients have the same coverage or benefits. Employers negotiate contracts individually with carriers and depending on the size of the employer, they may or may not have bargaining power to get access to as many benefits as possible at the cheapest premium.

Carriers dictate what services and procedures will be covered under their plans. A specific policy lists procedures and services—such as tests, drugs, surgeries, and treatments—referred to as covered benefits. Insurance **coverage** means that the carrier agrees to pay the cost of these items and services. The policy also lists services or items that are noncovered or **exclusions**. Exclusions are noncovered or uncovered and if received must be paid for by the patient, the **beneficiary**. A beneficiary is an individual covered under an insurance policy. The beneficiary may or may not be the subscriber of the policy. The **subscriber** is the holder or the guarantor of the policy. The subscriber is never a child, with the exception of Medicaid and Medicare (if they are disabled). The subscriber and the other members covered under the plan are also referred to as insured members. They are responsible for paying the premiums for the policy and any balance remaining on a claim after insurance has paid and contractual adjustments are made. Carriers also place **limitations** on policies whereby they cap the benefit at some level by placing limits either on the number of paid visits for a particular service or the dollar amount they will reimburse up to. For example, a plan may cover up to $500 per year for chiropractic benefits and nothing more. Insurance was never intended to cover 100% of charges incurred.

Employee Retirement Income Security Act (ERISA) is a federal law. It was enacted in 1974 to protect employees' pension plans. But as employers started to add health insurance as a benefit of employment, health benefit plans were placed under the protection of this law.

ERISA has jurisdiction over the claims process, payment of health benefits, and the appeals process of a denied or incorrectly paid health benefit. An incorrectly paid or denied health benefit is known as an **Adverse Benefit Determination**. The regulation provides that if an internal rule, guideline, protocol, or similar criterion was relied upon in making an adverse benefit determination, the notification of the adverse benefit determination must either set forth the rule, guideline, protocol, or criterion or indicate that such was relied upon and will be provided free of charge to the patient upon request. ERISA governs approximately 6 million private health and welfare plans. Health benefits provided by any government employer (federal, state, county, or city)—including Workers' Compensation and Medicare, individual plans, health benefits provided by a church employer, and hospitals that are owned by a church—are exempt from this law: this also includes hospitals that are owned by a church. ERISA works in the favor of healthcare providers by guaranteeing full and fair review when a claim is denied in part or in whole by a plan. It also requires that plans submit a copy of the SPD when requested by the patient or their representative.

One of the most important documents participants are entitled to receive automatically when they begin participating in an ERISA-covered retirement or health benefit plan or are a beneficiary receiving benefits under such a plan, is a summary of the plan, called the **summary plan description** or SPD. The plan administrator is legally obligated to provide to participants, free of charge, the SPD. The summary plan description is an important document that tells participants what the plan provides and how it operates. It provides information on when an employee can begin to participate in the plan, how services and benefits are calculated, when benefits become vested, when and in what form benefits are paid, and how to file a claim for benefits.

Office staff must be educated on Medicare coverage and exclusions. Medicare publishes coverage policies in the *National Coverage Determinations Manual* and the *Medicare Benefit Policy Manual*, both of which are available at the CMS website. Each state also publishes specific local carrier coverage policies on their respective websites. Outpatient providers (physicians, labs, suppliers, and hospitals) filing claims to Medicare for services that are likely noncovered must obtain signatures on an **Advance Beneficiary Notice (ABN)** (CMS-R-131) (Figure 3.2). This form serves as proof that the provider notified the Medicare beneficiary before treatment that the procedure will not be covered, and Medicare is expected to deny payment for certain services because they may not be deemed reasonable and necessary. Examples of services that may fall into this category are routine eye care, routine physicals and screening tests, care that is excluded from coverage (meaning it is never covered), custodial care, and routine foot care. The completed form should identify the service, state the reason Medicare will likely deny it, and an out-of-pocket cost estimate to the beneficiary. The cost estimate is a mandatory field. It is the provider's responsibility to discuss this amount with the patient when a service is likely to be denied and more importantly why. This must be explained to the patient *before* services are rendered. The patient can then make an informed decision regarding whether they want to proceed with treatment or services for which they may have to pay out of pocket. Patient signature on the ABN demonstrates that this discussion has taken place. A special modifier is then required to notify Medicare that an ABN or wavier was obtained when reporting a procedure code with a signed ABN on file. HCPCS level II modifier–GA is appended to the CPT code for the service that is likely to be denied for noncoverage. Once the service is provided and the claim is denied, then the provider can collect from the patient for these denied services.

Insurance Verification

Medical insurance coverage comes in all shapes and sizes. Some plans are designed to cover family planning services only while other plans exclude family planning and maternity services. Other plans provide coverage for medical, surgical, and preventative services. Most plans require the patient to be responsible for a co-pay for office visits and a co-insurance for outpatient testing, surgery, and inpatient services. A **co-payment** (co-pay) is a predetermined fixed amount that a patient must pay for an office visit each time they visit. It typically ranges from $2 to $50 depending on the insurance plan and benefits. **Co-insurance** is a shared portion of payment allowed by an insurance company for outpatient or inpatient services. It is typically a percentage of the reimbursable amount set by the insurance carrier. For example, if the insurance carrier allows $50 for a service and the plan covers 80% of this, the patient will be responsible for the other 20%, in this case $10. Not all insurance plans have a deductible. A **deductible** is a designated amount of out-of-pocket money a patient must pay before the insurance company will begin paying for covered services. Deductibles typically reset each January, requiring patients to pay out of pocket until their deductibles are fulfilled for the year.

(A) **Notifier(s):**

(B) **Patient Name:** *(C)* **Identification Number:**

ADVANCE BENEFICIARY NOTICE OF NONCOVERAGE (ABN)

NOTE: If Medicare doesn't pay for ***(D)***_____________ below, you may have to pay.

Medicare does not pay for everything, even some care that you or your health care provider have good reason to think you need. We expect Medicare may not pay for the ***(D)***_____________ below.

*(D)*_______________	*(E)* **Reason Medicare May Not Pay:**	*(F)* **Estimated Cost:**

WHAT YOU NEED TO DO NOW:

- Read this notice, so you can make an informed decision about your care.
- Ask us any questions that you may have after you finish reading.
- Choose an option below about whether to receive the ***(D)***_____________listed above.

Note: If you choose Option 1 or 2, we may help you to use any other insurance that you might have, but Medicare cannot require us to do this.

(G) **OPTIONS:** **Check only one box. We cannot choose a box for you.**
❑ **OPTION 1.** I want the ***(D)***__________ listed above. You may ask to be paid now, but I also want Medicare billed for an official decision on payment, which is sent to me on a Medicare Summary Notice (MSN). I understand that if Medicare doesn't pay, I am responsible for payment, but **I can appeal to Medicare** by following the directions on the MSN. If Medicare does pay, you will refund any payments I made to you, less co-pays or deductibles.
❑ **OPTION 2.** I want the ***(D)***__________ listed above, but do not bill Medicare. You may ask to be paid now as I am responsible for payment. **I cannot appeal if Medicare is not billed**.
❑ **OPTION 3.** I don't want the ***(D)***__________listed above. I understand with this choice I am **not** responsible for payment, and **I cannot appeal to see if Medicare would pay.**

(H) **Additional Information:**

This notice gives our opinion, not an official Medicare decision. If you have other questions on this notice or Medicare billing, call **1-800-MEDICARE** (1-800-633-4227/**TTY**: 1-877-486-2048).

Signing below means that you have received and understand this notice. You also receive a copy.

(I) **Signature:**	*(J)* **Date:**

According to the Paperwork Reduction Act of 1995, no persons are required to respond to a collection of information unless it displays a valid OMB control number. The valid OMB control number for this information collection is 0938-0566. The time required to complete this information collection is estimated to average 7 minutes per response, including the time to review instructions, search existing data resources, gather the data needed, and complete and review the information collection. If you have comments concerning the accuracy of the time estimate or suggestions for improving this form, please write to: CMS, 7500 Security Boulevard, Attn: PRA Reports Clearance Officer, Baltimore, Maryland 21244-1850.

Form CMS-R-131 (03/08) Form Approved OMB No. 0938-0566

Figure 3.2 Advance Beneficiary Notice (ABN)

When staff contacts the carrier or searches benefits and/or eligibility online, they complete the Insurance Verification form with all pertinent information. Refer to Figure 3.3. At DMA, insurance benefits and eligibility are routinely checked for:

- Every new patient to the practice
- First visit of the year for established patients
- When the patient notifies the office of an insurance change

DOUGLASVILLE MEDICINE ASSOCIATES

5076 BRAND BLVD, SUITE 401, DOUGLASVILLE, NY 01234

INSURANCE VERIFICATION

Date: ____________ **Initials:** ____________

Instructions: Call insurance company or check eligibility online. Obtain the following information. Depending on how far in advance information is verified, it can be mailed to the patient or the patient is called and benefits are explained. Do not leave this information on their answering machine unless you obtain permission from them ahead of time. For all inpatient admissions, in-office or outpatient surgery, benefits must be verified. Ask if surgery must be preauthorized. If so, give the insurance company all requested information (i.e., diagnosis, date of scheduled surgery, where surgery is scheduled, and planned surgical procedure). Some carriers want the ICD-9 and CPT codes at this time. Fill out demographic information before calling insurance carrier. Fill in sheet and file in the patient medical record.

Demographics:

Patient Name: ____________________ DOB: ____________________

Insurance Plan: ____________________ Insurance ID #: ____________________

Group # (if any): ____________________

Subscriber Name: ____________________ Subscriber DOB: ____________________

Subscriber SSN: ____________________

Benefits: (office visits/surgery/hospitalization)

Coverage dates: Effective from: __________ to __________

Deductible Met? Y/N Balance: __________ Copayment amt: __________ Coverage: __________

Limitations (if any): ____

Precertification/Preauthoriziation (Surgery/Hospitalization)

Co-insurance amount: __________ Preauthorization needed for surgery? Y/N

Facility Name: ____

Patient Diagnosis: ____________________ ICD-9: ____________________

Surgical Procedure: ____________________ CPT: ____________________

Authorization number: ____________________

Rep. spoke with: ____________________ Date patient informed: ____________________

Figure 3.3 Insurance Verification Form

Assignment of Benefits

An assignment of benefits by a patient is generally limited to assignment of the patient's right to receive a benefit payment under the terms of their insurance plan. When a patient is registered for the first time at DMA, the patient is asked to sign the Assignment of Benefits and Personal Representation form. Refer to Figure 3.4. DMA also requires established patients to sign this form annually to maintain a current

DOUGLASVILLE MEDICINE ASSOCIATES

5076 BRAND BLVD, SUITE 401, DOUGLASVILLE, NY 01234

ASSIGNMENT OF BENEFITS AND PATIENT REPRESENTATION

Patient Name: ______________________ Chart # ______________

Insured Name: ______________________________________

Insurance Company Name ______________________________

Policy # ______________________ Group # ______________

I hereby assign all medical and/or surgical benefits, to include major medical benefits to which I am entitled, to **Douglasville Medicine Associates.** This assignment will remain in effect until revoked by me in writing. A photocopy of this assignment is to be considered as valid as the original.

I understand that I am financially responsible for all charges whether or not paid by my insurance carrier. I understand that I will be responsible for any court costs or collection fees should it become necessary to take action to collect for services/supplies rendered.

I hereby authorize **Douglasville Medicine Associates** to release all medical information necessary to secure payment on my account.

I hereby authorize **Douglasville Medicine Associates** and medical billing staff members, to submit claims, on my behalf, to the insurance company listed on the copy of the current and valid insurance card I have provided to the Clinic in good faith. I fully agree and understand that the submission of a claim does not absolve me of my responsibility to ensure that the bill for medical services is paid in full.

I authorize **Douglasville Medicine Associates** and its medical billing representative, to be my personal representative, which allows the Clinic to: (1) submit any and all appeals when my insurance company performs an adverse benefit determination as defined in 29 CFR 2560-503-1, (2) submit any and all requests for benefit information from my employer and/or health insurance company, and (3) initiate formal complaints to any State or Federal agency that has jurisdiction over my benefits.

I fully understand and agree that I am responsible for full payment of the medical debt I owe the Clinic, if my insurance company has refused to pay 100% of my covered benefits, within ninety (90) days of any and all appeals or request for information. A photocopy of this document shall be considered as effective and valid as the original.

Patient ______________________________________

(signature) (date)

Patient Representative ______________________________

(date)

Relationship to Patient ______________________________

Witness ______________________________________

(signature) (date)

Figure 3.4 Assignment of Benefits and Patient Representation

signature on file. When this document is signed, it permits the carrier to send payments for services directly to the provider instead of to the patient, who would in turn then have to forward money to the provider. Typically assignment of benefits alone is not a grant of authority to act on a patient's behalf in pursuing and appealing a benefit determination under a plan. To appeal claims according to ERISA law, the practice must be able to demonstrate they are also the patient's personal representative and not just their provider.

The provider of services (facility or physician) or the provider's medical biller has no right to submit a claim for payment of health benefits, or appeal a denial or underpayment of a health benefit, unless the patient legally assigns their claims submission and/or appeals rights to the provider or medical biller. This makes the provider or medical biller the patient's personal representative.

Medical Insurance Review

Most insurance carriers require the provider to have a signed contract or agreement on file demonstrating that they are **participating** with that plan. Participating with a plan means that the provider agrees to treat patients with that insurance coverage at a negotiated rate. This negotiated payment rate is called a **fee schedule**. Fee schedules can be reimbursement at a percentage of the provider's charge for each CPT code or a negotiated set amount per procedure code like a price list. The provider accepts this negotiated rate and will not **balance bill** the patient the difference of the provider's charge and what is paid by the insurance plan. Balance billing is not permitted with any carrier where there is an agreement to accept a negotiated rate as payment in full minus any insurance plan co-payments or co-insurances. Once the insurance carrier has paid the designated allowed amount, the provider must perform a **contractual adjustment** or an insurance adjustment, writing off any difference between what the provider charged for a service and what was actually allowed and paid per the fee schedule. If a provider is **nonparticipating**, the provider has no agreement with the payer. Depending on the plan, patients may still seek treatment from a nonparticipating provider and have coverage, although the coverage will be less and the patient's out-of-pocket expense will be greater.

Most patients are covered by some type of prepaid health plan or federal health insurance, although the number of uninsured patients is on the rise due to the downswing of the economy and the high unemployment rate. Therefore, the largest part of healthcare expenses in the United States is reimbursed through third-party payers and not by the patients who received the services. The recipients (i.e., the patients) are considered the first parties and the providers the second parties. Third-party payers include:

- Medicare
- Medicaid
- Workers' Compensation
- Blue Cross/Blue Shield
- Federally funded health care programs
- Private commercial plans
- HMO/PPO prepaid plans
- Health care savings accounts
- Self-insured/individual plan

Insurance policies have exclusions and limitations for services and coverage. Physician office staff must work with patients and their carriers to determine coverage for proposed services. Determination of coverage needs to be performed before services are rendered. By doing so, the patient and the office staff can discuss payment options up front and the patient can better plan the timing of elective services. Insurance plans also vary widely with how they reimburse for services provided. Office staff should research this beforehand to determine how much the carrier will pay for the proposed service and consequently advise the patient of any financial responsibility they may have. It is conceivable that if three patients with three different insurance plans receive the exact same service, three different payments will be received by the provider.

Most commercial health insurance is provided in the form of group policies offered by employers as part of their fringe benefit packages for employees. The employer negotiates **group plans** on behalf of the entire organization, with premiums based on the size of the group. Organizations must have at least 10 employees to be eligible for a group plan. Generally group plans have lower rates than individual plans because of the number of covered lives. Unions also negotiate health insurance coverage during contract negotiations. In most cases, employees pay a share of the cost, and employers pay a share. The subscriber purchases **individual plans** directly from the insurance carrier. Individual health insurance plans are usually expensive, have limited coverage, and have high deductibles. Individuals with preexisting medical conditions often find it almost impossible to obtain individual coverage. **Government plans or programs** are state or federally funded plans such as Medicare, Medicaid, Tricare, and BlueCross Federal. **Self-funded** policies are funded by the employer. An employer will contract with an administrative services organization to process the claims and provide utilization review. Rather than paying premiums to an insurance carrier, the organization insures itself. It assumes the risk of paying directly for medical services and sets up a fund from which it pays for claims. This type of plan is not subject to most state laws or ERISA. These funds have more flexibility to tailor coverage to local needs and are not required to be consistent, that is, they do not have to provide the same coverage regardless of the state the employee lives in. To the insured this plan appears the same as the traditional group plan. Subscribers don't see the difference but employers do because it is cheaper and they get to keep any revenue at the end of the year rather than leaving the insurance company with the profit. Self-insured plans have more freedom to pick and choose what they want to cover.

Interpreting the Medicare Physician Fee Schedule (MPFS)

Coders, billers, practice managers, and physicians must be able to find, read, and interpret the **CMS Physician Fee Schedule (MPFS)** for many reasons—most importantly to know what Medicare covers and how much the provider will be compensated for his services. The MPFS is the physicians' official source of payment and coverage information for Medicare beneficiaries. It is more than just a payment schedule, it also includes all or nearly all of CMS's Medicare Part B rulemaking for the year, summarized from the *Federal Register*. There is a wealth of knowledge that comes with understanding all the elements of the schedule, such as knowing what the global days are for a certain procedure or what the technical component allows for a diagnostic procedure. This fee schedule is the nucleus of contracting negotiations and anticipating what other insurance carriers will allow. Most carriers mimic the basic concept of this fee schedule and base their allowed amounts at a percentage above what Medicare allows. Knowing how to read the fee schedule is important for practices that may provide only one of the following: preoperative care, intraoperative care, or postoperative care. Medicare assigns individual payments for these components, which are located on the MPFS.

This fee schedule is the cornerstone to determining Medicare coverage of physician services, projecting physician reimbursement, setting prices or fees for physician services, reconciling payments received to contracted amounts, calculating the Medicare patient co-insurance (20% of the allowed amount), determining global days, as well as a host of other uses.

For more than 10,000 physician services, the MPFS file contains the relative value units (RVUs), a fee schedule status indicator, and various payment policy indicators needed for reporting services and payment adjustment (e.g., payment of assistant at surgery, team surgery, bilateral surgery).

The MPFS is accessed on the CMS website and can be downloaded into an Excel document. Go to http://www.cms.hhs.gov, select *Medicare,* select *Medicare Fee for Service Payment,* select *Medicare Fee for Service Payment,* then select *Physician Fee Schedule.* Click on *PFS Relative Value File* and choose the year's current version. Save this to your desktop for future reference. A new fee schedule comes out each quarter, and each file is suffixed by the year and a letter. For example, PPRRVU09A would be for the fee schedule for first quarter 2009. There is also an option to select a state carrier–specific file instead of the national fee schedule. This is recommended once you are working and can be selective based on the state you are living in or the state for which a provider is working and you are processing payments. We will use Figure 3.5 as an example to discuss pertinent data elements that coding and billing staff use.

Let's talk about the most important elements of the fee schedule for the coder and biller and then use what we learn to do a few exercises. The first column lists the HCPCS/CPT code. The codes on this fee schedule are listed in alphabetical and then numerical order. The code descriptions are located in column 3.

Modifier Column

Column 2 is used to identify codes that can be reported with either the 26, TC, or 53 modifiers. Rows with codes for diagnostic tests will have a blank, TC, or 26 in this column. A blank in this field denotes the global service, meaning the physician will receive full payment for the service. Lines with component modifiers 26 and TC indicate that the provider will receive a portion of the full global payment for the component they provided. For services that do not contain a physician technical component, a blank will appear in this field. For example, 17110 does not have a separate line for the professional and technical components. This means that the payment for this service is for the skill of the professional alone.

Status Code

The *status code* column indicates whether the code is in the fee schedule and whether it is separately payable if the service is covered. The presence or absence of the HCPCS/CPT code doesn't reflect its coverage; the status indicator does. Only codes associated with status codes of A, R, or T, are used for Medicare payment. The indicators are as follows:

- A = Active Code. These codes are paid separately under the physician fee schedule, if covered.
- B = Bundled Code. Payments for covered services are always bundled into payments for other services not specified.
- C = Carriers price the code. Carriers will establish RVUs and payment amounts for these services, generally on an individual basis following review of documentation such as an operative report.
- E = Excluded from Physician Fee Schedule by regulation. These codes are for items and/or services that CMS chose to exclude from the fee schedule payment by regulation.
- G = Not valid for Medicare purposes. Medicare uses another code for reporting of, and payment for, these services.
- I = Not valid for Medicare purposes. Medicare uses another code for reporting of, and payment for, these services. Codes that are a status I usually have a HCPCS G code counterpart that CMS prefers over the CPT code. (Code *not* subject to a 90-day grace period.)
- M = Measurement codes. Used for reporting purposes only.
- N = Non-covered Services. These services are not covered by Medicare.
- P = Bundled/Excluded Codes. There are no RVUs and no payment amounts for these services. No separate payment should be made for them under the fee schedule.
- R = Restricted Coverage. Special coverage instructions apply. If no RVUs are shown, the service is carrier priced. (NOTE: The majority of codes to which this indicator will be assigned are the alphanumeric dental codes, which begin with D.)
- T = Injections. There are RVUs and payment amounts for these services, but they are paid only if there are no other services payable under the physician fee schedule billed on the same date by the same provider.
- X = Statutory Exclusion. These codes represent an item or service that is not in the statutory definition of "physician services" for fee schedule payment purposes and most likely reimbursed under a different fee schedule such as DME, Clinical Lab, Part B Drugs, or Medicare Part D.

HCPCS	MOD	DESCRIPTION	STATUS CODE	WORK RVU	TRANSITIONED NON-FAC PE RVU	FULLY IMPLEMENTED NON-FAC PE RVU	TRANSITIONED FACILITY PE RVU	FULLY IMPLEMENTED FACILITY PE RVU	MP RVU	TRANSITIONED NON-FACILITY TOTAL	FULLY IMPLEMENTED NON-FACILITY TOTAL	TRANSITIONED FACILITY TOTAL	FULLY IMPLEMENTED FACILITY TOTAL	PCTC IND	GLOB DAYS	PRE OP	INTRA OP	POST OP	MULT PROC	BILAT SURG	ASST SURG	CO-SURG	ENDO BASE	PHYSICIAN SUPERVISION OF DIAGNOSTIC PROCEDURES	DIAGNOSTIC IMAGING FAMILY INDICATOR
99213		Office/outpatient visit, est	A	0.92	0.75	0.77	0.29	0.30	0.03	1.70	1.72	1.24	1.25	0	XXX	0.00	0.00	0.00	0	0	0	0	0	09	99
11421		Exc h-f-nk-sp b9+marg 0.6-1	A	1.44	2.17	2.20	1.16	1.18	0.13	3.74	3.77	2.73	2.75	0	010	0.10	0.80	0.10	2	0	1	0	0	09	99
11900		Injection into skin lesions	A	0.52	0.85	0.91	0.25	0.26	0.02	1.39	1.45	0.79	0.80	0	000	0.00	0.00	0.00	2	0	1	0	0	09	99
11983		Remove/insert drug implant	A	3.30	2.61	2.71	1.44	1.43	0.23	6.14	6.24	4.97	4.96	0	XXX	0.00	0.00	0.00	2	0	0	0	0	09	99
12002		Repair superficial wound(s)	A	1.88	1.83	1.76	0.85	0.83	0.17	3.88	3.81	2.90	2.88	0	010	0.10	0.80	0.10	2	0	1	0	0	09	99

Figure 3.5 Medicare Physician Fee Schedule Excerpt

RVU

For coders to properly sequence the CPT codes on the claim, they have to know the values of the codes and where to locate these values. The values are located in the *RVU* columns on the MPFS. These decimal numbers are factored into a formula to derive the physician's reimbursement. Sequencing is done in accordance with the weight of the RVU. The code with the highest RVU is sequenced first as the primary procedure followed by the codes in descending RVU order. Some services, by the nature of their codes, are performed only in certain settings and will have only one level of practice expense RVU per code. Many of these are E/M services with code descriptions specific to the location of the service. Other services, such as most major surgical services with a 90-day global period, are performed almost entirely in the hospital, and generally will only have an RVU associated with the facility setting.

Facility and Nonfacility Payment

The facility practice expense RVUs are used to calculate payment for services performed in inpatient or outpatient hospital settings, emergency rooms, skilled nursing facilities, or ambulatory surgical centers (ASCs). This payment amount is located in the column *facility pymt.* The nonfacility practice expense relative value units are used to calculate payment for services furnished in all other settings. This is found in the column *non-facility pymt.* The RVU is higher for nonfacility because the physician, in providing his/her service, typically bears the cost of resources, such as labor, medical supplies, and medical equipment.

PC/TC Indicator

The *PC/TC* column indicates whether component billing applies to a service. This assists the coder in determining if it is appropriate to append the TC and 26 modifiers and if codes can be billed incident to the physician. Definitions of these indicators follow:

- *0* = Physician Service Codes. The concept of PC/TC does not apply because physician services cannot be split into professional and technical components. Modifiers 26 and TC cannot be used with these codes.
- *1* = Diagnostic Tests for Radiology Services. A *1* in this column identifies codes that describe diagnostic tests. Modifiers 26 and TC can be used with these codes.
- *2* = Professional Component Only Codes. A *2* in this column identifies stand-alone codes that describe the physician work portion of selected diagnostic tests for which there is an associated code that describes the technical component of the diagnostic test only and another associated code that describes the global test.
- *3* = Technical Component Only Codes. A *3* in this column identifies stand-alone codes that describe the technical component. Modifiers 26 and TC cannot be used with these codes.
- *4* = Global Test Only Codes. A *4* in this column identifies stand-alone codes that describe selected diagnostic tests for the total RVU for the 26 and TC components.
- 5 = Incident To Codes. A 5 in this column identifies codes that describe services covered incident to a physician's service when they are provided by auxiliary personnel employed by the physician and working under his/her direct personal supervision.
- 6 = Laboratory Physician Interpretation Codes. A 6 in this column identifies clinical laboratory codes for which separate payment for interpretations by laboratory physicians may be made. Modifier TC cannot be used with these codes.

Global Surgery Package

Pre, Intra, and *Post* columns assist the provider in calculating anticipated payment when only a portion of the global service was provided. Each of these columns lists a percentage of the total value that Medicare will reimburse. This concept is referred to as split billing. *Pre* is the percentage of the global fee for the preoperative portion of global package. *Intra* is the percentage of the global fee for the intraoperative portion of the global package, including postoperative work in the hospital. *Post* is the percentage of the global fee for the postoperative portion of care. When added together, these three columns should equal 1.00. Medicare assumes that the surgeon performing the surgery also performs the preoperative work, so they add these two percentages together. Notice that Medicare does not separate these percentages out for add-on codes because they are considered to be included in the value for the primary procedure. Codes that do not include separate pre-op, intra-op, and post-op values cannot be appended with modifiers 54, 55, or 56.

A patient injures himself while on vacation in California. He goes to the ER and the orthopedist on call says he immediately requires repair of one of the ligaments in his knee. This orthopedic surgeon evaluates him preoperatively, makes the decision for surgery, and performs the actual surgery. He reports 27405-54. He will receive 79% of $570.95. The patient is discharged and sent back home to Houston. He is instructed to follow up with an orthopedist in his home town four weeks after the surgery. The second orthopedist reports 27405-55. This provider will receive 21% of $570.95.

Global Days

One of the most common reasons E/M services are denied is because they are provided during the global period of a surgical procedure. Ways to avoid these denials is to schedule appointments outside this window of time or append appropriate modifiers. Neither of these can be accomplished if the practice doesn't know the global days for each procedure. CMS has assigned a postoperative window to each surgical procedure. The *global days* column will contain one of the following:

- 000 = Endoscopic or minor procedure with related preoperative and postoperative relative values on the day of the procedure only included in the fee schedule payment amount; evaluation and management services on the day of the procedure generally not payable.
- 10 = Minor procedure with preoperative relative values on the day of the procedure and postoperative relative values during a 10-day postoperative period included in the fee schedule amount; evaluation and management services on the day of the procedure and during the 10-day postoperative period generally not payable.
- 90 = Major surgery with a 1-day preoperative period and 90-day postoperative period included in the fee schedule amount.
- XXX = The global concept does not apply to the code.
- YYY = The carrier is to determine whether the global concept applies and establishes postoperative period, if appropriate, at time of pricing.
- ZZZ = The code is related to another service and is always included in the global period of the other service.

A patient underwent a total knee replacement on 2/1/xx. The surgeon cannot charge for follow-up visits within 90 days of 2/1/xx. The exception to this is if the surgeon submits a claim for care that is unrelated to this surgery and not considered to be normal surgical aftercare. A modifier is required to alert the carrier that the service is unrelated.

Assistant Surgeon and Co-surgeon

Payment for assistant surgeons is dependent on the indicator in the *Asst Surg* column. Assistant surgeons are usually PA-C or RN.P staff who work for the surgeon. They are paid 16% of the payment global fee. Indicators are:

- 0 = Payment restriction for assistants at surgery applies to this procedure unless supporting documentation is submitted to establish medical necessity.
- 1 = Statutory payment restriction for assistants at surgery applies to this procedure. Assistant at surgery may not be paid.
- 2 = Payment restriction for assistants at surgery does not apply, so billing for an assistant surgeon is allowed.
- 9 = Concept does not apply.

A co-surgeon is an MD who operates simultaneously with the primary surgeon. Each of these surgeons is of a different specialty. The *Cosurg* column delineates if the procedure qualifies for a co-surgeon. Indicators are:

- 0 = Co-surgeons not permitted for this procedure.
- 1 = Co-surgeons could be paid, though supporting documentation is required to establish the medical necessity of two surgeons for the procedure.
- 2 = Co-surgeons permitted and no documentation required if the two-specialty requirement is met.
- 9 = Concept does not apply.

Multiple Procedures

Claims that contain more than one code are subject to multiple procedure reductions. The *Mult Proc* column shows when a procedure is subject to a percentage reduction—either 50% or 25%. Indicators are as follows:

- 0 = No payment adjustment rules for multiple procedures apply. Payment is based on the payment on the lower of (a) the actual charge or (b) the fee schedule amount for the procedure.
- 2 = Standard payment adjustment rules for multiple procedures apply. If a procedure is reported on the same day as another procedure with an indicator of 1, 2, or 3, rank the procedures by fee schedule amount and apply the appropriate reduction to this code (100%, 50%, 50%, 50%, 50%, and by report). Base the payment on the lower of (a) the actual charge or (b) the fee schedule amount reduced by the appropriate percentage.
- 3 = Special rules for multiple endoscopic procedures apply if the procedure is billed with another endoscopy in the same family (i.e., another endoscopy that has the same base procedure). The base procedure for each code with this indicator is identified in the Endobase field of this file. Apply the multiple endoscopy rules to a family before ranking the family with the other procedures performed on the same day (e.g., if multiple endoscopies in the same family are reported on the same day as endoscopies in another family or on the same day as a nonendoscopic procedure). If an endoscopic procedure is reported with only its base procedure, do not pay separately for the base procedure. Payment for the base procedure is included in the payment for the other endoscopy.
- 4 = Special rules for the technical component (TC) of diagnostic imaging procedures apply if the procedure is billed with another diagnostic imaging procedure in the same family (per the diagnostic imaging family indicator, as follows). If the procedure is reported in the same session on the same day as another procedure with the same family indicator, rank the procedures by fee schedule amount for the TC. Pay 100% for the highest priced procedure and 75% for each subsequent procedure. Base the payment for subsequent procedures on the lower of (a) the actual charge or (b) the fee schedule amount reduced by the appropriate percentage. The professional component (PC) is paid at 100% for all procedures.
- 9 = Concept does not apply.

Bilateral Surgery

The indicators in the *Bilat Surg* column signify how the claim line will be paid when submitted with modifier 50 on the line or with LT and RT on two lines. The bilateral payment concept is based on whether the code reported represents a paired organ or body part and if the code is already valued as bilateral based on the code description. The indicators are as follows:

- 0 = 150% payment adjustment for bilateral procedures does not apply. This applies to codes that are not bilateral in nature. If the procedure is reported with modifier -50 or with modifiers RT and LT, the payment is based for the two sides on the lower of (a) the total actual charge for both sides or (b) 100% of the fee schedule amount for a *single* code.
- 1 = 150% payment adjustment for bilateral procedures applies. If the code is billed with the 50 modifier or is reported twice on the same day by any other means (e.g., with RT and LT modifiers,

or with a 2 in the units field), base the payment for these codes when reported as bilateral procedures on the lower of (a) the total actual charge for both sides or (b) 150% of the fee schedule amount for a single code.

- 2 = 150% payment adjustment does not apply. RVUs are already based on the procedure being performed as a bilateral procedure.
- 3 = The usual payment adjustment for bilateral procedures does not apply. If the procedure is reported with modifier -50 or is reported for both sides on the same day by any other means (e.g., with RT and LT modifiers or with a 2 in the units field), base the payment for each side or organ or site of a paired organ on the lower of (a) the actual charge for each side or (b) 100% of the fee schedule amount for *each* side.

Exercise 3.0 Your Turn to Try

Use the MPFS schedule located on the CMS website to answer the following questions.

1. A provider submits a claim with DOS 3/12/xx with the following codes: 99214-25, 17110. 17110 was denied. A previous claim for this patient was processed on 3/20/xx with DOS 3/2/xx with CPT codes 99214-25 and 17110. Think about the services provided and determine why 17110 was denied on 3/12/xx. ____________________
2. A physician performs a urine voiding pressure study in his office. He supplied the equipment and performed the interpretation of the findings. What code should he report? What is his expected payment from Medicare?

   ____
3. A patient comes to the office for suture removal. He sees the nurse and a claim is submitted with 15850. How much should the practice expect to be paid by Medicare?

   ____
4. What status indicator does G0009 have? Why do you think it has this status code? If it is not payable under the MPFS, then what fee schedule would it be paid under?

   ____
5. When reporting code 44393, would the physician append a -26 modifier? What column on the fee schedule tells you if you can report a code with a -26?

   ____
6. Why isn't there an allowed amount for nonfacility for code 27405?

   ____
7. Dr. Engle insists on taking his PA with him to assist in all surgeries he performs. The PA wants to know if he is going to get paid for assisting the tendon excision case tomorrow. CPT code 25109. What will you tell him? ____________________

Insurance Coverage

Families today commonly have medical coverage by more than one insurance carrier. There are more households today where both men and women are working, with each of them receiving benefits from their respective employer. Office staff routinely has difficulty in determining which insurance is primary or secondary for all family members covered by the plan. If both spouses are insured through their respective employers, then their company insurance plan would be their individual primary insurance; the other spouse's insurance would be secondary. For children, if both parents are insured and list their children as covered under both plans, staff must identify which of these plans is the child's primary insurance. According to the **birthday rule**, the parent with the earliest birthday in the year is designated as having the primary insurance. In the event the parents are divorced and they do not share joint custody, the plan of the custodial parent is primary and the plan of the other parent is secondary.

Insurance policies have contract provisions called **coordination of benefits (COB)** built in to explain how the policies will be listed when the patient has two or more insurances. This happens frequently when both husband and wife work and obtain insurance through both employers. These guidelines ensure that when a patient is covered by more than one policy, maximum appropriate benefits are paid up to 100% of usual and reasonable expenses between the benefits of all the plans. This way, neither carrier will pay more than 100% of the total charges incurred on the same claim. The balance of what the secondary insurance would have allowed and paid as primary then becomes a benefit savings and credited to the beneficiary to be applied in future claims. The credit can be used to provide benefits that would not otherwise have been paid.

Exercise 3.1 Your Turn to Try

From the following scenario, determine which insurance is primary and then determine the expected benefit from each carrier.

1. Lila is 10 years old and lives with her parents. Her mother works at Giant Cement and has family coverage with Aetna that has a deductible of $125. Aetna's plan pays 89% of the eligible expenses after a deductible. Her mother's date of birth is 09/16/1967. Her father works at Westwood Lumber Company and is also insured by his employer with family coverage through Great West. His plan pays at 75% after a deductible of $100. His date of birth is 09/15/1966. Both plans have coordination of benefits. The charges for the visit were $2400. The allowed amount is $2400. Whose insurance is primary? ______________________ How much will the primary insurance carrier reimburse? ______________________ How much will the secondary insurance carrier reimburse? ______________________

Credentialing

Physicians need to be affiliated with insurance carriers and hospitals to practice medicine. Physicians cannot admit patients to hospitals without having admitting privileges. Likewise, physicians cannot file claims to insurance carriers without being credentialed by the carrier. **Credentialing** is the process of collecting and validating data about a respective applicant for medical staff that includes examining the professional qualifications of a physician or licensed provider and comparing those qualifications against a facility's or carrier's requirements for medical staff. Carriers have standards of qualifications for participation in their provider networks. Credentialing is done to verify that a provider has completed all the necessary training, education, and certification to become a licensed M.D. and practice medicine. Investigations are carried out regarding the status of the physician's license, malpractice coverage, Controlled Substance Registration, and Federal Drug Enforcement Administration (DEA) Certificate Registration. This process is carried out to ensure enrollees and patients have adequate access to a legitimately qualified provider in good standing with the medical boards and board of licensure. As part of the credentialing process, the entity should search the CMS website to verify if the provider being credentialed has been excluded from the Medicare or Medicaid programs.

To credential a provider, an application must be completed with copies of important documents such as license; malpractice insurance; state and federal DEA certificates; diploma; certificates of completion of residency, internship, and fellowships; and so on. Credentials data also includes additional information and answers to questions on the application required by a carrier to complete the credentialing of a physician. Re-credentialing is the process by which a physician's information related to his/her credentials is updated and re-verified for purposes of determining whether the physician shall continue to participate in the carrier's healthcare provider network. This process typically occurs every two years and requires completing another application and copying the current license, DEAs, and malpractice insurance coverage.

Exercise 3.2 Your Turn to Try

Your task is to get Dr. Sally Kemper credentialed with Great West. She is a new doctor in our practice. The CD-ROM includes a blank application for Great West and a provider profile that includes necessary information for completing the application. Complete this application and attach any necessary documentation. Once this is done, the information will be mailed to Great West's provider enrollment department. Dr. Kemper will not be able to treat patients with Great West insurance or file claims to this carrier until credentialing is accomplished. It usually takes 60 days to become credentialed. Turn this application in to your instructor.

You will also need to confirm Dr. Kemper's provider information in MOSS. April Kennedy has already added her in the system.

Step 1 From the Main Menu, click on *File Maintenance*.

Step 2 Click on the *Lists* tab.

Step 3 Click on the box to the left of *Practice Physicians.* A yellow box will open. Use the scroll bar at the bottom of the screen and arrow over until you find her name.

Step 4 In fields 2–9 enter the information on Dr. Kemper's profile located on CD-ROM. In field 6 *Col. No.* enter 12. In *EIN/Tax ID* enter 045093221.

For field 10, *Practice Hours,* enter:

Start time: 9:00 a.m Stop time: 5:00 p.m. Lunch Starts: 12:00 p.m. Lunch Ends: 1:00 p.m.

Step 5 Save your work.

Government-Sponsored and Federal Health Care Programs

Federally funded programs fall under the auspices of the Correct Coding Initiative, and claims with multiple procedures on the same day must be checked against these edits. There are 13 federal health care programs. The three most common of these 13 are reviewed below. Table 3-1 provides examples of federally funded programs.

Medicare

Medicare is federal health insurance designed to help pay for medical care for retired persons 65-years-old and over and Americans with disabilities. It is available under two separate but coordinated programs: hospital insurance (known as Part A) and medical insurance (known as Part B). When a person turns 65, they automatically qualify for Part A. Part A covers hospital stays, home health, skilled nursing, and hospice care. Part B covers professional services, labs, x-rays, durable medical equipment, medical supplies, and outpatient care. To qualify for Part B, beneficiaries must be 65 years or older and must have worked for at least 10 years with an employer that is Medicare-covered or be disabled collecting Social Security or Railroad Retirement disability benefits for at least 24 months. Patients undergoing

Table 3-1 Federal Health Care Programs

Medicare Part A & B	Medicaid
Federal Prison Hospitals	Indian Health Services
OWCP (Workers' Compensation for federal employees)	Public Health Services
Railroad Retirement Board	Black Lung Program
Tricare	Veterans Administration
Health Benefits under Peace Corps Act	Title V and Title XX of Social Security Act for block grants

dialysis for kidney failure, those who require kidney transplantation, or those who have amyotrophic lateral sclerosis (ALS) also qualify. "Part C" Medicare refers to Medicare Managed Care plans. This is an option for Medicare beneficiaries that provides additional coverage for services not routinely covered by Medicare and that eliminates the annual deductible and co-insurance. These plans routinely require co-pays for each visit but no annual deductible. They replace the standard Medicare and eliminate the need for Medigap secondary insurance.

Medical insurance known as Part B is optional and requires monthly premiums paid by beneficiaries. Medicare pays 80% of the allowed charges and the patient pays the other 20%. Each year the patient has an annual deductible that must be met before Medicare awards benefits. This information can be located on CMS's website each year or on the state Medicare carrier website. Some Medicare patients have a supplemental insurance that helps cover the cost of the annual deductible and co-insurance. Once Medicare pays a claim as the primary insurance, in many cases it will automatically forward or cross over the claim to the secondary insurance. **Medigap**, a federally regulated plan sold to individuals, is common secondary insurance to Medicare. It is designed to supplement Medicare coverage. Medigap, like much other supplemental insurance, will pick up or pay the patient's deductible and co-insurance for covered services, eliminating the need to bill or collect from the patient.

Medicare is never the primary insurance in the following situations:

- Patient is receiving Black Lung benefits
- Workers' Compensation
- Automobile accidents where a no fault insurer or liability insurer is faulted for the accident
- If the Medicare recipient is still employed and has group health insurance
- If the Medicare recipient's spouse is still working and has coverage for both of them
- If the patient has end-stage renal disease (ESRD) and is within the 30-month coordination period

The Medicare Modernization Act of 2003 mandated that CMS replace the numerous carriers administering the Medicare Part A and Part B fee-for-service programs with entities known as **A/B MACs** (Medicare administrative contractors). Four DME MACs administer claims for durable medical equipment, supplies, and drugs billed by physicians, replacing the previously used DME regional carriers (DMERCs). Under this mandate, by 2011 seventeen A/B MACs will process and pay both Part A and Part B claims within specified multistate jurisdictions.

Medicare Benefit Policy Manual: Pub. No. 100-02 is located at http://www.cms.hhs.gov/Manuals/IOM/list.asp.

Medicare as a Secondary Payer (MSP)

Medicare secondary payer is a term used by Medicare to indicate that Medicare is not responsible for paying primary benefits. Fewer people are financially able to retire at age 65, so the number of Medicare beneficiaries working full-time is increasing. Many of these beneficiaries are also covered under group health plans by either their employer or their spouse's employer. It is our job at DMA to ascertain all information about our patients' coverage and determine if they or their spouse is still working. Use the following guidelines to help determine if Medicare is the primary or secondary insurance coverage. Medicare is a secondary insurance when:

- The beneficiary is working and covered by a group health plan
- The spouse is 65 or older and is working and covered by a group health plan
- The patient has with end stage renal disease (ESRD) and is covered by group health insurance
- The patient is 65 years or older with an injury or illness related to an automobile accident
- The patient is 65 or older, is working, and has suffered a work-related injury or illness
- A patient's injuries are covered by homeowner's, product liability, or malpractice insurance

Medicare provides a worksheet to help registration staff delineate primary and secondary insurance for Medicare beneficiaries. This Medicare secondary payer questionnaire is located on the CD-ROM. Carrier websites such as http://www.palmettogba.com have an online questionnaire that you can use.

Exercise 3.3 Your Turn to Try

Use the Medicare Secondary Payer questionnaire on the CD-ROM to determine if Medicare is primary or secondary insurance.

1. Marsha is 65-years-old and works for a DME supplier. The company offers Wellfix insurance and she is fully covered. The plan has a $50 deductible (met) and a $15 co-insurance for office visits. She plans on retiring at the end of the month. She received her Medicare card in the mail six months ago. This year the deductible is $135 (she has met $60 of this) and she has a 20% co-insurance. Which plan is her primary insurance?____________________ The charge for her visit was $95. The contractual allowable by Wellfix is $75. CPT code submitted was 99244. How much should the primary insurance reimburse for this visit?________________ How much should the secondary insurance reimburse for this visit?____________________
2. Bill is 67-years-old and retired twice. He retired from the Air Force 20 years ago and has recently retired from A&W Oil Company. He is covered by Medicare and Tricare for Life. His wife is still employed full-time as a school nurse and she is covered by a self-funded plan from her school district of 100 employees. Who is the primary insurance? ____________________

Medicaid

Medicaid is a medical assistance program designed to meet the needs of low income Americans. The program is funded partially by the federal government and partially by states and local governments. The federal government requires that certain services be covered by every state and sets specific eligibility requirements. Medicaid covers the following benefits:

- Inpatient hospital care
- Outpatient hospital care
- Laboratory and x-ray services
- Skilled nursing facility and home health services for persons over 21 years of age
- Physicians' services
- Family planning services
- Early and periodic screening, diagnosis, and treatment services

Medicaid is never primary if the patient has two insurances. Medicaid patients have a $2 co-pay at each visit.

Tricare/CHAMPVA

The federal government offers three health programs to address the needs of military personnel and their dependents. The Civilian Health and Medical Program–Veterans Administration (CHAMPVA) provides healthcare services for dependents and survivors of disabled veterans, survivors of veterans who died from service-related conditions, and survivors of military personnel who died in the line of duty. CHAMPVA is a voluntary program that allows beneficiaries to be treated for free at participating VA healthcare facilities.

TRICARE (formally CHAMPUS, the Civilian Health and Medical Program–Uniformed Services) provides coverage for active duty armed forces personnel, the dependents, and retirees receiving care outside a military treatment facility. The TRICARE program is administered by the Department of Defense. With Tricare, the patient's insurance ID number is the sponsor's social security number, which is located on the military ID card.

Workers' Compensation

Workers' compensation is an insurance system operated by the individual states. Each state has its own law and program to provide covered workers with some protection against the costs of medical care and loss of income resulting from work-related injuries and, in some cases, illnesses. When an individual is accidentally injured while working on the job or during a job-related duty for his/her employer or becomes ill as a result of a work-related exposure, the employee files an incident report (*First Report of Injury*) with his/her employer, who in turn files a claim with its workers' comp carrier. If the claim is deemed valid, these plans provide benefits for lost wages and permanent disabilities in addition to coverage of medical benefits.

Patients with workers' comp do not have any out-of-pocket expense. One note of caution: Bill workers' comp only for treatment received due to the accident or illness. If a patient is seen for a routine cold or condition unrelated to her workers' comp claim, then her private insurance would be billed in this instance. Providers are required to accept payment in full according to the workers' compensation allowable fee for services rendered. Any balance due on the account after this insurance has paid must be adjusted or charged off; it cannot be balance billed to the patient.

When registering patients who have workers' compensation benefits, it is important to obtain the date of injury because this information is required for claims processing. A claim number assigned by the workers' comp carrier is also needed to properly file the claim. This number goes in box 11 on the CMS-1500 claim form. The name of the patient's employer goes in box 11b, and the name of the workers' compensation carrier goes in box 11c. The CMS-1500 claim form is discussed later in this chapter.

Managed Care

Managed care is a broad term used to describe several types of prepaid healthcare plans. Common types of managed care plans include health maintenance organizations (HMOs), preferred provider organizations (PPOs), and point-of-service (POS) plans.

Members of HMOs pay a set premium and are entitled to receive a specific range of healthcare services. HMOs control costs by requiring members of the plan to seek services only from a pre-approved list of providers, who are reimbursed at discounted rates. The plans also control access to medical specialists, expensive diagnostic and treatment procedures, and high-cost pharmaceuticals. They generally require pre-approval for specialty consultations, inpatient care, and surgical procedures, and they require referrals for specialist visits. HMOs typically do not have an out-of-network option and if the patient chooses to see a provider that does not participate, then the patient will be responsible for all charges. PPOs allow patients more freedom of who they want to see without the need for a referral as long as the provider participates (in-network) with the plan. Like HMOs, PPOs also have a co-payment and deductible. Many PPOs have out-of-network options where the benefit is reduced, requiring the patient to pay a higher out-of-pocket expense.

Revenue Cycle

The revenue cycle actually begins when the physician signs a contract with the payer to accept *X* amount for services rendered and ends when the account is paid in full or zeroed out. Figures 3.6 and 3.7 illustrate the components of this cycle. Figure 3.7 lists each step in the cycle and helps demonstrate the importance of the information collected and the role of each staff member. It is important that the physician and the office staff understand what the contract includes and get questions answered in a timely manner and adequately. The following basic information must be made available to front desk and insurance department staff about each contract the clinic has agreed to with a carrier:

- **Fee schedule**. How much are they going to reimburse for services?
- **Timely filing parameters**. How long does the clinic have to file the claim with the carrier? Some carriers have deadlines as short as 60 days from the day of service to as long as 36 months after the day of service.
- **Payer ID**. This is required for electronic billing through the clearinghouse.
- **Claim form completion**. Do they have unique requirements for the completion of the CMS-1500?

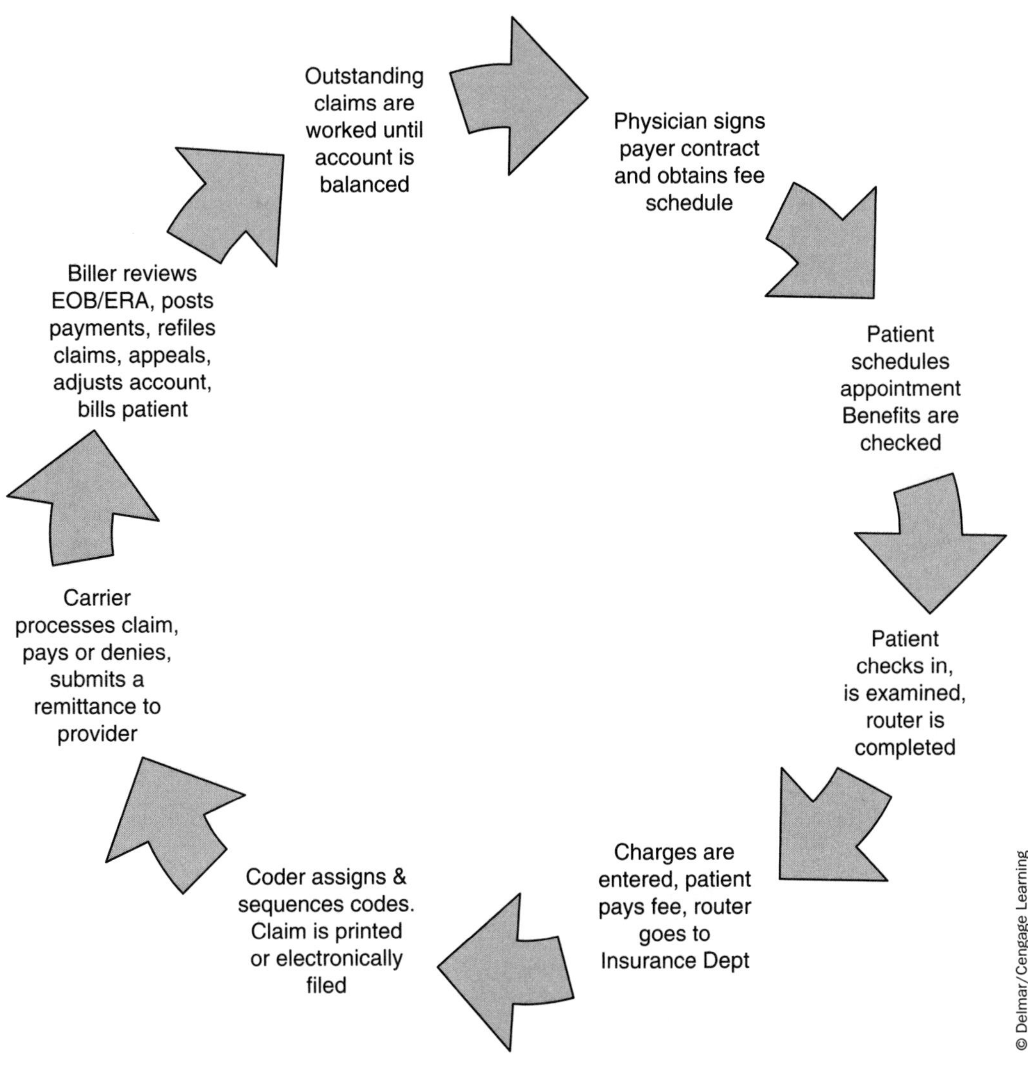

Figure 3.6 Revenue Cycle Components

- **Referral.** Is a referral required before we can treat the patient or send them to a specialist?
- **Area representative.** Who do we contact when we have questions or concerns? How do we get updates to the contract and covered services?
- **Payer policies.** Where do we go to get their specific policies on covered services?

This basic information about each contract should be made available to staff members who are responsible for scheduling, precerting, collecting patient co-pays and co-insurance, and posting payments.

It is important that office staff understand that reimbursement for health care services has steadily declined with the implementation of managed care. It is not unusual for a medical practice to report a gross collections rate of 60%, meaning that the office collects $0.60 out of every dollar billed. It is extremely important to bill the service correctly the first time to avoid additional lost revenue associated with resubmitting the claim or denials due to timely filing deadlines. Studies have shown that the cost of reworking and resubmitting a claim is approximately $25.

Scheduling

The next step in the process is patient scheduling. Contracts determine which patients may be seen in the office and outlines the terms of claims processing and reimbursement. Upon scheduling, the office staff member can begin the collections process by informing the patient that co-pays and co-insurances

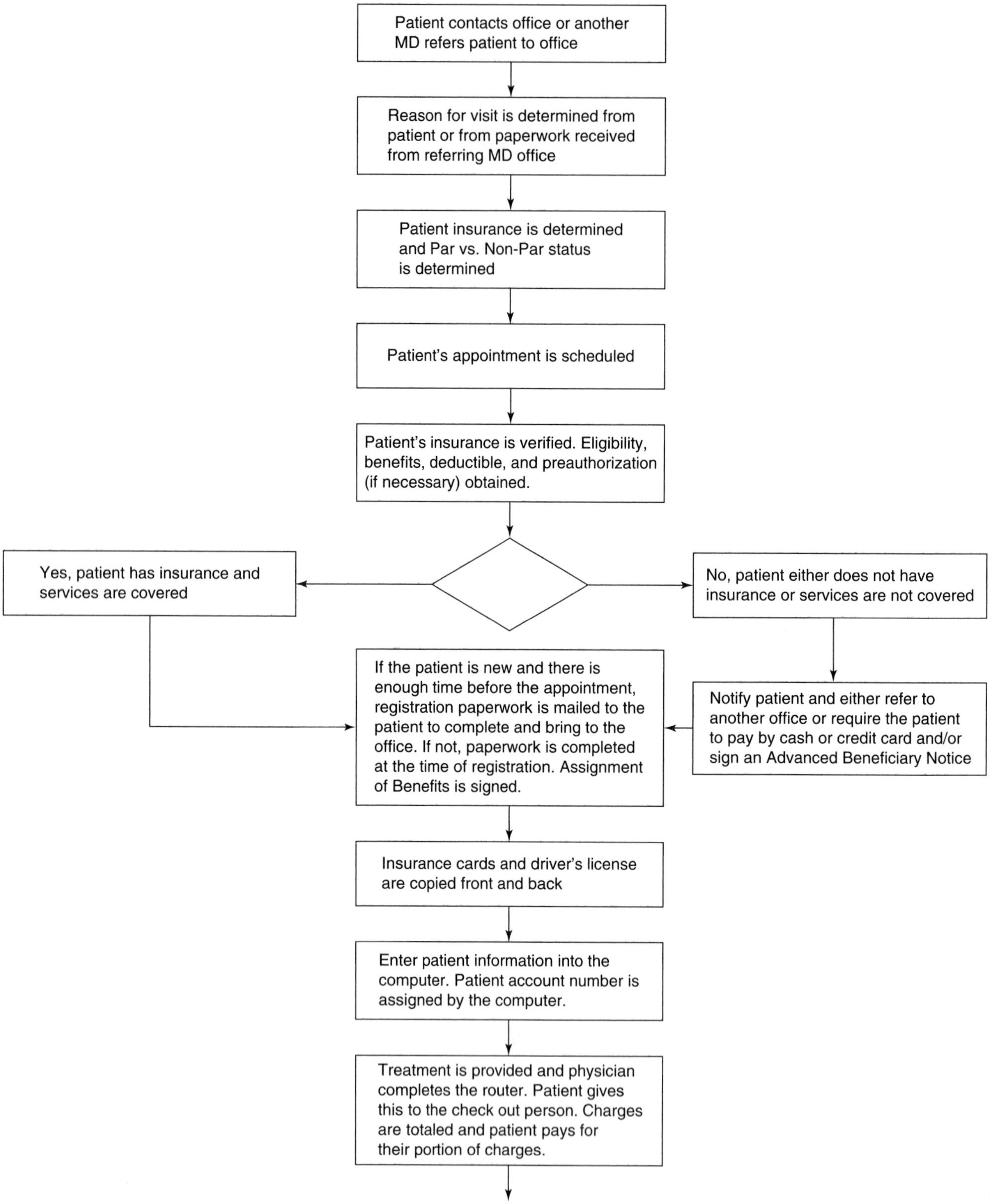

Patient contacts office or another MD refers patient to office

Reason for visit is determined from patient or from paperwork received from referring MD office

Patient insurance is determined and Par vs. Non-Par status is determined

Patient's appointment is scheduled

Patient's insurance is verified. Eligibility, benefits, deductible, and preauthorization (if necessary) obtained.

Yes, patient has insurance and services are covered

No, patient either does not have insurance or services are not covered

Notify patient and either refer to another office or require the patient to pay by cash or credit card and/or sign an Advanced Beneficiary Notice

If the patient is new and there is enough time before the appointment, registration paperwork is mailed to the patient to complete and bring to the office. If not, paperwork is completed at the time of registration. Assignment of Benefits is signed.

Insurance cards and driver's license are copied front and back

Enter patient information into the computer. Patient account number is assigned by the computer.

Treatment is provided and physician completes the router. Patient gives this to the check out person. Charges are totaled and patient pays for their portion of charges.

Figure 3.7 Revenue Cycle (continued)

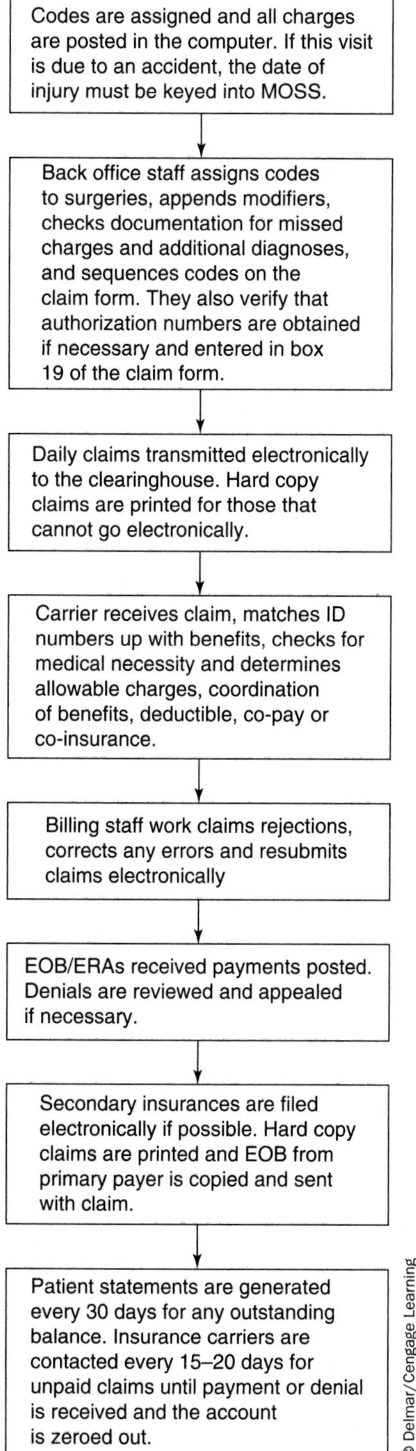

Codes are assigned and all charges are posted in the computer. If this visit is due to an accident, the date of injury must be keyed into MOSS.
Back office staff assigns codes to surgeries, appends modifiers, checks documentation for missed charges and additional diagnoses, and sequences codes on the claim form. They also verify that authorization numbers are obtained if necessary and entered in box 19 of the claim form.
Daily claims transmitted electronically to the clearinghouse. Hard copy claims are printed for those that cannot go electronically.
Carrier receives claim, matches ID numbers up with benefits, checks for medical necessity and determines allowable charges, coordination of benefits, deductible, co-pay or co-insurance.
Billing staff work claims rejections, corrects any errors and resubmits claims electronically
EOB/ERAs received payments posted. Denials are reviewed and appealed if necessary.
Secondary insurances are filed electronically if possible. Hard copy claims are printed and EOB from primary payer is copied and sent with claim.
Patient statements are generated every 30 days for any outstanding balance. Insurance carriers are contacted every 15–20 days for unpaid claims until payment or denial is received and the account is zeroed out.

Figure 3.7 Revenue Cycle

are due at the time of service. She should obtain pertinent insurance information from the patient or referring physician's office. This way, she can determine if the office is in or out of network and inform the patient of his/her financial obligations. At a minimum, the staff member must obtain the following elements from the patient at the time of scheduling:

- Patient full name, Social Security Number (SSN), and date of birth
- Primary insurance carrier and policy number
- Primary insurance subscriber's name, date of birth, and employer
- Secondary insurance carrier and policy number
- Secondary insurance subscriber's name, date of birth, and employer
- Referring physician's name (if applicable)
- Patient phone number

Registration

Front desk staff's ability to accurately obtain patient information is crucial to billing. Each year the patient should update personal and insurance information. Staff must be able to communicate financial policies to patients. While the patient is completing paperwork, staff verifies insurance benefits and eligibility if this was not done prior to patient arrival. At the time of check-in, staff should ask established patients if there are any changes to their personal or insurance information. If the guarantor's address is different from the patient's, update this in the patient registration screen. The guarantor's address is the address that statements and correspondence will be sent to. Registration staff is responsible for obtaining signatures from patients, making copies of insurance cards and driver's license, and collecting co-pays and outstanding balances. The patient will complete the Patient Registration Form, HIPAA Privacy Notice, and Assignment of Benefits and Patient Representation.

Exercise 3.4 Your Turn to Try

You are working the front desk today and will be collecting money from patients. In the following scenarios, determine what to collect from the patient at check-out.

1. Beth saw her family physician, Dr. Heath. She has a managed care plan and Dr. Heath is her primary care physician. Dr. Heath's charge for the office visit is $75. Her insurance card says she has a $10 co-pay for PCP and $20 co-pay for specialists. Dr. Heath knows that his office charge exceeds this managed care plan by $15. What will Beth pay at checkout? Is this a co-pay or co-insurance for the patient? What is the amount that Dr. Heath is expecting in reimbursement from Beth's managed care plan for this visit?

   ____

   ____

2. Susan's insurance benefits were verified. She has a co-insurance of 20%. Her initial office visit was billed at $200 to her insurance company. The contractual allowable for this service is $170. How much will Susan pay at checkout? How much should the check be that the insurance company sends the doctor? What is the contractual adjustment?

   ____

   ____

3. John saw Dr. Schwartz for his BP check and medication adjustment. He is self-pay. The router indicates 99212 with a fee of $59. He also wrote a check to us three months ago for $59 that was returned for insufficient funds. We assessed a $30 non-sufficient funds (NSF) fee to his account. How much do you collect from him today? ______________________________

Charge Entry

Each day charges for office visits are captured on the router and entered into MOSS. Charges for hospital visits are recorded on the Hospital Charge Form and entered into MOSS at least twice a week.

Coding

Coding staff compare charges and codes from routers and Hospital Charge Tickets with documentation confirming that all services have been accounted for. Coders have electronic access to the hospital's registration system and can retrieve operative reports, consults, path reports, H&Ps, and discharge summaries for accurate coding. Coding staff check NCDs, LCDs, global periods, CCI for Medicare, and federal programs, and assign modifiers. Coders also ensure that the sequencing of the codes on the claim form is in highest to lowest RVU order. RVU is a predetermined weight assigned to each CPT code used in calculating physician reimbursement. Elements factored into achieving this number are physician work, practice expense, and malpractice expense. This sequencing allows the services to be listed in descending order according to the anticipated payment. In other words, the code sequenced first should be the one that entails more physician work, practice expense, and malpractice expense; hence, greater payment. Many payers have a multiple procedure discount methodology whereby one procedure code is paid at 100% of the allowed amount and the others are paid at a portion thereof. By listing the highest paying service first, the clinic can expect to receive 100% of the allowed amount for that CPT code. The second service is paid at 50% of the allowed amount, and anything beyond the second service is paid at 25% of the allowed amount. By sequencing the most resource intensive service first, the clinic is optimizing the total amount payable. Codes and any missed charges are entered into MOSS, and a claim is generated.

Exercise 3.5 Your Turn to Try

Donald Blair is seen in the office on 11/1/09 for increased cough and fever. The patient has chronic asthma for which he takes medication and an inhaler. He is followed by Dr. Schwartz. After examining the patient, the doctor determines that Mr. Blair has viral pneumonia and a nebulizer treatment is performed in the office. The doctor lists the following codes on the router: 99214 Established patient Level IV, 94640 Nebulizer treatment, J7609 Albuterol 1mg INH. The router number is 15.

Use your CPT, ICD-9, and HCPCS books to assign the codes for the visit today. Enter the charges into MOSS.

Step 1 From the main menu in MOSS, select the *Procedure Posting* button. Search for Donald Blair's name. Select his name and click the *Add* button. This will allow you to add procedures to his account.

Step 2 A procedure window will pop up. You can use the Tab key to move from field to field. Enter the following information:

1. Router number 15 in field 1.
2. Select D.J. Schwartz as the provider in field 2.

3. In field 3, *POS,* use the dropdown arrow and choose *Office*. POS refers to the place where services were performed, place of service.
4. Leave field 4 blank. I does not apply because the POS was office.
5. Enter the DOS 11/1/2009 in field 5. Field 6 does not apply in this case because services occurred on one day only.
6. Enter the first CPT code 99214 in field 8. Once the Enter key is hit, the price of the procedure should display in field 10, *Charges: Ins:.*
7. Make sure field 11 is set to *Primary*. We want the bill to go to the primary insurance first.
8. In fields 12a–d enter the patient's diagnosis codes. There is room for only four codes on the claim form, so there are only four fields in which to enter information. The primary diagnosis code goes in Field 12a. You can either key the code directly into the field or use the magnifying search icon to the right of the field to search for the code. Only key in the ICD-9 codes that correspond with that CPT code. This is where you indicate which codes to link on the claim form.

   You will encounter two codes that are not listed in MOSS. When entering the codes into field 12, if MOSS does not recognize the code an error box will appear stating *Incorrect Diagnosis Code!* This does not mean the actual code is incorrect; it simply means the code has never been entered into MOSS before and must be added. You may do so by clicking on the magnifying glass. When the *ICD9 Code* box opens, click *Add.* Another box will appear with a list of codes and descriptions. Click *Add* again. Enter the code in its entirety (including the decimal point). Tab over to the description and type in the description. When you are done, choose *Close.* You can now enter this code and Tab to the next diagnosis box.
9. Field 13 should be checked *No* because this is not a visit related to an accident.
10. Click the *Post* button. This posts one charge line at a time to the patient's account. You should see this displayed in the *Posting Detail* section of the screen. Click the *Close* button and continue on with the same process described here until all CPT codes and charges have been entered. You will find two procedure codes that must be added to MOSS in the same way the ICD-9 codes were added previously. Next to field 8, *CPT Code,* there is a magnifying glass. When the *CPT Code* box opens, click *Add.* Another box will appear with a list of codes and descriptions. Click *Add* again. Enter the code. Tab over to the description and type in the description. You must also tab another field over to enter the fee for this service or supply. To find the fee for this code, you must refer to the procedure fee schedule on the CD-ROM. Locate this code on the fee schedule and obtain the price. Enter the dollar amount obtained from the fee schedule now. When you are done, choose *Close.* You can now enter this code and Tab to the next field.
11. When you have completed entering all ICD-9 and CPT codes, and you are sure the entry is correct, click on the *Post* button.

Check your work with Figure 3.8.

Billing

Billing is a three-fold process to file a clean claim to the insurance carrier for payment of services rendered. This process consists of claims preparation, claims editing, and claims submission. The goal is to submit a clean claim within a few days of the service being rendered. To keep cash flowing into the practice and to receive appropriate payment, the claims must be submitted in a timely manner and without errors. This cash flow is referred to as **accounts receivable** (it is more commonly referred to as A/R). A/R is monies that are outstanding from patients and insurance carriers. If the A/R is high, this means less money is coming in to the practice. When A/R is low, patients and insurance carriers are paying their portions on time, and more cash is flowing into the bank account. Lack of clean claims will choke off cash flow to the practice. The following are common billing errors that cause a claim to be denied or *kicked back* from a payer or clearinghouse:

- The referring (or ordering) physician's name/identification number was not listed in areas 17/17a of the claim forms. This is required when reporting diagnostic services and consults.

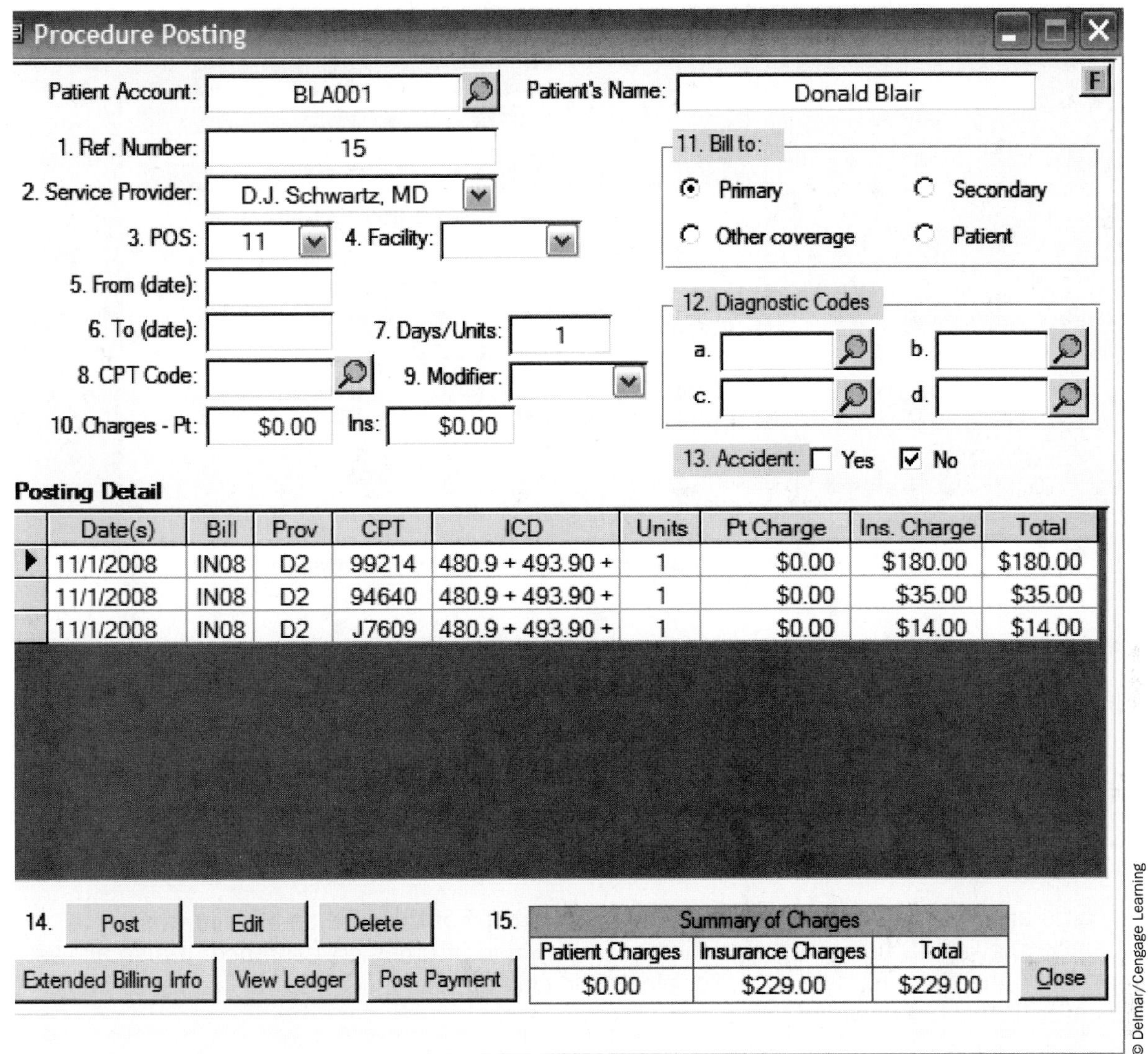

Procedure Posting

Patient Account: BLA001

Patient's Name: Donald Blair

1. Ref. Number: 15

2. Service Provider: D.J. Schwartz, MD

3. POS: 11

4. Facility:

5. From (date):

6. To (date):

7. Days/Units: 1

8. CPT Code:

9. Modifier:

10. Charges - Pt: $0.00 Ins: $0.00

11. Bill to: Primary / Secondary / Other coverage / Patient

12. Diagnostic Codes a. b. c. d.

13. Accident: Yes No

Posting Detail

Date(s)	Bill	Prov	CPT	ICD	Units	Pt Charge	Ins. Charge	Total
11/1/2008	IN08	D2	99214	480.9 + 493.90 +	1	$0.00	$180.00	$180.00
11/1/2008	IN08	D2	94640	480.9 + 493.90 +	1	$0.00	$35.00	$35.00
11/1/2008	IN08	D2	J7609	480.9 + 493.90 +	1	$0.00	$14.00	$14.00

14. Post Edit Delete

Extended Billing Info View Ledger Post Payment

15. Summary of Charges

Patient Charges	Insurance Charges	Total
$0.00	$229.00	$229.00

Close

Figure 3.8 Check Your Work for Step 11.

- E/M codes and their places of service didn't match.
- Diagnosis codes were invalid or missing a fifth digit.
- An inaccurate provider number was entered.
- The patient can't be identified in the payer system because of a nonmatching identification number.
- The patient is not identified because the name on the insurance card does not match the name on the claim. The name on the claim must be listed *exactly* as it appears on the insurance card.
- Field 32 on the claim form, which identifies where the service occurred, was not filled out properly, often excluding the site of service's street address, city, state, or zip code.
- The procedure code or modifier was invalid on or deleted prior to the date of service.
- Medicare was the secondary payer, but fields 11, 11a, 11b, and 11c were not filled out on the claim form.
- Missing date of birth and gender of subscriber.
- Punctuation such as hyphens, periods, and commas in the patient name and insurance ID.

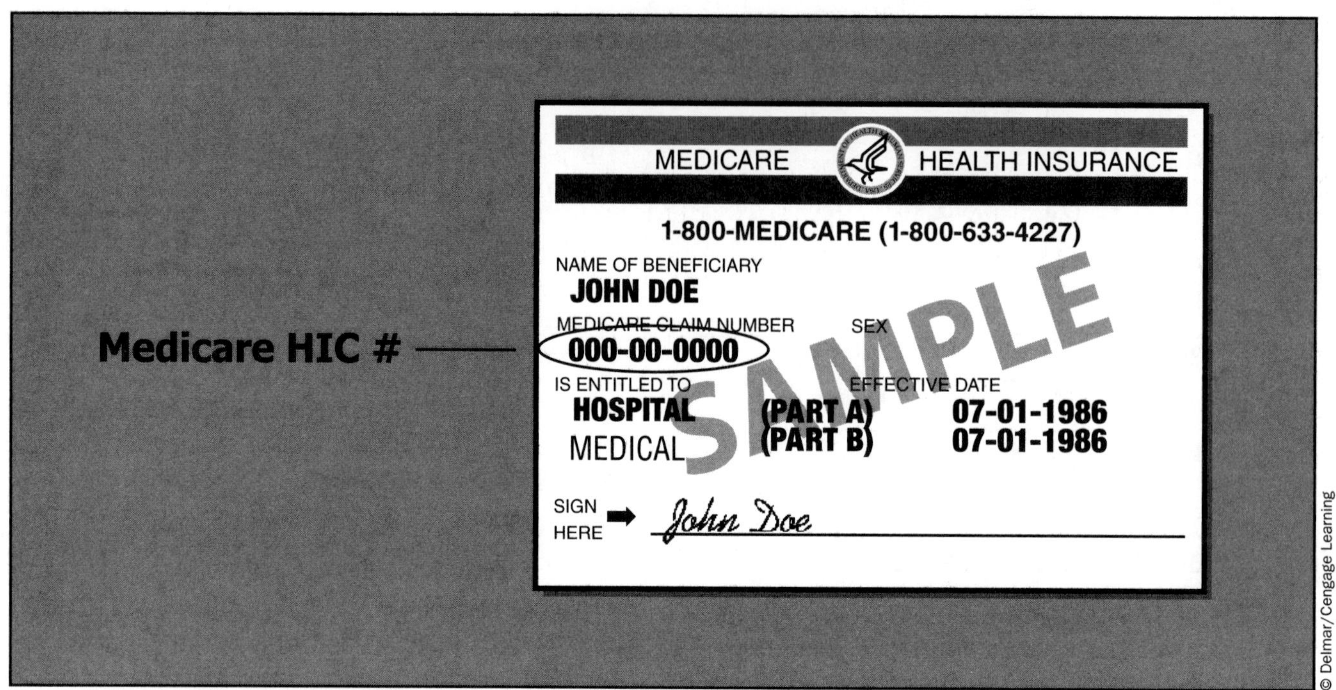

Figure 3.9 Sample Medicare Card

In this example, the patient's card in Figure 3.9 states John Doe and his ID number is 000-00-0000. The patient registers with DMA and indicates his name is John H. Doe. If a claim were submitted with his name as John H Doe, the claim would come back unpaid as not being able to identify the patient.

Insurance cards are crucial to the billing process. Having a copy of the card on file allows staff to check patient name spelling, ID number, group number, co-pay, and at times co-insurance. It also allows staff to confirm where the claim is to be sent. For electronic claims submission, some insurance cards even have the payer ID number provided.

CMS 1500 Claim Form Preparation

Patient data that is entered into MOSS along with charges, codes, rendering and referring provider, and service location all populate fields on the CMS 1500 claim form. MOSS is programmed to take the information keyed to print in the correct fields. The data elements located in Table 3-2 must be obtained from the medical record or router in order to input adequate information into MOSS to generate a complete claim. This information must be on every claim form regardless of payer. If any of this information is missing, you must seek it by contacting the patient or physician. A claim is considered unprocessable if it is submitted with incomplete or missing required information, or if it contains characters that are invalid. A claim returned as unprocessable for incomplete or invalid information does not meet the criteria to be considered a claim, is not denied, and, as such, is not afforded appeal rights.

The CMS 1500 is the paper claim form approved by CMS. The ANSI 837P is the electronic version of this claim that is submitted through a clearinghouse to a carrier for processing. Figure 3.10 shows this form. CMS has instructions in the *Medicare Carrier Manual* and on state Medicare carrier websites for completing this form correctly. The following list discusses fields on the claim form that are problematic.

- Boxes 10a–c are mandatory if the patient is being treated as a result of an accident.
- Boxes 12–13. The words *Signature on File* or *SOF* must be present to indicate that the patient authorizes the release of medical information to the insurance carrier as needed to get the claim paid and reimbursement to be directly paid to the provider and not the patient.

Table 3-2 Data Elements Required for Claims Submission

Patient Demographics	Insurance Information	Clinical Information
Patient name	Primary insurance	Name and NPI of referring MD
Date of birth	Secondary insurance	Name and NPI of rendering provider
Gender	Insurance ID number(s)	Address of rendering provider
Address	Relationship to policy holder (insured)	Place of service (location) where services were provided and address
Social Security Number	Insured's name, address, date of birth	Dates of service (To and From)
	Insured's Social Security Number	CPT and ICD-9 codes

- Box 14 needs a date to determine onset of the illness or injury being treated on that day.
- Box 15 is filled in if the patient has had the same or a similar illness related to the condition being treated at this visit. Date when the patient first consulted the provider for treatment is entered here. Otherwise, leave blank.
- Box 17 and 17b. The name is the referring provider, ordering provider, or supervising provider who referred, ordered, or supervised the service(s) or supply/supplies. The number is the NPI number. The **National Provider Identification (NPI)** number is a unique number assigned to each provider by the National Provider System. This 10-digit number replaces the former UPIN and Medicare PIN numbers effective 2007.
- Box 22 is populated if the patient's insurance plan required preauthorization and the provider was given a number.
- Box 24E. To demonstrate medical necessity, each procedure line must be linked to one or more ICD-9 codes in box 21.
- Box 24G. Enter the number of days or units. This field is most commonly used for multiple visits, units of supplies, anesthesia units or minutes, or oxygen volume. If only one service is performed, the numeral *1* must be entered.
- Box 33a–b. Enter the provider's or supplier's billing name, address, zip code, and phone number. The phone number is to be entered in the area to the right of the field title. Box 33a is the rendering providers' NPI number. Box 33b is the rendering provider's payer assigned unique identifier. Enter the name and address information in the following format:

First line: Name

Second line: Address

Third line: City, state, and zip code

Claim Rejects

There are two types of claim rejects: format and content. CPT code rejects occur at the clearinghouse and are considered to be pre-adjudicated errors, meaning the claim is rejected at the clearinghouse and not rejected from the payer. These rejections require staff to fix the transaction and resubmit. **Format rejects** are technical rejects that occur at the batch level and not at the claim level. Format rejects are comprised of claim form formatting errors where information must be populated in certain fields and loops of the electronic claim and relate to the initial practice management system setup. **Content rejects** are generated because of missing data elements from the claim form. These can occur from the clearinghouse or from the payer. These rejects can cause significant delays in claims processing, and providers may find themselves being penalized by state clean claims legislation and timely filing deadlines.

1500

HEALTH INSURANCE CLAIM FORM

APPROVED BY NATIONAL UNIFORM CLAIM COMMITTEE 08/05

PICA PICA

CARRIER

1. MEDICARE (Medicare #) MEDICAID (Medicaid #) TRICARE CHAMPUS (Sponsor's SSN) CHAMPVA (Member ID#) GROUP HEALTH PLAN (SSN or ID) FECA BLK LUNG (SSN) OTHER (ID)

1a. INSURED'S I.D. NUMBER (For Program in Item 1)

2. PATIENT'S NAME (Last Name, First Name, Middle Initial)

3. PATIENT'S BIRTH DATE MM DD YY SEX M F

4. INSURED'S NAME (Last Name, First Name, Middle Initial)

5. PATIENT'S ADDRESS (No., Street)

6. PATIENT RELATIONSHIP TO INSURED Self Spouse Child Other

7. INSURED'S ADDRESS (No., Street)

CITY STATE

8. PATIENT STATUS Single Married Other

CITY STATE

ZIP CODE TELEPHONE (Include Area Code) ( )

Employed Full-Time Student Part-Time Student

ZIP CODE TELEPHONE (Include Area Code) ( )

9. OTHER INSURED'S NAME (Last Name, First Name, Middle Initial)

10. IS PATIENT'S CONDITION RELATED TO:

11. INSURED'S POLICY GROUP OR FECA NUMBER

a. OTHER INSURED'S POLICY OR GROUP NUMBER

a. EMPLOYMENT? (Current or Previous) YES NO

a. INSURED'S DATE OF BIRTH MM DD YY SEX M F

b. OTHER INSURED'S DATE OF BIRTH MM DD YY SEX M F

b. AUTO ACCIDENT? YES NO PLACE (State)

b. EMPLOYER'S NAME OR SCHOOL NAME

c. EMPLOYER'S NAME OR SCHOOL NAME

c. OTHER ACCIDENT? YES NO

c. INSURANCE PLAN NAME OR PROGRAM NAME

d. INSURANCE PLAN NAME OR PROGRAM NAME

10d. RESERVED FOR LOCAL USE

d. IS THERE ANOTHER HEALTH BENEFIT PLAN? YES NO ***If yes,*** return to and complete item 9 a-d.

READ BACK OF FORM BEFORE COMPLETING & SIGNING THIS FORM.

12. PATIENT'S OR AUTHORIZED PERSON'S SIGNATURE I authorize the release of any medical or other information necessary to process this claim. I also request payment of government benefits either to myself or to the party who accepts assignment below.

SIGNED DATE

13. INSURED'S OR AUTHORIZED PERSON'S SIGNATURE I authorize payment of medical benefits to the undersigned physician or supplier for services described below.

SIGNED

PATIENT AND INSURED INFORMATION

14. DATE OF CURRENT: MM DD YY ILLNESS (First symptom) OR INJURY (Accident) OR PREGNANCY(LMP)

15. IF PATIENT HAS HAD SAME OR SIMILAR ILLNESS. GIVE FIRST DATE MM DD YY

16. DATES PATIENT UNABLE TO WORK IN CURRENT OCCUPATION FROM MM DD YY TO MM DD YY

17. NAME OF REFERRING PROVIDER OR OTHER SOURCE

17a.

17b. NPI

18. HOSPITALIZATION DATES RELATED TO CURRENT SERVICES FROM MM DD YY TO MM DD YY

19. RESERVED FOR LOCAL USE

20. OUTSIDE LAB? YES NO $ CHARGES

21. DIAGNOSIS OR NATURE OF ILLNESS OR INJURY (Relate Items 1, 2, 3 or 4 to Item 24E by Line)

1. ___ . ___

2. ___ . ___

3. ___ . ___

4. ___ . ___

22. MEDICAID RESUBMISSION CODE ORIGINAL REF. NO.

23. PRIOR AUTHORIZATION NUMBER

	24. A. DATE(S) OF SERVICE From MM DD YY	To MM DD YY	B. PLACE OF SERVICE	C. EMG	D. PROCEDURES, SERVICES, OR SUPPLIES (Explain Unusual Circumstances) CPT/HCPCS	MODIFIER	E. DIAGNOSIS POINTER	F. $ CHARGES	G. DAYS OR UNITS	H. EPSDT Family Plan	I. ID. QUAL.	J. RENDERING PROVIDER ID. #
1											NPI	
2											NPI	
3											NPI	
4											NPI	
5											NPI	
6											NPI	

25. FEDERAL TAX I.D. NUMBER SSN EIN

26. PATIENT'S ACCOUNT NO.

27. ACCEPT ASSIGNMENT? (For govt. claims, see back) YES NO

28. TOTAL CHARGE $

29. AMOUNT PAID $

30. BALANCE DUE $

31. SIGNATURE OF PHYSICIAN OR SUPPLIER INCLUDING DEGREES OR CREDENTIALS (I certify that the statements on the reverse apply to this bill and are made a part thereof.)

SIGNED DATE

32. SERVICE FACILITY LOCATION INFORMATION

a. NPI b.

33. BILLING PROVIDER INFO & PH # ( )

a. NPI b.

PHYSICIAN OR SUPPLIER INFORMATION

NUCC Instruction Manual available at: www.nucc.org

APPROVED OMB-0938-0999 FORM CMS-1500 (08-05)

Figure 3.10 CMS 1500 Claim Form

Interpreting an Explanation of Benefits (EOB)/Electronic Remittance Advice (ERA)

Reading the EOB or ERA is the responsibility of the person posting payments from the carriers. Any charge that is denied is researched to determine if it is necessary to appeal the denied charges, refer to the coder to make further recommendations for submitting a corrected claim, or confirm that the denial was appropriate. Payers often bundle separate codes together in an effort to pay the provider less. Just because the EOB says that certain code combinations are bundled doesn't mean the buck stops there and the charges should be adjusted. Bundling may be the result of a CPT code missing a modifier—typically -25 or -59. Does this mean that if a line comes back as bundled we automatically rebill with one of these modifiers? Of course not. We would review the documentation and have a coder determine if the documentation supports the services billed and confirm the need for a modifier. Figure 3.11 provides an example of a standard EOB. When posting payments from EOBs, look closely for coding changes such as adding or removing a modifier or recoding to a different code completely. Examine EOBs for the following red flags:

- Code omissions that look as though services were not performed. For example, on the claim filed, codes 99204-25 and 11740 were listed. When the EOB returned, 11740 was the only listed code.

EXPLANATION OF BENEFITS

PAGE 001 11/13/06 045093227

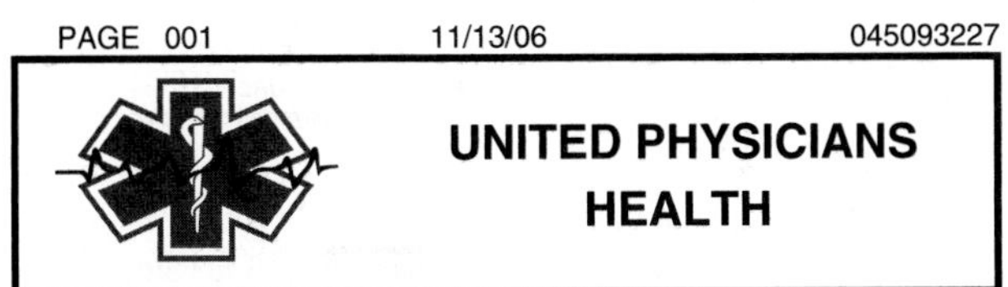

CHECK NUMBER: 0002033249

DOUGLASVILLE MEDICINE ASSOC.
5076 BRAND BLVD
DOUGLASVILLE, NY 01234

PHYSICIAN NUMBER OR EIN	DATE OF SERVICE (MON DAY YR)	PROCEDURE CODE	MOD	MOD	MOD	DAYS/ UNITS	CHARGE SUBMITTED	COVERED CHARGE	AMOUNT ALLOWED	PATIENT LIABILITY DEDUCT.	CO-PAY	COIN.	OTHER	PAYMENT	MESSAGE
ACCT# *		ID/CARD# 435605						NAME: DOE, JAYNE			CLAIM#: 11311C8020000				
045093227	080406	99213				1	80.00	80.00	47.00	.00	.00	.00	.00	15.00	SLM
		CLAIM TOTAL					80.00	80.00	47.00	.00	.00	.00	.00	15.00	
ACCT# *		ID/CARD# 777298						NAME: DOE, JOSEPH			CLAIM#: 11311C2990000				
045093227	072106	99244				1	260.00	.00	.00	.00	.00	.00	.00	.00	169
	072106	81000				1	17.00	.00	.00	.00	.00	.00	.00	.00	169
		CLAIM TOTAL					277.00	.00	.00	.00	.00	.00	.00	.00	
ACCT# *		ID/CARD# 777298						NAME: DOE, JOSEPH			CLAIM#: 11311C2990000			01	
045093227	072106	99244				1	260.00	260.00	140.00	.00	.00	.00	.00	25.00	ADJ SLM
	072106	81000				1	17.00	17.00	9.00	.00	.00	.00	.00	.00	ADJ SLM
		CLAIM TOTAL					277.00	277.00	149.00	.00	.00	.00	.00	25.00	
EOF 2354(02/05)						TOTAL	634.00							40.00	

ADJ THIS IS AN ADJUSTMENT OF A PREVIOUSLY PROCESSED SERVICE.

SLM COORDINATED WITH ANOTHER INSURANCE CONTRACT/POLICY. IF PRIMARY CARRIER PAYMENT EXCEEDS AMOUNT ALLOWED UNDER THIS SECONDARY PLAN, BENEFITS ARE NOT PAYABLE.

169 WE REQUESTED OTHER HEALTH INSURANCE INFORMATION FROM THE MEMBER. WE WILL REVIEW THE CLAIM FOR BENEFITS WHEN WE RECEIVE THIS INFORMATION.

Figure 3.11 Sample EOB

- Modifiers are stripped from the code submitted and there is no payment for the service.
- Bundling of charges into an unrelated procedure for a different diagnosis. EOB typically states: "Payment for this service is included in the fee for the procedure."
- Allowed amount is less than the provider's contracted amount.

Challenge the insurance carrier by appealing within the contract deadline and including all documentation. If there is no satisfaction or overturn, contact the carrier's medical director or provider relations.

Reading Explanation of Benefits

Careful attention is required when reading EOBs and posting payments. Keying errors, simple math mistakes, and lack of understanding of the terms encountered on the EOB are to blame for patient ledger mistakes. Patient names can look and sound familiar, numbers can be transposed, adjustments may not be taken correctly, and payments can be posted to the wrong date of service. Not all EOBs look alike, but they all have the same basic components. Once one's eye is trained to scan the document for these data elements, posting payments, taking adjustments, and balance billing patients will be done correctly.

EOBs/ERAs have the same core data elements. Table 3-3 defines these elements.

Table 3-3 EOB Data Elements Defined

Data Element	Definition/Use
Carrier	Insurance company's name and address.
Check number or EFT number	Number issued to check attached to the EOB. EFT number is the transaction number confirming electronic payment. It is listed on the deposit slip and is keyed into the system.
Check Amount	Total of all claim-level payments minus any provider contractual adjustments and patient responsibilities.
Physician Practice Name	Verify that the check belongs to the practice or facility before proceeding with posting payments.
Physician Provider Number/EIN/NPI number	Physician's unique number; used to confirm which provider to post the payment to.
Acct #/Name	Patient's name and/or practice-specific account number used to apply the payment to the correct patient account.
ICN/HICN Claim Number	Internal control number (ICN) 13-digit claim number assigned by the carrier upon receipt of the charges that were submitted for payment. Health insurance claim number (HICN) is the patient's insurance ID number.
Service Dates	Date of service corresponding the charges for services rendered.
Procedure Codes and Modifiers	CPT or HCPCS codes along with their respective modifiers assigned to the services rendered and submitted on the original claim.
Units	Units of service for each CPT/HCPCS code submitted.
Billed Amount	Charge submitted for each corresponding CPT/HCPCS code.
Allowed Amount	This amount is the cap the payer will pay any provider for that CPT code. Also called a maximum allowable fee, maximum charge, contracted fee, allowed fee, or allowable charge.
Covered Charge	Equals the billed amount if it is a service that is covered by the plan.

Data Element	Definition/Use
Patient Liability Deductible	This field shows how much of that payment was applied to the patient's deductible–meaning the patient owes this portion to the provider.
Co-pay	Set fee that the patient owes the provider per visit.
Co-insurance	Percentage of the allowed amount established by the patient's insurance benefits and owed by the patient to the provider.
Other	Amounts in this field are the responsibility of the patient and usually for noncovered services.
Payment	Amount paid to the provider for each service rendered.
Adj to Totals: Prev Paid	This field shows any previously paid amounts for this specific claim line and indicates that this line is adjusted.
Message/MOA	This field includes reason codes or remark codes and serves as communication to the provider about why payments were reduced, adjusted, or noncovered. The legend for these alpha or alphanumerical codes is located at the bottom of most EOBs.

Exercise 3.6 Your Turn to Try

Use the sample EOB in Figure 3.11 and answer the following questions.

1. What is the total amount paid to DMA? ________________
2. How much is the contractual adjustment for Jayne Doe's visit? ____________
3. Why is Joseph Doe's name appearing on this EOB twice for the same DOS, CPT codes, and charges? ____
4. How much does Jayne Doe owe for her visit? ______________________
5. Is United Physicians Health the primary or secondary insurance for Joseph Doe? ________________ ____
6. Why are the claim numbers different for Joseph Doe's visit on 7/21/06? ____________________ ____

Collections

The collections process encompasses many tasks such as account follow-up, denial management, patient statements (billing), and patient collections. Accounts that are "open" or have an outstanding insurance or patient balance are *worked* at least every 30 days. This step in the revenue cycle more than any other relies on the data that is acquired by running reports from *Reports Generation.* Here, business office staff and management can glean trends, track accounts receivable, and identify slow paying insurance carriers.

Insurance Follow-up

Billing staff are responsible for contacting insurance carriers to obtain claim status and inquire about payment. With the adoption of electronic claims filing, a clean claim should be processed and paid within 5 to 15 days from the time the claim was released. Providers are obligated to file claims within the payer's timely filing period. Payers in turn have a contractual obligation to pay clean claims in a timely fashion. Each state has its own rules and regulations with which coders and billers should become familiar.

Claims follow-up is a broad term used to refer to monitoring unpaid claims. Tasks built into this process include:

- Calling insurance carriers or visiting their websites to obtain a claim status. This confirms that the claim was received and is in the process of being paid or was denied.
- Reviewing all denied claims or claims paid at a reduced amount.
- Examining EOBs/ERAs and contacting the carrier for explanation when it is not clear why a claim is denied, what the carrier allowed for the service, and what the patient is responsible for.
- Appealing inappropriately denied or incorrectly paid claims.
- Communicating with carriers and complying with requests for additional information.
- Refiling claims that were not on file or were denied.
- Communicating with patients about their claims and statements.

If a claim is not paid or is denied, or if the insurance carrier has not requested additional information in a reasonable amount of time, typically 5 to 15 days, insurance staff follow up and determine the cause of the delay. A denied claim is not considered bad debt. Bad debt are charges that are unpaid by patients, not insurance carriers. Denied claims are also not the same as a rejected claim. Claims may be partially or completely denied. Reasons for denying claims include:

- Services not covered by the insurance carrier plan.
- Claim was not submitted within the timely filing requirements of the plan.
- The claim is a duplicate claim that was previously submitted and was either paid or denied.
- Services were billed but were not medically necessary.
- Services that were provided in the wrong place of service. Medicare has requirements that certain services be provided in the inpatient setting.
- Services may be denied for being performed during the global period of a procedure performed.
- Requested supporting documentation was not provided to carrier or was insufficient to support the services billed.

Staff is required to run the *Aging Report by Insurance Carrier* to track outstanding claims. This report groups all carriers with open claims and lists all patients with their respective account balance according to age of account. It is run once a week. This is a valuable report because offices can allocate insurance follow-up by carrier amongst staff, which reduces time spent searching for specific accounts. Focus can be on accounts in any age bracket or dollar value because this information is readily available on this report. It is run weekly to track payments received from the week prior and to ensure timely follow-up. This report makes follow-up simpler by listing all accounts for each carrier and the age of the account. From here, the biller can look up each account ledger and read any notes written by staff members. This is where notes will be written from conversations with carriers about claim status. Staff can also use the *Claims Tracking* option on the main menu. Here the insurance carrier is selected and the date range is entered, providing a similar report. This report can be seen as better because it shows the date of service and the procedure code. However, this report does not show the age of the claims by category (e.g., 0–30, 31–60). The staff member must consider this limitation when entering the date range. For example, if she wanted to determine all accounts for Great West that are over 30 days old but less than 60 days old, she would enter the *Start Date* 60 days prior to today's date, and the *End Date* would be 30 days prior to today's date. This query will bring up only outstanding accounts with dates of service that fall into the 31–60 day bucket.

Exercise 3.7 Your Turn to Try

Lindsay Morgan, your insurance supervisor, divided account follow-up by payer. She has assigned you Flexi-Health and Managed Med. This week your focus is following up on claims that are more than 60 days old. To know how many claims there are and what the account numbers are, you must first run your report.

Step 1 Click on the *Report Generation* button from the Main Menu (see Figure 3.12). This opens another window called the *Reports Panel* (see Figure 3.13).

Step 2 Five preloaded reports come standard with MOSS. Notice there is an Aging Date box in red. The date in this box should be 12/31/2009. Choose *Aging Report by Insurance Carriers & Patient Account No.* by clicking on the box to the right of number five.

Step 3 A separate window will pop up, previewing the report. Print the report. Notice that this report lists all payers, not just your assigned payers. To get a report with your assigned payers only, use the *Claim Tracking* option from the main menu as discussed earlier.

Step 4 Review the report. The main headings are Account Number, Patient Name, Age Delinquency Category (0-30, 31-60, 61-90, 91+), and Total Due. The insurance companies are listed in alphabetic order. Patient accounts associated with each payer are listed.

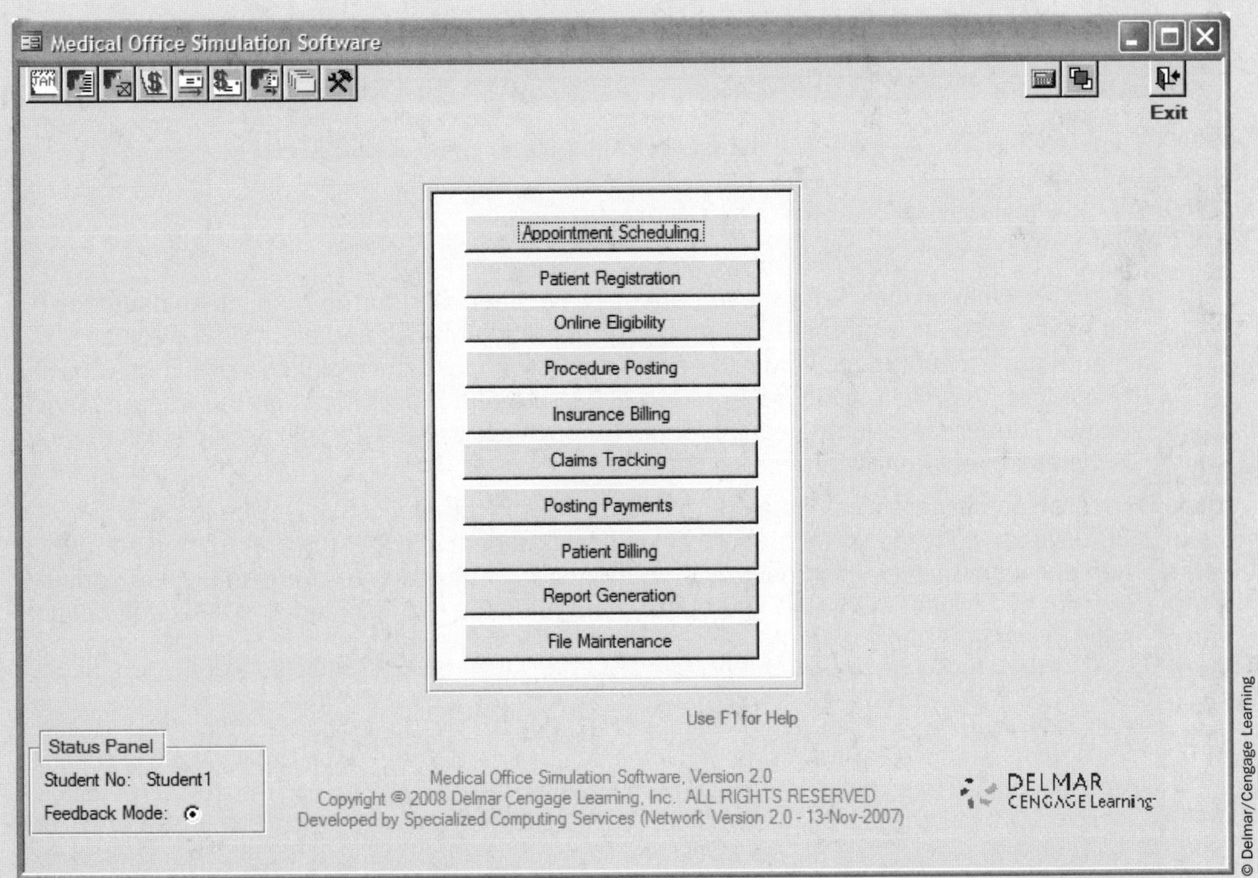

Figure 3.12 Main Menu

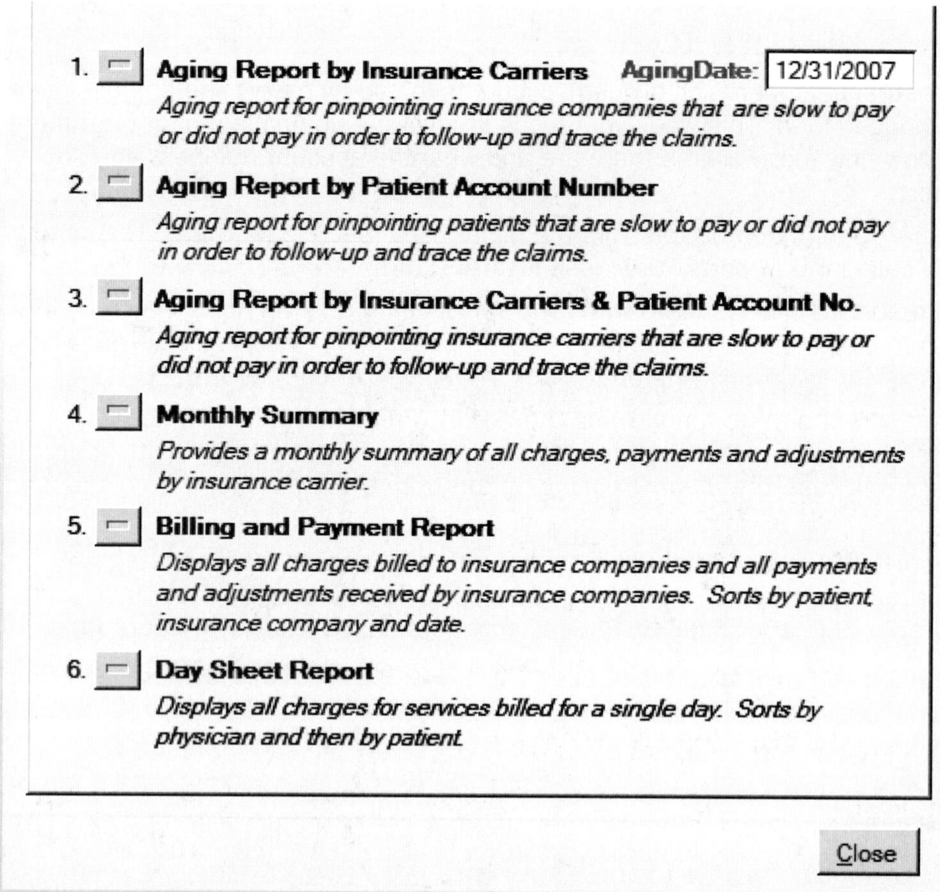

1. **Aging Report by Insurance Carriers** AgingDate: 12/31/2007
Aging report for pinpointing insurance companies that are slow to pay or did not pay in order to follow-up and trace the claims.

2. **Aging Report by Patient Account Number**
Aging report for pinpointing patients that are slow to pay or did not pay in order to follow-up and trace the claims.

3. **Aging Report by Insurance Carriers & Patient Account No.**
Aging report for pinpointing insurance carriers that are slow to pay or did not pay in order to follow-up and trace the claims.

4. **Monthly Summary**
Provides a monthly summary of all charges, payments and adjustments by insurance carrier.

5. **Billing and Payment Report**
Displays all charges billed to insurance companies and all payments and adjustments received by insurance companies. Sorts by patient, insurance company and date.

6. **Day Sheet Report**
Displays all charges for services billed for a single day. Sorts by physician and then by patient.

Close

Figure 3.13 Reports Panel

Step 5 Hypothetically, all claims for these patients have been filed to the respective insurance company, insurance payments received are posted in MOSS, and appropriate adjustments are accounted for. To double-check that these insurance claims were filed, you should run the *Billing and Payment* report. It is the fifth report listed on the *Reports Panel* screen. Under the column heading *Submitted by* the words *electronic* or *paper* will appear if the claim was generated and sent.

Step 6 Locate each patient who has an outstanding insurance balance for Flexihealth over 30 days as indicated on this report. Check each patient's ledger to confirm the information shown by checking for insurance payments and adjustments. You can access patient ledgers by clicking on the *Billing* dropdown menu on the main screen and selecting *patient ledger* (see in Figure 3.14).

Compare your findings with the following list:

1. **Stanley Kramer.** There is an insurance balance of $383 in the 61–90 day bucket. Check his account to see how many claims this entails and what the dates of service are. Upon viewing the ledger, you will see that he has three dates of service: 10/27/09, 10/29/09, 10/30/09. The 10/27/09 date of service (DOS) has charges of $145. The 10/29/09 DOS has a charge of $158 and the 10/30/09 DOS has an $80 charge. Next run the *Billing and Payment* report to see whether the claims were actually billed to the insurance carrier. You will find that the 10/29 and 10/30 DOS were not yet filed to the insurance company. According to this report, the 10/27/09 claim was filed electronically.

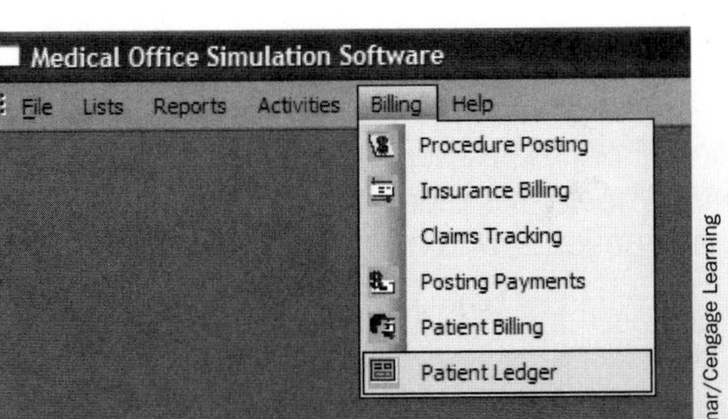

Figure 3.14 Selecting a Patient Ledger from the Pull Down Menu

Payment was not received for the charges that were submitted; therefore, follow-up is required. From the *Patient Ledger* screen, click on *Notes* and write a note about the actions you have taken.

2. **Elane Ybarra.** There is an insurance balance of $196 in the 61–90 day bucket. Upon checking her account and looking at the ledger, you see there were two charges for DOS 10/16/09, one charge for $16 and the other for $180. The *Billing and Payment* report does not show that either one of these charges was reported to the insurance company. From the *Patient Ledger* screen, click on *Notes* and place a note outlining the actions you have taken.
3. **Cynthia Worthington.** According to the *Aging Report* there is a $20 outstanding balance in the 91+ past due bucket.
   a. Look at the *Billing and Payment* report. Was the primary insurance billed?
   b. Was the claim sent electronically or on paper?
   c. What are the balance due totals for each procedure due from the insurance carrier?
   d. Does this total match the total from the *Aging Report?*
   e. What DOS is this balance for?
   f. Is this balance an insurance balance or a patient balance?

From the *Patient Ledger* screen, click on *Notes* and place a note regarding the actions you have taken.

Patient Statements

Patient statements for any patient balance (co-pay, co-insurance, deductible, noncovered service) are printed and mailed on the first of every month. A **statement** is a bill that itemizes a patient's account to include all charges, payments, and remaining balance. The **billing cycle** is the time between when one statement is sent and the next statement is sent. The typical lapse of time between statements is 30 days but may be as short as 15 days. Statements are mailed to patients after their primary and secondary insurances have paid. MOSS allows you to print statements with messages to the patients. These can be specific messages to a patient or group of patients, or you can include a standard message such as "Your insurance has paid. The balance due is your responsibility." This standard message is called a **dunning message** and will print on all statements. The message serves as a way of communicating with the patient, clarifying a situation, or explaining the reason for their balance. Statements should show recent account activity in addition to balance due such as insurance payments and contractual adjustments along with any patient payments.

Exercise 3.8 Your Turn to Try

Step 1 From the main menu, click on *Reports Generation*. From the *Reports Query* screen, select the number two report, *Aging Report by Account Number.* This report lists outstanding accounts for patient balances and is used to track patients who are slow to pay. Print this report.

Step 2 The balances on this report must be confirmed before printing patient statements. Refer to the *Insurance Billing and Payment* report printed for the previous exercise. Compare the names on *Aging Report by Account Number* to the names on the *Billing and Payment* report. Twenty-seven names are listed on the *Aging* report. For the purposes of this exercise, you will focus on the accounts that have a balance 61 to 90 days past due, bringing the count down to 12 names. We already worked the accounts for Flexihealth PPO in the previous exercise, so that leaves 9 accounts to review.

Step 3 The *Patient Ledger* can also be viewed while the *Aging* report is visible on the screen by using the pull-down menu called *Billing.* Search for this patient using the *Search* icon. Select the name and click on *View.* Compare the information and balance due on the ledger to the information and balance due on the *Aging* report. Determine that all claims were filed to the primary and secondary insurances (if applicable) and whether payments were received and posted. Determine the answers to the following questions for each account with a balance:

a. What is the actual balance due?

b. Is the outstanding balance pending an insurance payment? If so, which one and was it filed?

c. Is the balance due from the patient? How do you know?

d. If a patient statement is needed, what message would you want to provide on the statement?

Step 4 Compare your findings to Table 3-4. Determine which patients require a patient statement.

Step 5 From the Main Menu click on *Patient Billing.* Select the following settings to customize the patient statements:

1. In field 1, *Select Statement Type,* choose *Remainder Statement* to produce statements that show only the remaining balance due.
2. In field 2, *Provider,* choose *All*. This will allow statements to be produced for all doctors.
3. In field 3, *Settings,* use the dropdown box to select the patients to send statements to. If *All* is selected, this will print statements for all patients with a balance regardless of whether the balance is a true patient balance or an insurance balance. Because of this limitation, before statements can be mailed, you need to go through all the printed statements and discard the ones that are not true patient balances. The following patients are getting statements based on the information in Table 3-4:
   Vito Mangano, Robert Shinn, Eugene Sykes, Cynthia Worthington.
4. In field 4, *Process Type*, select *Preview on Screen.*
5. Field 5, *Global Dunning Message.* This message will be on all statements printed at this session. Type in this message: "Your insurance has been billed and paid. The balance shown is your responsibility. Please pay promptly."
6. Field 6, *Account Dunning Message.* Any message can be typed here to print on specific patient accounts. This is a unique dunning message that will not print on all patient statements.
7. Field 7, *Select Accounts for Message.* This box is used if you are sending statements to select patients with a message created in field 6. To select individual patients to receive this message, hold down the Ctrl (Control) key on the keyboard and click on the names from the list in the dropdown box in field 7. Do not let go of the Ctrl key until you have selected all the names you want.
8. Click on the *Process* button to create the statements. You can choose to save these statements to a file to print later, or you can bypass the *Save* feature and print immediately by clicking on the *Cancel* button.

Table 3-4 Patient Balance Analysis from Aging Report by Account Number

Name	Total Balance Due (from Aging report)	Insurance Balance?	Patient Balance?	Comments
Francois Blanc	$60.00	Yes. Medicare	No	Claim was filed electronically. Medicare will cross over the claim to Medicaid. No statement needed.
Xao Chang	$60.00	Yes. Medicare	No	Insurance needs billed. Not showing on Billing and Payment report. Medicare will cross over the claim to Medicaid. No statement needed.
Eric Gordon	$180.00	Yes. Consumer One HRA	No	According to the Billing and Payment report insurance was filed electronically.
Vito Mangano	$210.00	Yes. Medicare	No	There were three charges for the 10/27 DOS. All three show that they were filed electronically to Medicare.
Anna Pinkston	$78.00	Yes. Medicare	No	Insurance was filed electronically. Medicare will cross over the claim to Medicaid. No statement needed.
Manual Ramirez	$1,780.83	Yes. Medicare and Century Senior Gap	No	Insurance was filed for all three DOS. Payment received for 10/19/09. Secondary insurance needs filed for this DOS. No patient statement needed.
Robert Shinn	$181.00	Yes. Signal HMO	no- $10 co-pay collected	No patient statement needed.
Wilma Stearn	$14.49	No	Yes	Insurance paid $55.30 and $2.65. Patient balance is for co-insurance. Send statement.
Eugene Sykes	$300.00	Yes	No	Insurance filed for 10/21 and 10/30/09. Patient paid co-pay of $10.00 at each visit.

9. Preview the statements on the screen. The patient name should appear in the upper left corner. The clinic name appears in the upper right corner. The general dunning message appears at the bottom under *Important Note.*

   NOTE: For future reference when printing statements, co-pay and co-insurance are two different payment amounts. Co-insurance balances are not shown separately on the statement, but they are included in the current balance column.

10. Print the statements and turn them into your instructor.

Review Questions

Fill in the Blank

1. Search the Internet for insurance guidelines or laws requiring insurance carriers to pay clean insurance claims within a set timeframe. Visit the National Association of Insurance Commissioners website at http://www.naic.org. Under *NAIC States and Jurisdictions*, select New York. On the right side, click on *Site Map.* Under *Consumer Resources* click on *Health.* Under *General Information,* click on the link to *Health Care Provider Rights.* What is the prompt pay provision for this state?

   ____

2. Visit the MedLearn Matters website by accessing CMS's website at http://www.cms.hhs.gov. Click on *Outreach and Education* and then on *MLN Educational Webguides.* Next, click on *Web-based*

Training Modules. Select the *CMS Form 1500* course. Complete this course and give the certificate of completion to your instructor.

3. Visit CMS's website (http://www.cms.hhs.gov) and take the following web-based course: Understanding the Remittance Advice for Professional Providers. To locate the course, select *Outreach and Education* and then *MLN Educational Web Guides.* Select *Web Based Training (WBT) Modules.* Select *Understanding the Remittance Advice for Professional Providers*. Complete the course and give your certificate of completion to your instructor.

True/False

1. A Medicare patient missed her appointment yesterday. DMA has a policy that allows them to charge $20 for missed scheduled appointments. A missed appointment fee should be assessed to her account.

   T or **F**

2. An HMO is an example of a government-sponsored plan.

   T or **F**

3. The NPI number is a 10-digit number.

   T or **F**

4. Mary has had BCBS insurance with her employer since 2007. Effective 8/1/09 her husband added her to his insurance, Manage Med. Because his birthday is earliest in the year, Manage Med is now considered her primary insurance.

   T or **F**

5. A premium is a set amount that a patient pays at each office visit.

   T or **F**

6. Providers who participate with a plan are not permitted to bill the patient the difference between what they charge and what the plan allows.

   T or **F**

7. The goal of a practice is to have a high A/R to indicate the anticipated revenue.

   T or **F**

8. The order in which CPT codes are listed on the claim form will affect reimbursement.

   T or **F**

9. If a doctor does not participate with a plan, the patient has no choice but to see another provider who does participate.

   T or **F**

10. Exclusions are items or services that are not covered by a plan.

    T or **F**

11. Workers' Compensation covers medical expenses for all visits and services as long at the employee is out of work.

    T or **F**

12. If an insurance plan uses the patient's Social Security Number as the insurance ID, dashes should be used to separate the numbers in block 1a of the claim form (i.e. 111-11-1111).

    T or **F**

Multiple Choice

1. What modifier is necessary when submitting claims for Medicare patients that have an ABN on file?
   a. GZ
   b. GA
   c. GY
   d. 59

2. Many insurance plans require the patient to pay a ___________ at each office visit.
   a. deductible
   b. premium
   c. co-pay
   d. contractual adjustment

3. The name of the common paper claim form is:
   a. HIPAA 1500
   b. CMS 1500
   c. ANSI 837P
   d. ANSI 1500P

4. Freda Dish is a 66-year-old office worker. She has been working full-time as a coder for 25 years. She has Medicare and Signal HMO through her office. Which is her primary insurance?
   a. Medicare
   b. Signal HMO

5. Dr. Mendenhall charged $500 for a procedure. Because she is a participating provider the plan allows $360 for procedure. Mary's plan requires a $100 deductible (not met) and pays at 100%. How much is the check that the insurance company sends Dr. Mendenhall?
   a. $500
   b. $400
   c. $360
   d. $260

6. ERISA guidelines apply to all payers with the exception of:
   a. Government payers
   b. Church plans
   c. Individual plans
   d. All of the above

7. The term used to describe the person who is insured:
   a. Spouse
   b. Beneficiary
   c. Enrollee
   d. Subscriber

8. A ___________ allows the patient to seek services from a provider that is in network or to self-refer to an out-of-network provider at a greater cost.
   a. HMO
   b. PPO
   c. Fee for Service
   d. Tricare

9. Charges from an office visit are captured on this form:
   a. Hospital charge ticket
   b. Chargemaster
   c. Encounter Form
   d. Fee Schedule

10. What should be done if a claim denial is received because a billed service was not a program benefit?
   a. Rebill with a letter of explanation from the physician
   b. Write off the amount on the patient's ledger
   c. Send the patient a statement with a notation of the response from the insurance company
   d. Appeal the decision with a statement from the physician

11. Insurance follow-up on unpaid claims should be done at a minimum every:
   a. week
   b. 30 days
   c. 15 days
   d. day

12. Which of the following terms indicates that the patient has authorized insurance payments to be made directly to the provider?
   a. assignment of benefits
   b. coordination of benefits
   c. accepts assignment
   d. balance billing

13. Which of the following practices would be the best way to prevent a high A/R?
   a. Verify insurance benefits and eligibility on all patients prior to scheduled service
   b. Send all claims hardcopy with supporting documentation
   c. Send all claims electronically as the patient is checking out
   d. Call carriers and alert them that claims are in route to them and to pay them promptly

Fill in the Blank

1. What is the Medicare deductible for the current year? Where do you go to get this information?
   ____

2. Blake is a 9-year-old being seen for strep throat. He has two insurances: BCBS through his dad's work and Great West through his mom's work. His dad's birthday is 1/2/69 and his mother's birthday is 3/20/69. Which insurance is primary for Blake? ____________________

3. Gus saw Dr. Heath on 7/11/07. Dr. Heath's charge was $175. DMA is not in Gus's insurance network. This is the first time Gus has used an out-of-network provider. Gus's insurance company pays at 90% with no deductible for in-network physicians. Out-of-network benefits are reduced to 70% with a $200 deductible. What is Gus's financial responsibility for this visit? Is this co-pay or co-insurance for the patient? ____________________

4. A patient is seen in the office today, 2/15/xx, for right flank pain. Block 14 on the CMS 1500 requires entry of the date the patient first experienced signs or symptoms of the illness or injury for which they are seen for today. The doctor did not document the specific day but did indicate that the patient has had this pain for four consecutive days. What date goes in this box, or should it be left blank? ____________________

5. A patient was seen in the hospital on 3/24/xx for a subsequent visit. The patient was discharged on 3/26/xx. What date(s) go in box 24A (FROM: and TO:)? ____________________

6. Search the CMS website to complete the following statement.

   Physician assistants are paid at ____________% of the Medicare Physician Fee Schedule or the actual charge, whichever is ____________.

7. Search the CMS website to complete the following statements.

   Assistant surgeons are paid at ________% of the Medicare Physician Fee Schedule. Co-surgeon services are paid at ________% of the Medicare Physician Fee Schedule and reported with modifier ________.

8. Answer questions a–g by using the following EOB.

EXPLANATION OF BENEFITS

Wellness America

CHECK NUMBER: 0008480051

DOUGLASVILLE MEDICINE ASSOC.
5076 BRAND BLVD
DOUGLASVILLE, NY 01234

PHYSICIAN NUMBER OR EIN	DATE OF SERVICE (MON DAY YR)	PROCEDURE CODE	MOD	MOD	MOD	DAYS/ UNITS	CHARGE SUBMITTED	COVERED CHARGE	AMOUNT ALLOWED	PATIENT LIABILITY DEDUCT.	CO-PAY	COIN.	OTHER	PAYMENT	MESSAGE
ACCT#		ID/CARD# 34200901						NAME: SANDERS, AUBREY				CLAIM# 11276L9440000			
045086221	071006	55700				1	400.00	400.00	203.28	.00	.00	.00	.00	40.66	368 MED COB
	071006	76942				1	200.00	200.00	130.21	.00	.00	.00	.00	26.04	368 MED COB
	071006	76872				1	250.00	250.00	104.39	.00	.00	.00	.00	20.88	368 MED COB
		CLAIM TOTAL					850.00	850.00	437.88	.00	.00	.00	.00	87.58	

COB BENEFITS WERE COORDINATED WITH ANOTHER INSURANCE CONTRACT/POLICY. PATIENT IS LIABLE FOR TOTALS REFLECTED IN PATIENT LIABILITY COLUMNS (BALANCE REMAINING AFTER PRIMARY PAYMENT.)

MED MEDICARE ASSIGNMENT WAS ACCEPTED AND IS REFLECTED IN THE AMOUNT ALLOWED.

368 MAXIMUM BENEFITS PROVIDED BY MEDICARE.

EOF 2354(02/05) TOTAL 850.00 87.58

a. What is the DOS for Aubrey Sanders' visit? ____________
b. Who is the primary insurance? ____________
c. Did she have a co-pay for this date of service? ____________
d. How many units were submitted for 76872? ____________
e. Does this provider participate with the primary insurance? How do you know? ____________
f. The paid amount of $20.88 represents what? ____________
g. What is the contractual adjustment amount? ____________

CHAPTER

4 Moss Orientation and Training

Learning Objectives

When finished with this chapter, the student will be able to:

1. Describe the basic modules of the Medical Office Simulation Software (MOSS) and what they are used for.
2. Discuss the use of practice management software in the components of the revenue cycle.
3. Demonstrate how to log on and navigate within the Medical Office Simulation Software (MOSS).
4. Discuss the importance of properly maintaining files in practice management software.
5. Demonstrate how to perform in the Medical Office Simulation Software (MOSS) each of the following data entry functions: scheduling, registration, charge entry, payment posting, claims submission, patient eligibility, patient billing, account adjustments, and report generation.

Background Basics

- Students must have completed a basic computer course using a Windows environment. This book does not discuss how to use Windows.
- Students should have a general understanding of the job tasks of a coder/biller.

Competency Checklist

- Coders and billers must be savvy about the practice management software system they are working in. They tend to be troubleshooters and trainers on how and where to put information into the system to produce a clean claim.
- Coders and billers need to understand the logic of the system and how to perform each data entry function to be able to logically trace errors back through the software.
- Business office staff is responsible for maintaining the chargemaster; entering new insurance carriers, providers and fee schedules; and correcting data entry errors in the system.

Business demands in healthcare are increasing with the ever changing CMS regulations, payer policies and requests, HIPAA, and claim submission requirements; therefore, business transactions must be efficient and consistent. Administrative job duties have to be automated to accommodate increasing patient volume, physician scheduling at multiple locations, tracking referrals, claims submission, and operational data reporting. A systematic process to collect patient demographics, ensure complete charge capture, file claims in a timely manner, apply payments, and perform account follow-up will provide a consistent cash flow to the practice. By using a practice management system, these goals can be accomplished. First, staff must be thoroughly trained on how to use the software to perform their jobs. Second, they need a comprehensive understanding of where the data is collected and by whom.

This chapter focuses on providing an overview of all the general functions of the Medical Office Simulation Software (MOSS). There are hundreds of software programs marketed to practices promising efficiency, lower accounts receivable (A/R), and faster payments. The majority of them are Windows-based and can be easily navigated once one system is mastered. They all provide seven common features or functions. Though others are much more complex than MOSS, the core functions are the same and are easily learned. Remember, MOSS was developed strictly for educational purposes and is limited in reporting and the capacity to perform complex financial transactions but its functionality is comparable to the basic systems available in the work setting and provides the basis to practice your skills in the seven core functions.

Core Components of Practice Management Systems

The intent of practice management software is to automate key administrative data entry functions of the revenue cycle. Automation speeds up each job task and allows staff to easily identify missing charges, track claims, compare payments to carrier contracts, and recognize operational trends. All practice management systems offer the same core functions: scheduling, registration, charge entry, billing (insurance and patient), payment posting, file maintenance, and reports generation. Some systems are much more sophisticated and offer additional features such as online patient eligibility and claims status, audit trails, and claims scrubbing. Today most of these systems are Windows-based allowing staff to minimize and open many windows at a time. MOSS components are explained in the following sections. Details are provided on how to use each component with respect to the job function and revenue cycle impact. You will get to practice using the software at the end of each section.

Logging on to Moss

Delmar Cengage Learning's MOSS is developed for learning purposes only and is not marketed to the public. The goal is to provide the student with experience using a software product similar to what is used in the market. MOSS comes in two versions: a single user version and a network version. If you are working independently at home you will be using the single user version. If you are working in a computer classroom, check with your instructor before logging on. Your career school or college may have loaded this software on the campus network to access from the computer classroom only. For more information about how to Install MOSS, see Appendix E: Getting Started with MOSS 2.0.

Single User Version

Follow these steps to access the single user version of MOSS.

Step 1: Software for MOSS is located in the textbook package. Insert the CD-ROM and load the software onto your computer. An icon for MOSS will appear on your desktop.

Step 2: Double-click on the icon. A security warning may appear asking you if you want to continue opening this file. Click *Open.* See Figure 4.1 to check yourself.

Step 3: The logon screen will appear. The logon name and password will be auto-populated. The logon name is *Student 1.* The password will appear as asterisks. There is no reason to change this. See Figure 4.2 to check yourself. Click *OK* to continue to the *Main Menu Screen*. When the *Main Menu Screen* appears, you have successfully logged in.

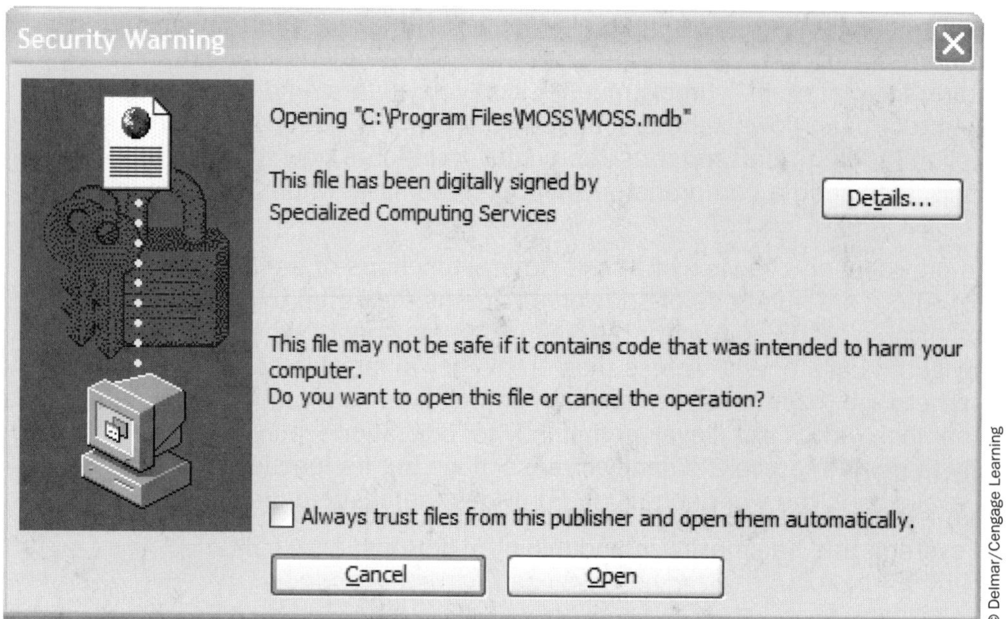

Figure 4.1 Security Screen

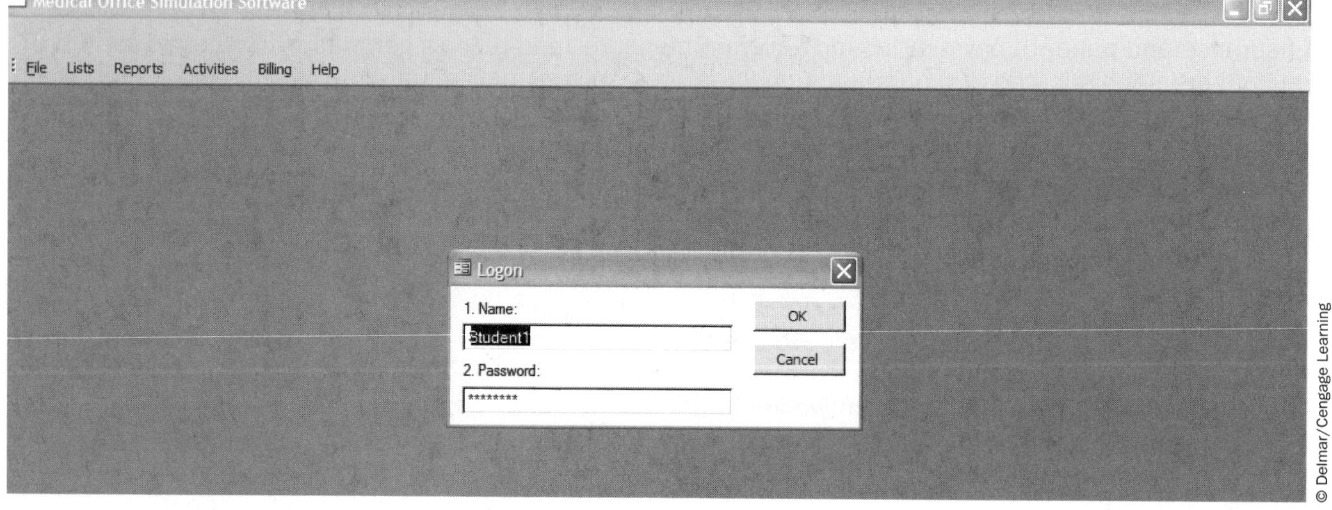

Figure 4.2 MOSS Login

Network Version

Logging on to the network version is slightly different from the single user version. You must first check with your instructor for specific directions for your school's network. Basic instructions are as follows:

Step 1: Click on the *Start* button in the lower left corner of your screen.

Step 2: Select *Programs* and find the software title *Medical Office Simulation Software*. Click on it. Your school may have loaded the software on the network and placed shortcut icons on each computer. If so, you may double-click on this icon.

Step 3: Your instructor will assign a specific student number to you. Logons and passwords are case sensitive. At the logon screen pictured in Figure 4.2, in field 1, enter *Student* and the number assigned to you like this: *Student5.* Do not put any spaces between the word Student and the number assigned to you. In field 2, enter this text again for your password. You will be asked to change this password shortly.

Step 4: A *New Student Form* screen will open. Complete the information required by tabbing through the fields. Check with your instructor to see which fields are required. Your instructor is the only person that will have access to this screen.

Step 5: Change your password by clicking on the *Change Password* button located on the bottom left of the *New Student Form.* A new *Change Password* window will open. Your student number should be displayed along the top of the window. In field 1, enter your old password. In field 2, enter a new password that is at least six characters long. Confirm this password by retyping it in field 3.

Step 6: Click *Close,* and the *Main Menu Screen* will appear.

Basic Tools for Navigating MOSS

As with most software, there is more than one way to maneuver from A to B. MOSS has all the components of a Windows-based system: title bar, maximize and minimize buttons, and dropdown menus. The *Main Menu Screen* is the hub of the program. From here, you can access all modules. You can also navigate through the software by using the dropdown menus in the title bar. If you make the MOSS screen smaller (you do not have to minimize it completely), the title bar will be visible. From here you can access everything you can from the *Main Menu Screen.* Browse through the dropdown menus, particularly the *Lists* menu. This menu is useful for quickly accessing tables located under *File Maintenance* in the *Main Menu.* See Figure 4.3 for an example of one of the dropdown menus.

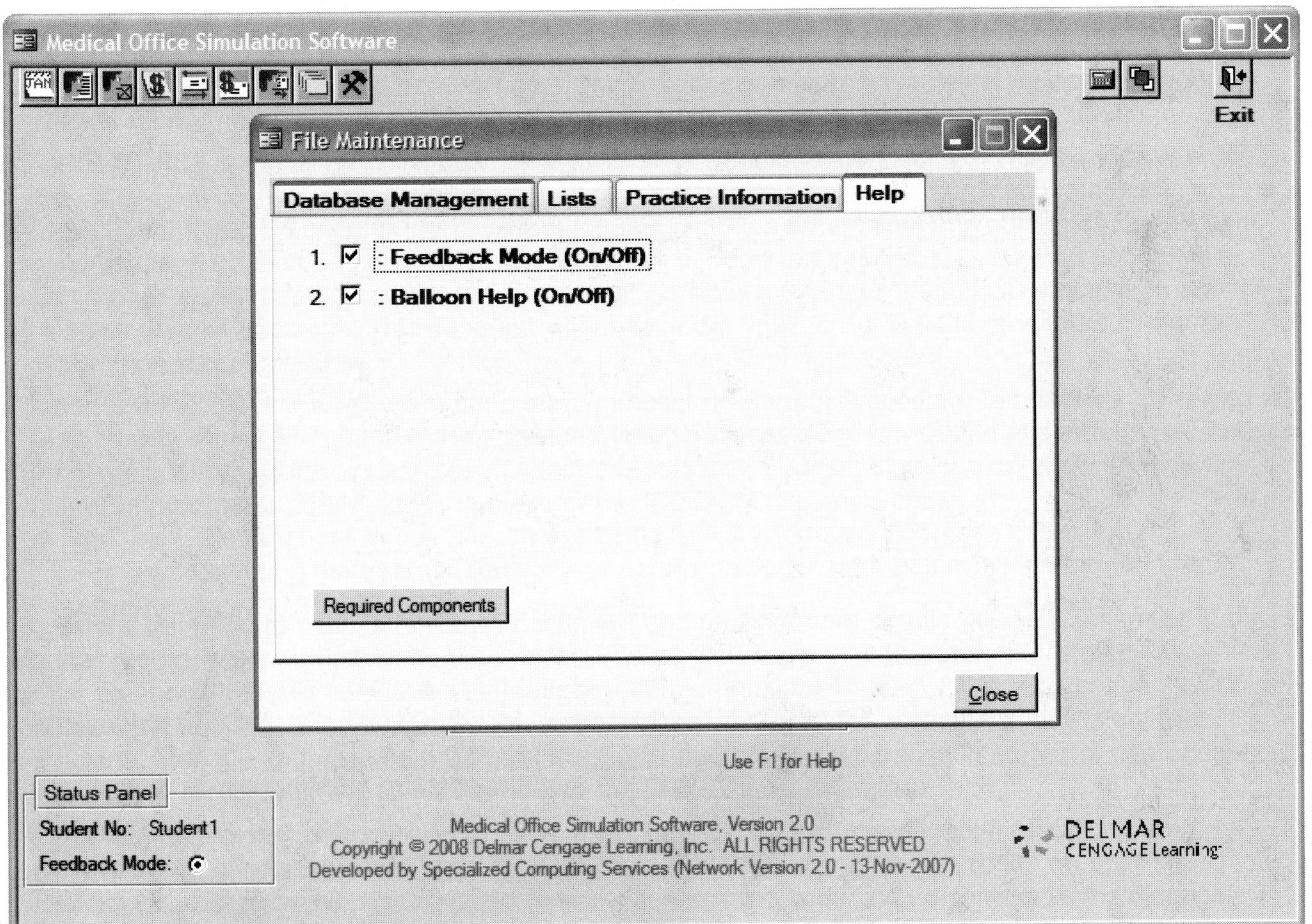

Figure 4.3 Dropdown Menu

Shortcut buttons on the *Main Menu Screen* are located to the top left. These take you to the same modules listed on the *Main Menu Screen.*

MOSS was developed for educational purposes and has some helpful features to use when first beginning to use the software to complete jobs. The software is designed to give advice and prompt students, along with feedback and balloon help captions. When first logging on to MOSS, be sure the software is set to *Feedback Mode.* You can determine this by checking in the lower left side of the *Main Menu Screen.* Under *Status Panel,* you will see your student number displayed. Directly beneath this, you will locate *Feedback Mode*. To take advantage of the messages and captions, make sure the radio button is selected. A black dot should appear. *Feedback Mode* alerts students as they try to exit a screen that information in required fields is missing. You can turn this off at any time while using the software by unclicking this button. If you are using the network version of MOSS, your instructor will have to do this for you.

Balloon Help provides additional explanation about a field. Not all fields have a balloon caption, but many of the more confusing or commonly misunderstood fields do. Check to see that the *Balloon Help* option is turned on by going to *File Maintenance* on the *Main Screen* and selecting the *Help* tab. If a check mark is in the box before the option, then it is turned on. If you want to turn it off, click on the box and the check mark will disappear. See Figure 4.4.

If *Balloon Help* is active, pressing F1 once you have clicked in a field you need assistance with will open up a feedback box with helpful information. You can always revert to the *Help* menu on the *Main Menu Screen* to assist you with this feature. Figure 4.5 shows a feedback box generated when clicking on field 20 and pressing F1 on the Patient Information Screen in Patient Registration.

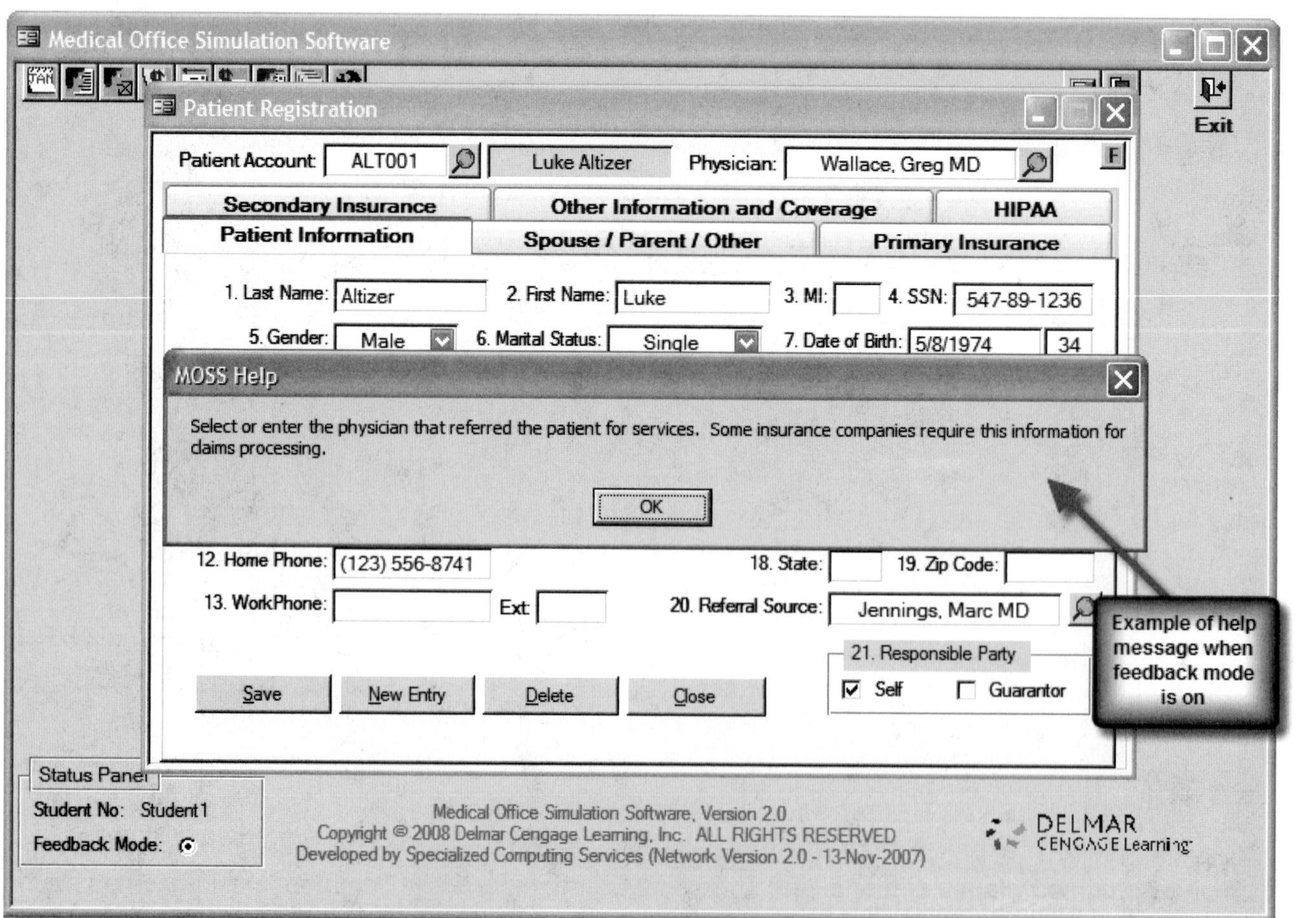

Figure 4.4 Options Feedback and Balloon Modes

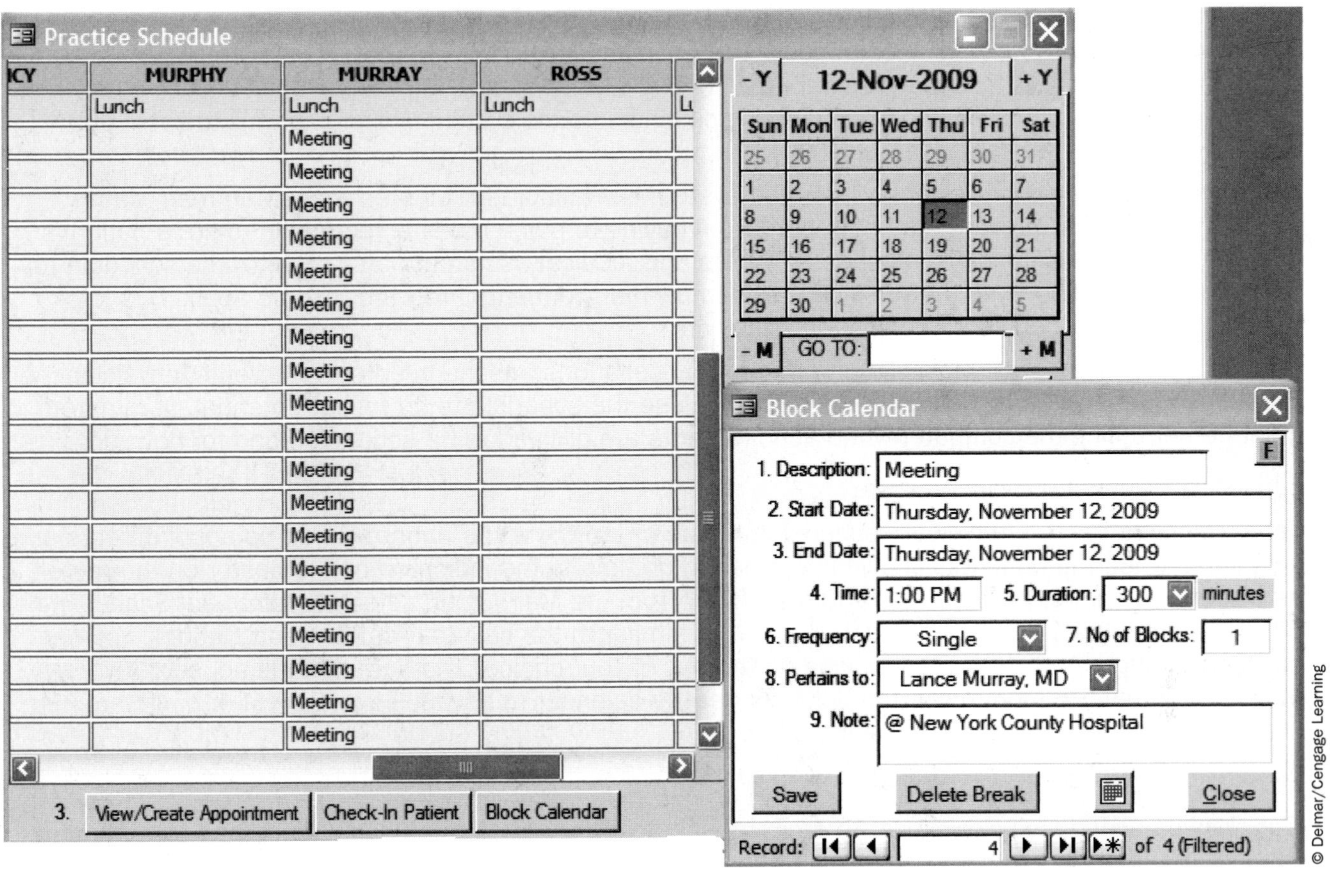

Figure 4.5 Feedback Mode

Appointment Scheduling

The office appointment schedule is the cornerstone of the practice. Without it, the office cannot staff or plan for the day. Physicians rely on this schedule to maximize time in the office by seeing as many patients as possible while providing adequate time to treat them according to their needs and coordinating visits at the hospital. The *Appointment Scheduling* module manages appointments in the office for all providers and allows for scheduling of time outside the office for hospital rounds, surgery, and so on. The days of using a day timer or traditional paper appointment book are long gone.

Scheduling has become an important task in the medical office and requires obtaining more information from patients prior to their arrival. Scheduling is the first point of contact and is the first step of the revenue cycle. Staff performing this task must be prudent in obtaining the information necessary to begin the precertification and eligibility processes. Patients are busy people and tend to schedule appointments around their work and home schedules. The scheduling module must be able to not only make appointments but to cancel and reschedule these appointments with ease. Patients commonly call and ask when their appointments are because they have lost their appointment cards.

In a computerized system, a search by name is done and the staff member can quickly locate a patient's scheduled appointment time. It should also be able to search for an available patient appointment quickly by time of day or type of visit. The computer is a useful tool for scheduling but staff must still use common sense when choosing appointments. They are required to use judgment when scheduling an appointment for an adequate amount of time depending on the patient's complaint and reason for visit. To allow for enough time, staff make the initial determination of whether the patient is new or established and whether the visit is a consultation or referral. At DMA new patients and consults are scheduled for 30 minutes. Established patient appointments are 15 minutes. Office procedures are scheduled for 30 minutes. (NOTE: if a patient is scheduled for 30 minutes, his/her name will appear twice—once for each 15-minute increment. This is not a duplicate appointment.) Scheduling staff also make judgment calls regarding routine appointments and those that require working in for immediate attention based on the medical problem and whether the appointment should be made that day or for the coming days or weeks. To avoid entering duplicate patients, scheduling staff should take heed when entering patients into the system by first checking to see if that patient is already in the database.

Information the scheduler enters into the system is available for all staff to view. In many cases, for example, this will prevent staff members from having to pull a medical record file to get a patient's phone number or insurance ID number. Providers and medical assistants also monitor the schedule to see who has checked in so that they can gauge how many patients are waiting to be seen. This lets them know how far behind in the schedule they are!

The schedule must be closely monitored for cancellations, rescheduled appointments, physician vacations, staff meetings, holidays, and so on. To use the schedule to its fullest potential, parameters must be set telling the computer when appointments are allowed to be scheduled and for how long.

Scheduling an Appointment

Patient appointments are typically scheduled ahead of time over the phone. Follow-up appointments are scheduled when the patient is checking out based on time frame indicated by the doctor on the router as to when the patient should return to the office. From the *Main Menu* select *Appointment Scheduling.* The appointment scheduling calendar in MOSS is similar to the calendar in Microsoft Outlook. You can navigate through the calendar by clicking on the day of your choice. The date box will appear gray. To move from month to month, use the boxes under the calendar to advance forward +**M** or backward –**M**; the same applies to moving from year to year.

Practice Schedule

The practice schedule looks similar to an Excel sheet with gridlines marking columns and rows. Each provider in the clinic has their own designated column to house their specific appointments. Each row represents 15 minutes of time. On the right side of the screen is a calendar box displaying an entire month. When a specific date is selected, the date in this box becomes highlighted and the left side of the screen displays time slots for that day. Available appointments will appear as blank fields. If a field is populated with a patient name, this means the appointment is assigned to that patient and is unavailable or "booked." Sometimes the office will *block out* available appointments for meetings, time off, holidays, lunch, and so on. If time is blocked, appointments cannot be scheduled during this time. Blocks are created in MOSS by going to *File Maintenance,* selecting *Practice Information,* and then choosing *Block Calendar.* Blocks can be added and changed at any time. From the *Practice Schedule*, a block can be deleted or changed by double-clicking on the blocked time slot. A *Block Calendar* dialogue box will open to allow the user to input or change information.

Exercise 4.0 Your Turn to Try

Let's practice using the block calendar. We are going to schedule a meeting for Dr. Murray at New York County Hospital at 1:30 p.m. on November 12, 2009. He will be in a meeting for the remainder of the afternoon.

Step 1 Go to *File Maintenance* and select *Practice Information* tab.

Step 2 Click on *Block Calendar*. A dialogue box will open.

Step 3 Use the arrow keys at the bottom of this dialogue box and click on the arrow for a new blank record. You can also arrow forward until you see a blank dialogue box.

Step 4 In field 1, *Description*, enter *Meeting.*

Step 5 In field 2, *Start Date*, enter *11/12/2009.*

Step 6 In field 3, *End Date*, will automatically populate with the same date as above.

Step 7 Field 4, *Time*, is the start time of the block. Lunch is from 12 p.m. to 1 p.m., so it's safe to say that Dr. Murray will not have time to see any patients after lunch and drive to the hospital for a 1:30 meeting. We will put the start time as *1:00 p.m.* Enter 01:00 p.m.

Step 8 Field 5, *Duration*, is how long the block is on this day. You must calculate the number of minutes from 1:00 p.m. to 6:00 p.m. so that all available appointment slots will be blocked for the rest of the afternoon. Enter 300 mins (5 hours × 60 mins).

Step 9 Field 6, *Frequency.* Because this meeting is a one time occurrence, choose *Single.* This field has the option to set blocks for the same day and time each week, month, and so on.

Step 10 In field 7, *No of Blocks* is 1. We are scheduling this meeting only one time on a nonrecurring basis.

Step 11 In field 8, *Pertains to*, select Lance Murray. This does not affect any of the other providers. However, if we were scheduling a block that applied to all providers in the office, *All* would be chosen.

Step 12 In field 9, *Note*, free text can be typed about what is taking place during the blocked time, where the meeting is, and so on. Enter @ *New York County Hospital.*

Step 13 Save your work.

Step 14 Check your work against Figure 4.6. You should also check the *Appointment Schedule* for this day and see that the afternoon is completely booked.

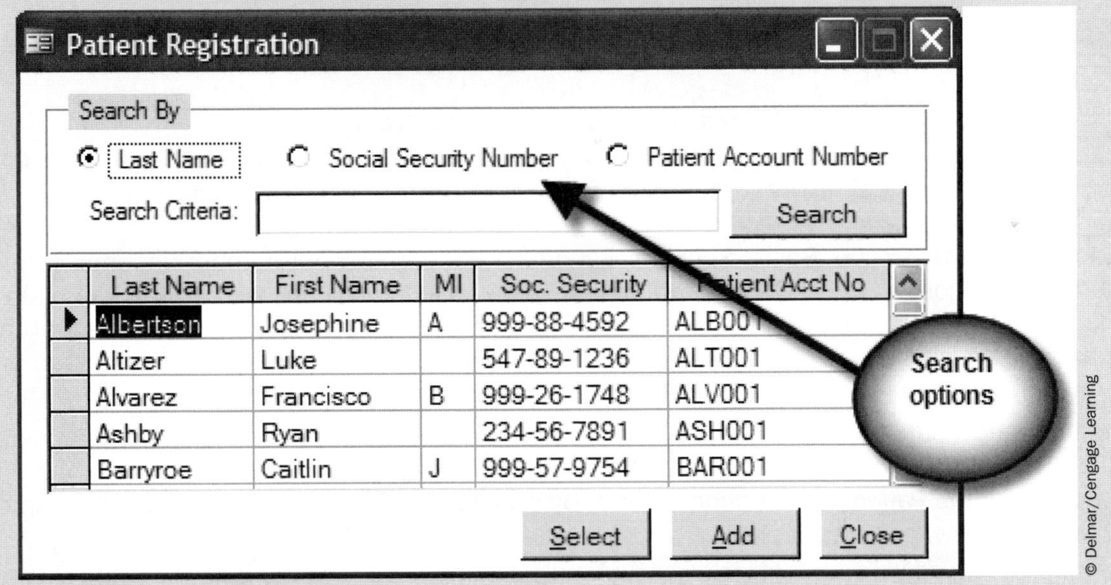

Figure 4.6 Block Schedule

Patient Registration

Patient registration is performed when the patient arrives for an appointment. Preregistration can occur by obtaining patient specific information over the phone and entering the information into MOSS prior to patient arrival. From the *Main Menu*, click on *Patient Registration.* A list of DMA patients displays in the dialog box in alphabetical order (Figure 4.7). From this box, you can search for the patient by last name, Social Security Number, or patient account number by selecting one of the radio buttons. In the

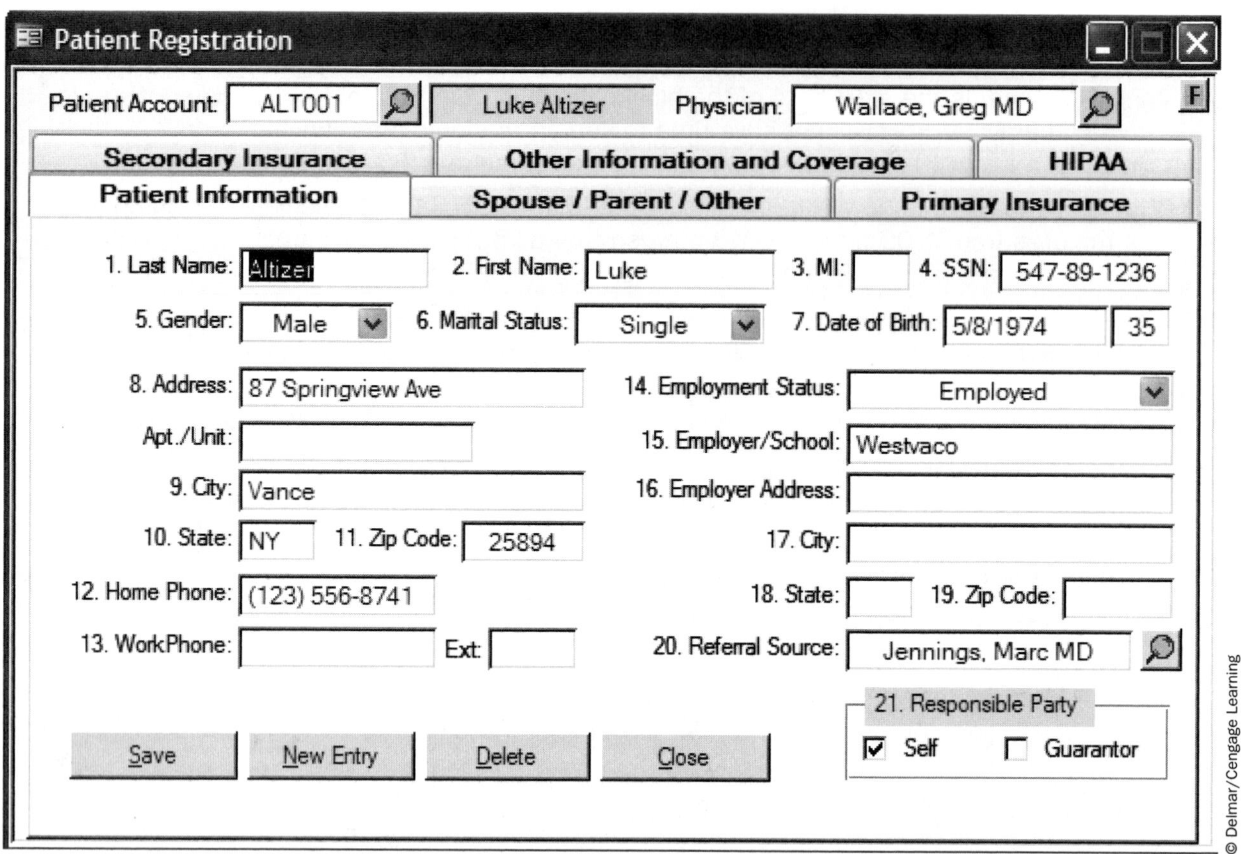

Figure 4.7 Patient Registration Dialog Box

Search Criteria box, enter the name, Social Security Number, or patient account number depending on which radio button was chosen. When the desired patient name is located there are two ways to open the patient's file: (1) double-click on the patient's name or (2) single click on the space to the left of the patient name and then click on the *Select* button at the base of the box. Once the patient's file is open, a patient information screen will appear (Figure 4.8) with six different tabs of information.

If the patient is a new patient, searching the database is not necessary unless the patient is unsure if they have ever been seen by one of our doctors in the past. To register a new patient, click on the *Add* button at the bottom of the *Patient Registration* screen. By clicking the *Add* button, you can enter demographic and insurance data for new patients.

The patient registration form completed by the patient upon checking in is used as the source for entering the pertinent data into MOSS. After reviewing the document for completion and accuracy, enter the data into MOSS. The patient account number is automatically assigned by MOSS after you enter the patient's last name. The account number consists of the first three characters of the patient's last name and three numbers. Select the physician that the patient is going to see by clicking on the magnifying glass and double-clicking the respective physician name.

The patient information screen houses all of the demographic information that is vitally important in patient record maintenance and claims processing. The goal of DMA is to have as many fields as possible completed to ensure accurate claims generation and record keeping. Ninety percent of the required claim form information is pulled from here, so it is important that the information keyed in is accurate and without spelling errors. The first tab, *Patient Information*, is where all of the patient-specific demographics are entered. MOSS doesn't require all 21 fields on this tab to be populated before saving. However, all fields with the exception of the work phone and employer address on this tab are key fields and

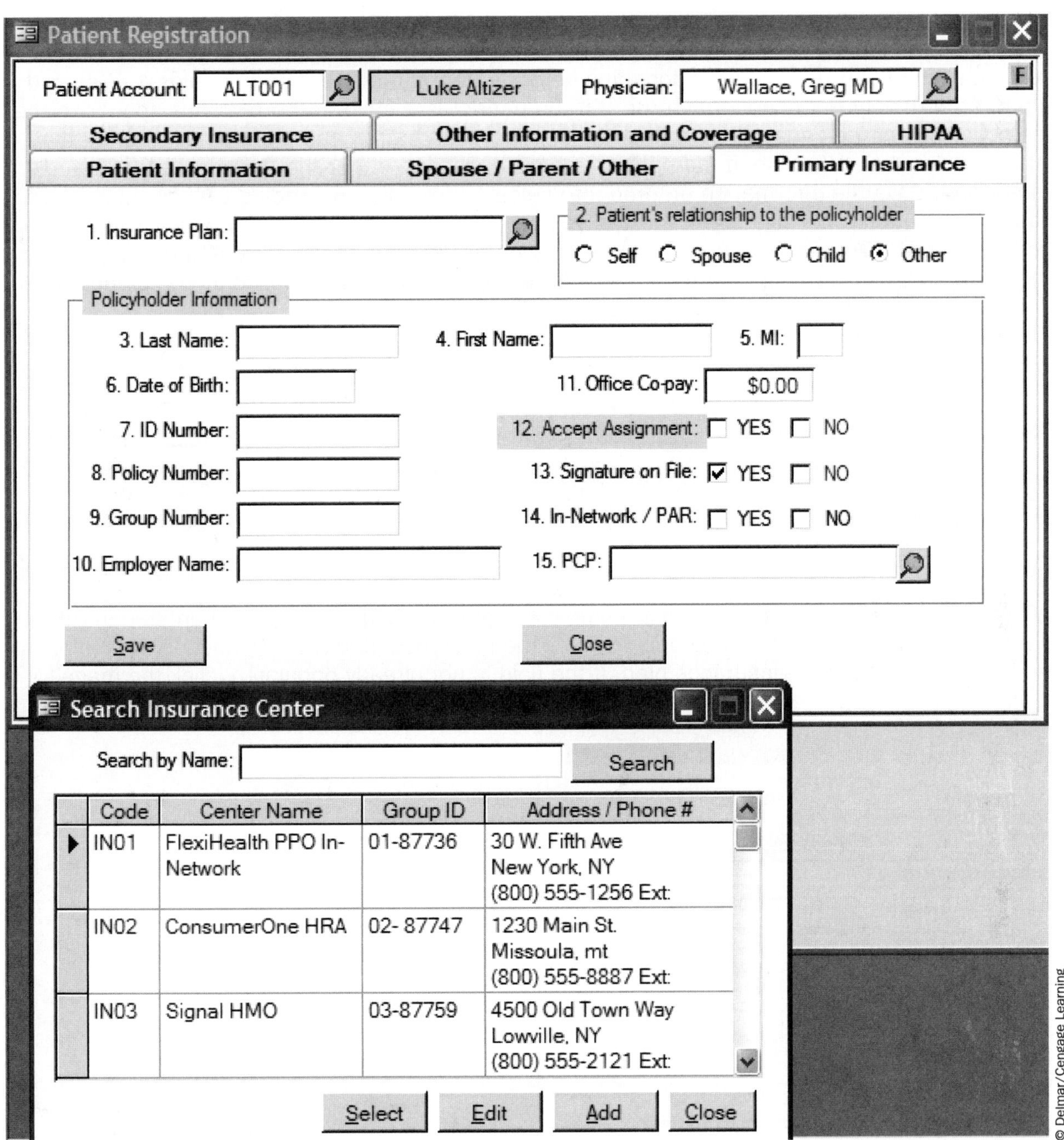

Figure 4.8 Patient Information Screen

should be populated. Field 21, *Responsible Party*, has two options to choose from: Self and Guarantor. For adult patients who are also the insurance policy holder, choose *Self*. For adult patients who are not the insurance policy holder and children, choose *Guarantor*.

Discussion:

Why is it necessary to complete the middle initial field? What about the employment status or employer fields?

The second tab, *Spouse/Parent/Other*, looks very much like the *Patient Information* tab but is specific to the patient's spouse, parent, or legal guardian. It is important to select the appropriate radio button to distinguish between these relationships before entering the information. Fields 1–7 should be filled out if the patient is the not guarantor or if the patient is a child. If the patient's spouse is the insurance policy holder (i.e., guarantor), select the *Spouse* radio button and proceed to entering the information in fields 1–7. Likewise, if the patient is a child, choose either the *Parent* or *Legal Guardian* radio buttons. Save the information entered into fields 1–7 before proceeding to the address and employment information. Clicking on the *Address* and *Employer* buttons opens a separate window, allowing you to enter the guarantor's address and employer information. If the patient and the guarantor live at the same address, clicking on the *Copy Pt Addr* auto-populates this field. After completing the information in each of these windows, click *Close*.

Discussion:

Why do you think there are two separate guarantor fields (1–8 and 9–16) on the *Spouse/Parent/Other* tab?

The *Primary Insurance* tab has 15 fields to complete (Figure 4.9). The information entered into this tab is also taken from the patient demographic sheet. The insurance plan (field 1) houses the patient's primary—and many times only—insurance plan. If the field is not already populated, click the magnifying

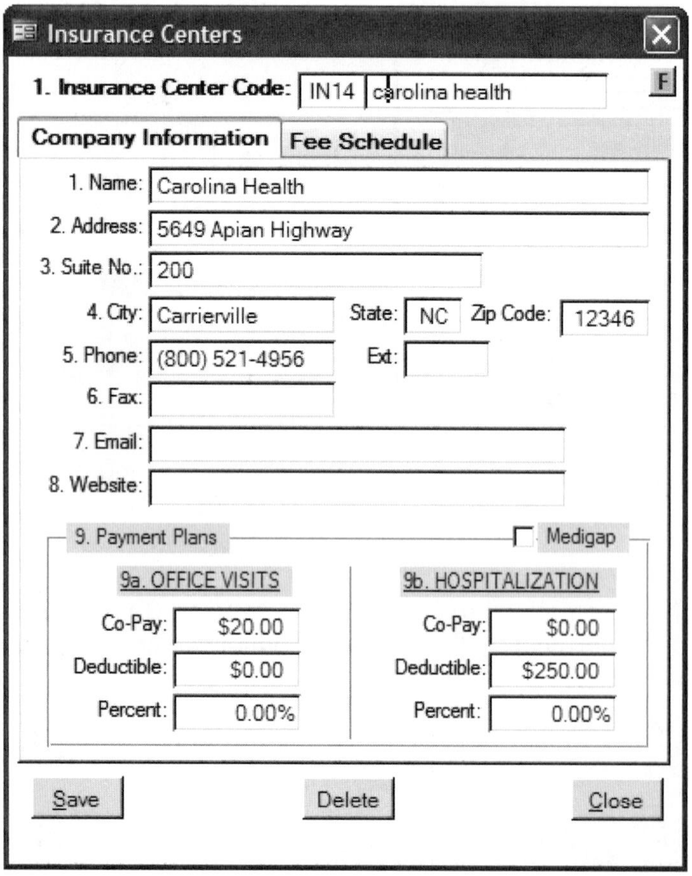

Insurance Centers
1. Insurance Center Code: IN14 carolina health
Company Information | Fee Schedule
1. Name: Carolina Health
2. Address: 5649 Apian Highway
3. Suite No.: 200
4. City: Carrierville State: NC Zip Code: 12346
5. Phone: (800) 521-4956 Ext:
6. Fax:
7. Email:
8. Website:
9. Payment Plans Medigap
9a. OFFICE VISITS — Co-Pay: $20.00 Deductible: $0.00 Percent: 0.00%
9b. HOSPITALIZATION — Co-Pay: $0.00 Deductible: $250.00 Percent: 0.00%
Save Delete Close

Figure 4.9 Searching and Entering Primary Insurance Information

glass to search the list of carriers already saved in the MOSS database and select the health plan name by either highlighting it and clicking on the *Select* button or double-clicking on the carrier name. The information entered on this tab primarily comes directly from the insurance card. The data in fields 7, 8, 9, 12, and 13 populate specific form fields on the CMS 1500 claim form. Registration paperwork allows DMA to check boxes 12 and 13. *Accept Assignment* (field 12), when checked, indicates that the insurance payment for provider services will go directly to the provider and not to the patient's home address. *Signature on File* (field 13) allows DMA to bill the patient's insurance company for services rendered. Field 14, *In Network/PAR*, is checked *Yes* when the provider has a contract with the carrier and *No* if they do not participate with or do not have a contract with the said carrier.

Discussion:

Why do you think it is important that the *In Network/PAR* field is checked?

If the required insurance carrier is not located here, you will have to enter it into MOSS by selecting the *Add* button. Another window opens (Figure 4.10) with two tabs on which to enter health plan–specific information and the health plan's fee schedule for services. Most of this information is obtained from the actual insurance card. The fee schedules are obtained either via the carrier's website or as an attachment to the provider contract. For the purposes of this simulation, insurance contracts and fee schedules for Douglasville Medical Clinic are located on the enclosed CD-ROM. Fee schedules are calculated by multiplying the percentage of Medicare allowable by the allowed amount located on the Medicare Fee Schedule. For example, if USA Insurance had a contract with DMA to pay at 145% of the Medicare allowable then for CPT code 99212 the contracted reimbursement to DMA would be \$49.30 (\$34.00 × 145%).

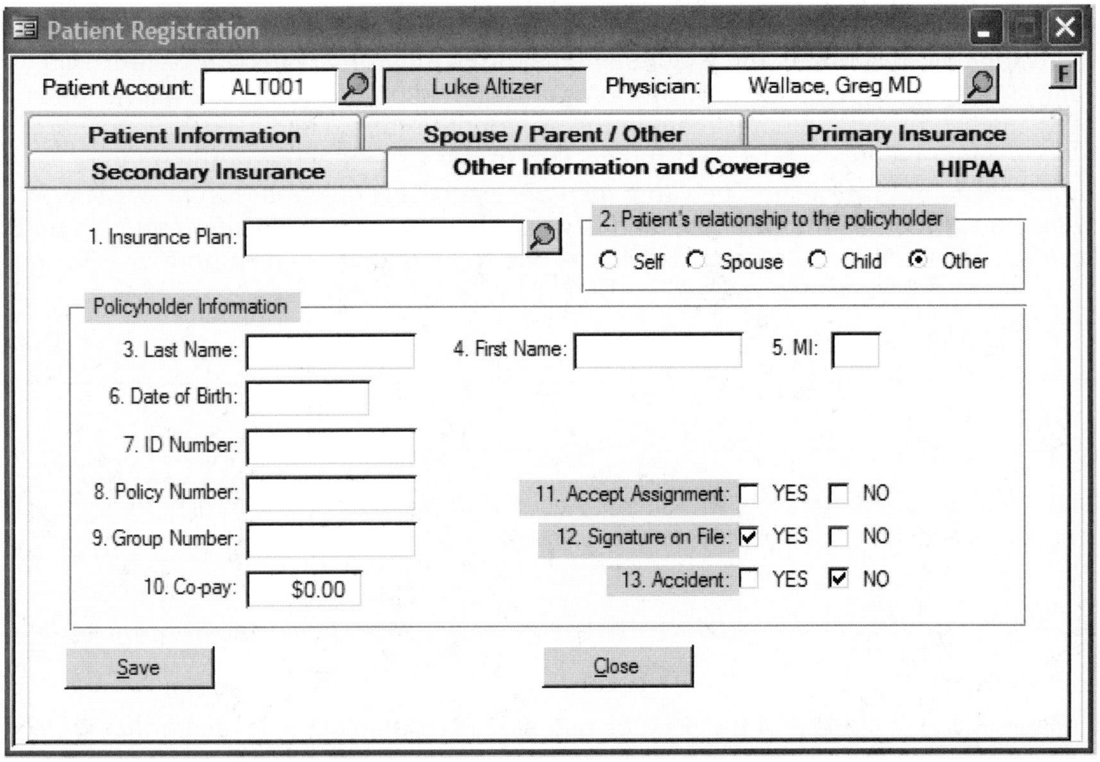

© Delmar/Cengage Learning

Figure 4.10 Adding New Insurance Carrier into MOSS

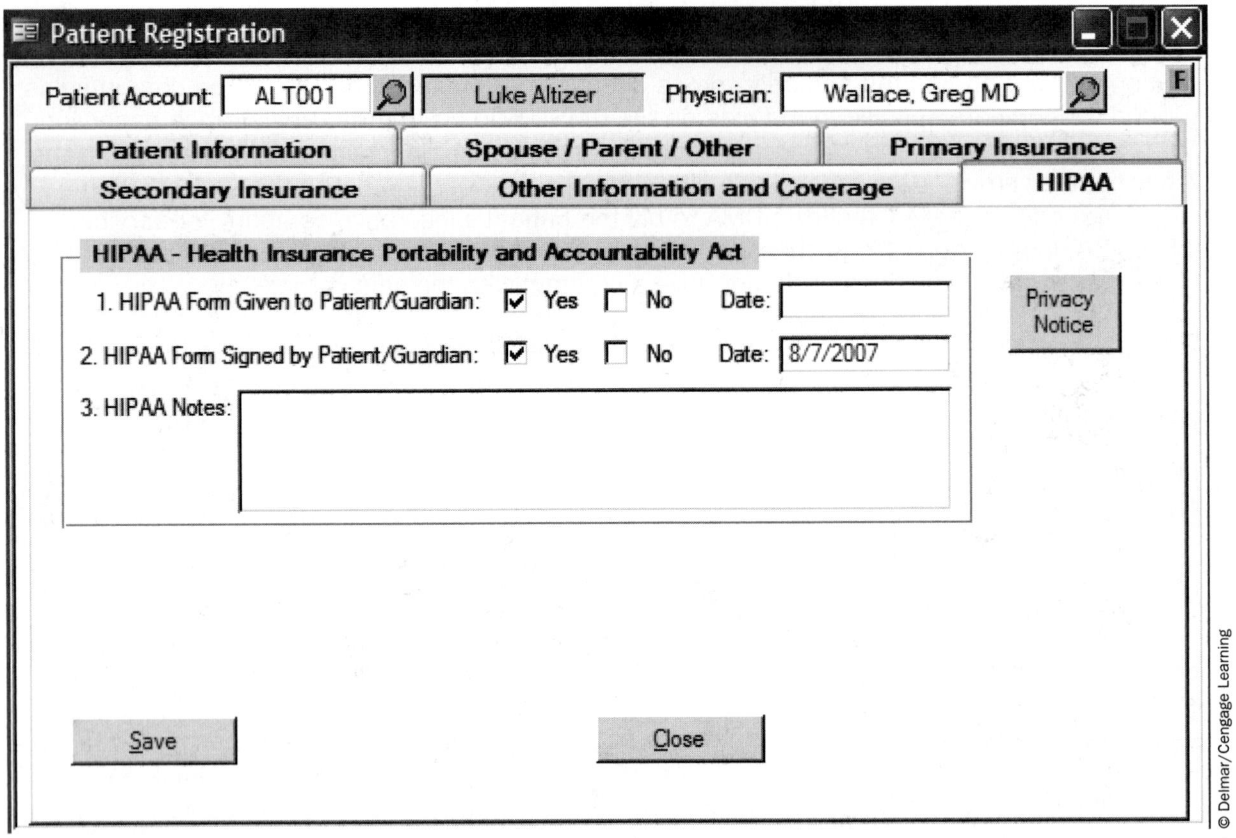

Figure 4.11 Other Insurance and Coverage

The *Secondary Insurance* tab contains the exact same fields as the *Primary Insurance* tab. This tab is necessary only if the patient has coverage by more than one insurance plan. You will need to differentiate between the two plans and enter them in the appropriate tabs. Field 10, *Bill Secondary Insurance after Primary*, must be checked to alert the system to generate a bill after the primary insurance has paid its portion of the claim. The *Other Insurance and Coverage* tab (Figure 4.11) will house any tertiary insurance the patient may have and is where third-party liability information is entered. Field 13, *Accident*, is checked if the patient's visit is due to an injury resulting from an accident of any nature.

Discussion:

Why do you think the coder needs to know what insurance the patient has? Do you think that if a patient has a third-party liability carrier that will impact how services are coded and the claim is submitted?

The *HIPPA* tab (Figure 4.12) is the last of the six tabs and serves as an electronic record that the practice provided the patient with the HIPAA notification, when it was provided, and when it was signed by the patient.

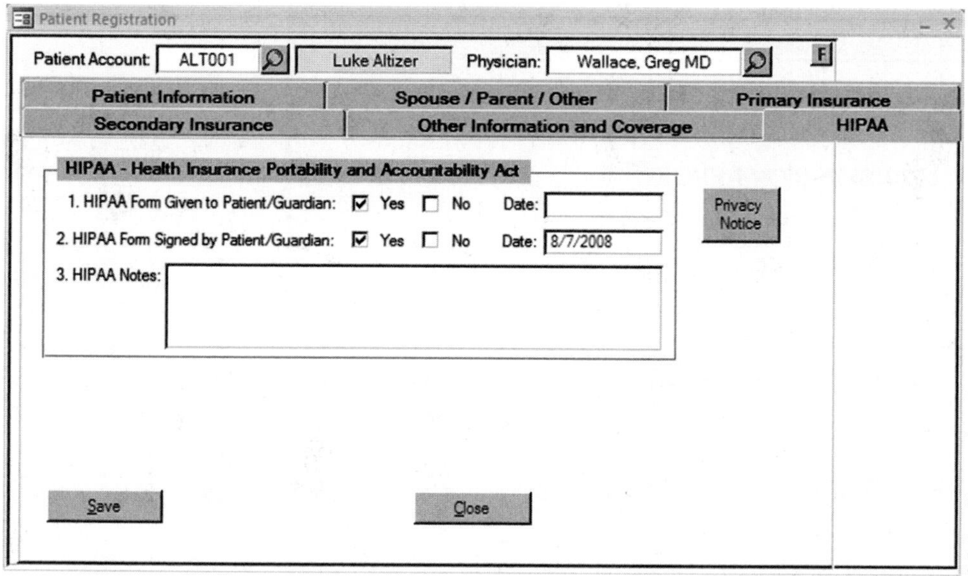

Figure 4.12 HIPAA Tab

Online Eligibility

As part of the preregistration or registration process, staff are required to verify insurance benefits and eligibility. It is important to wait to verify insurance until all patient registration information has been entered into MOSS. From the *Main Menu*, click on the *Online Eligibility* button. Search for the patient just as you did during the patient registration process by entering the patient's name, Social Security Number, or patient account number and clicking *Search*. Once the patient is located, click on *Select*. Another screen will appear showing the patient's account number and insurance carrier name. In the lower right corner of the screen select *Send to Payer* to transmit the eligibility query to the insurance carrier (Figure 4.13). A screen will appear showing the connection to the insurance carrier and the status of the transmission (Figure 4.14). From here, click on the *View* button to view the results of the inquiry from the carrier

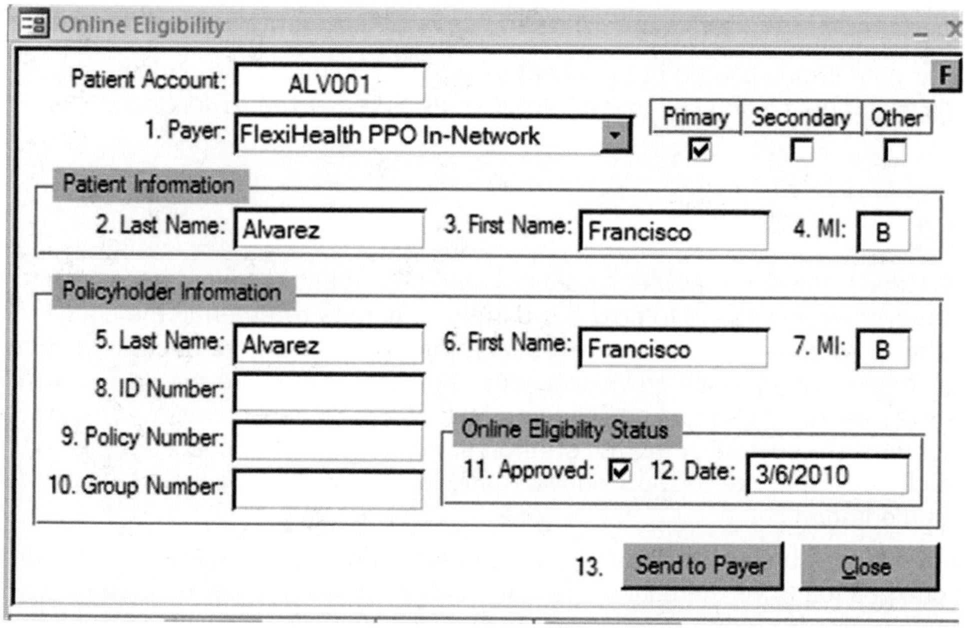

Figure 4.13 Online Eligibility

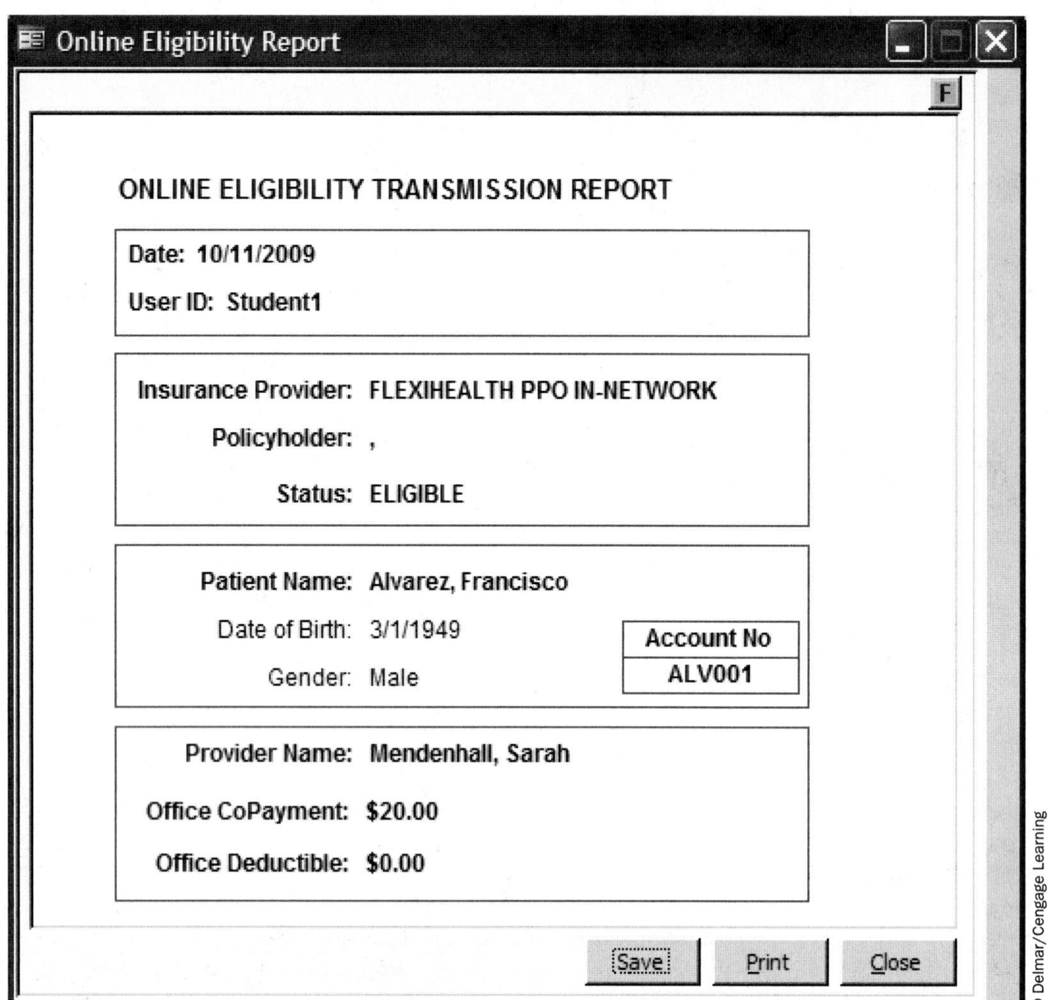
Online Eligibility Report

ONLINE ELIGIBILITY TRANSMISSION REPORT

Date: 10/11/2009
User ID: Student1

Insurance Provider: FLEXIHEALTH PPO IN-NETWORK
Policyholder: ,
Status: ELIGIBLE

Patient Name: Alvarez, Francisco
Date of Birth: 3/1/1949
Gender: Male
Account No
ALV001

Provider Name: Mendenhall, Sarah
Office CoPayment: $20.00
Office Deductible: $0.00

Save Print Close

Figure 4.14 Eligibility Transmission Status

(Figure 4.15). This sheet can be printed and placed in the patient's medical record. If the patient does not have insurance, a message will appear when you select their name that says *The patient does not have any insurance.*

Procedure Posting

After the patient has been registered, benefits have been verified, and the patient is seen and treated by the doctor, the next step in the revenue process is to post the patient's charges by entering the codes for all the services provided. The router, hospital charge sheets, and medical records are used as source documents to determine the date of service, which provider rendered the service, where the service was rendered, and which supplies were used. All charges entered into MOSS can be traced back to one of these documents. Some procedures are posted by the registration staff at the time of checkout. The coding or billing staff enters the others that are associated with office procedures and hospital encounters which require reading documentation.

To enter charges for procedures, click on the *Procedure Posting* button from the *Main Menu.* Search for the patient you need to enter charges for. Once the patient is located, click the *Add* button to add new procedures and charges to this patient account. Another procedure posting window will open with 15 fields. The patient's name and account number will be at the very top. Field 1 is *Ref. Number.* The ref number

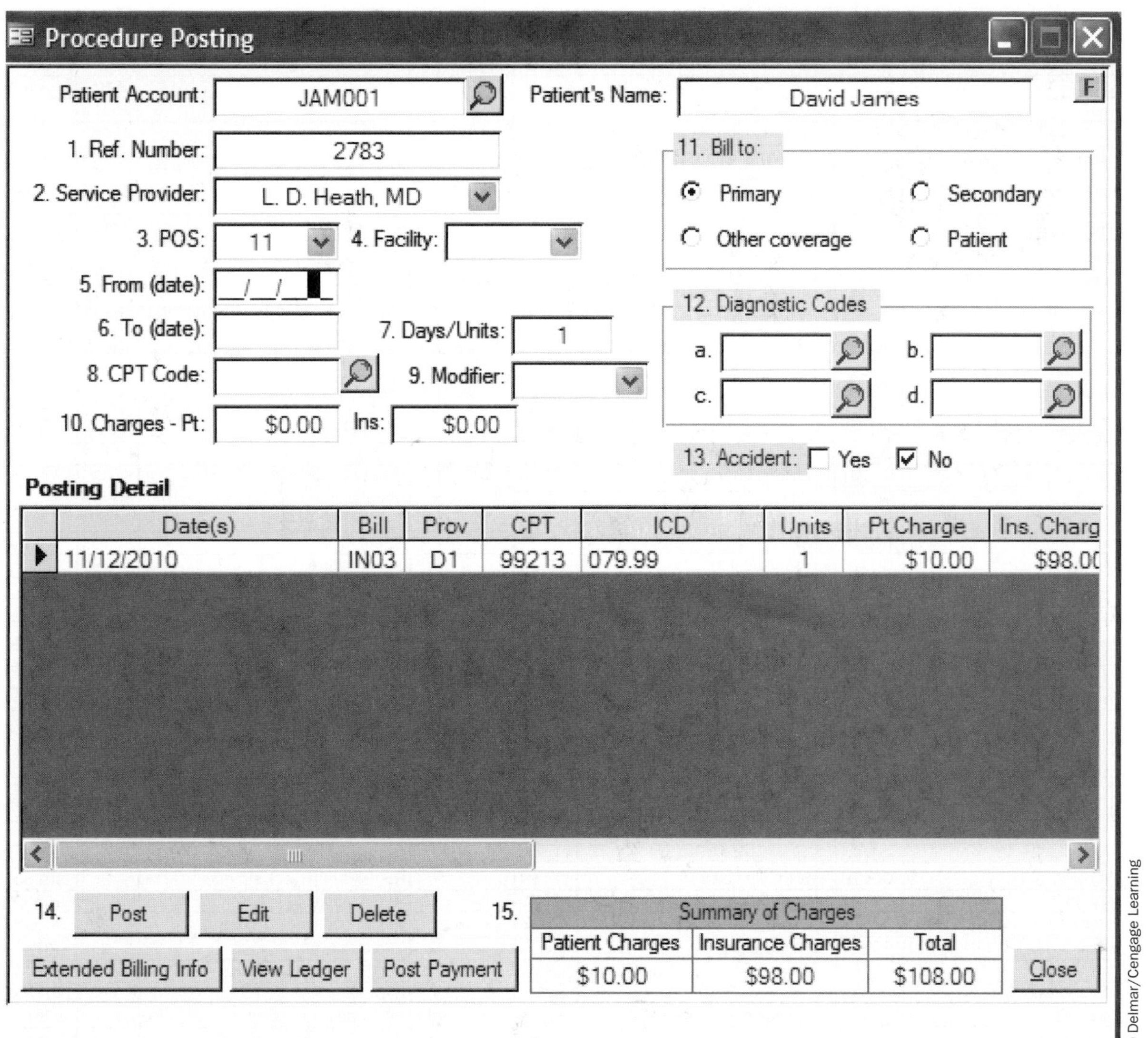

Figure 4.15 Online Eligibility Results

is the router number assigned for the day's visit. Figure 4.16 shows a router used to capture services performed in the office. Begin with field 1 and work through all the fields by inputting information from the documentation. Field 2, *Service Provider*, defaults to whomever the patient was last scheduled with. Should the provider need to change, use the dropdown arrow and select the appropriate provider name from the list. POS is the place where services were rendered. Select the appropriate POS by using the dropdown arrow. If charges are being keyed from a router, the services were rendered in POS 11, office. Field 4, *Facility*, is used only when the services were provided at the hospital or a facility other than the office. You will notice two date of service fields (fields 5 and 6). If the services are rendered on one date of service and do not span a date, then enter this date in field 5 only. Use field 6 only when billing for a span of dates with the same CPT code being submitted, such as subsequent hospital visits where the services were rendered on consecutive days. Enter the first CPT code for the visit in field 8 by either typing in the CPT code or clicking on the magnifying glass and searching for the respective code. Fields 7 and 9 correspond to the code entered in field 8. Field 11 defaults to *Primary* if the insurance has not already been billed for the particular date of service. This can be changed easily by clicking the appropriate radio button. Field 12 allows for four diagnoses codes to be entered in the same fashion as the CPT code in field 8 either by entering in the entire code or by searching (click on the magnifying glass). Don't forget about field 13 if the reason for the encounter was due to an accident. The default for this field is *No*. Once fields 1–13

Date of service: 11/12/2010	Insurance: **Signal HMO**				Router Number: 2783
Patient name: **David James**	Coinsurance:	Copay: 10.00			Physician Name: **HEATH**
Account #: **JAM001**	Noncovered Waiver?	yes	no	n/a	

x	**Office visit**	**New**	x	**Est**
	Minimal (RN only)			99211
	Problem focused	99201		99212
	Exp problem focused	99202		99213
	Detailed	99203	X	99214
	Comp	99204		99215
	Comprhen/Complex	99205		
	Well visit	**New**	x	**Est**
	< 1 y	99381		99391
	1-4 y	99382		99392
	5-11 y	99383		99393
	12-17 y	99384		99394
	18-39 y	99385		99395
	40-64 y	99386		99396
	65 y +	99387		99397
	Medicare preventive services			
	Pap			Q0091
	Pelvic & breast			G0101
	Prostate/PSA			G0103
	Tobacco couns/3-10 min			G0375
	Tobacco couns/>10 min			G0376
	Welcome to Medicare exam			G0344
	ECG w/Welcome to Medicare			G0366
	Hemoccult, guaiac			G0107
	Flu shot			G0008
	Pneumonia shot			G0009
	Consultation/preop clearance			
	Exp problem focused			99242
	Detailed			99243
	Comp/mod complex			99244
	Comp/high complex			99245
	Other services			
	After posted hours			99050
	Evening/weekend appointment			99051
	Home health certification			G0180
	Home health recertification			G0179
	Care Plan oversight			99374
	Care Plan Oversight >30 mins			99375
	Post-op follow-up			99024
	Prolonged/60min total			99354
	Prolonged/each add 30 mins			99355
	Special reports/forms			99080
	Disability/Workers comp			99455
	Smoking Cessation <10 mins			99406
	Smoking Cessation >10 mins			99407
	ETOH/SA screening <30 mins			99408
	Online E/M by MD			99444
	Phone E/M <10 mins			99441
	Phone E/M <20 mins			99442
	Phone E/M <30 mins			99443
	Anticoagulant Mgmt <90 days			99363
	Anticoagulant Mgmt >90 days			99364
	In office emergency serv			99058
	Other services			
	Supplies			
	Surgical Tray			99070
	Instructions:			
	Return in 7 days if not improved. Drink plenty of liquids Ibuprofen 400 mg q. 8 hrs for fever and aches.			

x	**Office procedures**		
	Cerumen removal		69210
	ECG, w/interpretation		93000
	ECG, rhythm strip		93040
	Endometrial biopsy		58100
	Fracture care, cast/splint		_____
	Site: ______________		
	Nebulizer		94640
	Nebulizer demo		94664
	Spirometry		94010
	Spirometry, pre and post		94060
	Vasectomy		55250
	Skin procedures		**Units**
	Foreign body, skin, simple	10120	
	Foreign body, skin, complex	10121	
	I&D, abscess	10060	
	I&D, hematoma/seroma	10140	
	Laceration repair, simple	120__	
	Site: _______ Size: ____		
	Laceration repair, layered	120__	
	Site: _______ Size: ____		
	Laser Light Tx	96597	
	Lesion, biopsy, one	11100	
	Lesion, biopsy, each add'l	11101	
	Lesion, excision, benign	114__	
	Site: _______ Size: ____		
	Lesion, excision, malignant	116__	
	Site: _______ Size: ____		
	Lesion, paring/cutting, one	11055	
	Lesion, paring/cutting, 2-4	11056	
	Lesion, shave	113__	
	Site: _______ Size: ____		
	Nail removal, partial (+T mod)	11730	
	Nail rem, w/matrix (+T mod)	11750	
	Skin tag, 1-15	11200	
	Wart, flat, 1-14	17110	
	Destruction lesion, 1st	17000	
	Destruct lesion, each addl 2-14	17003	
	Medications		**Units**
	Ampicillin, up to 500mg	J0290	
	B-12, up to 1,000 mcg	J3420	
	Epinephrine, up to 1ml	J0170	
	Kenalog, 10mg	J3301	
	Lidocaine, 10mg	J2001	
	Normal saline, 1000cc	J7030	
	Phenergan, up to 50mg	J2550	
	Progesterone, 150mg	J1055	
	Rocephin, 250mg	J0696	
	Testosterone, 200mg	J1080	
	Tigan, up to 200 mg	J3250	
	Toradol, 15mg	J1885	
	Albuterol	J7609	
	Depo-Provera 50 mg	J1055	
	Depo-Medrol 40 mg	J1030	
	Diagnoses		Code
	1. Viral Infection		TT079.99
	2		
	3		
	4		
	Next office visit:		
	Recheck • Preventative • PRN		
	Referral to:		
	Physician signature		
	X _L. D. Heath_______________		

x	**Laboratory**		-90
	Venipuncture	36415	
	Blood glucose, monitoring device	82962	
	Blood glucose, visual dipstick	82948	
	CBC, w/ auto differential	85025	
	CBC, w/o auto differential	85027	
	Cholesterol	82465	
	Hemoccult, guaiac	82270	
	Hemoccult, immunoassay	82274	
	Hemoglobin A1C	85018	
	Lipid panel	80061	
	Liver panel	80076	
	KOH prep (skin, hair, nails)	87220	
	Metabolic panel, basic	80048	
	Metabolic panel, comprehensive	80053	
	Mononucleosis	86308	
	Pregnancy, blood	84703	
	Pregnancy, urine	81025	
	Renal panel	80069	
	Sedimentation rate	85651	
	Strep, rapid	86403	
	Strep culture	87081	
	Strep A	87880	
	TB	86580	
	UA, complete, non-automated	81000	
	UA, w/o micro, non-automated	81002	
	UA, w/ micro, non-automated	81003	
	Urine colony count	87086	
	Urine culture, presumptive	87088	
	Wet mount/KOH	87210	
	Vaccines		
	DT, <7 y		90702
	DTP		90701
	DtaP, <7 y		90700
	Flu, 6-35 months		90657
	Flu, 3 y +		90658
	Hep A, adult		90632
	Hep A, ped/adol, 2 dose		90633
	Hep B, adult		90746
	Hep B, ped/adol 3 dose		90744
	Hep B-Hib		90748
	Hib, 4 dose		90645
	HPV		90649
	IPV		90713
	MMR		90707
	Pneumonia, >2 y		90732
	Pneumonia conjugate, <5 y		90669
	Td, >7 y		90718
	Varicella		90716
	Tetanus toxoid adsorbed, IM		90703
	Immunizations & Injections		**Units**
	Allergen, one	95115	
	Allergen, multiple	95117	
	Imm admn <8 yo 1st Inj	90465	
	Imm admn <8 yo each add inj	90466	
	Imm <8 yo oral or intranasal	90467	
	Imm admn <8 yo each add	90468	
	Imm admin, one vacc	90471	
	Imm admin, each add'l	90472	
	Imm admin, intranasal, one	90473	
	Imm admin, intranasal, each add'l	90474	
	Injection, joint, small	20600	
	Injection, joint, intermediate	20605	
	Today's charges:		98.00
	Today's payment:		10.00
	Balance due:		-0-

Figure 4.16 Sample Router. 2010 CPT © 2009 American Medical Association. All rights reserved.

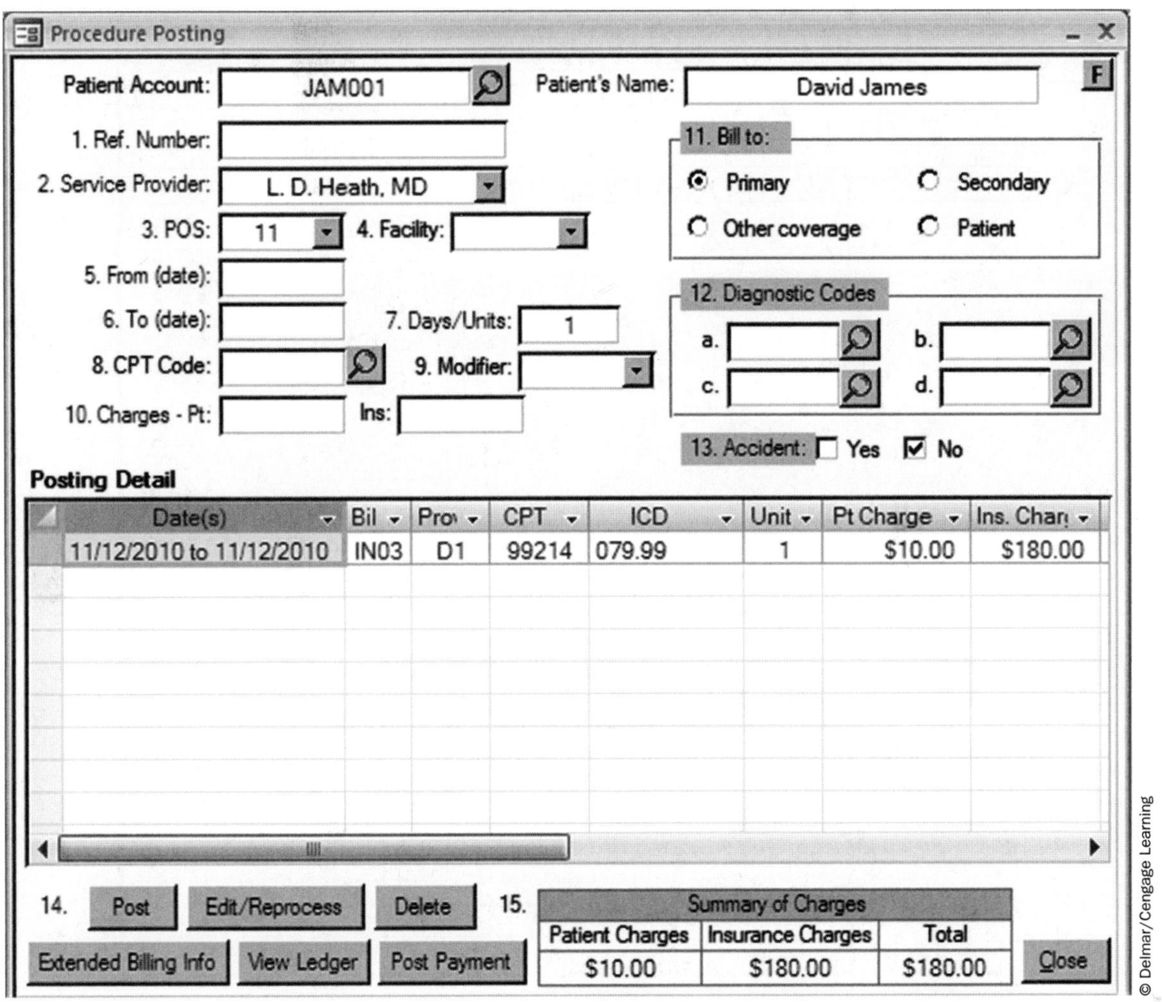

Figure 4.17 Procedure Posting

have been completed, click on the *Post* button. Continue entering codes in fields 8, 9, and 12 and clicking *Post* until all services are accounted for. You will notice in the *Posting Detail* area the details of the data entered in fields 1–13, including the fee or charge for the service and the patient's responsibility for these charges. The fee associated with the codes entered comes from DMA's fee schedule that is entered into MOSS and does not need to be keyed in each time charges are entered.

Use the router located in Figure 4.16 to enter charges for David James and check your work against Figure 4.17.

It is important to state that the *Procedure Posting* details screen shows only the current charges being entered for that specific posting session. To see previous charges, payments, and adjustments on the patient account, click on the *View Ledger* button at the bottom left of the *Procedure Entry* screen (Figure 4.17). The *Patient Ledger* screen is a read only screen and cannot be modified. It lists the activity on the patient's account with previous dates of service, CPT codes, charges, patient payments, insurance payments, adjustments, deductible, and account balance.

If the encounter for services was due to an accident or injury or the services required preauthorization, you must click on the *Extended Billing Information* button at the bottom left of this screen to enter additional required information (Figure 4.18). Here, you have 11 potential data fields to complete, depending on the individual circumstances. Field 1, *Patient's Condition Related To,* allows you to choose—in the case of a third-party liability—which type of claim this is: (1) *Auto Accident* (i.e., automotive insurance), (2) *Employment* (i.e., Workers' Compensation), or (3) *Other* (e.g., Third-party liability [i.e., fall on

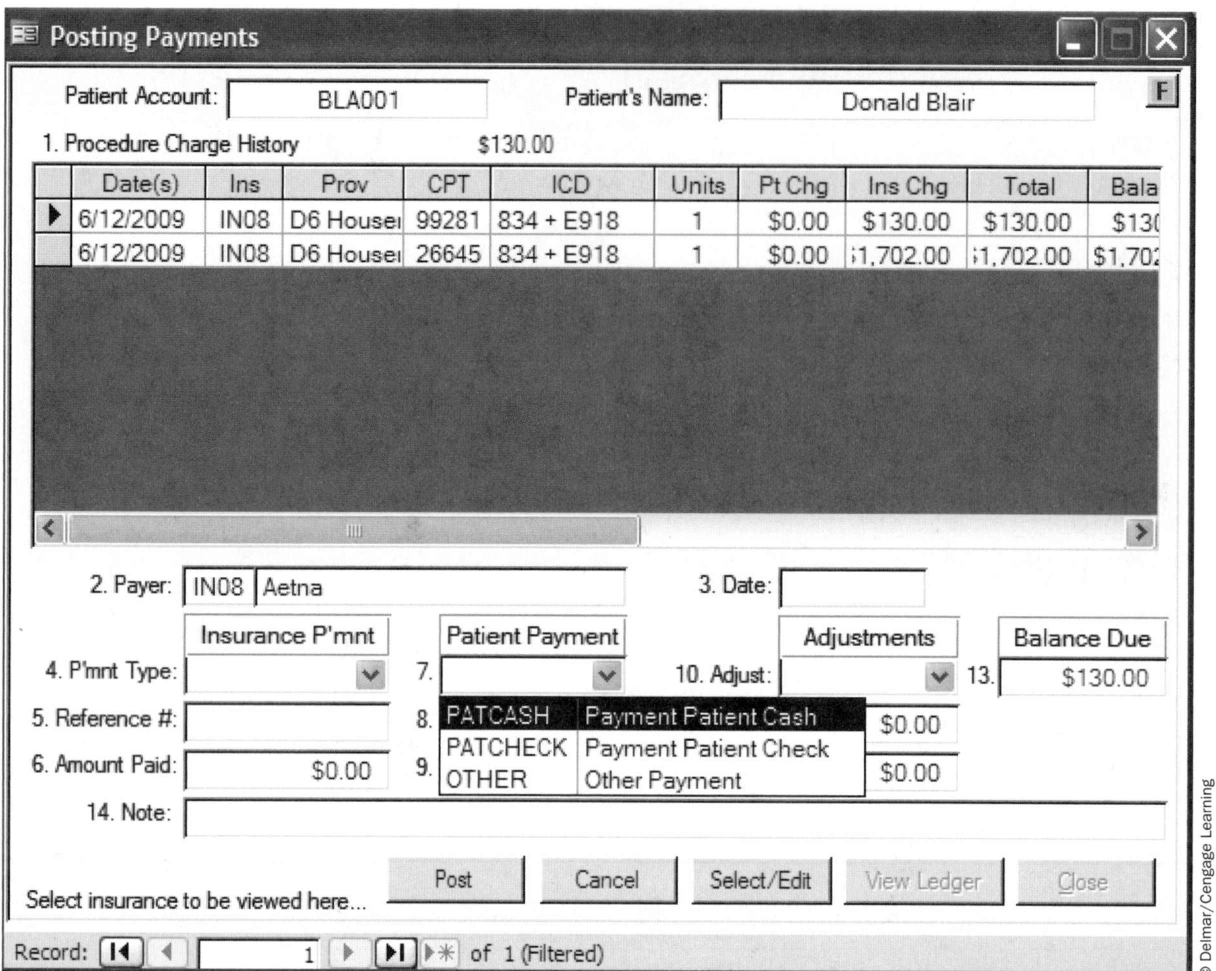

Figure 4.18 Extended Billing Information

someone else's property]). Field 2 is completed only if the patient is referred to the practice. Fields 3–6 are related to the injury or illness itself and when it occurred. The data in these fields are pulled directly into the CMS 1500. Fields 7–9 apply only if the practice is drawing labs and sending them to an outside lab they have paid to process. Field 10 is where DMA's CLIA number is entered if performing lab services and, finally, field 11 is for the preauthorization number obtained from the insurance carrier for services to be rendered.

Data Entry Errors

Data entry errors can be corrected in MOSS in the appointment scheduling, patient registration, and procedure posting modules. Procedure posting errors can be corrected at any time when the student realizes that an error was made. In the medical office, errors are not easily corrected and physically cannot be corrected once the claim for that particular date of service has been sent to the insurance carrier. In the office, the entry has to be voided and a corrected claim has to be generated. But because MOSS is a teaching tool, it offers the ability to delete entries and start over. If a data entry error is identified in the appointment scheduling or patient registration modules, the data field can be highlighted and typed over, or the cursor can be placed in a particular field and the text can be inserted. In the procedure posting module, search for the patient name. Open the patient's file and view the posting details. Double-click the entry with the error or highlight the line with the error and click on the *Edit* button. From here, edit the field with the error. Once the correction is made, click on the *Post* button. Entire lines may be deleted by highlighting the desired lines and pressing the *Delete* key. You will be prompted to confirm that you are deleting.

Insurance Billing

Insurance billing or medical claims management is the responsibility of the medical biller and/or the coder in the practice or facility, depending on the role of these individuals. Up to this point, the focus has been on how to enter the data and enter it correctly. Insurance billing, or the act of actually filing the claim to the insurance carrier, takes place once all patient demographic and insurance information is entered in the *Patient Registration* module and the charges and codes have been entered into the *Procedure Posting* module.

The claims management process encompasses three main steps: claims preparation, claims editing, and claims printing or electronic submission. Medical practices differ as to how and when claims are prepared. Electronic claims submission allows the biller to edit the claim and correct any obvious errors or omissions at that time in an effort to send a clean claim. Electronic claim submission enables practices and facilities to reduce their accounts receivable days by shortening by several weeks the time it takes the claim to be generated and sent to the carrier, and for payment to be received. Most offices prepare, print, and send claims daily. Some offices may prepare secondary claims only once a week. Claims can be submitted from the practice management system through a clearinghouse or directly to the insurance carrier.

Claim preparation begins with clicking on the *Insurance Billing* button on the *Main Menu.* MOSS allows you to print hard copy claims as well as submit claims electronically. A *Claims Preparation* window will open (Figure 4.19). There are five fields that require input and selection before the claims can be generated. Field 1, *Sort*, provides three options when you click on the dropdown arrow: patient name, service dates, and account number. Field 2, *Settings*, has 6 items to complete: (a) you must determine if this claim or claims are being generated for the first time or if the claim is being rebilled, (b) the provider field allows you to select a provider individually or choose *All* to generate claims for all providers at once, (c & d) service dates—you can generate claims for one date or a range of dates, (e) patient name allows you to choose a specific name or *All*, and (f) account number can be specifically designated or *All* can be selected to generate all patient account numbers. Field 3, *Transmit Type,* requires you to decide if the claims will be printed or sent electronically. Field 4, *Billing Options*, designates whether the batch of claims is being sent to the primary or secondary insurance carrier. Field 5, *Payer**, allows the student to select specific insurance carrier claims or all claims. The student can select more than one and not all payers by holding down the Shift or Ctrl (Control) key to select the specific payer names.

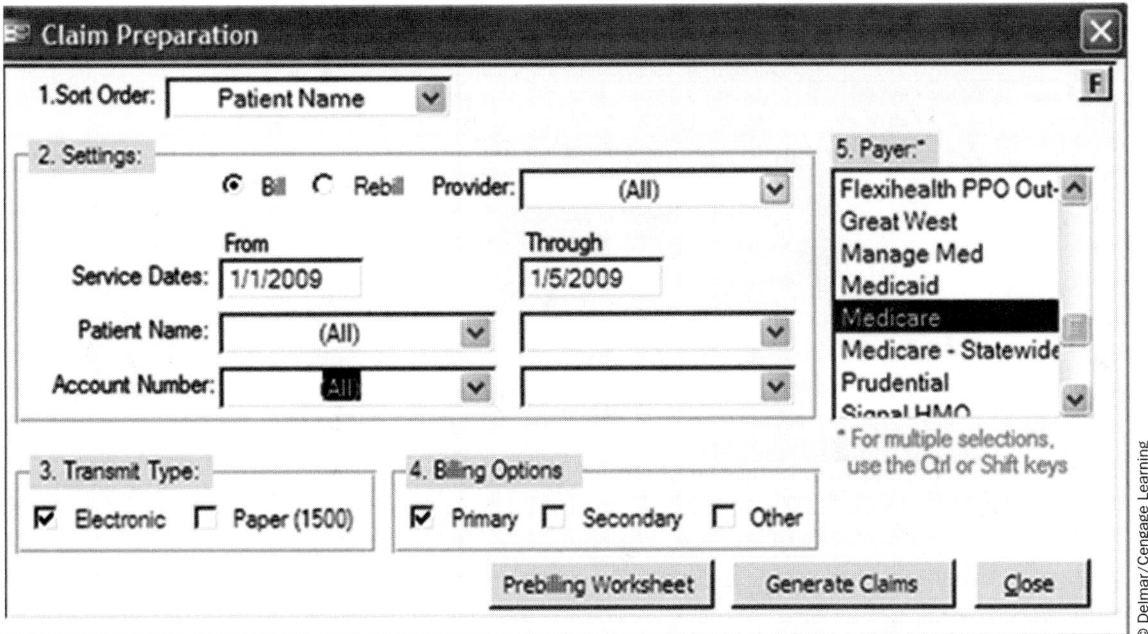

Figure 4.19 Claims Preparation

Once all six fields are completed, click on *Generate Claims.* The software will search for and display the claims in the CMS 1500 format according to the criteria selected in fields 1–6. For electronic claims, once the claims are generated and previewed, click on *Transmit EMC* at the bottom of the window. Doing so will electronically send the claim to the payer. When the transmission is complete, a transmission report shows a summary of each claim in the batch and the status of the claims as either accepted or rejected. It is a good idea to save the transmission report for future reference.

Payment Posting

Patient payments are collected at the time of service (cash, check, or credit/debit card) as well as received via postal mail. Insurance payments, depending on the carrier, can be in the form of either an electronic direct deposit to the practice's bank account or a paper check. Payments can be posted via two different avenues in MOSS depending on the type of payment being posted and the timing of the payment. The first, and most obvious, path to posting is taken by clicking on the *Posting Payments* button from the *Main Menu*. MOSS also allows for a payment to be posted to the account immediately after entering charges without you having to go the *Main Menu* to do so. This second path to posting payments is accessed from the *Procedure Posting* screen. For example, when a payment is collected at the time of service (typically when the patient is checking out) MOSS makes it convenient for the employee to enter the payment at the same time he/she is entering the charges for that day's visit. After you enter the charges into the *Procedure Posting* screen and before closing, you can click on the *Post Payment* button at the bottom of the screen (see Figure 4.17). When entering payments from the *Main Menu*, click on the *Posting Payments* button and select the patient account. Highlight the patient name and click on the *Apply Payment* button. Regardless of which avenue is chosen, you will begin entering the actual payment from the same *Payment Entry* screen (Figure 4.20).

Highlight the line to apply the payment to, taking caution to select the correct date of service to apply the payment to. Click the *Select/Edit* button. The balance due for that claim line should appear in the lower right of the screen in field 13, *Balance Due.* Enter the date the payment was received into field 3,

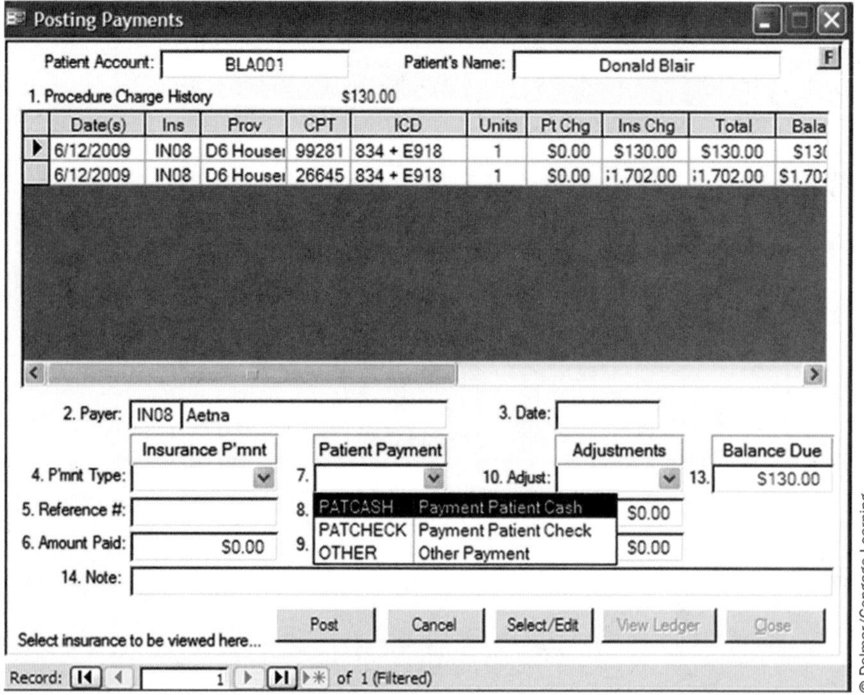

Figure 4.20 Payment Posting

Date. Fields 4–6 are specific to insurance payments only and do not apply at the time of posting patient payments. Field 4, *Insurance P'mnt,* has a dropdown with only one option: *PAYINS.* Field 5, *Reference #*, is the check number of the insurance check. Field 6, *Amount Paid*, is the amount paid to this particular patient's account, not the amount of the insurance check. Commonly more than one patient account is listed on an EOB and the amount of the check is the combined total of every patient account on the EOB. Field 7, *Patient Payment*, has a dropdown arrow option. When posting patient payments, one of these forms of payment must be selected: PATCASH, PATCHECK, OTHER. If the patient is paying by a credit or debit card, the correct payment option is *OTHER.* If the patient pays by check, enter the check number in field 8, which is the reference number for patient payments. Field 9, *Amount Paid*, equals the dollar amount collected from the patient over the counter, the amount of the check, or credit card payment.

Fields 10 and 11 are used when insurance payments are being posted and the payment does not equal 100% of the billed amount. These fields provide a way to capture the reason the entire billed amount isn't collected and to describe the specific adjustment reason. For example, if a patient does not have insurance and is given a self-pay discount, you will enter the patient payment, choose *ADJSP Self-pay Discount* from the dropdown menu in field 10, and enter the amount of the discount in field 11. When applying insurance payments and a portion of the insurance allowed amount is applied to the patient's deductible, this dollar amount is entered in field 12, *Deductible.* Notes can be entered into field 14, which is a free text field to provide space for documentation about patient conversations, messages

Exercise 4.1 Your Turn to Try

Use the following EOB to practice posting charges and making adjustments. The adjustment code to use for insurance contractual adjustments is ADJINS. Check your answer with Figure 4.21.

EXPLANATION OF BENEFITS

Managed Med

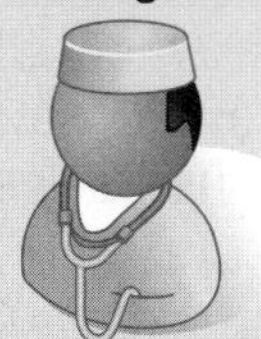

Date: 4/15/08

CHECK NUMBER: 0008480069

DOUGLASVILLE MEDICINE ASSOC.
5076 BRAND BLVD
DOUGLASVILLE, NY 01234

PHYSICIAN NUMBER OR EIN	DATE OF SERVICE (MON DAY YR)	PROCEDURE CODE	MOD	MOD	MOD	DAYS/UNITS	CHARGE SUBMITTED	COVERED CHARGE	AMOUNT ALLOWED	PATIENT LIABILITY DEDUCT.	CO-PAY	COIN.	OTHER	PAYMENT	MESSAGE
ACCT#		ID/CARD# 36914785						NAME:	LEIGHTON, LAURA			CLAIM# 11276L9440000			
045086221	031008	52000				1	713.00	713.00	631.01	.00	15.00	0.00	.00	616.01	
	032608	87086				1	24.00	24.00	21.24	.00	15.00	0.00	.00	6.24	
		CLAIM TOTAL					737.00	737.00	652.25	.00	30.00	0.00	.00	622.25	

EOF 2354(02/05) TOTAL 737.00 622.25

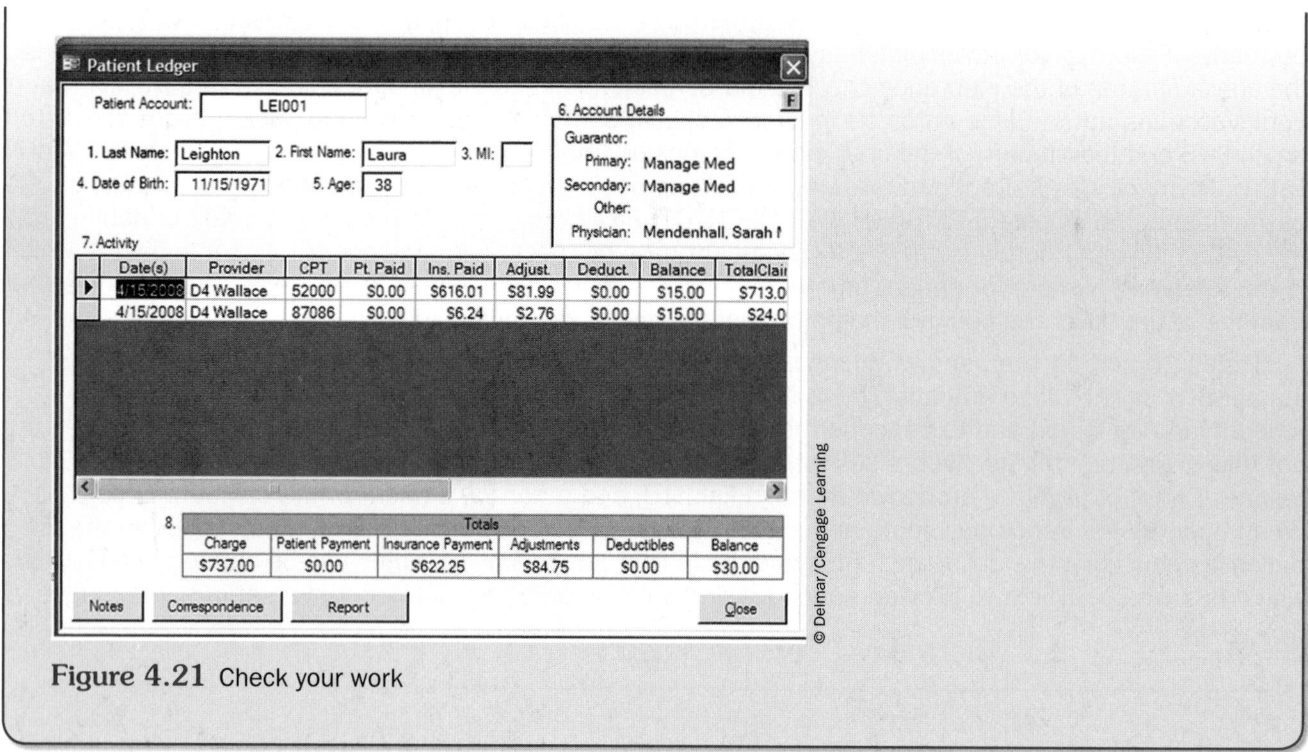

Figure 4.21 Check your work

to the patient, and so on. Once all payments are entered and adjustments accounted for, click on the *Post* button to finalize the transaction in the patient ledger.

Patient Billing

Practices have historically not done a good job of collecting patient responsibilities or the patient's portion of the fee for services, which results in a high (A/R). Many practices only collect patient co-pays up front or at the time of service and will bill the patient for coinsurance and deductibles on the back end after their insurance pays necessitating balance billing and generation of patient statements.

To properly bill a patient, the insurance plan contractual information, DMA's fee schedule, the insurance carrier allowed amounts, and payment fee schedules must be loaded into MOSS. Once the software is populated with this information, the software will do the math for you by taking the DMA charge for the service and subtracting the posted insurance plan paid amount and any patient deductible or patient payments made on the account. The difference between the DMA charge and the allowed amount minus the patient's responsibility (co-pay or co-insurance or deductible) is the contractual adjustment. The balance remaining will be the true patient balance. Patients are apt not to pay, particularly those with a percentage co-insurance, until insurance has paid.

Patient statements are prepared and sent in cycles. Cyclical billing generates and maintains a steady stream of practice income from outstanding patient balances throughout the month. Depending on the practice and its billing patterns, statements can be generated in various ways. For example, patients can receive a bill every 30 days after insurance has paid (30-, 60-, 90-day cycle), which means that statements are generated at the same time each month. This may mean that statements are generated during the same week each month (e.g., first week, second week, etc.) or on the first or fifteenth of each month. Accounts with patient balances can be divided up by alphabet. The first week (cycle 1) of the month, a segment of the alphabet is used to generate patient statements, such as A–G. Then the second week (or cycle 2) would generate statements for H–L, and so on.

Before statements are actually generated, most practices analyze outstanding balances and run reports from their practice management system. The conjecture here is that errors in payment posting may be identified before creating statements. Also, this process enables practices to adjust, or write off, small balances. In theory, it costs the practice more money—with administrative costs and postage—to bill patients for balances less than $9.99.

Reporting Used To Prepare Patient Statements

It is not necessary to analyze any reports before generating patient statements; however, reports can be useful in catching errors and providing the practice with an estimate of what is true patient A/R—that is, actual dollars the practice is expected to collect from the patient.

From the *Main Menu* select *Report Generation.* For our purposes here, enter the date 01/01/2008 in the *Aging Date* field in the upper right corner (Figure 4.22).

Select *Billing and Payment Report.* Enter start date 01/01/2008 at the prompt and then enter the end date 12/31/2009 at the next prompt. Figure 4.23 provides an excerpt from this report. Maximize

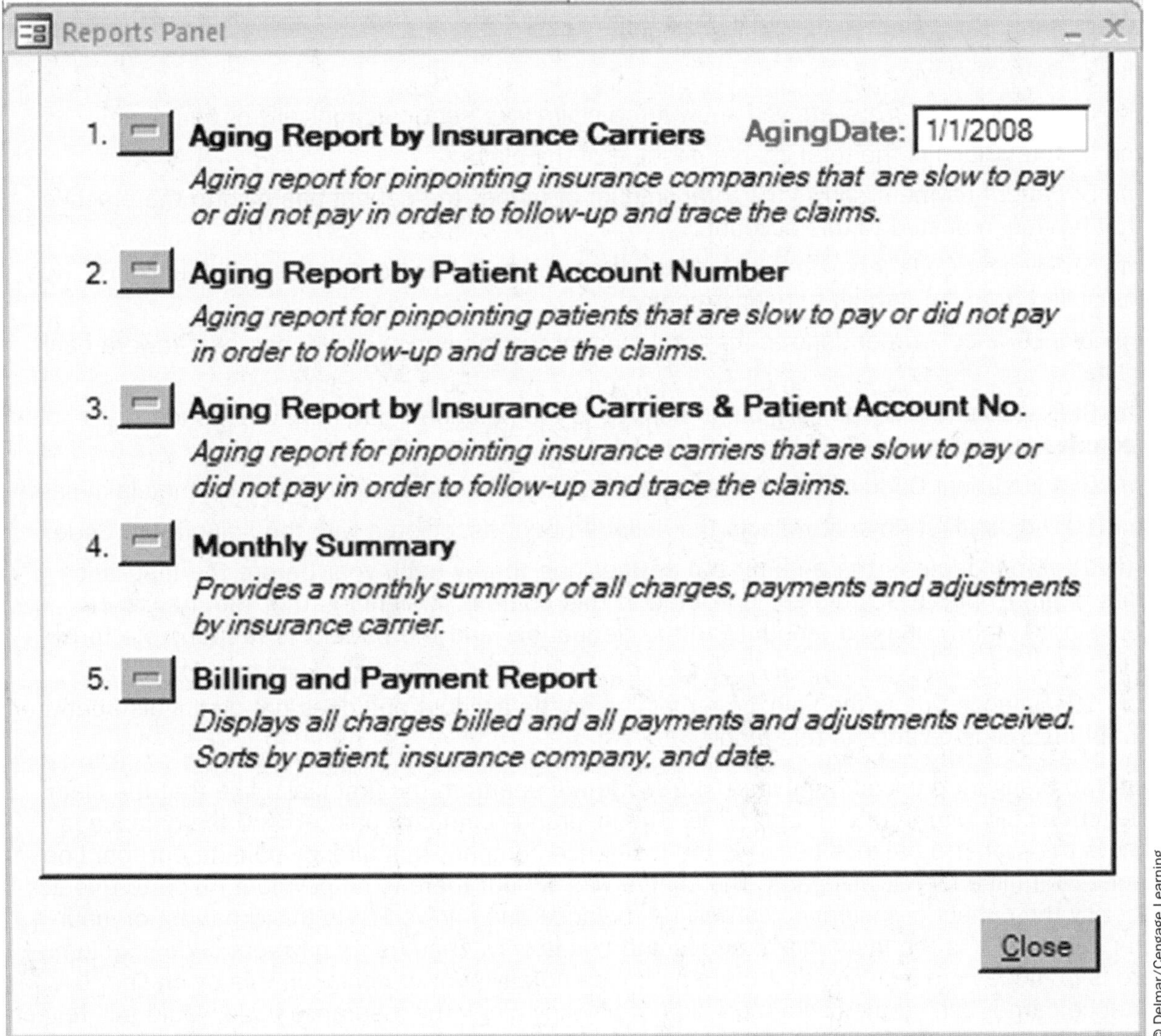

Figure 4.22 Standard Reporting Options

Insurance Billing & Payments for Student1

Account / Insurance Provider	Date of Service	Submitted By	Total Claim	Patient Payment	Payment Code	Insurance Payment	Dis-count	Adjust. Code	Adjust. Amount	Deduct-ible	Balance Due
LYN001 Mary Lynn											
IN09 GreatWest	25-Feb-08	Electronic	$6,544.00	$0.00		$0.00	0		$0.00	$0.00	$6,544.00
									Mary Lynn Balances:	$0.00	$6,544.00
MAN001 Vito Mangano											
IN04 Medicare - Statewide Corp.	23-Oct-09	Electronic	$6.00	$0.00	PAYINS	$5.00	0		$0.00	$0.00	$1.00
IN04 Medicare - Statewide Corp.	23-Oct-09	Electronic	$3.00	$0.00		$0.00	0		$0.00	$0.00	$3.00
									Vito Mangano Balances:	$0.00	$4.00

Figure 4.23 Excerpt Billing and Payment Report

the report on the screen to see all the columns. You can navigate from one page to the next by clicking the arrow keys at the bottom of the screen. This report, as well as all other MOSS reports, can be printed from your computer.

It is important that you understand how to read and interpret this report (Figure 4.23). The report is organized into 12 columns:

1. Column 1: Patient account number, name, and insurance carrier.
2. Column 2: Date of service.
3. Column 3: Submitted by. This lets you know if the claim was sent electronically or on paper.
4. Column 4: Total Claim is the total charge or value of the claim.
5. Column 5: Patient Payment shows the total amount of money the patient has paid to the practice and that has been posted to this account.
6. Column 6: Payment Code lets you know what kind of payment has been made to the account. This code is pulled from the payment posting module.
7. Column 7: Insurance Payment shows the total amount the insurance carrier has paid toward each claim line.
8. Column 8: Discount reflects any discounts applied to the balance aside from the standard contractual adjustment.
9. Column 9: Adjustment Code signifies what type of an adjustment was performed on the claim line.
10. Column 10: Adjustment Amount reflects the dollar amount associated with the Adjustment Code.
11. Column 11: Deductible is the amount the patient has to pay each year before the insurance benefits begin to pay. If any money is posted in this column, it signifies that the insurance carrier is posting any allowed amounts to the deductible and the patient is responsible for this amount.
12. Column 12: Balance Due is the balance remaining on the account and does not distinguish between patient or insurance balance in this report.

Look at Vito Mangano's account in Figure 4.23. You will see from the first claim line that the claim was sent electronically with a total charge of $6. The insurance company paid $5 and the balance is $1. This $1 is the patient's balance because the insurance company has already paid its portion. Look at the second claim line for Mr. Mangano. The charge was $3 but there is no payment made to this account, either by the patient or insurance carrier. The balance due shows $3. Is this a patient or insurance carrier balance? It is the insurance carrier's and this is why: There is no payment code in column 6. Since there is no code here signifies that there has been no payment or denial on this claim line. Even if the insurance carrier denied the claim (i.e., did not pay anything), the insurance code would still reflect PAYINS and the paid amount would equal $0.

For every patient account that has a balance, look up the patient ledger to compare with the information on this report. While performing this process and reviewing this report, answer these three questions for each patient account:

1. What is the balance due?
2. Is the balance an insurance balance or patient balance?
3. If the balance is due from the patient, what would the account dunning message tailored to the circumstances on the individual account say?

Exercise 4.2 Run the Insurance Billing and Payment Report and Answer the Following Questions

1. What should the balance due on Vito Mangano's statement reflect?
2. Will Mary Lynn receive a statement in this cycle? Why or why not?
3. Who else should receive a statement?

Preparing Patient Statements

A patient statement is an itemized bill for services in the date range selected. It shows all services provided in the date span chosen, including the procedure codes, total charges, patient co-pay, insurance payments, adjustments, deductible, and current balance. Everything that can be accessed from the patient ledger is summarized in the patient statement.

From the *Main Menu* select *Patient Billing*. A *Patient Billing* window opens and has seven fields to complete before statements can be generated (Figure 4.24). Input information into the following fields:

1. Field 1, *Select Statement Type*. There are two options to choose from: 30-60-90 and Remainder. The first option, 30-60-90, is chosen only when a practice wants to send a statement to the patient even if their insurance has not paid or paid the full allowed amount. The rationale behind sending a statement in such a situation is that the patient will see the lag in insurance company payment and take the initiative to contact it and potentially get the claim paid without practice intervention. *Remainder* statements are sent when the practice wants only patients with a genuine patient balance remaining to receive a statement. At DMA, we send only remainder statements.
2. Field 2, *Provider.* MOSS can print statements by individual provider or for all providers in one session. Some practices have a policy that the treating physician must review all patient statements before they are mailed out. This is done because they may want to apply additional discounts on balances for patients they know are financially strapped. In addition, physicians may have to authorize sending a patient to a collection agency and in some cases, physicians will direct the office staff to not schedule future appointments until the outstanding balance is satisfied (this is risky and does not often occur).
3. Field 3, *Settings. Service Dates* is the range of dates determined from the *Insurance Billing & Payment* report. *Patient Name* the drop down option allows you to select *All* or individual patient names. The routine choice is *All*, unless there is a reason to send a specific patient a statement with a custom message. *Account Number* does not need to be completed when the selection in patient name is *All.* It can be chosen if an individual patient is selected and the patient has more than one account number.
4. Field 4, *Process Type*. You are given the option to preview the statements on the screen or print them without previewing.

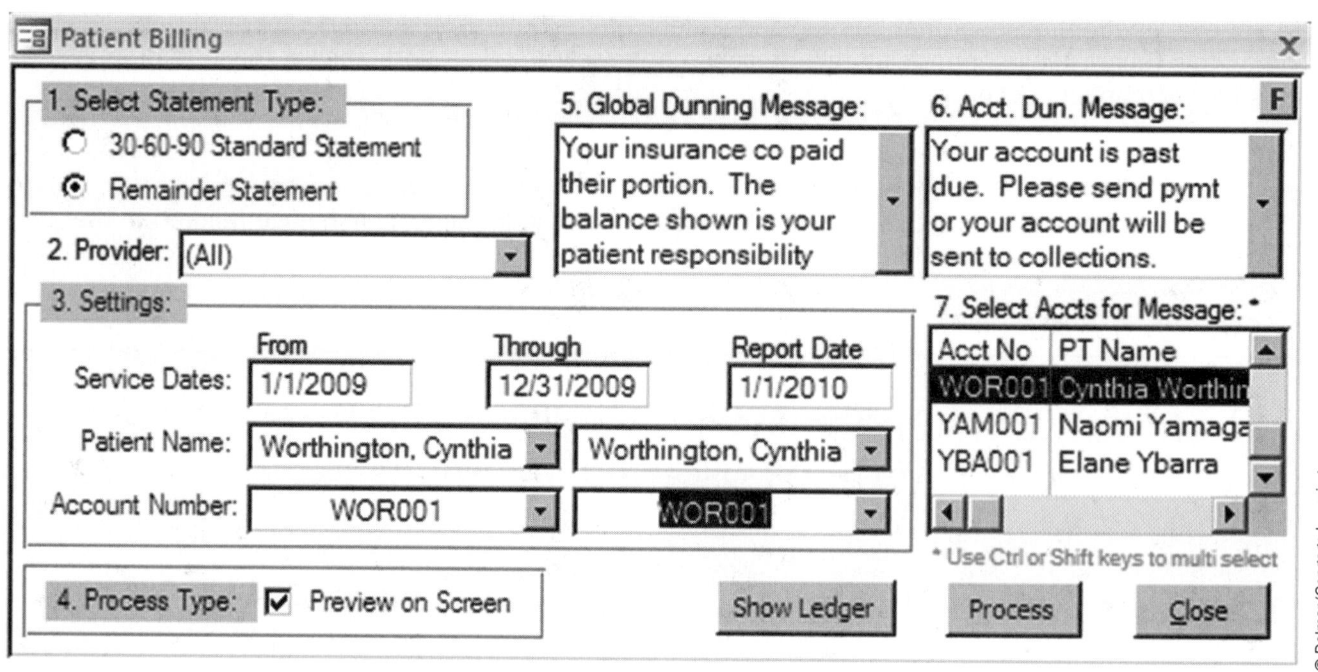

Figure 4.24 Patient Statement Creation

5. Field 5, *Global Dunning Message*. This message will appear on all statements generated in this batch. The user can create a message directly on this screen or the message can be created under *File Maintenance* from the *Main Menu*. If the messages are created here, you will use the dropdown menu in field 5 to select the global dunning version desired.
6. Field 6, *Account Dunning Message*. This field allows you to design a patient-specific message and is populated only when printing statements for a select group of patients or individual accounts. You can create a message directly on this screen or the message can be created under *File Maintenance* from the *Main Menu*. If the messages are created here, you will use the dropdown menu in field 6 to select the account Dunning version desired.
7. Field 7, *Select Accts for Message**. Here, you can select only the names of patients in which the account Dunning message should appear. This field is not used unless there is a message in field 6.

The Dunning message appears at the bottom of the statement. The balance that appears at the bottom right is the patient's balance after all insurance payments, adjustments, and previous patient payments are applied (Figure 4.25). Use the criteria in Figure 4.24 to practice preparing a statement. Compare your results with Figure 4.25.

Report Generation

The purpose of report generation is to retrieve and classify data from all the modules within MOSS. Electronic record keeping has made managing a practice much more efficient. With a few clicks of the mouse, practice management systems can generate a plethora of information to analyze, compare, and trend. Computerization not only saves time but also allows data to be manipulated and compared in ways that would be cost and time prohibitive to do manually. Most practice management systems have commonly used or standard preconfigured reports, and others allow for customization or ad hoc capability. Primary uses of reports are financially driven such as to track payments and outstanding balances, monitor medical billing activity, analyze income by physician, and assess carrier adherence to contracts.

Douglasville Medicine Associates
5076 Brand Blvd., Suite 401
Douglasville, NY 01234
Ph: (123) 456-7890
Fax: (123) 456-7891
Email: admin@dfma.com
Website: www.dfma.com

REMAINDER STATEMENT

CYNTHIA WORTHINGTON
5857 Granite Street
Douglasville, NY 01235

Date: 1/10/2010
Account No: WOR001
Student No: Student1

Date	Patient	Procedure	Total Charges	Patient Co-Pay	Insurance Payment	Adjust-ments	Deduct-ibles	Current Balance
27-Oct-09	Cynthia Worthington	99213	$111.00	$0.00	$88.80	$2.20	$0	$20.00
		Totals	$111.00	$0.00	$88.80	$2.20	$0	$20.00

Please make checks payable to:
Douglasville Medicine Associates

BALANCE DUE $20.00

Important Note:
Your account is past due. Please send pymt or your account will be sent to collections.
Your insurance co paid their portion. The balance shown is your patient responsibility.

1 No Filter

Figure 4.25 Patient Statement

Other uses are strategically based or for marketing purposes to learn more about practice patterns such as busiest providers, busiest times of day or week, and practice demographic trends.

MOSS comes preprogrammed with five standard reports (Figure 4.22). The following list provides a brief explanation of each report and its use:

1. *Aging Report by Insurance Carrier*. This report is used to track outstanding insurance payments and identify carriers that are slower to pay. This report assists insurance staff in targeting their efforts on the carriers with the most outstanding A/R. The staff will then contact the carriers and determine what the delay in payment is.

2. *Aging Report by Patient Account Number.* This report is used to track outstanding patient payments and identify those patients who are slow to pay or have high dollar outstanding balances. This report assists collection staff in targeting their efforts on the oldest patient accounts and those with the highest balances. The staff then contacts the patients by mail and/or phone to determine why there is a delay in payment.
3. *Aging Report by Insurance Carrier & Patient Account Number.* This report is better served when calling the insurance carrier because each patient with an outstanding insurance balance by payer is located on this report, and it allows the insurance staff member to have the patient account numbers on hand when speaking to the insurance carrier.
4. *Monthly Summary.* Provides a summary by month of all insurance payments, charges, and adjustments.
5. *Billing and Payment Report.* As discussed previously, this report is used to validate the balances on each account before sending patient statements.

Now that you have completed the MOSS training overview, you are ready to begin using the software and completing the tasks and jobs in chapters 5–9.

PART II

COMPUTER AND CODING ORIENTATION

CHAPTER 5

Coding from Source Documents

Learning Objectives

When finished with this chapter, the student will be able to:

1. Site specific coding guidelines regarding coding from documentation.
2. Identify medical record source documents.
3. Describe the standards for documentation.
4. List steps to code from documentation.
5. Describe incident-to billing.
6. Identify coding compliance plan features.
7. Discuss the purpose of the Correct Coding Initiative (CCI) and explain how to use edits.
8. Describe what Local Coverage Determinations are, their use, and how to locate them.
9. Assign codes to services routinely performed in a family practice setting.
10. Assess coding competency by completing the new hire coding test.
11. Utilize Use professional associations' and the CMS website to stay abreast of changes in coding guidelines and regulatory reporting.

Key Terms

Component Code
Comprehensive Code
Consent Form
Consult
Encounter Form
False Claims
History and Physical (H&P)
Incident-to Rule
Laboratory Report
Local Coverage Determination (LCD)
Medical Necessity
Medication List
Mutually Exclusive
National Correct Coding Initiative (NCCI)
Operative Report
Pathology Report
Patient Assessment
Patient Information Sheet
Pay-for-Performance
Physician Assistant (PA-C)
Physician Orders
Physician Quality Reporting Initiative (PQRI)
Progress Notes
Radiology Report
Recovery Audit Contractor Program (RAC)
Review of Systems
Significant Procedure
SOAP Notes
Source Documents
Unbundling

Background Basics

- Students should have completed a course in ICD-9-CM, CPT, and HCPCS coding methodologies.

Competency Checklist

- Coders must have a strong foundation in coding guidelines to properly assign codes for diagnoses and procedures.
- Coders are responsible for reading and interpreting medical information to justify medical necessity and assign codes to the highest specificity. They must be capable of navigating a medical record and identifying source documents.
- Coding and billing staff have to be fluent in Medicare payment policies, including the correct coding initiative and local coverage determinations to obtain optimal reimbursement and to maintain compliance. They must also be able to reference these sources quickly for use throughout the work day.

Coding Guidelines Review

The official ICD-9-CM outpatient coding guidelines published in the *Federal Register* are the basis for all coding at DMA. Guidelines are located in the front of the ICD-9-CM codebook. However, these are updated each April and October, and the updated guidelines must be obtained online. These can be downloaded from various cooperating party websites such as the American Health Information Management Association (AHIMA) (http://www.ahima.org) or the National Center for Health Statistics (NCHS) (http://www.cdc.gov/nchs/). Documentation must be available to report the primary or first-listed diagnosis and secondary diagnoses along with primary and secondary procedures. According to the guidelines, other diagnoses are interpreted as and reported if:

- The condition required a clinical evaluation
- The condition required therapeutic treatment
- Diagnostic procedures were performed to evaluate the condition
- The condition extended the hospital length of stay
- Additional nursing care or monitoring is required

The guidelines state that the "documentation should describe the patient's condition, using terminology which includes specific diagnoses as well as symptoms, problems, or reasons for the encounter." Codes for signs and symptoms are acceptable until a diagnosis is confirmed and established. Do not assign codes for conditions that were previously treated and no longer exist. However, do code all conditions that co-exist at the time of service that affect patient care or management.

For example, a diabetic patient was seen in the office for pneumonia two months ago and returns today for painful urination. Pneumonia would not be reported because this is not the reason the patient is seen today unless the doctor treats the pneumonia today. Painful urination is the primary diagnosis. The diabetes is reported because it affects the management and outcome of the patient's care.

V codes are assigned as the primary diagnosis for patients being seen for preventative visits, for immunizations, and for those who have been exposed to a disease but do not show signs at the time of the visit. We require that they be used as secondary diagnoses when a patient is either a carrier of a disease, has the sequelae or residual of a past disease, or is being treated with long-term drug therapy because these factors may affect the course of treatment.

Professional services provided by a physician (MD), a physician assistant (PA-C), a nurse, or a nurse practitioner (R.N.P.), are reported with CPT codes. Evaluation and Management (E/M) services are located in the index under the phrase *"Evaluation and Management* or *Consultation*. In family practice, at times it may be confusing to coders whether to classify a patient as a new patient or established patient. A new patient has not received any professional services from the physician within three years and has not received any professional services from another physician of the same specialty in the same group practice within three years. In our clinic, that would be six providers in addition to physicians who have left this practice in this time frame. All significant procedures are also assigned using CPT codes. **Significant procedures** or services:

1. Are surgical in nature
2. Carry a procedural risk
3. Carry an anesthetic risk
4. Are therapeutic in nature
5. Require specialized training

They are typically located under the terms: *incision, excision, repair, manipulation, amputation, endoscopy, destruction, suturing, injection*, and *introductions*. If more than one procedure is performed, a principal procedure must be chosen.

Coders should not choose a code because of its proven reimbursement record. Accurate and specific coding consists of choosing the most correct code available for the procedure or service rendered. Codes assigned must be justified by the documentation.

Discussion:

Based on the preceding discussion, is an injection a significant procedure? Why or why not?

Interpretations

To add to an already complex system of coding guidelines, there are discrepancies in interpretations of these guidelines between the American Medical Association (AMA) and CMS. Coders often struggle with why there are differences and when to apply which organization's interpretation. Keep it simple—if you are coding for services rendered to a government payer or Medicare beneficiary, heed the CMS interpretation. It is safe to employ the AMA interpretations for commercial claims. *CPT Assistant* provides the AMA's position for procedural guidelines. CMS publishes its guidelines in the *Correct Coding Initiative Manual*, *MLN Matters Articles*, and the *Medicare Claims Processing Manual.*

There are stark differences between CMS and AMA views regarding E/M Coding Guidelines, global periods, and reporting bilateral surgery. For example, CMS and the AMA differ when it comes to reporting bilateral procedures. Take a look at *52005 Cystourethroscopy, with ureteral catheterization, with or without irrigation, instillation, or ureteropyelography, exclusive of radiologic service.* The AMA allows this code to be reported bilaterally with a -50 modifier on the premise that the ureter is a paired body part—one from the left kidney and one from the right kidney. CMS does not allow this to be reported bilaterally. If you look at the MPFS for 52005, the indicator *0* denotes that a bilateral payment adjustment would not apply.

Exercise 5.0 Your Turn to Try

Read the following scenario and determine why the claim got denied. Then research the coding guidelines and determine what the diagnoses should be. Once you have done your research, prepare a document educating the physicians and coding staff about the importance of knowing and adhering to coding guidelines and how visits such as these should be coded and reported to avoid denials in the future. Be sure to site the authoritative sources from which you obtained your information.

Diagnosis reported: V58.69

PHYSICIAN NUMBER OR EIN	DATE OF SERVICE	PROCEDURE				DAYS/ UNITS	CHARGE SUBMITTED	COVERED CHARGE	AMOUNT ALLOWED	PATIENT LIABILITY				PAYMENT	MESSAGE
	MON DAY YR	CODE	MOD	MOD	MOD					DEDUCT.	COPAY	COIN.	OTHER		
ACCT#		ID/CARD# 777298						NAME:	DOE,	JOSEPH		CLAIM#: 11311C2990000WW			
045093227	072106	99212				1	55.00	55.00	45.06	.00	15.00	.00	.00	0.00	B52
	072106	85610				1	17.00	17.00	5.47	.00	.00	.00	.00	0.00	B52
	072106	36416				1	20.00	20.00	0.00					0.00	B52
		CLAIM TOTAL					277.00	277.00	149.00	.00	15.00	.00	.00	0.00	
B52	PRINCIPLE DIAGNOSIS WAS INAPPROPRIATELY CODED														

ICD-10-CM and ICD-10-PCS

On January 16, 2009 the *Federal Register CMS -0013-F 45 CFR Part 162* published the final rule to *HIPAA Administrative Simplification Modification to Medical Data Code Set Standardization to Adopt ICD-10-CM and ICD-10-PCS.* ICD-9-CM codes will not be accepted for services provided on or after October 1, 2013. This has been a long awaited decision by much of the health care industry because of inadequacies of the current ICD-9-CM. ICD-9-CM is running out of codes and cannot meet the demands of advances in medical technology. ICD-10 takes the ambiguity out of coding and will require providers to document essential details to properly assign these codes. Refer to Figure 5.1 for examples of each code set.

Some of you are saying, "Why make this change now? I am just learning ICD-9-CM"! Well, we have to let go of what is comfortable for the sake of progress. ICD-9 is 30 years old, and terminology and classification of some conditions are outdated and obsolete. Coders are often forced to choose a code that is unspecified or not elsewhere classified, which limits our ability to track and compare health care data. The anticipated benefits of the electronic health record (EHR) cannot be achieved without changing to ICD-10-CM. So change is here, like it or not.

The ICD–10 code set includes six-digit alphanumeric codes with a qualifier character. Codes can range from 3 to 7 characters in length. Digit 1 is alpha, digits 2 and 3 are numeric, and digits 4–7 are alpha or numeric. This code set provides a standard coding convention that is flexible with the capability of expansion while providing unique and specific codes for all health conditions. ICD–10–CM and ICD–10–PCS provide specific diagnosis and treatment information used by public health organizations to improve quality measurements and patient safety, as well as the assessment of medical processes and outcomes.

The ICD–10–CM code set provides much more information and detail within the codes than ICD–9–CM, facilitating timely electronic processing of claims by reducing requests for additional information such as

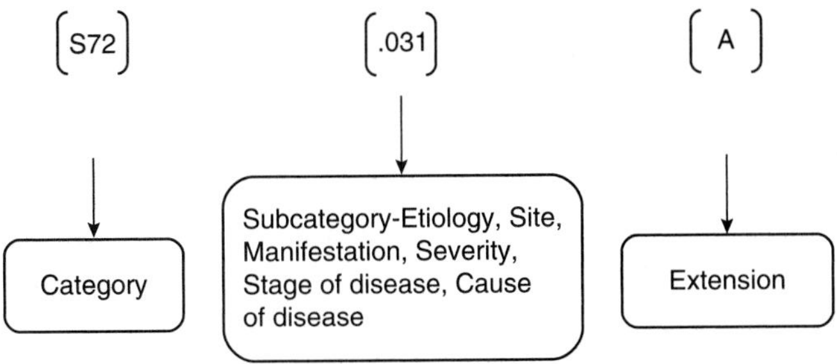

ICD-10-PCS

Dilation of the lacrimal duct right eye via probe into duct.
ICD-10-PCS Code: 087X7D

1	2	3	4	5	6	7
Section	Body System	Root operation	Body Part	Approach	Device	Qualifier
0	8	7	X	7	D	Z

Figure 5.1 Examples of ICD-10-CM and ICD-10-PCS

copies of the medical record. ICD–10–CM enables the coder to provide a more accurate depiction of the precise illness or disease such as mental disorders, neoplasms, cardiovascular disease, and infections as well as laterality for specifying which organ or part of the body is involved along with external causes of injury. The ICD–10–CM code set captures the details of advances in medicine and medical technology, as well as provides a means to capture more detail on socioeconomics, ambulatory care conditions, problems related to lifestyle, and the results of screening tests.

ICD–10–PCS is vastly more detailed than ICD-9 with the aim of describing complex medical procedures. ICD–10–PCS has unique, precise codes to differentiate body parts, surgical approaches, and devices used. It can be used to identify resource consumption differences and outcomes for different procedures, and it describes precisely what has been done to the patient. ICD–10–PCS codes have seven alphanumeric characters and group together services into approximately 30 procedures identified by a leading alpha character. This code set will replace the Volume 3 ICD-9-CM procedure codes for inpatient hospital procedures.

At the time of this writing, there is no stated impact on Current Procedural Terminology (CPT) and Health care Common Procedure Coding System (HCPCS) codes sets. Physicians and ambulatory outpatient centers will continue to use these codes to report their services. However, all provider types are required to report ICD-10-CM codes in place of the ICD-9-CM diagnosis codes.

Impact of Implementation

Physicians will need to change how they document and provide more details when documenting in the medical record, which will increase time spent on each patient. It is anticipated that practices will need to hire additional staff to handle the increased workload. Implementation of ICD-10 is costly. Health care entities must implement an electronic medical record with ICD-10-CM. Financial outlay is significant to physicians, health plans, facilities, clearinghouses, and the like on upgrades in software, new coding systems, and reprogramming to accommodate the new character lengths.

Something provider offices need to think about now is that with the adoption of ICD-10, it will be much harder for providers to list common diagnoses and their corresponding codes on their encounter forms (i.e., superbill, router). The days of having the diagnosis code and its corresponding diagnosis preprinted on this form and the ability to check it off will be a pastime. ICD-10 codes are much more specific and will require the documentation to assign the codes.

Not only will coders and providers need to be retrained in the new coding system, but many other systems will have to be updated to accommodate this change. Providers and facilities will need to work with virtually all of their software vendors to implement this change. One of the likely stumbling blocks of the transition will be the timely adoption of the new code set by insurance carriers, the adaptation of their claims processing systems, and the updating of their medical policies. For example, carrier medical policies, CMS's NCDs/LCDs, and associated carrier systems responsible for flagging claims and/or triggering an ABN are dependent on the current ICD-9-CM codes. These systems, forms, and related items will have to be updated to ICD-10 codes when updated policies are available from Medicare and its contractors. Understandably, updating medical necessity policies will not be at the top of carriers' priority lists when they are preparing for ICD-10, considering the number of other things in claims processing systems that have to be updated. It is anticipated that providers will be required to report both ICD-9 and ICD-10 codes for a period of time.

Physicians and coders need to start familiarizing themselves with the new code set now. According to the *Federal Register* both AHA and AHIMA will take lead roles in developing additional, more detailed technical training materials for coders. AHIMA has several links to valuable resources on their website as well as an *ICD-10 Checklist*, Practice Briefs, articles, seminar schedules, and frequently asked questions (FAQs). In addition, CMS has dedicated resources for ICD-10 on their website, http://www.cms.hhs.gov/ICD10, with links to the *Federal Register* and complete versions of both ICD-9-CM and ICD-10-PCS. AAPC also has free webinars and educational opportunities in addition to an ICD-10 plan for certified coders who are members of the AAPC. All AAPC members are required to take and pass an ICD-10-CM proficiency test between October 1, 2012 and September 30, 2014 to maintain their certifications.

Real World Application

Think about the transition to adopting ICD-10. What systems, forms, documents, and so on will need to be updated and revised? Will it be possible to use a physician office superbill in its current form? What about lab orders? Do some additional research on this topic and discuss it with your class.

Medical Record Contents

In this section, you should become familiar with the different components of a medical record. As a coder, you will need to be efficient at maneuvering around the record. The following text presents a list of forms you will see on an inpatient chart or physician office chart. When coding, you will be reviewing these key sections of the record to capture all that is going on with that patient. These are by no means all the forms you will see, but a good sampling of the most common ones. Forms from special testing departments such as graphic records, nerve conduction studies, or anesthesia/intraoperative reports are not covered here. Keep in mind that a physician's office receives copies of documentation generated from many settings, including other physicians' offices.

The medical record documentation truly originates when the patient schedules an appointment. Any referral information is obtained at this time either via fax or postal mail.

Patient Information Sheet

The **patient information sheet** is referred to by many names: admission/discharge sheet, summary sheet, demographic sheet, face sheet, or identification sheet. This sheet is usually computerized and generated upon registration in a facility. At DMA, the patient fills this out at their first visit and then this data is entered into MOSS (Figure 5.2). This information should be updated at each patient encounter or

DOUGLASVILLE MEDICINE ASSOCIATES
PATIENT REGISTRATION FORM

Patients must complete all information prior to seeing the physician. A copy of your insurance card(s) and driver's license will be made for your file.

Patient Name:________________________________ Date of Birth:____/____/____
Sex: Male or Female Social Security Number: ____-____-____ Marital Status:_____
Address Line 1:____
Address Line 2:____
City:__________________________________
State:______________________ Zip Code:____________
Home Telephone:(____)________________ Work Telephone:(____)______________
Cellular Telephone:(____)_______________ Email address:_________________________

Patient's Work Status (Full-Time, Part-Time, Retired, Student): ______________
Employer Name:____
Address Line 1:____
Address Line 2:____
City:____________________ State:__________ Zip:___________
Telephone:(_____)_____________________
If patient is a minor, who is the primary guardian?___________________________________

Primary Insurance Company:__________________________
Subscriber ID Number______________________ Policy Group #:___________
Subscriber Name:______________________________ Birth date:_______________
Subscriber Social Security Number:_____-____-_______ Relationship to patient:__________

Secondary Insurance Company:__________________________
Subscriber ID Number______________________ Policy Group #:___________
Subscriber Name:______________________________ Birth date:_______________
Subscriber Social Security Number:_____-____-_______ Relationship to patient:__________

Complete this Section if your Treatment is for an Injury or Accident.
Were you injured at work?______ Is this covered by Workers' Compensation?_______
If Yes, Contact person at your Employer____
Were you involved in an auto accident?_______ Provide insurance company, contact information, and claim number:____
____
Date & time of Accident___________________ Place of Accident_____________________
How did injury happen?____
Name of Physician who treated you at time of accident:_______________________________

Financial Responsibility Statement/Release of Information Authorization
"I authorize the release of any medical information necessary to my insurance company and the Payment of Benefits to the Physician for services provided."

X_______________________________________ Date_______________________
Signature of Patient or Legal Guardian

Figure 5.2 Patient Registration Form *(continued)*

DOUGLASVILLE MEDICINE ASSOCIATES
PATIENT REGISTRATION FORM

OUR FINANCIAL POLICY

By law, we must collect your carrier designated co-pay at the time of service. Please be prepared to pay that co-pay at each visit. We are also required to collect any portion of the deductible that has not been satisfied. If your plan requires a coinsurance instead of a co-pay and we participate with the plan, we will accept the designated payment and bill you accordingly for any deductible and coinsurance your plan indicates you are responsible for on their explanation of benefits.

Payment is expected at the time of service unless other financial arrangements have been made prior to your visit. If you are uninsured, you may qualify for a hardship discount. Ask one of our staff members for more information.

You are responsible for timely payment of your account. Douglasville Medicine Associates reserves the right to reschedule or deny a future appointment on delinquent accounts.

WE ACCEPT CASH, CHECKS, MASTERCARD AND VISA

THANK YOU for taking the time to review our policy.

______________________________ _______________

(Responsible Party Signature) (Date)

Figure 5.2 Patient Registration Form

at least annually. This sheet contains patient-specific information regarding insurance, name, address, employer, and so on. All of this information is used by the business office for printing on the CMS 1500 claim form or on the ANSI 837P.

Encounter Form (Router)

Encounter forms are preprinted and at times two-part forms that require the provider to check off services provided and supplies incurred during the patient encounter. These forms are also referred to as superbills, routers, charge tickets, or fee slips. For our purposes, we will refer to this document as a router (Figure 5.3). Routers provide a consistent method to substantiate claims for medically necessary services and supplies for our patients. They are used by medical offices and outpatient clinics only; they not used in the inpatient setting. Everything that is needed to post charges and file a claim, with the exception of insurance and policy holder information, is located on this router. All ICD-9, CPT, and HCPCS codes commonly used by our practice are located here. Sometimes a provider may have to handwrite a diagnosis code on this form if a specific code is missing. Each specialty has its own router tailored to its needs. Any follow-up visits needed are scheduled from this form as indicated by the physician who rendered services. We also provide a copy of this form to the patient to serve as a receipt for co-pays collected that day and as an appointment reminder for follow-ups. Coders at our clinic are not permitted

Date of service: 10/27/09	Insurance: **FLEXIHEALTH PPO**		Router Number: 2463
Patient name: **DEREK WALLACE**	Coinsurance:	Copay:	Physician Name: **MURRAY**
Account #: **WAL001**	Noncovered Waiver?	yes / no / n/a	

x	Office visit	New	x	Est
	Minimal (RN only)			99211
	Problem focused	99201		99212
	Exp problem focused	99202		99213
	Detailed	99203	X	99214
	Comp	99204		99215
	Comprhen/Complex	99205		
	Well visit	**New**	**x**	**Est**
	< 1 y	99381		99391
	1-4 y	99382		99392
	5-11 y	99383		99393
	12-17 y	99384		99394
	18-39 y	99385		99395
	40-64 y	99386		99396
	65 y +	99387		99397
	Medicare preventive services			
	Pap			Q0091
	Pelvic & breast			G0101
	Prostate/PSA			G0103
	Tobacco couns/3-10 min			G0375
	Tobacco couns/>10 min			G0376
	Welcome to Medicare exam			G0344
	ECG w/Welcome to Medicare			G0366
	Hemoccult, guaiac			G0107
	Flu shot			G0008
	Pneumonia shot			G0009
	Consultation/preop clearance			
	Exp problem focused			99242
	Detailed			99243
	Comp/mod complex			99244
	Comp/high complex			99245
	Other services			
	After posted hours			99050
	Evening/weekend appointment			99051
	Home health certification			G0180
	Home health recertification			G0179
	Care Plan oversight			99374
	Care Plan Oversight >30 mins			99375
	Post-op follow-up			99024
	Prolonged/60min total			99354
	Prolonged/each add 30 mins			99355
	Special reports/forms			99080
	Disability/Workers comp			99455
	Smoking Cessation <10 mins			99406
	Smoking Cessation >10 mins			99407
	ETOH/SA screening <30 mins			99408
	Online E/M by MD			99444
	Phone E/M <10 mins			99441
	Phone E/M <20 mins			99442
	Phone E/M <30 mins			99443
	Anticoagulant Mgmt <90 days			99363
	Anticoagulant Mgmt >90 days			99364
	In office emergency serv			99058
	Other services			
	Supplies			
	Surgical Tray			99070

x	Office procedures	Code	Units
	Cerumen removal		69210
	ECG, w/interpretation		93000
	ECG, rhythm strip		93040
	Endometrial biopsy		58100
	Fracture care, cast/splint		______
	Site: ________________		
	Nebulizer		94640
	Nebulizer demo		94664
	Spirometry		94010
	Spirometry, pre and post		94060
	Vasectomy		55250
	Skin procedures		**Units**
	Foreign body, skin, simple	10120	
	Foreign body, skin, complex	10121	
	I&D, abscess	10060	
	I&D, hematoma/seroma	10140	
	Laceration repair, simple	120__	
	Site: _______ Size: _____		
	Laceration repair, layered	120__	
	Site: _______ Size: _____		
	Laser Light Tx	96597	
	Lesion, biopsy, one	11100	
	Lesion, biopsy, each add'l	11101	
	Lesion, excision, benign	114__	
	Site: _______ Size: _____		
	Lesion, excision, malignant	116__	
	Site: _______ Size: _____		
	Lesion, paring/cutting, one	11055	
	Lesion, paring/cutting, 2-4	11056	
	Lesion, shave	113__	
	Site: _______ Size: _____		
	Nail removal, partial (+T mod)	11730	
	Nail rem, w/matrix (+T mod)	11750	
	Skin tag, 1-15	11200	
	Wart, flat, 1-14	17110	
	Destruction lesion, 1st	17000	
	Destruct lesion, each addl 2-14	17003	
	Medications		**Units**
	Ampicillin, up to 500mg	J0290	
	B-12, up to 1,000 mcg	J3420	
	Epinephrine, up to 1ml	J0170	
	Kenalog, 10mg	J3301	
	Lidocaine, 10mg	J2001	
	Normal saline, 1000cc	J7030	
	Phenergan, up to 50mg	J2550	
	Progesterone, 150mg	J1055	
	Rocephin, 250mg	J0696	
	Testosterone, 200mg	J1080	
	Tigan, up to 200 mg	J3250	
	Toradol, 15mg	J1885	
	Albuterol	J7609	
	Depo-Provera 50 mg	J1055	
	Depo-Medrol 40 mg	J1030	
	Diagnoses		**Code**
	1.		
	2		
	3		
	4		

x	Laboratory		-90
	Venipuncture	36415	
	Blood glucose, monitoring device	82962	
	Blood glucose, visual dipstick	82948	
	CBC, w/ auto differential	85025	
	CBC, w/o auto differential	85027	
	Cholesterol	82465	
	Hemoccult, guaiac	82270	
	Hemoccult, immunoassay	82274	
	Hemoglobin A1C	85018	
	Lipid panel	80061	
	Liver panel	80076	
	KOH prep (skin, hair, nails)	87220	
	Metabolic panel, basic	80048	
	Metabolic panel, comprehensive	80053	
	Mononucleosis	86308	
	Pregnancy, blood	84703	
	Pregnancy, urine	81025	
	Renal panel	80069	
	Sedimentation rate	85651	
	Strep, rapid	86403	
	Strep culture	87081	
	Strep A	87880	
	TB	86580	
	UA, complete, non-automated	81000	
	UA, w/o micro, non-automated	81002	
	UA, w/ micro, non-automated	81003	
	Urine colony count	87086	
	Urine culture, presumptive	87088	
	Wet mount/KOH	87210	
	Vaccines		
	DT, <7 y		90702
	DTP		90701
	DtaP, <7 y		90700
	Flu, 6-35 months		90657
	Flu, 3 y +		90658
	Hep A, adult		90632
	Hep A, ped/adol, 2 dose		90633
	Hep B, adult		90746
	Hep B, ped/adol 3 dose		90744
	Hep B-Hib		90748
	Hib, 4 dose		90645
	HPV		90649
	IPV		90713
	MMR		90707
	Pneumonia, >2 y		90732
	Pneumonia conjugate, <5 y		90669
	Td, >7 y		90718
	Varicella		90716
	Tetanus toxoid adsorbed, IM		90703
	Immunizations & Injections		**Units**
	Allergen, one	95115	
	Allergen, multiple	95117	
	Imm admn <8 yo 1st Inj	90465	
	Imm admn <8 yo each add inj	90466	
	Imm <8 yo oral or intranasal	90467	
	Imm admn <8 yo each add	90468	
	Imm admin, one vacc	90471	
	Imm admin, each add'l	90472	
	Imm admin, intranasal, one	90473	
	Imm admin, intranasal, each add'l	90474	
	Injection, joint, small	20600	
	Injection, joint, intermediate	20605	
	Injection, ther/proph/diag	90772	
	Injection, trigger pt 1-2 musc	20552	
	Today's charges:		
	Today's payment:		
	Balance due:		

Instructions:

Return in 7 days if not improved. Drink plenty of liquids Ibuprofen 400 mg q. 8 hrs for fever and aches.

Next office visit:

Recheck · Preventative · PRN

Referral to:

Physician signature

X ______________________________

Figure 5.3 Router *(continued)*

Infectious & Parasitic Diseases

053.9 Herpes zoster, NOS
054.9 Herpetic disease, uncomplicated
075 Mononucleosis
034.0 Strep throat
079.99 Viral infection, unspec.
078.10 Warts, all sites

Neoplasms

Benign Neoplasms
239.2 Skin, soft tissue neoplasm, unspec.
216.9 Skin, unspec.

Endocrine, Nutritional & Metabolic Disorders

Endocrine
250.01 Diabetes I, uncomplicated
250.91 Diabetes I, w/ unspec. complications
250.00 Diabetes II/unspec., w/o comp, not uncontrolled
250.90 Diabetes II, w/ unspec. complications
242.90 Hyperthyroidism, NOS
244.9 Hypothyroidism, unspec.
V58.67 Long term Insulin Use
Metabolic/Other
274.9 Gout, unspec.
272.0 Hypercholesterolemia
272.2 Hyperlipidemia, mixed
272.1 Hypertriglyceridemia
278.01 Obesity, morbid
278.00 Obesity, NOS
278.02 Overweight

Blood Diseases

285.9 Anemia, other, unspec.

Mental Disorders

300.00 Anxiety state, unspec.
314.00 Attention deficit, w/o hyperactivity
314.01 ADD w/ hyperactivity
290.00 Dementia, senile, NOS
311 Depression, NOS
305.1 Tobacco Abuse

Nervous System & Sense Organ Disorders

Nervous System Diseases
354.0 Carpal tunnel
345.90 Epilepsy, unspec., w/o status
346.90 Migraine, unspec., not intractable
Eye Diseases
372.30 Conjunctivitis, unspec.
368.10 Visual disturbance, unspec.
Ear Diseases
380.4 Cerumen impaction
389.9 Hearing loss, unspec.
380.10 Otitis externa, unspec.
382.00 Otitis media, acute

Circulatory System

Arrythmias
427.31 Atrial fibrillation
Cardiac
413.9 Angina pectoris, NOS
428.0 Heart failure, congestive, unspec.
414.9 Ischemic heart disease, chronic, unspec.
424.1 Valvular disorder, aortic, NOS
Vascular
796.2 Elevated BP w/o hypertension
401.1 Hypertension, benign
458.0 Hypotension, orthostatic
443.9 Peripheral vascular disease, unspec.
451.9 Thrombophlebitis, unspec.
459.81 Venous insufficiency, unspec.

Upper Respiratory Tract
462 Pharyngitis, acute
477.9 Rhinitis, allergic, cause unspec.
461.9 Sinusitis, acute, NOS
465.9 Upper respiratory infection, acute, NOS

Digestive System

564.00 Constipation, unspec.
562.10 Diverticulosis of colon
562.11 Diverticulitis of colon, NOS
535.50 Gastritis, unspec. w/o hemorrhage
558.9 Gastroenteritis, noninfectious, unspec.
530.81 GERD, no esophagitis
455.6 Hemorrhoids, NOS
564.1 Irritable bowel syndrome
578.1 Melena

Genitourinary System

Urinary System Diseases
592.9 Calculus, urinary, unspec.
595.0 Cystitis, acute
599.7 Hematuria
593.9 Renal insufficiency, acute
599.0 Urinary tract infection, unspec./pyuria
607.84 Impotence, organic
302.72 Impotence, psychosexual dysfunction
601.9 Prostatitis, NOS
257.2 Testicular hypofunction
098.0 Gonorrhea vagina/penis acute
091.0 Syphillis vagina/penis
611.72 Breast lump
616.0 Cervicitis
622.10 Dysplasia, cervix, unspec.
625.9 Pelvic pain, unspec. female disease
616.10 Vaginitis/vulvitis, unspec.
626.0 Amenorrhea
627.9 Menopausal disorders, unspec.
626.2 Menstruation, excessive/frequent
625.3 Menstruation, painful
626.6 Metrorrhagia

Skin, Subcutaneous Tissue

706.1 Acne
702.0 Actinic keratosis
682.9 Cellulitis/abscess, unspec.
692.9 Contact dermatitis, NOS
691.8 Eczema, atopic dermatitis
703.0 Ingrown nail
110.1 Onychomycosis
709.9 Other skin disease, unspec.
696.1 Psoriasis, other
695.3 Rosacea
706.2 Sebaceous cyst
702.19 Seborrheic keratosis, NOS
707.9 Ulcer, skin, chronic, unspec.
708.9 Urticaria, unspec.
078.10 Warts, viral

Musculoskeletal & Connective Tissue

General
716.9X Arthropathy, unspec.
729.1 Fibromyositis
703.8 Ingrown nail
715.90 Osteoarthrosis, unspec.
733.00 Osteoporosis, unspec.
714.0 Rheumatoid arthritis
727.00 Synovitis/tenosynovitis, unspec.
Lower Extremity
729.5 Pain in limb
728.71 Plantar fascitis
Spine/Torso

Signs & Symptoms

789.00 Abdominal pain, unspec.
795.01 Abnormal Pap, ASC-US
719.40 Arthralgia, unspec.
569.3 Bleeding, rectal
786.50 Chest pain, unspec.
786.2 Cough
787.91 Diarrhea, NOS
780.4 Dizziness/vertigo, NOS
787.2 Dysphagia
788.1 Dysuria
782.3 Edema, localized, NOS
783.3 Feeding problem, infant/elderly
780.6 Fever, nonperinatal
271.9 Glucose intolerance
784.0 Headache, unspec.
788.30 Incontinence/enuresis, NOS
782.2 Localized swelling/mass, superficial
785.6 Lymph nodes, enlarged
780.79 Malaise and fatigue, other
787.02 Nausea, alone
787.01 Nausea w/ vomiting
719.46 Pain, knee
724.2 Pain, low back
785.1 Palpitations
788.42 Polyuria
782.1 Rash, nonvesicular, unspec.
782.0 Sensory disturbance skin
786.05 Shortness of breath
780.2 Syncope
788.41 Urinary frequency
787.03 Vomiting, alone
783.21 Weight loss

Injuries & Adverse Effects

Dislocations, Sprains & Strains
845.00 Sprain/strain: ankle, unspec.
845.10 Sprain/strain: foot, unspec.
842.1 Sprain/strain: hand, unspec.
844.9 Sprain/strain: knee/leg, unspec.
847.0 Sprain/strain: neck, unspec.
840.9 Sprain/strain: shoulder/upper arm, unspec.
842.00 Sprain/strain: wrist, unspec.
Other Trauma, Adverse Effects
919.0 Abrasion, unspec.
924.9 Contusion, unspec.
919.4 Insect bite
894.0 Open wound, lower limb, unspec.
884.0 Open wound, upper limb, unspec.

Supplemental Classification

V72.32 Confirm norm Pap after initial abn
V25.01 Contraception, oral
V25.02 Contraception, other (diaphragm, etc.)
V25.2 Contraception, sterilization
V58.30 Dressing change, nonsurgical
V01.9 Exposure, infectious disease, unspec.
V72.31 Gynecological exam
V06.8 Immunization, combination, other
V06.1 Immunization, DTP
V04.81 Immunization, influenza
V70.0 Well adult check
V20.2 Well child check
V70.3 Sports Physical
V05.3 Hepatitis B
V58.61 Longterm Coumadin use
V58.65 Longterm Steroid use
V77.5 Screening for Gout
V77.0 Screening for Thyroid disorder
V79.1 Screening Alcoholism
V76.43 Screening skin cancer

Figure 5.3 Router

to assign codes directly from this form. Each record is reviewed before charges are finalized. Coders are expected to validate the level of E/M service provided, confirm that all services are captured, and append any necessary modifiers before releasing the claim.

Patient Assessment

The **patient assessment** is a nursing form used to document discussions and initial interviews with patients about their health status. The patients' physical, psychological, and social statuses are reviewed along with a detailed interview covering medications taken, habits (i.e., eating, sleeping, social), disabilities, allergies, health history, and so on. The constitutional elements of the exam—BP, height, weight—are recorded here as well. This information is a foundation for clinical staff to build on and allows them to get to know the patients and their needs. Doctors should refer to this form and make notations of this information in their progress note.

History and Physical (H&P)

A **history and physical (H&P)** is performed for every new patient that is seen in the practice. The H&P, as its name indicates, includes detailed information about a patient's health history and the physical examination performed by the physician (Figure 5.4). The history portion is information obtained from the patient about past and present illnesses, personal and family health histories, reason for visiting, habits (i.e. smoking, alcohol consumption, illicit drug use), medications and dosages, and allergies. Completing the H&P is the responsibility of the physician. It is not uncommon for a health history form to be completed by the patient himself in a physician's office. The physician should review this with the patient in detail to clarify answers or obtain additional information. During this interview, the physician will ask questions regarding the patient's body systems. This is referred to as **review of systems (ROS)**, and the physician will inventory each body system (e.g., gastrointestinal, neurological, genitourinary, respiratory) by asking questions about symptoms related to each site to determine the extent of a physical exam needed. The ROS may also be obtained from a patient questionnaire that is reviewed and signed by the physician. The physician's physical exam is hands-on. Depending on the nature of the visit, the physician will perform an exam specific to that body site or a detailed, comprehensive exam. Several elements must be present to make an H&P complete:

- Chief complaint (CC) (why is the patient here today?)
- History of present illness (HPI) (what has the patient done to alleviate the problem up to now? what treatments have been performed related to this problem?)
- Past medical history (PMH)(prior surgeries, history of cancer, chronic illnesses)
- Social history (SH)(smoker, occupation, drug use, habits)
- Family history (FH) (history of heart disease, cancer, mental health problems, etc.)
- Review of systems (questions to probe patient for signs or symptoms for each body system)
- Vital signs (blood pressure, weight, temperature, etc.)
- Exam specific to body parts and/or systems being treated (lungs, abdomen, genitourinary, etc.)
- Assessment/diagnosis (what is the doctor's conclusion of what is wrong with the patient?)
- Plan of treatment (what is the doctor going to do to rectify or further evaluate the problem?)

Assessment and Plan is where the doctor's medical decision making is documented with the number of diagnoses, management and treatment options, the amount and complexity of data to review to determine how to treat and assess the patient, and the overall risk to the patient.

The H&P holds the key to determining what level of E/M visit to assign. It should include all the elements needed to assign the correct E/M code.

NAME: Terri Haper Age: 35 Date: 10-18-02

CHIEF COMPLAINT: worsening sinusitis and nasal septal deviation.
PRESENT ILLNESS: The patient is a 35-year-old female who has experienced chronic nasal congestion, recurrent sinusitis and persistent headache which has intermittently been improved with the use of antibiotics. On office examination, a moderate to severe nasal septal deviation to the right is noted. On 10-15-02 CT evaluation of the sinuses revealed central nasal deviation with pneumotized right middle nasal turbinate and concha bullosa.

PAST MEDICAL HISTORY: chronic sinusitis

SURGERY: Non-contributory.

ALLERGIES: dust mites, pollen, cockroaches. NKDA.

PRESENT MEDICATIONS: Astelin spray 1-2 puffs b.i.d.

FAMILY HISTORY: N/A

SOCIAL HISTORY: non-smoker

REVIEW OF SYSTEMS: Respiratory: chronic cough and congestion. Neurological: no dizziness or loss of balance.

PHYSICAL EXAMINATION: blood pressure 122/80, Pulse 68, respirations 12, temperature 97.8.

GENERAL: The patient is a well-developed, well-nourished 35-year-old female in no acute distress.

SKIN: No rash evident.

HEENT: Normocephalic. Pupils equal, round, reactive to light and accommodation. Tympanic membranes intact bilaterally without discharge. Nose-nasal septal deviation with 3+ nasal turbinate enlargement. Throat- no obvious tonsillar enlargement noted.

NECK: No significant cervical node enlargement.

LUNGS: Clear to auscultation bilaterally without wheeze.

HEART: Regular rate and rhythm without murmur noted.

ABDOMEN: Deferred.

GENITOURINARY: Deferred.

NEUROLOGIC: Physiologic for age.

IMPRESSION: recurrent sinusitis and nasal septal deviation.

PLAN: Refer to Zach Mosley, MD ENT specialist for septoplasty and turbinate reduction.

____

Sally Kemper, M.D.

Figure 5.4 Sample History and Physical

Physician Orders

Physician orders represent the physician's plan for direction of the patient's therapeutic and diagnostic course (Figure 5.5). To have an ancillary test, consultation, or therapy, or to receive medication, an order must be present. To be carried out, orders must be clear, legible, precise, complete, and signed by the physician. Orders can be handwritten, computer generated, or simply marked off on a master order or standing order checklist sheet; but every order must be signed by the M.D., PA-C or R.N.P.

Medication List

Our practice uses a **medication list** (Figure 5.6) to compile and maintain a complete list of current medications the patient is consuming. This list is updated at each visit and changes are noted as needed. The physician can monitor any drug interactions by referring to this form. This form also has the patient's preferred pharmacy and phone number to make calling in prescriptions easier. Medication sheets are helpful to the coder to ensure they are capturing chronic illnesses that require monitoring and medication maintenance.

DOUGLASVILLE MEDICINE ASSOCIATES
5076 Brand Blvd, Suite 401, Douglasville, NY 01234
(123)456-7890 phone
(123)456-7891 fax

DEA:357923 *License #:753951*

9/5/xx

PA and Lateral chest x-ray, Hemoglobin A1C, CBC. Fax results to office.

Sally Kemper, MD

Sally Kemper

Figure 5.5 Sample Physician Order

MEDICATION SHEET

Patient Name: ____________________ DOB: __________ Allergies: __________

Pharmacy Name: ____________________________ Pharmacy Number: _________

Date	Medication (name, dose, frequency)	Continue	Discontinued	Comments

Figure 5.6 Sample Medication Sheet

Consultation

A consultation (consult) documents the services rendered by a specialist whose opinion or advice was requested by another physician in the treatment of a patient. *CPT Assistant*, July 2007, indicates that "there may be circumstances when a consultation is initiated by sources other than a physician, such as a physician assistant, nurse practitioner, doctor of chiropractic, . . . social worker, lawyer, or insurance company." The requesting physician should indicate in the patient record, either in the progress notes or in the orders, that a consult is requested and why it is sought. The specialist performing the consult must provide a report back to the requesting physician. To bill a consultation, the consulting physician must keep the requesting physician informed of the outcome of the visit. This report includes the date and time the consultation was performed, documentation reviewed regarding the history of the patient and past treatment, the examination performed and written findings with recommendations for further treatment.

Progress Notes

Progress notes can be notes from any clinical discipline but in the physician office typically only the physician and the nurses will document these. They are a means of communication between health care providers about the patient's course of treatment, changes in condition, responses to treatment, observations made, conversations with family members and patient, and so on. These notes are important because they may justify the level of care rendered for reimbursement purposes. In the office setting, this is where the physician documents discussions with the patient, examinations, treatment options, missed appointments, and so on.

SOAP Progress Notes

DMA uses the **SOAP note** format for physician progress notes. Each note is categorized into four consistent parts: Subjective, Objective, Assessment, and Plan; hence, SOAP.

S: Subjective information is the description of the patient's complaints, symptoms, and concerns in their own words. Past, family, and social history are also considered subjective because of the questions prompting the patient for answers.

O: Objective information is gleaned from a trained clinical person such as vital signs and physical examination. These are observations made by a clinician.

A: Assessment involves the clinician reviewing all patient information and test results, and forming an opinion or drawing a conclusion called a diagnosis.

P: Plan involves ordering further diagnostic tests to evaluate the problem, performing therapeutic procedures to treat the problem, or providing education to the patient on how to manage the problem.

This format allows us to assign a specific level of E/M service because the information flows in basic accordance with the seven key components of an E/M service. *Subjective* is listed first and essentially is the history. It includes chief complaint, past medical history, and history of present illness. *Objective* lists the constitutional items, nature of presenting problem, examination, and review of systems. *Assessment* is essentially the medical decision making. Once the physician has reviewed the patient's record, a diagnosis is achieved. Finally, *Plan* encompasses coordination of care and time involved if counseling is the driver of the level of service.

S: Patient says she has had a five-day history of cough, sinus congestion, and earache. Over the counter medications have not helped. Cough is non-productive. Patient complains of post-nasal drip and discolored mucous. Patient's history is significant for chronic sinusitis and allergies.

O: WT: 155lbs; BP 101/79; T: 99.7; P: 83 and regular. HEENT: PERRLA. Right ear drum is pink. Left ear drum is angry red and bulging. Nasal passages are red and irritated. Patient exhibits pain on face palpation. Neck: thyroid is mid-line. Slight cervical lymph node swelling. Lungs are clear to A&P. Heart: normal sinus rhythm.

A: Chronic sinusitis. Otitis media left ear.

P: Augmentin 500 mg twice a day for 10 days. Auralgan drops, two drops to left ear for seven days. Patient will return in 10 days if not resolved.

Laboratory Reports

Laboratory reports show results of laboratory tests performed per physician order. These could range from sputum cultures to blood work or urinalysis. These are typically computer-generated by the lab that is analyzing the specimen. Results must be reported to the ordering physician in a timely manner. Only final results need to be filed in the record. Any preliminary results may be discarded. The doctor will initial and date that the results were read. Any action necessary as a result of abnormal labs is recorded in the progress notes or orders. Diagnoses cannot be assigned directly from a lab report. To report it, the doctor must indicate the findings in the record.

It is important to note that if the lab tests are performed onsite, the CPT code for the test should be indicated on the router. If the clinic does not have the equipment in-house to conduct the test and sends the report to an outside lab, you need to consider whether the clinic has an agreement with the lab to bill the carrier on behalf of the lab and reimburse the lab when insurance pays. If so, modifier -90 must be appended to the lab test CPT code. If the clinic sends the specimens to an outside lab with no agreement for reimbursement, the clinic can bill only for the blood draw or collection of the specimen.

Radiology Reports

Radiology reports or x-ray reports document the radiologist's interpretation of radiologic and fluoroscopic diagnostic tests performed per physician order. For every order for a radiologic exam—whether it be x-ray, CT, MRI, and so on—a written report should be obtained with the findings of the exam. It should include the reason for the requested exam, type of exam done, findings, and at times recommendations for treatment. These are typically computer-generated with a computerized signature. Diagnoses cannot be coded directly from these reports. To report it, the doctor must indicate the findings in the record.

Consent Forms

Consent forms demonstrate proof of consent obtained from the patient for medical or surgical treatment. It should indicate that the patient was informed of the nature of the treatment, the risks, complications, alternatives to treatment, and consequences of the treatment or procedure. Consent is not valid if not signed by the patient or legal representative. Failure to obtain a informed consent my result in liability on the part of the physician.

Operative Report

Operative reports (Op notes) describe the surgical procedure itself and individuals who participated. These are referred to as procedure notes when surgical procedures are performed in the office. They are often dictated by the doctor and transcribed, but they may be handwritten. They contain details of the surgical procedure, including name of surgeon and any assistants, description of the procedure, type of anesthesia given, significant findings, any unusual events, specimens removed, pre- and postoperative diagnoses, and condition of patient at conclusion of case. These may also be referred to as a procedure note when the procedure was performed in the physician office setting. DMA has a minor procedure room where office procedures are performed such as small wound repair, lesion removal, foreign body removal, and vasectomy. Copies of operative reports for surgical procedures performed by a surgeon we referred to are obtained by DMA only at the request of one of our physicians.

Pathology Report

The **pathology report** describes the microscopic and macroscopic details of tissue removed surgically. A final diagnosis will be present once examination of the specimen is completed. It is important to wait for this report to obtain a final diagnosis when benign versus malignant is a question or when determination between a chronic versus acute condition is needed. Path reports also denote size of specimens, which is necessary in CPT coding for lesions. Be careful when coding lesion removals for Medicare patients. CMS states that if a lesion that is thought to be benign is excised and the final pathology report denotes a malignant or carcinoma in situ diagnosis for the lesion removed, the CPT code for a benign lesion is assigned because that was the original intent and preliminary diagnosis. The final pathology does not change the CPT code of the procedure performed. The best practice is to wait for the pathology report before assigning diagnoses codes as well as CPT codes for skin repairs and lesion sizes if this is not clearly documented in the operative report.

Source Documents

Coders must have access to pertinent documentation at the time of coding. Data may be in the form of paper records, electronic records, or a combination of both. Coders must be able to assess the completeness of the available documentation. At DMA, a policy is in place to consider situations when the documentation is not complete enough to code (missing an op note, etc.).

A coder can use only information documented in a **source document** by a physician or signed off by a physician. Coders cannot use information from a prior visit to fill in gaps when a current record is not complete. When coding from a medical record, the following reports are used (source documents). The following source documents make up the patient's record and are extremely important in the coding function:

- H&P
- Progress notes (MD, PA-C, R.N.P)
- Physician orders
- Consults
- OP reports (handwritten or typed)
- Pathology reports

Watch for symbols and color coding when assigning diagnosis codes. Depending on the publisher of the ICD-9 book you are using, codes that signify diagnoses as primary or secondary are identified. Do not make the mistake of using a secondary diagnosis as the primary diagnosis (first diagnosis position), because doing so will cause claim lines to deny. Sometimes the documentation in the record is mediocre at best. A coder cannot decide what a patient's condition is based on assumptions or whether a condition is complex, simple, or uncontrolled without the specific documentation by the physician. There may be evidence from ancillary documentation that points to a condition but it is not specifically documented in the record by the physician. Ancillary reports and nursing documentation can be used to support code assignment or to generate a physician query, but they cannot be used solely to code from without mention of that condition by a physician. When this is the case, physician querying is necessary. This entails the coder submitting questions to one of our physicians in writing. If the coder identifies a documentation deficiency, the physician should be asked to make a late entry in the record and include the missing information. DMA has a policy addressing physician querying.

How to Code a Diagnosis from a Record

1. Identify all main terms included in the diagnostic statement or report.
2. Locate each main term in the alphabetic index.
3. Refer to any sub terms indented under the main term in the index. The sub terms form individual line entries and describe the essential differences by site, etiology, or clinical type.
4. Follow cross-reference instructions if needed, especially if the code needed is not located under the first main entry that is looked up. Follow all directions for *see also*, *code also*, and so on.
5. Verify the code chosen in the tabular. Read and be guided by any instructions here. Pay attention to color coding and references to coding guidelines as to which codes can be used as principal or primary diagnoses and which codes are secondary diagnoses only.
6. Choose the most specific code. Assign three-digit codes only when no four-digit codes appear in that entry. Assign a fifth digit for any subcategory where a fifth digit is provided. Not all codes have four or five digits.

7. Continue coding until all independent diagnoses and procedures are captured and the reason for the service is fully identified. This includes any diagnoses that support the reason for the visit, such as V codes.

How to Assign CPT Codes from a Record

CPT codes are assigned to professional services, labs, x-rays, injections, and procedures. Progress notes, routers, and ancillary reports provide the necessary resources for nonsurgical services provided. Coding staff must review, at a minimum, the H&P, progress notes, procedure notes, and nursing assessment to accurately assign an E/M level of service. For non–face-to-face services such as telephone services, online medical evaluations and care plan oversight must be carefully documented with the following elements before consideration can be given for reporting these services:

- Total time spent communicating with the patient or other health care professionals.
- Previous E/M services rendered must be referenced to establish a timeline. If a patient received E/M services during the postoperative period or seven days prior to these services, they cannot be reported separately. Also, if as a result of communicating with a patient via Internet or telephone a patient is subsequently seen in the office within 24 hours or the next available appointment, these services cannot be reported.
- For reporting care plan oversight for Medicare patients or when reporting with a HCPCS G code to payers who accept them, a minimum of 30 minutes per month must be spent on reviewing charts, reports, and treatment plans; reviewing diagnostic studies if the review is not part of an E/M service; talking on the phone with other healthcare professionals who are not employees of the practice and are involved in the patient's care; conducting team conferences; discussing drug treatment and interactions (not routine prescription renewals) with a pharmacist; coordinating care if physician or nonphysician practitioner time is required; and making and implementing changes to the treatment plan. All other carriers abide by CPT instruction of every 15 minutes.

To determine the level of service, remember, for a code that requires all three key components, the key component at the lowest level controls the overall level of service. An E/M tool is helpful in methodically analyzing documentation and counting elements of the history, exam, and medical decision making. This tool is located in Appendix C of this manual. If a code requires only two of the three key components to be used in determining the level of service, disregard the lowest key component and base the level of service on the remaining two key components, still following the rule that the lowest key component of the remaining two controls the level of service. It is important to take into consideration counseling and/or coordination of care. When one of them dominates (is more than 50% of) the physician–patient and/or physician–family encounter, time is the key or controlling factor in determining the level of service. The extent of the counseling and/or coordination of care must be documented in the medical record. To accurately assign CPT codes to procedures and services, follow these steps:

1. Read the progress notes, router, and procedure notes for the date of service (DOS).
2. Verify the place of service (e.g., office, hospital, ER, nursing home).
3. Identify the content or level of service (i.e., minimal, consult, new patient).
4. Determine the nature of the presenting problems (i.e., disease, condition, illness).
5. Establish the level of HPI, ROS, PFSH, exam, MDM, and risk to determine level of E/M service.
6. Determine time involved in completing the service.
7. Locate all services and supplies provided by staff (e.g., injections, EKG, blood work, splints).
8. For office visits, compare the router to the medical record to ensure that diagnoses from previous visits are not coded unless they were conditions treated at this visit.
9. For procedure notes or operative reports, read the entire report. Identify any complications that may have occurred. If pre- and post-op diagnoses are different, use the post-op diagnosis because this was determined after surgery.

10. *Before* submitting a claim review the pathology report if specimens were removed to verify the diagnosis and size of lesion. If there is a discrepancy between the sizes documented by doctor and path report, use the doctor's codes.
11. Assign any applicable modifier (i.e., -25, -90).
12. Assign HCPCS codes to drugs and supplies used.

Exercise 5.1 Your Turn to Try

Read the office progress note in Figure 5.7 and assign CPT and ICD-9 codes for the visit.

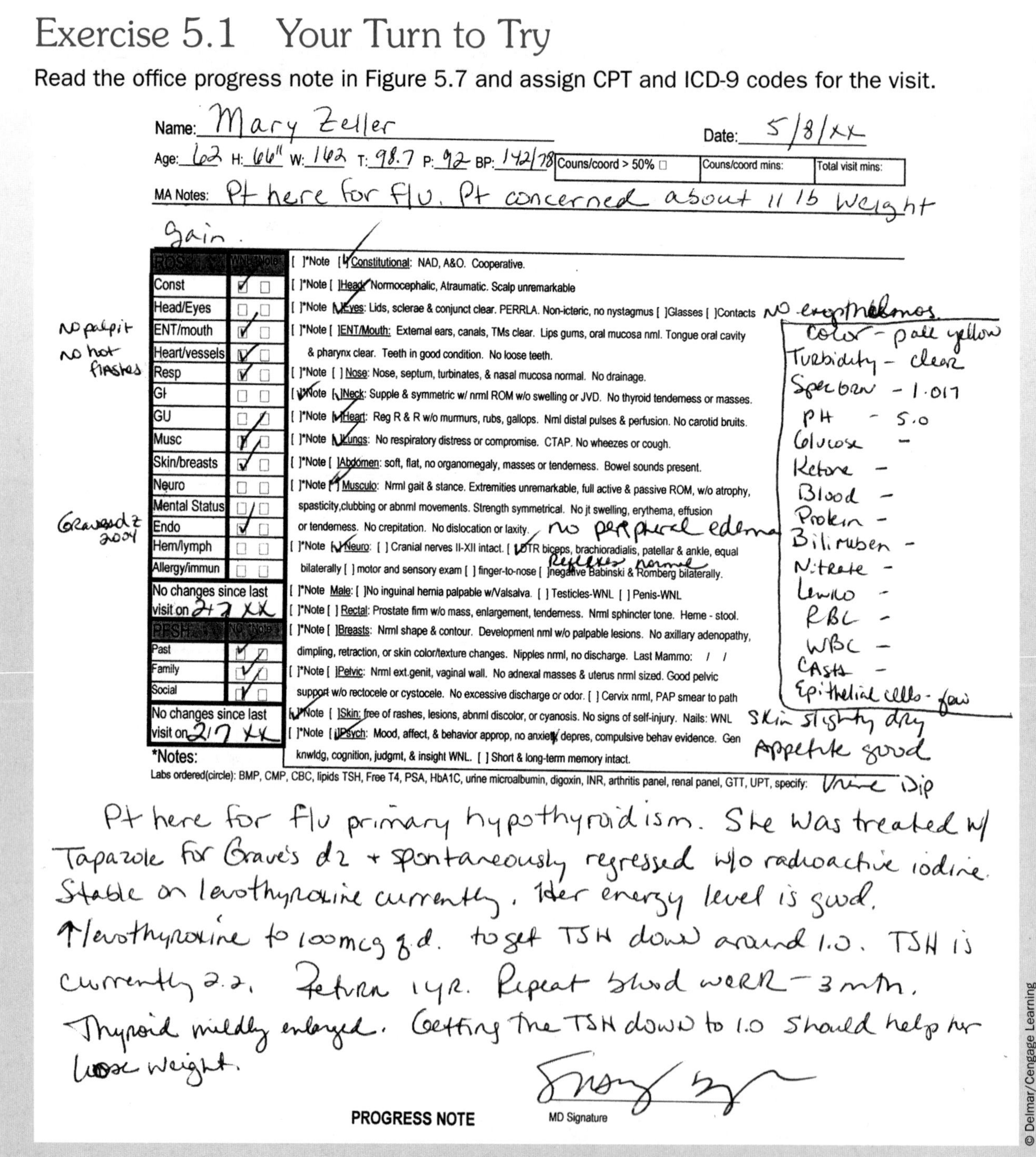

Name: Mary Zeller Date: 5/8/xx

Age: 62 H: 66" W: 162 T: 98.7 P: 92 BP: 142/78 Couns/coord > 50% □ Couns/coord mins: Total visit mins:

MA Notes: Pt here for f/u. Pt concerned about 11 lb weight gain.

ROS	WNL	Note
Const	☑	□
Head/Eyes	□	□
ENT/mouth	☑	□
Heart/vessels	☑	□
Resp	☑	□
GI	□	□
GU	□	✓
Musc	✓	□
Skin/breasts	☑	□
Neuro	□	□
Mental Status	✓	□
Endo	☑	□
Hem/lymph	□	□
Allergy/immun	□	□
No changes since last visit on 2/7 XX		
PFSH	**NC**	**Note**
Past	✓	□
Family	✓	□
Social	✓	□
No changes since last visit on 2/17 XX		

No palpit, no hot flashes

Graves dz 2004

[ ]*Note [✓]Constitutional: NAD, A&O. Cooperative.
[ ]*Note [ ]Head: Normocephalic, Atraumatic. Scalp unremarkable
[ ]*Note [✓]Eyes: Lids, sclerae & conjunct clear. PERRLA. Non-icteric, no nystagmus [ ]Glasses [ ]Contacts No exopthalmos.
[ ]*Note [ ]ENT/Mouth: External ears, canals, TMs clear. Lips gums, oral mucosa nml. Tongue oral cavity & pharynx clear. Teeth in good condition. No loose teeth.
[ ]*Note [ ] Nose: Nose, septum, turbinates, & nasal mucosa normal. No drainage.
[✓]*Note [✓]Neck: Supple & symmetric w/ nrml ROM w/o swelling or JVD. No thyroid tenderness or masses.
[ ]*Note [✓]Heart: Reg R & R w/o murmurs, rubs, gallops. Nml distal pulses & perfusion. No carotid bruits.
[ ]*Note [✓]Lungs: No respiratory distress or compromise. CTAP. No wheezes or cough.
[ ]*Note [ ]Abdomen: soft, flat, no organomegaly, masses or tenderness. Bowel sounds present.
[ ]*Note [✓]Musculo: Nrml gait & stance. Extremities unremarkable, full active & passive ROM, w/o atrophy, spasticity, clubbing or abnml movements. Strength symmetrical. No jt swelling, erythema, effusion or tenderness. No crepitation. No dislocation or laxity. no peripheral edema
[ ]*Note [✓]Neuro: [ ] Cranial nerves II-XII intact. [✓]DTR biceps, brachioradialis, patellar & ankle, equal bilaterally [ ] motor and sensory exam [ ] finger-to-nose [ ]negative Babinski & Romberg bilaterally. Reflexes normal
[ ]*Note Male: [ ]No inguinal hernia palpable w/Valsalva. [ ] Testicles-WNL [ ] Penis-WNL
[ ]*Note [ ] Rectal: Prostate firm w/o mass, enlargement, tenderness. Nrml sphincter tone. Heme - stool.
[ ]*Note [ ]Breasts: Nrml shape & contour. Development nml w/o palpable lesions. No axillary adenopathy, dimpling, retraction, or skin color/texture changes. Nipples nrml, no discharge. Last Mammo: / /
[ ]*Note [ ]Pelvic: Nrml ext.genit, vaginal wall. No adnexal masses & uterus nrml sized. Good pelvic support w/o rectocele or cystocele. No excessive discharge or odor. [ ] Cervix nrml, PAP smear to path
[✓]*Note [ ]Skin: free of rashes, lesions, abnml discolor, or cyanosis. No signs of self-injury. Nails: WNL Skin slightly dry
[ ]*Note [ ]Psych: Mood, affect, & behavior approp, no anxiety/depres, compulsive behav evidence. Gen knwldg, cognition, judgmt, & insight WNL. [ ] Short & long-term memory intact. Appetite good

Color - pale yellow
Turbidity - clear
Spec grav - 1.017
pH - 5.0
Glucose -
Ketone -
Blood -
Protein -
Bilirubin -
Nitrate -
Leuko -
RBC -
WBC -
Casts -
Epithelial cells - few

*Notes:

Labs ordered(circle): BMP, CMP, CBC, lipids TSH, Free T4, PSA, HbA1C, urine microalbumin, digoxin, INR, arthritis panel, renal panel, GTT, UPT, specify: Urine Dip

Pt here for f/u primary hypothyroidism. She was treated w/ Tapazole for Grave's dz + spontaneously regressed w/o radioactive iodine. Stable on levothyroxine currently. Her energy level is good. ↑levothyroxine to 100mcg q.d. to get TSH down around 1.0. TSH is currently 2.2. Return 1 yr. Repeat blood work - 3 mth. Thyroid mildly enlarged. Getting the TSH down to 1.0 should help her lose weight.

PROGRESS NOTE

MD Signature

© Delmar/Cengage Learning

Figure 5.7 Handwritten Office Note

Medical Necessity

Medicare, Medicaid, and other federally funded programs as well as many private payers pay only for services that are covered by their plan and for services that are deemed medically necessary as defined by each payer. Payers establish coverage criteria and policies to state their positions on coverage of specific tests and/or services. Payer definition of **medical necessity** is that services or supplies are in accordance with standards of good medical practice, that treatment is consistent with the diagnosis, and that the most appropriate level of care is provided in the most appropriate setting. CMS has its own set of national coverage policies that can be found in the Medicare Coverage Issues Manual (CIM). Medicare Part A fiscal intermediaries and Part B carriers (companies under contract with CMS to process and monitor claims) have the authority and responsibility to interpret these policies. Unfortunately everyone's interpretation of what is usual and customary is not the same.

Local Coverage Determinations (LCDs)

Local coverage determinations are state-specific CMS carrier policies regarding services provided to Medicare beneficiaries. LCDs indicate which services are restricted and list the criteria for coverage of such. It is a document drafted with the help of medical directors at the carrier level and the FI for each state. They get input from physicians practicing in the state to create a rule that fairly represents usual and customary medical management of a diagnosis or procedure in that state. LCDs contain ICD-9, CPT, and HCPCS codes representing a service with the corresponding ICD-9 codes that support medical necessity for the service. This is what Medicare is willing to reimburse for. The policy lists appropriate diagnoses and respective ICD-9 codes that will be covered for each restricted service. Some policies designate frequency guidelines that control the number of times a test will be reimbursed or in what time frame. Local carriers can develop local coverage determinations (LCDs) based on the following:

- Relevant medical literature
- Physician practice guidelines
- Policies from other carriers
- Outside consultants
- Acquired provider utilization data

What it boils down to is that Medicare is putting the onus on hospitals and doctors' offices to determine and prove medical necessity *before* a test or procedure is done. These rules vary from one local carrier to another; therefore, the carrier in Ohio may cover something that our local carrier in New York does not. Failure to comply with these medical necessity requirements on a regular basis can be defined as false claims and may result in fines up to $10,000 per claim.

It is extremely important that you know and understand how to appropriately link the diagnoses and procedures on the claim form. This process of linking or pointing shows a relationship between the test conducted or the procedure performed and *why.* Insurance companies are not going to pay every claim that is submitted unless it is justified and meets its requirements for what it feels is medically necessary.

For example, you would not link the diagnosis code for a UTI (599.0) with a procedure of appendectomy, would you? No, you would link it to a procedure that was related to the diagnosis, such as a cystoscopy or a urinalysis.

Look at the CMS 1500 claim form in Figure 3.11 (in Chapter 3). Refer to blocks 21 and 24E. Block 24E, the diagnosis pointer, would have a link to the numbered diagnosis in block 21. Block 21 allows for four diagnoses so, block 24E will have a 1, 2, 3, or 4 in it linking the procedure code in block 24D to the corresponding ICD-9 code in block 21. This must be done properly or claims will be denied.

Obtaining Copies of LCDs and Payer-Specific Coding Instructions

LCDs are published in newsletters distributed by state Medicare carriers. They are also published in the Medicare Advisory accessible online with CMS. The Medicare Part B Carrier Manual provides valuable information on how National Coverage Determinations (NCD) and LCDs are developed. You can also go to http://www.cms.hhs.gov, click on *Medicare,* and under *Coverage* click on *Medicare Coverage Determination Process* and then *Local Coverage Determinations.* It is a good idea to bookmark this site for future reference. You will need this to complete tasks in later chapters. Via the CMS website you can search for LCDs by state, topic, CPT code, and so on. You can also review all the local coverage policies by going to a state's local carrier website. Because DMA is located in New York, visit Empire Medicare Services Incorporated for LCDs specific to this state (http://www.empiremedicare.com).

Coder Responsibilities

The coder is involved in billing, precertification, and account follow-up responsibilities more than ever due to the impact that LCDs have had on practices and facilities. Coders should be aware of policies that impact their facilities for common services offered and hone in on *covered* diagnoses if documented in the record. The role of the coder is to assign ICD-9 diagnosis codes following coding guidelines to accurately report the reason for the visit (primary diagnosis) as well as any other secondary diagnoses. Sometimes a payer has specific guidelines for coding that differ from official coding guidelines. If this is the case, make sure you get a copy of that policy and maintain it for reference. All codes should be assigned based on the documentation provided in the medical record following official coding guidelines and payer-specific coding and reporting instructions. Assigning codes should never be based on what policies will cover. Consult the UB-04 and/or Medicare manuals for payer-specific billing instructions for inpatient or outpatient claims.

National Correct Coding Initiative (NCCI)

The **National Correct Coding Initiative (NCCI)** is a system of coding edits used nationally by Medicare. It is also known as the *National Correct Coding Policy for Part B Medicare Carriers*. The purpose of the initiative is to control improper coding that can lead to overpayments and to ensure uniform payment policies and procedures were followed. The edits determine appropriate billing of CPT and HCPCS codes. Accurate coding and reporting of services by physicians and facilities is of major concern to guarantee proper payment. The edits are designed to prevent fragmenting of services. Think back to the surgical package. Certain steps are performed in a procedure that make up the overall complete procedure. They are integral parts of the big picture. These little steps are called components of the comprehensive procedure. Many commercial payers have loaded these edits into their systems for use in claims review, so don't think these only apply to Medicare patients. Edits are published annually by CMS (formerly HCFA) and are updated quarterly. The NCCI applies when multiple procedures are conducted on the *same body site at the same time* and to services that should not be reported together. Physician advisors from CPT and AMA advisory committees, along with other special societies, submit comments to CMS before each update.

Use the following web address to access the NCCI: http://www.cms.hhs.gov. Select *Medicare* and under the *Coding* heading, choose *National Correct Coding Initiative Edits*. Be sure to choose *NCCI for Physicians* and not facilities. It is prudent to bookmark this site as well or download the edits to your computer each quarter.

Unbundling

Unbundling occurs when a component code is billed separately as a separate service instead of using the one comprehensive code that includes all related services. This is fraudulent billing. This can be done accidentally if you do not look up all the CPT codes used. *Intentionally* unbundling a code to increase payment and filing a claim is called *maximizing* (a form of fraud). Unintentional unbundling results from not knowing coding guidelines. Intentional unbundling occurs when providers purposely code integral components of a more comprehensive code for purposes of increasing reimbursement.

CCI Edits

CCI edits are pairs of CPT or HCPCS Level II codes that are not separately payable except under certain circumstances. The edits are applied to services billed by the same provider for the same beneficiary

Comprehensive/Component		Edits Mutually Exclusive Edits	
Column 1	Column 2	Column 1	Column 2

Figure 5.8 CCI Edit Columns

on the same date of service. All claims are processed against the CCI tables. When looking at the edits for the first time, they can appear cumbersome and overwhelming. Once the coder learns how to use the table, it will become an effective tool. Currently there are approximately 12,000 bundling edits.

The edits are arranged in two sets of tables. One table contains the comprehensive/component (correct coding) edits, and the other contains the mutually exclusive edits. Each table is arranged in two columns, as represented in Figure 5.8.

Note that column 2 codes in both tables are not payable with the column 1 codes unless the edit permits use of a modifier associated with CCI.

A **comprehensive code** represents the major procedure or service when reported with another code. The comprehensive code represents greater work, effort, and time as compared to the other code reported. A **component code** represents the lesser procedure or service when reported with another code. The component code is part of a major procedure or service and is often represented by a lower work relative value unit (RVU) under the Medicare Physician Fee Schedule as compared to the other code reported.

The NCCI edits are listed out in numerical order. There are two columns. One (1) = payable codes (comprehensive). Two (2) = components (integral). Column 1 has more complex or extensive procedures listed. Column 2 lists simpler procedures performed at the same site. When coding and billing multiple procedures, bill only codes from column 1. Anything that would fall in column 2 is bundled in to column 1. There are rare occasions when codes in column 2 can be billed separately. There is a modifier column located in this table (refer to Figure 5.9) that indicates whether or not a modifier can be used to bypass the edit. The values are: 0-no modifier bypass allowed; 1-allowed; 9-not applicable. If a 1 is located in the modifier column next to that code in the NCCI edits, it can be billed separately.

Column 1

Also known as the comprehensive code within the comprehensive/component (correct coding) edits table, this code represents the major procedure or service when reported with another code. When reported with another code, column 1 generally represents the code with the greater payment of the two codes.

However, within the mutually exclusive edits table, column 1 code generally represents the procedure or service with the lowest work RVU and is the payable procedure or service when reported with another code.

Column 2

Also known as the component code within the comprehensive/component (correct coding) edits table, this code represents the lesser procedure or service when reported with another code. When reported with another code, column 2 generally represents the code with the lower payment of the two codes.

However, within the mutually exclusive edits table, column 2 represents the procedure or service with the highest work RVU and is the nonpayable procedure or service when reported with another code.

Denials for Bundling Edits

If a denial is received for a procedure bundled into another service and this code pair can't be located in the comprehensive/component (correct coding) list of edits, the coder should also check the mutually exclusive code list. The mutually exclusive code edits are located in the same location on the CMS website. In Figure 5.10 a sample of this table is provided.

Column 1	Column 2	* = In existence prior to 1996	Effective Date	Deletion Date * = no data	Modifier 0 = not allowed 1 = allowed 9 = not applicable
29880	01995		20020701	*	0
29880	20610	*	19960101	*	1
29880	20680		19960101	19960101	9
29880	27347		20000605	*	1
29880	27570		19960101	*	1
29880	29870	*	19960101	*	1
29880	29871		19960101	*	1
29880	29874	*	19960101	*	0
29880	29875	*	19960101	*	1
29880	29877		20020101	20020101	9
29880	29877		20030301	*	0
29880	29881	*	19960101	*	1
29880	29884		19970101	*	1
29880	36000		20021001	*	1
29880	36410		20021001	*	1
29880	37202		20021001	*	1
29880	62318		20021001	*	1
29880	62319		20021001	*	1
29880	64415		20021001	*	1
29880	64416		20030101	*	1
29880	64417		20021001	*	1
29880	64450		20021001	*	1
29880	64470		20021001	*	1
29880	64475		20021001	*	1
29880	69990		20000605	*	0
29880	90780		20021001	*	1

**This table is an excerpt of the CCI edits. It shows that all codes listed in column 2 are part of the procedure 29880 in column 1 and only 29880 should be billed.*

For example, a patient has an arthroscopy with debridement of the left knee (29877) and a meniscectomy (29880). What codes are billed? You would assign only the code in column 1, which is 29880. 29877 is bundled into 29880 with no modifier allowed.

Figure 5.9 CCI Table Excerpt

Mutually Exclusive Edits					
Column 1	Column 2	* = In existence prior to 1996	Effective Date	Deletion Date * = no data	Modifier 0 = not allowed 1 = allowed 9 = not applicable
29880	29882		19960101	*	1
29880	29883		19960101	*	1
29880	29885		19960101	19960101	9
29880	29887		19960101	19960101	9

Figure 5.10 CCI Mutually Exclusive Edits

Mutually Exclusive Procedures

Mutually exclusive codes represent services that cannot be reasonably performed at the same session either by CPT definition or the medical impossibility or improbability that they could be performed at the same session (e.g., open and closed reduction of a fracture at the same time). Situations where two procedures representing two different methods to accomplish the same therapeutic result may have been used, but only the successful procedure should be reported (e.g., open cholecystectomy and laparoscopic cholecystectomy). You would bill only the open procedure. The billing of an initial service and a subsequent service together at the same time are also considered mutually exclusive.

In Figure 5.10, you will see that code 29882 is mutually exclusive of code 29880. When you look up the code definitions, you will find that 29880 is an arthroscopic meniscectomy and 29882 is an arthroscopic meniscal repair. What the table shows is that it does not make logical sense to remove the meniscus in 29880 and repair it in 29882 at the same time.

Steps to Follow when Coding and Using Bundling Edits

1. Read documentation and/or the operative note in its entirety and assign codes to encompass all procedures and services performed.
2. Review coding guidelines at the beginning of the respective section of the CPT book.
3. Refer to the NCCI edits. Look up each code you assigned and see if it falls into column 1 or column 2. The codes in the NCCI are in CPT code order. If the code is listed in column 1, it is a comprehensive code and can be coded. If it falls into column 2, it is an integral part of the code in column 1. Only assign codes from Column 1. If you don't have a hard copy of the CCI, you can also log onto the CMS website and type in each code to see what is bundled.

Let's try an example together. Use the link for the CMS website to reach the CCI edits and look up the following codes:

Determine what would be billed if a physician performs a laparoscopic cholecystectomy (47562) but must convert to an open cholecystectomy (47600). Check the table and see. 47562 is included in 47600, so only 47600 would be billed. Notice too that there is no modifier allowed, so they would never be reported separately.

Coding Compliance

At DMA our goal to is to be 100% compliant with ICD-9, CPT, HCPCS, and state and federal guidelines for coding and billing. As you may recall from Chapter 1, the compliance plan at DMA covers many topics. However, in this section, we will discuss only the coding and billing related items presented in the following list. Specific clinic policies and procedures are located in Appendix A of this manual.

Coding and Billing

- Waiving of co-pays. This is not permitted without determination of financial need.
- Adherence to coding guidelines. ICD-9, CPT, and HCPCS guidelines will be followed for proper code assignment.
- Billing for services not rendered. DMA will not bill the patient or the carrier for services that did not occur.
- Upcoding. We do not up code at DMA.
- Unbundling. This is avoided by using the CCI edits as a tool and using modifier 25 and 59 appropriately. Modifier -25 is applied to the E/M service if it is performed on the same day as a procedure.
- Double billing. Safeguards are in place to prevent this from occurring.
- Billing for physician services provided by nonphysicians (incident-to billing).
- Billing for non-covered services as if it were covered.
- Credit balances for patients and insurance carriers.
- Proper use of modifiers.
- Reasonable and necessary services.
- Misrepresenting diagnosis to justify services.
- Completing certificate of medical necessity for patients who are not known by the doctor.
- Obtaining Advanced Beneficiary Notices (ABN).
- Documentation.
- Record must indicate site of service, appropriateness of service.
- Claim form must link diagnoses with procedures with appropriate modifiers and correct patient demographics.

DMA attempts to code as accurately as possible to obtain the highest dollar amount justified by the insurance policy. This can be done by improving and optimizing access to documentation; providing education to coders, billers, and physicians; utilizing using coding tools; and reviewing claims to ensure proper payment for services rendered. Steps are taken to prevent false claims from being reported to any carrier by verifying documentation before coding and billing. **False claims** are those that are filed for services not provided or for items misrepresented in billing. They represent reckless disregard for the truth. False claims can prompt a lawsuit for knowingly presenting a false or fraudulent request for payment to the government or false record in support of a claim. Liability for false claims falls on both the physician and coder/biller. These individuals can assume civil monetary penalties for upcoding and assigning diagnoses not justified by documentation. Potential criminal liability for false claims and mail fraud must also be considered. Coders are liable for incorrect coding if it is proven that they acted outside their job description. They can also be held liable if they knowingly or should have known that codes were incorrect and if they benefited monetarily from filing incorrect codes. The OIG work plan is monitored annually to focus DMA's efforts on monitoring and auditing, problem areas, and education.

Previewing documentation before coding prevents billing for noncovered services, billing for services not rendered, upcoding, and billing the wrong rendering provider. To prevent upcoding, coders and billers are instructed to bill only for the level of service documented. DMA will not bill for services not rendered by one of our physicians, PAs, or R.N.Ps. Likewise, our practice will not bill noncovered services under another code that is covered by the patient's insurance carrier. Instead, we will notify the patient right away that their insurance will not cover the service, and then we will work out a payment arrangement.

We will also have them sign a document that they understand that their insurance benefits were verified and the service is not reimbursed by their carrier.

A **physician assistant (PA-C)** is a licensed health professional who practices medicine under the supervision of a physician. A physician assistant provides a broad range of healthcare services that were traditionally performed by a doctor, such as diagnosing and treating illnesses. PAs in New York are allowed to provide patient services in sites where the physician is not present all of the time, but they do not practice independently. PAs always have one or more supervising physicians. "Supervising" means overseeing the activities of, and accepting responsibility for, the medical services rendered by a physician assistant in a manner approved by the New York Labor Board. The supervising physician is responsible for all aspects of the physician assistant's practice. Supervision must be continuous but must not be construed as necessarily requiring the physical presence of the supervising physician at the time and place where the services are rendered, except as otherwise required for limited licensees. The supervising physician shall identify the physician assistant's scope of practice and determine the delegation of medical acts, tasks, or functions. At DMA, the supervising physician or alternate supervising physician physically must be present at the same location as the physician assistant at least 75% of the time each month the physician assistant is providing services at the same location as the supervising physician or alternate supervising physician. The physician assistant may not provide services in the absence of the supervising physician or alternate supervising physician for more than seven consecutive days each month without the prior written approval of the New York Labor Board. The supervising physician or alternate supervising physician must be physically present at the off-site location not less than 20% of the time each month the physician assistant is providing services there. The supervising physician or alternate must review, initial, and date the off-site physician assistant's charts not later than five working days from the date of service if not sooner in relation to the acuity of the patient's condition.

Caution must be exercised when coding and filing claims for physician assistants. PAs are considered physician extenders. Billing services rendered by physician extenders is an area that the OIG monitors for compliance with **"incident-to" rule** billing. Incident-to according to CMS is "the services or supplies furnished as an integral, although incidental, part of the physician's personal professional services in the course of diagnosis or treatment of an injury or illness." These services are commonly performed in the physician's office by a PA or nurse practitioner. When submitting claims under the incident-to rule, the rendering provider is the PA and the billable provider is the physician. Incident-to billing cannot be performed in the hospital. If the PA sees patients in the hospital, claims must be submitted under her own provider number. Under the incident-to rule, PAs cannot see a new patient without the patient first seeing a physician and having an established course of treatment. The exception is if the goal is to file a claim under the physician's provider number, the PA can perform only the ROS and past/family/social history portion of the encounter. The physician must perform the exam, history of present illness (HPI), chief complaint, medical decision making, and make references to the elements of the H&P the PA performed. However, if the PA is going to see the new patient, the claim must be filed under her own provider number and filed directly instead of under the incident-to rule. The physician's presence in the office at the time the PA renders services must be illustrated to be compliant with Medicare incident-to billing. The physician must stay actively involved in the patient's care. If the physician is not in the office at the time services are rendered by the PA or nurse practitioner, the claims should be billed under their respective NPI numbers and not the physician's. Under incident-to billing, the claim would be paid at 100% of the allowed amount. When the same service is performed and billed under the PA or nurse practitioner ID number, it is reimbursed at 85% of the allowed amount.

The practice manager and insurance supervisor are responsible for coding and billing compliance. Five claims per provider per month are audited for accuracy and appropriate payment. ICD-9-CM code selection follows the *Official Guidelines for Coding and Reporting*, developed by the cooperating parties and documented in *Coding Clinic* for ICD-9-CM, published by the American Hospital Association. CPT code selection follows the guidelines set forth in the CPT manual and in *CPT Assistant*, published by the American Medical Association. Coders are not permitted to code diagnoses treated and information documented in prior dates of service. For each encounter, the coder can code only conditions that are being monitored or treated at that particular encounter. The coder is responsible for updating the router as needed, at least annually, with revised and new ICD-9, CPT, and HCPCS codes to reduce the risk of filing deleted and inaccurate codes. The coder is also responsible for ordering new code books each year.

The ultimate responsibility for code assignment lies with the physician (provider). However, any coding assigned solely by physicians will be validated by our coder/biller using the CMS/AMA documentation guidelines. When a variance occurs, the following steps are taken for resolution:

1. Coder generates a physician query outlining the discrepancy.
2. Coder provides this along with the source documentation to the office manger to discuss with the physician and/or board.

To assign the correct code, the physician will also be queried when the clinical information is ambiguous or incomplete.

Diagnoses that are documented as *probable*, *suspected*, *questionable*, *rule-out*, *consistent with*, or *working diagnosis* are not coded as confirmed diagnoses. Instead, the code for the condition established at the visit is assigned, such as a symptom, sign, abnormal test result, or clinical finding.

In many cases Medicare requires that an HCPCS level II code be assigned rather than the CPT code for the service provided. Payer specifications must be adhered to or claims will not be paid correctly. Medicare coding/billing requirements are located at http://www.cms.hhs.gov. To receive proper payment from Medicare, submit the level I CPT code only when there is no directive to submit an HCPCS code.

Medical records are examined and codes selected only with complete and appropriate documentation by the available physician. The record is referenced for place of service (site where service was rendered), type of service (surgical or medical visit), patient insurance, demographics, rendering provider, modifier usage, and medical necessity justification. According to coding guidelines, codes are not assigned without physician documentation. On the claim form, each service provided is then linked to the diagnosis that is most related to it.

All rejected claims pertaining to diagnosis and procedure codes should be returned to coding staff for review or correction. All clinical codes, including modifiers, must never be changed or added without review by coding staff with access to the appropriate documentation. Coding resources should be utilized by coding professionals. Coders and billers have access to the following essential resources: current CPT Professional Version, current ICD-9-CM and HCPCS Level II code books, *Coders' Desk Reference for Procedures*, CCI edits, *CPT Assistant*, and an anatomy reference. These must be referred to during the coding process. CCI edits are checked prior to releasing all Medicare claims. Remember, these don't necessarily apply to all carriers but are mandatory for Medicare claims.

Co-pays are expected at the time of service. To prevent violations of the Stark Law, co-pays are not routinely waived. Co-pays may be waived if the patient is deemed a charity and meets the criteria for financial hardship.

If a service will not be covered by Medicare, Medicare beneficiaries are instructed before services are rendered. They are instructed to complete the Advanced Beneficiary Notice (ABN) acknowledging they will be responsible for noncovered services rendered. The claim will be filed to Medicare with the GA modifier indicating that DMA is aware that the service is noncovered and acknowledging that an ABN is on file. DMA will not misrepresent a diagnosis to receive payment for a service that would otherwise not be covered. Physicians will not complete certificates for medical necessity of equipment or supplies if documentation is not prevalent in order to falsely report need to purposely receive inappropriate payment from Medicare or any other insurance carrier.

Reports reflecting insurance and patient credit balances are generated monthly. Refunds will be processed for any legitimate credit balance once per month. Any insurance carrier request for refund is investigated and either appealed or processed within 14 days of receiving notice of overpayment.

DMA staff is required to participate in annual compliance training and sign a new code of conduct. This training and signing is done at the beginning of each calendar year. Coders and billers must abide by the AHIMA Standards of Ethical Coding. Refer to Appendix D of this manual to review these standards. The insurance supervisor provides education and training related to coding and billing changes and updates. Monthly business office staff meetings are held to provide carrier updates as well as *Coding Clinic* and *CPT Assistant* discussions. Coders and billers are required to receive 10 hours of annual continuing education in the form of seminars, Internet courses, conference calls, on-site training, and reading of periodicals. All certified staff is required to maintain continuing education as deemed appropriate by the national organization honoring their certification.

The Recovery Audit Contractor (RAC) Program

Recovery audit contractors (RACs) are companies that contract with Medicare to find and correct improper payments made to Medicare providers and suppliers. The RAC program was adopted because Medicare estimates that the national paid claims error rate is unacceptably large—between 6 and 10 percent. Four RACs are employed by CMS to audit, detect, and correct improper payments on Medicare claims. RACs apply statutes, regulations, billing policies, NCDs and LCDs approved by the respective regional Medicare carrier. RACs analyze claims data and identify claims suspect of improper payments. For claims that are flagged as possible overpayments, the RAC will request medical records from the provider, review the claim and the supporting documentation, and determine whether the claim was paid correctly or contained an overpayment. Depending on practice size, somewhere between 10 and 50 records per group NPI number can be requested every 45 days for RAC audits. During 2007 as part of the demonstration program, RACs succeeded in correcting more than $1.03 billion in Medicare overpayments. The majority of overpayments were recouped from inpatient hospitals and outpatient hospital providers. RACs are paid a percentage of the incorrect payments they recover. Overpayments are attributed to the following types of errors:

- Incorrectly coded records
- Medically unnecessary services
- Insufficient documentation

Investigators look for patterns in reporting the following:

- Intentionally coding services that were not performed or documented

  EXAMPLES

  A lab bills Medicare for tests that were not ordered or performed.

  A physician bills Medicare for drugs that were not administered.

- Coding services at a higher level than was carried out

  EXAMPLE: A provider bills the encounter for a BP check and weight check as a comprehensive physical examination.

- Performing and billing for procedures that are not related to the patient's condition and therefore are not medically necessary

  EXAMPLE: After reading an article about cancer screenings and how ovarian cancer is not detected until its final stages when symptoms present, the patient requests a CA-125 cancer screening blood test. Even though no symptoms or signs have been reported or observed, the physician orders and bills for the test.

Pay-for-Performance Programs

Coders need to keep abreast of updates and changes to **pay-for-performance** (P-4-P) programs and the requirements for reporting. CMS has launched a series of quality initiatives to encourage improved quality of care for patients in various healthcare settings. The intent of pay-for-performance programs is to reward the delivery of high-quality care with financial incentives.

For physician practices, providers can elect to participate in the Physician Quality Reporting Initiative (PQRI). Pay-for-performance programs consist of incentive payments to providers based on the performance of a specified set of quality measures, including:

- Quality of patient care
- Clinical outcomes
- Patient satisfaction
- Implementation of information technology

Physician Quality Reporting Initiative (PQRI)

The **Physician Quality Reporting Initiative (PQRI)** is a voluntary quality reporting program established by CMS in which physicians or other eligible professionals collect and report their practice data in relation to a set of patient care performance measures that are established annually. The program's goal is to determine best practices, define measures of quality, support improvement, and improve systems. For example, the 2009 PQRI program had 153 possible measurements. All of these measurements are located at the CMS website, http://www.cms.hhs.gov/PQRI.

CMS published *Physician Quality Reporting Initiative Specifications,* which describes specific measures and associated codes that address various aspects of care, such as prevention, management of chronic conditions, management of acute episodes of care, procedure-related care, resource utilization, and care coordination. Within this document, each PQRI quality measure is explained along with instructions on how to code each measure. Each measure has a reporting frequency requirement for each eligible patient seen during the reporting period (e.g., report one-time only, once for each procedure performed, once for each acute episode, per each eligible patient). Some measures also include specific performance timeframes related to the clinical action taken, which is distinct from the measure's reporting frequency requirement.

Physicians who successfully report PQRI codes are eligible for an additional 2% payment from CMS. The PQRI incentive is an all-or-nothing lump-sum payment. Even though this is a voluntary program, the provider must meet the basic requirement of reporting three measures applicable to the professional's practice at least 80% of the time. If more than three quality measures are applicable, the professional need report on only three.

Not every medical specialty has performance measures that apply. To implement the program, practices identify the measures that affect the greatest number of their patients. Once the measures are chosen, coders are trained to assign the applicable quality codes. These codes include CPT Category II codes, which are supplemental codes that can be used to facilitate data collection relating to certain quality of care indicators, such as prenatal care, tobacco use cessation, and assessment of hydration status. PQRI also requires using some HCPCS G codes to allow reporting of certain clinical topics that do not have CPT Category II codes assigned as yet.

PQRI codes do not have an associated RVU value and thus do not have a charge associated with the service provided. To receive payment, providers are required to report these codes on the claim form with either a $0.00 or a $0.01 charge, depending on the contractor.

The American Medical Association (AMA), along with CMS and other national associations such as the National Committee for Quality Assurance (NCQA), developed tools and references to assist providers eligible to participate in the program. The tools are designed to assist physicians in identifying measures appropriate to their practice, and collecting and reporting the required data. A coding specifications document is provided for use in collaboration with a data collection sheet to determine the appropriate code or combination of codes to be reported.

Exercise 5.2 Your Turn to Try

April Kennedy has asked you to research more about PQRI and how the practice can participate in this pay-for-performance program. Visit some of the sources mentioned previously, such as the AMA and CMS, and write a brief summary on how to enroll and which providers are eligible. Also make recommendations on which quality measures this practice should report and what codes to use to report each measure selected. Remember, providers are required to report only three.

Coding Exam

All new coders are required to complete a coding entrance exam. This exam is taken before newly hired coders are permitted to begin coding independently. The objective of the exam is to assess understanding of basic billing concepts, mastery of coding guidelines, and familiarity with available coding/billing resources. Coding staff must score a 95 or better on this exam within the first 30 days of employment. If the employee fails to reach a score of 95, he/she will be offered an available position within the practice not involving coding, or the staff member will be released. Complete the coding exam located at the end of this chapter. You will need your ICD-9-CM, CPT, and HCPCS code books. Your supervisor Lindsay Morgan will review the exam results with you.

This chapter concludes the orientation. Your orientation is now complete and you may begin working independently by completing the jobs in the following chapters.

Internet Exercise

1. AHIMA has a Practice Brief addressing physician querying. Go to its website and read it. Write a brief synopsis of what you found. *http://www.ahima.org*.
2. Go to the National Center for Health Statistics website and locate the most current version of the *ICD-9-CM Official Guidelines for Coding and Reporting.* Download these guidelines to your computer or flash drive for reference. These guidelines are located in the front of your ICD-9 book but may not be the most current version. Do not print this document because it is over 100 pages. *http://www.cdc.gov/nchs*.
3. Visit New York's Medicare carrier National Government Services, Inc. website at *http://www.ngsmedicare.com*. Choose Part B and the state of New York. Click on *Medical Policy Center*. Locate the list of local coverage policies for New York. Using this website, answer the following questions.
    1. How many active policies are there? ____________________
    2. Locate two policies that would impact a family medicine or general practice. List the policy number and title. ____________________
    3. According to policy L3726 would the diagnosis code V49.81 be a medically necessary condition to warrant a bone density scan on this procedure? ____________________
4. Visit the Office of the Inspector General website and list any items on their work plan for the current year that are related to coding or billing that the practice should be aware of. ____________________

____

Review Questions

True/False

1. Local carrier guidelines from state to state are consistent because the policy is implemented by CMS, which is a federal funded agency.

   T or **F**

2. Coders should focus on covered diagnoses and assign one to ensure payment if the documentation warrants this.

   T or **F**

3. Medicare, Medicaid, and other federally funded programs will pay only for services that are covered by their plan, but private payers have no requirements for claims submitted.

   T or **F**

4. It is not necessary to use the NCCI edits regularly when coding.

   T or **F**

5. The purpose of the CCI is to improve coding accuracy.

   T or **F**

6. NCCI edits are published by the CMS.

   T or **F**

7. It is not necessary to check the NCCI edits for each procedure code assigned.

   T or **F**

8. Services performed as part of the standards of medical/surgical practice are integral to the comprehensive procedure and should not be coded separately.

   T or **F**

9. CCI edits are updated annually.

   T or **F**

10. The NCCI Edits always agree with AMA coding guidelines.

    T or **F**

11. The history of the present illness is the patient's description of his current medical condition in his own words.

    T or **F**

12. The pathology report assists in the diagnosis and treatment of patients by documenting analysis of tissue removed surgically.

    T or **F**

13. A patient breaks out in hives after taking topical Erythromycin. The patient comes back to the office four days later. Two codes would be reported: 708.9 and E930.3.

    T or **F**

14. Sites in the neoplasm table marked with an asterisk (*) should be coded as a malignant neoplasm of the skin of these sites if the variety of neoplasm is a squamous cell carcinoma or an epidermoid carcinoma.

    T or **F**

15. The patient has been HIV positive for many years. The patient is seen today for viral gastroenteritis that is going around. Codes 487.8 and V08 are reported.

    T or **F**

Multiple Choice

1. What is the body that is contracted with CMS to process and monitor claims for each state?
   a. Part A FI
   b. Part B Carrier
   c. CIM
2. Examine each of the following code pairs. Indicate the one that is comprehensive by writing the code in the blank.
   a. 45378 and 45384 ____________
   b. 26700 and 26705 ____________
   c. 28070 and 28290 ____________
   d. 31505 and 31530 ____________
   e. 59120 and 59151 ____________
3. Suppose a physician plans to perform a laparoscopic tubal ligation to apply Falope rings. The patient has had several abdominal procedures in the past, and the physician is unable to do it laparoscopically. He commences to finish the procedure by abdominal approach. On his claim form, he lists 58671 and 58600. What do you think has happened? Do you think he
   a. Bundled
   b. Maximized
   c. Unbundled
4. The code pair 58672 and 58760 demonstrates what?
   a. Bundling
   b. Unbundling
   c. Mutually exclusive pair
5. Which column lists the comprehensive code that is reported alone?
   a. Column 1
   b. Column 2
   c. Mutually exclusive
   d. Column 3
6. What does the modifier *1* mean when it is listed next to a code in the CCI edits?
   a. It cannot be reported alone.
   b. It can be reported and billed separately by using a modifier.
   c. This is the modifier that is supposed to be appended to that code.
   d. This code must be reported first when sequencing code order.
7. What is a mutually exclusive procedure?
   a. Cannot be performed
   b. Is exclusive of the principal procedure and can be billed separately
   c. Reasonably cannot be performed at the same time as its code pair
8. Dr. Health completes a history and physical on Laura Bob, who states, "When I walk up stairs I have difficulty breathing." This statement is known as the patient's
   a. Chief complaint
   b. History of the present illness
   c. Past history
   d. Patient complaint

9. Dr. Mendenhall sees Megan in his office to monitor her blood chemistry. He completes an examination and orders blood tests. His medical assistant completes the venipuncture. Charges for these services would be recorded on a(n)

   a. Router
   b. Face sheet
   c. Fee schedule
   d. Superslip

10. Staff members at DMA are informed that failure to comply with the compliance plan and clinic P&Ps may result in

   a. Termination
   b. Disciplinary action
   c. Lawsuit
   d. All of the above

11. A patient with long-time diabetes opted for placement of an insulin pump. The pump was working fine until recently. The patient was feeling shaky and came to the office. The patient is not getting enough insulin. What diagnosis code(s) would be reported?

   a. 250.00
   b. 250.00, 996.57
   c. 996.57, 250.00, V58.67
   d. 996.57, 962.3

12. A 46-year-old female presents with swelling of the neck and lethargy for more than a month. She didn't think much of it because she was sick with the flu. The physician suspects lymphoma and decides to do a biopsy. A large hollow core needle is passed into the thyroid and a specimen is taken and sent to pathology for analysis. A diagnosis of non-Hodgkin's type lymphoma was confirmed.

   a. 202.01, 10021
   b. 202.81, 10021
   c. 202.01, 60100
   d. 202.81, 60100

13. An 11-year-old girl fell from her swing set and was seen in the office. An x-ray of the right arm confirmed a hairline fracture of the proximal radial shaft. No manipulation was needed with the closed reduction. She was fitted for a short-arm, fiberglass cast.

   a. 99213, 25500, Q4013
   b. 25500, Q4009
   c. 25500-RT, Q4010
   d. 99213, 25500-RT, Q4010

14. A 55-year-old male patient is seen today for a blood pressure check (BPC) and is asymptomatic, without hypertensive complications. He has had known hypertension for the past four years. He is being maintained on nifedipine 30 mg, one per day. BP 128/82. Pulse 80 and regular. He is to continue his medication along with 30 minutes of exercise per day. He is to return in one month. What is the E/M code for this visit?

   a. 99212
   b. 99213
   c. 99211
   d. 99214

15. A 13-year-old boy came to the office this morning for the treatment of a 3-cm laceration on his right forearm sustained when building a fort in the woods last night. The physician sutured his arm and administered a tetanus shot after realizing the boy was not current on his tetanus immunization. What E/M code would you assign for this case?

    a. 99211
    b. 99212
    c. 99212-25
    d. no E/M code would be assigned; only the codes for the repair and injection

Fill in the Blank

1. ____________ indicate which tests are restricted and list coverage requirements.

2. Local carriers develop guidelines based on what five elements? ______________________________
____

3. Name one publication that would have copies LCDs printed in it. ____________

4. ________________ diagnoses and procedures appropriately on the claim form assists in demonstrating medical necessity.

5. What does *CCI* stand for? ______________________________

6. Where do you go to review the CCI edits online? ______________________

7. Demonstrating ____________________ is accomplished when the physician documents in the medical record the need for each service, test, or supply.

8. Enforcing federal laws and adhering to a compliance plan is the responsibility of the ____________________.

9. A ____________________ oversees and is responsible for training, education, adherence, and maintenance of the compliance plan.

10. Training employees and physicians on HIPAA, compliance, and coding should occur at least ______________________.

11. What is the index entry that leads you to a code for the site where an accident happened? ______________________________

12. ______________________________ is more than one doctor providing similar services to the same patient on the same day.

13. To drive code assignment, counseling and coordination of care must dominate more than __________ of the visit.

14. Read the following office note and assign the CPT and ICD-9 codes for the visit.

Name: JOHN SMITH Date: 5/2/XX

Age: 52 H: 70" W: 254 T: 98.6 P: 87 BP: 120/74 Couns/coord > 50% ✓ Couns/coord mins: 15 Total visit mins: 30

MA Notes: Here for f/u. Wants refill on his Perocet due 6/9/XX.

ROS	WNL	Note
Const	✓	☐
Head/Eyes	☐	☐
ENT/mouth	☐	☐
Heart/vessels	✓	☐
Resp	☐	☐
GI	✓	☐
GU	✓	☐
Musc	✓	☐
Skin/breasts	☐	☐
Neuro	☐	☐
Mental Status	☐	☐
Endo	☐	☐
Hem/lymph	☐	☐
Allergy/immun	☐	☐
No changes since last visit on / /		
PFSH	**NC**	**Note**
Past	✓	☐
Family	✓	✓
Social	✓	☐
No changes since last visit on / /		

[ ]*Note [✓]Constitutional: NAD, A&O. Cooperative.
[ ]*Note [✓]Head: Normocephalic, Atraumatic. Scalp unremarkable
[ ]*Note [✓]Eyes: Lids, sclerae & conjunct clear. PERRLA. Non-icteric, no nystagmus [ ]Glasses [ ]Contacts
[ ]*Note [ ]ENT/Mouth: External ears, canals, TMs clear. Lips gums, oral mucosa nml. Tongue oral cavity & pharynx clear. Teeth in good condition. No loose teeth.
[ ]*Note [ ] Nose: Nose, septum, turbinates, & nasal mucosa normal. No drainage.
[ ]*Note [ ]Neck: Supple & symmetric w/ nrml ROM w/o swelling or JVD. No thyroid tenderness or masses.
[ ]*Note [✓]Heart: Reg R & R w/o murmurs, rubs, gallops. Nml distal pulses & perfusion. No carotid bruits.
[ ]*Note [✓]Lungs: No respiratory distress or compromise. CTAP. No wheezes or cough.
[ ]*Note [✓]Abdomen: soft, flat, no organomegaly, masses or tenderness. Bowel sounds present. Obese
[✓]*Note [ ] Musculo: Nrml gait & stance. Extremities unremarkable, full active & passive ROM, w/o atrophy, spasticity, clubbing or abnml movements. Strength symmetrical. No jt swelling, erythema, effusion or tenderness. No crepitation. No dislocation or laxity. crepitus (L) knee
[ ]*Note [ ] Neuro: [ ] Cranial nerves II-XII intact. [ ] DTR biceps, brachioradialis, patellar & ankle, equal bilaterally [ ] motor and sensory exam [ ] finger-to-nose [ ]negative Babinski & Romberg bilaterally.
[ ]*Note Male: [ ]No inguinal hernia palpable w/Valsalva. [ ] Testicles-WNL [ ] Penis-WNL
[ ]*Note [ ] Rectal: Prostate firm w/o mass, enlargement, tenderness. Nrml sphincter tone. Heme - stool.
[ ]*Note [ ]Breasts: Nrml shape & contour. Development nml w/o palpable lesions. No axillary adenopathy, dimpling, retraction, or skin color/texture changes. Nipples nrml, no discharge. Last Mammo: / /
[ ]*Note [ ]Pelvic: Nrml ext.genit, vaginal wall. No adnexal masses & uterus nrml sized. Good pelvic support w/o rectocele or cystocele. No excessive discharge or odor. [ ] Cervix nrml, PAP smear to path
[ ]*Note [✓]Skin: free of rashes, lesions, abnml discolor, or cyanosis. No signs of self-injury. Nails: WNL taut, no ulcerations
[ ]*Note [ ]Psych: Mood, affect, & behavior approp, no anxiety, depres, compulsive behav evidence. Gen knwldg, cognition, judgmt, & insight WNL. [ ] Short & long-term memory intact.

*Notes:

Labs ordered(circle): BMP, CMP, CBC, lipids TSH, Free T4, PSA, HbA1C, urine microalbumin, digoxin, (INR), arthritis panel, renal panel, GTT, UPT, specify:

(L) leg doing better. He went to Vascular sx + wearing support hose daily. Still has intermittent pain. Complains of (L) knee pain. Had cortisone shot by Dr. Jones.

Current Meds: Coumadin 12.5 mg Lasix 20mg as needed, Percocet 1 q.d. Flovent 44 mcg, Protonix 40mg, Neurontin 300mg q.h.s.

He had many questions about how to manage his Coumadin diet. Talked to him about staying away from foods w/ VIT K. Rather than avoid Vit K with foods - he is to be consistent w/ intake. Avg intake RDA Vit K is 120 mcg/day.

Instructed to avoid Green tea, ETOH, Cranberry juice. He is not to Δ his diet dramatically by eliminating all leafy greens.

Complains of erectile dysfunction. He is unable to obtain erection w/o Viagra.

(1) Chronic venous stasis. - Resolved. Ted hose. (2) OA (3) DVT - lifelong Rx. (4) GERD (5) Erectile dysfunction

PROGRESS NOTE

MD Signature

Figure 5.11 #14 Office Note

15. Read the following office note and assign the CPT and ICD-9 codes for the visit.

Name: Stella McVay Date: 6/18/XX

Age: 49 H: 66" W: 143 T: 98.1 P: 72 BP: 138/64 | Couns/coord > 50% ☐ | Couns/coord mins: | Total visit mins:

MA Notes: BP (L) arm sitting 138/64 138/64 (R) arm after 10 mins

ROS	WNL	*Note
Const	✓	☐
Head/Eyes	☐	☐
ENT/mouth	☐	☐
Heart/vessels	✓	☐
Resp	✓	☐
GI	✓	☐
GU	☐	☐
Musc	☐	☐
Skin/breasts	☐	☐
Neuro	☐	☐
Mental Status	☐	☐
Endo	☐	☐
Hem/lymph	☐	☐
Allergy/immun	☐	☐
No changes since last visit on / /		

NO CHEST PAIN
DENIES SOB
DYSPEPSIA

PFSH	NC	*Note
Past	✓	☐
Family	✓	☐
Social	☐	☐
No changes since last visit on / /		

[ ]*Note [ ] Constitutional: NAD, A&O. Cooperative.

[ ]*Note [ ]Head: Normocephalic, Atraumatic. Scalp unremarkable

[ ]*Note [ ]Eyes: Lids, sclerae & conjunct clear. PERRLA. Non-icteric, no nystagmus [ ]Glasses [ ]Contacts

[ ]*Note [ ]ENT/Mouth: External ears, canals, TMs clear. Lips gums, oral mucosa nml. Tongue oral cavity & pharynx clear. Teeth in good condition. No loose teeth.

[ ]*Note [ ] Nose: Nose, septum, turbinates, & nasal mucosa normal. No drainage.

[✓]*Note [ ]Neck: Supple & symmetric w/ nrml ROM w/o swelling or JVD. No thyroid tenderness or masses. WEAKENED CAROTID PULSES

[ ]*Note [✓]Heart: Reg R & R w/o murmurs, rubs, gallops. Nml distal pulses & perfusion. No carotid bruits. NO AUDIBLE BRUITS

[ ]*Note [ ]Lungs: No respiratory distress or compromise. CTAP. No wheezes or cough.

[ ]*Note [✓]Abdomen: soft, flat, no organomegaly, masses or tenderness. Bowel sounds present.

[✓]*Note [ ]Musculo: Nrml gait & stance. Extremities unremarkable, full active & passive ROM, w/o atrophy, spasticity, clubbing or abnml movements. Strength symmetrical. No jt swelling, erythema, effusion or tenderness. No crepitation. No dislocation or laxity. MILD SOCK EDEMA

[ ]*Note [ ] Neuro: [ ] Cranial nerves II-XII intact. [ ] DTR biceps, brachioradialis, patellar & ankle, equal bilaterally [ ] motor and sensory exam [ ] finger-to-nose [ ]negative Babinski & Romberg bilaterally.

[ ]*Note Male: [ ]No inguinal hernia palpable w/Valsalva. [ ] Testicles-WNL [ ] Penis-WNL

[ ]*Note [ ] Rectal: Prostate firm w/o mass, enlargement, tenderness. Nrml sphincter tone. Heme - stool.

[ ]*Note [ ]Breasts: Nrml shape & contour. Development nml w/o palpable lesions. No axillary adenopathy, dimpling, retraction, or skin color/texture changes. Nipples nrml, no discharge. Last Mammo: / /

[ ]*Note [ ]Pelvic: Nrml ext.genit, vaginal wall. No adnexal masses & uterus nrml sized. Good pelvic support w/o rectocele or cystocele. No excessive discharge or odor. [ ] Cervix nrml, PAP smear to path

[ ]*Note [✓]Skin: free of rashes, lesions, abnml discolor, or cyanosis. No signs of self-injury. Nails: WNL plethoric but clear

[ ]*Note [ ]Psych: Mood, affect, & behavior approp, no anxiety, depres, compulsive behav evidence. Gen knwldg, cognition, judgmt, & insight WNL. [ ] Short & long-term memory intact.

*Notes:

Labs ordered(circle): BMP, CMP, CBC, lipids TSH, Free T4, PSA, HbA1C, urine microalbumin, digoxin, INR, arthritis panel, renal panel, GTT, UPT, specify:

NO NEW SYMPTOMS. WALKS DAILY. USING ATKINS DIET

GU: FUNDI SHOW GRADE II ATHEROSCLEROTIC CHANGE, GRADE II KW ANTERIORLAR NARROWING. DISCS ARE SHARP.

MEDS: 1. USP THYROID EXTRACT + DRISDOL
2. HARMONE EXTRACT REPLACEMENT RX
3. DILTIAZEM SR 90 MG q. AM + PM.
4. ATENOLOL 50 MG Q AM

A: ① HTN 2° BILATERAL FIBROMUSCULAR DYSPLASIA - WELL CONTROLLED ON RX
② S/P (L) MASTECTOMY BREAST CA, STABLE
③ HYPOTHYROIDISM
④ OSTEOPENIA ON RX

PROGRESS NOTE MD Signature

F/U 4 mths CONTINUE PRESENT REGIMEN. DOING WELL.

Figure 5.12 #15 Office Note

Coding Exam

Multiple Choice

1. Which element is NOT considered a part of Nature of the Presenting Problem?
   a. Allergies
   b. Symptom
   c. Sign
   d. Complaint
2. Which of the following is NOT a part of Past History?
   a. Current medications
   b. Allergies
   c. Prior surgeries
   d. Employment history
3. Which of the following is NOT part of the Review of Systems?
   a. Ears
   b. Allergic/immunologic
   c. Psychiatric
   d. Weight
4. *Concurrent Care* is defined as:
   a. When a patient is being treated for more than one condition, by the same physician
   b. Similar services provided to the same patient by one or more physicians on the same day
   c. Oversight by a physician to provide ongoing review and revision of a patient's plan of care
   d. When two different specialists are treating a patient
5. What are the three key E/M components?
   a. Time, counseling, coordination of care
   b. History, medical decision making, review of systems
   c. History, exam, medical decision making
   d. Review of systems, nature of presenting problem, exam
6. What are the four E/M contributory factors?
   a. Time, counseling, coordination of care, history
   b. Exam, counseling, coordination of care, nature of the presenting problem
   c. History, exam, medical decision making, time
   d. Time, counseling, coordination of care, nature of the presenting problem
7. What is NOT a component for emergency department levels of E/M services?
   a. Exam
   b. Time
   c. Nature of the presenting problem
   d. Coordination of care
8. What is the difference between Past History and Social History?
   a. Past history is anything that happened in a previous admission.
   b. Social history is anything that has to do with pastimes and interaction with other people.
   c. Past history is concerned only with the patient's past experiences with illnesses, injuries, treatments, allergies, and medications.
   d. Social history focuses on occupational hazards.
9. Face-to-face time includes:
   a. Obtaining a history, performing an examination, and counseling a patient
   b. Taking phone calls from the patient, performing an examination, and counseling a patient

   c. Obtaining a history, reviewing test results, and counseling a patient
   d. Meeting with the patient's family, coordinating care with nursing staff, office time

10. What CPT codes are exempt from modifier -51?
   a. Unlisted codes
   b. Add-on codes
   c. V codes
   d. All of the above
11. E codes are used to indicate:
   a. Where an accident occurred
   b. How an accident occurred
   c. Adverse effects of drugs properly administered
   d. All of the above
12. Late effects are:
   a. The residual effects that remain from the acute phase of an injury or illness
   b. An E code to describe a fall ice skating
   c. Determined by a clinician if symptoms still persist 30 days after initial onset
   d. Not reported by physician offices, only inpatient hospitals
13. A crossover claim is:
   a. One that is sent back by the carrier for more information
   b. When Medicare forwards electronically secondary claim information
   c. A claim that is sent electronically to a payer via a clearing house
   d. A claim that has additional information electronically attached
14. The sequence of the procedures listed on the claim form can impact:
   a. Time period to get the claim paid
   b. Payment
   c. Procedure code usage that may trigger an audit by the OIG
   d. Sequence does not matter
15. A valid place of service code in box 24b for subsequent hospital visits is:
   a. 11
   b. 22
   c. 23
   d. 21
16. The term *linking* of codes refers to:
   a. Which CPT modifiers are linked to each procedure code in box 24D
   b. The number in box 24E that points to the one of four diagnoses codes in box 21 that supports the service
   c. The numbers in box 24E always being 1,2,3,4 for every CPT code in box 24D
   d. Providing the appropriate place of service code for each procedure performed
17. A "dirty" claim is:
   a. Is a slang term used by clearinghouses to describe a claim that was not electronically transmitted properly from the provider to the clearinghouse
   b. A hard copy claim that has unrecognizable marks on it
   c. A claim that has procedure codes not properly linked
   d. A claim that is missing required information
18. An EOB is:
   a. Explanation of Benefits
   b. Electronic Omission Bundle
   c. Examination of Beneficiary
   d. Explanation of Batch

19. Which carrier type always accepts all National HCPCS codes?
    a. Commercial carriers
    b. BC/BS
    c. Medicare
    d. None; these were eliminated with HIPAA
20. When a physician accepts assignment for a Medicare patient, the physician:
    a. Agrees to have Medicare pay him directly
    b. Agrees to bill the patient for the difference between the allowed amount and the limiting charge
    c. Must collect the patient's 20% co-pay up front
    d. Must charge 50% or less of his customary fee
21. Which of the following services are NOT covered by Part B Medicare?
    a. Physician office visits
    b. Inpatient admissions
    c. Outpatient visits
    d. Home health care
22. Tricare provides health care benefits for:
    a. All government employees currently employed
    b. The uniformed (armed) services and their dependents active or retired
    c. Only active duty military and their families
    d. Only retired military and their families
23. When coding a diagnostic statement that says the current condition is acute and chronic and the alphabetic index lists a separate code for each, what do you do?
    a. Code the acute and chronic codes separately
    b. Code acute only
    c. Code chronic only
24. A comorbity is not
    a. Coded when there is a principal diagnosis
    b. A condition that may influence the outcome of a patient's care
    c. An existing condition other than the principal diagnosis
    d. the principal diagnosis
25. A(n) ____________________ occurs when the wrong drug or an incorrect dosage of a correct drug is ingested.
    a. adverse reaction
    b. poisoning
    c. late effect
    d. neoplasm
26. For a condition to be considered a late effect, how much time must elapse between the acute event and the late effect?
    a. 24 hours
    b. 6 weeks
    c. 1 year
    d. no time limit
27. A physician writes an order for a drug; however, he does not indicate the condition or the diagnosis as to why the drug is given. The coder recognizes the drug as a well known medication for hypertension. What is the best action for the coder to take next?
    a. Code the hypertension since the medication is documented
    b. Document the hypertension in a progress note for the physician to sign

c. Code for the E/M service that day and any other diagnosis that is documented
d. Query the physician for further documentation

28. Which of the following professional's documentation may be used by a coder to report diagnoses and procedures?
    a. PA-C
    b. MD
    c. R.N.P
    d. All of the above

29. When reporting E/M services from the Initial Observation Care subcategory for an established patient, how many key components must be met or exceeded to qualify for a particular level of service?
    a. 4
    b. 7
    c. 3

30. For a Medicare patient, if a CPT code and a National code both exist to report a procedure, which one is assigned?
    a. the CPT code
    b. the National code
    c. both

31. Per CPT guidelines, if a lesion is biopsied and then the remainder of the lesion is removed, what code(s) is (are) assigned?
    a. a code for the biopsy and one for the lesion excision
    b. a code for the lesion excision only
    c. a code for the biopsy only

32. A patient returns to the office nine days after having a .5 cm lesion removed. Today he is complaining of a sinus infection. The physician may code the level of E/M service provided by attaching which modifier?
    a. 21
    b. 24
    c. 25

33. When the words *separate procedure* appear after the code description you know which of the following about that code?
    a. The procedure was the only service provided that day
    b. The procedure was provided on a day on which a major procedure was not provided
    c. The procedure was a minor procedure that would be coded only if it were the only service provided

34. What code(s) is submitted for the administration of the flu virus vaccine to a Medicare patient?
    a. G0001
    b. 90658, 90471
    c. G0008
    d. 90658

35. What code is submitted for a surgical tray for a laceration repair on a patient that has private insurance?
    a. A4550
    b. E0950
    c. 99070
    d. A4310

True/False

1. Coding for wound closures requires the following information: (1) location, (2) size (length), and (3) type of closure.

   T or **F**

2. Avoid coding from lab work, radiology reports, or special tests without additional supporting documentation from the attending physician.

   T or **F**

3. For both inpatient and outpatient settings, you may code conditions as ruled out.

   T or **F**

4. A symptom may be assigned as a principal diagnosis if a patient signs out of the hospital against medical advice before work-up is completed.

   T or **F**

5. Signs and symptoms that are part of the disease process should be coded separately.

   T or **F**

6. If a physician spends over a half hour on the phone with a patient, the call qualifies as face-to-face time.

   T or **F**

7. An established patient has received professional services from a particular physician within the past three years, or from another physician of the same specialty who belongs to the same group practice, within the past three years.

   T or **F**

8. Time is the most important factor during a counseling E/M visit.

   T or **F**

9. The review of systems recognizes over 13 body systems.

   T or **F**

10. Topics such as domestic violence and child abuse are not appropriate for inclusion in the family history record.

    T or **F**

11. It is sufficient to have history information taken by the staff or written by the patient without physician presence as long as the physician refers to it and reviews it with the patient.

    T or **F**

12. A comprehensive exam requires four or more body areas.

    T or **F**

13. If a patient has a chronic illness that is stable, this is not a factor when determining the level of medical decision making.

    T or **F**

14. According to the CPT guidelines, checkmarks or a notation indicating "normal" are not sufficient documentation in the medical record and can't be considered part of ROS.

    T or **F**

15. Constitutional items include sitting blood pressure, temperature, weight, and height.

    T or **F**

16. A preventative medicine service code cannot be submitted on the same day as an established patient sick visit.

    T or **F**

17. An E code can be listed as a principal diagnosis.

    T or **F**

18. NCCI edits are applicable only to hospital outpatient services; they do not apply to physician coding.

    T or **F**

19. If an endoscopic procedure fails, is terminated, and is converted to an open procedure, assign only the code for the open procedure.

    T or **F**

20. If a physician wishes to give a discount to a colleague or relative, then modifier -52 is appended to the code for that service.

    T or **F**

21. When performing endoscopic or laparoscopic procedures, if a biopsy is performed at the same site at which an excision is performed, it is appropriate to code both the biopsy and the excision.

    T or **F**

22. The emergency department services codes are restricted for use of emergency department physicians.

    T or **F**

23. When an adult patient presents to their primary care physician office for an annual physical, the diagnosis code of V70.0 is reported.

    T or **F**

24. A visit to an observation unit in a hospital is always reported with a V code as the first-listed diagnosis followed by the code for the medical condition.

    T or **F**

25. A physician who treats a patient in the office and sends the patient to the hospital for observation will report only the observation care codes and not the office visit codes.

    T or **F**

26. If a patient is age 65 or greater, Medicare is never a secondary insurance.

    T or **F**

27. CCI edits apply to all payer polices—private, commercial, and government.

    T or **F**

28. If a child is seen in the office and both parents have insured the child, the father's insurance is always considered primary.

    T or **F**

29. If a patient is seen in the office for a suspicious lesion and the doctor decides to perform a biopsy that day, the doctor would report the E/M code with a -57 modifier in addition to the code for the biopsy.

    T or **F**

30. A 66-year-old Medicare patient is seen by her family physician for a routine annual exam. A Waiver of Liability is signed by the patient instead of the ABN.

    T or **F**

Fill in the blank

Assign any ICD-9, CPT, and HCPCS codes as needed.

1. A Medicare patient is seen for a screening colonoscopy. The patient has a history of colon polyps. Internal hemorrhoids were identified. ______________________________
2. Incision and drainage of subcutaneous abscess of the penis. __________________

3. The patient presents to her internal medicine physician for a pneumonia vaccine. No other services were performed. ____________________

4. A 60-year-old patient recently moved to Maryland and is seeing a new practitioner there. The patient has a long history of gouty arthropathy and GERD, and is seen today for his annual exam. The physician completes a comprehensive H&P and counsels the patient on diet and medication and exercise. ____________________

5. An established patient came to the office complaining of sudden onset chest pain, nausea, and jaw pain. Per the patient, the pain is sharp and continuous in the chest but dull in the jaw. She woke up with it this morning and it has gotten progressively worse. She was not doing anything out of the ordinary this morning. She is currently under my care for HTN maintenance. Today her vitals are BP: 140/90, Temp: 99.3, Pulse: 120. An EKG was performed and interpreted. I ordered blood work to include cardiac enzymes. I reviewed her medical history and provided a brief exam to include heart and lungs. The pain is midsternal. Her family history is positive for heart disease. The patient is a long-time smoker. Because of her history and her current obesity and high blood pressure she was admitted to observation. I plan on having a Holter monitor placed, IV fluids, and nitroglycerin. I will arrange a cardiac consult. The patient was discharged the following day. Myocardial infarction was ruled out. ____________________

6. A patient has been in the hospital for four days. The admitting diagnosis was vertigo. He was admitted on 12/2 by Dr. A, another doctor in the practice. Dr. B saw him each day during rounds, performing a problem-focused exam and straightforward medical decision making. On 12/6 the patient is ready to be discharged. Dr. B provides all the discharge services and documents them in the hospital chart. He estimates that he spent 40 minutes providing the discharge care. Discharge diagnoses: Anemia and dehydration. Assign codes for Dr. B's services.
Codes: ____________________

7. Dr. Heath is called to the ER over the weekend to see an established patient.

S: She is a 47-year-old woman with Type II IDDM who went to the ER complaining of abdominal pain and dysuria. She states she had been feeling well until three days prior to admission, when she began to notice dysuria and urinary frequency. On the morning of admission she began to have nausea and abdominal pain, and because she was unable to eat, she stopped taking her insulin. Her abdominal pain became worse, so she came to the hospital.

O: The pain is in the epigastric region without radiation. She denies bloody diarrhea, fever, chills, sweats. She had not vomited as of yet, but feels severe nausea. She states that she was too busy getting ready for the holidays to check her finger sticks, but that she had been strict with her diet. SFH: She is married, has two children. She drinks a glass of wine a day and denies tobacco use. She has no allergies. Medications: NPH insulin 20u q a.m., 10u q p.m.

O: Physical exam reveals a woman, uncomfortable but in NAD.

Vital signs: Temp 99.3 degrees, RR 26 labored, supine BP: 102/62, HR 116, upright BP 92/60, HR 128

HEENT: NC/AT conjunctiva pink, anicteric, PEERLA, EOMI, fundi clear, TMs clear - oropharynx normal.

Chest: clear to A/P. Heart: S1 S2, no murmurs.

Abdomen: Normoactive bowel sounds, mild midepigastric tenderness and flank tenderness, no organomegaly or masses.

Extremities: No CCE.

Rectal: No masses, nontender, heme-negative.

A: Diabetic ketoacidosis.

P: EKG, CBC, urinalysis, chest-x-ray. Admit to observation.
Codes: ____________________

8. I am seeing this patient at the request of Dr. Hackney, his primary physician. Patient is a 59 y/o utility worker. He has been complaining of a bump on the back of his neck midline for the past three months. The bump has gradually grown in size and has begun to bleed. The bump is not painful but gets caught on his necklace and makes haircuts difficult. The patient has a family history of basal cell carcinoma. The patient has had moles removed prophylactically in the past.

   O: B/P: 120/80, Weight: 225, Temp: 98.6

   Patient is a pleasant male. He has not noticed any other suspicious lesions elsewhere on his body. Nodule is approximately 0.7 cm ulcerated with uneven borders. A central crust is present. Skin on the back, arms, face, and hands appears sun damaged from years of working outdoors.

   A: Basal cell carcinoma

   P: Electrodessication and curetting under local anesthesia. 1% Xylocaine injected in a pinwheel fashion. Polysporin cream applied. He is to take Advil for pain and reapply cream after showering. Return in 10 days for follow-up. A report will be sent to Dr. Hackney with the findings of this visit. Codes: ____________________

9. A 37 y/o patient visits the office for a routine annual exam. She is new to Dr. Case but saw Dr. Heath three years ago.

   PFSH: She has no general complaints. She is in good overall health. She exercises 3 × wk and watches her intake, keeping to a low-carb diet. Since she has a strong family history of diabetes and heart disease and she wants to be evaluated. She is a court reporter, works long hours, and is under a great deal of stress with working and raising a family. She drinks alcohol occasionally. She has a history of smoking since age 20. She smokes half a pack per day. She desires to quit smoking and inquired about patches and medication.

   ROS: According to her medical record, she has experienced a 10-lb weight gain over the past 3 years. Patient does not wear glasses. No problems with vision or hearing. She denies any shortness of breath, chest pain, dizziness, or headaches. She has no complaints with joint pain, urination, or bowel movements. Menstrual cycles are every 30 days.

   PHYSICAL EXAM:

   Patient appears to be well-nourished and in no distress. B/P: 120/70, Weight: 165lb, Temp: 98.7, Pulse: 105

   HEENT: PERRLA. TMs pink. Mucous membranes are pink and moist. Tongue is mid-line. Sinuses nontender.

   Neck: Supple; lymph nodes not palpable

   Chest: Clear. Heart: RRR No S1 or S2

   Abdomen: Soft and nontender; no organomegaly or mass

   Rectal: Normal; heme negative

   Extremities: Normal

   Skin: No rash or petechiae

   GYN: Exam deferred; patient has a gynecologist.

   P: Patient was counseled on smoking cessation methods and risk factor interventions. Spoke with patient for 20 mins about depression following quitting and local smoking cessation support groups. Prescribed Zyban 75 mg 2 × day and Nicotine patch 1 per day. Patch is placed in the morning and removed at bedtime.
   Codes: ____________________

10. Patient is seen in the office for his six-month diabetic foot check. Patient has been doing well since his last visit and is following his ADA diet. He says he thinks he has an ingrown toenail and wants me to look at it. His toe has been red and tender for the past three weeks. He has soaked it in Epson Salts. The toe is really painful when wearing dress shoes. Aside from ongoing onychomycosis, he has no other complaints. His blood sugars have been in the normal range, between 95 and 120. His current medications include Diabeta, Lantus, and Lasix.

O: BP: 140/80, Weight: 250lb, Temp: 98.5, Pulse: 110. Upon examination, his right great toe was swollen at the nail fold and was tender to touch. There was slight drainage of pus from the side of the nail.

A: Paronychia with ingrown nail.

P: Removal of ingrown nail with blunt dissection. Granulomatous tissue was removed and the abscess was drained. A partial matrixectomy was performed.
Codes: ______________________

PART III

OFFICE INTERNSHIP

CHAPTER

Working in the Clinic: Front Desk

6

Background Basics

- To complete this chapter successfully, students must have completed chapters 1–5 in their entirety.
- Students are required to access the Internet. Experience with conducting searches on the Internet is necessary.

Competency Checklist

- Coding staff have to be fluent in Medicare carrier policies and coverage to properly execute the ABN.
- Local Coverage Determinations (LCD) dictate what services will be covered for predetermined diagnoses. Staff must be cognizant of these policies and know where to go to research them prior to submitting claims.

Part III of this book is where all the background information and review covered in chapters 1–5 will be put to use. Part III, chapters 6–8, is comprised of work for your first week at DMA. Now that your orientation is complete and you know how to use MOSS, you can begin working in the clinic. The dates for this week's simulation are October 26–30, 2009. For the first two days, you will be working at the front desk to get a feel for the flow of patients and how data is collected, as well as to gain experience using the computer. You will learn firsthand the challenges of this position and accommodating patients, and the importance of an accurate schedule. You will also take part in communicating with the back office staff, contacting insurance carriers, processing required paperwork, and collecting money. While completing these jobs, think about how these tasks relate to or ultimately affect code assignments for services provided in the office or hospital.

To complete the jobs in Part III, you will be using Appendices A–D and the enclosed CD-ROM to access tools, fee schedules, and source documents fee schedules and source documents. When working at the front desk, you need guidance on how to handle certain situations and procedures for performing certain tasks. To collect the correct amount of money when the patient checks out, you need access to our price list (fee schedule) and insurance contracts. In this chapter, you will specifically be referring to Appendix A, Policies and Procedures; the CD-ROM for Insurance Contracts/Fee Schedules; the CD-ROM for the DMA Procedure Fee Schedule; and the CD-ROM for the Payment Plan Form.

There are approximately 30 jobs or tasks to perform each day. You must have access to the Internet to conduct research and carry out some of the assigned tasks for some of the jobs in this chapter.

In the office, at the end of each day, the routers are clipped to the patient's chart and placed in a bin for the billing staff to process the following day. New patients are scheduled for 30 minutes. Established patients are scheduled for 15 minutes. Office procedures are scheduled for 30 minutes. For new patients, charts must be made with the corresponding registration paperwork. When a patient reschedules, cancels, or misses an appointment you must document it in the *Appointment Scheduler* for medicolegal purposes. At the end of day two, turn your charts and routers in to your instructor to check your answers before proceeding to chapter 7.

When registering patients, check all tabs within the *Patient Registration* screen. It is crucial that all fields are filled in on the *Primary Insurance* and *Secondary Insurance* tabs. Otherwise, the claim will not transmit correctly in some cases and in others, checks will be mailed to patients and not the clinic if the *Assignment of Benefits* field is not checked. When registering new patients, complete the fields on the *HIPAA* tab with the date the notice was given to the patient and when they signed it. Print a copy of the *Privacy Notice* and give it to the patient. For our purposes, you can file it in their charts since you will not actually being having contact with patients. On each router, at the bottom right, indicate payments made. If the patient pays by check, write the check number next to the dollar amount. You don't need to total the charges unless it is a self-pay patient. All other patient balances are based on a set co-pay or a co-insurance depicted as a percentage of the allowed amount for each procedure code per carrier or contract negotiated by each payer after a co-pay (if applicable) is deducted.

REMINDER: When entering charges, posting payments, or registering patients, the documents needed to obtain this information are located at the end of this chapter.

WEEK 1

DAY ONE: MONDAY October 26, 2009

JOB 1: First read DMA's policy and procedure manual in Appendix A. This will get you grounded and acclimated to the way the clinic does business and will assist you in quickly locating the information you need for some of the jobs in this chapter. There is nothing to turn in to your instructor for this job.

JOB 2: The practice adopted a new fee schedule. Take the prices for each procedure code from the CD-ROM and compare them to what is in MOSS. Change any prices in MOSS that differ from the new Procedure Fee Schedule by going to the *File Maintenance*, *List* tab and then *CPT Code*. From here, you can add, delete, and change codes. Highlight the code you want to change a price for and tab across to the *Charge* column. You can also update the Medicare allowed amount while you are here. The CD-ROM houses all CPT codes and the Medicare allowed amounts. Updating the Medicare allowed amount must be done before proceeding to further jobs. To calculate account balances, co-insurances, and charges in future jobs, prices must be current. Any codes from the Procedure Fee Schedule not in MOSS can also be added at this time. Otherwise, you can add CPT codes and prices as you encounter them.

JOBS 3–5 Involve the schedule set up in MOSS.

JOB 3: Check the appointment calendar and make sure the following days have been blocked off because the office is closed. Print a copy of the schedule for these days and give it to your instructor.

December 24, 2009, December 25, 2009, January 1, 2010, May 31, 2010, July 2, 2010, September 6, 2010, November 25, 2010, December 24, 2010, and December 27, 2010.

JOB 4: The doctors have agreed to change the practice's office hours due to slow Friday afternoons. Fridays going forward, we will close at 1:00 p.m. We are going to change this for a trial period of one month beginning November 1 and ending November 30, 2009. The office will keep the scheduled hours of 9:00 a.m.–6:00 p.m. Monday through Thursday. After making these changes, print a copy of the schedule for November 6, 13, 20, and 27 reflecting this change.
HINT: Under *File Maintenance* select *Block Schedule* and block out the afternoon. Be sure to count the number of minutes to block off starting with the time in the time in field 4. The date the changes take effect is November 1, 2009. This date goes in field 2. Check to be sure that the changes take effect for all providers. You can also do this directly from the *Appointment Scheduler*.

JOB 5: In File Maintenance under Lists add Visit Code V10 for Office Consultation. Under Lists Cancellation Codes add C9 for No Show.

JOB 6: Francesco Alvarez left a message on the machine this morning asking for an appointment first thing this morning with Dr. Mendenhall. The patient is experiencing nausea/vomiting, fatigue, and heart palpitations. Schedule him for 9:30 a.m. *(See Job 6 & 9, Router- Francesco Alvarez)*

JOB 7: Gloria Morency called to schedule an appointment for her daughter Melissa Morency. She states that her daughter no longer wants to see a pediatrician and wants to see a female doctor in our group. She is concerned about her weight. She also wants to speak to the doctor about the HPV vaccine. She wants to come at 3:45 p.m. on October 27. DOB: 6/14/96, SSN: 214-60-3323, Phone number: (717)555-9964, Address: 121 Wellington Way, Ithaca, NY 14621. She is a full-time student. New patients are scheduled for 30 minutes. The father will be bringing her. Gloria has custody of Melissa but cannot leave work early to bring her. You assign her to Sally Kemper because she is new to the practice and is accepting new patients. Schedule this appointment now.

JOB 8: John Wittmer said he called this morning and scheduled an appointment for 9:00 a.m. to see Dr. Kemper. He checks in and says he has no changes to his insurance or demographic information. For some reason he is not on the schedule. Add him to the schedule and check him in. At this time, Mr. Alvarez arrives. Check him in as well. *(See Job 8 & 11, Router- John Wittmer)*

JOB 9: Mr. Alvarez is being admitted to the hospital for observation. Check him out. He pays his $20 co-pay in cash. *(See Job 6 & 9, Router- Francesco Alvarez)*

JOB 10: William Kostner is being referred by Dr. Ward Smith from Corning's Occupational Wellness Division (1234 Wingo Way, Monroe, CT, 06468; NPI #: 183459742) for vertigo. He is a new patient scheduled for October 27 at 1:00 p.m. with Dr. Heath. Dr. Ward wants to receive copies of notes and treatment records until the patient is released by Dr. Heath. Consultations are scheduled for 45 minutes. He works full-time and is insured with Galaxy Health Network. DOB: 2/13/59, SSN: 731-01-4513, Address: 47 Orangeman Way, N. Syracuse, NY 14871, Phone: (717)555-6271. Galaxy Health Network is not an insurance carrier listed in our system, so you must add it. We are in network and accept assignment. Schedule his appointment.
NOTE TO THE STUDENT: When entering new insurance carriers into MOSS, you must also enter the carrier's fee schedule or the claim will not process correctly in MOSS.

WEEK 1

DAY ONE: MONDAY October 26, 2009 (continued)

JOB 11: John Wittmer is checking out and does not need to return for a year. You notice in his *Patient Registration* screen that his $2 co-pay is not indicated. Update this and collect his $2 cash co-pay.

NOTE TO STUDENT: Because MOSS is not a provider patient management software, there are limitations to its ability to function as such. In a real office environment, the co-pay and/or coinsurance is typically collected when the patient checks in or checks out and the payment is immediately posted into the computer. MOSS does not have the ability to accept patient payments before charges are entered. Also, when scenarios state that a patient pays at the time of checkout, be sure to write that payment on the patient's respective router to track payment posting and deposit reconciliations in other jobs. *(See Job 8 & 11, Router- John Wittmer)*

JOB 12: Martin Beechwood called to schedule an appointment for his daughter Samantha. She was in an accident last night and is complaining of shoulder pain. She is scheduled for 4:00 p.m. tomorrow with Dr. Schwartz. He would like an x-ray of her shoulder taken. She has not seen Dr. Schwartz before. She is a full-time student at Baylor. DOB: 8/18/89, SSN: 619-51-4134, Address: 3615 Main St., Jamesville, NY 14691, Phone: (717)555-9274.

JOB 13: Hugh Williams is complaining of rectal bleeding and constipation. He has Medicare and Century Senior Gap. He wants to see Dr. Mendenhall at 10:00 a.m. on 10/28/09. He is new to the practice and was referred by John Conway, a current patient. DOB: 11/21/1934, SSN: 011-55-3261, Address: 220 Volunteer Way, Auburn, NY 14667, Phone: (717) 555-1122. He is married and retired from the pier.

JOB 14: Ryan Ashby called for an appointment. He injured his right hand. He sees Dr. Murray. He is scheduled for 10:15 a.m. today.

JOB 15: Brian McDonough called for an appointment. He is taking a mission trip overseas. He has elevated BP and asthma and wants to be evaluated before he leaves. He also wants to get a hepatitis booster. He did not care who he saw, so you scheduled him for 10:00 a.m. with Dr. Schwartz on 10/27/09. DOB: 6/26/66, SSN: 027-46-2232, Address: 26 Broad St., Syracuse, NY 14802, Phone: (717)555-2267. He has BC/BS. He is married and works full-time.

JOB 16: Ryan Ashby is checking out. He is to follow up in 10 days. Add up his charges and collect his payment. He says he can't pay more than $20 cash today and can afford only $25 per month. Write a payment plan for his balance. A blank payment plan form is located in on the CD-ROM.

HINT: Is his insurance the same since the last visit? If not, where should you go to update this information? *(See Job 16, Router- Ryan Ashby)*

JOB 17: You received notification from Signal HMO that the address to send secondary claims to has been changed. It is now Signal Secondary HMO, PO Box 4583, Talladega, MS 35842. Update the insurance carrier information in *File Maintenance*.

JOB 18: Naomi Yamagata called and wants an appointment today with Dr. Murray. She is having heavy periods. Schedule her appointment for 11:15 a.m.

JOB 19: Paul Morgan called and wants to schedule a vasectomy in the minor procedure room for 10/28/09 at 11:00 a.m. with Dr. Schwartz. Dr. Schwartz needs an hour for this office procedure. DOB: 8/18/68, SSN: 047-91-5571, Address: 47 Barrington Highway, Rochester, NY 14699, Phone: (717)555-4747. He has Aetna through his employer (ID# 4671921D) and Signal HMO through his wife.

JOB 20: Naomi Yamagata called back and needs to change her appointment time. She wants to move it to 4:00 p.m. today.

JOB 21: William Turner is a call-in patient today. He has a painful cold sore and wants to be seen. You put him on the schedule for 10:45 a.m. with Dr. Kemper. DOB: 10/16/73, SSN: 471-16-5555, Address: 16 Morgan Blvd, Apt B, Woliott, NY 14654, Phone: (717)555-1122. He is single and works full-time.

JOB 22: Schedule Laura Leighton for 2:00 p.m. today with Dr. Mendenhall. She has a lesion that she wants the doctor to look at.

JOB 23: Caitlin Barryroe called, and the reason for her appointment is personal. She wants an appointment with Dr. Heath at 10:45 a.m. today, but he is not available then. You tell her that Alberta Lynn, our PA, is available and she agrees to see her. When scheduling this appointment, you notice that Alberta's credential shows as M.D. in MOSS. She is not a physician. Correct this now.

JOB 24: William Turner checks in. Dr Kemper wants him back right away because he has to go back to the hospital. Make a new folder for him. Register him and mark him as *checked* in in MOSS. Check his insurance benefits. Print this out and put in his folder. *(See Job 24, Insurance Card and Registration Paper work- William Turner 1–5)*

JOB 25: Julius Washington wants to see Dr. Mendenhall tomorrow. He has had chronic asthma and is now complaining of shortness of breath and sinus congestion. He is scheduled for 11:15 a.m. His insurance is Great West (ID#4771651). DOB: 4/10/88, SSN: 707-51-1690, Address: 414 Maidstone Way, Auburn, NY 14616, Phone: (717) 555-7171. He is single and works full-time.

JOB 26: William Turner is checking out. You realize that he has Cigna insurance and DMA does not participate with that carrier. You inform him of this, and he is upset and demands to speak to the office manager. April speaks to him and calls his attention to the sign posted in the waiting room informing patients that the clinic does not participate with Cigna. He is angry and says he is going to call his insurance company. You tally up his charges and he insists he is only paying a $20 co-pay. Post his cash payment of $20. *(See Job 26, Insurance Card and Router- William Turner)*

WEEK 1

DAY ONE: MONDAY October 26, 2009 (continued)

a. What are his total charges for the day? (HINT: Use the CD-ROM and look up the charges for each CPT code.) ______________________

b. What insurance is entered in the computer for his visit today? ______________________

c. How could this situation be avoided in the future? Where were the breakdowns in communication?

____

d. What could April do to appease him or to offset some of his expense? (*HINT*: Check the Policy Manual.) ______________________

JOB 27: Caitlin Barrymore checks in. You notice that her name is misspelled in MOSS as Barrymore. Correct her name now in MOSS and on her router when she checks out. She sees the doctor and is ready to check out. She is to return in one week to discuss lab results. She pays her co-pay with check #425. Schedule her for November 3 at 10:45 a.m. with Alberta Lynn for follow-up. What is her co-insurance today?______________________ *(See Job 27, Router- Caitlin Barrymore)*

JOB 28: Each day the front desk staff calls patients to remind them of their appointments. Place a message in the *Note:* section of the appointment dialogue box indicating if you spoke to the patient to confirm (spoke w/pt) or if you left a message on machine (LMOM). Click the box to the left of *Confirmed.* This lets all staff know that a call was made and the appointment was confirmed for the following day. The *Date/Time* field will populate automatically. Print a copy of this appointment confirmation for each person on the schedule for October 27, 2009. When the appointment dialogue box is open, use the *Control P* shortcut to print this box. Turn these in to your instructor.

JOB 29: Laura Leighton is checking out. She is PRN. She pays $15 cash. *(See Job 29, Router- Laura Leighton)*

JOB 30: Naomi Yamagata is checking out. She needs to come back in 10 days for follow-up. Schedule this appointment for November 6 at 1:00 a.m. with Dr. Murray. Collect the patient's co-pay. She paid $10 in cash. *(See Job 30, Router- Naomi Yamagata)*

JOB 31: Isabel Durand is coming to see Dr. Kemper tomorrow for a pelvic exam and PAP. According to her, her last PAP and exam was in November 2007. Schedule her for 11:00 a.m.

JOB 32: Deanna Hartsfeld wants to see Dr. Murray tomorrow for a thorough physical at 1:15 p.m. He will need 30 minutes for the exam. She has Medicare and Century Senior Gap.

JOB 33: Wilma Stearn is being scheduled at 10:15 a.m. tomorrow in the minor procedure room for a phototherapy session on her actinic keratosis. Dr. Murray needs 30 minutes to complete this.

JOB 34: Check insurance benefits for each patient on the schedule for tomorrow. Print a copy of their eligibility reports. These will be filed in their charts when they check in tomorrow. Check with Medicare to see if they cover laser therapy for premalignant lesions (actinic keratosis) for Wilma Stearn. Also check to see if there is a national and/or local coverage determination about the pelvic exam and PAP on Isabel Durand.

HINT: Use the source documents for information you may be missing in order to run eligibility.

JOB 35: At the end of each day, it is the front desk's responsibility to tally up money collected over the counter and complete a deposit slip. Check all your routers and notes from the previous jobs and account for all money received today. Complete the deposit slip located on the CD-ROM Turn this in to your instructor.

JOB 36: Elane Ybarra called and wants to be seen tomorrow for her annual exam. She does not care who she sees. Schedule her with Dr. Schwartz at 4:00 p.m.

JOB 37: Print the schedule for tomorrow. Turn this schedule in to your instructor.

END OF DAY QUESTIONS

1. Were you able to check insurance eligibility benefits for Melissa Morency? ____________________
   Why or why not?____________________
2. When you checked benefits for Wilma Stearn what did you determine—is the laser therapy a covered service? ____________________
3. When you checked benefits for Isabel Durand what do you determine—is the pelvic exam and PAP a covered service? ________________ What form should be completed when she arrives tomorrow for her appointment? ____________________
4. Will Caitlin Barrymore's charges be filed under Dr. Heath's NPI number or Alberta Lynn's NPI number? Dr. Heath was in the office as well as other practice physicians. Dr. Heath was not available at the time Caitlin wanted. ____________________
5. Why is it important to document in the schedule and/or in the medical record when a patient misses, does not show up for, or cancels their appointment? ______________

WEEK 1

DAY TWO: TUESDAY October 27, 2009

JOB 1: Richard Manaly walks in at 8:30 a.m. and signs in. You check the schedule and see he is not on it. He says he was scheduled to come in for a Coumadin check. Add him to the schedule and let the lab know he is here. None of the doctors are here yet but Alberta Lynn the PA is. She will see him after he has his lab drawn. Check him in the system. Verify his insurance eligibility. Print this out for his file. Turn this into your instructor.

JOB 2: Brian McDonough arrives for his appointment. Check him in and make his folder. Update his registration information. *(See Job 2, Insurance Card and Router- Brian McDonough)*

JOB 3: Richard Manaly is checking out. He does not need to come back for one month. He says he will call back next week to schedule his appointment because he wants to check his calendar. How much does he owe for his visit today according to the insurance verification? He has a $400 deductible that has not been met. He pays by check #2367. (*HINT*: Use the CD-ROM to see what DMA's contract is with FlexiHealth and then calculate the amount due based on this.) ________________. *(See Job 3, Router- Richard Manaly)*

JOB 4: Elane Ybarra has arrived. Check her in and check her benefits.

JOB 5: Wilma Stearn has arrived. Check her in.

JOB 6: Mr. McDonough checks out. Calculate his charges for this visit. What is his co-insurance for the day? (*HINT*: Check the CD-ROM for the BC/BS contract and then calculate the allowed based on the negotiated rate.) He pays by check #4521. *(See Job 6, Registration paper work- Brian McDonough 1–5)*

Charges: ____________ Medicare Allowed: ____________ Blue Cross Allowed: ____________
Owed: ____________

Look at the router for his visit. Based on what you know about him and why he was being seen, is the visit coded correctly by Dr. Schwartz? Why/why not? ______________________
____

JOB 7: Isabel Durand arrives. You need to talk with her about her visit today. You must explain to her Medicare's coverage policy for pelvic exams and PAPs. Where do you find this information? When was her last PAP? What are you going to say to her? ______________________
____

What form must she sign before she can be seen today? ______________________

She wants to proceed with her scheduled appointment. Download the form from the Medicare website and complete it for her. Turn this into your instructor.

JOB 8: Elane Ybarra is checking out. What is her co-pay? ______________________
(See Job 8, Router- Elaine Ybarra 1–2)

JOB 9: Ms. Stearn is checking out. What is her coinsurance today for the phototherapy? She pays in cash. ______________________________
(See Job 9, Router- Wilma Stearn)

JOB 10: Julius Washington arrives for his appointment. Check him in and make a folder for him. Update his registration information. *(See Job 10, Insurance Card and Registration Paper work- Julius Washington 1–5)*

JOB 11: Ms. Durand checks out. How much money should you collect today for the services she received? ____________ She pays by check #654. *(See Job 11, Router- Isabel Durand)*

JOB 12: Russell Logan calls for an appointment tomorrow with Dr. Kemper. He is having right leg pain. Schedule him for 9:00 a.m.

JOB 13: Edward Gorman called and wants to schedule an appointment with Dr. Heath at 10:00 a.m. tomorrow. He is complaining of indigestion and food getting caught in his throat.

JOB 14: Mr. Washington is ready to check out. What is his coinsurance for today? (*HINT:* Go to the CD-ROM and see what our contract is with Great West. Calculate amount due based on contracted rate, not charges). He pays in cash. ____________ *(See Job 14, Insurance Card and Router- Julius Washington)*

JOB 15: William Kostner signs in. Check him in, update his registration information, and make a folder for him. *(See Job 15, Insurance Card and Registration Paper work- William Kostner 1–5)*

JOB 16: Ted Mosby called and wants to see Dr. Schwartz tomorrow. He has several skin tags he wants removed. He also says he has a few moles that are changing that he wants him to look at. Schedule him in the minor procedure room at 9:00 a.m. for 30 mins.

JOB 17: William Kostner is checking out. You notice on the Patient Registration Form that he indicated he was in an accident and is covered by Workers' Comp. Change this in the computer. This can be done when entering the charges later- just don't forget to! Does he owe any money before he checks out? ____________ *(See Job 17, Insurance Card and Router- William Kostner)*

JOB 18: Paul Morgan is having surgery tomorrow and you need to check vasectomy coverage with Aetna. Visit http://www.aetna.com. Click the *Health Care Professionals* link. Choose *Resource Center*. Select *Health Coverage Information*. Change the dropdown box to *Medical* and click on *Go*. Scroll down to *Precertification List* and click on *More*. Select *The Aetna National Participating Provider Precertification List*. Enter the CPT code for vasectomy and print the page that loads. File this in his chart.

JOB 19: Deanna Hartsfeld was checked in by someone else. She is ready to check out. What is her coinsurance for today? ____________ *(See Job 19, Router- Deanna Hartsfeld)*

WEEK 1

DAY TWO: TUESDAY October 27, 2009 (continued)

JOB 20: Derek Wallace walked in today at 2:00 p.m. and wants to be seen. He was working on his car today and the jack slipped and cut his hand. You add him to the schedule for Dr. Schwartz. He is taken to the back right away. Check his benefits now.

JOB 21: Vito Mangano checks out. When you checked his benefits yesterday, what did it say about his deductible? What is his co-pay today? He pays by check #845. ______________

____

(See Job 21, Router- Vito Mangano)

JOB 22: Mr. Wallace checks out. Collect his co-pay. He pays in cash. *(See Job 22, Router- Derek Wallace)*

JOB 23: Melissa Morency signs in. Check her in and make her a chart. You realize that her insurance information has not been verified because it was not obtained when her appointment was scheduled. Check her insurance benefits now. Print a copy for her chart. *(See Job 23, Insurance Card 1–2 and Registration Paper work- Melissa Morency 1–5)*

JOB 24: Barry Jurch calls and wants an appointment tomorrow with Dr. Heath. He has been complaining of fatigue and a sore throat for several days. Schedule him at 9:00 a.m.

JOB 25: Samantha Beechwood signs in. Register her and make her a chart. What is the problem with her registration paperwork?______________________________________ *(See Job 25, Insurance Card and Registration Form 1–5)*

JOB 26: Alan Shuman called and wants to come tomorrow to get his flu and pneumonia vaccines. He wants to come by at 9:00 a.m. He is not going to see the doctor. Schedule him on Alberta Lynn's calendar. She is giving injections today because the intake RN is off.

JOB 27: Melissa Morency checks out. Which insurance is primary for her? ______________

____

What is the co-insurance for Melissa's visit today? (*HINT*: You must check the CD-ROM for the contracts for her insurance carriers and the Medicare fee schedule allowable to calculate the percentage. Percentages are calculated from allowed amounts, not charges). She pays in cash.
____ *(See Job 27, Insurance Card 1–2 and Router- Melissa Morency)*

JOB 28: Samantha Beechwood checks out. What is her co-insurance for today? She pays by check #632.______________________________________ *(See Job 28, Insurance Card and Router- Samantha Beechwood)*

JOB 29: Mrs. Ramirez called to cancel her husband's appointment Friday. He was admitted to the hospital today for abdominal pain and rectal bleeding.

JOB 30: Mrs. Camille called about her daughter Emery. Emery is having bed wetting issues and Mrs. Camille wants her seen tomorrow at 2:30 p.m. with Dr. Kemper.

JOB 31: Diane Parker called for an appointment with Dr. Murray tomorrow at 1:00 p.m. She is having left heel pain. Her plantar fasciitis is back and she wants to have it injected again. She now has United Healthcare insurance (ID #U7568421).

JOB 32: Jordan Connell wants to have a physical tomorrow. He can't come before 3:00 p.m. He prefers a male physician. Schedule him with Dr. Murray at 3:15 p.m.

JOB 33: Check insurance benefits for each patient on the schedule for tomorrow. Print a copy of their eligibility reports. These will be filed in their charts when they check in tomorrow. Because Diane Parker just got United Healthcare, check their website for payment or reimbursement polices for injections. *(HINT:* You need to click on *Policies, Protocols and Administrative Guides*. Click on *Reimbursement Policies.* https://www.unitedhealthcareonline.com.)

JOB 34: Each day the front desk staff calls patients to remind them of their appointments. Place a message in the *Note:* section of the appointment dialogue box indicating if you spoke to the patient to confirm (spoke w/pt) or if you left a message on a machine (LMOM). Click the box to the left of *Confirmed*. This lets all staff know that a call was made and the appointment was confirmed for the following day. The *Date/Time* field will populate automatically. Print a copy of this appointment confirmation for each person on the schedule for October 28, 2009. When the appointment dialogue box is open, use the *Control P* short cut to print this box. Turn these appointment confirmation sheets in to your instructor.

JOB 35: Someone else checked Xao Chang in. Check him out. What is his coinsurance? He pays by check #7549. ______________________ *(See Job 35, Router- Xao Chang)*

JOB 36: Rose Vilas has been complaining of severe headaches and vertigo. Dr. Heath has ordered a CT scan of the brain without contrast to be performed ASAP. Because DMA owns the CT machine, we must notify the patient of this ownership and provide her with alternative locations to have the test performed. Two local area facilities that have CT scanners are New York County Hospital and Tri-City Radiology. Once you have written the notice explaining why she must be notified of this ownership, check the CMS carrier website for New York and see if this test has an LCD or prior authorization requirements. Is there an LCD, and will this test be covered with the diagnoses? ______________________

Check the MPFS and determine what the payment amount will be for this test so that you can let her know what her co-insurance will be. We have a contract with a radiologist that moonlights to do the readings of our CT scans. What is the allowed amount for this test? ______________ What will Ms. Vilas' co-insurance be? ______________ What is the Physician Supervision indicator for this test? If one of the doctors is in the office, can this test be performed?

WEEK 1

DAY TWO: TUESDAY October 27, 2009 (continued)

JOB 37: At the end of each day, it is the front desk's responsibility to tally up money collected over the counter and write up a deposit slip. Check all your routers and notes from the jobs above and account for all money received today. Complete the deposit slip located on the CD-ROM. Turn this in to your instructor.

JOB 38: The physicians are concerned that patients cannot get in touch with them when they need to. Patients have complained to them during visits that they can't return calls to the practice or reach the office at times that are convenient for them because they get the automated message to call back during normal business hours. It seems to them as though we are operating our phones at the convenience of the staff and not the patients. Our practice is busy and the physicians want to keep it that way. If patients can't reach us, they will go to a practice that they *can* reach. The staff complains that they are busy and overwhelmed and turn the phone on the service so that they can complete daily tasks. The physicians have asked that the phones not get forwarded to the answering service during daytime hours. April has asked each employee to offer suggestions on how to manage the telephone madness while not sacrificing productivity and customer service. Think creatively about how the office can answer incoming calls and manage to check patients in and out of the office while ensuring a continued smooth work flow at the front desk and clinical area, all while not jeopardizing customer service to the patients or fellow staff. Hiring additional staff members is not a current option. Write your suggestions and give rationale for your ideas. Turn these in to your instructor.

END OF DAY QUESTIONS

1. Does Paul Morgan's vasectomy procedure require precertification? ____________________
2. What NPI number will Richard Manaly's visit be billed under? ____________________
3. Does it matter if Isabel Durand has Medicaid as a secondary insurance? Will they pay if Medicare does not allow for a service? ____________________
4. Brian McDonough arrived 45 minutes before his scheduled appointment. At 9:45 a.m. he comes up to the front desk and begins to complain about having to wait. He states, "I have to be at work by 11:00 a.m. I've been waiting 30 minutes already. What is taking so long to call me back? There are only four other people waiting out here. I was here before that other lady and you took her back before me!" He is talking very loudly and waving his arm toward the waiting room. Patients are listening and watching him intently. What do you say to Brian and how do you diffuse his anger? ____________________
5. Look closely at Wilma Stearn's router. What do you find wrong with it? ____________________
6. What is United Healthcare's policy on injections for Diane Parker's appointment? Will her diagnosis be covered? Print it out and submit to your instructor. ____________________

The source documents located here represent forms and documents office staff use to record patient encounters, capture charges, and assign codes. Please note, not all jobs within this chapter require source documents.

The following table provides a summary of the Jobs in this chapter referencing their corresponding source documents. Note that jobs with N/A do not require source documents to complete the assignment.

WEEK 1

Day 1			Day 1		
Job No.	Patient Name	Documents	Job No.	Patient Name	Documents
Job 1	N/A	DMA Policy and Procedure Manual	Job 20	N/A	
Job 2	N/A	Fee Schedule from CD-rom	Job 21	N/A	
Job 3	N/A		Job 22	N/A	
Job 4	N/A		Job 23	N/A	
Job 5	N/A		Job 24	William Turner	Registration paperwork, Insurance card
Job 6	N/A		Job 25	N/A	
Job 7	N/A		Job 26	William Turner	Router
Job 8	N/A		Job 27	Caitlin Barrymore	Router
Job 9	Francesco Alvarez	Router	Job 28	N/A	
Job 10	N/A		Job 29	Laura Leighton	Router
Job 11	John Wittmer	Router	Job 30	Naomi Yamagata	Router
Job 12	N/A		Job 31	N/A	
Job 13	N/A		Job 32	N/A	
Job 14	N/A		Job 33	N/A	
Job 15	N/A		Job 34	N/A	
Job 16	Ryan Ashby	Router	Job 35	N/A	
Job 17	N/A		Job 36	N/A	
Job 18	N/A		Job 37	N/A	
Job 19	N/A				

(Continued)

Day 2			Day 2		
Job No.	Patient Name	Documents	Job No.	Patient Name	Documents
Job 1	N/A		Job 20	N/A	
Job 2	Brian McDonough	Registration paperwork, Insurance card	Job 21	Vito Mangano	Router
Job 3	Richard Manaly	Router	Job 22	Derek Wallace	Router
Job 4	N/A		Job 23	Melissa Morency	Registration paperwork, Insurance cards
Job 5	N/A		Job 24	N/A	
Job 6	Brian McDonough	Router	Job 25	Samantha Beechwood	Registration paperwork, Insurance card
Job 7	N/A		Job 26	N/A	
Job 8	Elane Ybarra	Router, Office note	Job 27	Melissa Morency	Router
Job 9	Wilma Stearn	Router	Job 28	Samantha Beechwood	Router
Job 10	Julius Washington	Registration paperwork, Insurance card	Job 29	N/A	
Job 11	Isabel Durand	Router	Job 30	N/A	
Job 12	N/A		Job 31	N/A	
Job 13	N/A		Job 32	N/A	
Job 14	Julius Washington	Router	Job 33	N/A	
Job 15	William Kostner	Registration paperwork, Insurance card	Job 34	N/A	
Job 16	N/A		Job 35	Xao Chang	Router
Job 17	William Kostner	Router	Job 36	N/A	
Job 18	N/A		Job 37	N/A	
Job 19	Deanna Hartsfeld	Router	Job 38	N/A	

Date of service: 10/26/09	Insurance: FLEXIHEALTH				Router #: 1497
Patient name: FRANCESCO ALVAREZ	Coinsurance:	Copay: 20.00			Physician Name: MENDENHALL
Account #: ALV001	Noncovered Waiver?	yes	no	n/a	

x	Office visit	New	x	Est
	Minimal (RN only)			99211
	Problem focused	99201		99212
	Exp problem focused	99202		99213
	Detailed	99203		99214
	Comp	99204	✓	99215
	Comprhen/Complex	99205		
	Well visit	**New**	**x**	**Est**
	< 1 y	99381		99391
	1-4 y	99382		99392
	5-11 y	99383		99393
	12-17 y	99384		99394
	18-39 y	99385		99395
	40-64 y	99386		99396
	65 y +	99387		99397

x	Medicare preventive services	
	Pap	Q0091
	Pelvic & breast	G0101
	Prostate/PSA	G0103
	Tobacco couns/3-10 min	G0375
	Tobacco couns/>10 min	G0376
	Welcome to Medicare exam	G0344
	ECG w/Welcome to Medicare	G0366
	Hemoccult, guaiac	G0107
	Flu shot	G0008
	Pneumonia shot	G0009
	Consultation/preop clearance	
	Exp problem focused	99242
	Detailed	99243
	Comp/mod complex	99244
	Comp/high complex	99245
	Other services	
	After posted hours	99050
	Evening/weekend appointment	99051
	Home health certification	G0180
	Home health recertification	G0179
	Care Plan oversight	99374
	Care Plan Oversight >30 mins	99375
	Post-op follow-up	99024
	Prolonged/60min total	99354
	Prolonged/each add 30 mins	99355
	Special reports/forms	99080
	Disability/Workers comp	99455
	Smoking Cessation <10 mins	99406
	Smoking Cessation >10 mins	99407
	ETOH/SA screening <30 mins	99408
	Online E/M by MD	99444
	Phone E/M <10 mins	99441
	Phone E/M <20 mins	99442
	Phone E/M <30 mins	99443
	Anticoagulant Mgmt <90 days	99363
	Anticoagulant Mgmt >90 days	99364
	In office emergency serv	99058
	Other services	
	Supplies	
	Surgical Tray	99070
	Instructions:	

Adx to observation today

x	Office procedures		
✓	Cerumen removal		69210
✓	ECG, w/interpretation		93000
	ECG, rhythm strip		93040
	Endometrial biopsy		58100
	Fracture care, cast/splint		
	Site: ______________		
	Nebulizer		94640
	Nebulizer demo		94664
	Spirometry		94010
	Spirometry, pre and post		94060
	Vasectomy		55250
	Skin procedures		**Units**
	Foreign body, skin, simple	10120	
	Foreign body, skin, complex	10121	
	I&D, abscess	10060	
	I&D, hematoma/seroma	10140	
	Laceration repair, simple	120__	
	Site: _______ Size: _____		
	Laceration repair, layered	120__	
	Site: _______ Size: _____		
	Laser Light Tx	96597	
	Lesion, biopsy, one	11100	
	Lesion, biopsy, each add'l	11101	
	Lesion, excision, benign	114__	
	Site: _______ Size: _____		
	Lesion, excision, malignant	116__	
	Site: _______ Size: _____		
	Lesion, paring/cutting, one	11055	
	Lesion, paring/cutting, 2-4	11056	
	Lesion, shave	113__	
	Site: _______ Size: _____		
	Nail removal, partial (+T mod)	11730	
	Nail rem, w/matrix (+T mod)	11750	
	Skin tag, 1-15	11200	
	Wart, flat, 1-14	17110	
	Destruction lesion, 1st	17000	
	Destruct lesion, each addl 2-14	17003	
	Medications		**Units**
	Ampicillin, up to 500mg	J0290	
	B-12, up to 1,000 mcg	J3420	
	Epinephrine, up to 1ml	J0170	
	Kenalog, 10mg	J3301	
	Lidocaine, 10mg	J2001	
	Normal saline, 1000cc	J7030	
	Phenergan, up to 50mg	J2550	
	Progesterone, 150mg	J1055	
	Rocephin, 250mg	J0696	
	Testosterone, 200mg	J1080	
	Tigan, up to 200 mg	J3250	
	Toradol, 15mg	J1885	
	Albuterol	J7609	
	Depo-Provera 50 mg	J1055	
	Depo-Medrol 40 mg	J1030	

Diagnoses		Code
1 A-fib		
2 ATN		
3		
4		

Next office visit:

Recheck • Preventative • PRN

Referral to:

Physician signature

X Sarah Mendenhall MD

x	Laboratory		-90
✓	Venipuncture	36415	
	Blood glucose, monitoring device	82962	
	Blood glucose, visual dipstick	82948	
✓	CBC, w/ auto differential	85025	
	CBC, w/o auto differential	85027	
	Cholesterol	82465	
	Hemoccult, guaiac	82270	
	Hemoccult, immunoassay	82274	
	Hemoglobin A1C	85018	
	Lipid panel	80061	
	Liver panel	80076	
	KOH prep (skin, hair, nails)	87220	
	Metabolic panel, basic	80048	
✓	Metabolic panel, comprehensive	80053	
	Mononucleosis	86308	
	Pregnancy, blood	84703	
	Pregnancy, urine	81025	
	Renal panel	80069	
	Sedimentation rate	85651	
	Strep, rapid	86403	
	Strep culture	87081	
	Strep A	87880	
	TB	86580	
	UA, complete, non-automated	81000	
	UA, w/o micro, non-automated	81002	
	UA, w/ micro, non-automated	81003	
	Urine colony count	87086	
	Urine culture, presumptive	87088	
	Wet mount/KOH	87210	

x	Vaccines	
	DT, <7 y	90702
	DTP	90701
	DtaP, <7 y	90700
	Flu, 6-35 months	90657
	Flu, 3 y +	90658
	Hep A, adult	90632
	Hep A, ped/adol, 2 dose	90633
	Hep B, adult	90746
	Hep B, ped/adol 3 dose	90744
	Hep B-Hib	90748
	Hib, 4 dose	90645
	HPV	90649
	IPV	90713
	MMR	90707
	Pneumonia, >2 y	90732
	Pneumonia conjugate, <5 y	90669
	Td, >7 y	90718
	Varicella	90716
	Tetanus toxoid adsorbed, IM	90703

x	Immunizations & Injections		Units
	Allergen, one	95115	
	Allergen, multiple	95117	
	Imm admn <8 yo 1st Inj	90465	
	Imm admn <8 yo each add inj	90466	
	Imm <8 yo oral or intranasal	90467	
	Imm admn <8 yo each add	90468	
	Imm admin, one vacc	90471	
	Imm admin, each add'l	90472	
	Imm admin, intranasal, one	90473	
	Imm admin, intranasal, each add'l	90474	
	Injection, joint, small	20600	
	Injection, joint, intermediate	20605	
	Injection, ther/proph/diag	90772	
	Injection, trigger pt 1-2 musc	20552	

Today's charges:		
Today's payment:		
Balance due:		

Job 6 & 9 Router- Francesco Alvarez

Date of service: 10/26/09	Insurance: MEDICAID		Superbill Number: 1490
Patient name: JOHN WITTMER	Coinsurance:	Copay: 2.00	Physician Name: KEMPER
Account #: WIT001	Noncovered Waiver?	yes / no / n/a	

X	Office visit	New	X	Est
	Minimal (RN only)			99211
	Problem focused	99201		99212
	Exp problem focused	99202		99213
	Detailed	99203		99214
	Comp	99204		99215
	Comprhen/Complex	99205		
	Well visit	**New**	**X**	**Est**
	< 1 y	99381		99391
	1-4 y	99382		99392
	5-11 y	99383		99393
	12-17 y	99384		99394
	18-39 y	99385		99395
	40-64 y	99386	✓	99396
	65 y +	99387		99397

X	Medicare preventive services	
	Pap	Q0091
	Pelvic & breast	G0101
	Prostate/PSA	G0103
	Tobacco couns/3-10 min	G0375
	Tobacco couns/>10 min	G0376
	Welcome to Medicare exam	G0344
	ECG w/Welcome to Medicare	G0366
	Hemoccult, guaiac	G0107
	Flu shot	G0008
	Pneumonia shot	G0009
	Consultation/preop clearance	
	Exp problem focused	99242
	Detailed	99243
	Comp/mod complex	99244
	Comp/high complex	99245
	Other services	
	After posted hours	99050
	Evening/weekend appointment	99051
	Home health certification	G0180
	Home health recertification	G0179
	Care Plan oversight	99374
	Care Plan Oversight >30 mins	99375
	Post-op follow-up	99024
	Prolonged/60min total	99354
	Prolonged/each add 30 mins	99355
	Special reports/forms	99080
	Disability/Workers comp	99455
✓	Smoking Cessation <10 mins	99406
	Smoking Cessation >10 mins	99407
	ETOH/SA screening <30 mins	99408
	Online E/M by MD	99444
	Phone E/M <10 mins	99441
	Phone E/M <20 mins	99442
	Phone E/M <30 mins	99443
	Anticoagulant Mgmt <90 days	99363
	Anticoagulant Mgmt >90 days	99364
	In office emergency serv	99058
	Other services	
	Supplies	
	Surgical Tray	99070

X	Office procedures		
	Cerumen removal		69210
	ECG, w/interpretation		93000
	ECG, rhythm strip		93040
	Endometrial biopsy		58100
	Fracture care, cast/splint Site: ______		____
	Nebulizer		94640
	Nebulizer demo		94664
	Spirometry		94010
	Spirometry, pre and post		94060
	Vasectomy		55250
	Skin procedures		**Units**
	Foreign body, skin, simple	10120	
	Foreign body, skin, complex	10121	
	I&D, abscess	10060	
	I&D, hematoma/seroma	10140	
	Laceration repair, simple Site: ______ Size: ____	120__	
	Laceration repair, layered Site: ______ Size: ____	120__	
	Laser Light Tx	96597	
	Lesion, biopsy, one	11100	
	Lesion, biopsy, each add'l	11101	
	Lesion, excision, benign Site: ______ Size: ____	114__	
	Lesion, excision, malignant Site: ______ Size: ____	116__	
	Lesion, paring/cutting, one	11055	
	Lesion, paring/cutting, 2-4	11056	
	Lesion, shave Site: ______ Size: ____	113__	
	Nail removal, partial (+T mod)	11730	
	Nail rem, w/matrix (+T mod)	11750	
	Skin tag, 1-15	11200	
	Wart, flat, 1-14	17110	
	Destruction lesion, 1st	17000	
	Destruct lesion, each addl 2-14	17003	
	Medications		**Units**
	Ampicillin, up to 500mg	J0290	
	B-12, up to 1,000 mcg	J3420	
	Epinephrine, up to 1ml	J0170	
	Kenalog, 10mg	J3301	
	Lidocaine, 10mg	J2001	
	Normal saline, 1000cc	J7030	
	Phenergan, up to 50mg	J2550	
	Progesterone, 150mg	J1055	
	Rocephin, 250mg	J0696	
	Testosterone, 200mg	J1080	
	Tigan, up to 200 mg	J3250	
	Toradol, 15mg	J1885	
	Albuterol	J7609	
	Depo-Provera 50 mg	J1055	
	Depo-Medrol 40 mg	J1030	

Diagnoses		Code
1 Well check		
2 Tobacco Abuse		
3		
4		

Next office visit: 1 yr

Recheck • Preventative • / PRN

Referral to:

X	Laboratory		-90
	Venipuncture	36415	
	Blood glucose, monitoring device	82962	
	Blood glucose, visual dipstick	82948	
	CBC, w/ auto differential	85025	
	CBC, w/o auto differential	85027	
	Cholesterol	82465	
	Hemoccult, guaiac	82270	
	Hemoccult, immunoassay	82274	
	Hemoglobin A1C	85018	
	Lipid panel	80061	
	Liver panel	80076	
	KOH prep (skin, hair, nails)	87220	
	Metabolic panel, basic	80048	
	Metabolic panel, comprehensive	80053	
	Mononucleosis	86308	
	Pregnancy, blood	84703	
	Pregnancy, urine	81025	
	Renal panel	80069	
	Sedimentation rate	85651	
	Strep, rapid	86403	
	Strep culture	87081	
	Strep A	87880	
	TB	86580	
	UA, complete, non-automated	81000	
	UA, w/o micro, non-automated	81002	
	UA, w/ micro, non-automated	81003	
	Urine colony count	87086	
	Urine culture, presumptive	87088	
	Wet mount/KOH	87210	
	Vaccines		
	DT, <7 y		90702
	DTP		90701
	DtaP, <7 y		90700
	Flu, 6-35 months		90657
	Flu, 3 y +		90658
	Hep A, adult		90632
	Hep A, ped/adol, 2 dose		90633
	Hep B, adult		90746
	Hep B, ped/adol 3 dose		90744
	Hep B-Hib		90748
	Hib, 4 dose		90645
	HPV		90649
	IPV		90713
	MMR		90707
	Pneumonia, >2 y		90732
	Pneumonia conjugate, <5 y		90669
	Td, >7 y		90718
	Varicella		90716
	Tetanus toxoid adsorbed, IM		90703
	Immunizations & Injections		**Units**
	Allergen, one	95115	
	Allergen, multiple	95117	
	Imm admn <8 yo 1st Inj	90465	
	Imm admn <8 yo each add inj	90466	
	Imm <8 yo oral or intranasal	90467	
	Imm admn <8 yo each add	90468	
	Imm admn, one vacc	90471	
	Imm admn, each add'l	90472	
	Imm admin, intranasal, one	90473	
	Imm admin, intranasal, each add'l	90474	
	Injection, joint, small	20600	
	Injection, joint, intermediate	20605	
	Injection, ther/proph/diag	90772	
	Injection, trigger pt 1-2 musc	20552	

Instructions:

Rx: Zyban

Physician signature	Today's charges:	
X Sally Kemper	Today's payment:	2.00 cash
	Balance due:	

Job 8 & 11 Router- John Wittmer

Date of service: 10/26/09	Insurance: SELF PAY	Superbill Number: 1494
Patient name: RYAN ASHBY	Coinsurance: / Copay:	Physician Name: MURRAY
Account #: ASH001	Noncovered Waiver? yes / no / n/a	

x	Office visit	New	x	Est
	Minimal (RN only)			99211
	Problem focused	99201		99212
	Exp problem focused	99202	✓	99213
	Detailed	99203		99214
	Comp	99204		99215
	Comprhen/Complex	99205		

x	Well visit	New	x	Est
	< 1 y	99381		99391
	1-4 y	99382		99392
	5-11 y	99383		99393
	12-17 y	99384		99394
	18-39 y	99385		99395
	40-64 y	99386		99396
	65 y +	99387		99397

x	Medicare preventive services	
	Pap	Q0091
	Pelvic & breast	G0101
	Prostate/PSA	G0103
	Tobacco couns/3-10 min	G0375
	Tobacco couns/>10 min	G0376
	Welcome to Medicare exam	G0344
	ECG w/Welcome to Medicare	G0366
	Hemoccult, guaiac	G0107
	Flu shot	G0008
	Pneumonia shot	G0009

x	Consultation/preop clearance	
	Exp problem focused	99242
	Detailed	99243
	Comp/mod complex	99244
	Comp/high complex	99245

x	Other services	
	After posted hours	99050
	Evening/weekend appointment	99051
	Home health certification	G0180
	Home health recertification	G0179
	Care Plan oversight	99374
	Care Plan Oversight >30 mins	99375
	Post-op follow-up	99024
	Prolonged/60min total	99354
	Prolonged/each add 30 mins	99355
	Special reports/forms	99080
	Disability/Workers comp	99455
	Smoking Cessation <10 mins	99406
	Smoking Cessation >10 mins	99407
	ETOH/SA screening <30 mins	99408
	Online E/M by MD	99444
	Phone E/M <10 mins	99441
	Phone E/M <20 mins	99442
	Phone E/M <30 mins	99443
	Anticoagulant Mgmt <90 days	99363
	Anticoagulant Mgmt >90 days	99364
	In office emergency serv	99058

x	Other services	

x	Supplies	
✓	Surgical Tray	99070

Instructions:

Return 10 days for suture removal

x	Office procedures	
	Cerumen removal	69210
	ECG, w/interpretation	93000
	ECG, rhythm strip	93040
	Endometrial biopsy	58100
	Fracture care, cast/splint	
	Site: ______________	
	Nebulizer	94640
	Nebulizer demo	94664
	Spirometry	94010
	Spirometry, pre and post	94060
	Vasectomy	55250

x	Skin procedures		Units
	Foreign body, skin, simple	10120	
	Foreign body, skin, complex	10121	
	I&D, abscess	10060	
	I&D, hematoma/seroma	10140	
✓	Laceration repair, simple	120__	
	Site: Rt hand Size: 3 cm		
	Laceration repair, layered	120__	
	Site: _______ Size: _____		
	Laser Light Tx	96597	
	Lesion, biopsy, one	11100	
	Lesion, biopsy, each add'l	11101	
	Lesion, excision, benign	114__	
	Site: _______ Size: _____		
	Lesion, excision, malignant	116__	
	Site: _______ Size: _____		
	Lesion, paring/cutting, one	11055	
	Lesion, paring/cutting, 2-4	11056	
	Lesion, shave	113__	
	Site: _______ Size: _____		
	Nail removal, partial (+T mod)	11730	
	Nail rem, w/matrix (+T mod)	11750	
	Skin tag, 1-15	11200	
	Wart, flat, 1-14	17110	
	Destruction lesion, 1st	17000	
	Destruct lesion, each addl 2-14	17003	

x	Medications		Units
	Ampicillin, up to 500mg	J0290	
	B-12, up to 1,000 mcg	J3420	
	Epinephrine, up to 1ml	J0170	
	Kenalog, 10mg	J3301	
	Lidocaine, 10mg	J2001	
	Normal saline, 1000cc	J7030	
	Phenergan, up to 50mg	J2550	
	Progesterone, 150mg	J1055	
	Rocephin, 250mg	J0696	
	Testosterone, 200mg	J1080	
	Tigan, up to 200 mg	J3250	
	Toradol, 15mg	J1885	
	Albuterol	J7609	
	Depo-Provera 50 mg	J1055	
	Depo-Medrol 40 mg	J1030	

Diagnoses	Code
1 Laceration Rt hand	
2	
3	
4	

Next office visit:

Recheck • Preventative • PRN

Referral to:

Physician signature

x [signature] MD

x	Laboratory		-90
	Venipuncture	36415	
	Blood glucose, monitoring device	82962	
	Blood glucose, visual dipstick	82948	
	CBC, w/ auto differential	85025	
	CBC, w/o auto differential	85027	
	Cholesterol	82465	
	Hemoccult, guaiac	82270	
	Hemoccult, immunoassay	82274	
	Hemoglobin A1C	85018	
	Lipid panel	80061	
	Liver panel	80076	
	KOH prep (skin, hair, nails)	87220	
	Metabolic panel, basic	80048	
	Metabolic panel, comprehensive	80053	
	Mononucleosis	86308	
	Pregnancy, blood	84703	
	Pregnancy, urine	81025	
	Renal panel	80069	
	Sedimentation rate	85651	
	Strep, rapid	86403	
	Strep culture	87081	
	Strep A	87880	
	TB	86580	
	UA, complete, non-automated	81000	
	UA, w/o micro, non-automated	81002	
	UA, w/ micro, non-automated	81003	
	Urine colony count	87086	
	Urine culture, presumptive	87088	
	Wet mount/KOH	87210	

x	Vaccines	
	DT, <7 y	90702
	DTP	90701
	DtaP, <7 y	90700
	Flu, 6-35 months	90657
	Flu, 3 y +	90658
	Hep A, adult	90632
	Hep A, ped/adol, 2 dose	90633
	Hep B, adult	90746
	Hep B, ped/adol 3 dose	90744
	Hep B-Hib	90748
	Hib, 4 dose	90645
	HPV	90649
	IPV	90713
	MMR	90707
	Pneumonia, >2 y	90732
	Pneumonia conjugate, <5 y	90669
	Td, >7 y	90718
	Varicella	90716
	Tetanus toxoid adsorbed, IM	90703

x	Immunizations & Injections		Units
	Allergen, one	95115	
	Allergen, multiple	95117	
	Imm admn <8 yo 1st Inj	90465	
	Imm admn <8 yo each add inj	90466	
	Imm <8 yo oral or intranasal	90467	
	Imm admn <8 yo each add	90468	
	Imm admin, one vacc	90471	
	Imm admin, each add'l	90472	
	Imm admin, intranasal, one	90473	
	Imm admin, intranasal, each add'l	90474	
	Injection, joint, small	20600	
	Injection, joint, intermediate	20605	
	Injection, ther/proph/diag	90772	
	Injection, trigger pt 1-2 musc	20552	

Today's charges:	
Today's payment:	
Balance due:	

Job 16 Router- Ryan Ashby

Cigna Health Network
Copay: $20.00 PCP/$30.00 Spec

William Turner
Policy No: 6161271B
Group No: H41776
PO Box 10520, Scranton, PA 17593 (800)555-8899

Job 24 & 26 Insurance Card

Douglasville Medicine Associates
Patient Registration Form

Patients must complete all information prior to seeing the physician. A copy of your insurance card(s) and driver's license will be made for your file.

Patient Name: WILLIAM TURNER Date of Birth: 10 / 16 / 73
Sex: (Male) or Female Social Security Number: 471 - 16 - 5555 Marital Status: S
Address Line 1: 16 MORGAN BLVD
Address Line 2: APT B
City: WOLCOTT
State: NY Zip Code: 14654
Home Telephone: (717) 555-1122 Work Telephone: (717) 555-6116
Cellular Telephone: (717) 555-4716 Email address: horsetrailer@ny.rr.com

Patient's Work Status (Full-Time, Part-Time, Retired, Student): ____________
Employer Name: CHARLIE'S STEAKHOUSE
Address Line 1: 417 ASHLEY AVENUE
Address Line 2: ____________
City: SYRACUSE State: NY Zip: 14816
Telephone: (SAME
If patient is a minor, who is the primary guardian? ____________

Primary Insurance Company: CIGNA
Subscriber ID Number 6161271B Policy Group #: H41776
Subscriber Name: SAME Birth date: SAME
Subscriber Social Security Number: SAME - Relationship to patient: SELF

Secondary Insurance Company: ____________
Subscriber ID Number ____________ Policy Group #: ____________
Subscriber Name: ____________ Birth date: ____________
Subscriber Social Security Number: ____-____-____ Relationship to patient: ____________

Complete this section if your treatment is for an injury or accident.
Were you injured at work? ______ Is this covered by Workers' Compensation? ______
If Yes, Contact person at your Employer ____________
Were you involved in an auto accident? ______ Provide insurance company, contact information, and claim number: ____________

Date & time of Accident ____________ Place of Accident ____________
How did injury happen? ____________
Name of Physician who treated you at time of accident: ____________

Financial Responsibility Statement/ Release of Information Authorization
"I authorize the release of any medical information necessary to my insurance company and the Payment of Benefits to the Physician for services provided.

X [signature] Date 10/26/09
Signature of Patient or Legal Guardian

Job 24 Registration Paper work- William Turner 1 of 5

Douglasville Medicine Associates
Patient Registration Form

OUR FINANCIAL POLICY

By law, we must collect your carrier designated co-pay at the time of service. Please be prepared to pay that co-pay at each visit. We are also required to collect any portion of the deductible that has not been satisfied. If your plan requires a coinsurance instead of a co-pay and we participate with the plan, we will accept the designated payment and bill you accordingly for any deductible and coinsurance your plan indicates you are responsible for on their explanation of benefits.

Payment is expected at the time of service unless other financial arrangements have been made prior to your visit. If you are uninsured, you may qualify for a hardship discount. Ask one of our staff members for more information.

You are responsible for timely payment of your account. Douglasville Medicine Associates reserves the right to reschedule or deny a future appointment on delinquent accounts.

WE ACCEPT CASH, CHECKS, MASTERCARD AND VISA

THANK YOU for taking the time to review our policy.

William Turner ______________________ 10/24/09 ____________

(Responsible Party Signature) (Date)

Job 24 Registration Paper work- William Turner 2 of 5

Douglasville Medicine Associates
5076 Brand Blvd., Suite 401•Douglasville, NY 01234 (123)456-7890

Patient Name:______________________________

Record #:_____________

I acknowledge that I have received a written copy of Douglasville Medicine Associates Notice of Patient Privacy Practices. I also acknowledge that I have been allowed to ask questions concerning this notice and my rights under this notice. I understand that this form will be part of my record until such time as I may choose to revoke this acknowledgement. If I am not the patient, I am the authorized representative of a minor child or authorized by law to act for and on the patient's behalf.

William Turner ____________________ 10/26/09 ______________

Signature of Patient or Authorized Agent Date

Patient (or authorized agent) refused to sign Notice of Privacy Practices.

Please describe events. ____

____

__________________________ ______________

Signature of DMA Employee Date

Job 24 Registration Paper work- William Turner 3 of 5

Douglasville Medicine Associates
5076 Brand Blvd., Suite 401▪Douglasville, NY 01234

CONSENT TO TREATMENT

Patient Name: ____________________ Date: 10/24/09

I, ____________________, hereby voluntarily consent to outpatient treatment and evaluation at Douglasville Medicine Associates for ____________________. This includes routine diagnostic procedures, examination and medical treatment including, but not limited to, routine laboratory work (such as blood, urine and other studies), x-rays, heart tracing and administration of medications prescribed by the physician.

I further consent to the performance of those diagnostic procedures, examinations and rendering of medical treatment by the medical staff and their assistants.

I understand that this consent form will be valid and remain in effect as long as I receive medical care at Douglasville Medicine Associates.

This form has been explained to me and I fully understand this Consent To Treatment and agree to its contents.

William Turner
____
Signature of Patient or
Person Authorized to consent for patient

____
Relationship to patient

____
Signature of Witness

Job 24 Registration Paper work- William Turner 4 of 5

Douglasville Medicine Associates
5076 Brand Blvd, Suite 401~ Douglasville, NY 01234

ASSIGNMENT OF BENEFITS AND PATIENT REPRESENTATION

Patient Name:______________________________ Chart # ________________

Insured Name:______________________________________

Insurance Company Name ______________________________________

Policy # ______________________ Group # ______________________

I hereby assign all medical and/or surgical benefits, to include major medical benefits to which I am entitled, to **Douglasville Medicine Associates**. This assignment will remain in effect until revoked by me in writing. A photocopy of this assignment is to be considered as valid as the original.

I understand that I am financially responsible for all charges whether or not paid by my insurance carrier. I understand that I will be responsible for any court costs or collection fees should it become necessary to take action to collect for services/supplies rendered.

I hereby authorize **Douglasville Medicine Associates** to release all medical information necessary to secure payment on my account.

I hereby authorize **Douglasville Medicine Associates** and medical billing staff members, to submit claims, on my behalf, to the insurance company listed on the copy of the current and valid insurance card I have provided to the Clinic in good faith. I fully agree and understand that the submission of a claim does not absolve me of my responsibility to ensure that the bill for medical services is paid in full.

I authorize **Douglasville Medicine Associates** and its medical billing representative, to be my personal representative, which allows the Clinic to: (1) submit any and all appeals when my insurance company performs an adverse benefit determination as defined in 29 CFR 2560-503-1, (2) submit any and all requests for benefit information from my employer and/or health insurance company, and (3) initiate formal complaints to any State or Federal agency that has jurisdiction over my benefits.

I fully understand and agree that I am responsible for full payment of the medical debt I owe the Clinic, if my insurance company has refused to pay 100% of my covered benefits, within ninety (90) days of any and all appeals or request for information. A photocopy of this document shall be considered as effective and valid as the original.

Patient ______________________ 10/24/09
(signature) (date)

Patient Representative ______________________
(date)

Relationship to Patient ______________________

Witness ______________________
(signature) (date)

Job 24 Registration Paper work- William Turner 5 of 5

Date of service: 10/26/09	Insurance: CIGNA				Superbill Number: 1492
Patient name: WILLIAM TURNER	Coinsurance:	Copay:			Physician Name: KEMPER
Account #: TUR001	Noncovered Waiver?	yes	no	n/a	

x	Office visit	New	x	Est
	Minimal (RN only)			99211
	Problem focused	99201		99212
✓	Exp problem focused	99202		99213
	Detailed	99203		99214
	Comp	99204		99215
	Comprhen/Complex	99205		
	Well visit	**New**	**x**	**Est**
	< 1 y	99381		99391
	1-4 y	99382		99392
	5-11 y	99383		99393
	12-17 y	99384		99394
	18-39 y	99385		99395
	40-64 y	99386		99396
	65 y +	99387		99397
	Medicare preventive services			
	Pap			Q0091
	Pelvic & breast			G0101
	Prostate/PSA			G0103
	Tobacco couns/3-10 min			G0375
	Tobacco couns/>10 min			G0376
	Welcome to Medicare exam			G0344
	ECG w/Welcome to Medicare			G0366
	Hemoccult, guaiac			G0107
	Flu shot			G0008
	Pneumonia shot			G0009
	Consultation/preop clearance			
	Exp problem focused			99242
	Detailed			99243
	Comp/mod complex			99244
	Comp/high complex			99245
	Other services			
	After posted hours			99050
	Evening/weekend appointment			99051
	Home health certification			G0180
	Home health recertification			G0179
	Care Plan oversight			99374
	Care Plan Oversight >30 mins			99375
	Post-op follow-up			99024
	Prolonged/60min total			99354
	Prolonged/each add 30 mins			99355
	Special reports/forms			99080
	Disability/Workers comp			99455
	Smoking Cessation <10 mins			99406
	Smoking Cessation >10 mins			99407
	ETOH/SA screening <30 mins			99408
	Online E/M by MD			99444
	Phone E/M <10 mins			99441
	Phone E/M <20 mins			99442
	Phone E/M <30 mins			99443
	Anticoagulant Mgmt <90 days			99363
	Anticoagulant Mgmt >90 days			99364
	In office emergency serv			99058
	Other services			
	PCR antigen amplified probe			
	Supplies			
	Surgical Tray			99070

x	Office procedures		
	Cerumen removal		69210
	ECG, w/interpretation		93000
	ECG, rhythm strip		93040
	Endometrial biopsy		58100
	Fracture care, cast/splint Site: ______________		
	Nebulizer		94640
	Nebulizer demo		94664
	Spirometry		94010
	Spirometry, pre and post		94060
	Vasectomy		55250
	Skin procedures		**Units**
	Foreign body, skin, simple	10120	
	Foreign body, skin, complex	10121	
	I&D, abscess	10060	
	I&D, hematoma/seroma	10140	
	Laceration repair, simple Site: _______ Size: _____	120__	
	Laceration repair, layered Site: _______ Size: _____	120__	
	Laser Light Tx	96597	
	Lesion, biopsy, one	11100	
	Lesion, biopsy, each add'l	11101	
	Lesion, excision, benign Site: _______ Size: _____	114__	
	Lesion, excision, malignant Site: _______ Size: _____	116__	
	Lesion, paring/cutting, one	11055	
	Lesion, paring/cutting, 2-4	11056	
	Lesion, shave Site: _______ Size: _____	113__	
	Nail removal, partial (+T mod)	11730	
	Nail rem, w/matrix (+T mod)	11750	
	Skin tag, 1-15	11200	
	Wart, flat, 1-14	17110	
	Destruction lesion, 1st	17000	
	Destruct lesion, each addl 2-14	17003	
	Medications		**Units**
	Ampicillin, up to 500mg	J0290	
	B-12, up to 1,000 mcg	J3420	
	Epinephrine, up to 1ml	J0170	
	Kenalog, 10mg	J3301	
	Lidocaine, 10mg	J2001	
	Normal saline, 1000cc	J7030	
	Phenergan, up to 50mg	J2550	
	Progesterone, 150mg	J1055	
	Rocephin, 250mg	J0696	
	Testosterone, 200mg	J1080	
	Tigan, up to 200 mg	J3250	
	Toradol, 15mg	J1885	
	Albuterol	J7609	
	Depo-Provera 50 mg	J1055	
	Depo-Medrol 40 mg	J1030	

Diagnoses	Code
1 Herpes Simplex Virus	
2	
3	
4	

x	Laboratory		-90
✓	Venipuncture	36415	
	Blood glucose, monitoring device	82962	
	Blood glucose, visual dipstick	82948	
	CBC, w/ auto differential	85025	
	CBC, w/o auto differential	85027	
	Cholesterol	82465	
	Hemoccult, guaiac	82270	
	Hemoccult, immunoassay	82274	
	Hemoglobin A1C	85018	
	Lipid panel	80061	
	Liver panel	80076	
	KOH prep (skin, hair, nails)	87220	
	Metabolic panel, basic	80048	
	Metabolic panel, comprehensive	80053	
	Mononucleosis	86308	
	Pregnancy, blood	84703	
	Pregnancy, urine	81025	
	Renal panel	80069	
	Sedimentation rate	85651	
	Strep, rapid	86403	
	Strep culture	87081	
	Strep A	87880	
	TB	86580	
	UA, complete, non-automated	81000	
	UA, w/o micro, non-automated	81002	
	UA, w/ micro, non-automated	81003	
	Urine colony count	87086	
	Urine culture, presumptive	87088	
	Wet mount/KOH	87210	
	Vaccines		
	DT, <7 y		90702
	DTP		90701
	DtaP, <7 y		90700
	Flu, 6-35 months		90657
	Flu, 3 y +		90658
	Hep A, adult		90632
	Hep A, ped/adol, 2 dose		90633
	Hep B, adult		90746
	Hep B, ped/adol 3 dose		90744
	Hep B-Hib		90748
	Hib, 4 dose		90645
	HPV		90649
	IPV		90713
	MMR		90707
	Pneumonia, >2 y		90732
	Pneumonia conjugate, <5 y		90669
	Td, >7 y		90718
	Varicella		90716
	Tetanus toxoid adsorbed, IM		90703
	Immunizations & Injections		**Units**
	Allergen, one	95115	
	Allergen, multiple	95117	
	Imm admn <8 yo 1st Inj	90465	
	Imm admn <8 yo each add inj	90466	
	Imm <8 yo oral or intranasal	90467	
	Imm admn <8 yo each add	90468	
	Imm admin, one vacc	90471	
	Imm admin, each add'l	90472	
	Imm admin, intranasal, one	90473	
	Imm admin, intranasal, each add'l	90474	
	Injection, joint, small	20600	
	Injection, joint, intermediate	20605	
	Injection, ther/proph/diag	90772	
	Injection, trigger pt 1-2 musc	20552	

Instructions:

Return 3wks F/U

Rx Viroxyn

Next office visit:
Recheck • Preventative • PRN

Referral to:

Physician signature

x [signature]

Today's charges:		
Today's payment:		
Balance due:		

Job 26 Router- William Turner

Date of service: 10/26/09	Insurance: FLEXIHEALTH PPO		Superbill Number: 1493
Patient name: CAITLIN BARRYMORE	Coinsurance:	Copay: 20.00	Physician Name: HEATH
Account #: BAR001	Noncovered Waiver?	yes / no / n/a	

X	Office visit	New	X	Est
	Minimal (RN only)			99211
	Problem focused	99201		99212
	Exp problem focused	99202		99213
	Detailed	99203	✓	99214
	Comp	99204		99215
	Comprhen/Complex	99205		
X	**Well visit**	**New**	**X**	**Est**
	< 1 y	99381		99391
	1-4 y	99382		99392
	5-11 y	99383		99393
	12-17 y	99384		99394
	18-39 y	99385		99395
	40-64 y	99386		99396
	65 y +	99387		99397

X	Medicare preventive services	
	Pap	Q0091
	Pelvic & breast	G0101
	Prostate/PSA	G0103
	Tobacco couns/3-10 min	G0375
	Tobacco couns/>10 min	G0376
	Welcome to Medicare exam	G0344
	ECG w/Welcome to Medicare	G0366
	Hemoccult, guaiac	G0107
	Flu shot	G0008
	Pneumonia shot	G0009
	Consultation/preop clearance	
	Exp problem focused	99242
	Detailed	99243
	Comp/mod complex	99244
	Comp/high complex	99245
	Other services	
	After posted hours	99050
	Evening/weekend appointment	99051
	Home health certification	G0180
	Home health recertification	G0179
	Care Plan oversight	99374
	Care Plan Oversight >30 mins	99375
	Post-op follow-up	99024
	Prolonged/60min total	99354
	Prolonged/each add 30 mins	99355
	Special reports/forms	99080
	Disability/Workers comp	99455
	Smoking Cessation <10 mins	99406
	Smoking Cessation >10 mins	99407
	ETOH/SA screening <30 mins	99408
	Online E/M by MD	99444
	Phone E/M <10 mins	99441
	Phone E/M <20 mins	99442
	Phone E/M <30 mins	99443
	Anticoagulant Mgmt <90 days	99363
	Anticoagulant Mgmt >90 days	99364
	In office emergency serv	99058
	Other services	
	VDRL	
	Pelvic Exam	
	Supplies	
	Surgical Tray	99070

Instructions:

F/U VDRL LAB

X	Office procedures		
	Cerumen removal		69210
	ECG, w/interpretation		93000
	ECG, rhythm strip		93040
	Endometrial biopsy		58100
	Fracture care, cast/splint Site: ________________		______
	Nebulizer		94640
	Nebulizer demo		94664
	Spirometry		94010
	Spirometry, pre and post		94060
	Vasectomy		55250
	Skin procedures		**Units**
	Foreign body, skin, simple	10120	
	Foreign body, skin, complex	10121	
	I&D, abscess	10060	
	I&D, hematoma/seroma	10140	
	Laceration repair, simple Site: _______ Size: _____	120__	
	Laceration repair, layered Site: _______ Size: _____	120__	
	Laser Light Tx	96597	
	Lesion, biopsy, one	11100	
	Lesion, biopsy, each add'l	11101	
	Lesion, excision, benign Site: _______ Size: _____	114__	
	Lesion, excision, malignant Site: _______ Size: _____	116__	
	Lesion, paring/cutting, one	11055	
	Lesion, paring/cutting, 2-4	11056	
	Lesion, shave Site: _______ Size: _____	113__	
	Nail removal, partial (+T mod)	11730	
	Nail rem, w/matrix (+T mod)	11750	
	Skin tag, 1-15	11200	
	Wart, flat, 1-14	17110	
	Destruction lesion, 1st	17000	
	Destruct lesion, each addl 2-14	17003	
	Medications		**Units**
	Ampicillin, up to 500mg	J0290	
	B-12, up to 1,000 mcg	J3420	
	Epinephrine, up to 1ml	J0170	
	Kenalog, 10mg	J3301	
	Lidocaine, 10mg	J2001	
	Normal saline, 1000cc	J7030	
	Phenergan, up to 50mg	J2550	
	Progesterone, 150mg	J1055	
	Rocephin, 250mg	J0696	
	Testosterone, 200mg	J1080	
	Tigan, up to 200 mg	J3250	
	Toradol, 15mg	J1885	
	Albuterol	J7609	
	Depo-Provera 50 mg	J1055	
	Depo-Medrol 40 mg	J1030	

Diagnoses	Code
1 Abdominal Pain	
2 Fatigue	
3 Possible VD	
4	

Next office visit: 1 wk
Recheck • Preventative • PRN
Referral to:

X	Laboratory		-90
✓	Venipuncture	36415	
	Blood glucose, monitoring device	82962	
	Blood glucose, visual dipstick	82948	
	CBC, w/ auto differential	85025	
	CBC, w/o auto differential	85027	
	Cholesterol	82465	
	Hemoccult, guaiac	82270	
	Hemoccult, immunoassay	82274	
	Hemoglobin A1C	85018	
	Lipid panel	80061	
	Liver panel	80076	
	KOH prep (skin, hair, nails)	87220	
	Metabolic panel, basic	80048	
	Metabolic panel, comprehensive	80053	
✓	Mononucleosis	86308	✓
	Pregnancy, blood	84703	
	Pregnancy, urine	81025	
	Renal panel	80069	
	Sedimentation rate	85651	
	Strep, rapid	86403	
	Strep culture	87081	
	Strep A	87880	
	TB	86580	
	UA, complete, non-automated	81000	
	UA, w/o micro, non-automated	81002	
✓	UA, w/ micro, non-automated	81003	✓
	Urine colony count	87086	
	Urine culture, presumptive	87088	
	Wet mount/KOH	87210	
	Vaccines		
	DT, <7 y		90702
	DTP		90701
	DtaP, <7 y		90700
	Flu, 6-35 months		90657
	Flu, 3 y +		90658
	Hep A, adult		90632
	Hep A, ped/adol, 2 dose		90633
	Hep B, adult		90746
	Hep B, ped/adol 3 dose		90744
	Hep B-Hib		90748
	Hib, 4 dose		90645
	HPV		90649
	IPV		90713
	MMR		90707
	Pneumonia, >2 y		90732
	Pneumonia conjugate, <5 y		90669
	Td, >7 y		90718
	Varicella		90716
	Tetanus toxoid adsorbed, IM		90703
	Immunizations & Injections		**Units**
	Allergen, one	95115	
	Allergen, multiple	95117	
	Imm admn <8 yo 1st Inj	90465	
	Imm admn <8 yo each add inj	90466	
	Imm <8 yo oral or intranasal	90467	
	Imm admn <8 yo each add	90468	
	Imm admn, one vacc	90471	
	Imm admn, each add'l	90472	
	Imm admn, intranasal, one	90473	
	Imm admn, intranasal, each add'l	90474	
	Injection, joint, small	20600	
	Injection, joint, intermediate	20605	
	Injection, ther/proph/diag	90772	
	Injection, trigger pt 1-2 musc	20552	

Physician signature		
x Alberta Lynn PA-C	Today's charges:	
	Today's payment:	20.00 #425
	Balance due:	

Job 27 Router- Caitlin Barrymore

Date of service: 10/26/09	Insurance: MANAGEMED				Superbill Number: 1495
Patient name: LAURA LEIGHTON	Coinsurance:	Copay: 15.00			Physician Name: MENDENHALL
Account #: LEI001	Noncovered Waiver?	yes	no	n/a	

x	Office visit	New	x	Est
	Minimal (RN only)			99211
	Problem focused	99201		99212
	Exp problem focused	99202		99213
	Detailed	99203	✓	99214
	Comp	99204		99215
	Comprhen/Complex	99205		
	Well visit	**New**	**x**	**Est**
	< 1 y	99381		99391
	1-4 y	99382		99392
	5-11 y	99383		99393
	12-17 y	99384		99394
	18-39 y	99385		99395
	40-64 y	99386		99396
	65 y +	99387		99397
	Medicare preventive services			
	Pap			Q0091
	Pelvic & breast			G0101
	Prostate/PSA			G0103
	Tobacco couns/3-10 min			G0375
	Tobacco couns/>10 min			G0376
	Welcome to Medicare exam			G0344
	ECG w/Welcome to Medicare			G0366
	Hemoccult, guaiac			G0107
	Flu shot			G0008
	Pneumonia shot			G0009
	Consultation/preop clearance			
	Exp problem focused			99242
	Detailed			99243
	Comp/mod complex			99244
	Comp/high complex			99245
	Other services			
	After posted hours			99050
	Evening/weekend appointment			99051
	Home health certification			G0180
	Home health recertification			G0179
	Care Plan oversight			99374
	Care Plan Oversight >30 mins			99375
	Post-op follow-up			99024
	Prolonged/60min total			99354
	Prolonged/each add 30 mins			99355
	Special reports/forms			99080
	Disability/Workers comp			99455
	Smoking Cessation <10 mins			99406
	Smoking Cessation >10 mins			99407
	ETOH/SA screening <30 mins			99408
	Online E/M by MD			99444
	Phone E/M <10 mins			99441
	Phone E/M <20 mins			99442
	Phone E/M <30 mins			99443
	Anticoagulant Mgmt <90 days			99363
	Anticoagulant Mgmt >90 days			99364
	In office emergency serv			99058
	Other services			
	Supplies			
	Surgical Tray			99070

Instructions:

Rx Refill

x	Office procedures		
	Cerumen removal		69210
	ECG, w/interpretation		93000
	ECG, rhythm strip		93040
	Endometrial biopsy		58100
	Fracture care, cast/splint Site: ____________		
	Nebulizer		94640
	Nebulizer demo		94664
	Spirometry		94010
	Spirometry, pre and post		94060
	Vasectomy		55250
	Skin procedures		**Units**
	Foreign body, skin, simple	10120	
	Foreign body, skin, complex	10121	
	I&D, abscess	10060	
	I&D, hematoma/seroma	10140	
	Laceration repair, simple Site: ______ Size: _____	120__	
	Laceration repair, layered Site: ______ Size: _____	120__	
	Laser Light Tx	96597	
	Lesion, biopsy, one	11100	
	Lesion, biopsy, each add'l	11101	
	Lesion, excision, benign Site: ______ Size: _____	114__	
	Lesion, excision, malignant Site: ______ Size: _____	116__	
	Lesion, paring/cutting, one	11055	
	Lesion, paring/cutting, 2-4	11056	
	Lesion, shave Site: ______ Size: _____	113__	
	Nail removal, partial (+T mod)	11730	
	Nail rem, w/matrix (+T mod)	11750	
	Skin tag, 1-15	11200	
	Wart, flat, 1-14	17110	
✓	Destruction lesion, 1st	17000	
	Destruct lesion, each addl 2-14	17003	
	Medications		**Units**
	Ampicillin, up to 500mg	J0290	
	B-12, up to 1,000 mcg	J3420	
	Epinephrine, up to 1ml	J0170	
	Kenalog, 10mg	J3301	
✓	Lidocaine, 10mg	J2001	
	Normal saline, 1000cc	J7030	
	Phenergan, up to 50mg	J2550	
	Progesterone, 150mg	J1055	
	Rocephin, 250mg	J0696	
	Testosterone, 200mg	J1080	
	Tigan, up to 200 mg	J3250	
	Toradol, 15mg	J1885	
	Albuterol	J7609	
	Depo-Provera 50 mg	J1055	
	Depo-Medrol 40 mg	J1030	

Diagnoses		Code
1 Migraine HA		
2 Dermatofibromas		
3		
4		

Next office visit:
Recheck • Preventative • (PRN)
Referral to:

x	Laboratory		-90
	Venipuncture	36415	
	Blood glucose, monitoring device	82962	
	Blood glucose, visual dipstick	82948	
	CBC, w/ auto differential	85025	
	CBC, w/o auto differential	85027	
	Cholesterol	82465	
	Hemoccult, guaiac	82270	
	Hemoccult, immunoassay	82274	
	Hemoglobin A1C	85018	
	Lipid panel	80061	
	Liver panel	80076	
	KOH prep (skin, hair, nails)	87220	
	Metabolic panel, basic	80048	
	Metabolic panel, comprehensive	80053	
	Mononucleosis	86308	
	Pregnancy, blood	84703	
	Pregnancy, urine	81025	
	Renal panel	80069	
	Sedimentation rate	85651	
	Strep, rapid	86403	
	Strep culture	87081	
	Strep A	87880	
	TB	86580	
	UA, complete, non-automated	81000	
	UA, w/o micro, non-automated	81002	
	UA, w/ micro, non-automated	81003	
	Urine colony count	87086	
	Urine culture, presumptive	87088	
	Wet mount/KOH	87210	
	Vaccines		
	DT, <7 y		90702
	DTP		90701
	DtaP, <7 y		90700
	Flu, 6-35 months		90657
	Flu, 3 y +		90658
	Hep A, adult		90632
	Hep A, ped/adol, 2 dose		90633
	Hep B, adult		90746
	Hep B, ped/adol 3 dose		90744
	Hep B-Hib		90748
	Hib, 4 dose		90645
	HPV		90649
	IPV		90713
	MMR		90707
	Pneumonia, >2 y		90732
	Pneumonia conjugate, <5 y		90669
	Td, >7 y		90718
	Varicella		90716
	Tetanus toxoid adsorbed, IM		90703
	Immunizations & Injections		**Units**
	Allergen, one	95115	
	Allergen, multiple	95117	
	Imm admn <8 yo 1st Inj	90465	
	Imm admn <8 yo each add inj	90466	
	Imm <8 yo oral or intranasal	90467	
	Imm admn <8 yo each add	90468	
	Imm admin, one vacc	90471	
	Imm admin, each add'l	90472	
	Imm admin, intranasal, one	90473	
	Imm admin, intranasal, each add'l	90474	
	Injection, joint, small	20600	
	Injection, joint, intermediate	20605	
	Injection, ther/proph/diag	90772	
	Injection, trigger pt 1-2 musc	20552	

Physician signature

x Sarah Mendenhall

Today's charges:	
Today's payment:	
Balance due:	

Job 29 Router- Laura Leighton

Date of service: 10/26/09	Insurance: SIGNAL HMO			Superbill Number: 1496
Patient name: NAOMI YAMAGATA	Coinsurance:	Copay: 10.00		Physician Name: MURRAY
Account #: YAM001	Noncovered Waiver?	yes	no	n/a

x	Office visit	New	x	Est
	Minimal (RN only)			99211
	Problem focused	99201		99212
	Exp problem focused	99202		99213
	Detailed	99203	✓	99214
	Comp	99204		99215
	Comprhen/Complex	99205		
	Well visit	**New**	**x**	**Est**
	< 1 y	99381		99391
	1-4 y	99382		99392
	5-11 y	99383		99393
	12-17 y	99384		99394
	18-39 y	99385		99395
	40-64 y	99386		99396
	65 y +	99387		99397
	Medicare preventive services			
	Pap			Q0091
	Pelvic & breast			G0101
	Prostate/PSA			G0103
	Tobacco couns/3-10 min			G0375
	Tobacco couns/>10 min			G0376
	Welcome to Medicare exam			G0344
	ECG w/Welcome to Medicare			G0366
	Hemoccult, guaiac			G0107
	Flu shot			G0008
	Pneumonia shot			G0009
	Consultation/preop clearance			
	Exp problem focused			99242
	Detailed			99243
	Comp/mod complex			99244
	Comp/high complex			99245
	Other services			
	After posted hours			99050
	Evening/weekend appointment			99051
	Home health certification			G0180
	Home health recertification			G0179
	Care Plan oversight			99374
	Care Plan Oversight >30 mins			99375
	Post-op follow-up			99024
	Prolonged/60min total			99354
	Prolonged/each add 30 mins			99355
	Special reports/forms			99080
	Disability/Workers comp			99455
	Smoking Cessation <10 mins			99406
	Smoking Cessation >10 mins			99407
	ETOH/SA screening <30 mins			99408
	Online E/M by MD			99444
	Phone E/M <10 mins			99441
	Phone E/M <20 mins			99442
	Phone E/M <30 mins			99443
	Anticoagulant Mgmt <90 days			99363
	Anticoagulant Mgmt >90 days			99364
	In office emergency serv			99058
	Other services			
	Supplies			
✓	Surgical Tray			99070

Instructions: Return f/u prn

x	Office procedures		
	Cerumen removal		69210
	ECG w/interpretation		93000
	ECG, rhythm strip		93040
✓	Endometrial biopsy		58100
	Fracture care, cast/splint Site: ________		____
	Nebulizer		94640
	Nebulizer demo		94664
	Spirometry		94010
	Spirometry, pre and post		94060
	Vasectomy		55250
	Skin procedures		**Units**
	Foreign body, skin, simple	10120	
	Foreign body, skin, complex	10121	
	I&D, abscess	10060	
	I&D, hematoma/seroma	10140	
	Laceration repair, simple Site: ____ Size: ____	120__	
	Laceration repair, layered Site: ____ Size: ____	120__	
	Laser Light Tx	96597	
	Lesion, biopsy, one	11100	
	Lesion, biopsy, each add'l	11101	
	Lesion, excision, benign Site: ____ Size: ____	114__	
	Lesion, excision, malignant Site: ____ Size: ____	116__	
	Lesion, paring/cutting, one	11055	
	Lesion, paring/cutting, 2-4	11056	
	Lesion, shave Site: ____ Size: ____	113__	
	Nail removal, partial (+T mod)	11730	
	Nail rem, w/matrix (+T mod)	11750	
	Skin tag, 1-15	11200	
	Wart, flat, 1-14	17110	
	Destruction lesion, 1st	17000	
	Destruct lesion, each addl 2-14	17003	
	Medications		**Units**
	Ampicillin, up to 500mg	J0290	
	B-12, up to 1,000 mcg	J3420	
	Epinephrine, up to 1ml	J0170	
	Kenalog, 10mg	J3301	
	Lidocaine, 10mg	J2001	
	Normal saline, 1000cc	J7030	
	Phenergan, up to 50mg	J2550	
	Progesterone, 150mg	J1055	
	Rocephin, 250mg	J0696	
	Testosterone, 200mg	J1080	
	Tigan, up to 200 mg	J3250	
	Toradol, 15mg	J1885	
	Albuterol	J7609	
	Depo-Provera 50 mg	J1055	
	Depo-Medrol 40 mg	J1030	

Diagnoses		Code
1 DUB		
2 Menorrhagia		
3		
4		

Next office visit: 10 days

Recheck (circled) • Preventative • PRN

Referral to:

x	Laboratory		-90
✓	Venipuncture	36415	
	Blood glucose, monitoring device	82962	
	Blood glucose, visual dipstick	82948	
	CBC, w/ auto differential	85025	
✓	CBC, w/o auto differential	85027	
	Cholesterol	82465	
	Hemoccult, guaiac	82270	
	Hemoccult, immunoassay	82274	
	Hemoglobin A1C	85018	
	Lipid panel	80061	
	Liver panel	80076	
	KOH prep (skin, hair, nails)	87220	
	Metabolic panel, basic	80048	
	Metabolic panel, comprehensive	80053	
	Mononucleosis	86308	
	Pregnancy, blood	84703	
✓	Pregnancy, urine	81025	
	Renal panel	80069	
	Sedimentation rate	85651	
	Strep, rapid	86403	
	Strep culture	87081	
	Strep A	87880	
	TB	86580	
	UA, complete, non-automated	81000	
	UA, w/o micro, non-automated	81002	
	UA, w/ micro, non-automated	81003	
	Urine colony count	87086	
	Urine culture, presumptive	87088	
	Wet mount/KOH	87210	
	Vaccines		
	DT, <7 y		90702
	DTP		90701
	DtaP, <7 y		90700
	Flu, 6-35 months		90657
	Flu, 3 y +		90658
	Hep A, adult		90632
	Hep A, ped/adol, 2 dose		90633
	Hep B, adult		90746
	Hep B, ped/adol 3 dose		90744
	Hep B-Hib		90748
	Hib, 4 dose		90645
	HPV		90649
	IPV		90713
	MMR		90707
	Pneumonia, >2 y		90732
	Pneumonia conjugate, <5 y		90669
	Td, >7 y		90718
	Varicella		90716
	Tetanus toxoid adsorbed, IM		90703
	Immunizations & Injections		**Units**
	Allergen, one	95115	
	Allergen, multiple	95117	
	Imm admn <8 yo 1st Inj	90465	
	Imm admn <8 yo each add inj	90466	
	Imm <8 yo oral or intranasal	90467	
	Imm admn <8 yo each add	90468	
	Imm admin, one vacc	90471	
	Imm admin, each add'l	90472	
	Imm admin, intranasal, one	90473	
	Imm admin, intranasal, each add'l	90474	
	Injection, joint, small	20600	
	Injection, joint, intermediate	20605	
	Injection, ther/proph/diag	90772	
	Injection, trigger pt 1-2 musc	20552	

Physician signature	Today's charges:	
x Laurie Murray MD	Today's payment:	10.00 cash
	Balance due:	

Job 30 Router- Naomi Yamagata

Blue Cross Blue Shield
Brian McDonough
ID No: B992796 Group No: G6722
Subscriber: Brian McDonough
20% coinsurance

PO Box 8212, New York, NY 01487 (800)888-5541

Job 2 Insurance Card

Date of service: 10/27/09	Insurance: BC/BS				Superbill Number: 2453
Patient name: BRIAN MCDONOUGH	Coinsurance: 20%	Copay:			Physician Name: SCHWARTZ
Account #: MCD001	Noncovered Waiver?	yes	no	n/a	

x	Office visit	New	x	Est
	Minimal (RN only)			99211
	Problem focused	99201		99212
	Exp problem focused	99202		99213
	Detailed	99203		99214
✓	Comp	99204		99215
	Comprhen/Complex	99205		
x	**Well visit**	**New**	x	**Est**
	< 1 y	99381		99391
	1-4 y	99382		99392
	5-11 y	99383		99393
	12-17 y	99384		99394
	18-39 y	99385		99395
	40-64 y	99386		99396
	65 y +	99387		99397

x	Medicare preventive services	
	Pap	Q0091
	Pelvic & breast	G0101
	Prostate/PSA	G0103
	Tobacco couns/3-10 min	G0375
	Tobacco couns/>10 min	G0376
	Welcome to Medicare exam	G0344
	ECG w/Welcome to Medicare	G0366
	Hemoccult, guaiac	G0107
	Flu shot	G0008
	Pneumonia shot	G0009
	Consultation/preop clearance	
	Exp problem focused	99242
	Detailed	99243
	Comp/mod complex	99244
	Comp/high complex	99245
	Other services	
	After posted hours	99050
	Evening/weekend appointment	99051
	Home health certification	G0180
	Home health recertification	G0179
	Care Plan oversight	99374
	Care Plan Oversight >30 mins	99375
	Post-op follow-up	99024
	Prolonged/60min total	99354
	Prolonged/each add 30 mins	99355
	Special reports/forms	99080
	Disability/Workers comp	99455
	Smoking Cessation <10 mins	99406
	Smoking Cessation >10 mins	99407
	ETOH/SA screening <30 mins	99408
	Online E/M by MD	99444
	Phone E/M <10 mins	99441
	Phone E/M <20 mins	99442
	Phone E/M <30 mins	99443
	Anticoagulant Mgmt <90 days	99363
	Anticoagulant Mgmt >90 days	99364
	In office emergency serv	99058
	Other services	
	Supplies	
	Surgical Tray	99070

Instructions:

x	Office procedures		
	Cerumen removal		69210
	ECG, w/interpretation		93000
	ECG, rhythm strip		93040
	Endometrial biopsy		58100
	Fracture care, cast/splint		
	Site: ____________		
	Nebulizer		94640
	Nebulizer demo		94664
	Spirometry		94010
	Spirometry, pre and post		94060
	Vasectomy		55250
	Skin procedures		**Units**
	Foreign body, skin, simple	10120	
	Foreign body, skin, complex	10121	
	I&D, abscess	10060	
	I&D, hematoma/seroma	10140	
	Laceration repair, simple	120__	
	Site: _______ Size: _____		
	Laceration repair, layered	120__	
	Site: _______ Size: _____		
	Laser Light Tx	96597	
	Lesion, biopsy, one	11100	
	Lesion, biopsy, each add'l	11101	
	Lesion, excision, benign	114__	
	Site: _______ Size: _____		
	Lesion, excision, malignant	116__	
	Site: _______ Size: _____		
	Lesion, paring/cutting, one	11055	
	Lesion, paring/cutting, 2-4	11056	
	Lesion, shave	113__	
	Site: _______ Size: _____		
	Nail removal, partial (+T mod)	11730	
	Nail rem, w/matrix (+T mod)	11750	
	Skin tag, 1-15	11200	
	Wart, flat, 1-14	17110	
	Destruction lesion, 1st	17000	
	Destruct lesion, each addl 2-14	17003	
	Medications		**Units**
	Ampicillin, up to 500mg	J0290	
	B-12, up to 1,000 mcg	J3420	
	Epinephrine, up to 1ml	J0170	
	Kenalog, 10mg	J3301	
	Lidocaine, 10mg	J2001	
	Normal saline, 1000cc	J7030	
	Phenergan, up to 50mg	J2550	
	Progesterone, 150mg	J1055	
	Rocephin, 250mg	J0696	
	Testosterone, 200mg	J1080	
	Tigan, up to 200 mg	J3250	
	Toradol, 15mg	J1885	
	Albuterol	J7609	
	Depo-Provera 50 mg	J1055	
	Depo-Medrol 40 mg	J1030	

Diagnoses	Code
1 Routine Physical	
2 Vaccination Update	
3	
4	

Next office visit:
Recheck • Preventative • PRN (circled)
Referral to:

Physician signature
x [signature] MD

x	Laboratory		-90
	Venipuncture	36415	
	Blood glucose, monitoring device	82962	
	Blood glucose, visual dipstick	82948	
	CBC, w/ auto differential	85025	
	CBC, w/o auto differential	85027	
	Cholesterol	82465	
	Hemoccult, guaiac	82270	
	Hemoccult, immunoassay	82274	
	Hemoglobin A1C	85018	
	Lipid panel	80061	
	Liver panel	80076	
	KOH prep (skin, hair, nails)	87220	
	Metabolic panel, basic	80048	
	Metabolic panel, comprehensive	80053	
	Mononucleosis	86308	
	Pregnancy, blood	84703	
	Pregnancy, urine	81025	
	Renal panel	80069	
	Sedimentation rate	85651	
	Strep, rapid	86403	
	Strep culture	87081	
	Strep A	87880	
	TB	86580	
	UA, complete, non-automated	81000	
	UA, w/o micro, non-automated	81002	
	UA, w/ micro, non-automated	81003	
	Urine colony count	87086	
	Urine culture, presumptive	87088	
	Wet mount/KOH	87210	
	Vaccines		
	DT, <7 y		90702
	DTP		90701
	DtaP, <7 y		90700
	Flu, 6-35 months		90657
	Flu, 3 y +		90658
	Hep A, adult		90632
	Hep A, ped/adol, 2 dose		90633
✓	Hep B, adult		90746
	Hep B, ped/adol 3 dose		90744
	Hep B-Hib		90748
	Hib, 4 dose		90645
	HPV		90649
	IPV		90713
	MMR		90707
	Pneumonia, >2 y		90732
	Pneumonia conjugate, <5 y		90669
	Td, >7 y		90718
	Varicella		90716
✓	Tetanus toxoid adsorbed, IM		90703
	Immunizations & Injections		**Units**
	Allergen, one	95115	
	Allergen, multiple	95117	
	Imm admn <8 yo 1st Inj	90465	
	Imm admn <8 yo each add inj	90466	
	Imm <8 yo oral or intranasal	90467	
	Imm admn <8 yo each add	90468	
✓	Imm admin, one vacc	90471	
✓	Imm admin, each add'l	90472	
	Imm admin, intranasal, one	90473	
	Imm admin, intranasal, each add'l	90474	
	Injection, joint, small	20600	
	Injection, joint, intermediate	20605	
	Injection, ther/proph/diag	90772	
	Injection, trigger pt 1-2 musc	20552	

Today's charges:	
Today's payment:	
Balance due:	

Job 2 Router- Brian McDonough

Date of service: 10/27/09	Insurance: FLEXIHEALTH				Superbill Number: 2459
Patient name: RICHARD MANALY	Coinsurance:	Copay: 20.00			Physician Name: LYNN
Account #: MAN001	Noncovered Waiver?	yes	no	n/a	

x	Office visit	New	x	Est
	Minimal (RN only)			99211
	Problem focused	99201		99212
	Exp problem focused	99202		99213
	Detailed	99203		99214
	Comp	99204		99215
	Comprhen/Complex	99205		
	Well visit	**New**	**x**	**Est**
	< 1 y	99381		99391
	1-4 y	99382		99392
	5-11 y	99383		99393
	12-17 y	99384		99394
	18-39 y	99385		99395
	40-64 y	99386		99396
	65 y +	99387		99397
	Medicare preventive services			
	Pap			Q0091
	Pelvic & breast			G0101
	Prostate/PSA			G0103
	Tobacco couns/3-10 min			G0375
	Tobacco couns/>10 min			G0376
	Welcome to Medicare exam			G0344
	ECG w/Welcome to Medicare			G0366
	Hemoccult, guaiac			G0107
	Flu shot			G0008
	Pneumonia shot			G0009
	Consultation/preop clearance			
	Exp problem focused			99242
	Detailed			99243
	Comp/mod complex			99244
	Comp/high complex			99245
	Other services			
	After posted hours			99050
	Evening/weekend appointment			99051
	Home health certification			G0180
	Home health recertification			G0179
	Care Plan oversight			99374
	Care Plan Oversight >30 mins			99375
	Post-op follow-up			99024
	Prolonged/60min total			99354
	Prolonged/each add 30 mins			99355
	Special reports/forms			99080
	Disability/Workers comp			99455
	Smoking Cessation <10 mins			99406
	Smoking Cessation >10 mins			99407
	ETOH/SA screening <30 mins			99408
	Online E/M by MD			99444
	Phone E/M <10 mins			99441
	Phone E/M <20 mins			99442
	Phone E/M <30 mins			99443
	Anticoagulant Mgmt <90 days			99363
✓	Anticoagulant Mgmt >90 days			99364
	In office emergency serv			99058
	Other services			
✓	Therapeutic Drug Assay-Carmadin			
	Supplies			
	Surgical Tray			99070
	Instructions:			

x	Office procedures		
	Cerumen removal		69210
	ECG, w/interpretation		93000
	ECG, rhythm strip		93040
	Endometrial biopsy		58100
	Fracture care, cast/splint Site: ________		____
	Nebulizer		94640
	Nebulizer demo		94664
	Spirometry		94010
	Spirometry, pre and post		94060
	Vasectomy		55250
	Skin procedures		**Units**
	Foreign body, skin, simple	10120	
	Foreign body, skin, complex	10121	
	I&D, abscess	10060	
	I&D, hematoma/seroma	10140	
	Laceration repair, simple Site: ______ Size: ____	120__	
	Laceration repair, layered Site: ______ Size: ____	120__	
	Laser Light Tx	96597	
	Lesion, biopsy, one	11100	
	Lesion, biopsy, each add'l	11101	
	Lesion, excision, benign Site: ______ Size: ____	114__	
	Lesion, excision, malignant Site: ______ Size: ____	116__	
	Lesion, paring/cutting, one	11055	
	Lesion, paring/cutting, 2-4	11056	
	Lesion, shave Site: ______ Size: ____	113__	
	Nail removal, partial (+T mod)	11730	
	Nail rem, w/matrix (+T mod)	11750	
	Skin tag, 1-15	11200	
	Wart, flat, 1-14	17110	
	Destruction lesion, 1st	17000	
	Destruct lesion, each addl 2-14	17003	
	Medications		**Units**
	Ampicillin, up to 500mg	J0290	
	B-12, up to 1,000 mcg	J3420	
	Epinephrine, up to 1ml	J0170	
	Kenalog, 10mg	J3301	
	Lidocaine, 10mg	J2001	
	Normal saline, 1000cc	J7030	
	Phenergan, up to 50mg	J2550	
	Progesterone, 150mg	J1055	
	Rocephin, 250mg	J0696	
	Testosterone, 200mg	J1080	
	Tigan, up to 200 mg	J3250	
	Toradol, 15mg	J1885	
	Albuterol	J7609	
	Depo-Provera 50 mg	J1055	
	Depo-Medrol 40 mg	J1030	

Diagnoses	Code
1 Arrhythmia	
2 HTN	
3 anticoagulation med use	
4	

Next office visit: 1 mon

Recheck • Preventative • PRN

Referral to:

Physician signature

x Albert Lynn PA-C

x	Laboratory		-90
✓	Venipuncture	36415	
	Blood glucose, monitoring device	82962	
	Blood glucose, visual dipstick	82948	
	CBC, w/ auto differential	85025	
	CBC, w/o auto differential	85027	
	Cholesterol	82465	
	Hemoccult, guaiac	82270	
	Hemoccult, immunoassay	82274	
	Hemoglobin A1C	85018	
	Lipid panel	80061	
	Liver panel	80076	
	KOH prep (skin, hair, nails)	87220	
	Metabolic panel, basic	80048	
	Metabolic panel, comprehensive	80053	
	Mononucleosis	86308	
	Pregnancy, blood	84703	
	Pregnancy, urine	81025	
	Renal panel	80069	
	Sedimentation rate	85651	
	Strep, rapid	86403	
	Strep culture	87081	
	Strep A	87880	
	TB	86580	
	UA, complete, non-automated	81000	
	UA, w/o micro, non-automated	81002	
	UA, w/ micro, non-automated	81003	
	Urine colony count	87086	
	Urine culture, presumptive	87088	
	Wet mount/KOH	87210	
	Vaccines		
	DT, <7 y		90702
	DTP		90701
	DtaP, <7 y		90700
	Flu, 6-35 months		90657
	Flu, 3 y +		90658
	Hep A, adult		90632
	Hep A, ped/adol, 2 dose		90633
	Hep B, adult		90746
	Hep B, ped/adol 3 dose		90744
	Hep B-Hib		90748
	Hib, 4 dose		90645
	HPV		90649
	IPV		90713
	MMR		90707
	Pneumonia, >2 y		90732
	Pneumonia conjugate, <5 y		90669
	Td, >7 y		90718
	Varicella		90716
	Tetanus toxoid adsorbed, IM		90703
	Immunizations & Injections		**Units**
	Allergen, one	95115	
	Allergen, multiple	95117	
	Imm admn <8 yo 1st Inj	90465	
	Imm admn <8 yo each add inj	90466	
	Imm <8 yo oral or intranasal	90467	
	Imm admn <8 yo each add	90468	
	Imm admin, one vacc	90471	
	Imm admin, each add'l	90472	
	Imm admin, intranasal, one	90473	
	Imm admin, intranasal, each add'l	90474	
	Injection, joint, small	20600	
	Injection, joint, intermediate	20605	
	Injection, ther/proph/diag	90772	
	Injection, trigger pt 1-2 musc	20552	

Today's charges:		
Today's payment:		
Balance due:		

Job 3 Router- Richard Manaly

Douglasville Medicine Associates
Patient Registration Form

Patients must complete all information prior to seeing the physician. A copy of your insurance card(s) and driver's license will be made for your file.

Patient Name: BRIAN McDONOUGH Date of Birth: 6/26/66
Sex: (Male) or Female Social Security Number: 027 - 46 - 2232 Marital Status: M
Address Line 1: 26 BROAD ST
Address Line 2: ______
City: SYRACUSE
State: NY Zip Code: 14802
Home Telephone: (717) 555-2267 Work Telephone: (717) 555-1926
Cellular Telephone: (717) 555-6198 Email address: 26broad@adelphia.net

Patient's Work Status (Full-Time, Part-Time, Retired, Student): ______
Employer Name: EMPIRE POWER AND GAS
Address Line 1: 11426 SMITHFIELD BLVD
Address Line 2: ______
City: SYRACUSE State: NY Zip: 14811
Telephone: (717) 555-1926
If patient is a minor, who is the primary guardian? ______

Primary Insurance Company: BLUE CROSS/BLUE SHIELD
Subscriber ID Number B992796 Policy Group #: G6722
Subscriber Name: SAME Birth date: 6/26/66
Subscriber Social Security Number: 027-46-2232 Relationship to patient: SAME

Secondary Insurance Company: ______
Subscriber ID Number ______ Policy Group #: ______
Subscriber Name: ______ Birth date: ______
Subscriber Social Security Number: ___-___-___ Relationship to patient: ______

Complete this section if your treatment is for an injury or accident.
Were you injured at work? NO Is this covered by Workers' Compensation? ______
If Yes, Contact person at your Employer ______
Were you involved in an auto accident? NO Provide insurance company, contact information, and claim number: ______

Date & time of Accident ______ Place of Accident ______
How did injury happen? ______
Name of Physician who treated you at time of accident: ______

Financial Responsibility Statement/ Release of Information Authorization
"I authorize the release of any medical information necessary to my insurance company and the Payment of Benefits to the Physician for services provided.

X Brian McDonough Date 10/27/09
Signature of Patient or Legal Guardian

Job 6 Registration Paper work- Brian McDonough 1 of 5

Douglasville Medicine Associates
Patient Registration Form

OUR FINANCIAL POLICY

By law, we must collect your carrier designated co-pay at the time of service. Please be prepared to pay that co-pay at each visit. We are also required to collect any portion of the deductible that has not been satisfied. If your plan requires a coinsurance instead of a co-pay and we participate with the plan, we will accept the designated payment and bill you accordingly for any deductible and coinsurance your plan indicates you are responsible for on their explanation of benefits.

Payment is expected at the time of service unless other financial arrangements have been made prior to your visit. If you are uninsured, you may qualify for a hardship discount. Ask one of our staff members for more information.

You are responsible for timely payment of your account. Douglasville Medicine Associates reserves the right to reschedule or deny a future appointment on delinquent accounts.

WE ACCEPT CASH, CHECKS, MASTERCARD AND VISA

THANK YOU for taking the time to review our policy.

Brian McDonough ______________________ 10/27/09 ______

(Responsible Party Signature) (Date)

Job 6 Registration Paper work- Brian McDonough 2 of 5

Douglasville Medicine Associates
5076 Brand Blvd., Suite 401▪Douglasville, NY 01234 (123)456-7890

Patient Name:_______________________________

Record #:____________

I acknowledge that I have received a written copy of Douglasville Medicine Associates Notice of Patient Privacy Practices. I also acknowledge that I have been allowed to ask questions concerning this notice and my rights under this notice. I understand that this form will be part of my record until such time as I may choose to revoke this acknowledgement. If I am not the patient, I am the authorized representative of a minor child or authorized by law to act for and on the patient's behalf.

Brian McDonough ______________________ 10/27/09 ____________

Signature of Patient or Authorized Agent Date

Patient (or authorized agent) refused to sign Notice of Privacy Practices.

Please describe events. ____

____

__________________________ ____________

Signature of DMA Employee Date

Job 6 Registration Paper work- Brian McDonough 3 of 5

Douglasville Medicine Associates
5076 Brand Blvd, Suite 401~ Douglasville, NY 01234

ASSIGNMENT OF BENEFITS AND PATIENT REPRESENTATION

Patient Name:________________________________ Chart # ________________

Insured Name:____

Insurance Company Name ____

Policy # ________________________ Group # ________________________

I hereby assign all medical and/or surgical benefits, to include major medical benefits to which I am entitled, to **Douglasville Medicine Associates**. This assignment will remain in effect until revoked by me in writing. A photocopy of this assignment is to be considered as valid as the original.

I understand that I am financially responsible for all charges whether or not paid by my insurance carrier. I understand that I will be responsible for any court costs or collection fees should it become necessary to take action to collect for services/supplies rendered.

I hereby authorize **Douglasville Medicine Associates** to release all medical information necessary to secure payment on my account.

I hereby authorize **Douglasville Medicine Associates** and medical billing staff members, to submit claims, on my behalf, to the insurance company listed on the copy of the current and valid insurance card I have provided to the Clinic in good faith. I fully agree and understand that the submission of a claim does not absolve me of my responsibility to ensure that the bill for medical services is paid in full.

I authorize **Douglasville Medicine Associates** and its medical billing representative, to be my personal representative, which allows the Clinic to: (1) submit any and all appeals when my insurance company performs an adverse benefit determination as defined in 29 CFR 2560-503-1, (2) submit any and all requests for benefit information from my employer and/or health insurance company, and (3) initiate formal complaints to any State or Federal agency that has jurisdiction over my benefits.

I fully understand and agree that I am responsible for full payment of the medical debt I owe the Clinic, if my insurance company has refused to pay 100% of my covered benefits, within ninety (90) days of any and all appeals or request for information. A photocopy of this document shall be considered as effective and valid as the original.

Patient Brian McDonough 12/27/09
(signature) (date)

Patient Representative ________________________________
(date)

Relationship to Patient ________________________________

Witness ________________________________
(signature) (date)

Job 6 Registration Paper work- Brian McDonough 4 of 5

Douglasville Medicine Associates
5076 Brand Blvd., Suite 401▪Douglasville, NY 01234

CONSENT TO TREATMENT

Patient Name: ______________________________ Date: 10/27/09

I, ______________________________, hereby voluntarily consent to outpatient treatment and evaluation at Douglasville Medicine Associates for ______________________________. This includes routine diagnostic procedures, examination and medical treatment including, but not limited to, routine laboratory work (such as blood, urine and other studies), x-rays, heart tracing and administration of medications prescribed by the physician.

I further consent to the performance of those diagnostic procedures, examinations and rendering of medical treatment by the medical staff and their assistants.

I understand that this consent form will be valid and remain in effect as long as I receive medical care at Douglasville Medicine Associates.

This form has been explained to me and I fully understand this Consent To Treatment and agree to its contents.

Brian McDonough
____
Signature of Patient or
Person Authorized to consent for patient

____
Relationship to patient

____
Signature of Witness

Job 6 Registration Paper work- Brian McDonough 5 of 5

Date of service: 10/27/09	PPO			Router Number: 2484
Patient name: ELANE YBARRA	Coinsurance:	Copay:		Physician Name: SCHWARTZ
Account #: YBA001	Noncovered Waiver?	yes	no	n/a

X	Office visit	New	X	Est
N/A	Minimal (RN only)	N/A		99211
	Problem focused	99201		99212
	Exp problem focused	99202		99213
	Detailed	99203		99214
	Comp	99204		99215
	Comprhen/Complex	99205		

X	Well visit	New	X	Est
	< 1 y	99381		99391
	1-4 y	99382		99392
	5-11 y	99383		99393
	12-17 y	99384		99394
	18-39 y	99385	✓	99395
	40-64 y	99386		99396
	65 y +	99387		99397

X	Medicare preventive services	
	Pap	Q0091
	Pelvic & breast	G0101
	Prostate/PSA	G0103
	Tobacco couns/3-10 min	G0375
	Tobacco couns/>10 min	G0376
	Welcome to Medicare exam	G0344
	ECG w/Welcome to Medicare	G0366
	Hemoccult, guaiac	G0107
	Flu shot	G0008
	Pneumonia shot	G0009

X	Consultation/preop clearance	
	Exp problem focused	99242
	Detailed	99243
	Comp/mod complex	99244
	Comp/high complex	99245

X	Other services	
	After posted hours	99050
	Evening/weekend appointment	99051
	Home health certification	G0180
	Home health recertification	G0179
	Care Plan oversight	99374
	Care Plan Oversight >30 mins	99375
	Post-op follow-up	99024
	Prolonged/60min total	99354
	Prolonged/each add 30 mins	99355
	Special reports/forms	99080
	Disability/Workers comp	99455
	Smoking Cessation <10 mins	99406
✓	Smoking Cessation >10 mins	99407
	ETOH/SA screening <30 mins	99408
	Online E/M by MD	99444
	Phone E/M <10 mins	99441
	Phone E/M <20 mins	99442
	Phone E/M <30 mins	99443
	Anticoagulant Mgmt <90 days	99363
	Anticoagulant Mgmt >90 days	99364
	In office emergency serv	99058

X	Other services	

X	Supplies	
	Surgical Tray	99070

Instructions:

Recommend getting mammogram

X	Office procedures		
	Cerumen removal		69210
✓	ECG, w/interpretation		93000
	ECG, rhythm strip		93040
	Endometrial biopsy		58100
	Fracture care, cast/splint Site: ________________		
	Nebulizer		94640
	Nebulizer demo		94664
	Spirometry		94010
	Spirometry, pre and post		94060
	Vasectomy		55250

X	Skin procedures		Units
	Foreign body, skin, simple	10120	
	Foreign body, skin, complex	10121	
	I&D, abscess	10060	
	I&D, hematoma/seroma	10140	
	Laceration repair, simple Site: _______ Size: _____	120__	
	Laceration repair, layered Site: _______ Size: _____	120__	
	Laser Light Tx	96597	
	Lesion, biopsy, one	11100	
	Lesion, biopsy, each add'l	11101	
	Lesion, excision, benign Site: _______ Size: _____	114__	
	Lesion, excision, malignant Site: _______ Size: _____	116__	
	Lesion, paring/cutting, one	11055	
	Lesion, paring/cutting, 2-4	11056	
	Lesion, shave Site: _______ Size: _____	113__	
	Nail removal, partial (+T mod)	11730	
	Nail rem, w/matrix (+T mod)	11750	
	Skin tag, 1-15	11200	
	Wart, flat, 1-14	17110	
	Destruction lesion, 1st	17000	
	Destruct lesion, each addl 2-14	17003	

X	Medications		Units
	Ampicillin, up to 500mg	J0290	
	B-12, up to 1,000 mcg	J3420	
	Epinephrine, up to 1ml	J0170	
	Kenalog, 10mg	J3301	
	Lidocaine, 10mg	J2001	
	Normal saline, 1000cc	J7030	
	Phenergan, up to 50mg	J2550	
	Progesterone, 150mg	J1055	
	Rocephin, 250mg	J0696	
	Testosterone, 200mg	J1080	
	Tigan, up to 200 mg	J3250	
	Toradol, 15mg	J1885	
	Albuterol	J7609	
	Depo-Provera 50 mg	J1055	
	Depo-Medrol 40 mg	J1030	

Diagnoses	Code
1 Annual Exam	
2 Hx Cigarette Smoking	
3	
4	

Next office visit:
Recheck • (Preventative) • PRN
Referral to:

Physician signature

X Schwartz MD

X	Laboratory		-90
✓	Venipuncture	36415	
	Blood glucose, monitoring device	82962	
✓	Blood glucose, visual dipstick	82948	
✓	CBC, w/ auto differential	85025	
	CBC, w/o auto differential	85027	
✓	Cholesterol	82465	
	Hemoccult, guaiac	82270	
	Hemoccult, immunoassay	82274	
	Hemoglobin A1C	85018	
✓	Lipid panel	80061	
	Liver panel	80076	
	KOH prep (skin, hair, nails)	87220	
✓	Metabolic panel, basic	80048	
	Metabolic panel, comprehensive	80053	
	Mononucleosis	86308	
	Pregnancy, blood	84703	
	Pregnancy, urine	81025	
	Renal panel	80069	
	Sedimentation rate	85651	
	Strep, rapid	86403	
	Strep culture	87081	
	Strep A	87880	
	TB	86580	
	UA, complete, non-automated	81000	
	UA, w/o micro, non-automated	81002	
	UA, w/ micro, non-automated	81003	
	Urine colony count	87086	
	Urine culture, presumptive	87088	
	Wet mount/KOH	87210	

X	Vaccines	
	DT, <7 y	90702
	DTP	90701
	DtaP, <7 y	90700
	Flu, 6-35 months	90657
	Flu, 3 y +	90658
	Hep A, adult	90632
	Hep A, ped/adol, 2 dose	90633
	Hep B, adult	90746
	Hep B, ped/adol 3 dose	90744
	Hep B-Hib	90748
	Hib, 4 dose	90645
	HPV	90649
	IPV	90713
	MMR	90707
	Pneumonia, >2 y	90732
	Pneumonia conjugate, <5 y	90669
	Td, >7 y	90718
	Varicella	90716
✓	Tetanus toxoid adsorbed, IM	90703

X	Immunizations & Injections		Units
	Allergen, one	95115	
	Allergen, multiple	95117	
	Imm admn <8 yo 1st Inj	90465	
	Imm admn <8 yo each add inj	90466	
	Imm <8 yo oral or intranasal	90467	
	Imm admn <8 yo each add	90468	
	Imm admin, one vacc	90471	
	Imm admin, each add'l	90472	
	Imm admin, intranasal, one	90473	
	Imm admin, intranasal, each add'l	90474	
	Injection, joint, small	20600	
	Injection, joint, intermediate	20605	
	Injection, ther/proph/diag	90772	
	Injection, trigger pt 1-2 musc	20552	

Today's charges:	
Today's payment:	
Balance due:	

Job 8 Router- Elaine Ybarra

Name: Elane Ybarra Date: 10/27/09

Age: 31 H: 5'4" W: 139 T: 98.7 P: 87 BP: 110/74

Couns/coord > 50% ☐	Couns/coord mins:	Total visit mins:

MA Notes: Here for annual check up. Per female annual exam protocol UPT. (Test +) LMP: 9/5/09 Blood draw.

ROS	WNL	*Note
Const	☑	☐
Head/Eyes	☐	☐
ENT/mouth	☐	☐
Heart/vessels	☑	☐
Resp	☑	☐
GI	☑	☐
GU	☑	☐
Musc	☐	☐
Skin/breasts	☑	☐
Neuro	☐	☐
Mental Status	☐	☐
Endo	☑	☐
Hem/lymph	☐	☐
Allergy/immun	☐	☐
No changes since last visit on / /		

PFSH	NO	*Note
Past	☑	☐
Family	☑	☐
Social	☑	☐
No changes since last visit on / /		

[ ]*Note [✓] Constitutional: NAD, A&O. Cooperative.

[ ]*Note [✓] Head: Normocephalic, Atraumatic. Scalp unremarkable

[ ]*Note [✓] Eyes: Lids, sclerae & conjunct clear. PERRLA. Non-icteric, no nystagmus [ ]Glasses [✓]Contacts

[ ]*Note [✓] ENT/Mouth: External ears, canals, TMs clear. Lips gums, oral mucosa nml. Tongue oral cavity & pharynx clear. Teeth in good condition. No loose teeth.

[ ]*Note [ ] Nose: Nose, septum, turbinates, & nasal mucosa normal. No drainage.

[ ]*Note [✓] Neck: Supple & symmetric w/ nrml ROM w/o swelling or JVD. No thyroid tenderness or masses.

[ ]*Note [✓] Heart: Reg R & R w/o murmurs, rubs, gallops. Nml distal pulses & perfusion. No carotid bruits. + Fm Hx ↑ chol. Lipid panel ordered.

[ ]*Note [✓] Lungs: No respiratory distress or compromise. CTAP. No wheezes or cough.

[ ]*Note [✓] Abdomen: soft, flat, no organomegaly, masses or tenderness. Bowel sounds present.

[ ]*Note [ ] Musculo: Nrml gait & stance. Extremities unremarkable, full active & passive ROM, w/o atrophy, spasticity, clubbing or abnml movements. Strength symmetrical. No jt swelling, erythema, effusion or tenderness. No crepitation. No dislocation or laxity.

[ ]*Note [ ] Neuro: [✓] Cranial nerves II-XII intact. [✓] DTR biceps, brachioradialis, patellar & ankle, equal bilaterally [ ] motor and sensory exam [ ] finger-to-nose [ ]negative Babinski & Romberg bilaterally.

[ ]*Note Male: [ ]No inguinal hernia palpable w/Valsalva. [ ] Testicles-WNL [ ] Penis-WNL

[ ]*Note [ ] Rectal: Prostate firm w/o mass, enlargement, tenderness. Nrml sphincter tone. Heme - stool.

[ ]*Note [✓] Breasts: Nrml shape & contour. Development nml w/o palpable lesions. No axillary adenopathy, dimpling, retraction, or skin color/texture changes. Nipples nrml, no discharge. Last Mammo: / /

[ ]*Note [✓] Pelvic: Nrml ext.genit, vaginal wall. No adnexal masses & uterus nrml sized. Good pelvic support w/o rectocele or cystocele. No excessive discharge or odor. [✓] Cervix nrml, PAP smear to path

[ ]*Note [ ] Skin: free of rashes, lesions, abnml discolor, or cyanosis. No signs of self-injury. Nails: WNL

[ ]*Note [ ] Psych: Mood, affect, & behavior approp, no anxiety, depres, compulsive behav evidence. Gen knwldg, cognition, judgmt, & insight WNL. [ ] Short & long-term memory intact.

*Notes:

Labs ordered(circle): BMP, CMP, CBC, (lipids) TSH, Free T4, PSA, HbA1C, urine microalbumin, digoxin, INR, arthritis panel, renal panel, GTT, (UPT), specify:

Pt here for annual checkup + GYN exam. Pt complaining of abdominal pain + sweating. Pts periods have been irregular. No change in bowel habits. NO loss of appetite. Pt not taking BC. Pt is G:0 P:0. Informed pt of (+) UPT. Referred her to OB/GYN. Suggested pt buy OTC prenatal vit.

[signature]

MD Signature

PROGRESS NOTE

Job 8 Office Note-Elane Ybarra

Date of service: 10/27/09	Insurance: MEDICARE				Superbill Number: 2460
Patient name: WILMA STEAM *Stearn*	Coinsurance: 20%	Copay:			Physician Name: MURRAY
Account #: STE001	Noncovered Waiver?	yes	no	n/a	

x	Office visit	New	x	Est
	Minimal (RN only)			99211
	Problem focused	99201		99212
	Exp problem focused	99202		99213
	Detailed	99203		99214
	Comp	99204		99215
	Comprhen/Complex	99205		
	Well visit	**New**	x	**Est**
	< 1 y	99381		99391
	1-4 y	99382		99392
	5-11 y	99383		99393
	12-17 y	99384		99394
	18-39 y	99385		99395
	40-64 y	99386		99396
	65 y +	99387		99397
	Medicare preventive services			
	Pap			Q0091
	Pelvic & breast			G0101
	Prostate/PSA			G0103
	Tobacco couns/3-10 min			G0375
	Tobacco couns/>10 min			G0376
	Welcome to Medicare exam			G0344
	ECG w/Welcome to Medicare			G0366
	Hemoccult, guaiac			G0107
	Flu shot			G0008
	Pneumonia shot			G0009
	Consultation/preop clearance			
	Exp problem focused			99242
	Detailed			99243
	Comp/mod complex			99244
	Comp/high complex			99245
	Other services			
	After posted hours			99050
	Evening/weekend appointment			99051
	Home health certification			G0180
	Home health recertification			G0179
	Care Plan oversight			99374
	Care Plan Oversight >30 mins			99375
	Post-op follow-up			99024
	Prolonged/60min total			99354
	Prolonged/each add 30 mins			99355
	Special reports/forms			99080
	Disability/Workers comp			99455
	Smoking Cessation <10 mins			99406
	Smoking Cessation >10 mins			99407
	ETOH/SA screening <30 mins			99408
	Online E/M by MD			99444
	Phone E/M <10 mins			99441
	Phone E/M <20 mins			99442
	Phone E/M <30 mins			99443
	Anticoagulant Mgmt <90 days			99363
	Anticoagulant Mgmt >90 days			99364
	In office emergency serv			99058
	Other services			
	Supplies			
	Surgical Tray			99070
	aminolevulinic acid (Levulan) HCL 20%			
	Instructions:			

x	Office procedures		
	Cerumen removal	69210	
	ECG, w/interpretation	93000	
	ECG, rhythm strip	93040	
	Endometrial biopsy	58100	
	Fracture care, cast/splint Site: ______________	______	
	Nebulizer	94640	
	Nebulizer demo	94664	
	Spirometry	94010	
	Spirometry, pre and post	94060	
	Vasectomy	55250	
	Skin procedures		**Units**
	Foreign body, skin, simple	10120	
	Foreign body, skin, complex	10121	
	I&D, abscess	10060	
	I&D, hematoma/seroma	10140	
	Laceration repair, simple Site: _______ Size: _____	120__	
	Laceration repair, layered Site: _______ Size: _____	120__	
✓	Laser Light Tx	96597	
	Lesion, biopsy, one	11100	
	Lesion, biopsy, each add'l	11101	
	Lesion, excision, benign Site: _______ Size: _____	114__	
	Lesion, excision, malignant Site: _______ Size: _____	116__	
	Lesion, paring/cutting, one	11055	
	Lesion, paring/cutting, 2-4	11056	
	Lesion, shave Site: _______ Size: _____	113__	
	Nail removal, partial (+T mod)	11730	
	Nail rem, w/matrix (+T mod)	11750	
	Skin tag, 1-15	11200	
	Wart, flat, 1-14	17110	
	Destruction lesion, 1st	17000	
	Destruct lesion, each addl 2-14	17003	
	Medications		**Units**
	Ampicillin, up to 500mg	J0290	
	B-12, up to 1,000 mcg	J3420	
	Epinephrine, up to 1ml	J0170	
	Kenalog, 10mg	J3301	
	Lidocaine, 10mg	J2001	
	Normal saline, 1000cc	J7030	
	Phenergan, up to 50mg	J2550	
	Progesterone, 150mg	J1055	
	Rocephin, 250mg	J0696	
	Testosterone, 200mg	J1080	
	Tigan, up to 200 mg	J3250	
	Toradol, 15mg	J1885	
	Albuterol	J7609	
	Depo-Provera 50 mg	J1055	
	Depo-Medrol 40 mg	J1030	

Diagnoses	Code
1 *actinic keratosis*	
2 *HTN*	
3 *DM*	
4	

Next office visit: *1 mth*

Recheck • Preventative • PRN

Referral to:

Physician signature

[signature]

x	Laboratory		-90
	Venipuncture	36415	
	Blood glucose, monitoring device	82962	
	Blood glucose, visual dipstick	82948	
	CBC, w/ auto differential	85025	
	CBC, w/o auto differential	85027	
	Cholesterol	82465	
	Hemoccult, guaiac	82270	
	Hemoccult, immunoassay	82274	
	Hemoglobin A1C	85018	
	Lipid panel	80061	
	Liver panel	80076	
	KOH prep (skin, hair, nails)	87220	
	Metabolic panel, basic	80048	
	Metabolic panel, comprehensive	80053	
	Mononucleosis	86308	
	Pregnancy, blood	84703	
	Pregnancy, urine	81025	
	Renal panel	80069	
	Sedimentation rate	85651	
	Strep, rapid	86403	
	Strep culture	87081	
	Strep A	87880	
	TB	86580	
	UA, complete, non-automated	81000	
	UA, w/o micro, non-automated	81002	
	UA, w/ micro, non-automated	81003	
	Urine colony count	87086	
	Urine culture, presumptive	87088	
	Wet mount/KOH	87210	

Vaccines	
DT, <7 y	90702
DTP	90701
DtaP, <7 y	90700
Flu, 6-35 months	90657
Flu, 3 y +	90658
Hep A, adult	90632
Hep A, ped/adol, 2 dose	90633
Hep B, adult	90746
Hep B, ped/adol 3 dose	90744
Hep B-Hib	90748
Hib, 4 dose	90645
HPV	90649
IPV	90713
MMR	90707
Pneumonia, >2 y	90732
Pneumonia conjugate, <5 y	90669
Td, >7 y	90718
Varicella	90716
Tetanus toxoid adsorbed, IM	90703

Immunizations & Injections		Units
Allergen, one	95115	
Allergen, multiple	95117	
Imm admn <8 yo 1st Inj	90465	
Imm admn <8 yo each add inj	90466	
Imm <8 yo oral or intranasal	90467	
Imm admn <8 yo each add	90468	
Imm admin, one vacc	90471	
Imm admin, each add'l	90472	
Imm admin, intranasal, one	90473	
Imm admin, intranasal, each add'l	90474	
Injection, joint, small	20600	
Injection, joint, intermediate	20605	
Injection, ther/proph/diag	90772	
Injection, trigger pt 1-2 musc	20552	

Today's charges:		
Today's payment:		
Balance due:		

Job 9 Router- Wilma Stearn

GREAT WEST

Julius A. Washington

ID No: 4771651 Group No: 91064

Subscriber: Julius A. Washington

Coinsurance: 20% /30%

Deductible: $150

PO Box 14785, Charlotte, NC 43695 (800)851-1236

Job 10 & 14 Insurance Card

Douglasville Medicine Associates
Patient Registration Form

Patients must complete all information prior to seeing the physician. A copy of your insurance card(s) and driver's license will be made for your file.

Patient Name: JULIUS WASHINGTON Date of Birth: 4 / 10 / 88
Sex: (Male) or Female Social Security Number: 707-51-1690 Marital Status: S
Address Line 1: 414 MAIDSTONE WAY
Address Line 2: ________
City: AUBURN
State: NY Zip Code: 14416
Home Telephone: (717) 555-7171 Work Telephone: (717) 555-9655
Cellular Telephone: (717) 555-3746 Email address: ________

Patient's Work Status (Full-Time, Part-Time, Retired, Student): ________
Employer Name: ELECTRONICS SUPER STORE
Address Line 1: 1600 JOHNSVILLE PIKE
Address Line 2: ________
City: AUBURN State: NY Zip: 14625
Telephone: (717) 555-9655
If patient is a minor, who is the primary guardian? ________

Primary Insurance Company: GREAT WEST
Subscriber ID Number 4771651 Policy Group #: 91064
Subscriber Name: SAME Birth date: SAME
Subscriber Social Security Number: ___-___-___ Relationship to patient: SELF

Secondary Insurance Company: ________
Subscriber ID Number ________ Policy Group #: ________
Subscriber Name: ________ Birth date: ________
Subscriber Social Security Number: ___-___-___ Relationship to patient: ________

Complete this section if your treatment is for an injury or accident.
Were you injured at work? ____ Is this covered by Workers' Compensation? ____
If Yes, Contact person at your Employer ________
Were you involved in an auto accident? ____ Provide insurance company, contact information, and claim number: ________

Date & time of Accident ________ Place of Accident ________
How did injury happen? ________
Name of Physician who treated you at time of accident: ________

Financial Responsibility Statement/ Release of Information Authorization
"I authorize the release of any medical information necessary to my insurance company and the Payment of Benefits to the Physician for services provided.

X Julius Washington Date 10/27/09
Signature of Patient or Legal Guardian

Job 10 Registration Paper work- Julius Washington 1 of 5

Douglasville Medicine Associates
Patient Registration Form

OUR FINANCIAL POLICY

By law, we must collect your carrier designated co-pay at the time of service. Please be prepared to pay that co-pay at each visit. We are also required to collect any portion of the deductible that has not been satisfied. If your plan requires a coinsurance instead of a co-pay and we participate with the plan, we will accept the designated payment and bill you accordingly for any deductible and coinsurance your plan indicates you are responsible for on their explanation of benefits.

Payment is expected at the time of service unless other financial arrangements have been made prior to your visit. If you are uninsured, you may qualify for a hardship discount. Ask one of our staff members for more information.

You are responsible for timely payment of your account. Douglasville Medicine Associates reserves the right to reschedule or deny a future appointment on delinquent accounts.

WE ACCEPT CASH, CHECKS, MASTERCARD AND VISA

THANK YOU for taking the time to review our policy.

Juli Wat ______________________ 10/27/09

(Responsible Party Signature) (Date)

Job 10 Registration Paper work- Julius Washington 2 of 5

Douglasville Medicine Associates
5076 Brand Blvd., Suite 401▪Douglasville, NY 01234 (123)456-7890

Patient Name:______________________________

Record #:_____________

I acknowledge that I have received a written copy of Douglasville Medicine Associates Notice of Patient Privacy Practices. I also acknowledge that I have been allowed to ask questions concerning this notice and my rights under this notice. I understand that this form will be part of my record until such time as I may choose to revoke this acknowledgement. If I am not the patient, I am the authorized representative of a minor child or authorized by law to act for and on the patient's behalf.

10/27/09

Signature of Patient or Authorized Agent Date

Patient (or authorized agent) refused to sign Notice of Privacy Practices.

Please describe events. ____

____

_________________________ ____________

Signature of DMA Employee Date

Job 10 Registration Paper work- Julius Washington 3 of 5

Douglasville Medicine Associates
5076 Brand Blvd., Suite 401▪Douglasville, NY 01234

CONSENT TO TREATMENT

Patient Name: ______________________________ Date: 10/27/05

I, ______________________________, hereby voluntarily consent to outpatient treatment and evaluation at Douglasville Medicine Associates for______________________________. This includes routine diagnostic procedures, examination and medical treatment including, but not limited to, routine laboratory work (such as blood, urine and other studies), x-rays, heart tracing and administration of medications prescribed by the physician.

I further consent to the performance of those diagnostic procedures, examinations and rendering of medical treatment by the medical staff and their assistants.

I understand that this consent form will be valid and remain in effect as long as I receive medical care at Douglasville Medicine Associates.

This form has been explained to me and I fully understand this Consent To Treatment and agree to its contents.

____
Signature of Patient or
Person Authorized to consent for patient

____
Relationship to patient

____
Signature of Witness

Job 10 Registration Paper work- Julius Washington 4 of 5

Douglasville Medicine Associates
5076 Brand Blvd, Suite 401~ Douglasville, NY 01234

ASSIGNMENT OF BENEFITS AND PATIENT REPRESENTATION

Patient Name:______________________________ Chart # ______________

Insured Name:____

Insurance Company Name ____________________________________

Policy # ____________________ Group # ____________________

I hereby assign all medical and/or surgical benefits, to include major medical benefits to which I am entitled, to **Douglasville Medicine Associates**. This assignment will remain in effect until revoked by me in writing. A photocopy of this assignment is to be considered as valid as the original.

I understand that I am financially responsible for all charges whether or not paid by my insurance carrier. I understand that I will be responsible for any court costs or collection fees should it become necessary to take action to collect for services/supplies rendered.

I hereby authorize **Douglasville Medicine Associates** to release all medical information necessary to secure payment on my account.

I hereby authorize **Douglasville Medicine Associates** and medical billing staff members, to submit claims, on my behalf, to the insurance company listed on the copy of the current and valid insurance card I have provided to the Clinic in good faith. I fully agree and understand that the submission of a claim does not absolve me of my responsibility to ensure that the bill for medical services is paid in full.

I authorize **Douglasville Medicine Associates** and its medical billing representative, to be my personal representative, which allows the Clinic to: (1) submit any and all appeals when my insurance company performs an adverse benefit determination as defined in 29 CFR 2560-503-1, (2) submit any and all requests for benefit information from my employer and/or health insurance company, and (3) initiate formal complaints to any State or Federal agency that has jurisdiction over my benefits.

I fully understand and agree that I am responsible for full payment of the medical debt I owe the Clinic, if my insurance company has refused to pay 100% of my covered benefits, within ninety (90) days of any and all appeals or request for information. A photocopy of this document shall be considered as effective and valid as the original.

Patient Julius Washington ____________________ 10/27/09
(signature) (date)

Patient Representative ______________________________
(date)

Relationship to Patient ______________________________

Witness ______________________________
(signature) (date)

Job 10 Registration Paper work- Julius Washington 5 of 5

Date of service: 10/27/09	Insurance: MEDICARE		Superbill Number: 2461
Patient name: ISABEL DURAND	Coinsurance: 20%	Copay:	Physician Name: KEMPER
Account #: DUR001	Noncovered Waiver?	yes / no / n/a	

X	Office visit	New	X	Est
	Minimal (RN only)			99211
	Problem focused	99201		99212
	Exp problem focused	99202		99213
	Detailed	99203		99214
	Comp	99204		99215
	Comprhen/Complex	99205		
	Well visit	**New**	**X**	**Est**
	< 1 y	99381		99391
	1-4 y	99382		99392
	5-11 y	99383		99393
	12-17 y	99384		99394
	18-39 y	99385		99395
	40-64 y	99386		99396
	65 y +	99387		99397

X	Medicare preventive services	
1 ✓	Pap	Q0091
1 ✓	Pelvic & breast	G0101
	Prostate/PSA	G0103
	Tobacco couns/3-10 min	G0375
	Tobacco couns/>10 min	G0376
	Welcome to Medicare exam	G0344
	ECG w/Welcome to Medicare	G0366
	Hemoccult, guaiac	G0107
	Flu shot	G0008
	Pneumonia shot	G0009
	Consultation/preop clearance	
	Exp problem focused	99242
	Detailed	99243
	Comp/mod complex	99244
	Comp/high complex	99245
	Other services	
	After posted hours	99050
	Evening/weekend appointment	99051
	Home health certification	G0180
	Home health recertification	G0179
	Care Plan oversight	99374
	Care Plan Oversight >30 mins	99375
	Post-op follow-up	99024
	Prolonged/60min total	99354
	Prolonged/each add 30 mins	99355
	Special reports/forms	99080
	Disability/Workers comp	99455
	Smoking Cessation <10 mins	99406
	Smoking Cessation >10 mins	99407
	ETOH/SA screening <30 mins	99408
	Online E/M by MD	99444
	Phone E/M <10 mins	99441
	Phone E/M <20 mins	99442
	Phone E/M <30 mins	99443
	Anticoagulant Mgmt <90 days	99363
	Anticoagulant Mgmt >90 days	99364
	In office emergency serv	99058
	Other services	
	Supplies	
	Surgical Tray	99070

Instructions:

Call w/ results if abnormal

X	Office procedures		
	Cerumen removal		69210
	ECG, w/interpretation		93000
	ECG, rhythm strip		93040
	Endometrial biopsy		58100
	Fracture care, cast/splint Site: ______________		____
	Nebulizer		94640
	Nebulizer demo		94664
	Spirometry		94010
	Spirometry, pre and post		94060
	Vasectomy		55250
	Skin procedures		**Units**
	Foreign body, skin, simple	10120	
	Foreign body, skin, complex	10121	
	I&D, abscess	10060	
	I&D, hematoma/seroma	10140	
	Laceration repair, simple Site: _______ Size: _____	120__	
	Laceration repair, layered Site: _______ Size: _____	120__	
	Laser Light Tx	96597	
	Lesion, biopsy, one	11100	
	Lesion, biopsy, each add'l	11101	
	Lesion, excision, benign Site: _______ Size: _____	114__	
	Lesion, excision, malignant Site: _______ Size: _____	116__	
	Lesion, paring/cutting, one	11055	
	Lesion, paring/cutting, 2-4	11056	
	Lesion, shave Site: _______ Size: _____	113__	
	Nail removal, partial (+T mod)	11730	
	Nail rem, w/matrix (+T mod)	11750	
	Skin tag, 1-15	11200	
	Wart, flat, 1-14	17110	
	Destruction lesion, 1st	17000	
	Destruct lesion, each addl 2-14	17003	
	Medications		**Units**
	Ampicillin, up to 500mg	J0290	
	B-12, up to 1,000 mcg	J3420	
	Epinephrine, up to 1ml	J0170	
	Kenalog, 10mg	J3301	
	Lidocaine, 10mg	J2001	
	Normal saline, 1000cc	J7030	
	Phenergan, up to 50mg	J2550	
	Progesterone, 150mg	J1055	
	Rocephin, 250mg	J0696	
	Testosterone, 200mg	J1080	
	Tigan, up to 200 mg	J3250	
	Toradol, 15mg	J1885	
	Albuterol	J7609	
	Depo-Provera 50 mg	J1055	
	Depo-Medrol 40 mg	J1030	

Diagnoses	Code
1 Annual Pelvic Exam	
2 Vaginal prolapse	
3	
4	

Next office visit:
Recheck • (Preventative) • PRN
Referral to:

Physician signature

x Sally Kemper MD

X	Laboratory		-90
	Venipuncture	36415	
	Blood glucose, monitoring device	82962	
	Blood glucose, visual dipstick	82948	
	CBC, w/ auto differential	85025	
	CBC, w/o auto differential	85027	
	Cholesterol	82465	
	Hemoccult, guaiac	82270	
	Hemoccult, immunoassay	82274	
	Hemoglobin A1C	85018	
	Lipid panel	80061	
	Liver panel	80076	
	KOH prep (skin, hair, nails)	87220	
	Metabolic panel, basic	80048	
	Metabolic panel, comprehensive	80053	
	Mononucleosis	86308	
	Pregnancy, blood	84703	
	Pregnancy, urine	81025	
	Renal panel	80069	
	Sedimentation rate	85651	
	Strep, rapid	86403	
	Strep culture	87081	
	Strep A	87880	
	TB	86580	
	UA, complete, non-automated	81000	
	UA, w/o micro, non-automated	81002	
	UA, w/ micro, non-automated	81003	
	Urine colony count	87086	
	Urine culture, presumptive	87088	
	Wet mount/KOH	87210	
	Vaccines		
	DT, <7 y		90702
	DTP		90701
	DtaP, <7 y		90700
	Flu, 6-35 months		90657
	Flu, 3 y +		90658
	Hep A, adult		90632
	Hep A, ped/adol, 2 dose		90633
	Hep B, adult		90746
	Hep B, ped/adol 3 dose		90744
	Hep B-Hib		90748
	Hib, 4 dose		90645
	HPV		90649
	IPV		90713
	MMR		90707
	Pneumonia, >2 y		90732
	Pneumonia conjugate, <5 y		90669
	Td, >7 y		90718
	Varicella		90716
	Tetanus toxoid adsorbed, IM		90703
	Immunizations & Injections		**Units**
	Allergen, one	95115	
	Allergen, multiple	95117	
	Imm admn <8 yo 1st Inj	90465	
	Imm admn <8 yo each add inj	90466	
	Imm <8 yo oral or intranasal	90467	
	Imm admn <8 yo each add	90468	
	Imm admin, one vacc	90471	
	Imm admin, each add'l	90472	
	Imm admin, intranasal, one	90473	
	Imm admin, intranasal, each add'l	90474	
	Injection, joint, small	20600	
	Injection, joint, intermediate	20605	
	Injection, ther/proph/diag	90772	
	Injection, trigger pt 1-2 musc	20552	

Today's charges:		
Today's payment:		
Balance due:		

Job 11 Router- Isabel Durand

Date of service: 10/27/09	Insurance: GREATWEST		Superbill Number: 2462
Patient name: JULIUS WASHINGTON	Coinsurance: 20%	Copay:	Physician Name: MENDENHALL
Account #: WAS001	Noncovered Waiver?	yes / no / n/a	

x	Office visit	New	x	Est
	Minimal (RN only)			99211
	Problem focused	99201		99212
	Exp problem focused	99202		99213
	Detailed	99203		99214
	Comp	99204	✓	99215
	Comprhen/Complex	99205		
	Well visit	**New**	**x**	**Est**
	< 1 y	99381		99391
	1-4 y	99382		99392
	5-11 y	99383		99393
	12-17 y	99384		99394
	18-39 y	99385		99395
	40-64 y	99386		99396
	65 y +	99387		99397
	Medicare preventive services			
	Pap			Q0091
	Pelvic & breast			G0101
	Prostate/PSA			G0103
	Tobacco couns/3-10 min			G0375
	Tobacco couns/>10 min			G0376
	Welcome to Medicare exam			G0344
	ECG w/Welcome to Medicare			G0366
	Hemoccult, guaiac			G0107
	Flu shot			G0008
	Pneumonia shot			G0009
	Consultation/preop clearance			
	Exp problem focused			99242
	Detailed			99243
	Comp/mod complex			99244
	Comp/high complex			99245
	Other services			
	After posted hours			99050
	Evening/weekend appointment			99051
	Home health certification			G0180
	Home health recertification			G0179
	Care Plan oversight			99374
	Care Plan Oversight >30 mins			99375
	Post-op follow-up			99024
	Prolonged/60min total			99354
	Prolonged/each add 30 mins			99355
	Special reports/forms			99080
	Disability/Workers comp			99455
	Smoking Cessation <10 mins			99406
	Smoking Cessation >10 mins			99407
	ETOH/SA screening <30 mins			99408
	Online E/M by MD			99444
	Phone E/M <10 mins			99441
	Phone E/M <20 mins			99442
	Phone E/M <30 mins			99443
	Anticoagulant Mgmt <90 days			99363
	Anticoagulant Mgmt >90 days			99364
	In office emergency serv			99058
	Other services			
✓	Chest x-ray front + lateral			
	Supplies			
	Surgical Tray			99070

x	Office procedures		
	Cerumen removal		69210
	ECG, w/interpretation		93000
	ECG, rhythm strip		93040
	Endometrial biopsy		58100
	Fracture care, cast/splint Site: ______		______
✓	Nebulizer		94640
	Nebulizer demo		94664
	Spirometry		94010
	Spirometry, pre and post		94060
	Vasectomy		55250
	Skin procedures		**Units**
	Foreign body, skin, simple	10120	
	Foreign body, skin, complex	10121	
	I&D, abscess	10060	
	I&D, hematoma/seroma	10140	
	Laceration repair, simple Site: ______ Size: ____	120__	
	Laceration repair, layered Site: ______ Size: ____	120__	
	Laser Light Tx	96597	
	Lesion, biopsy, one	11100	
	Lesion, biopsy, each add'l	11101	
	Lesion, excision, benign Site: ______ Size: ____	114__	
	Lesion, excision, malignant Site: ______ Size: ____	116__	
	Lesion, paring/cutting, one	11055	
	Lesion, paring/cutting, 2-4	11056	
	Lesion, shave Site: ______ Size: ____	113__	
	Nail removal, partial (+T mod)	11730	
	Nail rem, w/matrix (+T mod)	11750	
	Skin tag, 1-15	11200	
	Wart, flat, 1-14	17110	
	Destruction lesion, 1st	17000	
	Destruct lesion, each addl 2-14	17003	
	Medications		**Units**
	Ampicillin, up to 500mg	J0290	
	B-12, up to 1,000 mcg	J3420	
	Epinephrine, up to 1ml	J0170	
	Kenalog, 10mg	J3301	
	Lidocaine, 10mg	J2001	
	Normal saline, 1000cc	J7030	
	Phenergan, up to 50mg	J2550	
	Progesterone, 150mg	J1055	
	Rocephin, 250mg	J0696	
	Testosterone, 200mg	J1080	
	Tigan, up to 200 mg	J3250	
	Toradol, 15mg	J1885	
✓	Albuterol	J7609	
	Depo-Provera 50 mg	J1055	
	Depo-Medrol 40 mg	J1030	

Diagnoses	Code
1 Acute exacerbation asthma	
2 bronchitis	
3 sinusitis	
4	

Next office visit: 2 weeks

(Recheck) • Preventative • PRN

Referral to:

Instructions:

Rx Levaquin
po bid q day
10 days

Physician signature

x Sarah Mendenhall MD

x	Laboratory		-90
	Venipuncture	36415	
	Blood glucose, monitoring device	82962	
	Blood glucose, visual dipstick	82948	
	CBC, w/ auto differential	85025	
	CBC, w/o auto differential	85027	
	Cholesterol	82465	
	Hemoccult, guaiac	82270	
	Hemoccult, immunoassay	82274	
	Hemoglobin A1C	85018	
	Lipid panel	80061	
	Liver panel	80076	
	KOH prep (skin, hair, nails)	87220	
	Metabolic panel, basic	80048	
	Metabolic panel, comprehensive	80053	
	Mononucleosis	86308	
	Pregnancy, blood	84703	
	Pregnancy, urine	81025	
	Renal panel	80069	
	Sedimentation rate	85651	
	Strep, rapid	86403	
	Strep culture	87081	
	Strep A	87880	
	TB	86580	
	UA, complete, non-automated	81000	
	UA, w/o micro, non-automated	81002	
	UA, w/ micro, non-automated	81003	
	Urine colony count	87086	
	Urine culture, presumptive	87088	
	Wet mount/KOH	87210	
	Vaccines		
	DT, <7 y		90702
	DTP		90701
	DtaP, <7 y		90700
	Flu, 6-35 months		90657
	Flu, 3 y +		90658
	Hep A, adult		90632
	Hep A, ped/adol, 2 dose		90633
	Hep B, adult		90746
	Hep B, ped/adol 3 dose		90744
	Hep B-Hib		90748
	Hib, 4 dose		90645
	HPV		90649
	IPV		90713
	MMR		90707
	Pneumonia, >2 y		90732
	Pneumonia conjugate, <5 y		90669
	Td, >7 y		90718
	Varicella		90716
	Tetanus toxoid adsorbed, IM		90703
	Immunizations & Injections		**Units**
	Allergen, one	95115	
	Allergen, multiple	95117	
	Imm admn <8 yo 1st Inj	90465	
	Imm admn <8 yo each add inj	90466	
	Imm <8 yo oral or intranasal	90467	
	Imm admn <8 yo each add	90468	
	Imm admin, one vacc	90471	
	Imm admin, each add'l	90472	
	Imm admin, intranasal, one	90473	
	Imm admin, intranasal, each add'l	90474	
	Injection, joint, small	20600	
	Injection, joint, intermediate	20605	
	Injection, ther/proph/diag	90772	
	Injection, trigger pt 1-2 musc	20552	

Today's charges:	
Today's payment:	
Balance due:	

Job 14 Router- Julius Washington

Galaxy Health Network
William L. Kostner
ID No: 1167229B
Group No: 41997H
Coinsurance: 20% allowed amount
Deductible: $150

1999 Jupiter St. Suite 450, Atlanta, GA 74854 (800) 555-3369

Job 15 & 17 Insurance Card

Douglasville Medicine Associates
Patient Registration Form

Patients must complete all information prior to seeing the physician. A copy of your insurance card(s) and driver's license will be made for your file.

Patient Name: WILLIAM KOSTNER Date of Birth: 02/13/59
Sex: (Male) or Female Social Security Number: 731-01-4513 Marital Status: M
Address Line 1: 47 ORANGEMAN WAY
Address Line 2: ______
City: N. SYRACUSE
State: NY Zip Code: 14871
Home Telephone: (717) 555-6271 Work Telephone: (717) 555-4172
Cellular Telephone: (—) ______ Email address: william.kostner@corning.com

Patient's Work Status (Full-Time, Part-Time, Retired, Student): ______
Employer Name: CORNING
Address Line 1: 100 CORNING DRIVE
Address Line 2: ______
City: ROME State: NY Zip: 14644
Telephone: (717) 555-4172
If patient is a minor, who is the primary guardian? ______

Primary Insurance Company: GALAXY HEALTH NETWORK
Subscriber ID Number 11672293 Policy Group #: 41997H
Subscriber Name: SAME Birth date: SAME
Subscriber Social Security Number: ___-___-___ Relationship to patient: SAME

Secondary Insurance Company: ______
Subscriber ID Number ______ Policy Group #: ______
Subscriber Name: ______ Birth date: ______
Subscriber Social Security Number: ___-___-___ Relationship to patient: ______

Complete this section if your treatment is for an injury or accident.
Were you injured at work? YES Is this covered by Workers' Compensation? YES AFLAC
If Yes, Contact person at your Employer JACK WELLINGTON (717) 555-1236
Were you involved in an auto accident? ______ Provide insurance company, contact information, and claim number: ______

Date & time of Accident 6/19/09 Place of Accident Corning Warehouse
How did injury happen? Driving Forklift
Name of Physician who treated you at time of accident: Dr Smith

Financial Responsibility Statement/ Release of Information Authorization
"I authorize the release of any medical information necessary to my insurance company and the Payment of Benefits to the Physician for services provided.

X William Kostner Date 10/27/09
Signature of Patient or Legal Guardian

Job 15 Registration Paper work- William Kostner 1 of 5

Douglasville Medicine Associates
Patient Registration Form

OUR FINANCIAL POLICY

By law, we must collect your carrier designated co-pay at the time of service. Please be prepared to pay that co-pay at each visit. We are also required to collect any portion of the deductible that has not been satisfied. If your plan requires a coinsurance instead of a co-pay and we participate with the plan, we will accept the designated payment and bill you accordingly for any deductible and coinsurance your plan indicates you are responsible for on their explanation of benefits.

Payment is expected at the time of service unless other financial arrangements have been made prior to your visit. If you are uninsured, you may qualify for a hardship discount. Ask one of our staff members for more information.

You are responsible for timely payment of your account. Douglasville Medicine Associates reserves the right to reschedule or deny a future appointment on delinquent accounts.

WE ACCEPT CASH, CHECKS, MASTERCARD AND VISA

THANK YOU for taking the time to review our policy.

William Kostner ____________________ 10/27/09

(Responsible Party Signature) (Date)

Job 15 Registration Paper work- William Kostner 2 of 5

Douglasville Medicine Associates
5076 Brand Blvd., Suite 401▪Douglasville, NY 01234 (123)456-7890

Patient Name: William Kostner

Record #: KOS001

I acknowledge that I have received a written copy of Douglasville Medicine Associates Notice of Patient Privacy Practices. I also acknowledge that I have been allowed to ask questions concerning this notice and my rights under this notice. I understand that this form will be part of my record until such time as I may choose to revoke this acknowledgement. If I am not the patient, I am the authorized representative of a minor child or authorized by law to act for and on the patient's behalf.

William Kostner ______________ 10/27/09 ______________

Signature of Patient or Authorized Agent — Date

Patient (or authorized agent) refused to sign Notice of Privacy Practices.

Please describe events. ______________________________

____

______________________________ ______________

Signature of DMA Employee — Date

Douglasville Medicine Associates
5076 Brand Blvd., Suite 401▪Douglasville, NY 01234

CONSENT TO TREATMENT

Patient Name: ______________________ Date: 10/27/09

I, ______________________, hereby voluntarily consent to outpatient treatment and evaluation at Douglasville Medicine Associates for ______________________. This includes routine diagnostic procedures, examination and medical treatment including, but not limited to, routine laboratory work (such as blood, urine and other studies), x-rays, heart tracing and administration of medications prescribed by the physician.

I further consent to the performance of those diagnostic procedures, examinations and rendering of medical treatment by the medical staff and their assistants.

I understand that this consent form will be valid and remain in effect as long as I receive medical care at Douglasville Medicine Associates.

This form has been explained to me and I fully understand this Consent To Treatment and agree to its contents.

William Kostner
Signature of Patient or
Person Authorized to consent for patient

Self
Relationship to patient

____
Signature of Witness

Job 15 Registration Paper work- William Kostner 4 of 5

Douglasville Medicine Associates
5076 Brand Blvd, Suite 401~ Douglasville, NY 01234

ASSIGNMENT OF BENEFITS AND PATIENT REPRESENTATION

Patient Name:______________________________ Chart # ______________

Insured Name:____

Insurance Company Name ______________________________________

Policy # ____________________ Group # ____________________

I hereby assign all medical and/or surgical benefits, to include major medical benefits to which I am entitled, to **Douglasville Medicine Associates**. This assignment will remain in effect until revoked by me in writing. A photocopy of this assignment is to be considered as valid as the original.

I understand that I am financially responsible for all charges whether or not paid by my insurance carrier. I understand that I will be responsible for any court costs or collection fees should it become necessary to take action to collect for services/supplies rendered.

I hereby authorize **Douglasville Medicine Associates** to release all medical information necessary to secure payment on my account.

I hereby authorize **Douglasville Medicine Associates** and medical billing staff members, to submit claims, on my behalf, to the insurance company listed on the copy of the current and valid insurance card I have provided to the Clinic in good faith. I fully agree and understand that the submission of a claim does not absolve me of my responsibility to ensure that the bill for medical services is paid in full.

I authorize **Douglasville Medicine Associates** and its medical billing representative, to be my personal representative, which allows the Clinic to: (1) submit any and all appeals when my insurance company performs an adverse benefit determination as defined in 29 CFR 2560-503-1, (2) submit any and all requests for benefit information from my employer and/or health insurance company, and (3) initiate formal complaints to any State or Federal agency that has jurisdiction over my benefits.

I fully understand and agree that I am responsible for full payment of the medical debt I owe the Clinic, if my insurance company has refused to pay 100% of my covered benefits, within ninety (90) days of any and all appeals or request for information. A photocopy of this document shall be considered as effective and valid as the original.

Patient William Kost 10/27/09
(signature) (date)

Patient Representative ______________________________
(date)

Relationship to Patient ______________________________

Witness ______________________________
(signature) (date)

Job 15 Registration Paper work- William Kostner 5 of 5

Date of service: 10/27/09	Insurance: GALAXY HEALTH				Superbill Number: 2458
Patient name: WILLIAM KOSTNER	Coinsurance: 20%	Copay:			Physician Name: HEATH
Account #: KOS001	Noncovered Waiver?	yes	no	n/a	

x	Office visit	New	x	Est
	Minimal (RN only)			99211
	Problem focused	99201		99212
	Exp problem focused	99202		99213
	Detailed	99203		99214
	Comp	99204		99215
	Comprhen/Complex	99205		

x	Well visit	New	x	Est
	< 1 y	99381		99391
	1-4 y	99382		99392
	5-11 y	99383		99393
	12-17 y	99384		99394
	18-39 y	99385		99395
	40-64 y	99386		99396
	65 y +	99387		99397

x	Medicare preventive services	
	Pap	Q0091
	Pelvic & breast	G0101
	Prostate/PSA	G0103
	Tobacco couns/3-10 min	G0375
	Tobacco couns/>10 min	G0376
	Welcome to Medicare exam	G0344
	ECG w/Welcome to Medicare	G0366
	Hemoccult, guaiac	G0107
	Flu shot	G0008
	Pneumonia shot	G0009

x	Consultation/preop clearance	
	Exp problem focused	99242
	Detailed	99243
✓	Comp/mod complex	99244
	Comp/high complex	99245

x	Other services	
	After posted hours	99050
	Evening/weekend appointment	99051
	Home health certification	G0180
	Home health recertification	G0179
	Care Plan oversight	99374
	Care Plan Oversight >30 mins	99375
	Post-op follow-up	99024
	Prolonged/60min total	99354
	Prolonged/each add 30 mins	99355
	Special reports/forms	99080
	Disability/Workers comp	99455
	Smoking Cessation <10 mins	99406
	Smoking Cessation >10 mins	99407
	ETOH/SA screening <30 mins	99408
	Online E/M by MD	99444
	Phone E/M <10 mins	99441
	Phone E/M <20 mins	99442
	Phone E/M <30 mins	99443
	Anticoagulant Mgmt <90 days	99363
	Anticoagulant Mgmt >90 days	99364
	In office emergency serv	99058

x	Other services	

Supplies	
Surgical Tray	99070

Instructions:

x	Office procedures	
	Cerumen removal	69210
	ECG, w/interpretation	93000
	ECG, rhythm strip	93040
	Endometrial biopsy	58100
	Fracture care, cast/splint Site: ______	____
	Nebulizer	94640
	Nebulizer demo	94664
	Spirometry	94010
	Spirometry, pre and post	94060
	Vasectomy	55250

x	Skin procedures		Units
	Foreign body, skin, simple	10120	
	Foreign body, skin, complex	10121	
	I&D, abscess	10060	
	I&D, hematoma/seroma	10140	
	Laceration repair, simple Site: ______ Size: ____	120__	
	Laceration repair, layered Site: ______ Size: ____	120__	
	Laser Light Tx	96597	
	Lesion, biopsy, one	11100	
	Lesion, biopsy, each add'l	11101	
	Lesion, excision, benign Site: ______ Size: ____	114__	
	Lesion, excision, malignant Site: ______ Size: ____	116__	
	Lesion, paring/cutting, one	11055	
	Lesion, paring/cutting, 2-4	11056	
	Lesion, shave Site: ______ Size: ____	113__	
	Nail removal, partial (+T mod)	11730	
	Nail rem, w/matrix (+T mod)	11750	
	Skin tag, 1-15	11200	
	Wart, flat, 1-14	17110	
	Destruction lesion, 1st	17000	
	Destruct lesion, each addl 2-14	17003	

x	Medications		Units
	Ampicillin, up to 500mg	J0290	
	B-12, up to 1,000 mcg	J3420	
	Epinephrine, up to 1ml	J0170	
	Kenalog, 10mg	J3301	
✓	Lidocaine, 10mg	J2001	
	Normal saline, 1000cc	J7030	
	Phenergan, up to 50mg	J2550	
	Progesterone, 150mg	J1055	
	Rocephin, 250mg	J0696	
	Testosterone, 200mg	J1080	
	Tigan, up to 200 mg	J3250	
	Toradol, 15mg	J1885	
	Albuterol	J7609	
	Depo-Provera 50 mg	J1055	
✓	Depo-Medrol 40 mg	J1030	

Diagnoses		Code
1 Vertigo		
2 HA		
3 Myositis		
4		

Next office visit: 4 wks

Recheck • Preventative • PRN

Referral to:

Physician signature

X [signature]

x	Laboratory		-90
	Venipuncture	36415	
	Blood glucose, monitoring device	82962	
	Blood glucose, visual dipstick	82948	
	CBC, w/ auto differential	85025	
	CBC, w/o auto differential	85027	
	Cholesterol	82465	
	Hemoccult, guaiac	82270	
	Hemoccult, immunoassay	82274	
	Hemoglobin A1C	85018	
	Lipid panel	80061	
	Liver panel	80076	
	KOH prep (skin, hair, nails)	87220	
	Metabolic panel, basic	80048	
	Metabolic panel, comprehensive	80053	
	Mononucleosis	86308	
	Pregnancy, blood	84703	
	Pregnancy, urine	81025	
	Renal panel	80069	
	Sedimentation rate	85651	
	Strep, rapid	86403	
	Strep culture	87081	
	Strep A	87880	
	TB	86580	
	UA, complete, non-automated	81000	
	UA, w/o micro, non-automated	81002	
	UA, w/ micro, non-automated	81003	
	Urine colony count	87086	
	Urine culture, presumptive	87088	
	Wet mount/KOH	87210	

x	Vaccines	
	DT, <7 y	90702
	DTP	90701
	DtaP, <7 y	90700
	Flu, 6-35 months	90657
	Flu, 3 y +	90658
	Hep A, adult	90632
	Hep A, ped/adol, 2 dose	90633
	Hep B, adult	90746
	Hep B, ped/adol 3 dose	90744
	Hep B-Hib	90748
	Hib, 4 dose	90645
	HPV	90649
	IPV	90713
	MMR	90707
	Pneumonia, >2 y	90732
	Pneumonia conjugate, <5 y	90669
	Td, >7 y	90718
	Varicella	90716
	Tetanus toxoid adsorbed, IM	90703

x	Immunizations & Injections		Units
	Allergen, one	95115	
	Allergen, multiple	95117	
	Imm admn <8 yo 1st Inj	90465	
	Imm admn <8 yo each add inj	90466	
	Imm <8 yo oral or intranasal	90467	
	Imm admn <8 yo each add	90468	
	Imm admin, one vacc	90471	
	Imm admin, each add'l	90472	
	Imm admin, intranasal, one	90473	
	Imm admin, intranasal, each add'l	90474	
	Injection, joint, small	20600	
	Injection, joint, intermediate	20605	
	Injection, ther/proph/diag	90772	
✓	Injection, trigger pt 1-2 musc	20552	

Today's charges:		
Today's payment:		
Balance due:		

Job 17 Router- William Kostner

Date of service: 10/27/09	Insurance: MEDICARE SW/CENTURY SR				Superbill Number: 2457
Patient name: DEANNA HARTSFELD	Coinsurance: 20%	Copay:			Physician Name: MURRAY
Account #: HAR001	Noncovered Waiver?	yes	no	n/a	

X	Office visit	New	X	Est
	Minimal (RN only)			99211
	Problem focused	99201		99212
	Exp problem focused	99202		99213
	Detailed	99203		99214
	Comp	99204		99215
	Comprhen/Complex	99205		
	Well visit	**New**	**X**	**Est**
	< 1 y	99381		99391
	1-4 y	99382		99392
	5-11 y	99383		99393
	12-17 y	99384		99394
	18-39 y	99385		99395
	40-64 y	99386		99396
	65 y +	99387		99397
	Medicare preventive services			
✓	Pap			Q0091
	Pelvic & breast			G0101
	Prostate/PSA			G0103
	Tobacco couns/3-10 min			G0375
✓	Tobacco couns/>10 min			G0376
✓	Welcome to Medicare exam			G0344
	ECG w/Welcome to Medicare			G0366
	Hemoccult, guaiac			G0107
	Flu shot			G0008
	Pneumonia shot			G0009
	Consultation/preop clearance			
	Exp problem focused			99242
	Detailed			99243
	Comp/mod complex			99244
	Comp/high complex			99245
	Other services			
	After posted hours			99050
	Evening/weekend appointment			99051
	Home health certification			G0180
	Home health recertification			G0179
	Care Plan oversight			99374
	Care Plan Oversight >30 mins			99375
	Post-op follow-up			99024
	Prolonged/60min total			99354
	Prolonged/each add 30 mins			99355
	Special reports/forms			99080
	Disability/Workers comp			99455
	Smoking Cessation <10 mins			99406
	Smoking Cessation >10 mins			99407
	ETOH/SA screening <30 mins			99408
	Online E/M by MD			99444
	Phone E/M <10 mins			99441
	Phone E/M <20 mins			99442
	Phone E/M <30 mins			99443
	Anticoagulant Mgmt <90 days			99363
	Anticoagulant Mgmt >90 days			99364
	In office emergency serv			99058
	Other services			
✓	Dexa Scan			
	Supplies			
	Surgical Tray			99070

Instructions:

30 mins counseling diet/exercise/ Diabetes Risk

X	Office procedures		
	Cerumen removal	69210	
✓	ECG, w/interpretation	93000	
	ECG, rhythm strip	93040	
	Endometrial biopsy	58100	
	Fracture care, cast/splint Site: ________	____	
	Nebulizer	94640	
	Nebulizer demo	94664	
	Spirometry	94010	
	Spirometry, pre and post	94060	
	Vasectomy	55250	
	Skin procedures		**Units**
	Foreign body, skin, simple	10120	
	Foreign body, skin, complex	10121	
	I&D, abscess	10060	
	I&D, hematoma/seroma	10140	
	Laceration repair, simple Site: _______ Size: _____	120__	
	Laceration repair, layered Site: _______ Size: _____	120__	
	Laser Light Tx	96597	
	Lesion, biopsy, one	11100	
	Lesion, biopsy, each add'l	11101	
	Lesion, excision, benign Site: _______ Size: _____	114__	
	Lesion, excision, malignant Site: _______ Size: _____	116__	
	Lesion, paring/cutting, one	11055	
	Lesion, paring/cutting, 2-4	11056	
	Lesion, shave Site: _______ Size: _____	113__	
	Nail removal, partial (+T mod)	11730	
	Nail rem, w/matrix (+T mod)	11750	
	Skin tag, 1-15	11200	
	Wart, flat, 1-14	17110	
	Destruction lesion, 1st	17000	
	Destruct lesion, each addl 2-14	17003	
	Medications		**Units**
	Ampicillin, up to 500mg	J0290	
	B-12, up to 1,000 mcg	J3420	
	Epinephrine, up to 1ml	J0170	
	Kenalog, 10mg	J3301	
	Lidocaine, 10mg	J2001	
	Normal saline, 1000cc	J7030	
	Phenergan, up to 50mg	J2550	
	Progesterone, 150mg	J1055	
	Rocephin, 250mg	J0696	
	Testosterone, 200mg	J1080	
	Tigan, up to 200 mg	J3250	
	Toradol, 15mg	J1885	
	Albuterol	J7609	
	Depo-Provera 50 mg	J1055	
	Depo-Medrol 40 mg	J1030	

Diagnoses	Code
1 Elevated BP	
2 Well Check	
3 Obesity	
4	

Next office visit: 1 yr

Recheck (Preventative) PRN

Referral to:

Physician signature

x [signature] MD

X	Laboratory		-90
	Venipuncture	36415	
	Blood glucose, monitoring device	82962	
	Blood glucose, visual dipstick	82948	
	CBC, w/ auto differential	85025	
	CBC, w/o auto differential	85027	
	Cholesterol	82465	
	Hemoccult, guaiac	82270	
	Hemoccult, immunoassay	82274	
	Hemoglobin A1C	85018	
	Lipid panel	80061	
	Liver panel	80076	
	KOH prep (skin, hair, nails)	87220	
	Metabolic panel, basic	80048	
✓	Metabolic panel, comprehensive	80053	
	Mononucleosis	86308	
	Pregnancy, blood	84703	
	Pregnancy, urine	81025	
	Renal panel	80069	
	Sedimentation rate	85651	
	Strep, rapid	86403	
	Strep culture	87081	
	Strep A	87880	
	TB	86580	
	UA, complete, non-automated	81000	
	UA, w/o micro, non-automated	81002	
	UA, w/ micro, non-automated	81003	
	Urine colony count	87086	
	Urine culture, presumptive	87088	
	Wet mount/KOH	87210	

X	Vaccines	
	DT, <7 y	90702
	DTP	90701
	DtaP, <7 y	90700
	Flu, 6-35 months	90657
	Flu, 3 y +	90658
	Hep A, adult	90632
	Hep A, ped/adol, 2 dose	90633
	Hep B, adult	90746
	Hep B, ped/adol 3 dose	90744
	Hep B-Hib	90748
	Hib, 4 dose	90645
	HPV	90649
	IPV	90713
	MMR	90707
	Pneumonia, >2 y	90732
	Pneumonia conjugate, <5 y	90669
	Td, >7 y	90718
	Varicella	90716
	Tetanus toxoid adsorbed, IM	90703

X	Immunizations & Injections		Units
	Allergen, one	95115	
	Allergen, multiple	95117	
	Imm admn <8 yo 1st Inj	90465	
	Imm admn <8 yo each add inj	90466	
	Imm <8 yo oral or intranasal	90467	
	Imm admn <8 yo each add	90468	
	Imm admn, one vacc	90471	
	Imm admin, each add'l	90472	
	Imm admin, intranasal, one	90473	
	Imm admin, intranasal, each add'l	90474	
	Injection, joint, small	20600	
	Injection, joint, intermediate	20605	
	Injection, ther/proph/diag	90772	
	Injection, trigger pt 1-2 musc	20552	

Today's charges:	
Today's payment:	
Balance due:	

Job 19 Router- Deanna Hartsfeld

Date of service: 10/27/09	Insurance: MEDICARE STATE WIDE				Superbill Number: 2455
Patient name: VITO MANGANO	Coinsurance: 20%	Copay:			Physician Name: HEATH
Account #: MAN001	Noncovered Waiver?	yes	no	n/a	

x	Office visit	New	x	Est
	Minimal (RN only)			99211
	Problem focused	99201		99212
	Exp problem focused	99202		99213
	Detailed	99203		99214
	Comp	99204	✓	99215
	Comprhen/Complex	99205		
	Well visit	**New**	**x**	**Est**
	< 1 y	99381		99391
	1-4 y	99382		99392
	5-11 y	99383		99393
	12-17 y	99384		99394
	18-39 y	99385		99395
	40-64 y	99386		99396
	65 y +	99387		99397
	Medicare preventive services			
	Pap			Q0091
	Pelvic & breast			G0101
✓	Prostate/PSA			G0103
	Tobacco couns/3-10 min			G0375
	Tobacco couns/>10 min			G0376
	Welcome to Medicare exam			G0344
	ECG w/Welcome to Medicare			G0366
	Hemoccult, guaiac			G0107
	Flu shot			G0008
	Pneumonia shot			G0009
	Consultation/preop clearance			
	Exp problem focused			99242
	Detailed			99243
	Comp/mod complex			99244
	Comp/high complex			99245
	Other services			
	After posted hours			99050
	Evening/weekend appointment			99051
	Home health certification			G0180
	Home health recertification			G0179
	Care Plan oversight			99374
	Care Plan Oversight >30 mins			99375
	Post-op follow-up			99024
	Prolonged/60min total			99354
	Prolonged/each add 30 mins			99355
	Special reports/forms			99080
	Disability/Workers comp			99455
	Smoking Cessation <10 mins			99406
	Smoking Cessation >10 mins			99407
	ETOH/SA screening <30 mins			99408
	Online E/M by MD			99444
	Phone E/M <10 mins			99441
	Phone E/M <20 mins			99442
	Phone E/M <30 mins			99443
	Anticoagulant Mgmt <90 days			99363
	Anticoagulant Mgmt >90 days			99364
	In office emergency serv			99058
	Other services			
✓	U/S bladder & trans rectal prostate US			
	Supplies			
	Surgical Tray			99070
	Foley catheter			
	Bladder catheterization			

x	Office procedures		Code/Units
	Cerumen removal		69210
	ECG, w/interpretation		93000
	ECG, rhythm strip		93040
	Endometrial biopsy		58100
	Fracture care, cast/splint Site: ______		
	Nebulizer		94640
	Nebulizer demo		94664
	Spirometry		94010
	Spirometry, pre and post		94060
	Vasectomy		55250
	Skin procedures		**Units**
	Foreign body, skin, simple	10120	
	Foreign body, skin, complex	10121	
	I&D, abscess	10060	
	I&D, hematoma/seroma	10140	
	Laceration repair, simple Site: ______ Size: ______	120__	
	Laceration repair, layered Site: ______ Size: ______	120__	
	Laser Light Tx	96597	
	Lesion, biopsy, one	11100	
	Lesion, biopsy, each add'l	11101	
	Lesion, excision, benign Site: ______ Size: ______	114__	
	Lesion, excision, malignant Site: ______ Size: ______	116__	
	Lesion, paring/cutting, one	11055	
	Lesion, paring/cutting, 2-4	11056	
	Lesion, shave Site: ______ Size: ______	113__	
	Nail removal, partial (+T mod)	11730	
	Nail rem, w/matrix (+T mod)	11750	
	Skin tag, 1-15	11200	
	Wart, flat, 1-14	17110	
	Destruction lesion, 1st	17000	
	Destruct lesion, each addl 2-14	17003	
	Medications		**Units**
	Ampicillin, up to 500mg	J0290	
	B-12, up to 1,000 mcg	J3420	
	Epinephrine, up to 1ml	J0170	
	Kenalog, 10mg	J3301	
	Lidocaine, 10mg	J2001	
	Normal saline, 1000cc	J7030	
	Phenergan, up to 50mg	J2550	
	Progesterone, 150mg	J1055	
	Rocephin, 250mg	J0696	
	Testosterone, 200mg	J1080	
	Tigan, up to 200 mg	J3250	
	Toradol, 15mg	J1885	
	Albuterol	J7609	
	Depo-Provera 50 mg	J1055	
	Depo-Medrol 40 mg	J1030	
	Diagnoses		**Code**
	1 Enlarged prostate w/nodules		
	2 urinary outlet obstruction		
	3 urinary retention		
	4		

x	Laboratory		-90
✓	Venipuncture	36415	
	Blood glucose, monitoring device	82962	
	Blood glucose, visual dipstick	82948	
	CBC, w/ auto differential	85025	
	CBC, w/o auto differential	85027	
	Cholesterol	82465	
	Hemoccult, guaiac	82270	
	Hemoccult, immunoassay	82274	
	Hemoglobin A1C	85018	
	Lipid panel	80061	
	Liver panel	80076	
	KOH prep (skin, hair, nails)	87220	
	Metabolic panel, basic	80048	
	Metabolic panel, comprehensive	80053	
	Mononucleosis	86308	
	Pregnancy, blood	84703	
	Pregnancy, urine	81025	
	Renal panel	80069	
	Sedimentation rate	85651	
	Strep, rapid	86403	
	Strep culture	87081	
	Strep A	87880	
	TB	86580	
	UA, complete, non-automated	81000	
	UA, w/o micro, non-automated	81002	
✓	UA, w/ micro, non-automated	81003	
	Urine colony count	87086	
✓	Urine culture, presumptive	87088	
	Wet mount/KOH	87210	
	Vaccines		
	DT, <7 y		90702
	DTP		90701
	DtaP, <7 y		90700
	Flu, 6-35 months		90657
	Flu, 3 y +		90658
	Hep A, adult		90632
	Hep A, ped/adol, 2 dose		90633
	Hep B, adult		90746
	Hep B, ped/adol 3 dose		90744
	Hep B-Hib		90748
	Hib, 4 dose		90645
	HPV		90649
	IPV		90713
	MMR		90707
	Pneumonia, >2 y		90732
	Pneumonia conjugate, <5 y		90669
	Td, >7 y		90718
	Varicella		90716
	Tetanus toxoid adsorbed, IM		90703
	Immunizations & Injections		**Units**
	Allergen, one	95115	
	Allergen, multiple	95117	
	Imm admn <8 yo 1st Inj	90465	
	Imm admn <8 yo each add inj	90466	
	Imm <8 yo oral or intranasal	90467	
	Imm admn <8 yo each add	90468	
	Imm admin, one vacc	90471	
	Imm admin, each add'l	90472	
	Imm admin, intranasal, one	90473	
	Imm admin, intranasal, each add'l	90474	
	Injection, joint, small	20600	
	Injection, joint, intermediate	20605	
	Injection, ther/proph/diag	90772	
	Injection, trigger pt 1-2 musc	20552	

Next office visit: 1 mo

Recheck • Preventative • PRN

Referral to: Dr. Howard - urology

Instructions:

PSA - await results
Rx: alfuzosin
Finasteride

Physician signature

x [signature] MD

Today's charges:		
Today's payment:		
Balance due:		

Job 21 Router- Vito Mangano

Date of service: 10/27/09	Insurance: FLEXIHEALTH PPO			Router Number: 2463
Patient name: DEREK WALLACE	Coinsurance:	Copay:		Physician Name: MURRAY
Account #: WAL001	Noncovered Waiver?	yes	no	n/a

x	Office visit	New	x	Est
	Minimal (RN only)			99211
	Problem focused	99201		99212
	Exp problem focused	99202	*✓*	99213
	Detailed	99203		99214
	Comp	99204		99215
	Comprhen/Complex	99205		
	Well visit	**New**	**x**	**Est**
	< 1 y	99381		99391
	1-4 y	99382		99392
	5-11 y	99383		99393
	12-17 y	99384		99394
	18-39 y	99385		99395
	40-64 y	99386		99396
	65 y +	99387		99397
	Medicare preventive services			
	Pap			Q0091
	Pelvic & breast			G0101
	Prostate/PSA			G0103
	Tobacco couns/3-10 min			G0375
	Tobacco couns/>10 min			G0376
	Welcome to Medicare exam			G0344
	ECG w/Welcome to Medicare			G0366
	Hemoccult, guaiac			G0107
	Flu shot			G0008
	Pneumonia shot			G0009
	Consultation/preop clearance			
	Exp problem focused			99242
	Detailed			99243
	Comp/mod complex			99244
	Comp/high complex			99245
	Other services			
	After posted hours			99050
	Evening/weekend appointment			99051
	Home health certification			G0180
	Home health recertification			G0179
	Care Plan oversight			99374
	Care Plan Oversight >30 mins			99375
	Post-op follow-up			99024
	Prolonged/60min total			99354
	Prolonged/each add 30 mins			99355
	Special reports/forms			99080
	Disability/Workers comp			99455
	Smoking Cessation <10 mins			99406
	Smoking Cessation >10 mins			99407
	ETOH/SA screening <30 mins			99408
	Online E/M by MD			99444
	Phone E/M <10 mins			99441
	Phone E/M <20 mins			99442
	Phone E/M <30 mins			99443
	Anticoagulant Mgmt <90 days			99363
	Anticoagulant Mgmt >90 days			99364
✓	In office emergency serv			99058
	Other services			
	Repair nail bed			
	(R) index finger			
	Supplies			
✓	Surgical Tray			99070

Instructions:

Suture removal 10 days
Keep site dry

x	Office procedures		
	Cerumen removal	69210	
	ECG, w/interpretation	93000	
	ECG, rhythm strip	93040	
	Endometrial biopsy	58100	
	Fracture care, cast/splint Site: ______	______	
	Nebulizer	94640	
	Nebulizer demo	94664	
	Spirometry	94010	
	Spirometry, pre and post	94060	
	Vasectomy	55250	
	Skin procedures		**Units**
	Foreign body, skin, simple	10120	
	Foreign body, skin, complex	10121	
	I&D, abscess	10060	
	I&D, hematoma/seroma	10140	
	Laceration repair, simple Site: ______ Size: ____	120__	
✓	Laceration repair, layered Site: *(R) Hd* Size: *4.2cm*	120__	
	Laser Light Tx	96597	
	Lesion, biopsy, one	11100	
	Lesion, biopsy, each add'l	11101	
	Lesion, excision, benign Site: ______ Size: ____	114__	
	Lesion, excision, malignant Site: ______ Size: ____	116__	
	Lesion, paring/cutting, one	11055	
	Lesion, paring/cutting, 2-4	11056	
	Lesion, shave Site: ______ Size: ____	113__	
	Nail removal, partial (+T mod)	11730	
	Nail rem, w/matrix (+T mod)	11750	
	Skin tag, 1-15	11200	
	Wart, flat, 1-14	17110	
	Destruction lesion, 1st	17000	
	Destruct lesion, each addl 2-14	17003	
	Medications		**Units**
	Ampicillin, up to 500mg	J0290	
	B-12, up to 1,000 mcg	J3420	
	Epinephrine, up to 1ml	J0170	
	Kenalog, 10mg	J3301	
✓	Lidocaine, 10mg	J2001	
	Normal saline, 1000cc	J7030	
	Phenergan, up to 50mg	J2550	
	Progesterone, 150mg	J1055	
	Rocephin, 250mg	J0696	
	Testosterone, 200mg	J1080	
	Tigan, up to 200 mg	J3250	
	Toradol, 15mg	J1885	
	Albuterol	J7609	
	Depo-Provera 50 mg	J1055	
	Depo-Medrol 40 mg	J1030	

Diagnoses	Code
1 *Laceration (R) hand*	
2 *Crush injury fingernail*	
3	
4	

Next office visit: *10 days*

(Recheck) • Preventative • PRN

Referral to:

Physician signature

X *Lance Murray MD*

x	Laboratory		-90
	Venipuncture	36415	
	Blood glucose, monitoring device	82962	
	Blood glucose, visual dipstick	82948	
	CBC, w/ auto differential	85025	
	CBC, w/o auto differential	85027	
	Cholesterol	82465	
	Hemoccult, guaiac	82270	
	Hemoccult, immunoassay	82274	
	Hemoglobin A1C	85018	
	Lipid panel	80061	
	Liver panel	80076	
	KOH prep (skin, hair, nails)	87220	
	Metabolic panel, basic	80048	
	Metabolic panel, comprehensive	80053	
	Mononucleosis	86308	
	Pregnancy, blood	84703	
	Pregnancy, urine	81025	
	Renal panel	80069	
	Sedimentation rate	85651	
	Strep, rapid	86403	
	Strep culture	87081	
	Strep A	87880	
	TB	86580	
	UA, complete, non-automated	81000	
	UA, w/o micro, non-automated	81002	
	UA, w/ micro, non-automated	81003	
	Urine colony count	87086	
	Urine culture, presumptive	87088	
	Wet mount/KOH	87210	
	Vaccines		
	DT, <7 y		90702
	DTP		90701
	DtaP, <7 y		90700
	Flu, 6-35 months		90657
	Flu, 3 y +		90658
	Hep A, adult		90632
	Hep A, ped/adol, 2 dose		90633
	Hep B, adult		90746
	Hep B, ped/adol 3 dose		90744
	Hep B-Hib		90748
	Hib, 4 dose		90645
	HPV		90649
	IPV		90713
	MMR		90707
	Pneumonia, >2 y		90732
	Pneumonia conjugate, <5 y		90669
	Td, >7 y		90718
	Varicella		90716
	Tetanus toxoid adsorbed, IM		90703
	Immunizations & Injections		**Units**
	Allergen, one	95115	
	Allergen, multiple	95117	
	Imm admn <8 yo 1st Inj	90465	
	Imm admn <8 yo each add inj	90466	
	Imm <8 yo oral or intranasal	90467	
	Imm admn <8 yo each add	90468	
	Imm admin, one vacc	90471	
	Imm admin, each add'l	90472	
	Imm admin, intranasal, one	90473	
	Imm admin, intranasal, each add'l	90474	
	Injection, joint, small	20600	
	Injection, joint, intermediate	20605	
	Injection, ther/proph/diag	90772	
	Injection, trigger pt 1-2 musc	20552	

Today's charges:		
Today's payment:		
Balance due:		

Job 22 Router- Derek Wallace

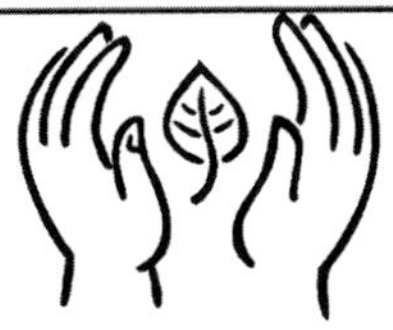

Consumer One HRA
Melissa Morency
ID No: 0016751 Group No: 6716
Subscriber: Victor Harris
Copay: $15/$25

1230 Main St. Missoula, MT 08896 (800) 555-8887

Job 23 & 27 Insurance Card 1 of 2

Prudential
Melissa Morency
ID No: 99612571 Group No: B1171

Subscriber: Gloria Morency
25% coinsurance

66653 Lansing Ave, Columbia, SC 45845 (800)888-7391

Job 23 & 27 Insurance Card 2 of 2

Douglasville Medicine Associates
Patient Registration Form

Patients must complete all information prior to seeing the physician. A copy of your insurance card(s) and driver's license will be made for your file.

Patient Name: Melissa Morency Date of Birth: 6 / 14 / 96
Sex: Male or (Female) Social Security Number: 214 - 60 - 3323 Marital Status: S
Address Line 1: 121 Wellington Way
Address Line 2:
City: Ithaca
State: NY Zip Code: 14621
Home Telephone: (717) 555-9964 Work Telephone: (—)
Cellular Telephone: (—) Email address: —

Patient's Work Status (Full-Time, Part-Time, Retired, (Student)):
Employer Name:
Address Line 1:
Address Line 2:
City: State: Zip:
Telephone: ( )
If patient is a minor, who is the primary guardian? Victor Harris

Primary Insurance Company: Consumer One HRA
Subscriber ID Number 0016751 Policy Group #: 6716
Subscriber Name: Victor Harris Birth date: 11/2/71
Subscriber Social Security Number: 330 - 24 - 1617 Relationship to patient: Father

Secondary Insurance Company: Prudential
Subscriber ID Number 99612571 Policy Group #: B1171
Subscriber Name: Gloria Morency Birth date: 11/19/74
Subscriber Social Security Number: 561 - 21 - 4136 Relationship to patient: Mother

Complete this section if your treatment is for an injury or accident.
Were you injured at work? Is this covered by Workers' Compensation?
If Yes, Contact person at your Employer
Were you involved in an auto accident? Provide insurance company, contact information, and claim number:

Date & time of Accident Place of Accident
How did injury happen?
Name of Physician who treated you at time of accident:

Financial Responsibility Statement/ Release of Information Authorization
"I authorize the release of any medical information necessary to my insurance company and the Payment of Benefits to the Physician for services provided.

X Victor Harris Date 10/27/09
Signature of Patient or Legal Guardian

Job 23 Registration Paper work- Melissa Morency 1 of 5

Douglasville Medicine Associates
Patient Registration Form

OUR FINANCIAL POLICY

By law, we must collect your carrier designated co-pay at the time of service. Please be prepared to pay that co-pay at each visit. We are also required to collect any portion of the deductible that has not been satisfied. If your plan requires a coinsurance instead of a co-pay and we participate with the plan, we will accept the designated payment and bill you accordingly for any deductible and coinsurance your plan indicates you are responsible for on their explanation of benefits.

Payment is expected at the time of service unless other financial arrangements have been made prior to your visit. If you are uninsured, you may qualify for a hardship discount. Ask one of our staff members for more information.

You are responsible for timely payment of your account. Douglasville Medicine Associates reserves the right to reschedule or deny a future appointment on delinquent accounts.

WE ACCEPT CASH, CHECKS, MASTERCARD AND VISA

THANK YOU for taking the time to review our policy.

Vit Harris ______________________ 10/27/09 __________

(Responsible Party Signature) (Date)

Job 23 Registration Paper work- Melissa Morency 2 of 5

Douglasville Medicine Associates
5076 Brand Blvd, Suite 401~ Douglasville, NY 01234

ASSIGNMENT OF BENEFITS AND PATIENT REPRESENTATION

Patient Name:______________________ Chart # ____________

Insured Name:______________________

Insurance Company Name ______________________

Policy # ______________ Group # ______________

I hereby assign all medical and/or surgical benefits, to include major medical benefits to which I am entitled, to **Douglasville Medicine Associates**. This assignment will remain in effect until revoked by me in writing. A photocopy of this assignment is to be considered as valid as the original.

I understand that I am financially responsible for all charges whether or not paid by my insurance carrier. I understand that I will be responsible for any court costs or collection fees should it become necessary to take action to collect for services/supplies rendered.

I hereby authorize **Douglasville Medicine Associates** to release all medical information necessary to secure payment on my account.

I hereby authorize **Douglasville Medicine Associates** and medical billing staff members, to submit claims, on my behalf, to the insurance company listed on the copy of the current and valid insurance card I have provided to the Clinic in good faith. I fully agree and understand that the submission of a claim does not absolve me of my responsibility to ensure that the bill for medical services is paid in full.

I authorize **Douglasville Medicine Associates** and its medical billing representative, to be my personal representative, which allows the Clinic to: (1) submit any and all appeals when my insurance company performs an adverse benefit determination as defined in 29 CFR 2560-503-1, (2) submit any and all requests for benefit information from my employer and/or health insurance company; and (3) initiate formal complaints to any State or Federal agency that has jurisdiction over my benefits.

I fully understand and agree that I am responsible for full payment of the medical debt I owe the Clinic, if my insurance company has refused to pay 100% of my covered benefits, within ninety (90) days of any and all appeals or request for information. A photocopy of this document shall be considered as effective and valid as the original.

Patient Victor Hari 10/27/09
(signature) (date)

Patient Representative ______________________
(date)

Relationship to Patient ______________________

Witness ______________________
(signature) (date)

Job 23 Registration Paper work- Melissa Morency 3 of 5

Douglasville Medicine Associates
5076 Brand Blvd., Suite 401▪Douglasville, NY 01234 (123)456-7890

Patient Name:______________________________

Record #:____________

I acknowledge that I have received a written copy of Douglasville Medicine Associates Notice of Patient Privacy Practices. I also acknowledge that I have been allowed to ask questions concerning this notice and my rights under this notice. I understand that this form will be part of my record until such time as I may choose to revoke this acknowledgement. If I am not the patient, I am the authorized representative of a minor child or authorized by law to act for and on the patient's behalf.

Vit Harris ______________________ 10/27/09 ____________

Signature of Patient or Authorized Agent Date

Patient (or authorized agent) refused to sign Notice of Privacy Practices.

Please describe events. ____

____

__________________________ ____________

Signature of DMA Employee Date

Job 23 Registration Paper work- Melissa Morency 4 of 5

Douglasville Medicine Associates
5076 Brand Blvd., Suite 401▪Douglasville, NY 01234

CONSENT TO TREATMENT

Patient Name: ______________________________ Date: 10/27/09

I, ______________________________, hereby voluntarily consent to outpatient treatment and evaluation at Douglasville Medicine Associates for______________________________. This includes routine diagnostic procedures, examination and medical treatment including, but not limited to, routine laboratory work (such as blood, urine and other studies), x-rays, heart tracing and administration of medications prescribed by the physician.

I further consent to the performance of those diagnostic procedures, examinations and rendering of medical treatment by the medical staff and their assistants.

I understand that this consent form will be valid and remain in effect as long as I receive medical care at Douglasville Medicine Associates.

This form has been explained to me and I fully understand this Consent To Treatment and agree to its contents.

Vict Hai______________________________
Signature of Patient or
Person Authorized to consent for patient

____
Relationship to patient

____
Signature of Witness

Job 23 Registration Paper work- Melissa Morency 5 of 5

Aetna
Samantha Beechwood
ID No: 476192TD
Group No: D6197
Subscriber: Martin Beechwood
25% coinsurance

159 Metro Dr, Milwaukee, WI 52631 (800)666-5584

Job 25 & 28 Insurance Card

Douglasville Medicine Associates
Patient Registration Form

Patients must complete all information prior to seeing the physician. A copy of your insurance card(s) and driver's license will be made for your file.

Patient Name: Samantha Beechwood Date of Birth: 8 / 18 / 89
Sex: Male or (Female) Social Security Number: 619 - 51 - 4134 Marital Status: S
Address Line 1: 3615 Main Street
Address Line 2: ____
City: Jamesville
State: NY Zip Code: 14691
Home Telephone: (717) 555-9274 Work Telephone: (—) ____
Cellular Telephone: (717) 555-4413 Email address: sbwood@aol.com

Patient's Work Status (Full-Time, Part-Time, Retired, (Student)): ____
Employer Name: ____
Address Line 1: ____
Address Line 2: ____
City: ____ State: ____ Zip: ____
Telephone: (____) ____
If patient is a minor, who is the primary guardian? Martin Beechwood

Primary Insurance Company: Aetna
Subscriber ID Number 476192TD Policy Group #: B6197
Subscriber Name: Martin Beechwood Birth date: 12/15/69
Subscriber Social Security Number: 147 - 99 - 1045 Relationship to patient: Father

Secondary Insurance Company: ____
Subscriber ID Number ____ Policy Group #: ____
Subscriber Name: ____ Birth date: ____
Subscriber Social Security Number: ____ - ____ - ____ Relationship to patient: ____

Complete this section if your treatment is for an injury or accident.
Were you injured at work? ____ Is this covered by Workers' Compensation? ____
If Yes, Contact person at your Employer ____
Were you involved in an auto accident? Yes Provide insurance company, contact information, and claim number: State Farm, 16900 Washington Blvd., Jamesville, NY 14692 clm # 0067221971
Date & time of Accident 10/25/09 6:30 PM Place of Accident Jamesville Mall
How did injury happen? rear-ended by another driver
Name of Physician who treated you at time of accident: Dr Bielstein – Jamesville Medical Center

Financial Responsibility Statement/ Release of Information Authorization
"I authorize the release of any medical information necessary to my insurance company and the Payment of Benefits to the Physician for services provided.

X Samantha Beechwood Date 10/27/09
Signature of Patient or Legal Guardian

Job 25 Registration Form 1 of 5

Douglasville Medicine Associates
Patient Registration Form

OUR FINANCIAL POLICY

By law, we must collect your carrier designated co-pay at the time of service. Please be prepared to pay that co-pay at each visit. We are also required to collect any portion of the deductible that has not been satisfied. If your plan requires a coinsurance instead of a co-pay and we participate with the plan, we will accept the designated payment and bill you accordingly for any deductible and coinsurance your plan indicates you are responsible for on their explanation of benefits.

Payment is expected at the time of service unless other financial arrangements have been made prior to your visit. If you are uninsured, you may qualify for a hardship discount. Ask one of our staff members for more information.

You are responsible for timely payment of your account. Douglasville Medicine Associates reserves the right to reschedule or deny a future appointment on delinquent accounts.

WE ACCEPT CASH, CHECKS, MASTERCARD AND VISA

THANK YOU for taking the time to review our policy.

Smith Buckland   10/27/09

(Responsible Party Signature)   (Date)

Job 25 Registration Form 2 of 5

Douglasville Medicine Associates
5076 Brand Blvd., Suite 401▪Douglasville, NY 01234 (123)456-7890

Patient Name:______________________

Record #:__________

I acknowledge that I have received a written copy of Douglasville Medicine Associates Notice of Patient Privacy Practices. I also acknowledge that I have been allowed to ask questions concerning this notice and my rights under this notice. I understand that this form will be part of my record until such time as I may choose to revoke this acknowledgement. If I am not the patient, I am the authorized representative of a minor child or authorized by law to act for and on the patient's behalf.

Scott Berland __________ 10/27/09 __________

Signature of Patient or Authorized Agent   Date

Patient (or authorized agent) refused to sign Notice of Privacy Practices.

Please describe events. ______________________________________

____

______________________   __________

Signature of DMA Employee   Date

Job 25 Registration Form 3 of 5

Douglasville Medicine Associates
5076 Brand Blvd., Suite 401▪Douglasville, NY 01234

CONSENT TO TREATMENT

Patient Name: ______________________________ Date: 10/27/09

I, ______________________________, hereby voluntarily consent to outpatient treatment and evaluation at Douglasville Medicine Associates for______________________________. This includes routine diagnostic procedures, examination and medical treatment including, but not limited to, routine laboratory work (such as blood, urine and other studies), x-rays, heart tracing and administration of medications prescribed by the physician.

I further consent to the performance of those diagnostic procedures, examinations and rendering of medical treatment by the medical staff and their assistants.

I understand that this consent form will be valid and remain in effect as long as I receive medical care at Douglasville Medicine Associates.

This form has been explained to me and I fully understand this Consent To Treatment and agree to its contents.

____
Signature of Patient or
Person Authorized to consent for patient

____
Relationship to patient

____
Signature of Witness

Job 25 Registration Form 4 of 5

Douglasville Medicine Associates
5076 Brand Blvd, Suite 401~ Douglasville, NY 01234

ASSIGNMENT OF BENEFITS AND PATIENT REPRESENTATION

Patient Name:________________________________ Chart # ________________

Insured Name:____

Insurance Company Name ____

Policy # ______________________ Group # ______________________

I hereby assign all medical and/or surgical benefits, to include major medical benefits to which I am entitled, to **Douglasville Medicine Associates**. This assignment will remain in effect until revoked by me in writing. A photocopy of this assignment is to be considered as valid as the original.

I understand that I am financially responsible for all charges whether or not paid by my insurance carrier. I understand that I will be responsible for any court costs or collection fees should it become necessary to take action to collect for services/supplies rendered.

I hereby authorize **Douglasville Medicine Associates** to release all medical information necessary to secure payment on my account.

I hereby authorize **Douglasville Medicine Associates** and medical billing staff members, to submit claims, on my behalf, to the insurance company listed on the copy of the current and valid insurance card I have provided to the Clinic in good faith. I fully agree and understand that the submission of a claim does not absolve me of my responsibility to ensure that the bill for medical services is paid in full.

I authorize **Douglasville Medicine Associates** and its medical billing representative, to be my personal representative, which allows the Clinic to: (1) submit any and all appeals when my insurance company performs an adverse benefit determination as defined in 29 CFR 2560-503-1, (2) submit any and all requests for benefit information from my employer and/or health insurance company, and (3) initiate formal complaints to any State or Federal agency that has jurisdiction over my benefits.

I fully understand and agree that I am responsible for full payment of the medical debt I owe the Clinic, if my insurance company has refused to pay 100% of my covered benefits, within ninety (90) days of any and all appeals or request for information. A photocopy of this document shall be considered as effective and valid as the original.

Patient Sunett Buchel ____________ 10/27/09
(signature) (date)

Patient Representative ________________________________
(date)

Relationship to Patient ________________________________

Witness ________________________________
(signature) (date)

Job 25 Registration Form 5 of 5

Date of service: 10/27/09	Insurance: CONSUMER ONE/PRUDENTIAL			Superbill Number: 2451
Patient name: MELISSA MORENCY	Coinsurance: 20%	Copay:		Physician Name: KEMPER
Account #: MOR001	Noncovered Waiver?	yes	no	n/a

x	Office visit	New	x	Est
	Minimal (RN only)			99211
	Problem focused	99201		99212
	Exp problem focused	99202		99213
	Detailed	99203		99214
	Comp	99204		99215
	Comprhen/Complex	99205		
	Well visit	**New**	**x**	**Est**
	< 1 y	99381		99391
	1-4 y	99382		99392
	5-11 y	99383		99393
✓	12-17 y	99384		99394
	18-39 y	99385		99395
	40-64 y	99386		99396
	65 y +	99387		99397
	Medicare preventive services			
	Pap			Q0091
	Pelvic & breast			G0101
	Prostate/PSA			G0103
	Tobacco couns/3-10 min			G0375
	Tobacco couns/>10 min			G0376
	Welcome to Medicare exam			G0344
	ECG w/Welcome to Medicare			G0366
	Hemoccult, guaiac			G0107
	Flu shot			G0008
	Pneumonia shot			G0009
	Consultation/preop clearance			
	Exp problem focused			99242
	Detailed			99243
	Comp/mod complex			99244
	Comp/high complex			99245
	Other services			
	After posted hours			99050
	Evening/weekend appointment			99051
	Home health certification			G0180
	Home health recertification			G0179
	Care Plan oversight			99374
	Care Plan Oversight >30 mins			99375
	Post-op follow-up			99024
	Prolonged/60min total			99354
	Prolonged/each add 30 mins			99355
	Special reports/forms			99080
	Disability/Workers comp			99455
	Smoking Cessation <10 mins			99406
	Smoking Cessation >10 mins			99407
	ETOH/SA screening <30 mins			99408
	Online E/M by MD			99444
	Phone E/M <10 mins			99441
	Phone E/M <20 mins			99442
	Phone E/M <30 mins			99443
	Anticoagulant Mgmt <90 days			99363
	Anticoagulant Mgmt >90 days			99364
	In office emergency serv			99058
	Other services			
✓	Preventative counseling 15 mins			
	Supplies			
	Surgical Tray			99070

Instructions: Weight Mgmt

Office procedures			x
Cerumen removal		69210	
ECG, w/interpretation		93000	
ECG, rhythm strip		93040	
Endometrial biopsy		58100	
Fracture care, cast/splint Site: ________________		____	
Nebulizer		94640	
Nebulizer demo		94664	
Spirometry		94010	
Spirometry, pre and post		94060	
Vasectomy		55250	
Skin procedures		**Units**	
Foreign body, skin, simple	10120		
Foreign body, skin, complex	10121		
I&D, abscess	10060		
I&D, hematoma/seroma	10140		
Laceration repair, simple Site: ________ Size: _____	120__		
Laceration repair, layered Site: ________ Size: _____	120__		
Laser Light Tx	96597		
Lesion, biopsy, one	11100		
Lesion, biopsy, each add'l	11101		
Lesion, excision, benign Site: ________ Size: _____	114__		
Lesion, excision, malignant Site: ________ Size: _____	116__		
Lesion, paring/cutting, one	11055		
Lesion, paring/cutting, 2-4	11056		
Lesion, shave Site: ________ Size: _____	113__		
Nail removal, partial (+T mod)	11730		
Nail rem, w/matrix (+T mod)	11750		
Skin tag, 1-15	11200		
Wart, flat, 1-14	17110		
Destruction lesion, 1st	17000		
Destruct lesion, each addl 2-14	17003		
Medications		**Units**	
Ampicillin, up to 500mg	J0290		
B-12, up to 1,000 mcg	J3420		
Epinephrine, up to 1ml	J0170		
Kenalog, 10mg	J3301		
Lidocaine, 10mg	J2001		
Normal saline, 1000cc	J7030		
Phenergan, up to 50mg	J2550		
Progesterone, 150mg	J1055		
Rocephin, 250mg	J0696		
Testosterone, 200mg	J1080		
Tigan, up to 200 mg	J3250		
Toradol, 15mg	J1885		
Albuterol	J7609		
Depo-Provera 50 mg	J1055		
Depo-Medrol 40 mg	J1030		

Diagnoses		Code
1	Vaccination update	
2	Obesity	
3		
4		

Next office visit:
Recheck • Preventative • PRN
Referral to:

Physician signature
X [signature: Sally Kemper MD]

x	Laboratory		-90
	Venipuncture	36415	
	Blood glucose, monitoring device	82962	
	Blood glucose, visual dipstick	82948	
	CBC, w/ auto differential	85025	
	CBC, w/o auto differential	85027	
	Cholesterol	82465	
	Hemoccult, guaiac	82270	
	Hemoccult, immunoassay	82274	
	Hemoglobin A1C	85018	
	Lipid panel	80061	
	Liver panel	80076	
	KOH prep (skin, hair, nails)	87220	
	Metabolic panel, basic	80048	
	Metabolic panel, comprehensive	80053	
	Mononucleosis	86308	
	Pregnancy, blood	84703	
	Pregnancy, urine	81025	
	Renal panel	80069	
	Sedimentation rate	85651	
	Strep, rapid	86403	
	Strep culture	87081	
	Strep A	87880	
	TB	86580	
	UA, complete, non-automated	81000	
	UA, w/o micro, non-automated	81002	
	UA, w/ micro, non-automated	81003	
	Urine colony count	87086	
	Urine culture, presumptive	87088	
	Wet mount/KOH	87210	
	Vaccines		
	DT, <7 y		90702
	DTP		90701
	DtaP, <7 y		90700
	Flu, 6-35 months		90657
	Flu, 3 y +		90658
	Hep A, adult		90632
	Hep A, ped/adol, 2 dose		90633
	Hep B, adult		90746
	Hep B, ped/adol 3 dose		90744
	Hep B-Hib		90748
	Hib, 4 dose		90645
✓	HPV		90649
	IPV		90713
	MMR		90707
	Pneumonia, >2 y		90732
	Pneumonia conjugate, <5 y		90669
	Td, >7 y		90718
	Varicella		90716
	Tetanus toxoid adsorbed, IM		90703
	Immunizations & Injections		**Units**
	Allergen, one	95115	
	Allergen, multiple	95117	
	Imm admn <8 yo 1st Inj	90465	
	Imm admn <8 yo each add inj	90466	
	Imm <8 yo oral or intranasal	90467	
	Imm admn <8 yo each add	90468	
✓	Imm admin, one vacc	90471	
	Imm admin, each add'l	90472	
	Imm admin, intranasal, one	90473	
	Imm admin, intranasal, each add'l	90474	
	Injection, joint, small	20600	
	Injection, joint, intermediate	20605	
	Injection, ther/proph/diag	90772	
	Injection, trigger pt 1-2 musc	20552	

Today's charges:		
Today's payment:		
Balance due:		

Job 27 Router- Melissa Morency

Date of service: 10/27/09	Insurance: AETNA		Superbill Number: 2452
Patient name: SAMANTHA BEECHWOOD	Coinsurance: 25%	Copay:	Physician Name: SCHWARTZ
Account #: BEE001	Noncovered Waiver?	yes / no / n/a	

x	Office visit	New	x	Est
	Minimal (RN only)			99211
	Problem focused	99201		99212
	Exp problem focused	99202		99213
	Detailed	99203		99214
✓	Comp	99204		99215
	Comprhen/Complex	99205		
	Well visit	**New**	**x**	**Est**
	< 1 y	99381		99391
	1-4 y	99382		99392
	5-11 y	99383		99393
	12-17 y	99384		99394
	18-39 y	99385		99395
	40-64 y	99386		99396
	65 y +	99387		99397
	Medicare preventive services			
	Pap			Q0091
	Pelvic & breast			G0101
	Prostate/PSA			G0103
	Tobacco couns/3-10 min			G0375
	Tobacco couns/>10 min			G0376
	Welcome to Medicare exam			G0344
	ECG w/Welcome to Medicare			G0366
	Hemoccult, guaiac			G0107
	Flu shot			G0008
	Pneumonia shot			G0009
	Consultation/preop clearance			
	Exp problem focused			99242
	Detailed			99243
	Comp/mod complex			99244
	Comp/high complex			99245
	Other services			
	After posted hours			99050
	Evening/weekend appointment			99051
	Home health certification			G0180
	Home health recertification			G0179
	Care Plan oversight			99374
	Care Plan Oversight >30 mins			99375
	Post-op follow-up			99024
	Prolonged/60min total			99354
	Prolonged/each add 30 mins			99355
	Special reports/forms			99080
	Disability/Workers comp			99455
	Smoking Cessation <10 mins			99406
	Smoking Cessation >10 mins			99407
	ETOH/SA screening <30 mins			99408
	Online E/M by MD			99444
	Phone E/M <10 mins			99441
	Phone E/M <20 mins			99442
	Phone E/M <30 mins			99443
	Anticoagulant Mgmt <90 days			99363
	Anticoagulant Mgmt >90 days			99364
	In office emergency serv			99058
	Other services			
✓	A/P + lateral shoulder xray			
✓	Injection @ shoulder			
	Supplies			
	Surgical Tray			99070
	Strapping @ shoulder			

x	Office procedures		
	Cerumen removal		69210
	ECG, w/interpretation		93000
	ECG, rhythm strip		93040
	Endometrial biopsy		58100
	Fracture care, cast/splint Site: _______		____
	Nebulizer		94640
	Nebulizer demo		94664
	Spirometry		94010
	Spirometry, pre and post		94060
	Vasectomy		55250
	Skin procedures		**Units**
	Foreign body, skin, simple	10120	
	Foreign body, skin, complex	10121	
	I&D, abscess	10060	
	I&D, hematoma/seroma	10140	
	Laceration repair, simple Site: _______ Size: _____	120__	
	Laceration repair, layered Site: _______ Size: _____	120__	
	Laser Light Tx	96597	
	Lesion, biopsy, one	11100	
	Lesion, biopsy, each add'l	11101	
	Lesion, excision, benign Site: _______ Size: _____	114__	
	Lesion, excision, malignant Site: _______ Size: _____	116__	
	Lesion, paring/cutting, one	11055	
	Lesion, paring/cutting, 2-4	11056	
	Lesion, shave Site: _______ Size: _____	113__	
	Nail removal, partial (+T mod)	11730	
	Nail rem, w/matrix (+T mod)	11750	
	Skin tag, 1-15	11200	
	Wart, flat, 1-14	17110	
	Destruction lesion, 1st	17000	
	Destruct lesion, each addl 2-14	17003	
	Medications		**Units**
	Ampicillin, up to 500mg	J0290	
	B-12, up to 1,000 mcg	J3420	
	Epinephrine, up to 1ml	J0170	
	Kenalog, 10mg	J3301	
✓	Lidocaine, 10mg	J2001	
	Normal saline, 1000cc	J7030	
	Phenergan, up to 50mg	J2550	
	Progesterone, 150mg	J1055	
	Rocephin, 250mg	J0696	
	Testosterone, 200mg	J1080	
	Tigan, up to 200 mg	J3250	
	Toradol, 15mg	J1885	
	Albuterol	J7609	
	Depo-Provera 50 mg	J1055	
✓	Depo-Medrol 40 mg	J1030	

Diagnoses		Code
1	Rt shoulder pain/ Strain	
2	Rt Shoulder dislocation	
3		
4		

x	Laboratory		-90
	Venipuncture	36415	
	Blood glucose, monitoring device	82962	
	Blood glucose, visual dipstick	82948	
	CBC, w/ auto differential	85025	
	CBC, w/o auto differential	85027	
	Cholesterol	82465	
	Hemoccult, guaiac	82270	
	Hemoccult, immunoassay	82274	
	Hemoglobin A1C	85018	
	Lipid panel	80061	
	Liver panel	80076	
	KOH prep (skin, hair, nails)	87220	
	Metabolic panel, basic	80048	
	Metabolic panel, comprehensive	80053	
	Mononucleosis	86308	
	Pregnancy, blood	84703	
	Pregnancy, urine	81025	
	Renal panel	80069	
	Sedimentation rate	85651	
	Strep, rapid	86403	
	Strep culture	87081	
	Strep A	87880	
	TB	86580	
	UA, complete, non-automated	81000	
	UA, w/o micro, non-automated	81002	
	UA, w/ micro, non-automated	81003	
	Urine colony count	87086	
	Urine culture, presumptive	87088	
	Wet mount/KOH	87210	
	Vaccines		
	DT, <7 y		90702
	DTP		90701
	DtaP, <7 y		90700
	Flu, 6-35 months		90657
	Flu, 3 y +		90658
	Hep A, adult		90632
	Hep A, ped/adol, 2 dose		90633
	Hep B, adult		90746
	Hep B, ped/adol 3 dose		90744
	Hep B-Hib		90748
	Hib, 4 dose		90645
	HPV		90649
	IPV		90713
	MMR		90707
	Pneumonia, >2 y		90732
	Pneumonia conjugate, <5 y		90669
	Td, >7 y		90718
	Varicella		90716
	Tetanus toxoid adsorbed, IM		90703
	Immunizations & Injections		**Units**
	Allergen, one	95115	
	Allergen, multiple	95117	
	Imm admn <8 yo 1st Inj	90465	
	Imm admn <8 yo each add inj	90466	
	Imm <8 yo oral or intranasal	90467	
	Imm admn <8 yo each add	90468	
	Imm admin, one vacc	90471	
	Imm admin, each add'l	90472	
	Imm admin, intranasal, one	90473	
	Imm admin, intranasal, each add'l	90474	
	Injection, joint, small	20600	
	Injection, joint, intermediate	20605	
	Injection, ther/proph/diag	90772	
	Injection, trigger pt 1-2 musc	20552	

Instructions: Keep shoulder strapped for 5 days.

Next office visit: Recheck • Preventative • PRN

Referral to: Dr. Alston - orthopedics

Physician signature

x DJ Schwartz MD

Today's charges:	
Today's payment:	
Balance due:	

Job 28 Router- Samantha Beechwood

Date of service: 10/27/09	Insurance: MEDICARE			Router Number: 2485
Patient name: XAO CHANG	Coinsurance:	Copay:		Physician Name: HEATH
Account #: CHA001	Noncovered Waiver?	yes	no	n/a

X	Office visit	New	X	Est
N/A	Minimal (RN only)	N/A		99211
	Problem focused	99201		99212
	Exp problem focused	99202	/	99213
	Detailed	99203	✓	99214
	Comp	99204		99215
	Comprhen/Complex	99205		
	Well visit	**New**	**X**	**Est**
	< 1 y	99381		99391
	1-4 y	99382		99392
	5-11 y	99383		99393
	12-17 y	99384		99394
	18-39 y	99385		99395
	40-64 y	99386		99396
	65 y +	99387		99397

X	Medicare preventive services	
	Pap	Q0091
	Pelvic & breast	G0101
	Prostate/PSA	G0103
	Tobacco couns/3-10 min	G0375
	Tobacco couns/>10 min	G0376
	Welcome to Medicare exam	G0344
	ECG w/Welcome to Medicare	G0366
	Hemoccult, guaiac	G0107
	Flu shot	G0008
	Pneumonia shot	G0009
	Consultation/preop clearance	
	Exp problem focused	99242
	Detailed	99243
	Comp/mod complex	99244
	Comp/high complex	99245
	Other services	
	After posted hours	99050
	Evening/weekend appointment	99051
	Home health certification	G0180
	Home health recertification	G0179
	Care Plan oversight	99374
	Care Plan Oversight >30 mins	99375
	Post-op follow-up	99024
	Prolonged/60min total	99354
	Prolonged/each add 30 mins	99355
	Special reports/forms	99080
	Disability/Workers comp	99455
	Smoking Cessation <10 mins	99406
	Smoking Cessation >10 mins	99407
	ETOH/SA screening <30 mins	99408
	Online E/M by MD	99444
	Phone E/M <10 mins	99441
	Phone E/M <20 mins	99442
	Phone E/M <30 mins	99443
	Anticoagulant Mgmt <90 days	99363
	Anticoagulant Mgmt >90 days	99364
	In office emergency serv	99058
	Other services	
✓	CT W/O CONTRAST Brain	
	Supplies	
	Surgical Tray	99070

X	Office procedures		
	Cerumen removal		69210
	ECG, w/interpretation		93000
	ECG, rhythm strip		93040
	Endometrial biopsy		58100
	Fracture care, cast/splint		
	Site: _______________		
	Nebulizer		94640
	Nebulizer demo		94664
	Spirometry		94010
	Spirometry, pre and post		94060
	Vasectomy		55250
	Skin procedures		**Units**
	Foreign body, skin, simple	10120	
	Foreign body, skin, complex	10121	
	I&D, abscess	10060	
	I&D, hematoma/seroma	10140	
	Laceration repair, simple	120__	
	Site: _______ Size: ____		
	Laceration repair, layered	120__	
	Site: _______ Size: ____		
	Laser Light Tx	96597	
	Lesion, biopsy, one	11100	
	Lesion, biopsy, each add'l	11101	
	Lesion, excision, benign	114__	
	Site: _______ Size: ____		
	Lesion, excision, malignant	116__	
	Site: _______ Size: ____		
	Lesion, paring/cutting, one	11055	
	Lesion, paring/cutting, 2-4	11056	
	Lesion, shave	113__	
	Site: _______ Size: ____		
	Nail removal, partial (+T mod)	11730	
	Nail rem, w/matrix (+T mod)	11750	
	Skin tag, 1-15	11200	
	Wart, flat, 1-14	17110	
	Destruction lesion, 1st	17000	
	Destruct lesion, each addl 2-14	17003	
	Medications		**Units**
	Ampicillin, up to 500mg	J0290	
	B-12, up to 1,000 mcg	J3420	
	Epinephrine, up to 1ml	J0170	
	Kenalog, 10mg	J3301	
	Lidocaine, 10mg	J2001	
	Normal saline, 1000cc	J7030	
	Phenergan, up to 50mg	J2550	
	Progesterone, 150mg	J1055	
	Rocephin, 250mg	J0696	
	Testosterone, 200mg	J1080	
	Tigan, up to 200 mg	J3250	
	Toradol, 15mg	J1885	
	Albuterol	J7609	
	Depo-Provera 50 mg	J1055	
	Depo-Medrol 40 mg	J1030	

Diagnoses	Code
1 HA / R/O Aneurysm	
2 HTN	
3 Vertigo	
4	

Next office visit:
Recheck • Preventative • PRN
Referral to:

X	Laboratory		-90
	Venipuncture	36415	
	Blood glucose, monitoring device	82962	
	Blood glucose, visual dipstick	82948	
	CBC, w/ auto differential	85025	
	CBC, w/o auto differential	85027	
	Cholesterol	82465	
	Hemoccult, guaiac	82270	
	Hemoccult, immunoassay	82274	
	Hemoglobin A1C	85018	
	Lipid panel	80061	
	Liver panel	80076	
	KOH prep (skin, hair, nails)	87220	
	Metabolic panel, basic	80048	
	Metabolic panel, comprehensive	80053	
	Mononucleosis	86308	
	Pregnancy, blood	84703	
	Pregnancy, urine	81025	
	Renal panel	80069	
	Sedimentation rate	85651	
	Strep, rapid	86403	
	Strep culture	87081	
	Strep A	87880	
	TB	86580	
	UA, complete, non-automated	81000	
	UA, w/o micro, non-automated	81002	
	UA, w/ micro, non-automated	81003	
	Urine colony count	87086	
	Urine culture, presumptive	87088	
	Wet mount/KOH	87210	
	Vaccines		
	DT, <7 y		90702
	DTP		90701
	DtaP, <7 y		90700
	Flu, 6-35 months		90657
	Flu, 3 y +		90658
	Hep A, adult		90632
	Hep A, ped/adol, 2 dose		90633
	Hep B, adult		90746
	Hep B, ped/adol 3 dose		90744
	Hep B-Hib		90748
	Hib, 4 dose		90645
	HPV		90649
	IPV		90713
	MMR		90707
	Pneumonia, >2 y		90732
	Pneumonia conjugate, <5 y		90669
	Td, >7 y		90718
	Varicella		90716
	Tetanus toxoid adsorbed, IM		90703
	Immunizations & Injections		**Units**
	Allergen, one	95115	
	Allergen, multiple	95117	
	Imm admn <8 yo 1st Inj	90465	
	Imm admn <8 yo each add inj	90466	
	Imm <8 yo oral or intranasal	90467	
	Imm admn <8 yo each add	90468	
	Imm admin, one vacc	90471	
	Imm admin, each add'l	90472	
	Imm admin, intranasal, one	90473	
	Imm admin, intranasal, each add'l	90474	
	Injection, joint, small	20600	
	Injection, joint, intermediate	20605	
	Injection, ther/proph/diag	90772	
	Injection, trigger pt 1-2 musc	20552	

Instructions:

CT image will be read by Radiologist CALL results to home

Physician signature	Today's charges:	
	Today's payment:	
X L D Heath MD	Balance due:	

Job 35 Router- Xao Chang

CHAPTER

7 Working in the Clinic: Charge Capture and Entry

Background Basics

- Students should have completed courses in ICD-9-CM, CPT-4, and HCPCS coding methodologies.
- Students will need current ICD-9, CPT-4, and HCPCS code books to complete this chapter.
- Students will need a calculator if they prefer not to use the one available in MOSS.
- To complete this chapter successfully, students must have completed chapters 1–6 in their entirety.

Competency Checklist

- Coders must have a strong foundation in coding guidelines to properly assign codes for diagnoses and procedures.
- Coders are responsible for reading and interpreting medical information to justify medical necessity and assign codes to the highest specificity. Judgment on when to query the physician is exercised.
- Coding staff have to be fluent in Medicare carrier coding requirements for reporting and the use of Correct Coding Edits.
- Local Coverage Determinations (LCDs) dictate what services will be covered for predetermined diagnoses. Staff must be cognizant of these policies and know where to go to research them prior to submitting claims.
- The Encounter Form must be updated at least annually, and coding staff play a vital role in maintaining these forms.
- Coding resources are essential to proper code assignment. Staff needs access to and experience with researching these resources.

In chapter 6, you worked the first two days of the job at the front desk performing registration and scheduling functions. In this chapter, you will spend the next two days focusing on the charge capture, coding, charge entry, and claims submission functions. You will enter the charges and code the visits for patients seen on Monday and Tuesday of this week. You will also create and submit the claims created for these visits. You will also assign codes for the services are our providers performed during hospital encounters in the past few days. It is important that the coder reviews the router carefully to be sure all charges are captured and the correct codes are assigned based on the site and available services. Keep in mind, modifiers may need to be appended to codes entered from the router. The source documents you need to complete these jobs are at the end of this chapter.

DAY THREE: WEDNESDAY, October 28, 2009

CODING

JOB 1: Take the routers from day 1 and day 2 and code the diagnoses and procedures. You can write the diagnosis codes in the right margin of the router. If a service was performed that did not have a prefilled field, it would have been entered under *Other Services* on the router. You can also record these codes in the margin. Check the end of this chapter to see if there are any additional progress notes to read for each patient visit before finalizing your codes. There are a total of 19 routers for these days. Turn these in to your instructor. *(See Job 1, Routers- 1–20)*

JOB 2: Derek Wallace had a laceration repair yesterday. The router indicates a surgical tray, Lidocaine, repair of the nail bed, Emergency Office Visit, and an E/M visit. Check the Physician CCI edits to determine if any of these services are bundled. If so, list what codes would be reported in column 1 and those that would not be reported in column 2. Search the CMS website for the physician CCI edits. You will need to look at the codes in the 90000–99999 range as well as 10000–19999. *(See Job 2, Router- Derek Wallace)*

Codes to be Reported	Bundled Codes

JOB 3: How is William Kostner's visit coded for 10/27/09? Do you agree or disagree? Is this a consult or referral? Write a memo to the doctor explaining the documentation requirements for consults and referrals. You should cite official sources such as *the Evaluation and Management Coding Guidelines* and/or the *Medicare Manual* or *Transmittals*. Use the letterhead paper located in Appendix K. *(See Job 3, Progress Report and Router- William Kostner)*

JOB 4: One of the physicians has recently read an article about capturing charges during "off hours" and the ability to report codes to capture services performed in the middle of the night. He has asked you to search specialty society websites and coding resources for direction on this. Prepare a draft policy to submit to April on what your research found and your recommendation on what code(s) can be reported, what must be documented, whether Medicare allows for this service, where the service must be rendered, and when our providers are able to bill for this service. Turn this in to your instructor.

JOB 5: Each day the doctors place their hospital charges in a bin on your desk. These charges are for patients seen in the ER, admitted to the hospital, or seen on the floors. Some of the doctors are better in keeping up with these visits than others. Code the visits you do have on the Hospital Charge Sheets. Record your codes directly on the sheets in the spaces provided. If the doctor already listed an E/M code, use that code and assign the ICD-9 codes. You should have 10 Hospital Charge Sheets. Turn these in to your instructor. *(See Job 5, Hospital Charge Sheets- 1–10)*

JOB 6: April Kennedy has asked you to research carriers to determine if they will reimburse for telemedicine services. Because our office is not located in a rural area, she is specifically interested in whether we can get paid for evaluations and instructions given over the phone or Internet. Our nursing staff in particular spends a fair amount of time providing this service, taking them away from duties in the office. Before you begin your inquiry, you need to locate the codes for telemedicine. These are broken out by who provides the service—physician or nonphysician. Check the following carrier sites to see what you can find: Medicare, United Healthcare, and Aetna. Turn in your findings to April (your instructor).

JOB 7: It is time again to audit the DMA router. Take a good look at it and check the codes to see if there are any changes necessary due to code additions/deletions. Highlight the codes that need changed/updated on your copy and indicate in the margin what the new code should be. Are any CPT codes missing that should be added because of additions to the CPT book or common use in the clinic?______________________________

____

(See Job 7, DMA Router)

JOB 8: Dr. Kemper would like to apply an automated continuous glucose biographer device to a patient with a 10-year history of Type I diabetes. She is 23 years old and is interested in having an insulin pump inserted. She has Carolina Care Plan insurance. She is having frequent hypoglycemic episodes and abnormal hemoglobin A1C tests even though her daily sugar tests are within a fairly normal range. Check to see if this service needs preauthorization. Is this a covered service? What would be the code for this service if performed? The physician would interpret the reading and dictate a report after the patient wears the device for 72 hours. ________________________

____

Entering Charges

JOB 9: To assess charges to patients' accounts for not showing up for an appointment or for writing checks with insufficient funds, we need to first create codes in MOSS. These are internal codes and not meant to be reported to insurance carriers or print on claim forms. Go to *File Maintenance* and click on the *Lists* tab. Select *CPT Codes*. Scroll down to the bottom of the screen until you see the * after the last CPT code. Click *Add*. Enter *99999* for No-Shows. Tab over to the *Charges* column and enter $20.00. On the next line click on *Add* and enter *88888* for NSF Fee. Tab over to the *Charges* column and enter $25.00. Close when you are done.

JOB 10: Samantha Beechwood was seen on 10/27/09. Because she was involved in an accident, what should the billing staff do before sending her claim? ________________________

____

(See Job 9, Router- Samantha Beechwood)

DAY THREE: WEDNESDAY, October 28, 2009 (continued)

JOB 11: Now that the office visits are coded from Monday and Tuesday, enter the charges for each. Click on *Procedure Posting* and search for the patient's name. Click on *Add* and begin entering your data. Remember, the reference number is the router number at the top right of the form. *Place of Service* is *(11) Office* for all office visits. You do not need to enter a *Facility* because this does not apply to office visits. The *From (date)* is the date of service. There is no need to enter a *To (date).* This date is only for hospital admissions and visits. *(See Job 11, Routers- 1–20)*

JOB 12: Now that the hospital visits you have to date are coded, enter the charges. The reference number for the hospital charges is the doctor's initials and the date of service. For example, if Dr. Murray saw a patient on 10/1/09, the reference number would be LM100109. If the doctor is providing charges for a range of days, the last day of the range would be the reference number. *(See Job 12, Hospital Charge Sheets- 1–10)*

JOB 13: Mr. Shinn was a no-show on 10/23/09. Assess his account with the no-show fee and print a patient statement. Enclose a letter explaining our office policy about missed appointments. Because he does not have a router, his reference number is NS102309. Refer to Appendix A for the policy on cancellations and no-shows. Enter the dummy diagnosis with the charge for no-showing. Use the letterhead paper located on the CD-ROM.

Claims Submission

JOB 14: Submit claims for all the charges entered today. From the *Main Menu*, select *Insurance Billing.* Sort the claims by service dates. Settings should be set to *Bill* and *Provider* to *All.* Service dates are 10/1/2009–10/27/2009 to capture all the hospital visits you entered today. It would probably be best to sort by Patient Name or Account Number to print the paper claims for the Workers' Comp and third-party payers first.

Transmit Type should be *Paper. Billing Options* should be set to *Other* in these cases. *Payer Selection* would be the Workers' Comp insurance carriers or small companies such as car insurance carriers. Once you are done setting up the parameters, choose *Prebilling Worksheet,* print and compare records to be sure all claims for Workers' Comp and third party payers have been prepped. When satisfied all are entered correctly, select *generate claims.* Use the record bar at the bottom of the screen to advance forward to view all your created claims. Click on *Print Forms* to print claims. Turn these in to your instructor.

The rest of the claims will be sent electronically. Keep provider set to *All* and the service dates at 10/1/09–10/27/09. Select *All* for *Patient Names* and *All* for *Payers. Transmit Type* should be *Electronic. Billing Options* is set to *Primary* because this is the first time we have submitted claims for these dates of service. Once you are done setting up the parameters, choose *Prebilling Worksheet,* print and compare records to be sure all claims have been prepped. When satisfied that all are entered correctly, select *generate claims.* Use the record bar at the bottom of the screen to advance forward to view all your created claims. Check for is patients with secondary insurance. For any new patients put in the system, make sure both primary and secondary (if any) insurances are entered. If you see any errors, you can go back to *Patient Registration* or *Procedure Posting* to make corrections. If you need to make corrections, do so and process the claims again for those individual claims. Do not select *Rebill.* If you are satisfied with the claims, click on the *Transmit EMC* button to submit the claims electronically. When the transmission is complete, print the *Transmission Report* and turn this in to your instructor.

DAY FOUR: THURSDAY, October 29, 2009
CODING

JOB 1: Code Wednesday's visits using the routers and notes from Wednesday located at the end of this chapter. Write your codes in the margin of the router and turn the routers in to your instructor. *(See Job 1, Insurance Cards 1–2, Registration Paper work- 1–5 and Routers- 1–6)*

JOB 2: Code the hospital charges that the doctors left you since yesterday. Write your codes on the sheet where indicated. *(See Job 2, Hospital Charge Sheets- 1–2)*

JOB 3: Hugh Williams was seen yesterday. He was complaining of rectal bleeding and constipation. Dr. Mendenhall performed a DRE and ordered a PSA. According to his history, he had a DRE and PSA drawn nine months ago. How should this encounter be coded and submitted? Is Mr. Williams responsible for any charges? Research Medicare's policies to determine your answer. *(See Job 3, Insurance Cards 1–2, Registration Paper work- 1–5 and Routers- Hugh Williams)*

____

JOB 4: Jordan Connell was seen yesterday for a physical. During the prostate exam, the doctor noted that his prostate was enlarged with nodularity and he ordered a PSA. He also biopsied a suspicious mole located on his right flank. Are all the services captured on the router? Can the charges be put in and the claim submitted without waiting for the path report? What would you recommend doing? ________________________________

____

(See Job 4, Router- Jordan Connell)

JOB 5: Chrissy Krouse is seen in the office today for her three-month diabetes follow-up. Her blood sugars are stable. When reviewing her chart, it appears she has gained 20 lbs since the last visit and her BP is elevated today at 159/92. Examination of the extremities shows 2+ pitting edema.

ASSESSMENT: HTN. Type II diabetes controlled. Fluid retention.

PLAN: Injection 10 mg of Lasix to initiate diuresis. Prescription oral Lasix for home use.

Codes: ________________________________

(See Job 5, Router- Chrissy Krouse)

JOB 6: Norman Johnson is seen today in the office accompanied by his mother who is his full-time caregiver. Norman is mentally retarded and autistic. His mother states he has been complaining of right ear pain and "noise" in his ear. Norman is loud and difficult to manage. He refuses to cooperate, keeps holding his hands over his ears, and shouts profanities. One of the nursing staff had to assist in restraining the patient long enough for me to look in his ear. Upon exam, his right TM is not visible. It is completely occluded with cerumen. The cerumen was impacted and required removal. I removed it by rolling the cerumen out of the ear canal with a blunt curet. Time spent with the patient was 30 minutes. Can the doctor bill prolonged services for this visit? Why or why not? Justify your reasoning. ________________________________

____

(See Job 6, Router- Norman Johnson)

JOB 7: Aimee Bradley presents today after having been bitten by a tick a month ago. She spends a great deal of time outdoors hiking and with her dogs. One day she noticed a small tick behind her right knee. She is not sure how long the tick was attached, but she thinks it could be as long as 48 hours. Her mother was able to remove it, but she then went on to develop a small area of redness around the bite. She had pruritus at the site of the tick bite, but otherwise felt well until recently.

Her physical examination reveals a 2-centimeter area of erythema migrans surrounding the site of the tick bite. There is no fluctuance or purulence at the site. Heart and lungs are normal. Her vital signs are normal. She is also complaining of joint pain and facial nerve numbness.

ASSESSMENT: Early onset Lymes Disease.

PLAN: Doxycycline 100 mg twice daily for 21 days. Order Lyme serology.

Codes:____

(See Job 7, Router- Aimee Bradley)

JOB 8: Paula Skektar injured her leg somehow but doesn't have an isolated incident other than falling at her daughter's home in September. She cannot leave the house because she can't walk. She has to be wheeled to the bathroom and cannot perform many of the activities of daily living. She is morbidly obese and her husband cannot carry her or assist her out of the house. She states that she has intense cramping in the back of her right calf. She has been receiving home health care for one month with marked improvement. Home health PT has been visiting her twice a week. Dr. Murray spends time reviewing her old records and notes the following diagnoses:

- Osteoarthritis right hip and bilateral knees
- At last visit in August, she was having difficulty ambulating with a cane
- Type II diabetes, fluctuating in and out of control
- Hypertension, controlled
- Sprain/strain right leg

Dr Murray discusses her case with the home health nurse who has been seeing her. He authorizes another month of home health. He wants continued PT as well as BP and blood sugar monitoring. If she is not completely recovered after another month, she must see an orthopaedist. He spent 30 minutes coordinating her care and reviewing her records this month.

Because she has Medicare, check the Medicare website to confirm how this treatment should be coded. ____

JOB 9: Nancy Herbert is seen in the office for a bone density study. She is postmenopausal and is not on HRT. It has been two years since her last scan. She is in great health and wants to be sure she does not have osteoporosis. She continues to exercise. She takes Arthrotec for her arthritis and a multivitamin along with extra vitamin D with calcium. The front desk staff has asked you to speak to the patient regarding Medicare coverage of this service. Research CMS's policies for bone density measurements. Print any supporting documentation you have about this coverage. What will you tell Ms. Herbert? What form must be signed prior to having the test performed? Download the form and complete it before talking with the patient. ____________________

____

(See Job 9, Router- Nancy Herbert)

DAY FOUR: THURSDAY, October 29, 2009 (continued)

JOB 10: April Kennedy has asked you to research on the Internet and obtain an updated CLIA Waived test list. The doctors are looking into performing the Phamatech At Home 12 Drug Test (Model 9308T) in the office, and she must determine if this is a CLIA-waived test. Print the requested list from the Medicare website and turn it into your instructor. Is this a waived test? What modifier must be appended to CLIA-waived tests?____________________

JOB 11: Enter the charges for all the routers from 10/28/09 visits you coded today. Also enter the visits you have coded from today. *(See Job 11, Router- Russell Logan)*

JOB 12: Now that the hospital visits you have to date are coded, enter the charges. The reference number for the hospital charges is the doctor's initials and the date of service. If the doctor is providing charges for a range of days, the last day of the range is the reference number.

Billing/Claims Submission

JOB 13: You discovered there is a Medicare claim from September 2007 that appears to have never been filed for a patient. Can you submit this claim now and receive payment? Search the Medicare website to find the terms of their timely filing deadline. What is their guideline for this situation? ____________________

____

JOB 14: Submit claims for all the charges entered today. Use the date range of 10/1/09–10/29/09 to capture all visits you coded today. When the transmission is complete, print the *Transmission Report* and turn this in to your instructor.

Chapter Exercises

1. Search the *Medicare Claims Processing Manual*. What is the timeline for them processing other than clean claims? ____________________
2. Diane Hartsfeld was seen on 10/27/09 for a physical exam. This was her first exam since receiving Medicare. Does her visit include all the elements that Medicare requires for the Welcome to Medicare exam? Visit Medicare's website and research preventative visits. ____________________

   ____
3. With respect to billing services provided in the hospital, describe span coding. Search the Internet and carrier websites to find information. ____________________

   ____

Day 3			Day 4		
Job No.	Patient Name	Documents	Job No.	Patient Name	Documents
Job 1	All patients seen in the office during days 1 and 2	Routers and typed progress notes	Job 1	Multiple patients	Routers from 10/28/09
Job 2	Derek Wallace	Router	Job 2	Julia Richard, Julius Washington	Hospital charge sheets
Job 3	William Kostner	Router 10/27/09	Job 3	Hugh Williams	Router
Job 4	N/A		Job 4	Jordon Connell	Router
Job 5	Robert Shinn, Manual Ramirez, Caroline Pratt, Tina Rizzo, John Conway, David James, Francesco Alvarez, Deanne Lloyd, Diane Parker, Abbey Taylor	Hospital Charge Sheets	Job 5	Chrissy Krouse	Router
Job 6	N/A		Job 6	Norman Johnson	Router
Job 7	N/A	DMA Router	Job 7	Aimee Bradley	Router
Job 8	N/A		Job 8	Paula Skektar	N/A
Job 9	N/A		Job 9	Nancy Herbert	Router
Job 10	Samantha Beechwood	Router 10/27/09	Job 10	N/A	N/A
Job 11	N/A	Routers from 10/26/09-10/27/09	Job 11	N/A	Routers from 10/28/09 from job 1
Job 12	N/A	Hospital Charge Sheets	Job 12	Julia Richard, Julius Washington	Hospital charge sheets from job 2
Job 13	N/A		Job 13	N/A	N/A
Job 14	N/A		Job 14	N/A	N/A

Date of service: 10/26/09	Insurance: FLEXIHEALTH		Router #: 1497
Patient name: FRANCESCO ALVAREZ	Coinsurance:	Copay: 20.00	Physician Name: MENDENHALL
Account #: ALV001	Noncovered Waiver?	yes / no / n/a	

X	Office visit	New	X	Est
	Minimal (RN only)			99211
	Problem focused	99201		99212
	Exp problem focused	99202		99213
	Detailed	99203		99214
	Comp	99204	✓	99215
	Comprhen/Complex	99205		

X	Well visit	New	X	Est
	< 1 y	99381		99391
	1-4 y	99382		99392
	5-11 y	99383		99393
	12-17 y	99384		99394
	18-39 y	99385		99395
	40-64 y	99386		99396
	65 y +	99387		99397

X	Medicare preventive services	
	Pap	Q0091
	Pelvic & breast	G0101
	Prostate/PSA	G0103
	Tobacco couns/3-10 min	G0375
	Tobacco couns/>10 min	G0376
	Welcome to Medicare exam	G0344
	ECG w/Welcome to Medicare	G0366
	Hemoccult, guaiac	G0107
	Flu shot	G0008
	Pneumonia shot	G0009

X	Consultation/preop clearance	
	Exp problem focused	99242
	Detailed	99243
	Comp/mod complex	99244
	Comp/high complex	99245

X	Other services	
	After posted hours	99050
	Evening/weekend appointment	99051
	Home health certification	G0180
	Home health recertification	G0179
	Care Plan oversight	99374
	Care Plan Oversight >30 mins	99375
	Post-op follow-up	99024
	Prolonged/60min total	99354
	Prolonged/each add 30 mins	99355
	Special reports/forms	99080
	Disability/Workers comp	99455
	Smoking Cessation <10 mins	99406
	Smoking Cessation >10 mins	99407
	ETOH/SA screening <30 mins	99408
	Online E/M by MD	99444
	Phone E/M <10 mins	99441
	Phone E/M <20 mins	99442
	Phone E/M <30 mins	99443
	Anticoagulant Mgmt <90 days	99363
	Anticoagulant Mgmt >90 days	99364
	In office emergency serv	99058

X	Other services	

X	Supplies	
	Surgical Tray	99070

Instructions:

Adx to observation today

X	Office procedures	
	Cerumen removal	69210
✓	ECG, w/interpretation	93000
	ECG, rhythm strip	93040
	Endometrial biopsy	58100
	Fracture care, cast/splint Site: ______________	
	Nebulizer	94640
	Nebulizer demo	94664
	Spirometry	94010
	Spirometry, pre and post	94060
	Vasectomy	55250

X	Skin procedures		Units
	Foreign body, skin, simple	10120	
	Foreign body, skin, complex	10121	
	I&D, abscess	10060	
	I&D, hematoma/seroma	10140	
	Laceration repair, simple Site: _______ Size: _____	120__	
	Laceration repair, layered Site: _______ Size: _____	120__	
	Laser Light Tx	96597	
	Lesion, biopsy, one	11100	
	Lesion, biopsy, each add'l	11101	
	Lesion, excision, benign Site: _______ Size: _____	114__	
	Lesion, excision, malignant Site: _______ Size: _____	116__	
	Lesion, paring/cutting, one	11055	
	Lesion, paring/cutting, 2-4	11056	
	Lesion, shave Site: _______ Size: _____	113__	
	Nail removal, partial (+T mod)	11730	
	Nail rem, w/matrix (+T mod)	11750	
	Skin tag, 1-15	11200	
	Wart, flat, 1-14	17110	
	Destruction lesion, 1st	17000	
	Destruct lesion, each addl 2-14	17003	

X	Medications		Units
	Ampicillin, up to 500mg	J0290	
	B-12, up to 1,000 mcg	J3420	
	Epinephrine, up to 1ml	J0170	
	Kenalog, 10mg	J3301	
	Lidocaine, 10mg	J2001	
	Normal saline, 1000cc	J7030	
	Phenergan, up to 50mg	J2550	
	Progesterone, 150mg	J1055	
	Rocephin, 250mg	J0696	
	Testosterone, 200mg	J1080	
	Tigan, up to 200 mg	J3250	
	Toradol, 15mg	J1885	
	Albuterol	J7609	
	Depo-Provera 50 mg	J1055	
	Depo-Medrol 40 mg	J1030	

Diagnoses		Code
1	A-fib	
2	ATN	
3		
4		

Next office visit:

Recheck • Preventative • PRN

Referral to:

Physician signature

X Sarah Mendenhall MD

X	Laboratory		-90
✓	Venipuncture	36415	
	Blood glucose, monitoring device	82962	
	Blood glucose, visual dipstick	82948	
✓	CBC, w/ auto differential	85025	
	CBC, w/o auto differential	85027	
	Cholesterol	82465	
	Hemoccult, guaiac	82270	
	Hemoccult, immunoassay	82274	
	Hemoglobin A1C	85018	
	Lipid panel	80061	
	Liver panel	80076	
	KOH prep (skin, hair, nails)	87220	
	Metabolic panel, basic	80048	
✓	Metabolic panel, comprehensive	80053	
	Mononucleosis	86308	
	Pregnancy, blood	84703	
	Pregnancy, urine	81025	
	Renal panel	80069	
	Sedimentation rate	85651	
	Strep, rapid	86403	
	Strep culture	87081	
	Strep A	87880	
	TB	86580	
	UA, complete, non-automated	81000	
	UA, w/o micro, non-automated	81002	
	UA, w/ micro, non-automated	81003	
	Urine colony count	87086	
	Urine culture, presumptive	87088	
	Wet mount/KOH	87210	

X	Vaccines	
	DT, <7 y	90702
	DTP	90701
	DtaP, <7 y	90700
	Flu, 6-35 months	90657
	Flu, 3 y +	90658
	Hep A, adult	90632
	Hep A, ped/adol, 2 dose	90633
	Hep B, adult	90746
	Hep B, ped/adol 3 dose	90744
	Hep B-Hib	90748
	Hib, 4 dose	90645
	HPV	90649
	IPV	90713
	MMR	90707
	Pneumonia, >2 y	90732
	Pneumonia conjugate, <5 y	90669
	Td, >7 y	90718
	Varicella	90716
	Tetanus toxoid adsorbed, IM	90703

X	Immunizations & Injections		Units
	Allergen, one	95115	
	Allergen, multiple	95117	
	Imm admn <8 yo 1st Inj	90465	
	Imm admn <8 yo each add inj	90466	
	Imm <8 yo oral or intranasal	90467	
	Imm admn <8 yo each add	90468	
	Imm admin, one vacc	90471	
	Imm admin, each add'l	90472	
	Imm admin, intranasal, one	90473	
	Imm admin, intranasal, each add'l	90474	
	Injection, joint, small	20600	
	Injection, joint, intermediate	20605	
	Injection, ther/proph/diag	90772	
	Injection, trigger pt 1-2 musc	20552	

Today's charges:		
Today's payment:		
Balance due:		

Job 1 Router- Francesco Alvarez 1 of 20

Date of service: 10/26/09	Insurance: MEDICAID				Superbill Number: 1490
Patient name: JOHN WITTMER	Coinsurance:	Copay: 2.00			Physician Name: KEMPER
Account #: WIT001	Noncovered Waiver?	yes	no	n/a	

x	Office visit	New	x	Est
	Minimal (RN only)			99211
	Problem focused	99201		99212
	Exp problem focused	99202		99213
	Detailed	99203		99214
	Comp	99204		99215
	Comprhen/Complex	99205		
	Well visit	**New**	**x**	**Est**
	< 1 y	99381		99391
	1-4 y	99382		99392
	5-11 y	99383		99393
	12-17 y	99384		99394
	18-39 y	99385		99395
	40-64 y	99386	✓	99396
	65 y +	99387		99397

x	Medicare preventive services	
	Pap	Q0091
	Pelvic & breast	G0101
	Prostate/PSA	G0103
	Tobacco couns/3-10 min	G0375
	Tobacco couns/>10 min	G0376
	Welcome to Medicare exam	G0344
	ECG w/Welcome to Medicare	G0366
	Hemoccult, guaiac	G0107
	Flu shot	G0008
	Pneumonia shot	G0009

x	Consultation/preop clearance	
	Exp problem focused	99242
	Detailed	99243
	Comp/mod complex	99244
	Comp/high complex	99245

x	Other services	
	After posted hours	99050
	Evening/weekend appointment	99051
	Home health certification	G0180
	Home health recertification	G0179
	Care Plan oversight	99374
	Care Plan Oversight >30 mins	99375
	Post-op follow-up	99024
	Prolonged/60min total	99354
	Prolonged/each add 30 mins	99355
	Special reports/forms	99080
	Disability/Workers comp	99455
✓	Smoking Cessation <10 mins	99406
	Smoking Cessation >10 mins	99407
	ETOH/SA screening <30 mins	99408
	Online E/M by MD	99444
	Phone E/M <10 mins	99441
	Phone E/M <20 mins	99442
	Phone E/M <30 mins	99443
	Anticoagulant Mgmt <90 days	99363
	Anticoagulant Mgmt >90 days	99364
	In office emergency serv	99058

x	Other services	

x	Supplies	
	Surgical Tray	99070

Instructions:

Rx: Zyban

x	Office procedures	
	Cerumen removal	69210
	ECG, w/interpretation	93000
	ECG, rhythm strip	93040
	Endometrial biopsy	58100
	Fracture care, cast/splint Site: ___________	___
	Nebulizer	94640
	Nebulizer demo	94664
	Spirometry	94010
	Spirometry, pre and post	94060
	Vasectomy	55250

x	Skin procedures		Units
	Foreign body, skin, simple	10120	
	Foreign body, skin, complex	10121	
	I&D, abscess	10060	
	I&D, hematoma/seroma	10140	
	Laceration repair, simple Site: _______ Size: _____	120__	
	Laceration repair, layered Site: _______ Size: _____	120__	
	Laser Light Tx	96597	
	Lesion, biopsy, one	11100	
	Lesion, biopsy, each add'l	11101	
	Lesion, excision, benign Site: _______ Size: _____	114__	
	Lesion, excision, malignant Site: _______ Size: _____	116__	
	Lesion, paring/cutting, one	11055	
	Lesion, paring/cutting, 2-4	11056	
	Lesion, shave Site: _______ Size: _____	113__	
	Nail removal, partial (+T mod)	11730	
	Nail rem, w/matrix (+T mod)	11750	
	Skin tag, 1-15	11200	
	Wart, flat, 1-14	17110	
	Destruction lesion, 1st	17000	
	Destruct lesion, each addl 2-14	17003	

x	Medications		Units
	Ampicillin, up to 500mg	J0290	
	B-12, up to 1,000 mcg	J3420	
	Epinephrine, up to 1ml	J0170	
	Kenalog, 10mg	J3301	
	Lidocaine, 10mg	J2001	
	Normal saline, 1000cc	J7030	
	Phenergan, up to 50mg	J2550	
	Progesterone, 150mg	J1055	
	Rocephin, 250mg	J0696	
	Testosterone, 200mg	J1080	
	Tigan, up to 200 mg	J3250	
	Toradol, 15mg	J1885	
	Albuterol	J7609	
	Depo-Provera 50 mg	J1055	
	Depo-Medrol 40 mg	J1030	

Diagnoses		Code
1 Well check		
2 Tobacco Abuse		
3		
4		

Next office visit: 1 yr

Recheck • Preventative • / PRN

Referral to:

Physician signature

x Sally Kemper

x	Laboratory		-90
	Venipuncture	36415	
	Blood glucose, monitoring device	82962	
	Blood glucose, visual dipstick	82948	
	CBC, w/ auto differential	85025	
	CBC, w/o auto differential	85027	
	Cholesterol	82465	
	Hemoccult, guaiac	82270	
	Hemoccult, immunoassay	82274	
	Hemoglobin A1C	85018	
	Lipid panel	80061	
	Liver panel	80076	
	KOH prep (skin, hair, nails)	87220	
	Metabolic panel, basic	80048	
	Metabolic panel, comprehensive	80053	
	Mononucleosis	86308	
	Pregnancy, blood	84703	
	Pregnancy, urine	81025	
	Renal panel	80069	
	Sedimentation rate	85651	
	Strep, rapid	86403	
	Strep culture	87081	
	Strep A	87880	
	TB	86580	
	UA, complete, non-automated	81000	
	UA, w/o micro, non-automated	81002	
	UA, w/ micro, non-automated	81003	
	Urine colony count	87086	
	Urine culture, presumptive	87088	
	Wet mount/KOH	87210	

x	Vaccines	
	DT, <7 y	90702
	DTP	90701
	DtaP, <7 y	90700
	Flu, 6-35 months	90657
	Flu, 3 y +	90658
	Hep A, adult	90632
	Hep A, ped/adol, 2 dose	90633
	Hep B, adult	90746
	Hep B, ped/adol 3 dose	90744
	Hep B-Hib	90748
	Hib, 4 dose	90645
	HPV	90649
	IPV	90713
	MMR	90707
	Pneumonia, >2 y	90732
	Pneumonia conjugate, <5 y	90669
	Td, >7 y	90718
	Varicella	90716
	Tetanus toxoid adsorbed, IM	90703

x	Immunizations & Injections		Units
	Allergen, one	95115	
	Allergen, multiple	95117	
	Imm admn <8 yo 1st Inj	90465	
	Imm admn <8 yo each add inj	90466	
	Imm <8 yo oral or intranasal	90467	
	Imm admn <8 yo each add	90468	
	Imm admin, one vacc	90471	
	Imm admin, each add'l	90472	
	Imm admin, intranasal, one	90473	
	Imm admin, intranasal, each add'l	90474	
	Injection, joint, small	20600	
	Injection, joint, intermediate	20605	
	Injection, ther/proph/diag	90772	
	Injection, trigger pt 1-2 musc	20552	

Today's charges:	
Today's payment:	2.00 cash
Balance due:	

Job 1 Router- John Wittmer 2 of 20

Date of service: 10/26/09	Insurance: SELF PAY				Superbill Number: 1494
Patient name: RYAN ASHBY	Coinsurance:	Copay:			Physician Name: MURRAY
Account #: ASH001	Noncovered Waiver?	yes	no	n/a	

x	Office visit	New	x	Est
	Minimal (RN only)			99211
	Problem focused	99201		99212
	Exp problem focused	99202	✓	99213
	Detailed	99203		99214
	Comp	99204		99215
	Comprhen/Complex	99205		
	Well visit	**New**	**x**	**Est**
	< 1 y	99381		99391
	1-4 y	99382		99392
	5-11 y	99383		99393
	12-17 y	99384		99394
	18-39 y	99385		99395
	40-64 y	99386		99396
	65 y +	99387		99397

x	Medicare preventive services	
	Pap	Q0091
	Pelvic & breast	G0101
	Prostate/PSA	G0103
	Tobacco couns/3-10 min	G0375
	Tobacco couns/>10 min	G0376
	Welcome to Medicare exam	G0344
	ECG w/Welcome to Medicare	G0366
	Hemoccult, guaiac	G0107
	Flu shot	G0008
	Pneumonia shot	G0009
	Consultation/preop clearance	
	Exp problem focused	99242
	Detailed	99243
	Comp/mod complex	99244
	Comp/high complex	99245
	Other services	
	After posted hours	99050
	Evening/weekend appointment	99051
	Home health certification	G0180
	Home health recertification	G0179
	Care Plan oversight	99374
	Care Plan Oversight >30 mins	99375
	Post-op follow-up	99024
	Prolonged/60min total	99354
	Prolonged/each add 30 mins	99355
	Special reports/forms	99080
	Disability/Workers comp	99455
	Smoking Cessation <10 mins	99406
	Smoking Cessation >10 mins	99407
	ETOH/SA screening <30 mins	99408
	Online E/M by MD	99444
	Phone E/M <10 mins	99441
	Phone E/M <20 mins	99442
	Phone E/M <30 mins	99443
	Anticoagulant Mgmt <90 days	99363
	Anticoagulant Mgmt >90 days	99364
	In office emergency serv	99058
	Other services	
	Supplies	
✓	Surgical Tray	99070

Instructions:

Return 10 days for suture removal

x	Office procedures		
	Cerumen removal		69210
	ECG, w/interpretation		93000
	ECG, rhythm strip		93040
	Endometrial biopsy		58100
	Fracture care, cast/splint Site: ________________		____
	Nebulizer		94640
	Nebulizer demo		94664
	Spirometry		94010
	Spirometry, pre and post		94060
	Vasectomy		55250
	Skin procedures		**Units**
	Foreign body, skin, simple	10120	
	Foreign body, skin, complex	10121	
	I&D, abscess	10060	
	I&D, hematoma/seroma	10140	
✓	Laceration repair, simple Site: Rt hand Size: 3cm	120__	
	Laceration repair, layered Site: _______ Size: _____	120__	
	Laser Light Tx	96597	
	Lesion, biopsy, one	11100	
	Lesion, biopsy, each add'l	11101	
	Lesion, excision, benign Site: _______ Size: _____	114__	
	Lesion, excision, malignant Site: _______ Size: _____	116__	
	Lesion, paring/cutting, one	11055	
	Lesion, paring/cutting, 2-4	11056	
	Lesion, shave Site: _______ Size: _____	113__	
	Nail removal, partial (+T mod)	11730	
	Nail rem, w/matrix (+T mod)	11750	
	Skin tag, 1-15	11200	
	Wart, flat, 1-14	17110	
	Destruction lesion, 1st	17000	
	Destruct lesion, each addl 2-14	17003	
	Medications		**Units**
	Ampicillin, up to 500mg	J0290	
	B-12, up to 1,000 mcg	J3420	
	Epinephrine, up to 1ml	J0170	
	Kenalog, 10mg	J3301	
	Lidocaine, 10mg	J2001	
	Normal saline, 1000cc	J7030	
	Phenergan, up to 50mg	J2550	
	Progesterone, 150mg	J1055	
	Rocephin, 250mg	J0696	
	Testosterone, 200mg	J1080	
	Tigan, up to 200 mg	J3250	
	Toradol, 15mg	J1885	
	Albuterol	J7609	
	Depo-Provera 50 mg	J1055	
	Depo-Medrol 40 mg	J1030	

Diagnoses		Code
1 Laceration Rt hand		
2		
3		
4		

Next office visit:

Recheck • Preventative • PRN

Referral to:

Physician signature

x [signature] MD

x	Laboratory		-90
	Venipuncture	36415	
	Blood glucose, monitoring device	82962	
	Blood glucose, visual dipstick	82948	
	CBC, w/ auto differential	85025	
	CBC, w/o auto differential	85027	
	Cholesterol	82465	
	Hemoccult, guaiac	82270	
	Hemoccult, immunoassay	82274	
	Hemoglobin A1C	85018	
	Lipid panel	80061	
	Liver panel	80076	
	KOH prep (skin, hair, nails)	87220	
	Metabolic panel, basic	80048	
	Metabolic panel, comprehensive	80053	
	Mononucleosis	86308	
	Pregnancy, blood	84703	
	Pregnancy, urine	81025	
	Renal panel	80069	
	Sedimentation rate	85651	
	Strep, rapid	86403	
	Strep culture	87081	
	Strep A	87880	
	TB	86580	
	UA, complete, non-automated	81000	
	UA, w/o micro, non-automated	81002	
	UA, w/ micro, non-automated	81003	
	Urine colony count	87086	
	Urine culture, presumptive	87088	
	Wet mount/KOH	87210	

Vaccines	
DT, <7 y	90702
DTP	90701
DtaP, <7 y	90700
Flu, 6-35 months	90657
Flu, 3 y +	90658
Hep A, adult	90632
Hep A, ped/adol, 2 dose	90633
Hep B, adult	90746
Hep B, ped/adol 3 dose	90744
Hep B-Hib	90748
Hib, 4 dose	90645
HPV	90649
IPV	90713
MMR	90707
Pneumonia, >2 y	90732
Pneumonia conjugate, <5 y	90669
Td, >7 y	90718
Varicella	90716
Tetanus toxoid adsorbed, IM	90703

Immunizations & Injections		Units
Allergen, one	95115	
Allergen, multiple	95117	
Imm admn <8 yo 1st Inj	90465	
Imm admn <8 yo each add inj	90466	
Imm <8 yo oral or intranasal	90467	
Imm admn <8 yo each add	90468	
Imm admin, one vacc	90471	
Imm admin, each add'l	90472	
Imm admin, intranasal, one	90473	
Imm admin, intranasal, each add'l	90474	
Injection, joint, small	20600	
Injection, joint, intermediate	20605	
Injection, ther/proph/diag	90772	
Injection, trigger pt 1-2 musc	20552	

Today's charges:	
Today's payment:	
Balance due:	

Job 1 Router- Ryan Ashby 3 of 20

Date of service: 10/26/09	Insurance: CIGNA				Superbill Number: 1492
Patient name: WILLIAM TURNER	Coinsurance:	Copay:			Physician Name: KEMPER
Account #: TUR001	Noncovered Waiver?	yes	no	n/a	

x	Office visit	New	x	Est
	Minimal (RN only)			99211
	Problem focused	99201		99212
✓	Exp problem focused	99202		99213
	Detailed	99203		99214
	Comp	99204		99215
	Comprhen/Complex	99205		
	Well visit	**New**	**x**	**Est**
	< 1 y	99381		99391
	1-4 y	99382		99392
	5-11 y	99383		99393
	12-17 y	99384		99394
	18-39 y	99385		99395
	40-64 y	99386		99396
	65 y +	99387		99397
	Medicare preventive services			
	Pap			Q0091
	Pelvic & breast			G0101
	Prostate/PSA			G0103
	Tobacco couns/3-10 min			G0375
	Tobacco couns/>10 min			G0376
	Welcome to Medicare exam			G0344
	ECG w/Welcome to Medicare			G0366
	Hemoccult, guaiac			G0107
	Flu shot			G0008
	Pneumonia shot			G0009
	Consultation/preop clearance			
	Exp problem focused			99242
	Detailed			99243
	Comp/mod complex			99244
	Comp/high complex			99245
	Other services			
	After posted hours			99050
	Evening/weekend appointment			99051
	Home health certification			G0180
	Home health recertification			G0179
	Care Plan oversight			99374
	Care Plan Oversight >30 mins			99375
	Post-op follow-up			99024
	Prolonged/60min total			99354
	Prolonged/each add 30 mins			99355
	Special reports/forms			99080
	Disability/Workers comp			99455
	Smoking Cessation <10 mins			99406
	Smoking Cessation >10 mins			99407
	ETOH/SA screening <30 mins			99408
	Online E/M by MD			99444
	Phone E/M <10 mins			99441
	Phone E/M <20 mins			99442
	Phone E/M <30 mins			99443
	Anticoagulant Mgmt <90 days			99363
	Anticoagulant Mgmt >90 days			99364
	In office emergency serv			99058
	Other services			
	PCR antigen amplified probe			
	Supplies			
	Surgical Tray			99070

Instructions:

Return 3wks F/U

Rx Viroxyn

x	Office procedures		
	Cerumen removal		69210
	ECG, w/interpretation		93000
	ECG, rhythm strip		93040
	Endometrial biopsy		58100
	Fracture care, cast/splint Site: ____________		____
	Nebulizer		94640
	Nebulizer demo		94664
	Spirometry		94010
	Spirometry, pre and post		94060
	Vasectomy		55250
	Skin procedures		**Units**
	Foreign body, skin, simple	10120	
	Foreign body, skin, complex	10121	
	I&D, abscess	10060	
	I&D, hematoma/seroma	10140	
	Laceration repair, simple Site: ______ Size: _____	120__	
	Laceration repair, layered Site: ______ Size: _____	120__	
	Laser Light Tx	96597	
	Lesion, biopsy, one	11100	
	Lesion, biopsy, each add'l	11101	
	Lesion, excision, benign Site: ______ Size: _____	114__	
	Lesion, excision, malignant Site: ______ Size: _____	116__	
	Lesion, paring/cutting, one	11055	
	Lesion, paring/cutting, 2-4	11056	
	Lesion, shave Site: ______ Size: _____	113__	
	Nail removal, partial (+T mod)	11730	
	Nail rem, w/matrix (+T mod)	11750	
	Skin tag, 1-15	11200	
	Wart, flat, 1-14	17110	
	Destruction lesion, 1st	17000	
	Destruct lesion, each addl 2-14	17003	
	Medications		**Units**
	Ampicillin, up to 500mg	J0290	
	B-12, up to 1,000 mcg	J3420	
	Epinephrine, up to 1ml	J0170	
	Kenalog, 10mg	J3301	
	Lidocaine, 10mg	J2001	
	Normal saline, 1000cc	J7030	
	Phenergan, up to 50mg	J2550	
	Progesterone, 150mg	J1055	
	Rocephin, 250mg	J0696	
	Testosterone, 200mg	J1080	
	Tigan, up to 200 mg	J3250	
	Toradol, 15mg	J1885	
	Albuterol	J7609	
	Depo-Provera 50 mg	J1055	
	Depo-Medrol 40 mg	J1030	

Diagnoses		Code
1 Herpes Simplex Virus 1		
2		
3		
4		

Next office visit:
Recheck • Preventative • PRN

Referral to:

Physician signature

x [signature]

x	Laboratory		-90
✓	Venipuncture	36415	
	Blood glucose, monitoring device	82962	
	Blood glucose, visual dipstick	82948	
	CBC, w/ auto differential	85025	
	CBC, w/o auto differential	85027	
	Cholesterol	82465	
	Hemoccult, guaiac	82270	
	Hemoccult, immunoassay	82274	
	Hemoglobin A1C	85018	
	Lipid panel	80061	
	Liver panel	80076	
	KOH prep (skin, hair, nails)	87220	
	Metabolic panel, basic	80048	
	Metabolic panel, comprehensive	80053	
	Mononucleosis	86308	
	Pregnancy, blood	84703	
	Pregnancy, urine	81025	
	Renal panel	80069	
	Sedimentation rate	85651	
	Strep, rapid	86403	
	Strep culture	87081	
	Strep A	87880	
	TB	86580	
	UA, complete, non-automated	81000	
	UA, w/o micro, non-automated	81002	
	UA, w/ micro, non-automated	81003	
	Urine colony count	87086	
	Urine culture, presumptive	87088	
	Wet mount/KOH	87210	
	Vaccines		
	DT, <7 y		90702
	DTP		90701
	DtaP, <7 y		90700
	Flu, 6-35 months		90657
	Flu, 3 y +		90658
	Hep A, adult		90632
	Hep A, ped/adol, 2 dose		90633
	Hep B, adult		90746
	Hep B, ped/adol 3 dose		90744
	Hep B-Hib		90748
	Hib, 4 dose		90645
	HPV		90649
	IPV		90713
	MMR		90707
	Pneumonia, >2 y		90732
	Pneumonia conjugate, <5 y		90669
	Td, >7 y		90718
	Varicella		90716
	Tetanus toxoid adsorbed, IM		90703
	Immunizations & Injections		**Units**
	Allergen, one	95115	
	Allergen, multiple	95117	
	Imm admn <8 yo 1st Inj	90465	
	Imm admn <8 yo each add inj	90466	
	Imm <8 yo oral or intranasal	90467	
	Imm admn <8 yo each add	90468	
	Imm admin, one vacc	90471	
	Imm admin, each add'l	90472	
	Imm admin, intranasal, one	90473	
	Imm admin, intranasal, each add'l	90474	
	Injection, joint, small	20600	
	Injection, joint, intermediate	20605	
	Injection, ther/proph/diag	90772	
	Injection, trigger pt 1-2 musc	20552	

Today's charges:		
Today's payment:		
Balance due:		

Job 1 Router- William Turner 4 of 20

Date of service: 10/26/09	Insurance: FLEXIHEALTH PPO				Superbill Number: 1493
Patient name: CAITLIN BARRYMORE	Coinsurance:	Copay: 20.00			Physician Name: HEATH
Account #: BAR001	Noncovered Waiver?	yes	no	n/a	

x	Office visit	New	x	Est
	Minimal (RN only)			99211
	Problem focused	99201		99212
	Exp problem focused	99202		99213
	Detailed	99203	✓	99214
	Comp	99204		99215
	Comprhen/Complex	99205		
	Well visit	**New**	**x**	**Est**
	< 1 y	99381		99391
	1-4 y	99382		99392
	5-11 y	99383		99393
	12-17 y	99384		99394
	18-39 y	99385		99395
	40-64 y	99386		99396
	65 y +	99387		99397
	Medicare preventive services			
	Pap			Q0091
	Pelvic & breast			G0101
	Prostate/PSA			G0103
	Tobacco couns/3-10 min			G0375
	Tobacco couns/>10 min			G0376
	Welcome to Medicare exam			G0344
	ECG w/Welcome to Medicare			G0366
	Hemoccult, guaiac			G0107
	Flu shot			G0008
	Pneumonia shot			G0009
	Consultation/preop clearance			
	Exp problem focused			99242
	Detailed			99243
	Comp/mod complex			99244
	Comp/high complex			99245
	Other services			
	After posted hours			99050
	Evening/weekend appointment			99051
	Home health certification			G0180
	Home health recertification			G0179
	Care Plan oversight			99374
	Care Plan Oversight >30 mins			99375
	Post-op follow-up			99024
	Prolonged/60min total			99354
	Prolonged/each add 30 mins			99355
	Special reports/forms			99080
	Disability/Workers comp			99455
	Smoking Cessation <10 mins			99406
	Smoking Cessation >10 mins			99407
	ETOH/SA screening <30 mins			99408
	Online E/M by MD			99444
	Phone E/M <10 mins			99441
	Phone E/M <20 mins			99442
	Phone E/M <30 mins			99443
	Anticoagulant Mgmt <90 days			99363
	Anticoagulant Mgmt >90 days			99364
	In office emergency serv			99058
	Other services			
	VDRL			
	Pelvic Exam			
	Supplies			
	Surgical Tray			99070

x	Office procedures		
	Cerumen removal		69210
	ECG, w/interpretation		93000
	ECG, rhythm strip		93040
	Endometrial biopsy		58100
	Fracture care, cast/splint		
	Site: ________		
	Nebulizer		94640
	Nebulizer demo		94664
	Spirometry		94010
	Spirometry, pre and post		94060
	Vasectomy		55250
	Skin procedures		**Units**
	Foreign body, skin, simple	10120	
	Foreign body, skin, complex	10121	
	I&D, abscess	10060	
	I&D, hematoma/seroma	10140	
	Laceration repair, simple	120__	
	Site: _______ Size: _____		
	Laceration repair, layered	120__	
	Site: _______ Size: _____		
	Laser Light Tx	96597	
	Lesion, biopsy, one	11100	
	Lesion, biopsy, each add'l	11101	
	Lesion, excision, benign	114__	
	Site: _______ Size: _____		
	Lesion, excision, malignant	116__	
	Site: _______ Size: _____		
	Lesion, paring/cutting, one	11055	
	Lesion, paring/cutting, 2-4	11056	
	Lesion, shave	113__	
	Site: _______ Size: _____		
	Nail removal, partial (+T mod)	11730	
	Nail rem, w/matrix (+T mod)	11750	
	Skin tag, 1-15	11200	
	Wart, flat, 1-14	17110	
	Destruction lesion, 1st	17000	
	Destruct lesion, each addl 2-14	17003	
	Medications		**Units**
	Ampicillin, up to 500mg	J0290	
	B-12, up to 1,000 mcg	J3420	
	Epinephrine, up to 1ml	J0170	
	Kenalog, 10mg	J3301	
	Lidocaine, 10mg	J2001	
	Normal saline, 1000cc	J7030	
	Phenergan, up to 50mg	J2550	
	Progesterone, 150mg	J1055	
	Rocephin, 250mg	J0696	
	Testosterone, 200mg	J1080	
	Tigan, up to 200 mg	J3250	
	Toradol, 15mg	J1885	
	Albuterol	J7609	
	Depo-Provera 50 mg	J1055	
	Depo-Medrol 40 mg	J1030	

Diagnoses		Code
1 Abdominal Pain		
2 fatigue		
3 Possible VD		
4		

Next office visit: 1 wk

Recheck • Preventative • PRN

Referral to:

x	Laboratory		-90
✓	Venipuncture	36415	
	Blood glucose, monitoring device	82962	
	Blood glucose, visual dipstick	82948	
	CBC, w/ auto differential	85025	
	CBC, w/o auto differential	85027	
	Cholesterol	82465	
	Hemoccult, guaiac	82270	
	Hemoccult, immunoassay	82274	
	Hemoglobin A1C	85018	
	Lipid panel	80061	
	Liver panel	80076	
	KOH prep (skin, hair, nails)	87220	
	Metabolic panel, basic	80048	
	Metabolic panel, comprehensive	80053	
✓	Mononucleosis	86308	✓
	Pregnancy, blood	84703	
	Pregnancy, urine	81025	
	Renal panel	80069	
	Sedimentation rate	85651	
	Strep, rapid	86403	
	Strep culture	87081	
	Strep A	87880	
	TB	86580	
	UA, complete, non-automated	81000	
	UA, w/o micro, non-automated	81002	
✓	UA, w/ micro, non-automated	81003	✓
	Urine colony count	87086	
	Urine culture, presumptive	87088	
	Wet mount/KOH	87210	
	Vaccines		
	DT, <7 y		90702
	DTP		90701
	DtaP, <7 y		90700
	Flu, 6-35 months		90657
	Flu, 3 y +		90658
	Hep A, adult		90632
	Hep A, ped/adol, 2 dose		90633
	Hep B, adult		90746
	Hep B, ped/adol 3 dose		90744
	Hep B-Hib		90748
	Hib, 4 dose		90645
	HPV		90649
	IPV		90713
	MMR		90707
	Pneumonia, >2 y		90732
	Pneumonia conjugate, <5 y		90669
	Td, >7 y		90718
	Varicella		90716
	Tetanus toxoid adsorbed, IM		90703
	Immunizations & Injections		**Units**
	Allergen, one	95115	
	Allergen, multiple	95117	
	Imm admn <8 yo 1st Inj	90465	
	Imm admn <8 yo each add inj	90466	
	Imm <8 yo oral or intranasal	90467	
	Imm admn <8 yo each add	90468	
	Imm admin, one vacc	90471	
	Imm admin, each add'l	90472	
	Imm admin, intranasal, one	90473	
	Imm admin, intranasal, each add'l	90474	
	Injection, joint, small	20600	
	Injection, joint, intermediate	20605	
	Injection, ther/proph/diag	90772	
	Injection, trigger pt 1-2 musc	20552	

Instructions:

F/U VDRL LAB

Physician signature

x Alberta Lynn PAC

Today's charges:		
Today's payment:	20	00 #425
Balance due:		

Job 1 Router- Caitlin Barrymore 5 of 20

Date of service: 10/26/09	Insurance: MANAGEMED		Superbill Number: 1495
Patient name: LAURA LEIGHTON	Coinsurance:	Copay: 15.00	Physician Name: MENDENHALL
Account #: LEI001	Noncovered Waiver?	yes / no / n/a	

x	Office visit	New	x	Est
	Minimal (RN only)			99211
	Problem focused	99201		99212
	Exp problem focused	99202		99213
	Detailed	99203	✓	99214
	Comp	99204		99215
	Comprhen/Complex	99205		
	Well visit	**New**	**x**	**Est**
	< 1 y	99381		99391
	1-4 y	99382		99392
	5-11 y	99383		99393
	12-17 y	99384		99394
	18-39 y	99385		99395
	40-64 y	99386		99396
	65 y +	99387		99397
	Medicare preventive services			
	Pap			Q0091
	Pelvic & breast			G0101
	Prostate/PSA			G0103
	Tobacco couns/3-10 min			G0375
	Tobacco couns/>10 min			G0376
	Welcome to Medicare exam			G0344
	ECG w/Welcome to Medicare			G0366
	Hemoccult, guaiac			G0107
	Flu shot			G0008
	Pneumonia shot			G0009
	Consultation/preop clearance			
	Exp problem focused			99242
	Detailed			99243
	Comp/mod complex			99244
	Comp/high complex			99245
	Other services			
	After posted hours			99050
	Evening/weekend appointment			99051
	Home health certification			G0180
	Home health recertification			G0179
	Care Plan oversight			99374
	Care Plan Oversight >30 mins			99375
	Post-op follow-up			99024
	Prolonged/60min total			99354
	Prolonged/each add 30 mins			99355
	Special reports/forms			99080
	Disability/Workers comp			99455
	Smoking Cessation <10 mins			99406
	Smoking Cessation >10 mins			99407
	ETOH/SA screening <30 mins			99408
	Online E/M by MD			99444
	Phone E/M <10 mins			99441
	Phone E/M <20 mins			99442
	Phone E/M <30 mins			99443
	Anticoagulant Mgmt <90 days			99363
	Anticoagulant Mgmt >90 days			99364
	In office emergency serv			99058
	Other services			
	Supplies			
	Surgical Tray			99070

x	Office procedures		
	Cerumen removal		69210
	ECG, w/interpretation		93000
	ECG, rhythm strip		93040
	Endometrial biopsy		58100
	Fracture care, cast/splint Site: ________		
	Nebulizer		94640
	Nebulizer demo		94664
	Spirometry		94010
	Spirometry, pre and post		94060
	Vasectomy		55250
	Skin procedures		**Units**
	Foreign body, skin, simple	10120	
	Foreign body, skin, complex	10121	
	I&D, abscess	10060	
	I&D, hematoma/seroma	10140	
	Laceration repair, simple Site: ______ Size: _____	120__	
	Laceration repair, layered Site: ______ Size: _____	120__	
	Laser Light Tx	96597	
	Lesion, biopsy, one	11100	
	Lesion, biopsy, each add'l	11101	
	Lesion, excision, benign Site: ______ Size: _____	114__	
	Lesion, excision, malignant Site: ______ Size: _____	116__	
	Lesion, paring/cutting, one	11055	
	Lesion, paring/cutting, 2-4	11056	
	Lesion, shave Site: ______ Size: _____	113__	
	Nail removal, partial (+T mod)	11730	
	Nail rem, w/matrix (+T mod)	11750	
	Skin tag, 1-15	11200	
	Wart, flat, 1-14	17110	
✓	Destruction lesion, 1st	17000	
✓	Destruct lesion, each addl 2-14	17003	
	Medications		**Units**
	Ampicillin, up to 500mg	J0290	
	B-12, up to 1,000 mcg	J3420	
	Epinephrine, up to 1ml	J0170	
	Kenalog, 10mg	J3301	
✓	Lidocaine, 10mg	J2001	
	Normal saline, 1000cc	J7030	
	Phenergan, up to 50mg	J2550	
	Progesterone, 150mg	J1055	
	Rocephin, 250mg	J0696	
	Testosterone, 200mg	J1080	
	Tigan, up to 200 mg	J3250	
	Toradol, 15mg	J1885	
	Albuterol	J7609	
	Depo-Provera 50 mg	J1055	
	Depo-Medrol 40 mg	J1030	

Diagnoses		Code
1 Migraine HA		
2 Dermatofibroma		
3		
4		

Next office visit:
Recheck • Preventative • (PRN)
Referral to:

x	Laboratory		-90
	Venipuncture	36415	
	Blood glucose, monitoring device	82962	
	Blood glucose, visual dipstick	82948	
	CBC, w/ auto differential	85025	
	CBC, w/o auto differential	85027	
	Cholesterol	82465	
	Hemoccult, guaiac	82270	
	Hemoccult, immunoassay	82274	
	Hemoglobin A1C	85018	
	Lipid panel	80061	
	Liver panel	80076	
	KOH prep (skin, hair, nails)	87220	
	Metabolic panel, basic	80048	
	Metabolic panel, comprehensive	80053	
	Mononucleosis	86308	
	Pregnancy, blood	84703	
	Pregnancy, urine	81025	
	Renal panel	80069	
	Sedimentation rate	85651	
	Strep, rapid	86403	
	Strep culture	87081	
	Strep A	87880	
	TB	86580	
	UA, complete, non-automated	81000	
	UA, w/o micro, non-automated	81002	
	UA, w/ micro, non-automated	81003	
	Urine colony count	87086	
	Urine culture, presumptive	87088	
	Wet mount/KOH	87210	
	Vaccines		
	DT, <7 y		90702
	DTP		90701
	DtaP, <7 y		90700
	Flu, 6-35 months		90657
	Flu, 3 y +		90658
	Hep A, adult		90632
	Hep A, ped/adol, 2 dose		90633
	Hep B, adult		90746
	Hep B, ped/adol 3 dose		90744
	Hep B-Hib		90748
	Hib, 4 dose		90645
	HPV		90649
	IPV		90713
	MMR		90707
	Pneumonia, >2 y		90732
	Pneumonia conjugate, <5 y		90669
	Td, >7 y		90718
	Varicella		90716
	Tetanus toxoid adsorbed, IM		90703
	Immunizations & Injections		**Units**
	Allergen, one	95115	
	Allergen, multiple	95117	
	Imm admn <8 yo 1st Inj	90465	
	Imm admn <8 yo each add inj	90466	
	Imm <8 yo oral or intranasal	90467	
	Imm admn <8 yo each add	90468	
	Imm admin, one vacc	90471	
	Imm admin, each add'l	90472	
	Imm admin, intranasal, one	90473	
	Imm admin, intranasal, each add'l	90474	
	Injection, joint, small	20600	
	Injection, joint, intermediate	20605	
	Injection, ther/proph/diag	90772	
	Injection, trigger pt 1-2 musc	20552	

Instructions:
Rx Refill

Physician signature
x Sarah Mendenhall

Today's charges:	
Today's payment:	
Balance due:	

Job 1 Router- Laura Leighton 6 of 20

Date of service: 10/26/09	Insurance: SIGNAL HMO				Superbill Number: 1496
Patient name: NAOMI YAMAGATA	Coinsurance:	Copay: 10.00			Physician Name: MURRAY
Account #: YAM001	Noncovered Waiver?	yes	no	n/a	

x	Office visit	New	x	Est
	Minimal (RN only)			99211
	Problem focused	99201		99212
	Exp problem focused	99202		99213
	Detailed	99203	✓	99214
	Comp	99204		99215
	Comprhen/Complex	99205		
	Well visit	**New**	**x**	**Est**
	< 1 y	99381		99391
	1-4 y	99382		99392
	5-11 y	99383		99393
	12-17 y	99384		99394
	18-39 y	99385		99395
	40-64 y	99386		99396
	65 y +	99387		99397
	Medicare preventive services			
	Pap			Q0091
	Pelvic & breast			G0101
	Prostate/PSA			G0103
	Tobacco couns/3-10 min			G0375
	Tobacco couns/>10 min			G0376
	Welcome to Medicare exam			G0344
	ECG w/Welcome to Medicare			G0366
	Hemoccult, guaiac			G0107
	Flu shot			G0008
	Pneumonia shot			G0009
	Consultation/preop clearance			
	Exp problem focused			99242
	Detailed			99243
	Comp/mod complex			99244
	Comp/high complex			99245
	Other services			
	After posted hours			99050
	Evening/weekend appointment			99051
	Home health certification			G0180
	Home health recertification			G0179
	Care Plan oversight			99374
	Care Plan Oversight >30 mins			99375
	Post-op follow-up			99024
	Prolonged/60min total			99354
	Prolonged/each add 30 mins			99355
	Special reports/forms			99080
	Disability/Workers comp			99455
	Smoking Cessation <10 mins			99406
	Smoking Cessation >10 mins			99407
	ETOH/SA screening <30 mins			99408
	Online E/M by MD			99444
	Phone E/M <10 mins			99441
	Phone E/M <20 mins			99442
	Phone E/M <30 mins			99443
	Anticoagulant Mgmt <90 days			99363
	Anticoagulant Mgmt >90 days			99364
	In office emergency serv			99058
	Other services			
	Supplies			
✓	Surgical Tray			99070

x	Office procedures		
	Cerumen removal		69210
	ECG, w/interpretation		93000
	ECG, rhythm strip		93040
✓	Endometrial biopsy		58100
	Fracture care, cast/splint		______
	Site: ______________		
	Nebulizer		94640
	Nebulizer demo		94664
	Spirometry		94010
	Spirometry, pre and post		94060
	Vasectomy		55250
	Skin procedures		**Units**
	Foreign body, skin, simple	10120	
	Foreign body, skin, complex	10121	
	I&D, abscess	10060	
	I&D, hematoma/seroma	10140	
	Laceration repair, simple	120__	
	Site: _______ Size: _____		
	Laceration repair, layered	120__	
	Site: _______ Size: _____		
	Laser Light Tx	96597	
	Lesion, biopsy, one	11100	
	Lesion, biopsy, each add'l	11101	
	Lesion, excision, benign	114__	
	Site: _______ Size: _____		
	Lesion, excision, malignant	116__	
	Site: _______ Size: _____		
	Lesion, paring/cutting, one	11055	
	Lesion, paring/cutting, 2-4	11056	
	Lesion, shave	113__	
	Site: _______ Size: _____		
	Nail removal, partial (+T mod)	11730	
	Nail rem, w/matrix (+T mod)	11750	
	Skin tag, 1-15	11200	
	Wart, flat, 1-14	17110	
	Destruction lesion, 1st	17000	
	Destruct lesion, each addl 2-14	17003	
	Medications		**Units**
	Ampicillin, up to 500mg	J0290	
	B-12, up to 1,000 mcg	J3420	
	Epinephrine, up to 1ml	J0170	
	Kenalog, 10mg	J3301	
	Lidocaine, 10mg	J2001	
	Normal saline, 1000cc	J7030	
	Phenergan, up to 50mg	J2550	
	Progesterone, 150mg	J1055	
	Rocephin, 250mg	J0696	
	Testosterone, 200mg	J1080	
	Tigan, up to 200 mg	J3250	
	Toradol, 15mg	J1885	
	Albuterol	J7609	
	Depo-Provera 50 mg	J1055	
	Depo-Medrol 40 mg	J1030	
	Diagnoses		**Code**
	1 DUB		
	2 Menorrhagia		
	3		
	4		

x	Laboratory		-90
✓	Venipuncture	36415	
	Blood glucose, monitoring device	82962	
	Blood glucose, visual dipstick	82948	
	CBC, w/ auto differential	85025	
✓	CBC, w/o auto differential	85027	
	Cholesterol	82465	
	Hemoccult, guaiac	82270	
	Hemoccult, immunoassay	82274	
	Hemoglobin A1C	85018	
	Lipid panel	80061	
	Liver panel	80076	
	KOH prep (skin, hair, nails)	87220	
	Metabolic panel, basic	80048	
	Metabolic panel, comprehensive	80053	
	Mononucleosis	86308	
	Pregnancy, blood	84703	
✓	Pregnancy, urine	81025	
	Renal panel	80069	
	Sedimentation rate	85651	
	Strep, rapid	86403	
	Strep culture	87081	
	Strep A	87880	
	TB	86580	
	UA, complete, non-automated	81000	
	UA, w/o micro, non-automated	81002	
	UA, w/ micro, non-automated	81003	
	Urine colony count	87086	
	Urine culture, presumptive	87088	
	Wet mount/KOH	87210	
	Vaccines		
	DT, <7 y		90702
	DTP		90701
	DtaP, <7 y		90700
	Flu, 6-35 months		90657
	Flu, 3 y +		90658
	Hep A, adult		90632
	Hep A, ped/adol, 2 dose		90633
	Hep B, adult		90746
	Hep B, ped/adol 3 dose		90744
	Hep B-Hib		90748
	Hib, 4 dose		90645
	HPV		90649
	IPV		90713
	MMR		90707
	Pneumonia, >2 y		90732
	Pneumonia conjugate, <5 y		90669
	Td, >7 y		90718
	Varicella		90716
	Tetanus toxoid adsorbed, IM		90703
	Immunizations & Injections		**Units**
	Allergen, one	95115	
	Allergen, multiple	95117	
	Imm admn <8 yo 1st Inj	90465	
	Imm admn <8 yo each add inj	90466	
	Imm <8 yo oral or intranasal	90467	
	Imm admn <8 yo each add	90468	
	Imm admin, one vacc	90471	
	Imm admin, each add'l	90472	
	Imm admin, intranasal, one	90473	
	Imm admin, intranasal, each add'l	90474	
	Injection, joint, small	20600	
	Injection, joint, intermediate	20605	
	Injection, ther/proph/diag	90772	
	Injection, trigger pt 1-2 musc	20552	

Next office visit: 10 days

(Recheck) • Preventative • PRN

Referral to:

Instructions:

Return F/U path

Physician signature

x [signature] MD

Today's charges:	
Today's payment:	10.00 cash
Balance due:	

Job 1 Router- Naomi Yamagata 7 of 20

Date of service: 10/27/09	Insurance: BC/BS		Superbill Number: 2453
Patient name: BRIAN MCDONOUGH	Coinsurance: 20%	Copay:	Physician Name: SCHWARTZ
Account #: MCD001	Noncovered Waiver?	yes / no / n/a	

x	Office visit	New	x	Est
	Minimal (RN only)			99211
	Problem focused	99201		99212
	Exp problem focused	99202		99213
	Detailed	99203		99214
✓	Comp	99204		99215
	Comprhen/Complex	99205		
	Well visit	**New**	x	**Est**
	< 1 y	99381		99391
	1-4 y	99382		99392
	5-11 y	99383		99393
	12-17 y	99384		99394
	18-39 y	99385		99395
	40-64 y	99386		99396
	65 y +	99387		99397
	Medicare preventive services			
	Pap			Q0091
	Pelvic & breast			G0101
	Prostate/PSA			G0103
	Tobacco couns/3-10 min			G0375
	Tobacco couns/>10 min			G0376
	Welcome to Medicare exam			G0344
	ECG w/Welcome to Medicare			G0366
	Hemoccult, guaiac			G0107
	Flu shot			G0008
	Pneumonia shot			G0009
	Consultation/preop clearance			
	Exp problem focused			99242
	Detailed			99243
	Comp/mod complex			99244
	Comp/high complex			99245
	Other services			
	After posted hours			99050
	Evening/weekend appointment			99051
	Home health certification			G0180
	Home health recertification			G0179
	Care Plan oversight			99374
	Care Plan Oversight >30 mins			99375
	Post-op follow-up			99024
	Prolonged/60min total			99354
	Prolonged/each add 30 mins			99355
	Special reports/forms			99080
	Disability/Workers comp			99455
	Smoking Cessation <10 mins			99406
	Smoking Cessation >10 mins			99407
	ETOH/SA screening <30 mins			99408
	Online E/M by MD			99444
	Phone E/M <10 mins			99441
	Phone E/M <20 mins			99442
	Phone E/M <30 mins			99443
	Anticoagulant Mgmt <90 days			99363
	Anticoagulant Mgmt >90 days			99364
	In office emergency serv			99058
	Other services			
	Supplies			
	Surgical Tray			99070
	Instructions:			

x	Office procedures		
	Cerumen removal		69210
	ECG, w/interpretation		93000
	ECG, rhythm strip		93040
	Endometrial biopsy		58100
	Fracture care, cast/splint		____
	Site: ____________		
	Nebulizer		94640
	Nebulizer demo		94664
	Spirometry		94010
	Spirometry, pre and post		94060
	Vasectomy		55250
	Skin procedures		**Units**
	Foreign body, skin, simple	10120	
	Foreign body, skin, complex	10121	
	I&D, abscess	10060	
	I&D, hematoma/seroma	10140	
	Laceration repair, simple	120__	
	Site: ________ Size: _____		
	Laceration repair, layered	120__	
	Site: ________ Size: _____		
	Laser Light Tx	96597	
	Lesion, biopsy, one	11100	
	Lesion, biopsy, each add'l	11101	
	Lesion, excision, benign	114__	
	Site: ________ Size: _____		
	Lesion, excision, malignant	116__	
	Site: ________ Size: _____		
	Lesion, paring/cutting, one	11055	
	Lesion, paring/cutting, 2-4	11056	
	Lesion, shave	113__	
	Site: ________ Size: _____		
	Nail removal, partial (+T mod)	11730	
	Nail rem, w/matrix (+T mod)	11750	
	Skin tag, 1-15	11200	
	Wart, flat, 1-14	17110	
	Destruction lesion, 1st	17000	
	Destruct lesion, each addl 2-14	17003	
	Medications		**Units**
	Ampicillin, up to 500mg	J0290	
	B-12, up to 1,000 mcg	J3420	
	Epinephrine, up to 1ml	J0170	
	Kenalog, 10mg	J3301	
	Lidocaine, 10mg	J2001	
	Normal saline, 1000cc	J7030	
	Phenergan, up to 50mg	J2550	
	Progesterone, 150mg	J1055	
	Rocephin, 250mg	J0696	
	Testosterone, 200mg	J1080	
	Tigan, up to 200 mg	J3250	
	Toradol, 15mg	J1885	
	Albuterol	J7609	
	Depo-Provera 50 mg	J1055	
	Depo-Medrol 40 mg	J1030	

Diagnoses		Code
1	Routine Physical	
2	Vaccination Update	
3		
4		

Next office visit:
Recheck • Preventative • PRN (circled)
Referral to:

Physician signature
x [signature] MD

x	Laboratory		-90
	Venipuncture	36415	
	Blood glucose, monitoring device	82962	
	Blood glucose, visual dipstick	82948	
	CBC, w/ auto differential	85025	
	CBC, w/o auto differential	85027	
	Cholesterol	82465	
	Hemoccult, guaiac	82270	
	Hemoccult, immunoassay	82274	
	Hemoglobin A1C	85018	
	Lipid panel	80061	
	Liver panel	80076	
	KOH prep (skin, hair, nails)	87220	
	Metabolic panel, basic	80048	
	Metabolic panel, comprehensive	80053	
	Mononucleosis	86308	
	Pregnancy, blood	84703	
	Pregnancy, urine	81025	
	Renal panel	80069	
	Sedimentation rate	85651	
	Strep, rapid	86403	
	Strep culture	87081	
	Strep A	87880	
	TB	86580	
	UA, complete, non-automated	81000	
	UA, w/o micro, non-automated	81002	
	UA, w/ micro, non-automated	81003	
	Urine colony count	87086	
	Urine culture, presumptive	87088	
	Wet mount/KOH	87210	
	Vaccines		
	DT, <7 y		90702
	DTP		90701
	DtaP, <7 y		90700
	Flu, 6-35 months		90657
	Flu, 3 y +		90658
	Hep A, adult		90632
	Hep A, ped/adol, 2 dose		90633
✓	Hep B, adult		90746
	Hep B, ped/adol 3 dose		90744
	Hep B-Hib		90748
	Hib, 4 dose		90645
	HPV		90649
	IPV		90713
	MMR		90707
	Pneumonia, >2 y		90732
	Pneumonia conjugate, <5 y		90669
	Td, >7 y		90718
	Varicella		90716
✓	Tetanus toxoid adsorbed, IM		90703
	Immunizations & Injections		**Units**
	Allergen, one	95115	
	Allergen, multiple	95117	
	Imm admn <8 yo 1st Inj	90465	
	Imm admn <8 yo each add inj	90466	
	Imm <8 yo oral or intranasal	90467	
	Imm admn <8 yo each add	90468	
✓	Imm admin, one vacc	90471	
✓	Imm admin, each add'l	90472	
	Imm admin, intranasal, one	90473	
	Imm admin, intranasal, each add'l	90474	
	Injection, joint, small	20600	
	Injection, joint, intermediate	20605	
	Injection, ther/proph/diag	90772	
	Injection, trigger pt 1-2 musc	20552	

Today's charges:		
Today's payment:		
Balance due:		

Job 1 Router- Brian McDonough 8 of 20

Date of service: 10/27/09	Insurance: FLEXIHEALTH				Superbill Number: 2459
Patient name: RICHARD MANALY	Coinsurance:	Copay: 20.00			Physician Name: LYNN
Account #: MAN001	Noncovered Waiver?	yes	no	n/a	

x	Office visit	New	x	Est
	Minimal (RN only)			99211
	Problem focused	99201		99212
	Exp problem focused	99202		99213
	Detailed	99203		99214
	Comp	99204		99215
	Comprhen/Complex	99205		
	Well visit	**New**	**x**	**Est**
	< 1 y	99381		99391
	1-4 y	99382		99392
	5-11 y	99383		99393
	12-17 y	99384		99394
	18-39 y	99385		99395
	40-64 y	99386		99396
	65 y +	99387		99397
	Medicare preventive services			
	Pap			Q0091
	Pelvic & breast			G0101
	Prostate/PSA			G0103
	Tobacco couns/3-10 min			G0375
	Tobacco couns/>10 min			G0376
	Welcome to Medicare exam			G0344
	ECG w/Welcome to Medicare			G0366
	Hemoccult, guaiac			G0107
	Flu shot			G0008
	Pneumonia shot			G0009
	Consultation/preop clearance			
	Exp problem focused			99242
	Detailed			99243
	Comp/mod complex			99244
	Comp/high complex			99245
	Other services			
	After posted hours			99050
	Evening/weekend appointment			99051
	Home health certification			G0180
	Home health recertification			G0179
	Care Plan oversight			99374
	Care Plan Oversight >30 mins			99375
	Post-op follow-up			99024
	Prolonged/60min total			99354
	Prolonged/each add 30 mins			99355
	Special reports/forms			99080
	Disability/Workers comp			99455
	Smoking Cessation <10 mins			99406
	Smoking Cessation >10 mins			99407
	ETOH/SA screening <30 mins			99408
	Online E/M by MD			99444
	Phone E/M <10 mins			99441
	Phone E/M <20 mins			99442
	Phone E/M <30 mins			99443
	Anticoagulant Mgmt <90 days			99363
✓	Anticoagulant Mgmt >90 days			99364
	In office emergency serv			99058
	Other services			
✓	Therapeutic Drug Assay-Carnidine			
	Supplies			
	Surgical Tray			99070
	Instructions:			

x	Office procedures		
	Cerumen removal		69210
	ECG, w/interpretation		93000
	ECG, rhythm strip		93040
	Endometrial biopsy		58100
	Fracture care, cast/splint Site: __________		____
	Nebulizer		94640
	Nebulizer demo		94664
	Spirometry		94010
	Spirometry, pre and post		94060
	Vasectomy		55250
	Skin procedures		**Units**
	Foreign body, skin, simple	10120	
	Foreign body, skin, complex	10121	
	I&D, abscess	10060	
	I&D, hematoma/seroma	10140	
	Laceration repair, simple Site: _______ Size: _____	120__	
	Laceration repair, layered Site: _______ Size: _____	120__	
	Laser Light Tx	96597	
	Lesion, biopsy, one	11100	
	Lesion, biopsy, each add'l	11101	
	Lesion, excision, benign Site: _______ Size: _____	114__	
	Lesion, excision, malignant Site: _______ Size: _____	116__	
	Lesion, paring/cutting, one	11055	
	Lesion, paring/cutting, 2-4	11056	
	Lesion, shave Site: _______ Size: _____	113__	
	Nail removal, partial (+T mod)	11730	
	Nail rem, w/matrix (+T mod)	11750	
	Skin tag, 1-15	11200	
	Wart, flat, 1-14	17110	
	Destruction lesion, 1st	17000	
	Destruct lesion, each addl 2-14	17003	
	Medications		**Units**
	Ampicillin, up to 500mg	J0290	
	B-12, up to 1,000 mcg	J3420	
	Epinephrine, up to 1ml	J0170	
	Kenalog, 10mg	J3301	
	Lidocaine, 10mg	J2001	
	Normal saline, 1000cc	J7030	
	Phenergan, up to 50mg	J2550	
	Progesterone, 150mg	J1055	
	Rocephin, 250mg	J0696	
	Testosterone, 200mg	J1080	
	Tigan, up to 200 mg	J3250	
	Toradol, 15mg	J1885	
	Albuterol	J7609	
	Depo-Provera 50 mg	J1055	
	Depo-Medrol 40 mg	J1030	

Diagnoses	Code
1 Arrhythmia	
2 HTN	
3 Coagulation mod use	
4	

Next office visit: 1 MN

Recheck • Preventative • PRN

Referral to:

x	Laboratory		-90
✓	Venipuncture	36415	
	Blood glucose, monitoring device	82962	
	Blood glucose, visual dipstick	82948	
	CBC, w/ auto differential	85025	
	CBC, w/o auto differential	85027	
	Cholesterol	82465	
	Hemoccult, guaiac	82270	
	Hemoccult, immunoassay	82274	
	Hemoglobin A1C	85018	
	Lipid panel	80061	
	Liver panel	80076	
	KOH prep (skin, hair, nails)	87220	
	Metabolic panel, basic	80048	
	Metabolic panel, comprehensive	80053	
	Mononucleosis	86308	
	Pregnancy, blood	84703	
	Pregnancy, urine	81025	
	Renal panel	80069	
	Sedimentation rate	85651	
	Strep, rapid	86403	
	Strep culture	87081	
	Strep A	87880	
	TB	86580	
	UA, complete, non-automated	81000	
	UA, w/o micro, non-automated	81002	
	UA, w/ micro, non-automated	81003	
	Urine colony count	87086	
	Urine culture, presumptive	87088	
	Wet mount/KOH	87210	

Vaccines	
DT, <7 y	90702
DTP	90701
DtaP, <7 y	90700
Flu, 6-35 months	90657
Flu, 3 y +	90658
Hep A, adult	90632
Hep A, ped/adol, 2 dose	90633
Hep B, adult	90746
Hep B, ped/adol 3 dose	90744
Hep B-Hib	90748
Hib, 4 dose	90645
HPV	90649
IPV	90713
MMR	90707
Pneumonia, >2 y	90732
Pneumonia conjugate, <5 y	90669
Td, >7 y	90718
Varicella	90716
Tetanus toxoid adsorbed, IM	90703

Immunizations & Injections		Units
Allergen, one	95115	
Allergen, multiple	95117	
Imm admn <8 yo 1st Inj	90465	
Imm admn <8 yo each add inj	90466	
Imm <8 yo oral or intranasal	90467	
Imm admn <8 yo each add	90468	
Imm admin, one vacc	90471	
Imm admin, each add'l	90472	
Imm admin, intranasal, one	90473	
Imm admin, intranasal, each add'l	90474	
Injection, joint, small	20600	
Injection, joint, intermediate	20605	
Injection, ther/proph/diag	90772	
Injection, trigger pt 1-2 musc	20552	

Physician signature

X Albert Lynn MD

Today's charges:		
Today's payment:		
Balance due:		

Job 1 Router- Richard Manaly 9 of 20

Date of service: 10/27/09	PPO				Router Number: 2484
Patient name: ELANE YBARRA	Coinsurance:	Copay:			Physician Name: SCHWARTZ
Account #: YBA001	Noncovered Waiver?	yes	no	n/a	

x	Office visit	New	x	Est
N/A	Minimal (RN only)	N/A		99211
	Problem focused	99201		99212
	Exp problem focused	99202		99213
	Detailed	99203		99214
	Comp	99204		99215
	Comprhen/Complex	99205		
x	**Well visit**	**New**	**x**	**Est**
	< 1 y	99381		99391
	1-4 y	99382		99392
	5-11 y	99383		99393
	12-17 y	99384		99394
	18-39 y	99385	✓	99395
	40-64 y	99386		99396
	65 y +	99387		99397
	Medicare preventive services			
	Pap			Q0091
	Pelvic & breast			G0101
	Prostate/PSA			G0103
	Tobacco couns/3-10 min			G0375
	Tobacco couns/>10 min			G0376
	Welcome to Medicare exam			G0344
	ECG w/Welcome to Medicare			G0366
	Hemoccult, guaiac			G0107
	Flu shot			G0008
	Pneumonia shot			G0009
	Consultation/preop clearance			
	Exp problem focused			99242
	Detailed			99243
	Comp/mod complex			99244
	Comp/high complex			99245
	Other services			
	After posted hours			99050
	Evening/weekend appointment			99051
	Home health certification			G0180
	Home health recertification			G0179
	Care Plan oversight			99374
	Care Plan Oversight >30 mins			99375
	Post-op follow-up			99024
	Prolonged/60min total			99354
	Prolonged/each add 30 mins			99355
	Special reports/forms			99080
	Disability/Workers comp			99455
	Smoking Cessation <10 mins			99406
✓	Smoking Cessation >10 mins			99407
	ETOH/SA screening <30 mins			99408
	Online E/M by MD			99444
	Phone E/M <10 mins			99441
	Phone E/M <20 mins			99442
	Phone E/M <30 mins			99443
	Anticoagulant Mgmt <90 days			99363
	Anticoagulant Mgmt >90 days			99364
	In office emergency serv			99058
	Other services			
	Supplies			
	Surgical Tray			99070

x	Office procedures		Code
	Cerumen removal		69210
✓	ECG, w/interpretation		93000
	ECG, rhythm strip		93040
	Endometrial biopsy		58100
	Fracture care, cast/splint Site: ______________		
	Nebulizer		94640
	Nebulizer demo		94664
	Spirometry		94010
	Spirometry, pre and post		94060
	Vasectomy		55250
	Skin procedures		**Units**
	Foreign body, skin, simple	10120	
	Foreign body, skin, complex	10121	
	I&D, abscess	10060	
	I&D, hematoma/seroma	10140	
	Laceration repair, simple Site: _______ Size: _____	120__	
	Laceration repair, layered Site: _______ Size: _____	120__	
	Laser Light Tx	96597	
	Lesion, biopsy, one	11100	
	Lesion, biopsy, each add'l	11101	
	Lesion, excision, benign Site: _______ Size: _____	114__	
	Lesion, excision, malignant Site: _______ Size: _____	116__	
	Lesion, paring/cutting, one	11055	
	Lesion, paring/cutting, 2-4	11056	
	Lesion, shave Site: _______ Size: _____	113__	
	Nail removal, partial (+T mod)	11730	
	Nail rem, w/matrix (+T mod)	11750	
	Skin tag, 1-15	11200	
	Wart, flat, 1-14	17110	
	Destruction lesion, 1st	17000	
	Destruct lesion, each addl 2-14	17003	
	Medications		**Units**
	Ampicillin, up to 500mg	J0290	
	B-12, up to 1,000 mcg	J3420	
	Epinephrine, up to 1ml	J0170	
	Kenalog, 10mg	J3301	
	Lidocaine, 10mg	J2001	
	Normal saline, 1000cc	J7030	
	Phenergan, up to 50mg	J2550	
	Progesterone, 150mg	J1055	
	Rocephin, 250mg	J0696	
	Testosterone, 200mg	J1080	
	Tigan, up to 200 mg	J3250	
	Toradol, 15mg	J1885	
	Albuterol	J7609	
	Depo-Provera 50 mg	J1055	
	Depo-Medrol 40 mg	J1030	

Diagnoses	Code
1 Annual Exam	
2 Hx Cigarette Smoking	
3	
4	

Next office visit:
Recheck • Preventative • PRN (Preventative circled)
Referral to:

x	Laboratory		-90
✓	Venipuncture	36415	
	Blood glucose, monitoring device	82962	
✓	Blood glucose, visual dipstick	82948	
✓	CBC, w/ auto differential	85025	
	CBC, w/o auto differential	85027	
✓	Cholesterol	82465	
	Hemoccult, guaiac	82270	
	Hemoccult, immunoassay	82274	
	Hemoglobin A1C	85018	
✓	Lipid panel	80061	
	Liver panel	80076	
	KOH prep (skin, hair, nails)	87220	
✓	Metabolic panel, basic	80048	
	Metabolic panel, comprehensive	80053	
	Mononucleosis	86308	
	Pregnancy, blood	84703	
	Pregnancy, urine	81025	
	Renal panel	80069	
	Sedimentation rate	85651	
	Strep, rapid	86403	
	Strep culture	87081	
	Strep A	87880	
	TB	86580	
	UA, complete, non-automated	81000	
	UA, w/o micro, non-automated	81002	
	UA, w/ micro, non-automated	81003	
	Urine colony count	87086	
	Urine culture, presumptive	87088	
	Wet mount/KOH	87210	
	Vaccines		
	DT, <7 y		90702
	DTP		90701
	DtaP, <7 y		90700
	Flu, 6-35 months		90657
	Flu, 3 y +		90658
	Hep A, adult		90632
	Hep A, ped/adol, 2 dose		90633
	Hep B, adult		90746
	Hep B, ped/adol 3 dose		90744
	Hep B-Hib		90748
	Hib, 4 dose		90645
	HPV		90649
	IPV		90713
	MMR		90707
	Pneumonia, >2 y		90732
	Pneumonia conjugate, <5 y		90669
	Td, >7 y		90718
	Varicella		90716
✓	Tetanus toxoid adsorbed, IM		90703
	Immunizations & Injections		**Units**
	Allergen, one	95115	
	Allergen, multiple	95117	
	Imm admn <8 yo 1st Inj	90465	
	Imm admn <8 yo each add inj	90466	
	Imm <8 yo oral or intranasal	90467	
	Imm admn <8 yo each add	90468	
	Imm admin, one vacc	90471	
	Imm admin, each add'l	90472	
	Imm admin, intranasal, one	90473	
	Imm admin, intranasal, each add'l	90474	
	Injection, joint, small	20600	
	Injection, joint, intermediate	20605	
	Injection, ther/proph/diag	90772	
	Injection, trigger pt 1-2 musc	20552	

Instructions:
Recommend getting mammogram

Physician signature
X Schwartz MD

Today's charges:	
Today's payment:	
Balance due:	

Job 1 Router- Elaine Ybarra 10 of 20

Date of service: 10/27/09	Insurance: MEDICARE		Superbill Number: 2460
Patient name: WILMA ~~STEAM~~ Stearn	Coinsurance: 20%	Copay:	Physician Name: MURRAY
Account #: STE001	Noncovered Waiver?	yes / no / n/a	

X	Office visit	New	X	Est
	Minimal (RN only)			99211
	Problem focused	99201		99212
	Exp problem focused	99202		99213
	Detailed	99203		99214
	Comp	99204		99215
	Comprhen/Complex	99205		
	Well visit	**New**	X	**Est**
	< 1 y	99381		99391
	1-4 y	99382		99392
	5-11 y	99383		99393
	12-17 y	99384		99394
	18-39 y	99385		99395
	40-64 y	99386		99396
	65 y +	99387		99397

	Medicare preventive services	
	Pap	Q0091
	Pelvic & breast	G0101
	Prostate/PSA	G0103
	Tobacco couns/3-10 min	G0375
	Tobacco couns/>10 min	G0376
	Welcome to Medicare exam	G0344
	ECG w/Welcome to Medicare	G0366
	Hemoccult, guaiac	G0107
	Flu shot	G0008
	Pneumonia shot	G0009
	Consultation/preop clearance	
	Exp problem focused	99242
	Detailed	99243
	Comp/mod complex	99244
	Comp/high complex	99245
	Other services	
	After posted hours	99050
	Evening/weekend appointment	99051
	Home health certification	G0180
	Home health recertification	G0179
	Care Plan oversight	99374
	Care Plan Oversight >30 mins	99375
	Post-op follow-up	99024
	Prolonged/60min total	99354
	Prolonged/each add 30 mins	99355
	Special reports/forms	99080
	Disability/Workers comp	99455
	Smoking Cessation <10 mins	99406
	Smoking Cessation >10 mins	99407
	ETOH/SA screening <30 mins	99408
	Online E/M by MD	99444
	Phone E/M <10 mins	99441
	Phone E/M <20 mins	99442
	Phone E/M <30 mins	99443
	Anticoagulant Mgmt <90 days	99363
	Anticoagulant Mgmt >90 days	99364
	In office emergency serv	99058
	Other services	
	Supplies	
	Surgical Tray	99070
	aminolevulinic acid (Levulan) HCL 20%	
	Instructions:	

X	Office procedures		
	Cerumen removal		69210
	ECG, w/interpretation		93000
	ECG, rhythm strip		93040
	Endometrial biopsy		58100
	Fracture care, cast/splint		____
	Site: ______________		
	Nebulizer		94640
	Nebulizer demo		94664
	Spirometry		94010
	Spirometry, pre and post		94060
	Vasectomy		55250
	Skin procedures		**Units**
	Foreign body, skin, simple	10120	
	Foreign body, skin, complex	10121	
	I&D, abscess	10060	
	I&D, hematoma/seroma	10140	
	Laceration repair, simple	120__	
	Site: ______ Size: _____		
	Laceration repair, layered	120__	
	Site: ______ Size: _____		
✓	Laser Light Tx	96597	
	Lesion, biopsy, one	11100	
	Lesion, biopsy, each add'l	11101	
	Lesion, excision, benign	114__	
	Site: ______ Size: _____		
	Lesion, excision, malignant	116__	
	Site: ______ Size: _____		
	Lesion, paring/cutting, one	11055	
	Lesion, paring/cutting, 2-4	11056	
	Lesion, shave	113__	
	Site: ______ Size: _____		
	Nail removal, partial (+T mod)	11730	
	Nail rem, w/matrix (+T mod)	11750	
	Skin tag, 1-15	11200	
	Wart, flat, 1-14	17110	
	Destruction lesion, 1st	17000	
	Destruct lesion, each addl 2-14	17003	
	Medications		**Units**
	Ampicillin, up to 500mg	J0290	
	B-12, up to 1,000 mcg	J3420	
	Epinephrine, up to 1ml	J0170	
	Kenalog, 10mg	J3301	
	Lidocaine, 10mg	J2001	
	Normal saline, 1000cc	J7030	
	Phenergan, up to 50mg	J2550	
	Progesterone, 150mg	J1055	
	Rocephin, 250mg	J0696	
	Testosterone, 200mg	J1080	
	Tigan, up to 200 mg	J3250	
	Toradol, 15mg	J1885	
	Albuterol	J7609	
	Depo-Provera 50 mg	J1055	
	Depo-Medrol 40 mg	J1030	

Diagnoses	Code
1 actinic keratosis	
2 HTN	
3 DM	
4	

Next office visit: 1 mo

Recheck • Preventative • PRN

Referral to:

Physician signature

[signature]

X	Laboratory		-90
	Venipuncture	36415	
	Blood glucose, monitoring device	82962	
	Blood glucose, visual dipstick	82948	
	CBC, w/ auto differential	85025	
	CBC, w/o auto differential	85027	
	Cholesterol	82465	
	Hemoccult, guaiac	82270	
	Hemoccult, immunoassay	82274	
	Hemoglobin A1C	85018	
	Lipid panel	80061	
	Liver panel	80076	
	KOH prep (skin, hair, nails)	87220	
	Metabolic panel, basic	80048	
	Metabolic panel, comprehensive	80053	
	Mononucleosis	86308	
	Pregnancy, blood	84703	
	Pregnancy, urine	81025	
	Renal panel	80069	
	Sedimentation rate	85651	
	Strep, rapid	86403	
	Strep culture	87081	
	Strep A	87880	
	TB	86580	
	UA, complete, non-automated	81000	
	UA, w/o micro, non-automated	81002	
	UA, w/ micro, non-automated	81003	
	Urine colony count	87086	
	Urine culture, presumptive	87088	
	Wet mount/KOH	87210	

	Vaccines	
	DT, <7 y	90702
	DTP	90701
	DtaP, <7 y	90700
	Flu, 6-35 months	90657
	Flu, 3 y +	90658
	Hep A, adult	90632
	Hep A, ped/adol, 2 dose	90633
	Hep B, adult	90746
	Hep B, ped/adol 3 dose	90744
	Hep B-Hib	90748
	Hib, 4 dose	90645
	HPV	90649
	IPV	90713
	MMR	90707
	Pneumonia, >2 y	90732
	Pneumonia conjugate, <5 y	90669
	Td, >7 y	90718
	Varicella	90716
	Tetanus toxoid adsorbed, IM	90703

	Immunizations & Injections		Units
	Allergen, one	95115	
	Allergen, multiple	95117	
	Imm admn <8 yo 1st Inj	90465	
	Imm admn <8 yo each add inj	90466	
	Imm <8 yo oral or intranasal	90467	
	Imm admn <8 yo each add	90468	
	Imm admin, one vacc	90471	
	Imm admin, each add'l	90472	
	Imm admin, intranasal, one	90473	
	Imm admin, intranasal, each add'l	90474	
	Injection, joint, small	20600	
	Injection, joint, intermediate	20605	
	Injection, ther/proph/diag	90772	
	Injection, trigger pt 1-2 musc	20552	

Today's charges:		
Today's payment:		
Balance due:		

Job 1 Router- Wilma Stearn 11 of 20

Date of service: 10/27/09	Insurance: MEDICARE				Superbill Number: 2461
Patient name: ISABEL DURAND	Coinsurance: 20%	Copay:			Physician Name: KEMPER
Account #: DUR001	Noncovered Waiver?	yes	no	n/a	

X	Office visit	New	X	Est
	Minimal (RN only)			99211
	Problem focused	99201		99212
	Exp problem focused	99202		99213
	Detailed	99203		99214
	Comp	99204		99215
	Comprhen/Complex	99205		
	Well visit	**New**	X	**Est**
	< 1 y	99381		99391
	1-4 y	99382		99392
	5-11 y	99383		99393
	12-17 y	99384		99394
	18-39 y	99385		99395
	40-64 y	99386		99396
	65 y +	99387		99397
	Medicare preventive services			
1 ✓	Pap			Q0091
1 ✓	Pelvic & breast			G0101
	Prostate/PSA			G0103
	Tobacco couns/3-10 min			G0375
	Tobacco couns/>10 min			G0376
	Welcome to Medicare exam			G0344
	ECG w/Welcome to Medicare			G0366
	Hemoccult, guaiac			G0107
	Flu shot			G0008
	Pneumonia shot			G0009
	Consultation/preop clearance			
	Exp problem focused			99242
	Detailed			99243
	Comp/mod complex			99244
	Comp/high complex			99245
	Other services			
	After posted hours			99050
	Evening/weekend appointment			99051
	Home health certification			G0180
	Home health recertification			G0179
	Care Plan oversight			99374
	Care Plan Oversight >30 mins			99375
	Post-op follow-up			99024
	Prolonged/60min total			99354
	Prolonged/each add 30 mins			99355
	Special reports/forms			99080
	Disability/Workers comp			99455
	Smoking Cessation <10 mins			99406
	Smoking Cessation >10 mins			99407
	ETOH/SA screening <30 mins			99408
	Online E/M by MD			99444
	Phone E/M <10 mins			99441
	Phone E/M <20 mins			99442
	Phone E/M <30 mins			99443
	Anticoagulant Mgmt <90 days			99363
	Anticoagulant Mgmt >90 days			99364
	In office emergency serv			99058
	Other services			
	Supplies			
	Surgical Tray			99070
	Instructions:			

Call w/ results if abnormal

X	Office procedures		
	Cerumen removal		69210
	ECG, w/interpretation		93000
	ECG, rhythm strip		93040
	Endometrial biopsy		58100
	Fracture care, cast/splint		____
	Site: ______________		
	Nebulizer		94640
	Nebulizer demo		94664
	Spirometry		94010
	Spirometry, pre and post		94060
	Vasectomy		55250
	Skin procedures		**Units**
	Foreign body, skin, simple	10120	
	Foreign body, skin, complex	10121	
	I&D, abscess	10060	
	I&D, hematoma/seroma	10140	
	Laceration repair, simple	120__	
	Site: _______ Size: _____		
	Laceration repair, layered	120__	
	Site: _______ Size: _____		
	Laser Light Tx	96597	
	Lesion, biopsy, one	11100	
	Lesion, biopsy, each add'l	11101	
	Lesion, excision, benign	114__	
	Site: _______ Size: _____		
	Lesion, excision, malignant	116__	
	Site: _______ Size: _____		
	Lesion, paring/cutting, one	11055	
	Lesion, paring/cutting, 2-4	11056	
	Lesion, shave	113__	
	Site: _______ Size: _____		
	Nail removal, partial (+T mod)	11730	
	Nail rem, w/matrix (+T mod)	11750	
	Skin tag, 1-15	11200	
	Wart, flat, 1-14	17110	
	Destruction lesion, 1st	17000	
	Destruct lesion, each addl 2-14	17003	
	Medications		**Units**
	Ampicillin, up to 500mg	J0290	
	B-12, up to 1,000 mcg	J3420	
	Epinephrine, up to 1ml	J0170	
	Kenalog, 10mg	J3301	
	Lidocaine, 10mg	J2001	
	Normal saline, 1000cc	J7030	
	Phenergan, up to 50mg	J2550	
	Progesterone, 150mg	J1055	
	Rocephin, 250mg	J0696	
	Testosterone, 200mg	J1080	
	Tigan, up to 200 mg	J3250	
	Toradol, 15mg	J1885	
	Albuterol	J7609	
	Depo-Provera 50 mg	J1055	
	Depo-Medrol 40 mg	J1030	

Diagnoses	Code
1 Annual Pelvic Exam	
2 Vaginal prolapse	
3	
4	

Next office visit:
Recheck • (Preventative) • PRN
Referral to:

Physician signature

X Sally Kemper MD

X	Laboratory		-90
	Venipuncture	36415	
	Blood glucose, monitoring device	82962	
	Blood glucose, visual dipstick	82948	
	CBC, w/ auto differential	85025	
	CBC, w/o auto differential	85027	
	Cholesterol	82465	
	Hemoccult, guaiac	82270	
	Hemoccult, immunoassay	82274	
	Hemoglobin A1C	85018	
	Lipid panel	80061	
	Liver panel	80076	
	KOH prep (skin, hair, nails)	87220	
	Metabolic panel, basic	80048	
	Metabolic panel, comprehensive	80053	
	Mononucleosis	86308	
	Pregnancy, blood	84703	
	Pregnancy, urine	81025	
	Renal panel	80069	
	Sedimentation rate	85651	
	Strep, rapid	86403	
	Strep culture	87081	
	Strep A	87880	
	TB	86580	
	UA, complete, non-automated	81000	
	UA, w/o micro, non-automated	81002	
	UA, w/ micro, non-automated	81003	
	Urine colony count	87086	
	Urine culture, presumptive	87088	
	Wet mount/KOH	87210	
	Vaccines		
	DT, <7 y		90702
	DTP		90701
	DtaP, <7 y		90700
	Flu, 6-35 months		90657
	Flu, 3 y +		90658
	Hep A, adult		90632
	Hep A, ped/adol, 2 dose		90633
	Hep B, adult		90746
	Hep B, ped/adol 3 dose		90744
	Hep B-Hib		90748
	Hib, 4 dose		90645
	HPV		90649
	IPV		90713
	MMR		90707
	Pneumonia, >2 y		90732
	Pneumonia conjugate, <5 y		90669
	Td, >7 y		90718
	Varicella		90716
	Tetanus toxoid adsorbed, IM		90703
	Immunizations & Injections		**Units**
	Allergen, one	95115	
	Allergen, multiple	95117	
	Imm admn <8 yo 1st Inj	90465	
	Imm admn <8 yo each add inj	90466	
	Imm <8 yo oral or intranasal	90467	
	Imm admn <8 yo each add	90468	
	Imm admin, one vacc	90471	
	Imm admin, each add'l	90472	
	Imm admin, intranasal, one	90473	
	Imm admin, intranasal, each add'l	90474	
	Injection, joint, small	20600	
	Injection, joint, intermediate	20605	
	Injection, ther/proph/diag	90772	
	Injection, trigger pt 1-2 musc	20552	

Today's charges:		
Today's payment:		
Balance due:		

Job 1 Router- Isabel Durand 12 of 20

Date of service: 10/27/09	Insurance: GREATWEST		Superbill Number: 2462
Patient name: JULIUS WASHINGTON	Coinsurance: 20%	Copay:	Physician Name: MENDENHALL
Account #: WAS001	Noncovered Waiver?	yes / no / n/a	

x	Office visit	New	x	Est
	Minimal (RN only)			99211
	Problem focused	99201		99212
	Exp problem focused	99202		99213
	Detailed	99203		99214
✓	Comp	99204		99215
	Comprhen/Complex	99205		

x	Well visit	New	x	Est
	< 1 y	99381		99391
	1-4 y	99382		99392
	5-11 y	99383		99393
	12-17 y	99384		99394
	18-39 y	99385		99395
	40-64 y	99386		99396
	65 y +	99387		99397

x	Medicare preventive services	
	Pap	Q0091
	Pelvic & breast	G0101
	Prostate/PSA	G0103
	Tobacco couns/3-10 min	G0375
	Tobacco couns/>10 min	G0376
	Welcome to Medicare exam	G0344
	ECG w/Welcome to Medicare	G0366
	Hemoccult, guaiac	G0107
	Flu shot	G0008
	Pneumonia shot	G0009

x	Consultation/preop clearance	
	Exp problem focused	99242
	Detailed	99243
	Comp/mod complex	99244
	Comp/high complex	99245

x	Other services	
	After posted hours	99050
	Evening/weekend appointment	99051
	Home health certification	G0180
	Home health recertification	G0179
	Care Plan oversight	99374
	Care Plan Oversight >30 mins	99375
	Post-op follow-up	99024
	Prolonged/60min total	99354
	Prolonged/each add 30 mins	99355
	Special reports/forms	99080
	Disability/Workers comp	99455
	Smoking Cessation <10 mins	99406
	Smoking Cessation >10 mins	99407
	ETOH/SA screening <30 mins	99408
	Online E/M by MD	99444
	Phone E/M <10 mins	99441
	Phone E/M <20 mins	99442
	Phone E/M <30 mins	99443
	Anticoagulant Mgmt <90 days	99363
	Anticoagulant Mgmt >90 days	99364
	In office emergency serv	99058

x	Other services	
✓	Chest x-ray front + lateral	

x	Supplies	
	Surgical Tray	99070

Instructions:

Rx Levaquin po bid q day 10 days

x	Office procedures	
	Cerumen removal	69210
	ECG, w/interpretation	93000
	ECG, rhythm strip	93040
	Endometrial biopsy	58100
	Fracture care, cast/splint Site: ______	____
✓	Nebulizer	94640
	Nebulizer demo	94664
	Spirometry	94010
	Spirometry, pre and post	94060
	Vasectomy	55250

x	Skin procedures		Units
	Foreign body, skin, simple	10120	
	Foreign body, skin, complex	10121	
	I&D, abscess	10060	
	I&D, hematoma/seroma	10140	
	Laceration repair, simple Site: ______ Size: ____	120__	
	Laceration repair, layered Site: ______ Size: ____	120__	
	Laser Light Tx	96597	
	Lesion, biopsy, one	11100	
	Lesion, biopsy, each add'l	11101	
	Lesion, excision, benign Site: ______ Size: ____	114__	
	Lesion, excision, malignant Site: ______ Size: ____	116__	
	Lesion, paring/cutting, one	11055	
	Lesion, paring/cutting, 2-4	11056	
	Lesion, shave Site: ______ Size: ____	113__	
	Nail removal, partial (+T mod)	11730	
	Nail rem, w/matrix (+T mod)	11750	
	Skin tag, 1-15	11200	
	Wart, flat, 1-14	17110	
	Destruction lesion, 1st	17000	
	Destruct lesion, each addl 2-14	17003	

x	Medications		Units
	Ampicillin, up to 500mg	J0290	
	B-12, up to 1,000 mcg	J3420	
	Epinephrine, up to 1ml	J0170	
	Kenalog, 10mg	J3301	
	Lidocaine, 10mg	J2001	
	Normal saline, 1000cc	J7030	
	Phenergan, up to 50mg	J2550	
	Progesterone, 150mg	J1055	
	Rocephin, 250mg	J0696	
	Testosterone, 200mg	J1080	
	Tigan, up to 200 mg	J3250	
	Toradol, 15mg	J1885	
✓	Albuterol	J7609	
	Depo-Provera 50 mg	J1055	
	Depo-Medrol 40 mg	J1030	

Diagnoses	Code
1 Acute exacerbation asthma	
2 bronchitis	
3 sinusitis	
4	

Next office visit: 2 weeks

(Recheck) • Preventative • PRN

Referral to:

Physician signature

x Sarah Mendenhall MD

x	Laboratory		-90
	Venipuncture	36415	
	Blood glucose, monitoring device	82962	
	Blood glucose, visual dipstick	82948	
	CBC, w/ auto differential	85025	
	CBC, w/o auto differential	85027	
	Cholesterol	82465	
	Hemoccult, guaiac	82270	
	Hemoccult, immunoassay	82274	
	Hemoglobin A1C	85018	
	Lipid panel	80061	
	Liver panel	80076	
	KOH prep (skin, hair, nails)	87220	
	Metabolic panel, basic	80048	
	Metabolic panel, comprehensive	80053	
	Mononucleosis	86308	
	Pregnancy, blood	84703	
	Pregnancy, urine	81025	
	Renal panel	80069	
	Sedimentation rate	85651	
	Strep, rapid	86403	
	Strep culture	87081	
	Strep A	87880	
	TB	86580	
	UA, complete, non-automated	81000	
	UA, w/o micro, non-automated	81002	
	UA, w/ micro, non-automated	81003	
	Urine colony count	87086	
	Urine culture, presumptive	87088	
	Wet mount/KOH	87210	

x	Vaccines	
	DT, <7 y	90702
	DTP	90701
	DtaP, <7 y	90700
	Flu, 6-35 months	90657
	Flu, 3 y +	90658
	Hep A, adult	90632
	Hep A, ped/adol, 2 dose	90633
	Hep B, adult	90746
	Hep B, ped/adol 3 dose	90744
	Hep B-Hib	90748
	Hib, 4 dose	90645
	HPV	90649
	IPV	90713
	MMR	90707
	Pneumonia, >2 y	90732
	Pneumonia conjugate, <5 y	90669
	Td, >7 y	90718
	Varicella	90716
	Tetanus toxoid adsorbed, IM	90703

x	Immunizations & Injections		Units
	Allergen, one	95115	
	Allergen, multiple	95117	
	Imm admn <8 yo 1st Inj	90465	
	Imm admn <8 yo each add inj	90466	
	Imm <8 yo oral or intranasal	90467	
	Imm admn <8 yo each add	90468	
	Imm admin, one vacc	90471	
	Imm admin, each add'l	90472	
	Imm admin, intranasal, one	90473	
	Imm admin, intranasal, each add'l	90474	
	Injection, joint, small	20600	
	Injection, joint, intermediate	20605	
	Injection, ther/proph/diag	90772	
	Injection, trigger pt 1-2 musc	20552	

Today's charges:		
Today's payment:		
Balance due:		

Job 1 Router- Julius Washington 13 of 20

Date of service: 10/27/09	Insurance: GALAXY HEALTH	Superbill Number: 2458
Patient name: WILLIAM KOSTNER	Coinsurance: 20% Copay:	Physician Name: HEATH
Account #: KOS001	Noncovered Waiver? yes / no / n/a	

x	Office visit	New	x	Est
	Minimal (RN only)			99211
	Problem focused	99201		99212
	Exp problem focused	99202		99213
	Detailed	99203		99214
	Comp	99204		99215
	Comprhen/Complex	99205		
	Well visit	**New**	x	**Est**
	< 1 y	99381		99391
	1-4 y	99382		99392
	5-11 y	99383		99393
	12-17 y	99384		99394
	18-39 y	99385		99395
	40-64 y	99386		99396
	65 y +	99387		99397

	Medicare preventive services	
	Pap	Q0091
	Pelvic & breast	G0101
	Prostate/PSA	G0103
	Tobacco couns/3-10 min	G0375
	Tobacco couns/>10 min	G0376
	Welcome to Medicare exam	G0344
	ECG w/Welcome to Medicare	G0366
	Hemoccult, guaiac	G0107
	Flu shot	G0008
	Pneumonia shot	G0009
	Consultation/preop clearance	
	Exp problem focused	99242
	Detailed	99243
✓	Comp/mod complex	99244
	Comp/high complex	99245
	Other services	
	After posted hours	99050
	Evening/weekend appointment	99051
	Home health certification	G0180
	Home health recertification	G0179
	Care Plan oversight	99374
	Care Plan Oversight >30 mins	99375
	Post-op follow-up	99024
	Prolonged/60min total	99354
	Prolonged/each add 30 mins	99355
	Special reports/forms	99080
	Disability/Workers comp	99455
	Smoking Cessation <10 mins	99406
	Smoking Cessation >10 mins	99407
	ETOH/SA screening <30 mins	99408
	Online E/M by MD	99444
	Phone E/M <10 mins	99441
	Phone E/M <20 mins	99442
	Phone E/M <30 mins	99443
	Anticoagulant Mgmt <90 days	99363
	Anticoagulant Mgmt >90 days	99364
	In office emergency serv	99058
	Other services	
	Supplies	
	Surgical Tray	99070

Instructions:

x	Office procedures		
	Cerumen removal		69210
	ECG, w/interpretation		93000
	ECG, rhythm strip		93040
	Endometrial biopsy		58100
	Fracture care, cast/splint		____
	Site: ______________		
	Nebulizer		94640
	Nebulizer demo		94664
	Spirometry		94010
	Spirometry, pre and post		94060
	Vasectomy		55250
	Skin procedures		**Units**
	Foreign body, skin, simple	10120	
	Foreign body, skin, complex	10121	
	I&D, abscess	10060	
	I&D, hematoma/seroma	10140	
	Laceration repair, simple	120__	
	Site: _______ Size: _____		
	Laceration repair, layered	120__	
	Site: _______ Size: _____		
	Laser Light Tx	96597	
	Lesion, biopsy, one	11100	
	Lesion, biopsy, each add'l	11101	
	Lesion, excision, benign	114__	
	Site: _______ Size: _____		
	Lesion, excision, malignant	116__	
	Site: _______ Size: _____		
	Lesion, paring/cutting, one	11055	
	Lesion, paring/cutting, 2-4	11056	
	Lesion, shave	113__	
	Site: _______ Size: _____		
	Nail removal, partial (+T mod)	11730	
	Nail rem, w/matrix (+T mod)	11750	
	Skin tag, 1-15	11200	
	Wart, flat, 1-14	17110	
	Destruction lesion, 1st	17000	
	Destruct lesion, each addl 2-14	17003	
	Medications		**Units**
	Ampicillin, up to 500mg	J0290	
	B-12, up to 1,000 mcg	J3420	
	Epinephrine, up to 1ml	J0170	
	Kenalog, 10mg	J3301	
✓	Lidocaine, 10mg	J2001	
	Normal saline, 1000cc	J7030	
	Phenergan, up to 50mg	J2550	
	Progesterone, 150mg	J1055	
	Rocephin, 250mg	J0696	
	Testosterone, 200mg	J1080	
	Tigan, up to 200 mg	J3250	
	Toradol, 15mg	J1885	
	Albuterol	J7609	
	Depo-Provera 50 mg	J1055	
✓	Depo-Medrol 40 mg	J1030	

Diagnoses		Code
1 Vertigo		
2 HA		
3 Myospasm		
4		

Next office visit: 4 wks
Recheck • Preventative • PRN
Referral to:

Physician signature
X [signature]

x	Laboratory		-90
	Venipuncture	36415	
	Blood glucose, monitoring device	82962	
	Blood glucose, visual dipstick	82948	
	CBC, w/ auto differential	85025	
	CBC, w/o auto differential	85027	
	Cholesterol	82465	
	Hemoccult, guaiac	82270	
	Hemoccult, immunoassay	82274	
	Hemoglobin A1C	85018	
	Lipid panel	80061	
	Liver panel	80076	
	KOH prep (skin, hair, nails)	87220	
	Metabolic panel, basic	80048	
	Metabolic panel, comprehensive	80053	
	Mononucleosis	86308	
	Pregnancy, blood	84703	
	Pregnancy, urine	81025	
	Renal panel	80069	
	Sedimentation rate	85651	
	Strep, rapid	86403	
	Strep culture	87081	
	Strep A	87880	
	TB	86580	
	UA, complete, non-automated	81000	
	UA, w/o micro, non-automated	81002	
	UA, w/ micro, non-automated	81003	
	Urine colony count	87086	
	Urine culture, presumptive	87088	
	Wet mount/KOH	87210	

	Vaccines	
	DT, <7 y	90702
	DTP	90701
	DtaP, <7 y	90700
	Flu, 6-35 months	90657
	Flu, 3 y +	90658
	Hep A, adult	90632
	Hep A, ped/adol, 2 dose	90633
	Hep B, adult	90746
	Hep B, ped/adol 3 dose	90744
	Hep B-Hib	90748
	Hib, 4 dose	90645
	HPV	90649
	IPV	90713
	MMR	90707
	Pneumonia, >2 y	90732
	Pneumonia conjugate, <5 y	90669
	Td, >7 y	90718
	Varicella	90716
	Tetanus toxoid adsorbed, IM	90703

	Immunizations & Injections		Units
	Allergen, one	95115	
	Allergen, multiple	95117	
	Imm admn <8 yo 1st Inj	90465	
	Imm admn <8 yo each add Inj	90466	
	Imm <8 yo oral or intranasal	90467	
	Imm admn <8 yo each add	90468	
	Imm admin, one vacc	90471	
	Imm admin, each add'l	90472	
	Imm admin, intranasal, one	90473	
	Imm admin, intranasal, each add'l	90474	
	Injection, joint, small	20600	
	Injection, joint, intermediate	20605	
	Injection, ther/proph/diag	90772	
✓	Injection, trigger pt 1-2 musc	20552	

Today's charges:		
Today's payment:		
Balance due:		

Job 1 Router- William Kostner 14 of 20

Date of service: 10/27/09	Insurance: MEDICARE SW/CENTURY SR			Superbill Number: 2457
Patient name: DEANNA HARTSFELD	Coinsurance: 20%	Copay:		Physician Name: MURRAY
Account #: HAR001	Noncovered Waiver?	yes	no	n/a

x	Office visit	New	x	Est
	Minimal (RN only)			99211
	Problem focused	99201		99212
	Exp problem focused	99202		99213
	Detailed	99203		99214
	Comp	99204		99215
	Comprhen/Complex	99205		
	Well visit	**New**	**x**	**Est**
	< 1 y	99381		99391
	1-4 y	99382		99392
	5-11 y	99383		99393
	12-17 y	99384		99394
	18-39 y	99385		99395
	40-64 y	99386		99396
	65 y +	99387		99397

x	Medicare preventive services	
✓	Pap	Q0091
	Pelvic & breast	G0101
	Prostate/PSA	G0103
	Tobacco couns/3-10 min	G0375
	Tobacco couns/>10 min	G0376
✓	Welcome to Medicare exam	G0344
	ECG w/Welcome to Medicare	G0366
	Hemoccult, guaiac	G0107
	Flu shot	G0008
	Pneumonia shot	G0009
	Consultation/preop clearance	
	Exp problem focused	99242
	Detailed	99243
	Comp/mod complex	99244
	Comp/high complex	99245
	Other services	
	After posted hours	99050
	Evening/weekend appointment	99051
	Home health certification	G0180
	Home health recertification	G0179
	Care Plan oversight	99374
	Care Plan Oversight >30 mins	99375
	Post-op follow-up	99024
	Prolonged/60min total	99354
	Prolonged/each add 30 mins	99355
	Special reports/forms	99080
	Disability/Workers comp	99455
	Smoking Cessation <10 mins	99406
	Smoking Cessation >10 mins	99407
	ETOH/SA screening <30 mins	99408
	Online E/M by MD	99444
	Phone E/M <10 mins	99441
	Phone E/M <20 mins	99442
	Phone E/M <30 mins	99443
	Anticoagulant Mgmt <90 days	99363
	Anticoagulant Mgmt >90 days	99364
	In office emergency serv	99058
	Other services	
✓	*Dexa Scan*	
	Supplies	
	Surgical Tray	99070

Instructions:

20 mins counseling diet / exercise / Diabetes Risk

x	Office procedures		
	Cerumen removal		69210
✓	ECG, w/interpretation		93000
	ECG, rhythm strip		93040
	Endometrial biopsy		58100
	Fracture care, cast/splint Site: ______		____
	Nebulizer		94640
	Nebulizer demo		94664
	Spirometry		94010
	Spirometry, pre and post		94060
	Vasectomy		55250
	Skin procedures		**Units**
	Foreign body, skin, simple	10120	
	Foreign body, skin, complex	10121	
	I&D, abscess	10060	
	I&D, hematoma/seroma	10140	
	Laceration repair, simple Site: ______ Size: ____	120__	
	Laceration repair, layered Site: ______ Size: ____	120__	
	Laser Light Tx	96597	
	Lesion, biopsy, one	11100	
	Lesion, biopsy, each add'l	11101	
	Lesion, excision, benign Site: ______ Size: ____	114__	
	Lesion, excision, malignant Site: ______ Size: ____	116__	
	Lesion, paring/cutting, one	11055	
	Lesion, paring/cutting, 2-4	11056	
	Lesion, shave Site: ______ Size: ____	113__	
	Nail removal, partial (+T mod)	11730	
	Nail rem, w/matrix (+T mod)	11750	
	Skin tag, 1-15	11200	
	Wart, flat, 1-14	17110	
	Destruction lesion, 1st	17000	
	Destruct lesion, each addl 2-14	17003	
	Medications		**Units**
	Ampicillin, up to 500mg	J0290	
	B-12, up to 1,000 mcg	J3420	
	Epinephrine, up to 1ml	J0170	
	Kenalog, 10mg	J3301	
	Lidocaine, 10mg	J2001	
	Normal saline, 1000cc	J7030	
	Phenergan, up to 50mg	J2550	
	Progesterone, 150mg	J1055	
	Rocephin, 250mg	J0696	
	Testosterone, 200mg	J1080	
	Tigan, up to 200 mg	J3250	
	Toradol, 15mg	J1885	
	Albuterol	J7609	
	Depo-Provera 50 mg	J1055	
	Depo-Medrol 40 mg	J1030	

Diagnoses	Code
1 *Elevated BP*	
2 *Well Check*	
3 *Obesity*	
4	

Next office visit: *1 yr*

Recheck • (Preventative) • PRN

Referral to:

Physician signature

x *Jamie Murray MD*

x	Laboratory		-90
	Venipuncture	36415	
	Blood glucose, monitoring device	82962	
	Blood glucose, visual dipstick	82948	
	CBC, w/ auto differential	85025	
	CBC, w/o auto differential	85027	
	Cholesterol	82465	
	Hemoccult, guaiac	82270	
	Hemoccult, immunoassay	82274	
	Hemoglobin A1C	85018	
	Lipid panel	80061	
	Liver panel	80076	
	KOH prep (skin, hair, nails)	87220	
	Metabolic panel, basic	80048	
✓	Metabolic panel, comprehensive	80053	
	Mononucleosis	86308	
	Pregnancy, blood	84703	
	Pregnancy, urine	81025	
	Renal panel	80069	
	Sedimentation rate	85651	
	Strep, rapid	86403	
	Strep culture	87081	
	Strep A	87880	
	TB	86580	
	UA, complete, non-automated	81000	
	UA, w/o micro, non-automated	81002	
	UA, w/ micro, non-automated	81003	
	Urine colony count	87086	
	Urine culture, presumptive	87088	
	Wet mount/KOH	87210	
	Vaccines		
	DT, <7 y		90702
	DTP		90701
	DtaP, <7 y		90700
	Flu, 6-35 months		90657
	Flu, 3 y +		90658
	Hep A, adult		90632
	Hep A, ped/adol, 2 dose		90633
	Hep B, adult		90746
	Hep B, ped/adol 3 dose		90744
	Hep B-Hib		90748
	Hib, 4 dose		90645
	HPV		90649
	IPV		90713
	MMR		90707
	Pneumonia, >2 y		90732
	Pneumonia conjugate, <5 y		90669
	Td, >7 y		90718
	Varicella		90716
	Tetanus toxoid adsorbed, IM		90703
	Immunizations & Injections		**Units**
	Allergen, one	95115	
	Allergen, multiple	95117	
	Imm admn <8 yo 1st Inj	90465	
	Imm admn <8 yo each add inj	90466	
	Imm <8 yo oral or intranasal	90467	
	Imm admn <8 yo each add	90468	
	Imm admin, one vacc	90471	
	Imm admin, each add'l	90472	
	Imm admin, intranasal, one	90473	
	Imm admin, intranasal, each add'l	90474	
	Injection, joint, small	20600	
	Injection, joint, intermediate	20605	
	Injection, ther/proph/diag	90772	
	Injection, trigger pt 1-2 musc	20552	

Today's charges:		
Today's payment:		
Balance due:		

Job 1 Router- Deanna Hartsfeld 15 of 20

Date of service: 10/27/09	Insurance: MEDICARE STATE WIDE		Superbill Number: 2455
Patient name: VITO MANGANO	Coinsurance: 20%	Copay:	Physician Name: HEATH
Account #: MAN001	Noncovered Waiver?	yes / no / n/a	

x	Office visit	New	x	Est
	Minimal (RN only)			99211
	Problem focused	99201		99212
	Exp problem focused	99202		99213
	Detailed	99203		99214
	Comp	99204	✓	99215
	Comprhen/Complex	99205		

x	Well visit	New	x	Est
	< 1 y	99381		99391
	1-4 y	99382		99392
	5-11 y	99383		99393
	12-17 y	99384		99394
	18-39 y	99385		99395
	40-64 y	99386		99396
	65 y +	99387		99397

x	Medicare preventive services	
	Pap	Q0091
	Pelvic & breast	G0101
✓	Prostate/PSA	G0103
	Tobacco couns/3-10 min	G0375
	Tobacco couns/>10 min	G0376
	Welcome to Medicare exam	G0344
	ECG w/Welcome to Medicare	G0366
	Hemoccult, guaiac	G0107
	Flu shot	G0008
	Pneumonia shot	G0009

x	Consultation/preop clearance	
	Exp problem focused	99242
	Detailed	99243
	Comp/mod complex	99244
	Comp/high complex	99245

x	Other services	
	After posted hours	99050
	Evening/weekend appointment	99051
	Home health certification	G0180
	Home health recertification	G0179
	Care Plan oversight	99374
	Care Plan Oversight >30 mins	99375
	Post-op follow-up	99024
	Prolonged/60min total	99354
	Prolonged/each add 30 mins	99355
	Special reports/forms	99080
	Disability/Workers comp	99455
	Smoking Cessation <10 mins	99406
	Smoking Cessation >10 mins	99407
	ETOH/SA screening <30 mins	99408
	Online E/M by MD	99444
	Phone E/M <10 mins	99441
	Phone E/M <20 mins	99442
	Phone E/M <30 mins	99443
	Anticoagulant Mgmt <90 days	99363
	Anticoagulant Mgmt >90 days	99364
	In office emergency serv	99058

Other services

✓ U/S bladder + trans prostate US

Supplies

Surgical Tray	99070

- Foley catheter
- Bladder catheterization

Instructions:

PSA - await results
Rx: alfuzosin
Finasteride

x	Office procedures	
	Cerumen removal	69210
	ECG, w/interpretation	93000
	ECG, rhythm strip	93040
	Endometrial biopsy	58100
	Fracture care, cast/splint	______
	Site: ____________	
	Nebulizer	94640
	Nebulizer demo	94664
	Spirometry	94010
	Spirometry, pre and post	94060
	Vasectomy	55250

x	Skin procedures		Units
	Foreign body, skin, simple	10120	
	Foreign body, skin, complex	10121	
	I&D, abscess	10060	
	I&D, hematoma/seroma	10140	
	Laceration repair, simple	120__	
	Site: _______ Size: _____		
	Laceration repair, layered	120__	
	Site: _______ Size: _____		
	Laser Light Tx	96597	
	Lesion, biopsy, one	11100	
	Lesion, biopsy, each add'l	11101	
	Lesion, excision, benign	114__	
	Site: _______ Size: _____		
	Lesion, excision, malignant	116__	
	Site: _______ Size: _____		
	Lesion, paring/cutting, one	11055	
	Lesion, paring/cutting, 2-4	11056	
	Lesion, shave	113__	
	Site: _______ Size: _____		
	Nail removal, partial (+T mod)	11730	
	Nail rem, w/matrix (+T mod)	11750	
	Skin tag, 1-15	11200	
	Wart, flat, 1-14	17110	
	Destruction lesion, 1st	17000	
	Destruct lesion, each addl 2-14	17003	

x	Medications		Units
	Ampicillin, up to 500mg	J0290	
	B-12, up to 1,000 mcg	J3420	
	Epinephrine, up to 1ml	J0170	
	Kenalog, 10mg	J3301	
	Lidocaine, 10mg	J2001	
	Normal saline, 1000cc	J7030	
	Phenergan, up to 50mg	J2550	
	Progesterone, 150mg	J1055	
	Rocephin, 250mg	J0696	
	Testosterone, 200mg	J1080	
	Tigan, up to 200 mg	J3250	
	Toradol, 15mg	J1885	
	Albuterol	J7609	
	Depo-Provera 50 mg	J1055	
	Depo-Medrol 40 mg	J1030	

Diagnoses	Code
1 Enlarged prostate w/nodules	
2 urinary outlet obstruction	
3 urinary retention	
4	

Next office visit: 1 mo

Recheck • Preventative • PRN

Referral to: Dr. Howard - urology

Physician signature

x [signature] MD

x	Laboratory		-90
✓	Venipuncture	36415	
	Blood glucose, monitoring device	82962	
	Blood glucose, visual dipstick	82948	
	CBC, w/ auto differential	85025	
	CBC, w/o auto differential	85027	
	Cholesterol	82465	
	Hemoccult, guaiac	82270	
	Hemoccult, immunoassay	82274	
	Hemoglobin A1C	85018	
	Lipid panel	80061	
	Liver panel	80076	
	KOH prep (skin, hair, nails)	87220	
	Metabolic panel, basic	80048	
	Metabolic panel, comprehensive	80053	
	Mononucleosis	86308	
	Pregnancy, blood	84703	
	Pregnancy, urine	81025	
	Renal panel	80069	
	Sedimentation rate	85651	
	Strep, rapid	86403	
	Strep culture	87081	
	Strep A	87880	
	TB	86580	
	UA, complete, non-automated	81000	
	UA, w/o micro, non-automated	81002	
✓	UA, w/ micro, non-automated	81003	
	Urine colony count	87086	
✓	Urine culture, presumptive	87088	
	Wet mount/KOH	87210	

x	Vaccines	
	DT, <7 y	90702
	DTP	90701
	DtaP, <7 y	90700
	Flu, 6-35 months	90657
	Flu, 3 y +	90658
	Hep A, adult	90632
	Hep A, ped/adol, 2 dose	90633
	Hep B, adult	90746
	Hep B, ped/adol 3 dose	90744
	Hep B-Hib	90748
	Hib, 4 dose	90645
	HPV	90649
	IPV	90713
	MMR	90707
	Pneumonia, >2 y	90732
	Pneumonia conjugate, <5 y	90669
	Td, >7 y	90718
	Varicella	90716
	Tetanus toxoid adsorbed, IM	90703

x	Immunizations & Injections		Units
	Allergen, one	95115	
	Allergen, multiple	95117	
	Imm admn <8 yo 1st Inj	90465	
	Imm admn <8 yo each add inj	90466	
	Imm <8 yo oral or intranasal	90467	
	Imm admn <8 yo each add	90468	
	Imm admin, one vacc	90471	
	Imm admin, each add'l	90472	
	Imm admin, intranasal, one	90473	
	Imm admin, intranasal, each add'l	90474	
	Injection, joint, small	20600	
	Injection, joint, intermediate	20605	
	Injection, ther/proph/diag	90772	
	Injection, trigger pt 1-2 musc	20552	

Today's charges:	
Today's payment:	
Balance due:	

Job 1 Router- Vito Mangano 16 of 20

Date of service: 10/27/09	Insurance: FLEXIHEALTH PPO		Router Number: 2463
Patient name: DEREK WALLACE	Coinsurance:	Copay:	Physician Name: MURRAY
Account #: WAL001	Noncovered Waiver?	yes / no / n/a	

x	Office visit	New	x	Est
	Minimal (RN only)			99211
	Problem focused	99201		99212
	Exp problem focused	99202	✓	99213
	Detailed	99203		99214
	Comp	99204		99215
	Comprhen/Complex	99205		
	Well visit	**New**	**x**	**Est**
	< 1 y	99381		99391
	1-4 y	99382		99392
	5-11 y	99383		99393
	12-17 y	99384		99394
	18-39 y	99385		99395
	40-64 y	99386		99396
	65 y +	99387		99397

x	Medicare preventive services	
	Pap	Q0091
	Pelvic & breast	G0101
	Prostate/PSA	G0103
	Tobacco couns/3-10 min	G0375
	Tobacco couns/>10 min	G0376
	Welcome to Medicare exam	G0344
	ECG w/Welcome to Medicare	G0366
	Hemoccult, guaiac	G0107
	Flu shot	G0008
	Pneumonia shot	G0009
	Consultation/preop clearance	
	Exp problem focused	99242
	Detailed	99243
	Comp/mod complex	99244
	Comp/high complex	99245
	Other services	
	After posted hours	99050
	Evening/weekend appointment	99051
	Home health certification	G0180
	Home health recertification	G0179
	Care Plan oversight	99374
	Care Plan Oversight >30 mins	99375
	Post-op follow-up	99024
	Prolonged/60min total	99354
	Prolonged/each add 30 mins	99355
	Special reports/forms	99080
	Disability/Workers comp	99455
	Smoking Cessation <10 mins	99406
	Smoking Cessation >10 mins	99407
	ETOH/SA screening <30 mins	99408
	Online E/M by MD	99444
	Phone E/M <10 mins	99441
	Phone E/M <20 mins	99442
	Phone E/M <30 mins	99443
	Anticoagulant Mgmt <90 days	99363
	Anticoagulant Mgmt >90 days	99364
✓	In office emergency serv	99058
	Other services	
	Repair nail bed (R) index finger	
	Supplies	
✓	Surgical Tray	99070

x	Office procedures	
	Cerumen removal	69210
	ECG, w/interpretation	93000
	ECG, rhythm strip	93040
	Endometrial biopsy	58100
	Fracture care, cast/splint Site: ______	
	Nebulizer	94640
	Nebulizer demo	94664
	Spirometry	94010
	Spirometry, pre and post	94060
	Vasectomy	55250

x	Skin procedures		Units
	Foreign body, skin, simple	10120	
	Foreign body, skin, complex	10121	
	I&D, abscess	10060	
	I&D, hematoma/seroma	10140	
	Laceration repair, simple Site: ______ Size: ______	120__	
✓	Laceration repair, layered Site: (R) Hd Size: 4.2cm	120__	
	Laser Light Tx	96597	
	Lesion, biopsy, one	11100	
	Lesion, biopsy, each add'l	11101	
	Lesion, excision, benign Site: ______ Size: ______	114__	
	Lesion, excision, malignant Site: ______ Size: ______	116__	
	Lesion, paring/cutting, one	11055	
	Lesion, paring/cutting, 2-4	11056	
	Lesion, shave Site: ______ Size: ______	113__	
	Nail removal, partial (+T mod)	11730	
	Nail rem, w/matrix (+T mod)	11750	
	Skin tag, 1-15	11200	
	Wart, flat, 1-14	17110	
	Destruction lesion, 1st	17000	
	Destruct lesion, each addl 2-14	17003	

x	Medications		Units
	Ampicillin, up to 500mg	J0290	
	B-12, up to 1,000 mcg	J3420	
	Epinephrine, up to 1ml	J0170	
	Kenalog, 10mg	J3301	
✓	Lidocaine, 10mg	J2001	
	Normal saline, 1000cc	J7030	
	Phenergan, up to 50mg	J2550	
	Progesterone, 150mg	J1055	
	Rocephin, 250mg	J0696	
	Testosterone, 200mg	J1080	
	Tigan, up to 200 mg	J3250	
	Toradol, 15mg	J1885	
	Albuterol	J7609	
	Depo-Provera 50 mg	J1055	
	Depo-Medrol 40 mg	J1030	

Diagnoses	Code
1 Laceration (R) hand	
2 Crush injury fingernail	
3	
4	

Next office visit: 10 days

(Recheck) • Preventative • PRN

Referral to:

x	Laboratory		-90
	Venipuncture	36415	
	Blood glucose, monitoring device	82962	
	Blood glucose, visual dipstick	82948	
	CBC, w/ auto differential	85025	
	CBC, w/o auto differential	85027	
	Cholesterol	82465	
	Hemoccult, guaiac	82270	
	Hemoccult, immunoassay	82274	
	Hemoglobin A1C	85018	
	Lipid panel	80061	
	Liver panel	80076	
	KOH prep (skin, hair, nails)	87220	
	Metabolic panel, basic	80048	
	Metabolic panel, comprehensive	80053	
	Mononucleosis	86308	
	Pregnancy, blood	84703	
	Pregnancy, urine	81025	
	Renal panel	80069	
	Sedimentation rate	85651	
	Strep, rapid	86403	
	Strep culture	87081	
	Strep A	87880	
	TB	86580	
	UA, complete, non-automated	81000	
	UA, w/o micro, non-automated	81002	
	UA, w/ micro, non-automated	81003	
	Urine colony count	87086	
	Urine culture, presumptive	87088	
	Wet mount/KOH	87210	

x	Vaccines	
	DT, <7 y	90702
	DTP	90701
	DtaP, <7 y	90700
	Flu, 6-35 months	90657
	Flu, 3 y +	90658
	Hep A, adult	90632
	Hep A, ped/adol, 2 dose	90633
	Hep B, adult	90746
	Hep B, ped/adol 3 dose	90744
	Hep B-Hib	90748
	Hib, 4 dose	90645
	HPV	90649
	IPV	90713
	MMR	90707
	Pneumonia, >2 y	90732
	Pneumonia conjugate, <5 y	90669
	Td, >7 y	90718
	Varicella	90716
	Tetanus toxoid adsorbed, IM	90703

x	Immunizations & Injections		Units
	Allergen, one	95115	
	Allergen, multiple	95117	
	Imm admn <8 yo 1st Inj	90465	
	Imm admn <8 yo each add inj	90466	
	Imm <8 yo oral or intranasal	90467	
	Imm admn <8 yo each add	90468	
	Imm admin, one vacc	90471	
	Imm admin, each add'l	90472	
	Imm admin, intranasal, one	90473	
	Imm admin, intranasal, each add'l	90474	
	Injection, joint, small	20600	
	Injection, joint, intermediate	20605	
	Injection, ther/proph/diag	90772	
	Injection, trigger pt 1-2 musc	20552	

Instructions:

Suture removal 10 days

Keep site dry

Physician signature

X Lance Murray MD

Today's charges:	
Today's payment:	
Balance due:	

Job 1 Router- Derek Wallace 17 of 20

Date of service: 10/27/09	Insurance: CONSUMER ONE/PRUDENTIAL				Superbill Number: 2451
Patient name: MELISSA MORENCY	Coinsurance: 20%	Copay:			Physician Name: KEMPER
Account #: MOR001	Noncovered Waiver?	yes	no	n/a	

X	Office visit	New	X	Est
	Minimal (RN only)			99211
	Problem focused	99201		99212
	Exp problem focused	99202		99213
	Detailed	99203		99214
	Comp	99204		99215
	Comprhen/Complex	99205		
	Well visit	**New**	**X**	**Est**
	< 1 y	99381		99391
	1-4 y	99382		99392
	5-11 y	99383		99393
✓	12-17 y	99384		99394
	18-39 y	99385		99395
	40-64 y	99386		99396
	65 y +	99387		99397
	Medicare preventive services			
	Pap			Q0091
	Pelvic & breast			G0101
	Prostate/PSA			G0103
	Tobacco couns/3-10 min			G0375
	Tobacco couns/>10 min			G0376
	Welcome to Medicare exam			G0344
	ECG w/Welcome to Medicare			G0366
	Hemoccult, guaiac			G0107
	Flu shot			G0008
	Pneumonia shot			G0009
	Consultation/preop clearance			
	Exp problem focused			99242
	Detailed			99243
	Comp/mod complex			99244
	Comp/high complex			99245
	Other services			
	After posted hours			99050
	Evening/weekend appointment			99051
	Home health certification			G0180
	Home health recertification			G0179
	Care Plan oversight			99374
	Care Plan Oversight >30 mins			99375
	Post-op follow-up			99024
	Prolonged/60min total			99354
	Prolonged/each add 30 mins			99355
	Special reports/forms			99080
	Disability/Workers comp			99455
	Smoking Cessation <10 mins			99406
	Smoking Cessation >10 mins			99407
	ETOH/SA screening <30 mins			99408
	Online E/M by MD			99444
	Phone E/M <10 mins			99441
	Phone E/M <20 mins			99442
	Phone E/M <30 mins			99443
	Anticoagulant Mgmt <90 days			99363
	Anticoagulant Mgmt >90 days			99364
	In office emergency serv			99058
	Other services			
✓	Preventative counseling 15 mins			
	Supplies			
	Surgical Tray			99070

Instructions:

Weight Mgmt

X	Office procedures		
	Cerumen removal		69210
	ECG, w/interpretation		93000
	ECG, rhythm strip		93040
	Endometrial biopsy		58100
	Fracture care, cast/splint Site: ________		
	Nebulizer		94640
	Nebulizer demo		94664
	Spirometry		94010
	Spirometry, pre and post		94060
	Vasectomy		55250
	Skin procedures		**Units**
	Foreign body, skin, simple	10120	
	Foreign body, skin, complex	10121	
	I&D, abscess	10060	
	I&D, hematoma/seroma	10140	
	Laceration repair, simple Site: ______ Size: ____	120__	
	Laceration repair, layered Site: ______ Size: ____	120__	
	Laser Light Tx	96597	
	Lesion, biopsy, one	11100	
	Lesion, biopsy, each add'l	11101	
	Lesion, excision, benign Site: ______ Size: ____	114__	
	Lesion, excision, malignant Site: ______ Size: ____	116__	
	Lesion, paring/cutting, one	11055	
	Lesion, paring/cutting, 2-4	11056	
	Lesion, shave Site: ______ Size: ____	113__	
	Nail removal, partial (+T mod)	11730	
	Nail rem, w/matrix (+T mod)	11750	
	Skin tag, 1-15	11200	
	Wart, flat, 1-14	17110	
	Destruction lesion, 1st	17000	
	Destruct lesion, each addl 2-14	17003	
	Medications		**Units**
	Ampicillin, up to 500mg	J0290	
	B-12, up to 1,000 mcg	J3420	
	Epinephrine, up to 1ml	J0170	
	Kenalog, 10mg	J3301	
	Lidocaine, 10mg	J2001	
	Normal saline, 1000cc	J7030	
	Phenergan, up to 50mg	J2550	
	Progesterone, 150mg	J1055	
	Rocephin, 250mg	J0696	
	Testosterone, 200mg	J1080	
	Tigan, up to 200 mg	J3250	
	Toradol, 15mg	J1885	
	Albuterol	J7609	
	Depo-Provera 50 mg	J1055	
	Depo-Medrol 40 mg	J1030	

Diagnoses	Code
1 Vaccination update	
2 Obesity	
3	
4	

Next office visit:
Recheck • Preventative • PRN
Referral to:

Physician signature
X Sally Kemper MD

X	Laboratory		-90
	Venipuncture	36415	
	Blood glucose, monitoring device	82962	
	Blood glucose, visual dipstick	82948	
	CBC, w/ auto differential	85025	
	CBC, w/o auto differential	85027	
	Cholesterol	82465	
	Hemoccult, guaiac	82270	
	Hemoccult, immunoassay	82274	
	Hemoglobin A1C	85018	
	Lipid panel	80061	
	Liver panel	80076	
	KOH prep (skin, hair, nails)	87220	
	Metabolic panel, basic	80048	
	Metabolic panel, comprehensive	80053	
	Mononucleosis	86308	
	Pregnancy, blood	84703	
	Pregnancy, urine	81025	
	Renal panel	80069	
	Sedimentation rate	85651	
	Strep, rapid	86403	
	Strep culture	87081	
	Strep A	87880	
	TB	86580	
	UA, complete, non-automated	81000	
	UA, w/o micro, non-automated	81002	
	UA, w/ micro, non-automated	81003	
	Urine colony count	87086	
	Urine culture, presumptive	87088	
	Wet mount/KOH	87210	
	Vaccines		
	DT, <7 y		90702
	DTP		90701
	DtaP, <7 y		90700
	Flu, 6-35 months		90657
	Flu, 3 y +		90658
	Hep A, adult		90632
	Hep A, ped/adol, 2 dose		90633
	Hep B, adult		90746
	Hep B, ped/adol 3 dose		90744
	Hep B-Hib		90748
	Hib, 4 dose		90645
✓	HPV		90649
	IPV		90713
	MMR		90707
	Pneumonia, >2 y		90732
	Pneumonia conjugate, <5 y		90669
	Td, >7 y		90718
	Varicella		90716
	Tetanus toxoid adsorbed, IM		90703
	Immunizations & Injections		**Units**
	Allergen, one	95115	
	Allergen, multiple	95117	
	Imm admn <8 yo 1st Inj	90465	
	Imm admn <8 yo each add inj	90466	
	Imm <8 yo oral or intranasal	90467	
	Imm admn <8 yo each add	90468	
✓	Imm admin, one vacc	90471	
	Imm admin, each add'l	90472	
	Imm admin, intranasal, one	90473	
	Imm admin, intranasal, each add'l	90474	
	Injection, joint, small	20600	
	Injection, joint, intermediate	20605	
	Injection, ther/proph/diag	90772	
	Injection, trigger pt 1-2 musc	20552	

Today's charges:		
Today's payment:		
Balance due:		

Job 1 Router- Melissa Morency 18 of 20

Date of service: 10/27/09	Insurance: AETNA		Superbill Number: 2452
Patient name: SAMANTHA BEECHWOOD	Coinsurance: 25%	Copay:	Physician Name: SCHWARTZ
Account #: BEE001	Noncovered Waiver?	yes / no / n/a	

x	Office visit	New	x	Est
	Minimal (RN only)			99211
	Problem focused	99201		99212
	Exp problem focused	99202		99213
	Detailed	99203		99214
✓	Comp	99204		99215
	Comprhen/Complex	99205		
	Well visit	**New**	**x**	**Est**
	< 1 y	99381		99391
	1-4 y	99382		99392
	5-11 y	99383		99393
	12-17 y	99384		99394
	18-39 y	99385		99395
	40-64 y	99386		99396
	65 y +	99387		99397

x	Medicare preventive services	
	Pap	Q0091
	Pelvic & breast	G0101
	Prostate/PSA	G0103
	Tobacco couns/3-10 min	G0375
	Tobacco couns/>10 min	G0376
	Welcome to Medicare exam	G0344
	ECG w/Welcome to Medicare	G0366
	Hemoccult, guaiac	G0107
	Flu shot	G0008
	Pneumonia shot	G0009
	Consultation/preop clearance	
	Exp problem focused	99242
	Detailed	99243
	Comp/mod complex	99244
	Comp/high complex	99245
	Other services	
	After posted hours	99050
	Evening/weekend appointment	99051
	Home health certification	G0180
	Home health recertification	G0179
	Care Plan oversight	99374
	Care Plan Oversight >30 mins	99375
	Post-op follow-up	99024
	Prolonged/60min total	99354
	Prolonged/each add 30 mins	99355
	Special reports/forms	99080
	Disability/Workers comp	99455
	Smoking Cessation <10 mins	99406
	Smoking Cessation >10 mins	99407
	ETOH/SA screening <30 mins	99408
	Online E/M by MD	99444
	Phone E/M <10 mins	99441
	Phone E/M <20 mins	99442
	Phone E/M <30 mins	99443
	Anticoagulant Mgmt <90 days	99363
	Anticoagulant Mgmt >90 days	99364
	In office emergency serv	99058
	Other services	
✓	AP + Lateral Shoulder xray	
✓	Injection R shoulder	
	Supplies	
	Surgical Tray	99070
	Strapping R shoulder	

Instructions:

Keep shoulder strapped for 5 days.

x	Office procedures		
	Cerumen removal		69210
	ECG, w/interpretation		93000
	ECG, rhythm strip		93040
	Endometrial biopsy		58100
	Fracture care, cast/splint Site: ________		____
	Nebulizer		94640
	Nebulizer demo		94664
	Spirometry		94010
	Spirometry, pre and post		94060
	Vasectomy		55250
	Skin procedures		**Units**
	Foreign body, skin, simple	10120	
	Foreign body, skin, complex	10121	
	I&D, abscess	10060	
	I&D, hematoma/seroma	10140	
	Laceration repair, simple Site: ______ Size: _____	120__	
	Laceration repair, layered Site: ______ Size: _____	120__	
	Laser Light Tx	96597	
	Lesion, biopsy, one	11100	
	Lesion, biopsy, each add'l	11101	
	Lesion, excision, benign Site: ______ Size: _____	114__	
	Lesion, excision, malignant Site: ______ Size: _____	116__	
	Lesion, paring/cutting, one	11055	
	Lesion, paring/cutting, 2-4	11056	
	Lesion, shave Site: ______ Size: _____	113__	
	Nail removal, partial (+T mod)	11730	
	Nail rem, w/matrix (+T mod)	11750	
	Skin tag, 1-15	11200	
	Wart, flat, 1-14	17110	
	Destruction lesion, 1st	17000	
	Destruct lesion, each addl 2-14	17003	
	Medications		**Units**
	Ampicillin, up to 500mg	J0290	
	B-12, up to 1,000 mcg	J3420	
	Epinephrine, up to 1ml	J0170	
	Kenalog, 10mg	J3301	
✓	Lidocaine, 10mg	J2001	
	Normal saline, 1000cc	J7030	
	Phenergan, up to 50mg	J2550	
	Progesterone, 150mg	J1055	
	Rocephin, 250mg	J0696	
	Testosterone, 200mg	J1080	
	Tigan, up to 200 mg	J3250	
	Toradol, 15mg	J1885	
	Albuterol	J7609	
	Depo-Provera 50 mg	J1055	
✓	Depo-Medrol 40 mg	J1030	

Diagnoses		Code
1 Rt shoulder pain/ Strain		
2 Rt Shoulder dislocation		
3		
4		

Next office visit:

Recheck • Preventative • PRN

Referral to: Dr. Alston - Orthopaedics

Physician signature

X DJ Schwartz MD

x	Laboratory		-90
	Venipuncture	36415	
	Blood glucose, monitoring device	82962	
	Blood glucose, visual dipstick	82948	
	CBC, w/ auto differential	85025	
	CBC, w/o auto differential	85027	
	Cholesterol	82465	
	Hemoccult, guaiac	82270	
	Hemoccult, immunoassay	82274	
	Hemoglobin A1C	85018	
	Lipid panel	80061	
	Liver panel	80076	
	KOH prep (skin, hair, nails)	87220	
	Metabolic panel, basic	80048	
	Metabolic panel, comprehensive	80053	
	Mononucleosis	86308	
	Pregnancy, blood	84703	
	Pregnancy, urine	81025	
	Renal panel	80069	
	Sedimentation rate	85651	
	Strep, rapid	86403	
	Strep culture	87081	
	Strep A	87880	
	TB	86580	
	UA, complete, non-automated	81000	
	UA, w/o micro, non-automated	81002	
	UA, w/ micro, non-automated	81003	
	Urine colony count	87086	
	Urine culture, presumptive	87088	
	Wet mount/KOH	87210	

x	Vaccines	
	DT, <7 y	90702
	DTP	90701
	DtaP, <7 y	90700
	Flu, 6-35 months	90657
	Flu, 3 y +	90658
	Hep A, adult	90632
	Hep A, ped/adol, 2 dose	90633
	Hep B, adult	90746
	Hep B, ped/adol 3 dose	90744
	Hep B-Hib	90748
	Hib, 4 dose	90645
	HPV	90649
	IPV	90713
	MMR	90707
	Pneumonia, >2 y	90732
	Pneumonia conjugate, <5 y	90669
	Td, >7 y	90718
	Varicella	90716
	Tetanus toxoid adsorbed, IM	90703

x	Immunizations & Injections		Units
	Allergen, one	95115	
	Allergen, multiple	95117	
	Imm admn <8 yo 1st Inj	90465	
	Imm admn <8 yo each add inj	90466	
	Imm <8 yo oral or intranasal	90467	
	Imm admn <8 yo each add	90468	
	Imm admin, one vacc	90471	
	Imm admin, each add'l	90472	
	Imm admin, intranasal, one	90473	
	Imm admin, intranasal, each add'l	90474	
	Injection, joint, small	20600	
	Injection, joint, intermediate	20605	
	Injection, ther/proph/diag	90772	
	Injection, trigger pt 1-2 musc	20552	

Today's charges:	
Today's payment:	
Balance due:	

Job 1 Router- Samantha Beechwood 19 of 20

Date of service: 10/27/09	Insurance: MEDICARE	Router Number: 2485
Patient name: XAO CHANG	Coinsurance: / Copay:	Physician Name: HEATH
Account #: CHA001	Noncovered Waiver? yes / no / n/a	

x	Office visit	New	x	Est
N/A	Minimal (RN only)	N/A		99211
	Problem focused	99201		99212
	Exp problem focused	99202		99213
	Detailed	99203	✓	99214
	Comp	99204		99215
	Comprhen/Complex	99205		
	Well visit	**New**	**x**	**Est**
	< 1 y	99381		99391
	1-4 y	99382		99392
	5-11 y	99383		99393
	12-17 y	99384		99394
	18-39 y	99385		99395
	40-64 y	99386		99396
	65 y +	99387		99397

x	Medicare preventive services	
	Pap	Q0091
	Pelvic & breast	G0101
	Prostate/PSA	G0103
	Tobacco couns/3-10 min	G0375
	Tobacco couns/>10 min	G0376
	Welcome to Medicare exam	G0344
	ECG w/Welcome to Medicare	G0366
	Hemoccult, guaiac	G0107
	Flu shot	G0008
	Pneumonia shot	G0009
	Consultation/preop clearance	
	Exp problem focused	99242
	Detailed	99243
	Comp/mod complex	99244
	Comp/high complex	99245
	Other services	
	After posted hours	99050
	Evening/weekend appointment	99051
	Home health certification	G0180
	Home health recertification	G0179
	Care Plan oversight	99374
	Care Plan Oversight >30 mins	99375
	Post-op follow-up	99024
	Prolonged/60min total	99354
	Prolonged/each add 30 mins	99355
	Special reports/forms	99080
	Disability/Workers comp	99455
	Smoking Cessation <10 mins	99406
	Smoking Cessation >10 mins	99407
	ETOH/SA screening <30 mins	99408
	Online E/M by MD	99444
	Phone E/M <10 mins	99441
	Phone E/M <20 mins	99442
	Phone E/M <30 mins	99443
	Anticoagulant Mgmt <90 days	99363
	Anticoagulant Mgmt >90 days	99364
	In office emergency serv	99058
	Other services	
✓	CT W/O Contrast Brain	
	Supplies	
	Surgical Tray	99070

x	Office procedures	
	Cerumen removal	69210
	ECG, w/interpretation	93000
	ECG, rhythm strip	93040
	Endometrial biopsy	58100
	Fracture care, cast/splint Site: ______	
	Nebulizer	94640
	Nebulizer demo	94664
	Spirometry	94010
	Spirometry, pre and post	94060
	Vasectomy	55250

Skin procedures		Units
Foreign body, skin, simple	10120	
Foreign body, skin, complex	10121	
I&D, abscess	10060	
I&D, hematoma/seroma	10140	
Laceration repair, simple Site: ______ Size: ____	120__	
Laceration repair, layered Site: ______ Size: ____	120__	
Laser Light Tx	96597	
Lesion, biopsy, one	11100	
Lesion, biopsy, each add'l	11101	
Lesion, excision, benign Site: ______ Size: ____	114__	
Lesion, excision, malignant Site: ______ Size: ____	116__	
Lesion, paring/cutting, one	11055	
Lesion, paring/cutting, 2-4	11056	
Lesion, shave Site: ______ Size: ____	113__	
Nail removal, partial (+T mod)	11730	
Nail rem, w/matrix (+T mod)	11750	
Skin tag, 1-15	11200	
Wart, flat, 1-14	17110	
Destruction lesion, 1st	17000	
Destruct lesion, each addl 2-14	17003	

Medications		Units
Ampicillin, up to 500mg	J0290	
B-12, up to 1,000 mcg	J3420	
Epinephrine, up to 1ml	J0170	
Kenalog, 10mg	J3301	
Lidocaine, 10mg	J2001	
Normal saline, 1000cc	J7030	
Phenergan, up to 50mg	J2550	
Progesterone, 150mg	J1055	
Rocephin, 250mg	J0696	
Testosterone, 200mg	J1080	
Tigan, up to 200 mg	J3250	
Toradol, 15mg	J1885	
Albuterol	J7609	
Depo-Provera 50 mg	J1055	
Depo-Medrol 40 mg	J1030	

Diagnoses	Code
1 HA / R/O Aneurysm	
2 HTN	
3 Vertigo	
4	

Next office visit:
Recheck • Preventative • PRN
Referral to:

x	Laboratory		-90
	Venipuncture	36415	
	Blood glucose, monitoring device	82962	
	Blood glucose, visual dipstick	82948	
	CBC, w/ auto differential	85025	
	CBC, w/o auto differential	85027	
	Cholesterol	82465	
	Hemoccult, guaiac	82270	
	Hemoccult, immunoassay	82274	
	Hemoglobin A1C	85018	
	Lipid panel	80061	
	Liver panel	80076	
	KOH prep (skin, hair, nails)	87220	
	Metabolic panel, basic	80048	
	Metabolic panel, comprehensive	80053	
	Mononucleosis	86308	
	Pregnancy, blood	84703	
	Pregnancy, urine	81025	
	Renal panel	80069	
	Sedimentation rate	85651	
	Strep, rapid	86403	
	Strep culture	87081	
	Strep A	87880	
	TB	86580	
	UA, complete, non-automated	81000	
	UA, w/o micro, non-automated	81002	
	UA, w/ micro, non-automated	81003	
	Urine colony count	87086	
	Urine culture, presumptive	87088	
	Wet mount/KOH	87210	

Vaccines	
DT, <7 y	90702
DTP	90701
DtaP, <7 y	90700
Flu, 6-35 months	90657
Flu, 3 y +	90658
Hep A, adult	90632
Hep A, ped/adol, 2 dose	90633
Hep B, adult	90746
Hep B, ped/adol 3 dose	90744
Hep B-Hib	90748
Hib, 4 dose	90645
HPV	90649
IPV	90713
MMR	90707
Pneumonia, >2 y	90732
Pneumonia conjugate, <5 y	90669
Td, >7 y	90718
Varicella	90716
Tetanus toxoid adsorbed, IM	90703

Immunizations & Injections		Units
Allergen, one	95115	
Allergen, multiple	95117	
Imm admn <8 yo 1st Inj	90465	
Imm admn <8 yo each add inj	90466	
Imm <8 yo oral or intranasal	90467	
Imm admn <8 yo each add	90468	
Imm admin, one vacc	90471	
Imm admin, each add'l	90472	
Imm admin, intranasal, one	90473	
Imm admin, intranasal, each add'l	90474	
Injection, joint, small	20600	
Injection, joint, intermediate	20605	
Injection, ther/proph/diag	90772	
Injection, trigger pt 1-2 musc	20552	

Instructions:
CT image will be read by [illegible] Radiologist call results to home

Physician signature
X L D Heath MD

Today's charges:	
Today's payment:	
Balance due:	

Job 1 Router- Xao Chang 20 of 20

Date of service: 10/27/09	Insurance: FLEXIHEALTH PPO		Router Number: 2463
Patient name: DEREK WALLACE	Coinsurance:	Copay:	Physician Name: MURRAY
Account #: WAL001	Noncovered Waiver?	yes / no / n/a	

x	Office visit	New	x	Est
	Minimal (RN only)			99211
	Problem focused	99201		99212
	Exp problem focused	99202	✓	99213
	Detailed	99203		99214
	Comp	99204		99215
	Comprhen/Complex	99205		
	Well visit	**New**	**x**	**Est**
	< 1 y	99381		99391
	1-4 y	99382		99392
	5-11 y	99383		99393
	12-17 y	99384		99394
	18-39 y	99385		99395
	40-64 y	99386		99396
	65 y +	99387		99397

x	Medicare preventive services	
	Pap	Q0091
	Pelvic & breast	G0101
	Prostate/PSA	G0103
	Tobacco couns/3-10 min	G0375
	Tobacco couns/>10 min	G0376
	Welcome to Medicare exam	G0344
	ECG w/Welcome to Medicare	G0366
	Hemoccult, guaiac	G0107
	Flu shot	G0008
	Pneumonia shot	G0009
	Consultation/preop clearance	
	Exp problem focused	99242
	Detailed	99243
	Comp/mod complex	99244
	Comp/high complex	99245
	Other services	
	After posted hours	99050
	Evening/weekend appointment	99051
	Home health certification	G0180
	Home health recertification	G0179
	Care Plan oversight	99374
	Care Plan Oversight >30 mins	99375
	Post-op follow-up	99024
	Prolonged/60min total	99354
	Prolonged/each add 30 mins	99355
	Special reports/forms	99080
	Disability/Workers comp	99455
	Smoking Cessation <10 mins	99406
	Smoking Cessation >10 mins	99407
	ETOH/SA screening <30 mins	99408
	Online E/M by MD	99444
	Phone E/M <10 mins	99441
	Phone E/M <20 mins	99442
	Phone E/M <30 mins	99443
	Anticoagulant Mgmt <90 days	99363
	Anticoagulant Mgmt >90 days	99364
✓	In office emergency serv	99058
	Other services	
	Repair nail bed (R) index finger	
	Supplies	
✓	Surgical Tray	99070
	Instructions:	
	Suture removal 10 days Keep site dry	

x	Office procedures		
	Cerumen removal		69210
	ECG, w/interpretation		93000
	ECG, rhythm strip		93040
	Endometrial biopsy		58100
	Fracture care, cast/splint		
	Site:		
	Nebulizer		94640
	Nebulizer demo		94664
	Spirometry		94010
	Spirometry, pre and post		94060
	Vasectomy		55250
	Skin procedures		**Units**
	Foreign body, skin, simple	10120	
	Foreign body, skin, complex	10121	
	I&D, abscess	10060	
	I&D, hematoma/seroma	10140	
	Laceration repair, simple	120__	
	Site: ______ Size: ____		
✓	Laceration repair, layered	120__	
	Site: (R) Hd Size: 4.2cm		
	Laser Light Tx	96597	
	Lesion, biopsy, one	11100	
	Lesion, biopsy, each add'l	11101	
	Lesion, excision, benign	114__	
	Site: ______ Size: ____		
	Lesion, excision, malignant	116__	
	Site: ______ Size: ____		
	Lesion, paring/cutting, one	11055	
	Lesion, paring/cutting, 2-4	11056	
	Lesion, shave	113__	
	Site: ______ Size: ____		
	Nail removal, partial (+T mod)	11730	
	Nail rem, w/matrix (+T mod)	11750	
	Skin tag, 1-15	11200	
	Wart, flat, 1-14	17110	
	Destruction lesion, 1st	17000	
	Destruct lesion, each addl 2-14	17003	
	Medications		**Units**
	Ampicillin, up to 500mg	J0290	
	B-12, up to 1,000 mcg	J3420	
	Epinephrine, up to 1ml	J0170	
	Kenalog, 10mg	J3301	
✓	Lidocaine, 10mg	J2001	
	Normal saline, 1000cc	J7030	
	Phenergan, up to 50mg	J2550	
	Progesterone, 150mg	J1055	
	Rocephin, 250mg	J0696	
	Testosterone, 200mg	J1080	
	Tigan, up to 200 mg	J3250	
	Toradol, 15mg	J1885	
	Albuterol	J7609	
	Depo-Provera 50 mg	J1055	
	Depo-Medrol 40 mg	J1030	

Diagnoses	Code
1 Laceration (R) hand	
2 Crush injury finger nail	
3	
4	

Next office visit: 10 days

(Recheck) • Preventative • PRN

Referral to:

Physician signature

x Lance Murray MD

x	Laboratory		-90
	Venipuncture	36415	
	Blood glucose, monitoring device	82962	
	Blood glucose, visual dipstick	82948	
	CBC, w/ auto differential	85025	
	CBC, w/o auto differential	85027	
	Cholesterol	82465	
	Hemoccult, guaiac	82270	
	Hemoccult, immunoassay	82274	
	Hemoglobin A1C	85018	
	Lipid panel	80061	
	Liver panel	80076	
	KOH prep (skin, hair, nails)	87220	
	Metabolic panel, basic	80048	
	Metabolic panel, comprehensive	80053	
	Mononucleosis	86308	
	Pregnancy, blood	84703	
	Pregnancy, urine	81025	
	Renal panel	80069	
	Sedimentation rate	85651	
	Strep, rapid	86403	
	Strep culture	87081	
	Strep A	87880	
	TB	86580	
	UA, complete, non-automated	81000	
	UA, w/o micro, non-automated	81002	
	UA, w/ micro, non-automated	81003	
	Urine colony count	87086	
	Urine culture, presumptive	87088	
	Wet mount/KOH	87210	
	Vaccines		
	DT, <7 y		90702
	DTP		90701
	DtaP, <7 y		90700
	Flu, 6-35 months		90657
	Flu, 3 y +		90658
	Hep A, adult		90632
	Hep A, ped/adol, 2 dose		90633
	Hep B, adult		90746
	Hep B, ped/adol 3 dose		90744
	Hep B-Hib		90748
	Hib, 4 dose		90645
	HPV		90649
	IPV		90713
	MMR		90707
	Pneumonia, >2 y		90732
	Pneumonia conjugate, <5 y		90669
	Td, >7 y		90718
	Varicella		90716
	Tetanus toxoid adsorbed, IM		90703
	Immunizations & Injections		**Units**
	Allergen, one	95115	
	Allergen, multiple	95117	
	Imm admn <8 yo 1st Inj	90465	
	Imm admn <8 yo each add inj	90466	
	Imm <8 yo oral or intranasal	90467	
	Imm admn <8 yo each add	90468	
	Imm admin, one vacc	90471	
	Imm admin, each add'l	90472	
	Imm admin, intranasal, one	90473	
	Imm admin, intranasal, each add'l	90474	
	Injection, joint, small	20600	
	Injection, joint, intermediate	20605	
	Injection, ther/proph/diag	90772	
	Injection, trigger pt 1-2 musc	20552	

Today's charges:	
Today's payment:	
Balance due:	

Job 2 Router- Derek Wallace

Date of service: 10/27/09	Insurance: GALAXY HEALTH				Superbill Number: 2458
Patient name: WILLIAM KOSTNER	Coinsurance: 20%	Copay:			Physician Name: HEATH
Account #: KOS001	Noncovered Waiver?	yes	no	n/a	

x	Office visit	New	x	Est
	Minimal (RN only)			99211
	Problem focused	99201		99212
	Exp problem focused	99202		99213
	Detailed	99203		99214
	Comp	99204		99215
	Comprhen/Complex	99205		
	Well visit	**New**	**x**	**Est**
	< 1 y	99381		99391
	1-4 y	99382		99392
	5-11 y	99383		99393
	12-17 y	99384		99394
	18-39 y	99385		99395
	40-64 y	99386		99396
	65 y +	99387		99397
	Medicare preventive services			
	Pap			Q0091
	Pelvic & breast			G0101
	Prostate/PSA			G0103
	Tobacco couns/3-10 min			G0375
	Tobacco couns/>10 min			G0376
	Welcome to Medicare exam			G0344
	ECG w/Welcome to Medicare			G0366
	Hemoccult, guaiac			G0107
	Flu shot			G0008
	Pneumonia shot			G0009
	Consultation/preop clearance			
	Exp problem focused			99242
	Detailed			99243
✓	Comp/mod complex			99244
	Comp/high complex			99245
	Other services			
	After posted hours			99050
	Evening/weekend appointment			99051
	Home health certification			G0180
	Home health recertification			G0179
	Care Plan oversight			99374
	Care Plan Oversight >30 mins			99375
	Post-op follow-up			99024
	Prolonged/60min total			99354
	Prolonged/each add 30 mins			99355
	Special reports/forms			99080
	Disability/Workers comp			99455
	Smoking Cessation <10 mins			99406
	Smoking Cessation >10 mins			99407
	ETOH/SA screening <30 mins			99408
	Online E/M by MD			99444
	Phone E/M <10 mins			99441
	Phone E/M <20 mins			99442
	Phone E/M <30 mins			99443
	Anticoagulant Mgmt <90 days			99363
	Anticoagulant Mgmt >90 days			99364
	In office emergency serv			99058
	Other services			
	Supplies			
	Surgical Tray			99070
	Instructions:			

x	Office procedures		
	Cerumen removal		69210
	ECG, w/interpretation		93000
	ECG, rhythm strip		93040
	Endometrial biopsy		58100
	Fracture care, cast/splint		____
	Site: ______________		
	Nebulizer		94640
	Nebulizer demo		94664
	Spirometry		94010
	Spirometry, pre and post		94060
	Vasectomy		55250
	Skin procedures		**Units**
	Foreign body, skin, simple	10120	
	Foreign body, skin, complex	10121	
	I&D, abscess	10060	
	I&D, hematoma/seroma	10140	
	Laceration repair, simple	120__	
	Site: ________ Size: _____		
	Laceration repair, layered	120__	
	Site: ________ Size: _____		
	Laser Light Tx	96597	
	Lesion, biopsy, one	11100	
	Lesion, biopsy, each add'l	11101	
	Lesion, excision, benign	114__	
	Site: ________ Size: _____		
	Lesion, excision, malignant	116__	
	Site: ________ Size: _____		
	Lesion, paring/cutting, one	11055	
	Lesion, paring/cutting, 2-4	11056	
	Lesion, shave	113__	
	Site: ________ Size: _____		
	Nail removal, partial (+T mod)	11730	
	Nail rem, w/matrix (+T mod)	11750	
	Skin tag, 1-15	11200	
	Wart, flat, 1-14	17110	
	Destruction lesion, 1st	17000	
	Destruct lesion, each addl 2-14	17003	
	Medications		**Units**
	Ampicillin, up to 500mg	J0290	
	B-12, up to 1,000 mcg	J3420	
	Epinephrine, up to 1ml	J0170	
	Kenalog, 10mg	J3301	
✓	Lidocaine, 10mg	J2001	
	Normal saline, 1000cc	J7030	
	Phenergan, up to 50mg	J2550	
	Progesterone, 150mg	J1055	
	Rocephin, 250mg	J0696	
	Testosterone, 200mg	J1080	
	Tigan, up to 200 mg	J3250	
	Toradol, 15mg	J1885	
	Albuterol	J7609	
	Depo-Provera 50 mg	J1055	
✓	Depo-Medrol 40 mg	J1030	

Diagnoses		Code
1	Vertigo	
2	HA	
3	Myospasm	
4		

Next office visit: 4 wks

Recheck • Preventative • PRN

Referral to:

Physician signature

X [signature]

x	Laboratory		-90
	Venipuncture	36415	
	Blood glucose, monitoring device	82962	
	Blood glucose, visual dipstick	82948	
	CBC, w/ auto differential	85025	
	CBC, w/o auto differential	85027	
	Cholesterol	82465	
	Hemoccult, guaiac	82270	
	Hemoccult, immunoassay	82274	
	Hemoglobin A1C	85018	
	Lipid panel	80061	
	Liver panel	80076	
	KOH prep (skin, hair, nails)	87220	
	Metabolic panel, basic	80048	
	Metabolic panel, comprehensive	80053	
	Mononucleosis	86308	
	Pregnancy, blood	84703	
	Pregnancy, urine	81025	
	Renal panel	80069	
	Sedimentation rate	85651	
	Strep, rapid	86403	
	Strep culture	87081	
	Strep A	87880	
	TB	86580	
	UA, complete, non-automated	81000	
	UA, w/o micro, non-automated	81002	
	UA, w/ micro, non-automated	81003	
	Urine colony count	87086	
	Urine culture, presumptive	87088	
	Wet mount/KOH	87210	
	Vaccines		
	DT, <7 y		90702
	DTP		90701
	DtaP, <7 y		90700
	Flu, 6-35 months		90657
	Flu, 3 y +		90658
	Hep A, adult		90632
	Hep A, ped/adol, 2 dose		90633
	Hep B, adult		90746
	Hep B, ped/adol 3 dose		90744
	Hep B-Hib		90748
	Hib, 4 dose		90645
	HPV		90649
	IPV		90713
	MMR		90707
	Pneumonia, >2 y		90732
	Pneumonia conjugate, <5 y		90669
	Td, >7 y		90718
	Varicella		90716
	Tetanus toxoid adsorbed, IM		90703
	Immunizations & Injections		**Units**
	Allergen, one	95115	
	Allergen, multiple	95117	
	Imm admn <8 yo 1st Inj	90465	
	Imm admn <8 yo each add inj	90466	
	Imm <8 yo oral or intranasal	90467	
	Imm admn <8 yo each add	90468	
	Imm admn, one vacc	90471	
	Imm admn, each add'l	90472	
	Imm admn, intranasal, one	90473	
	Imm admn, intranasal, each add'l	90474	
	Injection, joint, small	20600	
	Injection, joint, intermediate	20605	
	Injection, ther/proph/diag	90772	
✓	Injection, trigger pt 1-2 musc	20552	

Today's charges:		
Today's payment:		
Balance due:		

Job 3 Router- William Kostner

10/27/xx

HPI: William Kostner was injured at work. He works in the warehouse and was driving a fork lift when a crate unknowingly broke free. He drove over it and was ejected from his seat. He hit his head on the floor, suffering whiplash. He states he never lost consciousness and was wearing a helmet. Evaluation in the New York County ER was positive for concussion. He has not returned to work because he has intermittent debilitating headaches, back spasms, and vertigo and is not cleared by the company doctor to drive a fork lift. Up to this point, William did not have a family physician.

PAST MEDICAL HISTORY: Negative. He is allergic to nuts. He takes 150 mg of Ultram daily along with Flexeril as needed. He also takes Lipitor for his cholesterol.

FAMILY HISTORY: Both parents are still living. History of CVD in father. Maternal aunt had multiple sclerosis.

SOCIAL HISTORY: Married for 25 yrs. Two children. Nonsmoker. Drinks a beer a day.

ROS:

ENT: Slight hearing loss with ringing in both ears.

Neuro: Headaches daily, no changes in speech, dizziness particularly in the morning or riding in the car.

MS: No joint pain, swelling, or weakness. Back spasms.

CV: No chest pain, no numbness in extremities, no palpitations.

EXAM:

BP: 138/75 Weight: 225 lb Height: 6'1".

HEENT: Normal, pupils equal and reactive. No lesions or masses palpated. Thyroid normal.

Chest: Normal. Normal S1. No wheezing.

Abdomen: No masses or tenderness.

Back: Spasm of mid-back T2–T4.

Extremities: No weakness or tenderness bilaterally. No edema.

Neuro: Slight decreased sensation in fingers.

ASSESSMENT: Cervical vertigo, headaches, myospasm.

PLAN: PT twice a week for six weeks.

Trigger point injection.

Addition of Zanaflex for myospasm.

Return in 4 weeks.

PROCEDURE NOTE:

Patient was taken to the minor procedure room and placed in the supine position. One mL Lidocaine mixed with 1 mL triamcinolone acetonide 40 mg/mL and 1mL dexamethasone 4mg/mL were injected in the soft tissue of the T2–T4 areas using a 1-inch 25-gauge needle. The area was infiltrated repeatedly, withdrawing and redirecting the needle in a 2-cm circle. Patient tolerated procedure well.

L.D. Heath, MD

Job 3 Progress Note- William Kostner

Douglasville Medicine Associates

HOSPITAL CHARGE SHEET

☐Sarah Mendenhall, M.D. ☒D.J. Schwartrz, M.D. ☐L.D. Heath, M.D.
☐Sally Kemper, M.D. ☐Alberta Lynn, P.A.C. ☐Lance Murray, M.D.

Patient's Name: Robert Shinn **Date(s) of Service:** 10/27/09

Place of Service: ☐ New York County Hospital ☐Community General Hospital ☐Beaufort Regional Hospital ☒County Memorial Hospital

Hospital Visit Type: ☐Observation ☐Inpatient ☐Subsequent Visit ☒Emergency Room ☐Consultation ☐Initial Admission ☐Discharge Planning ☐Critical Care

Insurance Carrier: Signal HMO **Insurance ID#** ____________

Diagnosis/ICD-9: Gastroenteritis, Bactrim Allergy

Procedure/Service Performed/CPT:
Pt seen in ER N/V (gradual onset). Tx w/ Bactrim by Dr Heath for rash 10/26/09. Moderate Nausea - vomited 1-2 x last 24 hrs. Diarrhea. ⊖ blood in stool. Rash + Apparent spider bite visualized by me. ⊖ SOB. Complains of fatigue. HR 108 NKDA. Mother said rash worse than yesterday. HEENT, Heart, Lungs, Normal. He is alert + oriented x 3. ROS - GU - normal, RESP - OK, no fever, GI - diarrhea. Stop Bactrim. Motrin prn for aches. Phenergan 25 mg IM, Rx 25 mg P.O. Q 8 #12

Signature: DJ Schwartz MD **Date given to biller:** 10/28/09

Notes: F/U w/ Heath. Discharged to home - stable

Job 5 Hospital Charge Sheet- Robert Shinn 1 of 10

Douglasville Medicine Associates

HOSPITAL CHARGE SHEET

☐Sarah Mendenhall, M.D. ☐Sally Kemper, M.D.
☐D.J. Schwartrz, M.D. ☐Alberta Lynn, P.A.C.
☐L.D. Heath, M.D. ☐Lance Murray, M.D.

Patient's Name: Manuel Ramirez **Date(s) of Service:** 10/24 -10/26/09

Place of Service: ☐ New York County Hospital ☐Community General Hospital

☐Beaufort Regional Hospital ☐County Memorial Hospital

Hospital Visit Type: ☐Observation ☐Inpatient ☐Subsequent Visit ☐Emergency Room

☐Consultation ☐Initial Admission ☐Discharge Planning ☐Critical Care

Insurance Carrier: Medicare **Insurance ID#** __________

Diagnosis/ICD-9: Abd pain Rectal Bleeding IBS Erosive gastritis

Procedure/Service Performed/CPT:
Pt Adm for eval of Abd pain, N/V, + emesis by Dr Ramsey. Shortly after EGD + colonoscopy (10/22/09) Pt developed LUQ pain + hematemesis. He was Adm to GI specialty, I was asked to follow pt for medical maintenance.

Signature: LD Heath MD **Date given to biller:** 10/27/09

Notes:
10/25 SUBSEQ VISIT
10/26 SUBSEQ VISIT

Job 5 Hospital Charge Sheet- Manual Ramirez 2 of 10

Douglasville Medicine Associates

HOSPITAL CHARGE SHEET

☐Sarah Mendenhall, M.D.
☐D.J. Schwartrz, M.D.
☒L.D. Heath, M.D.

☐Sally Kemper, M.D.
☐Alberta Lynn, P.A.C.
☐Lance Murray, M.D.

Patient's Name: CAROLINE PRATT **Date(s) of Service:** 10/25 - 10/26

Place of Service: ☒New York County Hospital ☐Community General Hospital

☐Beaufort Regional Hospital ☐County Memorial Hospital

Hospital Visit Type: ☐Observation ☐Inpatient ☐Subsequent Visit ☐Emergency Room

☐Consultation ☐Initial Admission ☐Discharge Planning ☒Critical Care

Insurance Carrier: SELF **Insurance ID#** ______

Diagnosis/ICD-9: SUICIDE ATTEMPT, CARBON MONOXIDE INHALATION POISONING, CARDIAC ARREST - RESOLVED

Procedure/Service Performed/CPT:
ER SERVICE CALLED ME AT 6:30 PM 10/25 + GAVE ME A REPORT. PT WAS TRANSPORTED TO THE ER VIA LIFE-FLIGHT. PT WAS INTUBATED + RESUSCITATED. I ARRIVED AT THE ER AT 6:30 + ASSUMED CARE. WHILE PREPARING FOR TRANSFER TO ICU PT WENT INTO CARDIAC ARREST. SHE WAS DEFIBRILLATED X2. SHE WAS TRANSFERRED

Signature: LD Heath **Date given to biller:** 10/27/09

TO ICU IN UNSTABLE CONDITION WHERE I STAYED IN CONSTANT ATTENDANCE UNTIL 8:00 PM.

Notes:
I WAS CALLED BACK TO ICU @ 1:00 AM BECAUSE PTS CONDITION WORSENED WHERE I STAYED IN CONSTANT ATTENDANCE UNTIL 2:00 AM WHEN SHE STABILIZED

Job 5 Hospital Charge Sheet- Caroline Pratt 3 of 10

Douglasville Medicine Associates

HOSPITAL CHARGE SHEET

☐Sarah Mendenhall, M.D.
☐D.J. Schwartrz, M.D.
☑L.D. Heath, M.D.

☐Sally Kemper, M.D.
☐Alberta Lynn, P.A.C.
☐Lance Murray, M.D.

Patient's Name: Tina Rizzo **Date(s) of Service:** 10/26/09

Place of Service: ☐ New York County Hospital ☐Community General Hospital ☐Beaufort Regional Hospital ☑County Memorial Hospital

Hospital Visit Type: ☐Observation ☐Inpatient ☐Subsequent Visit ☑Emergency Room ☐Consultation ☐Initial Admission ☐Discharge Planning ☐Critical Care

Insurance Carrier: Consumer One **Insurance ID#** ____________

Diagnosis/ICD-9: ____________

Procedure/Service Performed/CPT: Pt seen in ER. Complained of severe flank pain, N/V, dysuria. On exam Abd non-tender w/o masses. Discomfort to suprapubic palpation. U/S showed adnexal torsion findings also consistent w/ cystourethritis. 99284

Signature: LD Heath **Date given to biller:** 10/27/09

Notes:

Job 5 Hospital Charge Sheet- Tina Rizzo 4 of 10

Douglasville Medicine Associates

HOSPITAL CHARGE SHEET

☐Sarah Mendenhall, M.D.
☐D.J. Schwartrz, M.D.
☑L.D. Heath, M.D.

☐Sally Kemper, M.D.
☐Alberta Lynn, P.A.C.
☐Lance Murray, M.D.

Patient's Name: JOHN CONWAY **Date(s) of Service:** 10/24/09

Place of Service: ☑New York County Hospital ☐Community General Hospital

☐Beaufort Regional Hospital ☐County Memorial Hospital

Hospital Visit Type: ☐Observation ☐Inpatient ☐Subsequent Visit ☐Emergency Room

☑Consultation ☐Initial Admission ☐Discharge Planning ☐Critical Care

Insurance Carrier: CONSUMER ONE **Insurance ID#** ____________

Diagnosis/ICD-9: Abd pain, R/O gallstone vs bowel obstr.

Procedure/Service Performed/CPT:
Pt adx by Schwartz on 10/23/09 on call coverage.
GI consult ordered.

Signature: LD Heath **Date given to biller:** 10/27/09

Notes:

Job 5 Hospital Charge Sheet- John Conway 5 of 10

Douglasville Medicine Associates

HOSPITAL CHARGE SHEET

☐Sarah Mendenhall, M.D.
☐D.J. Schwartrz, M.D.
☒L.D. Heath, M.D.
☐Sally Kemper, M.D.
☐Alberta Lynn, P.A.C.
☐Lance Murray, M.D.

Patient's Name: DAVID JAMES **Date(s) of Service:** 10/19/09

Place of Service: ☒New York County Hospital ☐Community General Hospital ☐Beaufort Regional Hospital ☐County Memorial Hospital

Hospital Visit Type: ☒Observation ☐Inpatient ☐Subsequent Visit ☐Emergency Room ☐Consultation ☐Initial Admission ☐Discharge Planning ☐Critical Care

Insurance Carrier: SIGNAL HMO **Insurance ID#** ____________

Diagnosis/ICD-9: Type I DM Uncontrolled R/O diabetic Ketoacidosis.

Procedure/Service Performed/CPT: PT experienced dizziness + disorientation. His mother called + reported he has been drinking + not taking his insulin regularly. Glucose was 350. I admitted him to OBS w/ IV fluids + short acting insulin. 99219

Signature: LD Heath **Date given to biller:** 10/26/09

Notes:

Job 5 Hospital Charge Sheet- David James 6 of 10

Douglasville Medicine Associates

HOSPITAL CHARGE SHEET

☑ Sarah Mendenhall, M.D.
☐ D.J. Schwartrz, M.D.
☐ L.D. Heath, M.D.
☐ Sally Kemper, M.D.
☐ Alberta Lynn, P.A.C.
☐ Lance Murray, M.D.

Patient's Name: Francesco Alvarez **Date(s) of Service:** 10/26/09

Place of Service: ☑ New York County Hospital ☐ Community General Hospital ☐ Beaufort Regional Hospital ☐ County Memorial Hospital

Hospital Visit Type: ☑ Observation ~~☑ Inpatient~~ ☐ Subsequent Visit ☐ Emergency Room ☐ Consultation ☑ Initial Admission ☐ Discharge Planning ☐ Critical Care

Insurance Carrier: FlexiHealth PPO **Insurance ID#** __________

Diagnosis/ICD-9: N/V, fatigue, heart palpitations
Tachycardia

Procedure/Service Performed/CPT: 99220
10/26 - Adx Obs - telemetry, cardiology consult ordered
10/27 - Subseq visit

Signature: Sarah Mendenhall MD **Date given to biller:** 10/28/09

Notes:

Job 5 Hospital Charge Sheet- Francesco Alvarez 7 of 10

Douglasville Medicine Associates

HOSPITAL CHARGE SHEET

☐Sarah Mendenhall, M.D.
☐D.J. Schwartrz, M.D.
☐L.D. Heath, M.D.
☑Sally Kemper, M.D.
☐Alberta Lynn, P.A.C.
☐Lance Murray, M.D.

Patient's Name: Deanne Lloyd **Date(s) of Service:** 10/12/09

Place of Service: ☑New York County Hospital ☐Community General Hospital ☐Beaufort Regional Hospital ☐County Memorial Hospital

Hospital Visit Type: ☐Observation ☐Inpatient ☐Subsequent Visit ☐Emergency Room ☐Consultation ☐Initial Admission ☐Discharge Planning ☐Critical Care

Insurance Carrier: ______ **Insurance ID#** ______

Diagnosis/ICD-9: Asthma acute exacerbation, URI, fever

Procedure/Service Performed/CPT:
Pt seen in ER for 2 day h/o cough + rhinorrhea + congestion. Now c/o chest tightness. Pt is asthmatic + takes Albuterol + Flovent. Pt also has SC trait. Pt rec'vd Albuterol @ 1400 + Flovent @ 1500 w/ slight relief of tightness. Pt has fever of 100.9. NKDA. Pt does not smoke. ROS - eyes, ENT, CV, GI, GU, MS, Skin, Neuro, Endo, Psych - All WNL. Pt has obvious rhinorrhea + looks ill but in NAD.

Signature: Sally Kemper **Date given to biller:** 10/24/09

HEENT - clear nasal drainage. Neck - NML. Chest (B) wheezes - expiratory. Heart - RRR. Extrem - no cyanosis or edema. Neuro - NML. Skin - warm + dry.

Notes:
Respiratory performed peak flows + nebulizer tx + Asthma education.

Job 5 Hospital Charge Sheet- Deanne Lloyd 8 of 10

Douglasville Medicine Associates

HOSPITAL CHARGE SHEET

☒Sarah Mendenhall, M.D.
☐D.J. Schwartrz, M.D.
☐L.D. Heath, M.D.
☐Sally Kemper, M.D.
☐Alberta Lynn, P.A.C.
☐Lance Murray, M.D.

Patient's Name: Diane Parker **Date(s) of Service:** 10/25/09

Place of Service: ☒New York County Hospital ☐Community General Hospital ☐Beaufort Regional Hospital ☐County Memorial Hospital

Hospital Visit Type: ☐Observation ☐Inpatient ☐Subsequent Visit ☐Emergency Room ☐Consultation ☒Initial Admission ☐Discharge Planning ☐Critical Care

Insurance Carrier: Flexi Health PPO **Insurance ID#** __________

Diagnosis/ICD-9: DVT

Procedure/Service Performed/CPT:
Pt went to ER for pain + swelling in her (L) lower leg. ER service called me after performing doppler in ER stating she required adm for DVT & further w/u. Adm w/ IV Heparin drip, ECHO, chest x-ray, D-dimer, Chem 7, PT + INR, + CBC.

Signature: Sarah Mendenhall MD **Date given to biller:** 10/26/09

Notes: 99220

Job 5 Hospital Charge Sheet- Diane Parker 9 of 10

Douglasville Medicine Associates

HOSPITAL CHARGE SHEET

☐Sarah Mendenhall, M.D.
☐D.J. Schwartrz, M.D.
☐L.D. Heath, M.D.
☒Sally Kemper, M.D.
☐Alberta Lynn, P.A.C.
☐Lance Murray, M.D.

Patient's Name: Abbey Taylor **Date(s) of Service:** 10/27/09

Place of Service: ☐ New York County Hospital ☒Community General Hospital

☐Beaufort Regional Hospital ☐County Memorial Hospital

Hospital Visit Type: ☐Observation ☐Inpatient ☐Subsequent Visit ☐Emergency Room

☒Consultation ☐Initial Admission ☐Discharge Planning ☐Critical Care

Insurance Carrier: SIGNAL HMO **Insurance ID#** 87135249

Diagnosis/ICD-9: Sarcoidosis, Erythema Nodosum

Procedure/Service Performed/CPT:
I was asked to consult on this pt by Dr. Ramsey to render an opinion + confirm his initial Dx + treatment plan. 99254

Signature: Sally Kemper MD **Date given to biller:** 10/28/09

Notes:
PT DOB- 3/14/59
ADDRESS - 3121 Line Dr, Douglasville, NY

Job 5 Hospital Charge Sheet- Abbey Taylor 10 of 10

Date of service:	Insurance:		Router Number:
Patient name:	Coinsurance:	Copay:	Physician Name:
Account #:	Noncovered Waiver?	yes / no / n/a	

X	Office visit	New	X	Est
N/A	Minimal (RN only)	N/A		99211
	Problem focused	99201		99212
	Exp problem focused	99202		99213
	Detailed	99203		99214
	Comp	99204		99215
	Comprhen/Complex	99205		
	Well visit	**New**	**X**	**Est**
	< 1 y	99381		99391
	1-4 y	99382		99392
	5-11 y	99383		99393
	12-17 y	99384		99394
	18-39 y	99385		99395
	40-64 y	99386		99396
	65 y +	99387		99397

X	Medicare preventive services	
	Pap	Q0091
	Pelvic & breast	G0101
	Prostate/PSA	G0103
	Tobacco couns/3-10 min	G0375
	Tobacco couns/>10 min	G0376
	Welcome to Medicare exam	G0344
	ECG w/Welcome to Medicare	G0366
	Hemoccult, guaiac	G0107
	Flu shot	G0008
	Pneumonia shot	G0009
	Consultation/preop clearance	
	Exp problem focused	99242
	Detailed	99243
	Comp/mod complex	99244
	Comp/high complex	99245
	Other services	
	After posted hours	99050
	Evening/weekend appointment	99051
	Home health certification	G0180
	Home health recertification	G0179
	Care Plan oversight	99374
	Care Plan Oversight >30 mins	99375
	Post-op follow-up	99024
	Prolonged/60min total	99354
	Prolonged/each add 30 mins	99355
	Special reports/forms	99080
	Disability/Workers comp	99455
	Smoking Cessation <10 mins	99406
	Smoking Cessation >10 mins	99407
	ETOH/SA screening <30 mins	99408
	Online E/M by MD	99444
	Phone E/M <10 mins	99441
	Phone E/M <20 mins	99442
	Phone E/M <30 mins	99443
	Anticoagulant Mgmt <90 days	99363
	Anticoagulant Mgmt >90 days	99364
	In office emergency serv	99058
	Other services	
	Supplies	
	Surgical Tray	99070

Instructions:

X	Office procedures		
	Cerumen removal		69210
	ECG, w/interpretation		93000
	ECG, rhythm strip		93040
	Endometrial biopsy		58100
	Fracture care, cast/splint Site: ______________		
	Nebulizer		94640
	Nebulizer demo		94664
	Spirometry		94010
	Spirometry, pre and post		94060
	Vasectomy		55250
	Skin procedures		**Units**
	Foreign body, skin, simple	10120	
	Foreign body, skin, complex	10121	
	I&D, abscess	10060	
	I&D, hematoma/seroma	10140	
	Laceration repair, simple Site: _______ Size: _____	120__	
	Laceration repair, layered Site: _______ Size: _____	120__	
	Laser Light Tx	96597	
	Lesion, biopsy, one	11100	
	Lesion, biopsy, each add'l	11101	
	Lesion, excision, benign Site: _______ Size: _____	114__	
	Lesion, excision, malignant Site: _______ Size: _____	116__	
	Lesion, paring/cutting, one	11055	
	Lesion, paring/cutting, 2-4	11056	
	Lesion, shave Site: _______ Size: _____	113__	
	Nail removal, partial (+T mod)	11730	
	Nail rem, w/matrix (+T mod)	11750	
	Skin tag, 1-15	11200	
	Wart, flat, 1-14	17110	
	Destruction lesion, 1st	17000	
	Destruct lesion, each addl 2-14	17003	
	Medications		**Units**
	Ampicillin, up to 500mg	J0290	
	B-12, up to 1,000 mcg	J3420	
	Epinephrine, up to 1ml	J0170	
	Kenalog, 10mg	J3301	
	Lidocaine, 10mg	J2001	
	Normal saline, 1000cc	J7030	
	Phenergan, up to 50mg	J2550	
	Progesterone, 150mg	J1055	
	Rocephin, 250mg	J0696	
	Testosterone, 200mg	J1080	
	Tigan, up to 200 mg	J3250	
	Toradol, 15mg	J1885	
	Albuterol	J7609	
	Depo-Provera 50 mg	J1055	
	Depo-Medrol 40 mg	J1030	

Diagnoses	Code
1	
2	
3	
4	

Next office visit:

Recheck • Preventative • PRN

Referral to:

Physician signature

X ______________________________

X	Laboratory		-90
	Venipuncture	36415	
	Blood glucose, monitoring device	82962	
	Blood glucose, visual dipstick	82948	
	CBC, w/ auto differential	85025	
	CBC, w/o auto differential	85027	
	Cholesterol	82465	
	Hemoccult, guaiac	82270	
	Hemoccult, immunoassay	82274	
	Hemoglobin A1C	85018	
	Lipid panel	80061	
	Liver panel	80076	
	KOH prep (skin, hair, nails)	87220	
	Metabolic panel, basic	80048	
	Metabolic panel, comprehensive	80053	
	Mononucleosis	86308	
	Pregnancy, blood	84703	
	Pregnancy, urine	81025	
	Renal panel	80069	
	Sedimentation rate	85651	
	Strep, rapid	86403	
	Strep culture	87081	
	Strep A	87880	
	TB	86580	
	UA, complete, non-automated	81000	
	UA, w/o micro, non-automated	81002	
	UA, w/ micro, non-automated	81003	
	Urine colony count	87086	
	Urine culture, presumptive	87088	
	Wet mount/KOH	87210	
	Vaccines		
	DT, <7 y		90702
	DTP		90701
	DtaP, <7 y		90700
	Flu, 6-35 months		90657
	Flu, 3 y +		90658
	Hep A, adult		90632
	Hep A, ped/adol, 2 dose		90633
	Hep B, adult		90746
	Hep B, ped/adol 3 dose		90744
	Hep B-Hib		90748
	Hib, 4 dose		90645
	HPV		90649
	IPV		90713
	MMR		90707
	Pneumonia, >2 y		90732
	Pneumonia conjugate, <5 y		90669
	Td, >7 y		90718
	Varicella		90716
	Tetanus toxoid adsorbed, IM		90703
	Immunizations & Injections		**Units**
	Allergen, one	95115	
	Allergen, multiple	95117	
	Imm admn <8 yo 1st Inj	90465	
	Imm admn <8 yo each add inj	90466	
	Imm <8 yo oral or intranasal	90467	
	Imm admn <8 yo each add	90468	
	Imm admin, one vacc	90471	
	Imm admin, each add'l	90472	
	Imm admin, intranasal, one	90473	
	Imm admin, intranasal, each add'l	90474	
	Injection, joint, small	20600	
	Injection, joint, intermediate	20605	
	Injection, ther/proph/diag	90772	
	Injection, trigger pt 1-2 musc	20552	

Today's charges:		
Today's payment:		
Balance due:		

Job 7 DMA Router

Date of service: 10/27/09	Insurance: AETNA				Superbill Number: 2452
Patient name: SAMANTHA BEECHWOOD	Coinsurance: 25%	Copay:			Physician Name: SCHWARTZ
Account #: BEE001	Noncovered Waiver?	yes	no	n/a	

x	Office visit	New	x	Est
	Minimal (RN only)			99211
	Problem focused	99201		99212
	Exp problem focused	99202		99213
	Detailed	99203		99214
✓	Comp	99204		99215
	Comprhen/Complex	99205		
	Well visit	**New**	**x**	**Est**
	< 1 y	99381		99391
	1-4 y	99382		99392
	5-11 y	99383		99393
	12-17 y	99384		99394
	18-39 y	99385		99395
	40-64 y	99386		99396
	65 y +	99387		99397
	Medicare preventive services			
	Pap			Q0091
	Pelvic & breast			G0101
	Prostate/PSA			G0103
	Tobacco couns/3-10 min			G0375
	Tobacco couns/>10 min			G0376
	Welcome to Medicare exam			G0344
	ECG w/Welcome to Medicare			G0366
	Hemoccult, guaiac			G0107
	Flu shot			G0008
	Pneumonia shot			G0009
	Consultation/preop clearance			
	Exp problem focused			99242
	Detailed			99243
	Comp/mod complex			99244
	Comp/high complex			99245
	Other services			
	After posted hours			99050
	Evening/weekend appointment			99051
	Home health certification			G0180
	Home health recertification			G0179
	Care Plan oversight			99374
	Care Plan Oversight >30 mins			99375
	Post-op follow-up			99024
	Prolonged/60min total			99354
	Prolonged/each add 30 mins			99355
	Special reports/forms			99080
	Disability/Workers comp			99455
	Smoking Cessation <10 mins			99406
	Smoking Cessation >10 mins			99407
	ETOH/SA screening <30 mins			99408
	Online E/M by MD			99444
	Phone E/M <10 mins			99441
	Phone E/M <20 mins			99442
	Phone E/M <30 mins			99443
	Anticoagulant Mgmt <90 days			99363
	Anticoagulant Mgmt >90 days			99364
	In office emergency serv			99058
	Other services			
✓	AP + Lateral Shoulder xray			
✓	Injection @ shoulder			
	Supplies			
	Surgical Tray			99070
	Strapping @ shoulder			

x	Office procedures	
	Cerumen removal	69210
	ECG, w/interpretation	93000
	ECG, rhythm strip	93040
	Endometrial biopsy	58100
	Fracture care, cast/splint Site: ______	
	Nebulizer	94640
	Nebulizer demo	94664
	Spirometry	94010
	Spirometry, pre and post	94060
	Vasectomy	55250

x	Skin procedures		Units
	Foreign body, skin, simple	10120	
	Foreign body, skin, complex	10121	
	I&D, abscess	10060	
	I&D, hematoma/seroma	10140	
	Laceration repair, simple Site: ______ Size: ____	120__	
	Laceration repair, layered Site: ______ Size: ____	120__	
	Laser Light Tx	96597	
	Lesion, biopsy, one	11100	
	Lesion, biopsy, each add'l	11101	
	Lesion, excision, benign Site: ______ Size: ____	114__	
	Lesion, excision, malignant Site: ______ Size: ____	116__	
	Lesion, paring/cutting, one	11055	
	Lesion, paring/cutting, 2-4	11056	
	Lesion, shave Site: ______ Size: ____	113__	
	Nail removal, partial (+T mod)	11730	
	Nail rem, w/matrix (+T mod)	11750	
	Skin tag, 1-15	11200	
	Wart, flat, 1-14	17110	
	Destruction lesion, 1st	17000	
	Destruct lesion, each addl 2-14	17003	

x	Medications		Units
	Ampicillin, up to 500mg	J0290	
	B-12, up to 1,000 mcg	J3420	
	Epinephrine, up to 1ml	J0170	
	Kenalog, 10mg	J3301	
✓	Lidocaine, 10mg	J2001	
	Normal saline, 1000cc	J7030	
	Phenergan, up to 50mg	J2550	
	Progesterone, 150mg	J1055	
	Rocephin, 250mg	J0696	
	Testosterone, 200mg	J1080	
	Tigan, up to 200 mg	J3250	
	Toradol, 15mg	J1885	
	Albuterol	J7609	
	Depo-Provera 50 mg	J1055	
✓	Depo-Medrol 40 mg	J1030	

Diagnoses	Code
1 Rt shoulder pain/ Strain	
2 Rt Shoulder dislocation	
3	
4	

x	Laboratory		-90
	Venipuncture	36415	
	Blood glucose, monitoring device	82962	
	Blood glucose, visual dipstick	82948	
	CBC, w/ auto differential	85025	
	CBC, w/o auto differential	85027	
	Cholesterol	82465	
	Hemoccult, guaiac	82270	
	Hemoccult, immunoassay	82274	
	Hemoglobin A1C	85018	
	Lipid panel	80061	
	Liver panel	80076	
	KOH prep (skin, hair, nails)	87220	
	Metabolic panel, basic	80048	
	Metabolic panel, comprehensive	80053	
	Mononucleosis	86308	
	Pregnancy, blood	84703	
	Pregnancy, urine	81025	
	Renal panel	80069	
	Sedimentation rate	85651	
	Strep, rapid	86403	
	Strep culture	87081	
	Strep A	87880	
	TB	86580	
	UA, complete, non-automated	81000	
	UA, w/o micro, non-automated	81002	
	UA, w/ micro, non-automated	81003	
	Urine colony count	87086	
	Urine culture, presumptive	87088	
	Wet mount/KOH	87210	

x	Vaccines	
	DT, <7 y	90702
	DTP	90701
	DtaP, <7 y	90700
	Flu, 6-35 months	90657
	Flu, 3 y +	90658
	Hep A, adult	90632
	Hep A, ped/adol, 2 dose	90633
	Hep B, adult	90746
	Hep B, ped/adol 3 dose	90744
	Hep B-Hib	90748
	Hib, 4 dose	90645
	HPV	90649
	IPV	90713
	MMR	90707
	Pneumonia, >2 y	90732
	Pneumonia conjugate, <5 y	90669
	Td, >7 y	90718
	Varicella	90716
	Tetanus toxoid adsorbed, IM	90703

x	Immunizations & Injections		Units
	Allergen, one	95115	
	Allergen, multiple	95117	
	Imm admn <8 yo 1st Inj	90465	
	Imm admn <8 yo each add inj	90466	
	Imm <8 yo oral or intranasal	90467	
	Imm admn <8 yo each add	90468	
	Imm admin, one vacc	90471	
	Imm admin, each add'l	90472	
	Imm admin, intranasal, one	90473	
	Imm admin, intranasal, each add'l	90474	
	Injection, joint, small	20600	
	Injection, joint, intermediate	20605	
	Injection, ther/proph/diag	90772	
	Injection, trigger pt 1-2 musc	20552	

Instructions: Keep shoulder strapped for 5 days.

Next office visit:
Recheck • Preventative • PRN

Referral to: Dr. Alston - orthopedics

Physician signature
X DO Schwartz MD

Today's charges:		
Today's payment:		
Balance due:		

Job 10 Router- Samantha Beechwood

Date of service: 10/26/09	Insurance: FLEXIHEALTH			Router #: 1497
Patient name: FRANCESCO ALVAREZ	Coinsurance:	Copay: 20.00		Physician Name: MENDENHALL
Account #: ALV001	Noncovered Waiver?	yes	no	n/a

x	Office visit	New	x	Est
	Minimal (RN only)			99211
	Problem focused	99201		99212
	Exp problem focused	99202		99213
	Detailed	99203		99214
	Comp	99204	✓	99215
	Comprhen/Complex	99205		
	Well visit	**New**	**x**	**Est**
	< 1 y	99381		99391
	1-4 y	99382		99392
	5-11 y	99383		99393
	12-17 y	99384		99394
	18-39 y	99385		99395
	40-64 y	99386		99396
	65 y +	99387		99397

x	Medicare preventive services	
	Pap	Q0091
	Pelvic & breast	G0101
	Prostate/PSA	G0103
	Tobacco couns/3-10 min	G0375
	Tobacco couns/>10 min	G0376
	Welcome to Medicare exam	G0344
	ECG w/Welcome to Medicare	G0366
	Hemoccult, guaiac	G0107
	Flu shot	G0008
	Pneumonia shot	G0009
	Consultation/preop clearance	
	Exp problem focused	99242
	Detailed	99243
	Comp/mod complex	99244
	Comp/high complex	99245
	Other services	
	After posted hours	99050
	Evening/weekend appointment	99051
	Home health certification	G0180
	Home health recertification	G0179
	Care Plan oversight	99374
	Care Plan Oversight >30 mins	99375
	Post-op follow-up	99024
	Prolonged/60min total	99354
	Prolonged/each add 30 mins	99355
	Special reports/forms	99080
	Disability/Workers comp	99455
	Smoking Cessation <10 mins	99406
	Smoking Cessation >10 mins	99407
	ETOH/SA screening <30 mins	99408
	Online E/M by MD	99444
	Phone E/M <10 mins	99441
	Phone E/M <20 mins	99442
	Phone E/M <30 mins	99443
	Anticoagulant Mgmt <90 days	99363
	Anticoagulant Mgmt >90 days	99364
	In office emergency serv	99058
	Other services	
	Supplies	
	Surgical Tray	99070

Instructions: Adx to observation today

x	Office procedures		
	Cerumen removal	69210	
✓	ECG, w/interpretation	93000	
	ECG, rhythm strip	93040	
	Endometrial biopsy	58100	
	Fracture care, cast/splint Site: ________	____	
	Nebulizer	94640	
	Nebulizer demo	94664	
	Spirometry	94010	
	Spirometry, pre and post	94060	
	Vasectomy	55250	
	Skin procedures		**Units**
	Foreign body, skin, simple	10120	
	Foreign body, skin, complex	10121	
	I&D, abscess	10060	
	I&D, hematoma/seroma	10140	
	Laceration repair, simple Site: ______ Size: _____	120__	
	Laceration repair, layered Site: ______ Size: _____	120__	
	Laser Light Tx	96597	
	Lesion, biopsy, one	11100	
	Lesion, biopsy, each add'l	11101	
	Lesion, excision, benign Site: ______ Size: _____	114__	
	Lesion, excision, malignant Site: ______ Size: _____	116__	
	Lesion, paring/cutting, one	11055	
	Lesion, paring/cutting, 2-4	11056	
	Lesion, shave Site: ______ Size: _____	113__	
	Nail removal, partial (+T mod)	11730	
	Nail rem, w/matrix (+T mod)	11750	
	Skin tag, 1-15	11200	
	Wart, flat, 1-14	17110	
	Destruction lesion, 1st	17000	
	Destruct lesion, each addl 2-14	17003	
	Medications		**Units**
	Ampicillin, up to 500mg	J0290	
	B-12, up to 1,000 mcg	J3420	
	Epinephrine, up to 1ml	J0170	
	Kenalog, 10mg	J3301	
	Lidocaine, 10mg	J2001	
	Normal saline, 1000cc	J7030	
	Phenergan, up to 50mg	J2550	
	Progesterone, 150mg	J1055	
	Rocephin, 250mg	J0696	
	Testosterone, 200mg	J1080	
	Tigan, up to 200 mg	J3250	
	Toradol, 15mg	J1885	
	Albuterol	J7609	
	Depo-Provera 50 mg	J1055	
	Depo-Medrol 40 mg	J1030	

Diagnoses	Code
1 A fib	
2 ATN	
3	
4	

Next office visit:
Recheck • Preventative • PRN

Referral to:

Physician signature

x Sarah Mendenhall MD

x	Laboratory		-90
✓	Venipuncture	36415	
	Blood glucose, monitoring device	82962	
	Blood glucose, visual dipstick	82948	
✓	CBC, w/ auto differential	85025	
	CBC, w/o auto differential	85027	
	Cholesterol	82465	
	Hemoccult, guaiac	82270	
	Hemoccult, immunoassay	82274	
	Hemoglobin A1C	85018	
	Lipid panel	80061	
	Liver panel	80076	
	KOH prep (skin, hair, nails)	87220	
	Metabolic panel, basic	80048	
✓	Metabolic panel, comprehensive	80053	
	Mononucleosis	86308	
	Pregnancy, blood	84703	
	Pregnancy, urine	81025	
	Renal panel	80069	
	Sedimentation rate	85651	
	Strep, rapid	86403	
	Strep culture	87081	
	Strep A	87880	
	TB	86580	
	UA, complete, non-automated	81000	
	UA, w/o micro, non-automated	81002	
	UA, w/ micro, non-automated	81003	
	Urine colony count	87086	
	Urine culture, presumptive	87088	
	Wet mount/KOH	87210	

x	Vaccines	
	DT, <7 y	90702
	DTP	90701
	DtaP, <7 y	90700
	Flu, 6-35 months	90657
	Flu, 3 y +	90658
	Hep A, adult	90632
	Hep A, ped/adol, 2 dose	90633
	Hep B, adult	90746
	Hep B, ped/adol 3 dose	90744
	Hep B-Hib	90748
	Hib, 4 dose	90645
	HPV	90649
	IPV	90713
	MMR	90707
	Pneumonia, >2 y	90732
	Pneumonia conjugate, <5 y	90669
	Td, >7 y	90718
	Varicella	90716
	Tetanus toxoid adsorbed, IM	90703

x	Immunizations & Injections		Units
	Allergen, one	95115	
	Allergen, multiple	95117	
	Imm admn <8 yo 1st Inj	90465	
	Imm admn <8 yo each add inj	90466	
	Imm <8 yo oral or intranasal	90467	
	Imm admn <8 yo each add	90468	
	Imm admin, one vacc	90471	
	Imm admin, each add'l	90472	
	Imm admin, intranasal, one	90473	
	Imm admin, intranasal, each add'l	90474	
	Injection, joint, small	20600	
	Injection, joint, intermediate	20605	
	Injection, ther/proph/diag	90772	
	Injection, trigger pt 1-2 musc	20552	

Today's charges:	
Today's payment:	
Balance due:	

Job 11 Router- Francesco Alvarez 1 of 20

Date of service: 10/26/09	Insurance: MEDICAID				Superbill Number: 1490
Patient name: JOHN WITTMER	Coinsurance:	Copay: 2.00			Physician Name: KEMPER
Account #: WIT001	Noncovered Waiver?	yes	no	n/a	

x	Office visit	New	x	Est
	Minimal (RN only)			99211
	Problem focused	99201		99212
	Exp problem focused	99202		99213
	Detailed	99203		99214
	Comp	99204		99215
	Comprhen/Complex	99205		
	Well visit	**New**	**x**	**Est**
	< 1 y	99381		99391
	1-4 y	99382		99392
	5-11 y	99383		99393
	12-17 y	99384		99394
	18-39 y	99385		99395
	40-64 y	99386	✓	99396
	65 y +	99387		99397
	Medicare preventive services			
	Pap			Q0091
	Pelvic & breast			G0101
	Prostate/PSA			G0103
	Tobacco couns/3-10 min			G0375
	Tobacco couns/>10 min			G0376
	Welcome to Medicare exam			G0344
	ECG w/Welcome to Medicare			G0366
	Hemoccult, guaiac			G0107
	Flu shot			G0008
	Pneumonia shot			G0009
	Consultation/preop clearance			
	Exp problem focused			99242
	Detailed			99243
	Comp/mod complex			99244
	Comp/high complex			99245
	Other services			
	After posted hours			99050
	Evening/weekend appointment			99051
	Home health certification			G0180
	Home health recertification			G0179
	Care Plan oversight			99374
	Care Plan Oversight >30 mins			99375
	Post-op follow-up			99024
	Prolonged/60min total			99354
	Prolonged/each add 30 mins			99355
	Special reports/forms			99080
	Disability/Workers comp			99455
✓	Smoking Cessation <10 mins			99406
	Smoking Cessation >10 mins			99407
	ETOH/SA screening <30 mins			99408
	Online E/M by MD			99444
	Phone E/M <10 mins			99441
	Phone E/M <20 mins			99442
	Phone E/M <30 mins			99443
	Anticoagulant Mgmt <90 days			99363
	Anticoagulant Mgmt >90 days			99364
	In office emergency serv			99058
	Other services			
	Supplies			
	Surgical Tray			99070

Instructions:

Rx: Zyban

x	Office procedures		
	Cerumen removal		69210
	ECG, w/interpretation		93000
	ECG, rhythm strip		93040
	Endometrial biopsy		58100
	Fracture care, cast/splint Site: ______		____
	Nebulizer		94640
	Nebulizer demo		94664
	Spirometry		94010
	Spirometry, pre and post		94060
	Vasectomy		55250
	Skin procedures		**Units**
	Foreign body, skin, simple	10120	
	Foreign body, skin, complex	10121	
	I&D, abscess	10060	
	I&D, hematoma/seroma	10140	
	Laceration repair, simple Site: ______ Size: ____	120__	
	Laceration repair, layered Site: ______ Size: ____	120__	
	Laser Light Tx	96597	
	Lesion, biopsy, one	11100	
	Lesion, biopsy, each add'l	11101	
	Lesion, excision, benign Site: ______ Size: ____	114__	
	Lesion, excision, malignant Site: ______ Size: ____	116__	
	Lesion, paring/cutting, one	11055	
	Lesion, paring/cutting, 2-4	11056	
	Lesion, shave Site: ______ Size: ____	113__	
	Nail removal, partial (+T mod)	11730	
	Nail rem, w/matrix (+T mod)	11750	
	Skin tag, 1-15	11200	
	Wart, flat, 1-14	17110	
	Destruction lesion, 1st	17000	
	Destruct lesion, each addl 2-14	17003	
	Medications		**Units**
	Ampicillin, up to 500mg	J0290	
	B-12, up to 1,000 mcg	J3420	
	Epinephrine, up to 1ml	J0170	
	Kenalog, 10mg	J3301	
	Lidocaine, 10mg	J2001	
	Normal saline, 1000cc	J7030	
	Phenergan, up to 50mg	J2550	
	Progesterone, 150mg	J1055	
	Rocephin, 250mg	J0696	
	Testosterone, 200mg	J1080	
	Tigan, up to 200 mg	J3250	
	Toradol, 15mg	J1885	
	Albuterol	J7609	
	Depo-Provera 50 mg	J1055	
	Depo-Medrol 40 mg	J1030	

Diagnoses		Code
1	Well Check	
2	Tobacco Abuse	
3		
4		

Next office visit: 1 yr

Recheck • Preventative • / PRN

Referral to:

x	Laboratory		-90
	Venipuncture	36415	
	Blood glucose, monitoring device	82962	
	Blood glucose, visual dipstick	82948	
	CBC, w/ auto differential	85025	
	CBC, w/o auto differential	85027	
	Cholesterol	82465	
	Hemoccult, guaiac	82270	
	Hemoccult, immunoassay	82274	
	Hemoglobin A1C	85018	
	Lipid panel	80061	
	Liver panel	80076	
	KOH prep (skin, hair, nails)	87220	
	Metabolic panel, basic	80048	
	Metabolic panel, comprehensive	80053	
	Mononucleosis	86308	
	Pregnancy, blood	84703	
	Pregnancy, urine	81025	
	Renal panel	80069	
	Sedimentation rate	85651	
	Strep, rapid	86403	
	Strep culture	87081	
	Strep A	87880	
	TB	86580	
	UA, complete, non-automated	81000	
	UA, w/o micro, non-automated	81002	
	UA, w/ micro, non-automated	81003	
	Urine colony count	87086	
	Urine culture, presumptive	87088	
	Wet mount/KOH	87210	
	Vaccines		
	DT, <7 y		90702
	DTP		90701
	DtaP, <7 y		90700
	Flu, 6-35 months		90657
	Flu, 3 y +		90658
	Hep A, adult		90632
	Hep A, ped/adol, 2 dose		90633
	Hep B, adult		90746
	Hep B, ped/adol 3 dose		90744
	Hep B-Hib		90748
	Hib, 4 dose		90645
	HPV		90649
	IPV		90713
	MMR		90707
	Pneumonia, >2 y		90732
	Pneumonia conjugate, <5 y		90669
	Td, >7 y		90718
	Varicella		90716
	Tetanus toxoid adsorbed, IM		90703
	Immunizations & Injections		**Units**
	Allergen, one	95115	
	Allergen, multiple	95117	
	Imm admn <8 yo 1st Inj	90465	
	Imm admn <8 yo each add inj	90466	
	Imm <8 yo oral or intranasal	90467	
	Imm admn <8 yo each add	90468	
	Imm admin, one vacc	90471	
	Imm admin, each add'l	90472	
	Imm admin, intranasal, one	90473	
	Imm admin, intranasal, each add'l	90474	
	Injection, joint, small	20600	
	Injection, joint, intermediate	20605	
	Injection, ther/proph/diag	90772	
	Injection, trigger pt 1-2 musc	20552	

Physician signature	Today's charges:	
X Sally Kemper	Today's payment:	2.00 cash
	Balance due:	

Job 11 Router- John Wittmer 2 of 20

Date of service: 10/26/09	Insurance: SELF PAY				Superbill Number: 1494
Patient name: RYAN ASHBY	Coinsurance:	Copay:			Physician Name: MURRAY
Account #: ASH001	Noncovered Waiver?	yes	no	n/a	

x	Office visit	New	x	Est
	Minimal (RN only)			99211
	Problem focused	99201		99212
	Exp problem focused	99202	✓	99213
	Detailed	99203		99214
	Comp	99204		99215
	Comprhen/Complex	99205		
	Well visit	**New**	**x**	**Est**
	< 1 y	99381		99391
	1-4 y	99382		99392
	5-11 y	99383		99393
	12-17 y	99384		99394
	18-39 y	99385		99395
	40-64 y	99386		99396
	65 y +	99387		99397
	Medicare preventive services			
	Pap			Q0091
	Pelvic & breast			G0101
	Prostate/PSA			G0103
	Tobacco couns/3-10 min			G0375
	Tobacco couns/>10 min			G0376
	Welcome to Medicare exam			G0344
	ECG w/Welcome to Medicare			G0366
	Hemoccult, guaiac			G0107
	Flu shot			G0008
	Pneumonia shot			G0009
	Consultation/preop clearance			
	Exp problem focused			99242
	Detailed			99243
	Comp/mod complex			99244
	Comp/high complex			99245
	Other services			
	After posted hours			99050
	Evening/weekend appointment			99051
	Home health certification			G0180
	Home health recertification			G0179
	Care Plan oversight			99374
	Care Plan Oversight >30 mins			99375
	Post-op follow-up			99024
	Prolonged/60min total			99354
	Prolonged/each add 30 mins			99355
	Special reports/forms			99080
	Disability/Workers comp			99455
	Smoking Cessation <10 mins			99406
	Smoking Cessation >10 mins			99407
	ETOH/SA screening <30 mins			99408
	Online E/M by MD			99444
	Phone E/M <10 mins			99441
	Phone E/M <20 mins			99442
	Phone E/M <30 mins			99443
	Anticoagulant Mgmt <90 days			99363
	Anticoagulant Mgmt >90 days			99364
	In office emergency serv			99058
	Other services			
	Supplies			
✓	Surgical Tray			99070
	Instructions:			

Return 10 days for suture removal

x	Office procedures		
	Cerumen removal		69210
	ECG, w/interpretation		93000
	ECG, rhythm strip		93040
	Endometrial biopsy		58100
	Fracture care, cast/splint		____
	Site: ______________		
	Nebulizer		94640
	Nebulizer demo		94664
	Spirometry		94010
	Spirometry, pre and post		94060
	Vasectomy		55250
	Skin procedures		**Units**
	Foreign body, skin, simple	10120	
	Foreign body, skin, complex	10121	
	I&D, abscess	10060	
	I&D, hematoma/seroma	10140	
✓	Laceration repair, simple	120__	
	Site: Rt hand Size: 3 cm		
	Laceration repair, layered	120__	
	Site: _______ Size: _____		
	Laser Light Tx	96597	
	Lesion, biopsy, one	11100	
	Lesion, biopsy, each add'l	11101	
	Lesion, excision, benign	114__	
	Site: _______ Size: _____		
	Lesion, excision, malignant	116__	
	Site: _______ Size: _____		
	Lesion, paring/cutting, one	11055	
	Lesion, paring/cutting, 2-4	11056	
	Lesion, shave	113__	
	Site: _______ Size: _____		
	Nail removal, partial (+T mod)	11730	
	Nail rem, w/matrix (+T mod)	11750	
	Skin tag, 1-15	11200	
	Wart, flat, 1-14	17110	
	Destruction lesion, 1st	17000	
	Destruct lesion, each addl 2-14	17003	
	Medications		**Units**
	Ampicillin, up to 500mg	J0290	
	B-12, up to 1,000 mcg	J3420	
	Epinephrine, up to 1ml	J0170	
	Kenalog, 10mg	J3301	
	Lidocaine, 10mg	J2001	
	Normal saline, 1000cc	J7030	
	Phenergan, up to 50mg	J2550	
	Progesterone, 150mg	J1055	
	Rocephin, 250mg	J0696	
	Testosterone, 200mg	J1080	
	Tigan, up to 200 mg	J3250	
	Toradol, 15mg	J1885	
	Albuterol	J7609	
	Depo-Provera 50 mg	J1055	
	Depo-Medrol 40 mg	J1030	
	Diagnoses		**Code**
	1 Laceration Rt hand		
	2		
	3		
	4		

Next office visit:

Recheck • Preventative • PRN

Referral to:

Physician signature

x [signature] MD

x	Laboratory		-90
	Venipuncture	36415	
	Blood glucose, monitoring device	82962	
	Blood glucose, visual dipstick	82948	
	CBC, w/ auto differential	85025	
	CBC, w/o auto differential	85027	
	Cholesterol	82465	
	Hemoccult, guaiac	82270	
	Hemoccult, immunoassay	82274	
	Hemoglobin A1C	85018	
	Lipid panel	80061	
	Liver panel	80076	
	KOH prep (skin, hair, nails)	87220	
	Metabolic panel, basic	80048	
	Metabolic panel, comprehensive	80053	
	Mononucleosis	86308	
	Pregnancy, blood	84703	
	Pregnancy, urine	81025	
	Renal panel	80069	
	Sedimentation rate	85651	
	Strep, rapid	86403	
	Strep culture	87081	
	Strep A	87880	
	TB	86580	
	UA, complete, non-automated	81000	
	UA, w/o micro, non-automated	81002	
	UA, w/ micro, non-automated	81003	
	Urine colony count	87086	
	Urine culture, presumptive	87088	
	Wet mount/KOH	87210	
	Vaccines		
	DT, <7 y		90702
	DTP		90701
	DtaP, <7 y		90700
	Flu, 6-35 months		90657
	Flu, 3 y +		90658
	Hep A, adult		90632
	Hep A, ped/adol, 2 dose		90633
	Hep B, adult		90746
	Hep B, ped/adol 3 dose		90744
	Hep B-Hib		90748
	Hib, 4 dose		90645
	HPV		90649
	IPV		90713
	MMR		90707
	Pneumonia, >2 y		90732
	Pneumonia conjugate, <5 y		90669
	Td, >7 y		90718
	Varicella		90716
	Tetanus toxoid adsorbed, IM		90703
	Immunizations & Injections		**Units**
	Allergen, one	95115	
	Allergen, multiple	95117	
	Imm admn <8 yo 1st Inj	90465	
	Imm admn <8 yo each add inj	90466	
	Imm <8 yo oral or intranasal	90467	
	Imm admn <8 yo each add	90468	
	Imm admin, one vacc	90471	
	Imm admin, each add'l	90472	
	Imm admin, intranasal, one	90473	
	Imm admin, intranasal, each add'l	90474	
	Injection, joint, small	20600	
	Injection, joint, intermediate	20605	
	Injection, ther/proph/diag	90772	
	Injection, trigger pt 1-2 musc	20552	

Today's charges:	
Today's payment:	
Balance due:	

Job 11 Router- Ryan Ashby 3 of 20

Date of service: 10/26/09	Insurance: CIGNA				Superbill Number: 1492
Patient name: WILLIAM TURNER	Coinsurance:	Copay:			Physician Name: KEMPER
Account #: TUR001	Noncovered Waiver?	yes	no	n/a	

x	Office visit	New	x	Est
	Minimal (RN only)			99211
	Problem focused	99201		99212
✓	Exp problem focused	99202		99213
	Detailed	99203		99214
	Comp	99204		99215
	Comprhen/Complex	99205		
	Well visit	**New**	**x**	**Est**
	< 1 y	99381		99391
	1-4 y	99382		99392
	5-11 y	99383		99393
	12-17 y	99384		99394
	18-39 y	99385		99395
	40-64 y	99386		99396
	65 y +	99387		99397

x	Medicare preventive services	
	Pap	Q0091
	Pelvic & breast	G0101
	Prostate/PSA	G0103
	Tobacco couns/3-10 min	G0375
	Tobacco couns/>10 min	G0376
	Welcome to Medicare exam	G0344
	ECG w/Welcome to Medicare	G0366
	Hemoccult, guaiac	G0107
	Flu shot	G0008
	Pneumonia shot	G0009
	Consultation/preop clearance	
	Exp problem focused	99242
	Detailed	99243
	Comp/mod complex	99244
	Comp/high complex	99245
	Other services	
	After posted hours	99050
	Evening/weekend appointment	99051
	Home health certification	G0180
	Home health recertification	G0179
	Care Plan oversight	99374
	Care Plan Oversight >30 mins	99375
	Post-op follow-up	99024
	Prolonged/60min total	99354
	Prolonged/each add 30 mins	99355
	Special reports/forms	99080
	Disability/Workers comp	99455
	Smoking Cessation <10 mins	99406
	Smoking Cessation >10 mins	99407
	ETOH/SA screening <30 mins	99408
	Online E/M by MD	99444
	Phone E/M <10 mins	99441
	Phone E/M <20 mins	99442
	Phone E/M <30 mins	99443
	Anticoagulant Mgmt <90 days	99363
	Anticoagulant Mgmt >90 days	99364
	In office emergency serv	99058
	Other services	
	PCR Antigen amplified probe	
	Supplies	
	Surgical Tray	99070

x	Office procedures		
	Cerumen removal		69210
	ECG, w/interpretation		93000
	ECG, rhythm strip		93040
	Endometrial biopsy		58100
	Fracture care, cast/splint Site: ________		____
	Nebulizer		94640
	Nebulizer demo		94664
	Spirometry		94010
	Spirometry, pre and post		94060
	Vasectomy		55250
	Skin procedures		**Units**
	Foreign body, skin, simple	10120	
	Foreign body, skin, complex	10121	
	I&D, abscess	10060	
	I&D, hematoma/seroma	10140	
	Laceration repair, simple Site: _______ Size: _____	120__	
	Laceration repair, layered Site: _______ Size: _____	120__	
	Laser Light Tx	96597	
	Lesion, biopsy, one	11100	
	Lesion, biopsy, each add'l	11101	
	Lesion, excision, benign Site: _______ Size: _____	114__	
	Lesion, excision, malignant Site: _______ Size: _____	116__	
	Lesion, paring/cutting, one	11055	
	Lesion, paring/cutting, 2-4	11056	
	Lesion, shave Site: _______ Size: _____	113__	
	Nail removal, partial (+T mod)	11730	
	Nail rem, w/matrix (+T mod)	11750	
	Skin tag, 1-15	11200	
	Wart, flat, 1-14	17110	
	Destruction lesion, 1st	17000	
	Destruct lesion, each addl 2-14	17003	
	Medications		**Units**
	Ampicillin, up to 500mg	J0290	
	B-12, up to 1,000 mcg	J3420	
	Epinephrine, up to 1ml	J0170	
	Kenalog, 10mg	J3301	
	Lidocaine, 10mg	J2001	
	Normal saline, 1000cc	J7030	
	Phenergan, up to 50mg	J2550	
	Progesterone, 150mg	J1055	
	Rocephin, 250mg	J0696	
	Testosterone, 200mg	J1080	
	Tigan, up to 200 mg	J3250	
	Toradol, 15mg	J1885	
	Albuterol	J7609	
	Depo-Provera 50 mg	J1055	
	Depo-Medrol 40 mg	J1030	

Diagnoses		Code
1 Herpes Simplex virus 1		
2		
3		
4		

x	Laboratory		-90
✓	Venipuncture	36415	
	Blood glucose, monitoring device	82962	
	Blood glucose, visual dipstick	82948	
	CBC, w/ auto differential	85025	
	CBC, w/o auto differential	85027	
	Cholesterol	82465	
	Hemoccult, guaiac	82270	
	Hemoccult, immunoassay	82274	
	Hemoglobin A1C	85018	
	Lipid panel	80061	
	Liver panel	80076	
	KOH prep (skin, hair, nails)	87220	
	Metabolic panel, basic	80048	
	Metabolic panel, comprehensive	80053	
	Mononucleosis	86308	
	Pregnancy, blood	84703	
	Pregnancy, urine	81025	
	Renal panel	80069	
	Sedimentation rate	85651	
	Strep, rapid	86403	
	Strep culture	87081	
	Strep A	87880	
	TB	86580	
	UA, complete, non-automated	81000	
	UA, w/o micro, non-automated	81002	
	UA, w/ micro, non-automated	81003	
	Urine colony count	87086	
	Urine culture, presumptive	87088	
	Wet mount/KOH	87210	

x	Vaccines		
	DT, <7 y		90702
	DTP		90701
	DtaP, <7 y		90700
	Flu, 6-35 months		90657
	Flu, 3 y +		90658
	Hep A, adult		90632
	Hep A, ped/adol, 2 dose		90633
	Hep B, adult		90746
	Hep B, ped/adol 3 dose		90744
	Hep B-Hib		90748
	Hib, 4 dose		90645
	HPV		90649
	IPV		90713
	MMR		90707
	Pneumonia, >2 y		90732
	Pneumonia conjugate, <5 y		90669
	Td, >7 y		90718
	Varicella		90716
	Tetanus toxoid adsorbed, IM		90703
	Immunizations & Injections		**Units**
	Allergen, one	95115	
	Allergen, multiple	95117	
	Imm admn <8 yo 1st Inj	90465	
	Imm admn <8 yo each add inj	90466	
	Imm <8 yo oral or intranasal	90467	
	Imm admn <8 yo each add	90468	
	Imm admin, one vacc	90471	
	Imm admin, each add'l	90472	
	Imm admin, intranasal, one	90473	
	Imm admin, intranasal, each add'l	90474	
	Injection, joint, small	20600	
	Injection, joint, intermediate	20605	
	Injection, ther/proph/diag	90772	
	Injection, trigger pt 1-2 musc	20552	

Instructions:

Return 3wks F/U

Rx Viroxyn

Next office visit:
Recheck • Preventative • PRN

Referral to:

Physician signature

x

Today's charges:		
Today's payment:		
Balance due:		

Job 11 Router- William Turner 4 of 20

Date of service: 10/26/09	Insurance: FLEXIHEALTH PPO			Superbill Number: 1493
Patient name: CAITLIN BARRYMORE	Coinsurance:	Copay: 20.00		Physician Name: HEATH
Account #: BAR001	Noncovered Waiver?	yes	no	n/a

X	Office visit	New	X	Est
	Minimal (RN only)			99211
	Problem focused	99201		99212
	Exp problem focused	99202		99213
	Detailed	99203	✓	99214
	Comp	99204		99215
	Comprhen/Complex	99205		
	Well visit	**New**	**X**	**Est**
	< 1 y	99381		99391
	1-4 y	99382		99392
	5-11 y	99383		99393
	12-17 y	99384		99394
	18-39 y	99385		99395
	40-64 y	99386		99396
	65 y +	99387		99397
	Medicare preventive services			
	Pap			Q0091
	Pelvic & breast			G0101
	Prostate/PSA			G0103
	Tobacco couns/3-10 min			G0375
	Tobacco couns/>10 min			G0376
	Welcome to Medicare exam			G0344
	ECG w/Welcome to Medicare			G0366
	Hemoccult, guaiac			G0107
	Flu shot			G0008
	Pneumonia shot			G0009
	Consultation/preop clearance			
	Exp problem focused			99242
	Detailed			99243
	Comp/mod complex			99244
	Comp/high complex			99245
	Other services			
	After posted hours			99050
	Evening/weekend appointment			99051
	Home health certification			G0180
	Home health recertification			G0179
	Care Plan oversight			99374
	Care Plan Oversight >30 mins			99375
	Post-op follow-up			99024
	Prolonged/60min total			99354
	Prolonged/each add 30 mins			99355
	Special reports/forms			99080
	Disability/Workers comp			99455
	Smoking Cessation <10 mins			99406
	Smoking Cessation >10 mins			99407
	ETOH/SA screening <30 mins			99408
	Online E/M by MD			99444
	Phone E/M <10 mins			99441
	Phone E/M <20 mins			99442
	Phone E/M <30 mins			99443
	Anticoagulant Mgmt <90 days			99363
	Anticoagulant Mgmt >90 days			99364
	In office emergency serv			99058
	Other services			
	VDRL			
	Pelvic Exam			
	Supplies			
	Surgical Tray			99070

X	Office procedures		
	Cerumen removal		69210
	ECG, w/interpretation		93000
	ECG, rhythm strip		93040
	Endometrial biopsy		58100
	Fracture care, cast/splint Site: ______		____
	Nebulizer		94640
	Nebulizer demo		94664
	Spirometry		94010
	Spirometry, pre and post		94060
	Vasectomy		55250
	Skin procedures		**Units**
	Foreign body, skin, simple	10120	
	Foreign body, skin, complex	10121	
	I&D, abscess	10060	
	I&D, hematoma/seroma	10140	
	Laceration repair, simple Site: ______ Size: ______	120__	
	Laceration repair, layered Site: ______ Size: ______	120__	
	Laser Light Tx	96597	
	Lesion, biopsy, one	11100	
	Lesion, biopsy, each add'l	11101	
	Lesion, excision, benign Site: ______ Size: ______	114__	
	Lesion, excision, malignant Site: ______ Size: ______	116__	
	Lesion, paring/cutting, one	11055	
	Lesion, paring/cutting, 2-4	11056	
	Lesion, shave Site: ______ Size: ______	113__	
	Nail removal, partial (+T mod)	11730	
	Nail rem, w/matrix (+T mod)	11750	
	Skin tag, 1-15	11200	
	Wart, flat, 1-14	17110	
	Destruction lesion, 1st	17000	
	Destruct lesion, each addl 2-14	17003	
	Medications		**Units**
	Ampicillin, up to 500mg	J0290	
	B-12, up to 1,000 mcg	J3420	
	Epinephrine, up to 1ml	J0170	
	Kenalog, 10mg	J3301	
	Lidocaine, 10mg	J2001	
	Normal saline, 1000cc	J7030	
	Phenergan, up to 50mg	J2550	
	Progesterone, 150mg	J1055	
	Rocephin, 250mg	J0696	
	Testosterone, 200mg	J1080	
	Tigan, up to 200 mg	J3250	
	Toradol, 15mg	J1885	
	Albuterol	J7609	
	Depo-Provera 50 mg	J1055	
	Depo-Medrol 40 mg	J1030	

Diagnoses	Code
1 Abdominal Pain	
2 Fatigue	
3 Possible VD	
4	

Next office visit: 1 wk

Recheck • Preventative • PRN

Referral to:

X	Laboratory		-90
✓	Venipuncture	36415	
	Blood glucose, monitoring device	82962	
	Blood glucose, visual dipstick	82948	
	CBC, w/ auto differential	85025	
	CBC, w/o auto differential	85027	
	Cholesterol	82465	
	Hemoccult, guaiac	82270	
	Hemoccult, immunoassay	82274	
	Hemoglobin A1C	85018	
	Lipid panel	80061	
	Liver panel	80076	
	KOH prep (skin, hair, nails)	87220	
	Metabolic panel, basic	80048	
	Metabolic panel, comprehensive	80053	
✓	Mononucleosis	86308	✓
	Pregnancy, blood	84703	
	Pregnancy, urine	81025	
	Renal panel	80069	
	Sedimentation rate	85651	
	Strep, rapid	86403	
	Strep culture	87081	
	Strep A	87880	
	TB	86580	
	UA, complete, non-automated	81000	
	UA, w/o micro, non-automated	81002	
✓	UA, w/ micro, non-automated	81003	✓
	Urine colony count	87086	
	Urine culture, presumptive	87088	
	Wet mount/KOH	87210	

	Vaccines		
	DT, <7 y		90702
	DTP		90701
	DtaP, <7 y		90700
	Flu, 6-35 months		90657
	Flu, 3 y +		90658
	Hep A, adult		90632
	Hep A, ped/adol, 2 dose		90633
	Hep B, adult		90746
	Hep B, ped/adol 3 dose		90744
	Hep B-Hib		90748
	Hib, 4 dose		90645
	HPV		90649
	IPV		90713
	MMR		90707
	Pneumonia, >2 y		90732
	Pneumonia conjugate, <5 y		90669
	Td, >7 y		90718
	Varicella		90716
	Tetanus toxoid adsorbed, IM		90703
	Immunizations & Injections		**Units**
	Allergen, one	95115	
	Allergen, multiple	95117	
	Imm admn <8 yo 1st Inj	90465	
	Imm admn <8 yo each add inj	90466	
	Imm <8 yo oral or intranasal	90467	
	Imm admn <8 yo each add	90468	
	Imm admin, one vacc	90471	
	Imm admin, each add'l	90472	
	Imm admin, intranasal, one	90473	
	Imm admin, intranasal, each add'l	90474	
	Injection, joint, small	20600	
	Injection, joint, intermediate	20605	
	Injection, ther/proph/diag	90772	
	Injection, trigger pt 1-2 musc	20552	

Instructions:

F/U VDRL LAB

Physician signature

X Alberta Lynn PA-C

Today's charges:	
Today's payment:	20.00 #425
Balance due:	

Job 11 Router- Caitlin Barrymore 5 of 20

Date of service: 10/26/09	Insurance: MANAGEMED				Superbill Number: 1495
Patient name: LAURA LEIGHTON	Coinsurance:	Copay: 15.00			Physician Name: MENDENHALL
Account #: LEI001	Noncovered Waiver?	yes	no	n/a	

X	Office visit	New	X	Est
	Minimal (RN only)			99211
	Problem focused	99201		99212
	Exp problem focused	99202		99213
	Detailed	99203	√	99214
	Comp	99204		99215
	Comprhen/Complex	99205		
	Well visit	**New**	**X**	**Est**
	< 1 y	99381		99391
	1-4 y	99382		99392
	5-11 y	99383		99393
	12-17 y	99384		99394
	18-39 y	99385		99395
	40-64 y	99386		99396
	65 y +	99387		99397
	Medicare preventive services			
	Pap			Q0091
	Pelvic & breast			G0101
	Prostate/PSA			G0103
	Tobacco couns/3-10 min			G0375
	Tobacco couns/>10 min			G0376
	Welcome to Medicare exam			G0344
	ECG w/Welcome to Medicare			G0366
	Hemoccult, guaiac			G0107
	Flu shot			G0008
	Pneumonia shot			G0009
	Consultation/preop clearance			
	Exp problem focused			99242
	Detailed			99243
	Comp/mod complex			99244
	Comp/high complex			99245
	Other services			
	After posted hours			99050
	Evening/weekend appointment			99051
	Home health certification			G0180
	Home health recertification			G0179
	Care Plan oversight			99374
	Care Plan Oversight >30 mins			99375
	Post-op follow-up			99024
	Prolonged/60min total			99354
	Prolonged/each add 30 mins			99355
	Special reports/forms			99080
	Disability/Workers comp			99455
	Smoking Cessation <10 mins			99406
	Smoking Cessation >10 mins			99407
	ETOH/SA screening <30 mins			99408
	Online E/M by MD			99444
	Phone E/M <10 mins			99441
	Phone E/M <20 mins			99442
	Phone E/M <30 mins			99443
	Anticoagulant Mgmt <90 days			99363
	Anticoagulant Mgmt >90 days			99364
	In office emergency serv			99058
	Other services			
	Supplies			
	Surgical Tray			99070

X	Office procedures		
	Cerumen removal		69210
	ECG, w/interpretation		93000
	ECG, rhythm strip		93040
	Endometrial biopsy		58100
	Fracture care, cast/splint Site: _______________		
	Nebulizer		94640
	Nebulizer demo		94664
	Spirometry		94010
	Spirometry, pre and post		94060
	Vasectomy		55250
	Skin procedures		**Units**
	Foreign body, skin, simple	10120	
	Foreign body, skin, complex	10121	
	I&D, abscess	10060	
	I&D, hematoma/seroma	10140	
	Laceration repair, simple Site: _______ Size: _____	120__	
	Laceration repair, layered Site: _______ Size: _____	120__	
	Laser Light Tx	96597	
	Lesion, biopsy, one	11100	
	Lesion, biopsy, each add'l	11101	
	Lesion, excision, benign Site: _______ Size: _____	114__	
	Lesion, excision, malignant Site: _______ Size: _____	116__	
	Lesion, paring/cutting, one	11055	
	Lesion, paring/cutting, 2-4	11056	
	Lesion, shave Site: _______ Size: _____	113__	
	Nail removal, partial (+T mod)	11730	
	Nail rem, w/matrix (+T mod)	11750	
	Skin tag, 1-15	11200	
	Wart, flat, 1-14	17110	
√	Destruction lesion, 1st	17000	
	Destruct lesion, each addl 2-14	17003	
	Medications		**Units**
	Ampicillin, up to 500mg	J0290	
	B-12, up to 1,000 mcg	J3420	
	Epinephrine, up to 1ml	J0170	
	Kenalog, 10mg	J3301	
√	Lidocaine, 10mg	J2001	
	Normal saline, 1000cc	J7030	
	Phenergan, up to 50mg	J2550	
	Progesterone, 150mg	J1055	
	Rocephin, 250mg	J0696	
	Testosterone, 200mg	J1080	
	Tigan, up to 200 mg	J3250	
	Toradol, 15mg	J1885	
	Albuterol	J7609	
	Depo-Provera 50 mg	J1055	
	Depo-Medrol 40 mg	J1030	

Diagnoses		Code
1 Migraine [illegible]		
2 Dermatofibromas		
3		
4		

X	Laboratory		-90
	Venipuncture	36415	
	Blood glucose, monitoring device	82962	
	Blood glucose, visual dipstick	82948	
	CBC, w/ auto differential	85025	
	CBC, w/o auto differential	85027	
	Cholesterol	82465	
	Hemoccult, guaiac	82270	
	Hemoccult, immunoassay	82274	
	Hemoglobin A1C	85018	
	Lipid panel	80061	
	Liver panel	80076	
	KOH prep (skin, hair, nails)	87220	
	Metabolic panel, basic	80048	
	Metabolic panel, comprehensive	80053	
	Mononucleosis	86308	
	Pregnancy, blood	84703	
	Pregnancy, urine	81025	
	Renal panel	80069	
	Sedimentation rate	85651	
	Strep, rapid	86403	
	Strep culture	87081	
	Strep A	87880	
	TB	86580	
	UA, complete, non-automated	81000	
	UA, w/o micro, non-automated	81002	
	UA, w/ micro, non-automated	81003	
	Urine colony count	87086	
	Urine culture, presumptive	87088	
	Wet mount/KOH	87210	
	Vaccines		
	DT, <7 y		90702
	DTP		90701
	DtaP, <7 y		90700
	Flu, 6-35 months		90657
	Flu, 3 y +		90658
	Hep A, adult		90632
	Hep A, ped/adol, 2 dose		90633
	Hep B, adult		90746
	Hep B, ped/adol 3 dose		90744
	Hep B-Hib		90748
	Hib, 4 dose		90645
	HPV		90649
	IPV		90713
	MMR		90707
	Pneumonia, >2 y		90732
	Pneumonia conjugate, <5 y		90669
	Td, >7 y		90718
	Varicella		90716
	Tetanus toxoid adsorbed, IM		90703
	Immunizations & injections		**Units**
	Allergen, one	95115	
	Allergen, multiple	95117	
	Imm admn <8 yo 1st Inj	90465	
	Imm admn <8 yo each add inj	90466	
	Imm <8 yo oral or intranasal	90467	
	Imm admn <8 yo each add	90468	
	Imm admin, one vacc	90471	
	Imm admin, each add'l	90472	
	Imm admin, intranasal, one	90473	
	Imm admin, intranasal, each add'l	90474	
	Injection, joint, small	20600	
	Injection, joint, intermediate	20605	
	Injection, ther/proph/diag	90772	
	Injection, trigger pt 1-2 musc	20552	

Instructions: Rx Refill

Next office visit:
Recheck • Preventative • PRN (circled)

Referral to:

Physician signature
x Sarah Mendenhall

Today's charges:	
Today's payment:	
Balance due:	

Job 11 Router- Laura Leighton 6 of 20

Date of service: 10/26/09	Insurance: SIGNAL HMO			Superbill Number: 1496
Patient name: NAOMI YAMAGATA	Coinsurance:	Copay: 10.00		Physician Name: MURRAY
Account #: YAM001	Noncovered Waiver?	yes	no	n/a

x	Office visit	New	x	Est
	Minimal (RN only)			99211
	Problem focused	99201		99212
	Exp problem focused	99202		99213
	Detailed	99203	✓	99214
	Comp	99204		99215
	Comprhen/Complex	99205		
	Well visit	**New**	**x**	**Est**
	< 1 y	99381		99391
	1-4 y	99382		99392
	5-11 y	99383		99393
	12-17 y	99384		99394
	18-39 y	99385		99395
	40-64 y	99386		99396
	65 y +	99387		99397
	Medicare preventive services			
	Pap			Q0091
	Pelvic & breast			G0101
	Prostate/PSA			G0103
	Tobacco couns/3-10 min			G0375
	Tobacco couns/>10 min			G0376
	Welcome to Medicare exam			G0344
	ECG w/Welcome to Medicare			G0366
	Hemoccult, guaiac			G0107
	Flu shot			G0008
	Pneumonia shot			G0009
	Consultation/preop clearance			
	Exp problem focused			99242
	Detailed			99243
	Comp/mod complex			99244
	Comp/high complex			99245
	Other services			
	After posted hours			99050
	Evening/weekend appointment			99051
	Home health certification			G0180
	Home health recertification			G0179
	Care Plan oversight			99374
	Care Plan Oversight >30 mins			99375
	Post-op follow-up			99024
	Prolonged/60min total			99354
	Prolonged/each add 30 mins			99355
	Special reports/forms			99080
	Disability/Workers comp			99455
	Smoking Cessation <10 mins			99406
	Smoking Cessation >10 mins			99407
	ETOH/SA screening <30 mins			99408
	Online E/M by MD			99444
	Phone E/M <10 mins			99441
	Phone E/M <20 mins			99442
	Phone E/M <30 mins			99443
	Anticoagulant Mgmt <90 days			99363
	Anticoagulant Mgmt >90 days			99364
	In office emergency serv			99058
	Other services			
	Supplies			
✓	Surgical Tray			99070

x	Office procedures		
	Cerumen removal		69210
	ECG, w/interpretation		93000
	ECG, rhythm strip		93040
✓	Endometrial biopsy		58100
	Fracture care, cast/splint Site: ____________		____
	Nebulizer		94640
	Nebulizer demo		94664
	Spirometry		94010
	Spirometry, pre and post		94060
	Vasectomy		55250
	Skin procedures		**Units**
	Foreign body, skin, simple	10120	
	Foreign body, skin, complex	10121	
	I&D, abscess	10060	
	I&D, hematoma/seroma	10140	
	Laceration repair, simple Site: ________ Size: _____	120__	
	Laceration repair, layered Site: ________ Size: _____	120__	
	Laser Light Tx	96597	
	Lesion, biopsy, one	11100	
	Lesion, biopsy, each add'l	11101	
	Lesion, excision, benign Site: ________ Size: _____	114__	
	Lesion, excision, malignant Site: ________ Size: _____	116__	
	Lesion, paring/cutting, one	11055	
	Lesion, paring/cutting, 2-4	11056	
	Lesion, shave Site: ________ Size: _____	113__	
	Nail removal, partial (+T mod)	11730	
	Nail rem, w/matrix (+T mod)	11750	
	Skin tag, 1-15	11200	
	Wart, flat, 1-14	17110	
	Destruction lesion, 1st	17000	
	Destruct lesion, each addl 2-14	17003	
	Medications		**Units**
	Ampicillin, up to 500mg	J0290	
	B-12, up to 1,000 mcg	J3420	
	Epinephrine, up to 1ml	J0170	
	Kenalog, 10mg	J3301	
	Lidocaine, 10mg	J2001	
	Normal saline, 1000cc	J7030	
	Phenergan, up to 50mg	J2550	
	Progesterone, 150mg	J1055	
	Rocephin, 250mg	J0696	
	Testosterone, 200mg	J1080	
	Tigan, up to 200 mg	J3250	
	Toradol, 15mg	J1885	
	Albuterol	J7609	
	Depo-Provera 50 mg	J1055	
	Depo-Medrol 40 mg	J1030	
	Diagnoses		**Code**
	1 DUB		
	2 Menorrhagia		
	3		
	4		

x	Laboratory		-90
✓	Venipuncture	36415	
	Blood glucose, monitoring device	82962	
	Blood glucose, visual dipstick	82948	
	CBC, w/ auto differential	85025	
✓	CBC, w/o auto differential	85027	
	Cholesterol	82465	
	Hemoccult, guaiac	82270	
	Hemoccult, immunoassay	82274	
	Hemoglobin A1C	85018	
	Lipid panel	80061	
	Liver panel	80076	
	KOH prep (skin, hair, nails)	87220	
	Metabolic panel, basic	80048	
	Metabolic panel, comprehensive	80053	
	Mononucleosis	86308	
	Pregnancy, blood	84703	
✓	Pregnancy, urine	81025	
	Renal panel	80069	
	Sedimentation rate	85651	
	Strep, rapid	86403	
	Strep culture	87081	
	Strep A	87880	
	TB	86580	
	UA, complete, non-automated	81000	
	UA, w/o micro, non-automated	81002	
	UA, w/ micro, non-automated	81003	
	Urine colony count	87086	
	Urine culture, presumptive	87088	
	Wet mount/KOH	87210	
	Vaccines		
	DT, <7 y		90702
	DTP		90701
	DtaP, <7 y		90700
	Flu, 6-35 months		90657
	Flu, 3 y +		90658
	Hep A, adult		90632
	Hep A, ped/adol, 2 dose		90633
	Hep B, adult		90746
	Hep B, ped/adol 3 dose		90744
	Hep B-Hib		90748
	Hib, 4 dose		90645
	HPV		90649
	IPV		90713
	MMR		90707
	Pneumonia, >2 y		90732
	Pneumonia conjugate, <5 y		90669
	Td, >7 y		90718
	Varicella		90716
	Tetanus toxoid adsorbed, IM		90703
	Immunizations & Injections		**Units**
	Allergen, one	95115	
	Allergen, multiple	95117	
	Imm admn <8 yo 1st Inj	90465	
	Imm admn <8 yo each add inj	90466	
	Imm <8 yo oral or intranasal	90467	
	Imm admn <8 yo each add	90468	
	Imm admin, one vacc	90471	
	Imm admin, each add'l	90472	
	Imm admin, intranasal, one	90473	
	Imm admin, intranasal, each add'l	90474	
	Injection, joint, small	20600	
	Injection, joint, intermediate	20605	
	Injection, ther/proph/diag	90772	
	Injection, trigger pt 1-2 musc	20552	

Next office visit: 10 days

(Recheck) • Preventative • PRN

Referral to:

Instructions: Return F/U path

Physician signature

x [signature] MD

Today's charges:	
Today's payment:	10.00 cash
Balance due:	

Job 11 Router- Naomi Yamagata 7 of 20

Date of service: 10/27/09	Insurance: BC/BS				Superbill Number: 2453
Patient name: BRIAN MCDONOUGH	Coinsurance: 20%	Copay:			Physician Name: SCHWARTZ
Account #: MCD001	Noncovered Waiver?	yes	no	n/a	

x	Office visit	New	x	Est
	Minimal (RN only)			99211
	Problem focused	99201		99212
	Exp problem focused	99202		99213
	Detailed	99203		99214
✓	Comp	99204		99215
	Comprhen/Complex	99205		
x	**Well visit**	**New**	**x**	**Est**
	< 1 y	99381		99391
	1-4 y	99382		99392
	5-11 y	99383		99393
	12-17 y	99384		99394
	18-39 y	99385		99395
	40-64 y	99386		99396
	65 y +	99387		99397

x	Medicare preventive services	
	Pap	Q0091
	Pelvic & breast	G0101
	Prostate/PSA	G0103
	Tobacco couns/3-10 min	G0375
	Tobacco couns/>10 min	G0376
	Welcome to Medicare exam	G0344
	ECG w/Welcome to Medicare	G0366
	Hemoccult, guaiac	G0107
	Flu shot	G0008
	Pneumonia shot	G0009
	Consultation/preop clearance	
	Exp problem focused	99242
	Detailed	99243
	Comp/mod complex	99244
	Comp/high complex	99245
	Other services	
	After posted hours	99050
	Evening/weekend appointment	99051
	Home health certification	G0180
	Home health recertification	G0179
	Care Plan oversight	99374
	Care Plan Oversight >30 mins	99375
	Post-op follow-up	99024
	Prolonged/60min total	99354
	Prolonged/each add 30 mins	99355
	Special reports/forms	99080
	Disability/Workers comp	99455
	Smoking Cessation <10 mins	99406
	Smoking Cessation >10 mins	99407
	ETOH/SA screening <30 mins	99408
	Online E/M by MD	99444
	Phone E/M <10 mins	99441
	Phone E/M <20 mins	99442
	Phone E/M <30 mins	99443
	Anticoagulant Mgmt <90 days	99363
	Anticoagulant Mgmt >90 days	99364
	In office emergency serv	99058
	Other services	
	Supplies	
	Surgical Tray	99070

Instructions:

x	Office procedures		
	Cerumen removal		69210
	ECG, w/interpretation		93000
	ECG, rhythm strip		93040
	Endometrial biopsy		58100
	Fracture care, cast/splint		______
	Site: ________________		
	Nebulizer		94640
	Nebulizer demo		94664
	Spirometry		94010
	Spirometry, pre and post		94060
	Vasectomy		55250
	Skin procedures		**Units**
	Foreign body, skin, simple	10120	
	Foreign body, skin, complex	10121	
	I&D, abscess	10060	
	I&D, hematoma/seroma	10140	
	Laceration repair, simple	120__	
	Site: _______ Size: _____		
	Laceration repair, layered	120__	
	Site: _______ Size: _____		
	Laser Light Tx	96597	
	Lesion, biopsy, one	11100	
	Lesion, biopsy, each add'l	11101	
	Lesion, excision, benign	114__	
	Site: _______ Size: _____		
	Lesion, excision, malignant	116__	
	Site: _______ Size: _____		
	Lesion, paring/cutting, one	11055	
	Lesion, paring/cutting, 2-4	11056	
	Lesion, shave	113__	
	Site: _______ Size: _____		
	Nail removal, partial (+T mod)	11730	
	Nail rem, w/matrix (+T mod)	11750	
	Skin tag, 1-15	11200	
	Wart, flat, 1-14	17110	
	Destruction lesion, 1st	17000	
	Destruct lesion, each addl 2-14	17003	
	Medications		**Units**
	Ampicillin, up to 500mg	J0290	
	B-12, up to 1,000 mcg	J3420	
	Epinephrine, up to 1ml	J0170	
	Kenalog, 10mg	J3301	
	Lidocaine, 10mg	J2001	
	Normal saline, 1000cc	J7030	
	Phenergan, up to 50mg	J2550	
	Progesterone, 150mg	J1055	
	Rocephin, 250mg	J0696	
	Testosterone, 200mg	J1080	
	Tigan, up to 200 mg	J3250	
	Toradol, 15mg	J1885	
	Albuterol	J7609	
	Depo-Provera 50 mg	J1055	
	Depo-Medrol 40 mg	J1030	

Diagnoses		Code
1 Routine Physical		
2 Vaccination Update		
3		
4		

Next office visit:
Recheck • Preventative • (PRN)
Referral to:

Physician signature
x [signature] MD

x	Laboratory		-90
	Venipuncture	36415	
	Blood glucose, monitoring device	82962	
	Blood glucose, visual dipstick	82948	
	CBC, w/ auto differential	85025	
	CBC, w/o auto differential	85027	
	Cholesterol	82465	
	Hemoccult, guaiac	82270	
	Hemoccult, immunoassay	82274	
	Hemoglobin A1C	85018	
	Lipid panel	80061	
	Liver panel	80076	
	KOH prep (skin, hair, nails)	87220	
	Metabolic panel, basic	80048	
	Metabolic panel, comprehensive	80053	
	Mononucleosis	86308	
	Pregnancy, blood	84703	
	Pregnancy, urine	81025	
	Renal panel	80069	
	Sedimentation rate	85651	
	Strep, rapid	86403	
	Strep culture	87081	
	Strep A	87880	
	TB	86580	
	UA, complete, non-automated	81000	
	UA, w/o micro, non-automated	81002	
	UA, w/ micro, non-automated	81003	
	Urine colony count	87086	
	Urine culture, presumptive	87088	
	Wet mount/KOH	87210	
	Vaccines		
	DT, <7 y		90702
	DTP		90701
	DtaP, <7 y		90700
	Flu, 6-35 months		90657
	Flu, 3 y +		90658
	Hep A, adult		90632
	Hep A, ped/adol, 2 dose		90633
✓	Hep B, adult		90746
	Hep B, ped/adol 3 dose		90744
	Hep B-Hib		90748
	Hib, 4 dose		90645
	HPV		90649
	IPV		90713
	MMR		90707
	Pneumonia, >2 y		90732
	Pneumonia conjugate, <5 y		90669
	Td, >7 y		90718
	Varicella		90716
✓	Tetanus toxoid adsorbed, IM		90703
	Immunizations & Injections		**Units**
	Allergen, one	95115	
	Allergen, multiple	95117	
	Imm admn <8 yo 1st Inj	90465	
	Imm admn <8 yo each add inj	90466	
	Imm <8 yo oral or intranasal	90467	
	Imm admn <8 yo each add	90468	
✓	Imm admin, one vacc	90471	
✓	Imm admin, each add'l	90472	
	Imm admin, intranasal, one	90473	
	Imm admin, intranasal, each add'l	90474	
	Injection, joint, small	20600	
	Injection, joint, intermediate	20605	
	Injection, ther/proph/diag	90772	
	Injection, trigger pt 1-2 musc	20552	
	Today's charges:		
	Today's payment:		
	Balance due:		

Job 11 Router- Brian McDonough 8 of 20

Date of service: 10/27/09	Insurance: FLEXIHEALTH				Superbill Number: 2459
Patient name: RICHARD MANALY	Coinsurance:	Copay: 20.00			Physician Name: LYNN
Account #: MAN001	Noncovered Waiver?	yes	no	n/a	

x	Office visit	New	x	Est
	Minimal (RN only)			99211
	Problem focused	99201		99212
	Exp problem focused	99202		99213
	Detailed	99203		99214
	Comp	99204		99215
	Comprhen/Complex	99205		
	Well visit	**New**	**x**	**Est**
	< 1 y	99381		99391
	1-4 y	99382		99392
	5-11 y	99383		99393
	12-17 y	99384		99394
	18-39 y	99385		99395
	40-64 y	99386		99396
	65 y +	99387		99397
	Medicare preventive services			
	Pap			Q0091
	Pelvic & breast			G0101
	Prostate/PSA			G0103
	Tobacco couns/3-10 min			G0375
	Tobacco couns/>10 min			G0376
	Welcome to Medicare exam			G0344
	ECG w/Welcome to Medicare			G0366
	Hemoccult, guaiac			G0107
	Flu shot			G0008
	Pneumonia shot			G0009
	Consultation/preop clearance			
	Exp problem focused			99242
	Detailed			99243
	Comp/mod complex			99244
	Comp/high complex			99245
	Other services			
	After posted hours			99050
	Evening/weekend appointment			99051
	Home health certification			G0180
	Home health recertification			G0179
	Care Plan oversight			99374
	Care Plan Oversight >30 mins			99375
	Post-op follow-up			99024
	Prolonged/60min total			99354
	Prolonged/each add 30 mins			99355
	Special reports/forms			99080
	Disability/Workers comp			99455
	Smoking Cessation <10 mins			99406
	Smoking Cessation >10 mins			99407
	ETOH/SA screening <30 mins			99408
	Online E/M by MD			99444
	Phone E/M <10 mins			99441
	Phone E/M <20 mins			99442
	Phone E/M <30 mins			99443
	Anticoagulant Mgmt <90 days			99363
✓	Anticoagulant Mgmt >90 days			99364
	In office emergency serv			99058
	Other services			
✓	Therapeutic Drug Assay - Carnatin			
	Supplies			
	Surgical Tray			99070
	Instructions:			

x	Office procedures		
	Cerumen removal		69210
	ECG, w/interpretation		93000
	ECG, rhythm strip		93040
	Endometrial biopsy		58100
	Fracture care, cast/splint		_____
	Site: _______________		
	Nebulizer		94640
	Nebulizer demo		94664
	Spirometry		94010
	Spirometry, pre and post		94060
	Vasectomy		55250
	Skin procedures		**Units**
	Foreign body, skin, simple	10120	
	Foreign body, skin, complex	10121	
	I&D, abscess	10060	
	I&D, hematoma/seroma	10140	
	Laceration repair, simple	120__	
	Site: ________ Size: _____		
	Laceration repair, layered	120__	
	Site: ________ Size: _____		
	Laser Light Tx	96597	
	Lesion, biopsy, one	11100	
	Lesion, biopsy, each add'l	11101	
	Lesion, excision, benign	114__	
	Site: ________ Size: _____		
	Lesion, excision, malignant	116__	
	Site: ________ Size: _____		
	Lesion, paring/cutting, one	11055	
	Lesion, paring/cutting, 2-4	11056	
	Lesion, shave	113__	
	Site: ________ Size: _____		
	Nail removal, partial (+T mod)	11730	
	Nail rem, w/matrix (+T mod)	11750	
	Skin tag, 1-15	11200	
	Wart, flat, 1-14	17110	
	Destruction lesion, 1st	17000	
	Destruct lesion, each addl 2-14	17003	
	Medications		**Units**
	Ampicillin, up to 500mg	J0290	
	B-12, up to 1,000 mcg	J3420	
	Epinephrine, up to 1ml	J0170	
	Kenalog, 10mg	J3301	
	Lidocaine, 10mg	J2001	
	Normal saline, 1000cc	J7030	
	Phenergan, up to 50mg	J2550	
	Progesterone, 150mg	J1055	
	Rocephin, 250mg	J0696	
	Testosterone, 200mg	J1080	
	Tigan, up to 200 mg	J3250	
	Toradol, 15mg	J1885	
	Albuterol	J7609	
	Depo-Provera 50 mg	J1055	
	Depo-Medrol 40 mg	J1030	
	Diagnoses		**Code**
	1 Arrhythmia		
	2 HTN		
	3 Coagulation mgt use		
	4		

Next office visit: 1 mth

Recheck • Preventative • PRN

Referral to:

Physician signature

x Alberta Lynn PA-C

x	Laboratory		-90
✓	Venipuncture	36415	
	Blood glucose, monitoring device	82962	
	Blood glucose, visual dipstick	82948	
	CBC, w/ auto differential	85025	
	CBC, w/o auto differential	85027	
	Cholesterol	82465	
	Hemoccult, guaiac	82270	
	Hemoccult, immunoassay	82274	
	Hemoglobin A1C	85018	
	Lipid panel	80061	
	Liver panel	80076	
	KOH prep (skin, hair, nails)	87220	
	Metabolic panel, basic	80048	
	Metabolic panel, comprehensive	80053	
	Mononucleosis	86308	
	Pregnancy, blood	84703	
	Pregnancy, urine	81025	
	Renal panel	80069	
	Sedimentation rate	85651	
	Strep, rapid	86403	
	Strep culture	87081	
	Strep A	87880	
	TB	86580	
	UA, complete, non-automated	81000	
	UA, w/o micro, non-automated	81002	
	UA, w/ micro, non-automated	81003	
	Urine colony count	87086	
	Urine culture, presumptive	87088	
	Wet mount/KOH	87210	
	Vaccines		
	DT, <7 y		90702
	DTP		90701
	DtaP, <7 y		90700
	Flu, 6-35 months		90657
	Flu, 3 y +		90658
	Hep A, adult		90632
	Hep A, ped/adol, 2 dose		90633
	Hep B, adult		90746
	Hep B, ped/adol 3 dose		90744
	Hep B-Hib		90748
	Hib, 4 dose		90645
	HPV		90649
	IPV		90713
	MMR		90707
	Pneumonia, >2 y		90732
	Pneumonia conjugate, <5 y		90669
	Td, >7 y		90718
	Varicella		90716
	Tetanus toxoid adsorbed, IM		90703
	Immunizations & Injections		**Units**
	Allergen, one	95115	
	Allergen, multiple	95117	
	Imm admn <8 yo 1st Inj	90465	
	Imm admn <8 yo each add inj	90466	
	Imm <8 yo oral or intranasal	90467	
	Imm admn <8 yo each add	90468	
	Imm admin, one vacc	90471	
	Imm admin, each add'l	90472	
	Imm admin, intranasal, one	90473	
	Imm admin, intranasal, each add'l	90474	
	Injection, joint, small	20600	
	Injection, joint, intermediate	20605	
	Injection, ther/proph/diag	90772	
	Injection, trigger pt 1-2 musc	20552	

Today's charges:	
Today's payment:	
Balance due:	

Job 11 Router- Richard Manaly 9 of 20

Date of service: 10/27/09	PPO				Router Number: 2484
Patient name: ELANE YBARRA	Coinsurance:	Copay:			Physician Name: SCHWARTZ
Account #: YBA001	Noncovered Waiver?	yes	no	n/a	

X	Office visit	New	X	Est
N/A	Minimal (RN only)	N/A		99211
	Problem focused	99201		99212
	Exp problem focused	99202		99213
	Detailed	99203		99214
	Comp	99204		99215
	Comprhen/Complex	99205		
	Well visit	**New**	**X**	**Est**
	< 1 y	99381		99391
	1-4 y	99382		99392
	5-11 y	99383		99393
	12-17 y	99384		99394
	18-39 y	99385	✓	99395
	40-64 y	99386		99396
	65 y +	99387		99397

X	Medicare preventive services	
	Pap	Q0091
	Pelvic & breast	G0101
	Prostate/PSA	G0103
	Tobacco couns/3-10 min	G0375
	Tobacco couns/>10 min	G0376
	Welcome to Medicare exam	G0344
	ECG w/Welcome to Medicare	G0366
	Hemoccult, guaiac	G0107
	Flu shot	G0008
	Pneumonia shot	G0009
	Consultation/preop clearance	
	Exp problem focused	99242
	Detailed	99243
	Comp/mod complex	99244
	Comp/high complex	99245
	Other services	
	After posted hours	99050
	Evening/weekend appointment	99051
	Home health certification	G0180
	Home health recertification	G0179
	Care Plan oversight	99374
	Care Plan Oversight >30 mins	99375
	Post-op follow-up	99024
	Prolonged/60min total	99354
	Prolonged/each add 30 mins	99355
	Special reports/forms	99080
	Disability/Workers comp	99455
	Smoking Cessation <10 mins	99406
✓	Smoking Cessation >10 mins	99407
	ETOH/SA screening <30 mins	99408
	Online E/M by MD	99444
	Phone E/M <10 mins	99441
	Phone E/M <20 mins	99442
	Phone E/M <30 mins	99443
	Anticoagulant Mgmt <90 days	99363
	Anticoagulant Mgmt >90 days	99364
	In office emergency serv	99058
	Other services	
	Supplies	
	Surgical Tray	99070

Instructions:

Recommend getting mammogram

X	Office procedures		
	Cerumen removal		69210
✓	ECG, w/interpretation		93000
	ECG, rhythm strip		93040
	Endometrial biopsy		58100
	Fracture care, cast/splint Site: ________________		
	Nebulizer		94640
	Nebulizer demo		94664
	Spirometry		94010
	Spirometry, pre and post		94060
	Vasectomy		55250
	Skin procedures		**Units**
	Foreign body, skin, simple	10120	
	Foreign body, skin, complex	10121	
	I&D, abscess	10060	
	I&D, hematoma/seroma	10140	
	Laceration repair, simple Site: _______ Size: _____	120__	
	Laceration repair, layered Site: _______ Size: _____	120__	
	Laser Light Tx	96597	
	Lesion, biopsy, one	11100	
	Lesion, biopsy, each add'l	11101	
	Lesion, excision, benign Site: _______ Size: _____	114__	
	Lesion, excision, malignant Site: _______ Size: _____	116__	
	Lesion, paring/cutting, one	11055	
	Lesion, paring/cutting, 2-4	11056	
	Lesion, shave Site: _______ Size: _____	113__	
	Nail removal, partial (+T mod)	11730	
	Nail rem, w/matrix (+T mod)	11750	
	Skin tag, 1-15	11200	
	Wart, flat, 1-14	17110	
	Destruction lesion, 1st	17000	
	Destruct lesion, each addl 2-14	17003	
	Medications		**Units**
	Ampicillin, up to 500mg	J0290	
	B-12, up to 1,000 mcg	J3420	
	Epinephrine, up to 1ml	J0170	
	Kenalog, 10mg	J3301	
	Lidocaine, 10mg	J2001	
	Normal saline, 1000cc	J7030	
	Phenergan, up to 50mg	J2550	
	Progesterone, 150mg	J1055	
	Rocephin, 250mg	J0696	
	Testosterone, 200mg	J1080	
	Tigan, up to 200 mg	J3250	
	Toradol, 15mg	J1885	
	Albuterol	J7609	
	Depo-Provera 50 mg	J1055	
	Depo-Medrol 40 mg	J1030	

Diagnoses	Code
1 Annual Exam	
2 Hx Cigarette Smoking	
3	
4	

Next office visit:
Recheck • (Preventative) • PRN
Referral to:

Physician signature

X Schwartz MD

X	Laboratory		-90
✓	Venipuncture	36415	
	Blood glucose, monitoring device	82962	
✓	Blood glucose, visual dipstick	82948	
✓	CBC, w/ auto differential	85025	
	CBC, w/o auto differential	85027	
✓	Cholesterol	82465	
	Hemoccult, guaiac	82270	
	Hemoccult, immunoassay	82274	
	Hemoglobin A1C	85018	
✓	Lipid panel	80061	
	Liver panel	80076	
	KOH prep (skin, hair, nails)	87220	
✓	Metabolic panel, basic	80048	
	Metabolic panel, comprehensive	80053	
	Mononucleosis	86308	
	Pregnancy, blood	84703	
	Pregnancy, urine	81025	
	Renal panel	80069	
	Sedimentation rate	85651	
	Strep, rapid	86403	
	Strep culture	87081	
	Strep A	87880	
	TB	86580	
	UA, complete, non-automated	81000	
	UA, w/o micro, non-automated	81002	
	UA, w/ micro, non-automated	81003	
	Urine colony count	87086	
	Urine culture, presumptive	87088	
	Wet mount/KOH	87210	
	Vaccines		
	DT, <7 y		90702
	DTP		90701
	DtaP, <7 y		90700
	Flu, 6-35 months		90657
	Flu, 3 y +		90658
	Hep A, adult		90632
	Hep A, ped/adol, 2 dose		90633
	Hep B, adult		90746
	Hep B, ped/adol 3 dose		90744
	Hep B-Hib		90748
	Hib, 4 dose		90645
	HPV		90649
	IPV		90713
	MMR		90707
	Pneumonia, >2 y		90732
	Pneumonia conjugate, <5 y		90669
	Td, >7 y		90718
	Varicella		90716
✓	Tetanus toxoid adsorbed, IM		90703
	Immunizations & Injections		**Units**
	Allergen, one	95115	
	Allergen, multiple	95117	
	Imm admn <8 yo 1st Inj	90465	
	Imm admn <8 yo each add inj	90466	
	Imm <8 yo oral or intranasal	90467	
	Imm admn <8 yo each add	90468	
	Imm admin, one vacc	90471	
	Imm admin, each add'l	90472	
	Imm admin, intranasal, one	90473	
	Imm admin, intranasal, each add'l	90474	
	Injection, joint, small	20600	
	Injection, joint, intermediate	20605	
	Injection, ther/proph/diag	90772	
	Injection, trigger pt 1-2 musc	20552	

Today's charges:		
Today's payment:		
Balance due:		

Job 11 Router- Elaine Ybarra 10 of 20

Date of service: 10/27/09	Insurance: MEDICARE				Superbill Number: 2460
Patient name: WILMA STEAM Stearn	Coinsurance: 20%	Copay:			Physician Name: MURRAY
Account #: STE001	Noncovered Waiver?	yes	no	n/a	

X	Office visit	New	X	Est
	Minimal (RN only)			99211
	Problem focused	99201		99212
	Exp problem focused	99202		99213
	Detailed	99203		99214
	Comp	99204		99215
	Comprhen/Complex	99205		
	Well visit	**New**	**X**	**Est**
	< 1 y	99381		99391
	1-4 y	99382		99392
	5-11 y	99383		99393
	12-17 y	99384		99394
	18-39 y	99385		99395
	40-64 y	99386		99396
	65 y +	99387		99397

	Medicare preventive services	
	Pap	Q0091
	Pelvic & breast	G0101
	Prostate/PSA	G0103
	Tobacco couns/3-10 min	G0375
	Tobacco couns/>10 min	G0376
	Welcome to Medicare exam	G0344
	ECG w/Welcome to Medicare	G0366
	Hemoccult, guaiac	G0107
	Flu shot	G0008
	Pneumonia shot	G0009
	Consultation/preop clearance	
	Exp problem focused	99242
	Detailed	99243
	Comp/mod complex	99244
	Comp/high complex	99245
	Other services	
	After posted hours	99050
	Evening/weekend appointment	99051
	Home health certification	G0180
	Home health recertification	G0179
	Care Plan oversight	99374
	Care Plan Oversight >30 mins	99375
	Post-op follow-up	99024
	Prolonged/60min total	99354
	Prolonged/each add 30 mins	99355
	Special reports/forms	99080
	Disability/Workers comp	99455
	Smoking Cessation <10 mins	99406
	Smoking Cessation >10 mins	99407
	ETOH/SA screening <30 mins	99408
	Online E/M by MD	99444
	Phone E/M <10 mins	99441
	Phone E/M <20 mins	99442
	Phone E/M <30 mins	99443
	Anticoagulant Mgmt <90 days	99363
	Anticoagulant Mgmt >90 days	99364
	In office emergency serv	99058
	Other services	
	Supplies	
	Surgical Tray	99070
	Aminolevulinic acid (Levulan) HCL 20%	
	Instructions:	

X	Office procedures		
	Cerumen removal		69210
	ECG, w/interpretation		93000
	ECG, rhythm strip		93040
	Endometrial biopsy		58100
	Fracture care, cast/splint Site: ________		____
	Nebulizer		94640
	Nebulizer demo		94664
	Spirometry		94010
	Spirometry, pre and post		94060
	Vasectomy		55250
	Skin procedures		**Units**
	Foreign body, skin, simple	10120	
	Foreign body, skin, complex	10121	
	I&D, abscess	10060	
	I&D, hematoma/seroma	10140	
	Laceration repair, simple Site: _______ Size: _____	120__	
	Laceration repair, layered Site: _______ Size: _____	120__	
✓	Laser Light Tx	96597	
	Lesion, biopsy, one	11100	
	Lesion, biopsy, each add'l	11101	
	Lesion, excision, benign Site: _______ Size: _____	114__	
	Lesion, excision, malignant Site: _______ Size: _____	116__	
	Lesion, paring/cutting, one	11055	
	Lesion, paring/cutting, 2-4	11056	
	Lesion, shave Site: _______ Size: _____	113__	
	Nail removal, partial (+T mod)	11730	
	Nail rem, w/matrix (+T mod)	11750	
	Skin tag, 1-15	11200	
	Wart, flat, 1-14	17110	
	Destruction lesion, 1st	17000	
	Destruct lesion, each addl 2-14	17003	
	Medications		**Units**
	Ampicillin, up to 500mg	J0290	
	B-12, up to 1,000 mcg	J3420	
	Epinephrine, up to 1ml	J0170	
	Kenalog, 10mg	J3301	
	Lidocaine, 10mg	J2001	
	Normal saline, 1000cc	J7030	
	Phenergan, up to 50mg	J2550	
	Progesterone, 150mg	J1055	
	Rocephin, 250mg	J0696	
	Testosterone, 200mg	J1080	
	Tigan, up to 200 mg	J3250	
	Toradol, 15mg	J1885	
	Albuterol	J7609	
	Depo-Provera 50 mg	J1055	
	Depo-Medrol 40 mg	J1030	

Diagnoses	Code
1 actinic keratosis	
2 HTN	
3 DM	
4	

Next office visit: 1 mth

Recheck • Preventative • PRN

Referral to:

Physician signature

[signature] MD

X	Laboratory		-90
	Venipuncture	36415	
	Blood glucose, monitoring device	82962	
	Blood glucose, visual dipstick	82948	
	CBC, w/ auto differential	85025	
	CBC, w/o auto differential	85027	
	Cholesterol	82465	
	Hemoccult, guaiac	82270	
	Hemoccult, immunoassay	82274	
	Hemoglobin A1C	85018	
	Lipid panel	80061	
	Liver panel	80076	
	KOH prep (skin, hair, nails)	87220	
	Metabolic panel, basic	80048	
	Metabolic panel, comprehensive	80053	
	Mononucleosis	86308	
	Pregnancy, blood	84703	
	Pregnancy, urine	81025	
	Renal panel	80069	
	Sedimentation rate	85651	
	Strep, rapid	86403	
	Strep culture	87081	
	Strep A	87880	
	TB	86580	
	UA, complete, non-automated	81000	
	UA, w/o micro, non-automated	81002	
	UA, w/ micro, non-automated	81003	
	Urine colony count	87086	
	Urine culture, presumptive	87088	
	Wet mount/KOH	87210	

	Vaccines	
	DT, <7 y	90702
	DTP	90701
	DtaP, <7 y	90700
	Flu, 6-35 months	90657
	Flu, 3 y +	90658
	Hep A, adult	90632
	Hep A, ped/adol, 2 dose	90633
	Hep B, adult	90746
	Hep B, ped/adol 3 dose	90744
	Hep B-Hib	90748
	Hib, 4 dose	90645
	HPV	90649
	IPV	90713
	MMR	90707
	Pneumonia, >2 y	90732
	Pneumonia conjugate, <5 y	90669
	Td, >7 y	90718
	Varicella	90716
	Tetanus toxoid adsorbed, IM	90703

	Immunizations & Injections		Units
	Allergen, one	95115	
	Allergen, multiple	95117	
	Imm admn <8 yo 1st Inj	90465	
	Imm admn <8 yo each add inj	90466	
	Imm <8 yo oral or intranasal	90467	
	Imm admn <8 yo each add	90468	
	Imm admin, one vacc	90471	
	Imm admin, each add'l	90472	
	Imm admin, intranasal, one	90473	
	Imm admin, intranasal, each add'l	90474	
	Injection, joint, small	20600	
	Injection, joint, intermediate	20605	
	Injection, ther/proph/diag	90772	
	Injection, trigger pt 1-2 musc	20552	

Today's charges:		
Today's payment:		
Balance due:		

Job 11 Router- Wilma Stearn 11 of 20

Date of service: 10/27/09	Insurance: MEDICARE				Superbill Number: 2461
Patient name: ISABEL DURAND	Coinsurance: 20%	Copay:			Physician Name: KEMPER
Account #: DUR001	Noncovered Waiver?	yes	no	n/a	

x	Office visit	New	x	Est
	Minimal (RN only)			99211
	Problem focused	99201		99212
	Exp problem focused	99202		99213
	Detailed	99203		99214
	Comp	99204		99215
	Comprhen/Complex	99205		
	Well visit	**New**	**x**	**Est**
	< 1 y	99381		99391
	1-4 y	99382		99392
	5-11 y	99383		99393
	12-17 y	99384		99394
	18-39 y	99385		99395
	40-64 y	99386		99396
	65 y +	99387		99397
	Medicare preventive services			
1 ✓	Pap			Q0091
1 ✓	Pelvic & breast			G0101
	Prostate/PSA			G0103
	Tobacco couns/3-10 min			G0375
	Tobacco couns/>10 min			G0376
	Welcome to Medicare exam			G0344
	ECG w/Welcome to Medicare			G0366
	Hemoccult, guaiac			G0107
	Flu shot			G0008
	Pneumonia shot			G0009
	Consultation/preop clearance			
	Exp problem focused			99242
	Detailed			99243
	Comp/mod complex			99244
	Comp/high complex			99245
	Other services			
	After posted hours			99050
	Evening/weekend appointment			99051
	Home health certification			G0180
	Home health recertification			G0179
	Care Plan oversight			99374
	Care Plan Oversight >30 mins			99375
	Post-op follow-up			99024
	Prolonged/60min total			99354
	Prolonged/each add 30 mins			99355
	Special reports/forms			99080
	Disability/Workers comp			99455
	Smoking Cessation <10 mins			99406
	Smoking Cessation >10 mins			99407
	ETOH/SA screening <30 mins			99408
	Online E/M by MD			99444
	Phone E/M <10 mins			99441
	Phone E/M <20 mins			99442
	Phone E/M <30 mins			99443
	Anticoagulant Mgmt <90 days			99363
	Anticoagulant Mgmt >90 days			99364
	In office emergency serv			99058
	Other services			
	Supplies			
	Surgical Tray			99070

x	Office procedures		
	Cerumen removal		69210
	ECG, w/interpretation		93000
	ECG, rhythm strip		93040
	Endometrial biopsy		58100
	Fracture care, cast/splint		____
	Site: ____________		
	Nebulizer		94640
	Nebulizer demo		94664
	Spirometry		94010
	Spirometry, pre and post		94060
	Vasectomy		55250
	Skin procedures		**Units**
	Foreign body, skin, simple	10120	
	Foreign body, skin, complex	10121	
	I&D, abscess	10060	
	I&D, hematoma/seroma	10140	
	Laceration repair, simple	120__	
	Site: _______ Size: ____		
	Laceration repair, layered	120__	
	Site: _______ Size: ____		
	Laser Light Tx	96597	
	Lesion, biopsy, one	11100	
	Lesion, biopsy, each add'l	11101	
	Lesion, excision, benign	114__	
	Site: _______ Size: ____		
	Lesion, excision, malignant	116__	
	Site: _______ Size: ____		
	Lesion, paring/cutting, one	11055	
	Lesion, paring/cutting, 2-4	11056	
	Lesion, shave	113__	
	Site: _______ Size: ____		
	Nail removal, partial (+T mod)	11730	
	Nail rem, w/matrix (+T mod)	11750	
	Skin tag, 1-15	11200	
	Wart, flat, 1-14	17110	
	Destruction lesion, 1st	17000	
	Destruct lesion, each addl 2-14	17003	
	Medications		**Units**
	Ampicillin, up to 500mg	J0290	
	B-12, up to 1,000 mcg	J3420	
	Epinephrine, up to 1ml	J0170	
	Kenalog, 10mg	J3301	
	Lidocaine, 10mg	J2001	
	Normal saline, 1000cc	J7030	
	Phenergan, up to 50mg	J2550	
	Progesterone, 150mg	J1055	
	Rocephin, 250mg	J0696	
	Testosterone, 200mg	J1080	
	Tigan, up to 200 mg	J3250	
	Toradol, 15mg	J1885	
	Albuterol	J7609	
	Depo-Provera 50 mg	J1055	
	Depo-Medrol 40 mg	J1030	

Diagnoses	Code
1 Annual Pelvic Exam	
2 Vaginal prolapse	
3	
4	

Next office visit:
Recheck • Preventative (circled) • PRN
Referral to:

x	Laboratory		-90
	Venipuncture	36415	
	Blood glucose, monitoring device	82962	
	Blood glucose, visual dipstick	82948	
	CBC, w/ auto differential	85025	
	CBC, w/o auto differential	85027	
	Cholesterol	82465	
	Hemoccult, guaiac	82270	
	Hemoccult, immunoassay	82274	
	Hemoglobin A1C	85018	
	Lipid panel	80061	
	Liver panel	80076	
	KOH prep (skin, hair, nails)	87220	
	Metabolic panel, basic	80048	
	Metabolic panel, comprehensive	80053	
	Mononucleosis	86308	
	Pregnancy, blood	84703	
	Pregnancy, urine	81025	
	Renal panel	80069	
	Sedimentation rate	85651	
	Strep, rapid	86403	
	Strep culture	87081	
	Strep A	87880	
	TB	86580	
	UA, complete, non-automated	81000	
	UA, w/o micro, non-automated	81002	
	UA, w/ micro, non-automated	81003	
	Urine colony count	87086	
	Urine culture, presumptive	87088	
	Wet mount/KOH	87210	
	Vaccines		
	DT, <7 y		90702
	DTP		90701
	DtaP, <7 y		90700
	Flu, 6-35 months		90657
	Flu, 3 y +		90658
	Hep A, adult		90632
	Hep A, ped/adol, 2 dose		90633
	Hep B, adult		90746
	Hep B, ped/adol 3 dose		90744
	Hep B-Hib		90748
	Hib, 4 dose		90645
	HPV		90649
	IPV		90713
	MMR		90707
	Pneumonia, >2 y		90732
	Pneumonia conjugate, <5 y		90669
	Td, >7 y		90718
	Varicella		90716
	Tetanus toxoid adsorbed, IM		90703
	Immunizations & Injections		**Units**
	Allergen, one	95115	
	Allergen, multiple	95117	
	Imm admn <8 yo 1st Inj	90465	
	Imm admn <8 yo each add inj	90466	
	Imm <8 yo oral or intranasal	90467	
	Imm admn <8 yo each add	90468	
	Imm admin, one vacc	90471	
	Imm admin, each add'l	90472	
	Imm admin, intranasal, one	90473	
	Imm admin, intranasal, each add'l	90474	
	Injection, joint, small	20600	
	Injection, joint, intermediate	20605	
	Injection, ther/proph/diag	90772	
	Injection, trigger pt 1-2 musc	20552	

Instructions:

Call w/ results if abnormal

Physician signature

X Sally Kemper MD

Today's charges:		
Today's payment:		
Balance due:		

Job 11 Router- Isabel Durand 12 of 20

Date of service: 10/27/09	Insurance: GREATWEST			Superbill Number: 2462
Patient name: JULIUS WASHINGTON	Coinsurance: 20%	Copay:		Physician Name: MENDENHALL
Account #: WAS001	Noncovered Waiver?	yes	no	n/a

x	Office visit	New	x	Est
	Minimal (RN only)			99211
	Problem focused	99201		99212
	Exp problem focused	99202		99213
	Detailed	99203		99214
✓	Comp	99204		99215
	Comprhen/Complex	99205		
x	**Well visit**	**New**	**x**	**Est**
	< 1 y	99381		99391
	1-4 y	99382		99392
	5-11 y	99383		99393
	12-17 y	99384		99394
	18-39 y	99385		99395
	40-64 y	99386		99396
	65 y +	99387		99397

	Medicare preventive services	
	Pap	Q0091
	Pelvic & breast	G0101
	Prostate/PSA	G0103
	Tobacco couns/3-10 min	G0375
	Tobacco couns/>10 min	G0376
	Welcome to Medicare exam	G0344
	ECG w/Welcome to Medicare	G0366
	Hemoccult, guaiac	G0107
	Flu shot	G0008
	Pneumonia shot	G0009
	Consultation/preop clearance	
	Exp problem focused	99242
	Detailed	99243
	Comp/mod complex	99244
	Comp/high complex	99245
	Other services	
	After posted hours	99050
	Evening/weekend appointment	99051
	Home health certification	G0180
	Home health recertification	G0179
	Care Plan oversight	99374
	Care Plan Oversight >30 mins	99375
	Post-op follow-up	99024
	Prolonged/60min total	99354
	Prolonged/each add 30 mins	99355
	Special reports/forms	99080
	Disability/Workers comp	99455
	Smoking Cessation <10 mins	99406
	Smoking Cessation >10 mins	99407
	ETOH/SA screening <30 mins	99408
	Online E/M by MD	99444
	Phone E/M <10 mins	99441
	Phone E/M <20 mins	99442
	Phone E/M <30 mins	99443
	Anticoagulant Mgmt <90 days	99363
	Anticoagulant Mgmt >90 days	99364
	In office emergency serv	99058
	Other services	
✓	Chest x-ray front + lateral	
	Supplies	
	Surgical Tray	99070

Instructions:

Rx Levaquin po bid q day 10 days

x	Office procedures		
	Cerumen removal		69210
	ECG, w/interpretation		93000
	ECG, rhythm strip		93040
	Endometrial biopsy		58100
	Fracture care, cast/splint		____
	Site: ______________		
✓	Nebulizer		94640
	Nebulizer demo		94664
	Spirometry		94010
	Spirometry, pre and post		94060
	Vasectomy		55250
	Skin procedures		**Units**
	Foreign body, skin, simple	10120	
	Foreign body, skin, complex	10121	
	I&D, abscess	10060	
	I&D, hematoma/seroma	10140	
	Laceration repair, simple	120__	
	Site: _______ Size: _____		
	Laceration repair, layered	120__	
	Site: _______ Size: _____		
	Laser Light Tx	96597	
	Lesion, biopsy, one	11100	
	Lesion, biopsy, each add'l	11101	
	Lesion, excision, benign	114__	
	Site: _______ Size: _____		
	Lesion, excision, malignant	116__	
	Site: _______ Size: _____		
	Lesion, paring/cutting, one	11055	
	Lesion, paring/cutting, 2-4	11056	
	Lesion, shave	113__	
	Site: _______ Size: _____		
	Nail removal, partial (+T mod)	11730	
	Nail rem, w/matrix (+T mod)	11750	
	Skin tag, 1-15	11200	
	Wart, flat, 1-14	17110	
	Destruction lesion, 1st	17000	
	Destruct lesion, each addl 2-14	17003	
	Medications		**Units**
	Ampicillin, up to 500mg	J0290	
	B-12, up to 1,000 mcg	J3420	
	Epinephrine, up to 1ml	J0170	
	Kenalog, 10mg	J3301	
	Lidocaine, 10mg	J2001	
	Normal saline, 1000cc	J7030	
	Phenergan, up to 50mg	J2550	
	Progesterone, 150mg	J1055	
	Rocephin, 250mg	J0696	
	Testosterone, 200mg	J1080	
	Tigan, up to 200 mg	J3250	
	Toradol, 15mg	J1885	
✓	Albuterol	J7609	
	Depo-Provera 50 mg	J1055	
	Depo-Medrol 40 mg	J1030	

Diagnoses	Code
1 Acute exacerbation asthma	
2 bronchitis	
3 sinusitis	
4	

Next office visit: 2 weeks

(Recheck) • Preventative • PRN

Referral to:

Physician signature

x Sarah Mendenhall MD

x	Laboratory		-90
	Venipuncture	36415	
	Blood glucose, monitoring device	82962	
	Blood glucose, visual dipstick	82948	
	CBC, w/ auto differential	85025	
	CBC, w/o auto differential	85027	
	Cholesterol	82465	
	Hemoccult, guaiac	82270	
	Hemoccult, immunoassay	82274	
	Hemoglobin A1C	85018	
	Lipid panel	80061	
	Liver panel	80076	
	KOH prep (skin, hair, nails)	87220	
	Metabolic panel, basic	80048	
	Metabolic panel, comprehensive	80053	
	Mononucleosis	86308	
	Pregnancy, blood	84703	
	Pregnancy, urine	81025	
	Renal panel	80069	
	Sedimentation rate	85651	
	Strep, rapid	86403	
	Strep culture	87081	
	Strep A	87880	
	TB	86580	
	UA, complete, non-automated	81000	
	UA, w/o micro, non-automated	81002	
	UA, w/ micro, non-automated	81003	
	Urine colony count	87086	
	Urine culture, presumptive	87088	
	Wet mount/KOH	87210	
	Vaccines		
	DT, <7 y		90702
	DTP		90701
	DtaP, <7 y		90700
	Flu, 6-35 months		90657
	Flu, 3 y +		90658
	Hep A, adult		90632
	Hep A, ped/adol, 2 dose		90633
	Hep B, adult		90746
	Hep B, ped/adol 3 dose		90744
	Hep B-Hib		90748
	Hib, 4 dose		90645
	HPV		90649
	IPV		90713
	MMR		90707
	Pneumonia, >2 y		90732
	Pneumonia conjugate, <5 y		90669
	Td, >7 y		90718
	Varicella		90716
	Tetanus toxoid adsorbed, IM		90703
	Immunizations & Injections		**Units**
	Allergen, one	95115	
	Allergen, multiple	95117	
	Imm admn <8 yo 1st Inj	90465	
	Imm admn <8 yo each add inj	90466	
	Imm <8 yo oral or intranasal	90467	
	Imm admn <8 yo each add	90468	
	Imm admin, one vacc	90471	
	Imm admin, each add'l	90472	
	Imm admin, intranasal, one	90473	
	Imm admin, intranasal, each add'l	90474	
	Injection, joint, small	20600	
	Injection, joint, intermediate	20605	
	Injection, ther/proph/diag	90772	
	Injection, trigger pt 1-2 musc	20552	

Today's charges:	
Today's payment:	
Balance due:	

Job 11 Router- Julius Washington 13 of 20

Date of service: 10/27/09	Insurance: GALAXY HEALTH				Superbill Number: 2458
Patient name: WILLIAM KOSTNER	Coinsurance: 20%	Copay:			Physician Name: HEATH
Account #: KOS001	Noncovered Waiver?	yes	no	n/a	

x	Office visit	New	x	Est
	Minimal (RN only)			99211
	Problem focused	99201		99212
	Exp problem focused	99202		99213
	Detailed	99203		99214
	Comp	99204		99215
	Comprhen/Complex	99205		
	Well visit	**New**	x	**Est**
	< 1 y	99381		99391
	1-4 y	99382		99392
	5-11 y	99383		99393
	12-17 y	99384		99394
	18-39 y	99385		99395
	40-64 y	99386		99396
	65 y +	99387		99397
	Medicare preventive services			
	Pap			Q0091
	Pelvic & breast			G0101
	Prostate/PSA			G0103
	Tobacco couns/3-10 min			G0375
	Tobacco couns/>10 min			G0376
	Welcome to Medicare exam			G0344
	ECG w/Welcome to Medicare			G0366
	Hemoccult, guaiac			G0107
	Flu shot			G0008
	Pneumonia shot			G0009
	Consultation/preop clearance			
	Exp problem focused			99242
	Detailed			99243
✓	Comp/mod complex			99244
	Comp/high complex			99245
	Other services			
	After posted hours			99050
	Evening/weekend appointment			99051
	Home health certification			G0180
	Home health recertification			G0179
	Care Plan oversight			99374
	Care Plan Oversight >30 mins			99375
	Post-op follow-up			99024
	Prolonged/60min total			99354
	Prolonged/each add 30 mins			99355
	Special reports/forms			99080
	Disability/Workers comp			99455
	Smoking Cessation <10 mins			99406
	Smoking Cessation >10 mins			99407
	ETOH/SA screening <30 mins			99408
	Online E/M by MD			99444
	Phone E/M <10 mins			99441
	Phone E/M <20 mins			99442
	Phone E/M <30 mins			99443
	Anticoagulant Mgmt <90 days			99363
	Anticoagulant Mgmt >90 days			99364
	In office emergency serv			99058
	Other services			
	Supplies			
	Surgical Tray			99070
	Instructions:			

x	Office procedures		
	Cerumen removal		69210
	ECG, w/interpretation		93000
	ECG, rhythm strip		93040
	Endometrial biopsy		58100
	Fracture care, cast/splint		____
	Site: ________________		
	Nebulizer		94640
	Nebulizer demo		94664
	Spirometry		94010
	Spirometry, pre and post		94060
	Vasectomy		55250
	Skin procedures		**Units**
	Foreign body, skin, simple	10120	
	Foreign body, skin, complex	10121	
	I&D, abscess	10060	
	I&D, hematoma/seroma	10140	
	Laceration repair, simple	120__	
	Site: _______ Size: _____		
	Laceration repair, layered	120__	
	Site: _______ Size: _____		
	Laser Light Tx	96597	
	Lesion, biopsy, one	11100	
	Lesion, biopsy, each add'l	11101	
	Lesion, excision, benign	114__	
	Site: _______ Size: _____		
	Lesion, excision, malignant	116__	
	Site: _______ Size: _____		
	Lesion, paring/cutting, one	11055	
	Lesion, paring/cutting, 2-4	11056	
	Lesion, shave	113__	
	Site: _______ Size: _____		
	Nail removal, partial (+T mod)	11730	
	Nail rem, w/matrix (+T mod)	11750	
	Skin tag, 1-15	11200	
	Wart, flat, 1-14	17110	
	Destruction lesion, 1st	17000	
	Destruct lesion, each addl 2-14	17003	
	Medications		**Units**
	Ampicillin, up to 500mg	J0290	
	B-12, up to 1,000 mcg	J3420	
	Epinephrine, up to 1ml	J0170	
	Kenalog, 10mg	J3301	
✓	Lidocaine, 10mg	J2001	
	Normal saline, 1000cc	J7030	
	Phenergan, up to 50mg	J2550	
	Progesterone, 150mg	J1055	
	Rocephin, 250mg	J0696	
	Testosterone, 200mg	J1080	
	Tigan, up to 200 mg	J3250	
	Toradol, 15mg	J1885	
	Albuterol	J7609	
	Depo-Provera 50 mg	J1055	
✓	Depo-Medrol 40 mg	J1030	
	Diagnoses		**Code**
	1 Vertigo		
	2 HA		
	3 Myospasm		
	4		

Next office visit: 4 wks

Recheck • Preventative • PRN

Referral to:

x	Laboratory		-90
	Venipuncture	36415	
	Blood glucose, monitoring device	82962	
	Blood glucose, visual dipstick	82948	
	CBC, w/ auto differential	85025	
	CBC, w/o auto differential	85027	
	Cholesterol	82465	
	Hemoccult, guaiac	82270	
	Hemoccult, immunoassay	82274	
	Hemoglobin A1C	85018	
	Lipid panel	80061	
	Liver panel	80076	
	KOH prep (skin, hair, nails)	87220	
	Metabolic panel, basic	80048	
	Metabolic panel, comprehensive	80053	
	Mononucleosis	86308	
	Pregnancy, blood	84703	
	Pregnancy, urine	81025	
	Renal panel	80069	
	Sedimentation rate	85651	
	Strep, rapid	86403	
	Strep culture	87081	
	Strep A	87880	
	TB	86580	
	UA, complete, non-automated	81000	
	UA, w/o micro, non-automated	81002	
	UA, w/ micro, non-automated	81003	
	Urine colony count	87086	
	Urine culture, presumptive	87088	
	Wet mount/KOH	87210	
	Vaccines		
	DT, <7 y		90702
	DTP		90701
	DtaP, <7 y		90700
	Flu, 6-35 months		90657
	Flu, 3 y +		90658
	Hep A, adult		90632
	Hep A, ped/adol, 2 dose		90633
	Hep B, adult		90746
	Hep B, ped/adol 3 dose		90744
	Hep B-Hib		90748
	Hib, 4 dose		90645
	HPV		90649
	IPV		90713
	MMR		90707
	Pneumonia, >2 y		90732
	Pneumonia conjugate, <5 y		90669
	Td, >7 y		90718
	Varicella		90716
	Tetanus toxoid adsorbed, IM		90703
	Immunizations & Injections		**Units**
	Allergen, one	95115	
	Allergen, multiple	95117	
	Imm admn <8 yo 1st Inj	90465	
	Imm admn <8 yo each add inj	90466	
	Imm <8 yo oral or intranasal	90467	
	Imm admn <8 yo each add	90468	
	Imm admin, one vacc	90471	
	Imm admin, each add'l	90472	
	Imm admin, intranasal, one	90473	
	Imm admin, intranasal, each add'l	90474	
	Injection, joint, small	20600	
	Injection, joint, intermediate	20605	
	Injection, ther/proph/diag	90772	
✓	Injection, trigger pt 1-2 musc	20552	

Physician signature	Today's charges:		
x [signature]	Today's payment:		
	Balance due:		

Job 11 Router- William Kostner 14 of 20

Date of service: 10/27/09	Insurance: MEDICARE SW/CENTURY SR				Superbill Number: 2457
Patient name: DEANNA HARTSFELD	Coinsurance: 20%	Copay:			Physician Name: MURRAY
Account #: HAR001	Noncovered Waiver?	yes	no	n/a	

x	Office visit	New	x	Est
	Minimal (RN only)			99211
	Problem focused	99201		99212
	Exp problem focused	99202		99213
	Detailed	99203		99214
	Comp	99204		99215
	Comprhen/Complex	99205		
	Well visit	**New**	**x**	**Est**
	< 1 y	99381		99391
	1-4 y	99382		99392
	5-11 y	99383		99393
	12-17 y	99384		99394
	18-39 y	99385		99395
	40-64 y	99386		99396
	65 y +	99387		99397
	Medicare preventive services			
✓	Pap			Q0091
	Pelvic & breast			G0101
	Prostate/PSA			G0103
	Tobacco couns/3-10 min			G0375
✓	Tobacco couns/>10 min			G0376
✓	Welcome to Medicare exam			G0344
	ECG w/Welcome to Medicare			G0366
	Hemoccult, guaiac			G0107
	Flu shot			G0008
	Pneumonia shot			G0009
	Consultation/preop clearance			
	Exp problem focused			99242
	Detailed			99243
	Comp/mod complex			99244
	Comp/high complex			99245
	Other services			
	After posted hours			99050
	Evening/weekend appointment			99051
	Home health certification			G0180
	Home health recertification			G0179
	Care Plan oversight			99374
	Care Plan Oversight >30 mins			99375
	Post-op follow-up			99024
	Prolonged/60min total			99354
	Prolonged/each add 30 mins			99355
	Special reports/forms			99080
	Disability/Workers comp			99455
	Smoking Cessation <10 mins			99406
	Smoking Cessation >10 mins			99407
	ETOH/SA screening <30 mins			99408
	Online E/M by MD			99444
	Phone E/M <10 mins			99441
	Phone E/M <20 mins			99442
	Phone E/M <30 mins			99443
	Anticoagulant Mgmt <90 days			99363
	Anticoagulant Mgmt >90 days			99364
	In office emergency serv			99058
	Other services			
✓	Neck Scan			
	Supplies			
	Surgical Tray			99070
	Instructions:			

20 mins counseling diet/exercise/ Diabetes Risk

x	Office procedures		
	Cerumen removal		69210
✓	ECG, w/interpretation		93000
	ECG, rhythm strip		93040
	Endometrial biopsy		58100
	Fracture care, cast/splint Site: ________		____
	Nebulizer		94640
	Nebulizer demo		94664
	Spirometry		94010
	Spirometry, pre and post		94060
	Vasectomy		55250
	Skin procedures		**Units**
	Foreign body, skin, simple	10120	
	Foreign body, skin, complex	10121	
	I&D, abscess	10060	
	I&D, hematoma/seroma	10140	
	Laceration repair, simple Site: _____ Size: ____	120__	
	Laceration repair, layered Site: _____ Size: ____	120__	
	Laser Light Tx	96597	
	Lesion, biopsy, one	11100	
	Lesion, biopsy, each add'l	11101	
	Lesion, excision, benign Site: _____ Size: ____	114__	
	Lesion, excision, malignant Site: _____ Size: ____	116__	
	Lesion, paring/cutting, one	11055	
	Lesion, paring/cutting, 2-4	11056	
	Lesion, shave Site: _____ Size: ____	113__	
	Nail removal, partial (+T mod)	11730	
	Nail rem, w/matrix (+T mod)	11750	
	Skin tag, 1-15	11200	
	Wart, flat, 1-14	17110	
	Destruction lesion, 1st	17000	
	Destruct lesion, each addl 2-14	17003	
	Medications		**Units**
	Ampicillin, up to 500mg	J0290	
	B-12, up to 1,000 mcg	J3420	
	Epinephrine, up to 1ml	J0170	
	Kenalog, 10mg	J3301	
	Lidocaine, 10mg	J2001	
	Normal saline, 1000cc	J7030	
	Phenergan, up to 50mg	J2550	
	Progesterone, 150mg	J1055	
	Rocephin, 250mg	J0696	
	Testosterone, 200mg	J1080	
	Tigan, up to 200 mg	J3250	
	Toradol, 15mg	J1885	
	Albuterol	J7609	
	Depo-Provera 50 mg	J1055	
	Depo-Medrol 40 mg	J1030	
	Diagnoses		**Code**
	1 Elevated BP		
	2 Well Check		
	3 Obesity		
	4		
	Next office visit: 1 yr		
	Recheck • Preventative • PRN		
	Referral to:		
	Physician signature		
	x Renee Murray MD		

x	Laboratory		-90
	Venipuncture	36415	
	Blood glucose, monitoring device	82962	
	Blood glucose, visual dipstick	82948	
	CBC, w/ auto differential	85025	
	CBC, w/o auto differential	85027	
	Cholesterol	82465	
	Hemoccult, guaiac	82270	
	Hemoccult, immunoassay	82274	
	Hemoglobin A1C	85018	
	Lipid panel	80061	
	Liver panel	80076	
	KOH prep (skin, hair, nails)	87220	
	Metabolic panel, basic	80048	
✓	Metabolic panel, comprehensive	80053	
	Mononucleosis	86308	
	Pregnancy, blood	84703	
	Pregnancy, urine	81025	
	Renal panel	80069	
	Sedimentation rate	85651	
	Strep, rapid	86403	
	Strep culture	87081	
	Strep A	87880	
	TB	86580	
	UA, complete, non-automated	81000	
	UA, w/o micro, non-automated	81002	
	UA, w/ micro, non-automated	81003	
	Urine colony count	87086	
	Urine culture, presumptive	87088	
	Wet mount/KOH	87210	
	Vaccines		
	DT, <7 y		90702
	DTP		90701
	DtaP, <7 y		90700
	Flu, 6-35 months		90657
	Flu, 3 y +		90658
	Hep A, adult		90632
	Hep A, ped/adol, 2 dose		90633
	Hep B, adult		90746
	Hep B, ped/adol 3 dose		90744
	Hep B-Hib		90748
	Hib, 4 dose		90645
	HPV		90649
	IPV		90713
	MMR		90707
	Pneumonia, >2 y		90732
	Pneumonia conjugate, <5 y		90669
	Td, >7 y		90718
	Varicella		90716
	Tetanus toxoid adsorbed, IM		90703
	Immunizations & Injections		**Units**
	Allergen, one	95115	
	Allergen, multiple	95117	
	Imm admn <8 yo 1st Inj	90465	
	Imm admn <8 yo each add inj	90466	
	Imm <8 yo oral or intranasal	90467	
	Imm admn <8 yo each add	90468	
	Imm admin, one vacc	90471	
	Imm admin, each add'l	90472	
	Imm admin, intranasal, one	90473	
	Imm admin, intranasal, each add'l	90474	
	Injection, joint, small	20600	
	Injection, joint, intermediate	20605	
	Injection, ther/proph/diag	90772	
	Injection, trigger pt 1-2 musc	20552	
	Today's charges:		
	Today's payment:		
	Balance due:		

Job 11 Router- Deanna Hartsfeld 15 of 20

Date of service: 10/27/09	Insurance: MEDICARE STATE WIDE				Superbill Number: 2455
Patient name: VITO MANGANO	Coinsurance: 20%	Copay:			Physician Name: HEATH
Account #: MAN001	Noncovered Waiver?	yes	no	n/a	

x	Office visit	New	x	Est
	Minimal (RN only)			99211
	Problem focused	99201		99212
	Exp problem focused	99202		99213
	Detailed	99203		99214
	Comp	99204	✓	99215
	Comprhen/Complex	99205		
	Well visit	**New**	**x**	**Est**
	< 1 y	99381		99391
	1-4 y	99382		99392
	5-11 y	99383		99393
	12-17 y	99384		99394
	18-39 y	99385		99395
	40-64 y	99386		99396
	65 y +	99387		99397
	Medicare preventive services			
	Pap			Q0091
	Pelvic & breast			G0101
✓	Prostate/PSA			G0103
	Tobacco couns/3-10 min			G0375
	Tobacco couns/>10 min			G0376
	Welcome to Medicare exam			G0344
	ECG w/Welcome to Medicare			G0366
	Hemoccult, guaiac			G0107
	Flu shot			G0008
	Pneumonia shot			G0009
	Consultation/preop clearance			
	Exp problem focused			99242
	Detailed			99243
	Comp/mod complex			99244
	Comp/high complex			99245
	Other services			
	After posted hours			99050
	Evening/weekend appointment			99051
	Home health certification			G0180
	Home health recertification			G0179
	Care Plan oversight			99374
	Care Plan Oversight >30 mins			99375
	Post-op follow-up			99024
	Prolonged/60min total			99354
	Prolonged/each add 30 mins			99355
	Special reports/forms			99080
	Disability/Workers comp			99455
	Smoking Cessation <10 mins			99406
	Smoking Cessation >10 mins			99407
	ETOH/SA screening <30 mins			99408
	Online E/M by MD			99444
	Phone E/M <10 mins			99441
	Phone E/M <20 mins			99442
	Phone E/M <30 mins			99443
	Anticoagulant Mgmt <90 days			99363
	Anticoagulant Mgmt >90 days			99364
	In office emergency serv			99058
	Other services			
✓	U/S bladder +			
	Trans rectal prostate US			
	Supplies			
	Surgical Tray			99070
	Foley catheter			
	Bladder catheterization			

x	Office procedures		
	Cerumen removal		69210
	ECG, w/interpretation		93000
	ECG, rhythm strip		93040
	Endometrial biopsy		58100
	Fracture care, cast/splint		
	Site: ________________		
	Nebulizer		94640
	Nebulizer demo		94664
	Spirometry		94010
	Spirometry, pre and post		94060
	Vasectomy		55250
	Skin procedures		**Units**
	Foreign body, skin, simple	10120	
	Foreign body, skin, complex	10121	
	I&D, abscess	10060	
	I&D, hematoma/seroma	10140	
	Laceration repair, simple	120__	
	Site: _______ Size: _____		
	Laceration repair, layered	120__	
	Site: _______ Size: _____		
	Laser Light Tx	96597	
	Lesion, biopsy, one	11100	
	Lesion, biopsy, each add'l	11101	
	Lesion, excision, benign	114__	
	Site: _______ Size: _____		
	Lesion, excision, malignant	116__	
	Site: _______ Size: _____		
	Lesion, paring/cutting, one	11055	
	Lesion, paring/cutting, 2-4	11056	
	Lesion, shave	113__	
	Site: _______ Size: _____		
	Nail removal, partial (+T mod)	11730	
	Nail rem, w/matrix (+T mod)	11750	
	Skin tag, 1-15	11200	
	Wart, flat, 1-14	17110	
	Destruction lesion, 1st	17000	
	Destruct lesion, each addl 2-14	17003	
	Medications		**Units**
	Ampicillin, up to 500mg	J0290	
	B-12, up to 1,000 mcg	J3420	
	Epinephrine, up to 1ml	J0170	
	Kenalog, 10mg	J3301	
	Lidocaine, 10mg	J2001	
	Normal saline, 1000cc	J7030	
	Phenergan, up to 50mg	J2550	
	Progesterone, 150mg	J1055	
	Rocephin, 250mg	J0696	
	Testosterone, 200mg	J1080	
	Tigan, up to 200 mg	J3250	
	Toradol, 15mg	J1885	
	Albuterol	J7609	
	Depo-Provera 50 mg	J1055	
	Depo-Medrol 40 mg	J1030	

Diagnoses		Code
1 Enlarged prostate w/ nodules		
2 Urinary outlet obstruction		
3 Urinary retention		
4		

Next office visit: 1 mo

Recheck • Preventative • PRN

Referral to: Dr. Howard - urology

x	Laboratory		-90
✓	Venipuncture	36415	
	Blood glucose, monitoring device	82962	
	Blood glucose, visual dipstick	82948	
	CBC, w/ auto differential	85025	
	CBC, w/o auto differential	85027	
	Cholesterol	82465	
	Hemoccult, guaiac	82270	
	Hemoccult, immunoassay	82274	
	Hemoglobin A1C	85018	
	Lipid panel	80061	
	Liver panel	80076	
	KOH prep (skin, hair, nails)	87220	
	Metabolic panel, basic	80048	
	Metabolic panel, comprehensive	80053	
	Mononucleosis	86308	
	Pregnancy, blood	84703	
	Pregnancy, urine	81025	
	Renal panel	80069	
	Sedimentation rate	85651	
	Strep, rapid	86403	
	Strep culture	87081	
	Strep A	87880	
	TB	86580	
	UA, complete, non-automated	81000	
	UA, w/o micro, non-automated	81002	
✓	UA, w/ micro, non-automated	81003	
	Urine colony count	87086	
✓	Urine culture, presumptive	87088	
	Wet mount/KOH	87210	
	Vaccines		
	DT, <7 y		90702
	DTP		90701
	DtaP, <7 y		90700
	Flu, 6-35 months		90657
	Flu, 3 y +		90658
	Hep A, adult		90632
	Hep A, ped/adol, 2 dose		90633
	Hep B, adult		90746
	Hep B, ped/adol 3 dose		90744
	Hep B-Hib		90748
	Hib, 4 dose		90645
	HPV		90649
	IPV		90713
	MMR		90707
	Pneumonia, >2 y		90732
	Pneumonia conjugate, <5 y		90669
	Td, >7 y		90718
	Varicella		90716
	Tetanus toxoid adsorbed, IM		90703
	Immunizations & Injections		**Units**
	Allergen, one	95115	
	Allergen, multiple	95117	
	Imm admn <8 yo 1st Inj	90465	
	Imm admn <8 yo each add inj	90466	
	Imm <8 yo oral or intranasal	90467	
	Imm admn <8 yo each add	90468	
	Imm admin, one vacc	90471	
	Imm admin, each add'l	90472	
	Imm admin, intranasal, one	90473	
	Imm admin, intranasal, each add'l	90474	
	Injection, joint, small	20600	
	Injection, joint, intermediate	20605	
	Injection, ther/proph/diag	90772	
	Injection, trigger pt 1-2 musc	20552	

Instructions:

PSA - await results
Rx: alfuzosin
Finasteride

Physician signature	Today's charges:		
X [signature] MD	Today's payment:		
	Balance due:		

Job 11 Router- Vito Mangano 16 of 20

Date of service: 10/27/09	Insurance: FLEXIHEALTH PPO		Router Number: 2463
Patient name: DEREK WALLACE	Coinsurance:	Copay:	Physician Name: MURRAY
Account #: WAL001	Noncovered Waiver?	yes / no / n/a	

x	Office visit	New	x	Est
	Minimal (RN only)			99211
	Problem focused	99201		99212
	Exp problem focused	99202	✓	99213
	Detailed	99203		99214
	Comp	99204		99215
	Comprhen/Complex	99205		
	Well visit	**New**	**x**	**Est**
	< 1 y	99381		99391
	1-4 y	99382		99392
	5-11 y	99383		99393
	12-17 y	99384		99394
	18-39 y	99385		99395
	40-64 y	99386		99396
	65 y +	99387		99397
	Medicare preventive services			
	Pap			Q0091
	Pelvic & breast			G0101
	Prostate/PSA			G0103
	Tobacco couns/3-10 min			G0375
	Tobacco couns/>10 min			G0376
	Welcome to Medicare exam			G0344
	ECG w/Welcome to Medicare			G0366
	Hemoccult, guaiac			G0107
	Flu shot			G0008
	Pneumonia shot			G0009
	Consultation/preop clearance			
	Exp problem focused			99242
	Detailed			99243
	Comp/mod complex			99244
	Comp/high complex			99245
	Other services			
	After posted hours			99050
	Evening/weekend appointment			99051
	Home health certification			G0180
	Home health recertification			G0179
	Care Plan oversight			99374
	Care Plan Oversight >30 mins			99375
	Post-op follow-up			99024
	Prolonged/60min total			99354
	Prolonged/each add 30 mins			99355
	Special reports/forms			99080
	Disability/Workers comp			99455
	Smoking Cessation <10 mins			99406
	Smoking Cessation >10 mins			99407
	ETOH/SA screening <30 mins			99408
	Online E/M by MD			99444
	Phone E/M <10 mins			99441
	Phone E/M <20 mins			99442
	Phone E/M <30 mins			99443
	Anticoagulant Mgmt <90 days			99363
	Anticoagulant Mgmt >90 days			99364
✓	In office emergency serv			99058
	Other services			
	[Repair nail bed (R) index finger]			
	Supplies			
✓	Surgical Tray			99070

Instructions:

[Suture removal 10 days
Keep site dry]

x	Office procedures		
	Cerumen removal		69210
	ECG, w/interpretation		93000
	ECG, rhythm strip		93040
	Endometrial biopsy		58100
	Fracture care, cast/splint Site: ________		______
	Nebulizer		94640
	Nebulizer demo		94664
	Spirometry		94010
	Spirometry, pre and post		94060
	Vasectomy		55250
	Skin procedures		**Units**
	Foreign body, skin, simple	10120	
	Foreign body, skin, complex	10121	
	I&D, abscess	10060	
	I&D, hematoma/seroma	10140	
	Laceration repair, simple Site: ______ Size: _____	120__	
✓	Laceration repair, layered Site: [(R) Hd] Size: [4.2cm]	120__	
	Laser Light Tx	96597	
	Lesion, biopsy, one	11100	
	Lesion, biopsy, each add'l	11101	
	Lesion, excision, benign Site: ______ Size: _____	114__	
	Lesion, excision, malignant Site: ______ Size: _____	116__	
	Lesion, paring/cutting, one	11055	
	Lesion, paring/cutting, 2-4	11056	
	Lesion, shave Site: ______ Size: _____	113__	
	Nail removal, partial (+T mod)	11730	
	Nail rem, w/matrix (+T mod)	11750	
	Skin tag, 1-15	11200	
	Wart, flat, 1-14	17110	
	Destruction lesion, 1st	17000	
	Destruct lesion, each addl 2-14	17003	
	Medications		**Units**
	Ampicillin, up to 500mg	J0290	
	B-12, up to 1,000 mcg	J3420	
	Epinephrine, up to 1ml	J0170	
	Kenalog, 10mg	J3301	
✓	Lidocaine, 10mg	J2001	
	Normal saline, 1000cc	J7030	
	Phenergan, up to 50mg	J2550	
	Progesterone, 150mg	J1055	
	Rocephin, 250mg	J0696	
	Testosterone, 200mg	J1080	
	Tigan, up to 200 mg	J3250	
	Toradol, 15mg	J1885	
	Albuterol	J7609	
	Depo-Provera 50 mg	J1055	
	Depo-Medrol 40 mg	J1030	
	Diagnoses		**Code**
	1 [Laceration (R) hand]		
	2 [Crush injury fingernail]		
	3		
	4		

Next office visit: [10 days]
(Recheck) • Preventative • PRN
Referral to:

Physician signature
X [Lance Murray MD]

x	Laboratory		-90
	Venipuncture	36415	
	Blood glucose, monitoring device	82962	
	Blood glucose, visual dipstick	82948	
	CBC, w/ auto differential	85025	
	CBC, w/o auto differential	85027	
	Cholesterol	82465	
	Hemoccult, guaiac	82270	
	Hemoccult, immunoassay	82274	
	Hemoglobin A1C	85018	
	Lipid panel	80061	
	Liver panel	80076	
	KOH prep (skin, hair, nails)	87220	
	Metabolic panel, basic	80048	
	Metabolic panel, comprehensive	80053	
	Mononucleosis	86308	
	Pregnancy, blood	84703	
	Pregnancy, urine	81025	
	Renal panel	80069	
	Sedimentation rate	85651	
	Strep, rapid	86403	
	Strep culture	87081	
	Strep A	87880	
	TB	86580	
	UA, complete, non-automated	81000	
	UA, w/o micro, non-automated	81002	
	UA, w/ micro, non-automated	81003	
	Urine colony count	87086	
	Urine culture, presumptive	87088	
	Wet mount/KOH	87210	
	Vaccines		
	DT, <7 y		90702
	DTP		90701
	DtaP, <7 y		90700
	Flu, 6-35 months		90657
	Flu, 3 y +		90658
	Hep A, adult		90632
	Hep A, ped/adol, 2 dose		90633
	Hep B, adult		90746
	Hep B, ped/adol 3 dose		90744
	Hep B-Hib		90748
	Hib, 4 dose		90645
	HPV		90649
	IPV		90713
	MMR		90707
	Pneumonia, >2 y		90732
	Pneumonia conjugate, <5 y		90669
	Td, >7 y		90718
	Varicella		90716
	Tetanus toxoid adsorbed, IM		90703
	Immunizations & Injections		**Units**
	Allergen, one	95115	
	Allergen, multiple	95117	
	Imm admn <8 yo 1st Inj	90465	
	Imm admn <8 yo each add inj	90466	
	Imm <8 yo oral or intranasal	90467	
	Imm admn <8 yo each add	90468	
	Imm admin, one vacc	90471	
	Imm admin, each add'l	90472	
	Imm admin, intranasal, one	90473	
	Imm admin, intranasal, each add'l	90474	
	Injection, joint, small	20600	
	Injection, joint, intermediate	20605	
	Injection, ther/proph/diag	90772	
	Injection, trigger pt 1-2 musc	20552	

Today's charges:	
Today's payment:	
Balance due:	

Job 11 Router- Derek Wallace 17 of 20

Date of service: 10/27/09	Insurance: CONSUMER ONE/PRUDENTIAL				Superbill Number: 2451
Patient name: MELISSA MORENCY	Coinsurance: 20%	Copay:			Physician Name: KEMPER
Account #: MOR001	Noncovered Waiver?	yes	no	n/a	

x	Office visit	New	x	Est
	Minimal (RN only)			99211
	Problem focused	99201		99212
	Exp problem focused	99202		99213
	Detailed	99203		99214
	Comp	99204		99215
	Comprhen/Complex	99205		
	Well visit	**New**	**x**	**Est**
	< 1 y	99381		99391
	1-4 y	99382		99392
	5-11 y	99383		99393
✓	12-17 y	99384		99394
	18-39 y	99385		99395
	40-64 y	99386		99396
	65 y +	99387		99397

x	Medicare preventive services	
	Pap	Q0091
	Pelvic & breast	G0101
	Prostate/PSA	G0103
	Tobacco couns/3-10 min	G0375
	Tobacco couns/>10 min	G0376
	Welcome to Medicare exam	G0344
	ECG w/Welcome to Medicare	G0366
	Hemoccult, guaiac	G0107
	Flu shot	G0008
	Pneumonia shot	G0009
	Consultation/preop clearance	
	Exp problem focused	99242
	Detailed	99243
	Comp/mod complex	99244
	Comp/high complex	99245
	Other services	
	After posted hours	99050
	Evening/weekend appointment	99051
	Home health certification	G0180
	Home health recertification	G0179
	Care Plan oversight	99374
	Care Plan Oversight >30 mins	99375
	Post-op follow-up	99024
	Prolonged/60min total	99354
	Prolonged/each add 30 mins	99355
	Special reports/forms	99080
	Disability/Workers comp	99455
	Smoking Cessation <10 mins	99406
	Smoking Cessation >10 mins	99407
	ETOH/SA screening <30 mins	99408
	Online E/M by MD	99444
	Phone E/M <10 mins	99441
	Phone E/M <20 mins	99442
	Phone E/M <30 mins	99443
	Anticoagulant Mgmt <90 days	99363
	Anticoagulant Mgmt >90 days	99364
	In office emergency serv	99058
	Other services	
✓	Preventative counseling 15 mins	
	Supplies	
	Surgical Tray	99070

x	Office procedures		
	Cerumen removal		69210
	ECG, w/interpretation		93000
	ECG, rhythm strip		93040
	Endometrial biopsy		58100
	Fracture care, cast/splint		____
	Site: ____________		
	Nebulizer		94640
	Nebulizer demo		94664
	Spirometry		94010
	Spirometry, pre and post		94060
	Vasectomy		55250
	Skin procedures		**Units**
	Foreign body, skin, simple	10120	
	Foreign body, skin, complex	10121	
	I&D, abscess	10060	
	I&D, hematoma/seroma	10140	
	Laceration repair, simple	120__	
	Site: ________ Size: _____		
	Laceration repair, layered	120__	
	Site: ________ Size: _____		
	Laser Light Tx	96597	
	Lesion, biopsy, one	11100	
	Lesion, biopsy, each add'l	11101	
	Lesion, excision, benign	114__	
	Site: ________ Size: _____		
	Lesion, excision, malignant	116__	
	Site: ________ Size: _____		
	Lesion, paring/cutting, one	11055	
	Lesion, paring/cutting, 2-4	11056	
	Lesion, shave	113__	
	Site: ________ Size: _____		
	Nail removal, partial (+T mod)	11730	
	Nail rem, w/matrix (+T mod)	11750	
	Skin tag, 1-15	11200	
	Wart, flat, 1-14	17110	
	Destruction lesion, 1st	17000	
	Destruct lesion, each addl 2-14	17003	
	Medications		**Units**
	Ampicillin, up to 500mg	J0290	
	B-12, up to 1,000 mcg	J3420	
	Epinephrine, up to 1ml	J0170	
	Kenalog, 10mg	J3301	
	Lidocaine, 10mg	J2001	
	Normal saline, 1000cc	J7030	
	Phenergan, up to 50mg	J2550	
	Progesterone, 150mg	J1055	
	Rocephin, 250mg	J0696	
	Testosterone, 200mg	J1080	
	Tigan, up to 200 mg	J3250	
	Toradol, 15mg	J1885	
	Albuterol	J7609	
	Depo-Provera 50 mg	J1055	
	Depo-Medrol 40 mg	J1030	

Diagnoses		Code
1 Vaccination update		
2 Obesity		
3		
4		

x	Laboratory		-90
	Venipuncture	36415	
	Blood glucose, monitoring device	82962	
	Blood glucose, visual dipstick	82948	
	CBC, w/ auto differential	85025	
	CBC, w/o auto differential	85027	
	Cholesterol	82465	
	Hemoccult, guaiac	82270	
	Hemoccult, immunoassay	82274	
	Hemoglobin A1C	85018	
	Lipid panel	80061	
	Liver panel	80076	
	KOH prep (skin, hair, nails)	87220	
	Metabolic panel, basic	80048	
	Metabolic panel, comprehensive	80053	
	Mononucleosis	86308	
	Pregnancy, blood	84703	
	Pregnancy, urine	81025	
	Renal panel	80069	
	Sedimentation rate	85651	
	Strep, rapid	86403	
	Strep culture	87081	
	Strep A	87880	
	TB	86580	
	UA, complete, non-automated	81000	
	UA, w/o micro, non-automated	81002	
	UA, w/ micro, non-automated	81003	
	Urine colony count	87086	
	Urine culture, presumptive	87088	
	Wet mount/KOH	87210	

x	Vaccines	
	DT, <7 y	90702
	DTP	90701
	DtaP, <7 y	90700
	Flu, 6-35 months	90657
	Flu, 3 y +	90658
	Hep A, adult	90632
	Hep A, ped/adol, 2 dose	90633
	Hep B, adult	90746
	Hep B, ped/adol 3 dose	90744
	Hep B-Hib	90748
	Hib, 4 dose	90645
✓	HPV	90649
	IPV	90713
	MMR	90707
	Pneumonia, >2 y	90732
	Pneumonia conjugate, <5 y	90669
	Td, >7 y	90718
	Varicella	90716
	Tetanus toxoid adsorbed, IM	90703

x	Immunizations & Injections		Units
	Allergen, one	95115	
	Allergen, multiple	95117	
	Imm admn <8 yo 1st Inj	90465	
	Imm admn <8 yo each add inj	90466	
	Imm <8 yo oral or intranasal	90467	
	Imm admn <8 yo each add	90468	
✓	Imm admin, one vacc	90471	
	Imm admin, each add'l	90472	
	Imm admin, intranasal, one	90473	
	Imm admin, intranasal, each add'l	90474	
	Injection, joint, small	20600	
	Injection, joint, intermediate	20605	
	Injection, ther/proph/diag	90772	
	Injection, trigger pt 1-2 musc	20552	

Instructions:

Weight Mgmt

Next office visit:
Recheck • Preventative • PRN

Referral to:

Physician signature

x Sally Kemper MD

Today's charges:	
Today's payment:	
Balance due:	

Job 11 Router- Melissa Morency 18 of 20

Date of service: 10/27/09	Insurance: AETNA				Superbill Number: 2452
Patient name: SAMANTHA BEECHWOOD	Coinsurance: 25%	Copay:			Physician Name: SCHWARTZ
Account #: BEE001	Noncovered Waiver?	yes	no	n/a	

x	Office visit	New	x	Est
	Minimal (RN only)			99211
	Problem focused	99201		99212
	Exp problem focused	99202		99213
	Detailed	99203		99214
✓	Comp	99204		99215
	Comprhen/Complex	99205		
	Well visit	**New**	**x**	**Est**
	< 1 y	99381		99391
	1-4 y	99382		99392
	5-11 y	99383		99393
	12-17 y	99384		99394
	18-39 y	99385		99395
	40-64 y	99386		99396
	65 y +	99387		99397

x	Medicare preventive services	
	Pap	Q0091
	Pelvic & breast	G0101
	Prostate/PSA	G0103
	Tobacco couns/3-10 min	G0375
	Tobacco couns/>10 min	G0376
	Welcome to Medicare exam	G0344
	ECG w/Welcome to Medicare	G0366
	Hemoccult, guaiac	G0107
	Flu shot	G0008
	Pneumonia shot	G0009
	Consultation/preop clearance	
	Exp problem focused	99242
	Detailed	99243
	Comp/mod complex	99244
	Comp/high complex	99245
	Other services	
	After posted hours	99050
	Evening/weekend appointment	99051
	Home health certification	G0180
	Home health recertification	G0179
	Care Plan oversight	99374
	Care Plan Oversight >30 mins	99375
	Post-op follow-up	99024
	Prolonged/60min total	99354
	Prolonged/each add 30 mins	99355
	Special reports/forms	99080
	Disability/Workers comp	99455
	Smoking Cessation <10 mins	99406
	Smoking Cessation >10 mins	99407
	ETOH/SA screening <30 mins	99408
	Online E/M by MD	99444
	Phone E/M <10 mins	99441
	Phone E/M <20 mins	99442
	Phone E/M <30 mins	99443
	Anticoagulant Mgmt <90 days	99363
	Anticoagulant Mgmt >90 days	99364
	In office emergency serv	99058
	Other services	
✓	A/P + lateral shoulder xray	
✓	Injection ® shoulder	
	Supplies	
	Surgical Tray	99070
	Strapping ® shoulder	

Instructions:

Keep shoulder strapped for 5 days.

x	Office procedures		
	Cerumen removal		69210
	ECG, w/interpretation		93000
	ECG, rhythm strip		93040
	Endometrial biopsy		58100
	Fracture care, cast/splint		______
	Site: ______________		
	Nebulizer		94640
	Nebulizer demo		94664
	Spirometry		94010
	Spirometry, pre and post		94060
	Vasectomy		55250
	Skin procedures		**Units**
	Foreign body, skin, simple	10120	
	Foreign body, skin, complex	10121	
	I&D, abscess	10060	
	I&D, hematoma/seroma	10140	
	Laceration repair, simple	120__	
	Site: _______ Size: _____		
	Laceration repair, layered	120__	
	Site: _______ Size: _____		
	Laser Light Tx	96597	
	Lesion, biopsy, one	11100	
	Lesion, biopsy, each add'l	11101	
	Lesion, excision, benign	114__	
	Site: _______ Size: _____		
	Lesion, excision, malignant	116__	
	Site: _______ Size: _____		
	Lesion, paring/cutting, one	11055	
	Lesion, paring/cutting, 2-4	11056	
	Lesion, shave	113__	
	Site: _______ Size: _____		
	Nail removal, partial (+T mod)	11730	
	Nail rem, w/matrix (+T mod)	11750	
	Skin tag, 1-15	11200	
	Wart, flat, 1-14	17110	
	Destruction lesion, 1st	17000	
	Destruct lesion, each addl 2-14	17003	
	Medications		**Units**
	Ampicillin, up to 500mg	J0290	
	B-12, up to 1,000 mcg	J3420	
	Epinephrine, up to 1ml	J0170	
	Kenalog, 10mg	J3301	
✓	Lidocaine, 10mg	J2001	
	Normal saline, 1000cc	J7030	
	Phenergan, up to 50mg	J2550	
	Progesterone, 150mg	J1055	
	Rocephin, 250mg	J0696	
	Testosterone, 200mg	J1080	
	Tigan, up to 200 mg	J3250	
	Toradol, 15mg	J1885	
	Albuterol	J7609	
	Depo-Provera 50 mg	J1055	
✓	Depo-Medrol 40 mg	J1030	

Diagnoses		Code
1	Rt shoulder pain/ Strain	
2	Rt shoulder dislocation	
3		
4		

Next office visit:
Recheck • Preventative • PRN

Referral to: Dr. Alston - orthopedics

Physician signature

X D J Schwartz MD

x	Laboratory		-90
	Venipuncture	36415	
	Blood glucose, monitoring device	82962	
	Blood glucose, visual dipstick	82948	
	CBC, w/ auto differential	85025	
	CBC, w/o auto differential	85027	
	Cholesterol	82465	
	Hemoccult, guaiac	82270	
	Hemoccult, immunoassay	82274	
	Hemoglobin A1C	85018	
	Lipid panel	80061	
	Liver panel	80076	
	KOH prep (skin, hair, nails)	87220	
	Metabolic panel, basic	80048	
	Metabolic panel, comprehensive	80053	
	Mononucleosis	86308	
	Pregnancy, blood	84703	
	Pregnancy, urine	81025	
	Renal panel	80069	
	Sedimentation rate	85651	
	Strep, rapid	86403	
	Strep culture	87081	
	Strep A	87880	
	TB	86580	
	UA, complete, non-automated	81000	
	UA, w/o micro, non-automated	81002	
	UA, w/ micro, non-automated	81003	
	Urine colony count	87086	
	Urine culture, presumptive	87088	
	Wet mount/KOH	87210	
	Vaccines		
	DT, <7 y		90702
	DTP		90701
	DtaP, <7 y		90700
	Flu, 6-35 months		90657
	Flu, 3 y +		90658
	Hep A, adult		90632
	Hep A, ped/adol, 2 dose		90633
	Hep B, adult		90746
	Hep B, ped/adol 3 dose		90744
	Hep B-Hib		90748
	Hib, 4 dose		90645
	HPV		90649
	IPV		90713
	MMR		90707
	Pneumonia, >2 y		90732
	Pneumonia conjugate, <5 y		90669
	Td, >7 y		90718
	Varicella		90716
	Tetanus toxoid adsorbed, IM		90703
	Immunizations & Injections		**Units**
	Allergen, one	95115	
	Allergen, multiple	95117	
	Imm admn <8 yo 1st Inj	90465	
	Imm admn <8 yo each add inj	90466	
	Imm <8 yo oral or intranasal	90467	
	Imm admn <8 yo each add	90468	
	Imm admin, one vacc	90471	
	Imm admin, each add'l	90472	
	Imm admin, intranasal, one	90473	
	Imm admin, intranasal, each add'l	90474	
	Injection, joint, small	20600	
	Injection, joint, intermediate	20605	
	Injection, ther/proph/diag	90772	
	Injection, trigger pt 1-2 musc	20552	

Today's charges:	
Today's payment:	
Balance due:	

Job 11 Router- Samantha Beechwood 19 of 20

Date of service: 10/27/09	Insurance: MEDICARE			Router Number: 2485
Patient name: XAO CHANG	Coinsurance:	Copay:		Physician Name: HEATH
Account #: CHA001	Noncovered Waiver?	yes	no	n/a

x	Office visit	New	x	Est
N/A	Minimal (RN only)	N/A		99211
	Problem focused	99201		99212
	Exp problem focused	99202		99213
	Detailed	99203	✓	99214
	Comp	99204		99215
	Comprhen/Complex	99205		
	Well visit	**New**	**x**	**Est**
	< 1 y	99381		99391
	1-4 y	99382		99392
	5-11 y	99383		99393
	12-17 y	99384		99394
	18-39 y	99385		99395
	40-64 y	99386		99396
	65 y +	99387		99397

x	Medicare preventive services	
	Pap	Q0091
	Pelvic & breast	G0101
	Prostate/PSA	G0103
	Tobacco couns/3-10 min	G0375
	Tobacco couns/>10 min	G0376
	Welcome to Medicare exam	G0344
	ECG w/Welcome to Medicare	G0366
	Hemoccult, guaiac	G0107
	Flu shot	G0008
	Pneumonia shot	G0009
	Consultation/preop clearance	
	Exp problem focused	99242
	Detailed	99243
	Comp/mod complex	99244
	Comp/high complex	99245
	Other services	
	After posted hours	99050
	Evening/weekend appointment	99051
	Home health certification	G0180
	Home health recertification	G0179
	Care Plan oversight	99374
	Care Plan Oversight >30 mins	99375
	Post-op follow-up	99024
	Prolonged/60min total	99354
	Prolonged/each add 30 mins	99355
	Special reports/forms	99080
	Disability/Workers comp	99455
	Smoking Cessation <10 mins	99406
	Smoking Cessation >10 mins	99407
	ETOH/SA screening <30 mins	99408
	Online E/M by MD	99444
	Phone E/M <10 mins	99441
	Phone E/M <20 mins	99442
	Phone E/M <30 mins	99443
	Anticoagulant Mgmt <90 days	99363
	Anticoagulant Mgmt >90 days	99364
	In office emergency serv	99058
	Other services	
✓	CT W/O CONTRAST Brain	
	Supplies	
	Surgical Tray	99070

Instructions: CT image will be read by Radiologist CALL results to home

x	Office procedures	
	Cerumen removal	69210
	ECG, w/interpretation	93000
	ECG, rhythm strip	93040
	Endometrial biopsy	58100
	Fracture care, cast/splint	
	Site: ___________	
	Nebulizer	94640
	Nebulizer demo	94664
	Spirometry	94010
	Spirometry, pre and post	94060
	Vasectomy	55250

Skin procedures		Units
Foreign body, skin, simple	10120	
Foreign body, skin, complex	10121	
I&D, abscess	10060	
I&D, hematoma/seroma	10140	
Laceration repair, simple	120__	
Site: _______ Size: ____		
Laceration repair, layered	120__	
Site: _______ Size: ____		
Laser Light Tx	96597	
Lesion, biopsy, one	11100	
Lesion, biopsy, each add'l	11101	
Lesion, excision, benign	114__	
Site: _______ Size: ____		
Lesion, excision, malignant	116__	
Site: _______ Size: ____		
Lesion, paring/cutting, one	11055	
Lesion, paring/cutting, 2-4	11056	
Lesion, shave	113__	
Site: _______ Size: ____		
Nail removal, partial (+T mod)	11730	
Nail rem, w/matrix (+T mod)	11750	
Skin tag, 1-15	11200	
Wart, flat, 1-14	17110	
Destruction lesion, 1st	17000	
Destruct lesion, each addl 2-14	17003	

Medications		Units
Ampicillin, up to 500mg	J0290	
B-12, up to 1,000 mcg	J3420	
Epinephrine, up to 1ml	J0170	
Kenalog, 10mg	J3301	
Lidocaine, 10mg	J2001	
Normal saline, 1000cc	J7030	
Phenergan, up to 50mg	J2550	
Progesterone, 150mg	J1055	
Rocephin, 250mg	J0696	
Testosterone, 200mg	J1080	
Tigan, up to 200 mg	J3250	
Toradol, 15mg	J1885	
Albuterol	J7609	
Depo-Provera 50 mg	J1055	
Depo-Medrol 40 mg	J1030	

Diagnoses	Code
1 HA / R/O Aneurysm	
2 HTN	
3 Vertigo	
4	

Next office visit:
Recheck • Preventative • PRN

Referral to:

Physician signature

x LD Heath MD (signature)

x	Laboratory		-90
	Venipuncture	36415	
	Blood glucose, monitoring device	82962	
	Blood glucose, visual dipstick	82948	
	CBC, w/ auto differential	85025	
	CBC, w/o auto differential	85027	
	Cholesterol	82465	
	Hemoccult, guaiac	82270	
	Hemoccult, immunoassay	82274	
	Hemoglobin A1C	85018	
	Lipid panel	80061	
	Liver panel	80076	
	KOH prep (skin, hair, nails)	87220	
	Metabolic panel, basic	80048	
	Metabolic panel, comprehensive	80053	
	Mononucleosis	86308	
	Pregnancy, blood	84703	
	Pregnancy, urine	81025	
	Renal panel	80069	
	Sedimentation rate	85651	
	Strep, rapid	86403	
	Strep culture	87081	
	Strep A	87880	
	TB	86580	
	UA, complete, non-automated	81000	
	UA, w/o micro, non-automated	81002	
	UA, w/ micro, non-automated	81003	
	Urine colony count	87086	
	Urine culture, presumptive	87088	
	Wet mount/KOH	87210	

x	Vaccines	
	DT, <7 y	90702
	DTP	90701
	DtaP, <7 y	90700
	Flu, 6-35 months	90657
	Flu, 3 y +	90658
	Hep A, adult	90632
	Hep A, ped/adol, 2 dose	90633
	Hep B, adult	90746
	Hep B, ped/adol 3 dose	90744
	Hep B-Hib	90748
	Hib, 4 dose	90645
	HPV	90649
	IPV	90713
	MMR	90707
	Pneumonia, >2 y	90732
	Pneumonia conjugate, <5 y	90669
	Td, >7 y	90718
	Varicella	90716
	Tetanus toxoid adsorbed, IM	90703

x	Immunizations & Injections		Units
	Allergen, one	95115	
	Allergen, multiple	95117	
	Imm admn <8 yo 1st Inj	90465	
	Imm admn <8 yo each add inj	90466	
	Imm <8 yo oral or intranasal	90467	
	Imm admn <8 yo each add	90468	
	Imm admin, one vacc	90471	
	Imm admin, each add'l	90472	
	Imm admin, intranasal, one	90473	
	Imm admin, intranasal, each add'l	90474	
	Injection, joint, small	20600	
	Injection, joint, intermediate	20605	
	Injection, ther/proph/diag	90772	
	Injection, trigger pt 1-2 musc	20552	

Today's charges:		
Today's payment:		
Balance due:		

Job 11 Router- Xao Chang 20 of 20

Douglasville Medicine Associates

HOSPITAL CHARGE SHEET

☐Sarah Mendenhall, M.D.
☒D.J. Schwartrz, M.D.
☐L.D. Heath, M.D.
☐Sally Kemper, M.D.
☐Alberta Lynn, P.A.C.
☐Lance Murray, M.D.

Patient's Name: Robert Shinn **Date(s) of Service:** 10/27/09

Place of Service: ☐ New York County Hospital ☐Community General Hospital ☐Beaufort Regional Hospital ☑County Memorial Hospital

Hospital Visit Type: ☐Observation ☐Inpatient ☐Subsequent Visit ☑Emergency Room ☐Consultation ☐Initial Admission ☐Discharge Planning ☐Critical Care

Insurance Carrier: Signal HMO **Insurance ID#** ________

Diagnosis/ICD-9: Gastroenteritis, Bactrim Allergy

Procedure/Service Performed/CPT:
Pt seen in ER N/V (gradual onset). Tx w/ Bactrim by Dr Heath for rash 10/26/09. Moderate Nausea - vomited 1-2 x last 24 hrs. Diarrhea. ⊝ blood in stool. Rash + Apparent spider bite visualized by me. ⊝ SOB. Complains of fatigue. HR 108. NKDA. Mother said rash worse than yesterday. HEENT, Heart, Lungs, Normal. He is alert + oriented x 3. ROS - GU - normal, RESP - OK, No fever, GI - diarrhea. Stop Bactrim. Motrin prn for aches. Phenergan 25 mg IM, Rx 25 mg p.o. Q8 #12

Signature: DJ Schwartz MD **Date given to biller:** 10/28/09

Notes: F/U w/ Heath. Discharged to home - stable

Job 12 Hospital Charge Sheet- Robert Shinn 1 of 10

Douglasville Medicine Associates

HOSPITAL CHARGE SHEET

☐Sarah Mendenhall, M.D. **☐Sally Kemper, M.D.**
☐D.J. Schwartrz, M.D. **☐Alberta Lynn, P.A.C.**
☑L.D. Heath, M.D. **☐Lance Murray, M.D.**

Patient's Name: Manuel Ramirez **Date(s) of Service:** 10/24 -10/26/09

Place of Service: ☑ New York County Hospital ☐Community General Hospital ☐Beaufort Regional Hospital ☐County Memorial Hospital

Hospital Visit Type: ☐Observation ☑Inpatient ☑Subsequent Visit ☐Emergency Room ☐Consultation ☐Initial Admission ☐Discharge Planning ☐Critical Care

Insurance Carrier: Medicare **Insurance ID#** ____________

Diagnosis/ICD-9: Abd pain Rectal Bleeding IBS Erosive gastritis

Procedure/Service Performed/CPT:
Pt Adm for eval of Abd pain, N/V, + emesis by Dr Ramsey. Shortly after EGD + colonoscopy (10/22/09) Pt developed LUQ pain + hematemesis. He was Adm to GI specialty, I was asked to follow pt for medical maintenance.

Signature: LD Heath MD **Date given to biller:** 10/27/09

Notes:
10/25 SUBSEQ VISIT
10/26 SUBSEQ VISIT

Job 12 Hospital Charge Sheet- Manual Ramirez 2 of 10

Douglasville Medicine Associates

HOSPITAL CHARGE SHEET

☐Sarah Mendenhall, M.D.
☐D.J. Schwartrz, M.D.
☒L.D. Heath, M.D.
☐Sally Kemper, M.D.
☐Alberta Lynn, P.A.C.
☐Lance Murray, M.D.

Patient's Name: CAROLINE PRATT **Date(s) of Service:** 10/25 - 10/26

Place of Service: ☒New York County Hospital ☐Community General Hospital ☐Beaufort Regional Hospital ☐County Memorial Hospital

Hospital Visit Type: ☐Observation ☐Inpatient ☐Subsequent Visit ☐Emergency Room ☐Consultation ☐Initial Admission ☐Discharge Planning ☒Critical Care

Insurance Carrier: SELF **Insurance ID#** ______

Diagnosis/ICD-9: SUICIDE ATTEMPT, CARBON MONOXIDE INHALATION POISONING, CARDIAC ARREST - RESOLVED

Procedure/Service Performed/CPT:
ER SERVICE CALLED ME AT 6:30 PM 10/25 + GAVE ME A REPORT. PT WAS TRANSPORTED TO THE ER VIA LIFE-FLIGHT. PT WAS INTUBATED + RESUSCITATED. I ARRIVED AT THE ER AT 6:30 & ASSUMED CARE. WHILE PREPARING FOR TRANSFER TO ICU PT WENT INTO CARDIAC ARREST. SHE WAS DEFIBRILLATED X2. SHE WAS TRANSFERRED TO ICU IN UNSTABLE CONDITION WHERE I STAYED IN CONSTANT ATTENDANCE UNTIL 8:00 PM.

Signature: LD Heath **Date given to biller:** 10/27/09

Notes:
I WAS CALLED BACK TO ICU @ 1:00 AM BECAUSE PTS CONDITION WORSENED WHERE I STAYED IN CONSTANT ATTENDANCE UNTIL 2:00 AM WHEN SHE STABILIZED

Job 12 Hospital Charge Sheet- Caroline Pratt 3 of 10

Douglasville Medicine Associates

HOSPITAL CHARGE SHEET

☐Sarah Mendenhall, M.D.
☐D.J. Schwartrz, M.D.
☑L.D. Heath, M.D.

☐Sally Kemper, M.D.
☐Alberta Lynn, P.A.C.
☐Lance Murray, M.D.

Patient's Name: Tina Rizzo **Date(s) of Service:** 10/26/09

Place of Service: ☐ New York County Hospital ☐Community General Hospital

☐Beaufort Regional Hospital ☑County Memorial Hospital

Hospital Visit Type: ☐Observation ☐Inpatient ☐Subsequent Visit ☑Emergency Room

☐Consultation ☐Initial Admission ☐Discharge Planning ☐Critical Care

Insurance Carrier: Consumer One **Insurance ID#** ____________

Diagnosis/ICD-9: ____________

Procedure/Service Performed/CPT:
Pt seen in ER. Complained of severe flank pain, N/V, dysuria. On exam Abd non-tender w/o masses. Discomfort to suprapubic palpation. U/S showed adrenal torsion findings also consistent w/ cystourethritis. 99284

Signature: LD Heath **Date given to biller:** 10/27/09

Notes:

Job 12 Hospital Charge Sheet- Tina Rizzo 4 of 10

Douglasville Medicine Associates

HOSPITAL CHARGE SHEET

☐Sarah Mendenhall, M.D.
☐D.J. Schwartrz, M.D.
☑L.D. Heath, M.D.

☐Sally Kemper, M.D.
☐Alberta Lynn, P.A.C.
☐Lance Murray, M.D.

Patient's Name: JOHN CONWAY **Date(s) of Service:** 10/24/09

Place of Service: ☑New York County Hospital ☐Community General Hospital

☐Beaufort Regional Hospital ☐County Memorial Hospital

Hospital Visit Type: ☐Observation ☐Inpatient ☐Subsequent Visit ☐Emergency Room

☑Consultation ☐Initial Admission ☐Discharge Planning ☐Critical Care

Insurance Carrier: CONSUMER ONE **Insurance ID#** ____________

Diagnosis/ICD-9: Abd pain, R/O gallstone vs bowel obstr.

Procedure/Service Performed/CPT:
Pt adx by Schwartz on 10/23/09 on call coverage.
GI consult ordered.

Signature: LD Heath **Date given to biller:** 10/27/09

Notes:

Job 12 Hospital Charge Sheet- John Conway 5 of 10

Douglasville Medicine Associates

HOSPITAL CHARGE SHEET

☐Sarah Mendenhall, M.D.
☐D.J. Schwartrz, M.D.
☒L.D. Heath, M.D.

☐Sally Kemper, M.D.
☐Alberta Lynn, P.A.C.
☐Lance Murray, M.D.

Patient's Name: DAVID JAMES **Date(s) of Service:** 10/19/09

Place of Service: ☑New York County Hospital ☐Community General Hospital

☐Beaufort Regional Hospital ☐County Memorial Hospital

Hospital Visit Type: ☒Observation ☐Inpatient ☐Subsequent Visit ☐Emergency Room

☐Consultation ☐Initial Admission ☐Discharge Planning ☐Critical Care

Insurance Carrier: SIGNAL HMO **Insurance ID#** ____________

Diagnosis/ICD-9: Type I DM Uncontrolled R/O diabetic Ketoacidosis.

Procedure/Service Performed/CPT:
PT experienced dizziness + disorientation. His mother called + reported he has been drinking + NOT taking his insulin regularly. Glucose was 350. I admitted him to OBS w/ IV fluids + short acting insulin. 99219

Signature: LD Heath **Date given to biller:** 10/26/09

Notes:

Job 12 Hospital Charge Sheet- David James 6 of 10

Douglasville Medicine Associates

HOSPITAL CHARGE SHEET

☑ Sarah Mendenhall, M.D.
☐ D.J. Schwartrz, M.D.
☐ L.D. Heath, M.D.
☐ Sally Kemper, M.D.
☐ Alberta Lynn, P.A.C.
☐ Lance Murray, M.D.

Patient's Name: Francesco Alvarez **Date(s) of Service:** 10/26/09

Place of Service: ☑ New York County Hospital ☐ Community General Hospital ☐ Beaufort Regional Hospital ☐ County Memorial Hospital

Hospital Visit Type: ☑ Observation ☐ ~~Inpatient~~ ☐ Subsequent Visit ☐ Emergency Room ☐ Consultation ☑ Initial Admission ☐ Discharge Planning ☐ Critical Care

Insurance Carrier: FlexiHealth PPO **Insurance ID#** __________

Diagnosis/ICD-9: N/V, fatigue, heart palpitations Tachycardia

Procedure/Service Performed/CPT: 99220
10/26 - Adx Obs - telemetry, cardiology consult ordered
10/27 - Subseq visit

Signature: Sarah Mendenhall MD **Date given to biller:** 10/28/09

Notes:

Job 12 Hospital Charge Sheet- Francesco Alvarez 7 of 10

Douglasville Medicine Associates

HOSPITAL CHARGE SHEET

☐Sarah Mendenhall, M.D.
☐D.J. Schwartrz, M.D.
☐L.D. Heath, M.D.

☑Sally Kemper, M.D.
☐Alberta Lynn, P.A.C.
☐Lance Murray, M.D.

Patient's Name: Deanne Lloyd **Date(s) of Service:** 10/12/09

Place of Service: ☑New York County Hospital ☐Community General Hospital

☐Beaufort Regional Hospital ☐County Memorial Hospital

Hospital Visit Type: ☐Observation ☐Inpatient ☐Subsequent Visit ☐Emergency Room

☐Consultation ☐Initial Admission ☐Discharge Planning ☐Critical Care

Insurance Carrier: ______________________ **Insurance ID#** ________________

Diagnosis/ICD-9: Asthma acute exacerbation, URI, fever

Procedure/Service Performed/CPT:

Pt seen in ER for 2 day h/o cough + rhinorrhea + congestion. Now c/o chest tightness. Pt is asthmatic + takes Albuterol + Flovent. Pt also has SC trait. Pt rec'vd Albuterol @ 1400 + Flovent @ 1500 w/ slight relief of tightness. Pt has fever of 100.9. NKDA. Pt does not smoke. ROS - eyes, ENT, CV, GI, GU, MS, Skin, Neuro, Endo, Psych - All WNL. Pt has obvious rhinorrhea + looks ill but in NAD.

Signature: Sally Kemper **Date given to biller:** 10/24/09

HEENT - clear nasal drainage. Neck - nml. Chest Ⓑ wheezes - expiratory. Heart - RRR. Extrem - no cyanosis or edema. Neuro - nml. Skin - warm + dry.

Notes:

Respiratory performed peak flows + nebulizer tx + Asthma education.

Job 12 Hospital Charge Sheet- Deanne Lloyd 8 of 10

Douglasville Medicine Associates

HOSPITAL CHARGE SHEET

☑Sarah Mendenhall, M.D.
☐D.J. Schwartrz, M.D.
☐L.D. Heath, M.D.
☐Sally Kemper, M.D.
☐Alberta Lynn, P.A.C.
☐Lance Murray, M.D.

Patient's Name: Diane Parker **Date(s) of Service:** 10/25/09

Place of Service: ☑New York County Hospital ☐Community General Hospital ☐Beaufort Regional Hospital ☐County Memorial Hospital

Hospital Visit Type: ☐Observation ☐Inpatient ☐Subsequent Visit ☐Emergency Room ☐Consultation ☑Initial Admission ☐Discharge Planning ☐Critical Care

Insurance Carrier: Flexi Health PPO **Insurance ID#** ________________

Diagnosis/ICD-9: DVT

Procedure/Service Performed/CPT:
Pt went to ER for pain + swelling in her (L) lower leg. ER service called me after performing doppler in ER stating she required adm for DVT & further w/u. Adm w/ IV Heparin drip; ECHO, chest x-ray, D-dimer, Chem 7, PT + INR, + CBC.

Signature: Sarah Mendenhall MD **Date given to biller:** 10/26/09

Notes: 99222

Job 12 Hospital Charge Sheet- Diane Parker 9 of 10

Douglasville Medicine Associates

HOSPITAL CHARGE SHEET

☐Sarah Mendenhall, M.D.
☐D.J. Schwartrz, M.D.
☐L.D. Heath, M.D.
☒Sally Kemper, M.D.
☐Alberta Lynn, P.A.C.
☐Lance Murray, M.D.

Patient's Name: Abbey Taylor **Date(s) of Service:** 10/27/09

Place of Service: ☐ New York County Hospital ☒Community General Hospital

☐Beaufort Regional Hospital ☐County Memorial Hospital

Hospital Visit Type: ☐Observation ☐Inpatient ☐Subsequent Visit ☐Emergency Room

☒Consultation ☐Initial Admission ☐Discharge Planning ☐Critical Care

Insurance Carrier: SIGNAL HMO **Insurance ID#** 87135249

Diagnosis/ICD-9: Sarcoidosis, Erythema Nodosum

Procedure/Service Performed/CPT:
I was asked to consult on this pt by Dr. Ramsey to render an opinion + confirm his initial Dx + treatment plan. 99254

Signature: Sally Kemper MD **Date given to biller:** 10/28/09

Notes:
PT DOB- 3/14/59
ADDRESS - 3121 Line Dr, Douglasville, NY

Job 12 Hospital Charge Sheet- Abbey Taylor 10 of 10

Date of service: 10/28/09	Insurance: SELF PAY				Router Number: 2470
Patient name: RUSSELL LOGAN	Coinsurance:	Copay:			Physician Name: KEMPER
Account #: LOG001	Noncovered Waiver?	yes	no	n/a	

x	Office visit	New	x	Est
N/A	Minimal (RN only)	N/A		99211
	Problem focused	99201		99212
	Exp problem focused	99202		99213
	Detailed	99203	✓	99214
	Comp	99204		99215
	Comprhen/Complex	99205		
	Well visit	**New**	**x**	**Est**
	< 1 y	99381		99391
	1-4 y	99382		99392
	5-11 y	99383		99393
	12-17 y	99384		99394
	18-39 y	99385		99395
	40-64 y	99386		99396
	65 y +	99387		99397

x	Medicare preventive services	
	Pap	Q0091
	Pelvic & breast	G0101
	Prostate/PSA	G0103
	Tobacco couns/3-10 min	G0375
	Tobacco couns/>10 min	G0376
	Welcome to Medicare exam	G0344
	ECG w/Welcome to Medicare	G0366
	Hemoccult, guaiac	G0107
	Flu shot	G0008
	Pneumonia shot	G0009
	Consultation/preop clearance	
	Exp problem focused	99242
	Detailed	99243
	Comp/mod complex	99244
	Comp/high complex	99245
	Other services	
	After posted hours	99050
	Evening/weekend appointment	99051
	Home health certification	G0180
	Home health recertification	G0179
	Care Plan oversight	99374
	Care Plan Oversight >30 mins	99375
	Post-op follow-up	99024
	Prolonged/60min total	99354
	Prolonged/each add 30 mins	99355
	Special reports/forms	99080
	Disability/Workers comp	99455
	Smoking Cessation <10 mins	99406
	Smoking Cessation >10 mins	99407
	ETOH/SA screening <30 mins	99408
	Online E/M by MD	99444
	Phone E/M <10 mins	99441
	Phone E/M <20 mins	99442
	Phone E/M <30 mins	99443
	Anticoagulant Mgmt <90 days	99363
	Anticoagulant Mgmt >90 days	99364
	In office emergency serv	99058
	Other services	
✓	U/S (R) Leg	
	Supplies	
	Surgical Tray	99070
	Instructions:	

x	Office procedures		
	Cerumen removal		69210
	ECG, w/interpretation		93000
	ECG, rhythm strip		93040
	Endometrial biopsy		58100
	Fracture care, cast/splint		
	Site: ________________		
	Nebulizer		94640
	Nebulizer demo		94664
	Spirometry		94010
	Spirometry, pre and post		94060
	Vasectomy		55250
	Skin procedures		**Units**
	Foreign body, skin, simple	10120	
	Foreign body, skin, complex	10121	
	I&D, abscess	10060	
	I&D, hematoma/seroma	10140	
	Laceration repair, simple Site: ________ Size: _____	120__	
	Laceration repair, layered Site: ________ Size: _____	120__	
	Laser Light Tx	96597	
	Lesion, biopsy, one	11100	
	Lesion, biopsy, each add'l	11101	
	Lesion, excision, benign Site: ________ Size: _____	114__	
	Lesion, excision, malignant Site: ________ Size: _____	116__	
	Lesion, paring/cutting, one	11055	
	Lesion, paring/cutting, 2-4	11056	
	Lesion, shave Site: ________ Size: _____	113__	
	Nail removal, partial (+T mod)	11730	
	Nail rem, w/matrix (+T mod)	11750	
	Skin tag, 1-15	11200	
	Wart, flat, 1-14	17110	
	Destruction lesion, 1st	17000	
	Destruct lesion, each addl 2-14	17003	
	Medications		**Units**
	Ampicillin, up to 500mg	J0290	
	B-12, up to 1,000 mcg	J3420	
	Epinephrine, up to 1ml	J0170	
	Kenalog, 10mg	J3301	
	Lidocaine, 10mg	J2001	
	Normal saline, 1000cc	J7030	
	Phenergan, up to 50mg	J2550	
	Progesterone, 150mg	J1055	
	Rocephin, 250mg	J0696	
	Testosterone, 200mg	J1080	
	Tigan, up to 200 mg	J3250	
	Toradol, 15mg	J1885	
	Albuterol	J7609	
	Depo-Provera 50 mg	J1055	
	Depo-Medrol 40 mg	J1030	

Diagnoses	Code
1 (R) leg pain	
2 Lymphedema	
3 (+) Stemmer Sign	
4 Lipedema	
5. HTN	

Next office visit:

Recheck • Preventative • PRN

Referral to:

x	Laboratory		-90
	Venipuncture	36415	
	Blood glucose, monitoring device	82962	
	Blood glucose, visual dipstick	82948	
	CBC, w/ auto differential	85025	
	CBC, w/o auto differential	85027	
	Cholesterol	82465	
	Hemoccult, guaiac	82270	
	Hemoccult, immunoassay	82274	
	Hemoglobin A1C	85018	
	Lipid panel	80061	
	Liver panel	80076	
	KOH prep (skin, hair, nails)	87220	
	Metabolic panel, basic	80048	
	Metabolic panel, comprehensive	80053	
	Mononucleosis	86308	
	Pregnancy, blood	84703	
	Pregnancy, urine	81025	
	Renal panel	80069	
	Sedimentation rate	85651	
	Strep, rapid	86403	
	Strep culture	87081	
	Strep A	87880	
	TB	86580	
	UA, complete, non-automated	81000	
	UA, w/o micro, non-automated	81002	
	UA, w/ micro, non-automated	81003	
	Urine colony count	87086	
	Urine culture, presumptive	87088	
	Wet mount/KOH	87210	
	Vaccines		
	DT, <7 y		90702
	DTP		90701
	DtaP, <7 y		90700
	Flu, 6-35 months		90657
	Flu, 3 y +		90658
	Hep A, adult		90632
	Hep A, ped/adol, 2 dose		90633
	Hep B, adult		90746
	Hep B, ped/adol 3 dose		90744
	Hep B-Hib		90748
	Hib, 4 dose		90645
	HPV		90649
	IPV		90713
	MMR		90707
	Pneumonia, >2 y		90732
	Pneumonia conjugate, <5 y		90669
	Td, >7 y		90718
	Varicella		90716
	Tetanus toxoid adsorbed, IM		90703
	Immunizations & Injections		**Units**
	Allergen, one	95115	
	Allergen, multiple	95117	
	Imm admn <8 yo 1st Inj	90465	
	Imm admn <8 yo each add inj	90466	
	Imm <8 yo oral or intranasal	90467	
	Imm admn <8 yo each add	90468	
	Imm admin, one vacc	90471	
	Imm admin, each add'l	90472	
	Imm admn, intranasal, one	90473	
	Imm admin, intranasal, each add'l	90474	
	Injection, joint, small	20600	
	Injection, joint, intermediate	20605	
	Injection, ther/proph/diag	90772	
	Injection, trigger pt 1-2 musc	20552	

Physician signature	Today's charges:		
X S. Kemper MD	Today's payment:		
	Balance due:		

Job 1 Router- Russell Logan 1 of 6

Date of service: 10/28/09	Insurance: FLEXIHEALTH PPO				Router Number: 2467
Patient name: EDWARD GORMAN	Coinsurance:	Copay:			Physician Name: HEATH
Account #: GOR001	Noncovered Waiver?	yes	no	n/a	

X	Office visit	New	X	Est
	Minimal (RN only)			99211
	Problem focused	99201		99212
	Exp problem focused	99202		99213
	Detailed	99203	✓	99214
	Comp	99204		99215
	Comprhen/Complex	99205		
	Well visit	**New**	**X**	**Est**
	< 1 y	99381		99391
	1-4 y	99382		99392
	5-11 y	99383		99393
	12-17 y	99384		99394
	18-39 y	99385		99395
	40-64 y	99386		99396
	65 y +	99387		99397

	Medicare preventive services	
	Pap	Q0091
	Pelvic & breast	G0101
	Prostate/PSA	G0103
	Tobacco couns/3-10 min	G0375
	Tobacco couns/>10 min	G0376
	Welcome to Medicare exam	G0344
	ECG w/Welcome to Medicare	G0366
	Hemoccult, guaiac	G0107
	Flu shot	G0008
	Pneumonia shot	G0009
	Consultation/preop clearance	
	Exp problem focused	99242
	Detailed	99243
	Comp/mod complex	99244
	Comp/high complex	99245
	Other services	
	After posted hours	99050
	Evening/weekend appointment	99051
	Home health certification	G0180
	Home health recertification	G0179
	Care Plan oversight	99374
	Care Plan Oversight >30 mins	99375
	Post-op follow-up	99024
	Prolonged/60min total	99354
	Prolonged/each add 30 mins	99355
	Special reports/forms	99080
	Disability/Workers comp	99455
	Smoking Cessation <10 mins	99406
	Smoking Cessation >10 mins	99407
	ETOH/SA screening <30 mins	99408
	Online E/M by MD	99444
	Phone E/M <10 mins	99441
	Phone E/M <20 mins	99442
	Phone E/M <30 mins	99443
	Anticoagulant Mgmt <90 days	99363
	Anticoagulant Mgmt >90 days	99364
	In office emergency serv	99058
	Other services	
	Supplies	
	Surgical Tray	99070

Instructions:

Refer to GI for upper endos. + stretching

X	Office procedures		
	Cerumen removal		69210
	ECG, w/interpretation		93000
	ECG, rhythm strip		93040
	Endometrial biopsy		58100
	Fracture care, cast/splint Site: ______		____
	Nebulizer		94640
	Nebulizer demo		94664
	Spirometry		94010
	Spirometry, pre and post		94060
	Vasectomy		55250
	Skin procedures		**Units**
	Foreign body, skin, simple	10120	
	Foreign body, skin, complex	10121	
	I&D, abscess	10060	
	I&D, hematoma/seroma	10140	
	Laceration repair, simple Site: ____ Size: ____	120__	
	Laceration repair, layered Site: ____ Size: ____	120__	
	Laser Light Tx	96597	
	Lesion, biopsy, one	11100	
	Lesion, biopsy, each add'l	11101	
	Lesion, excision, benign Site: ____ Size: ____	114__	
	Lesion, excision, malignant Site: ____ Size: ____	116__	
	Lesion, paring/cutting, one	11055	
	Lesion, paring/cutting, 2-4	11056	
	Lesion, shave Site: ____ Size: ____	113__	
	Nail removal, partial (+T mod)	11730	
	Nail rem, w/matrix (+T mod)	11750	
	Skin tag, 1-15	11200	
	Wart, flat, 1-14	17110	
	Destruction lesion, 1st	17000	
	Destruct lesion, each addl 2-14	17003	
	Medications		**Units**
	Ampicillin, up to 500mg	J0290	
	B-12, up to 1,000 mcg	J3420	
	Epinephrine, up to 1ml	J0170	
	Kenalog, 10mg	J3301	
	Lidocaine, 10mg	J2001	
	Normal saline, 1000cc	J7030	
	Phenergan, up to 50mg	J2550	
	Progesterone, 150mg	J1055	
	Rocephin, 250mg	J0696	
	Testosterone, 200mg	J1080	
	Tigan, up to 200 mg	J3250	
	Toradol, 15mg	J1885	
	Albuterol	J7609	
	Depo-Provera 50 mg	J1055	
	Depo-Medrol 40 mg	J1030	

Diagnoses	Code
1 Indigestion	
2 food caught in	
3 throat	
4 Esophageal stricture	

Next office visit: 3 mos

Recheck • Preventative • PRN (circled)

Referral to: Paul Snyder MD

Physician signature

X [signature]

X	Laboratory		-90
	Venipuncture	36415	
	Blood glucose, monitoring device	82962	
	Blood glucose, visual dipstick	82948	
	CBC, w/ auto differential	85025	
	CBC, w/o auto differential	85027	
	Cholesterol	82465	
	Hemoccult, guaiac	82270	
	Hemoccult, immunoassay	82274	
	Hemoglobin A1C	85018	
	Lipid panel	80061	
	Liver panel	80076	
	KOH prep (skin, hair, nails)	87220	
	Metabolic panel, basic	80048	
	Metabolic panel, comprehensive	80053	
	Mononucleosis	86308	
	Pregnancy, blood	84703	
	Pregnancy, urine	81025	
	Renal panel	80069	
	Sedimentation rate	85651	
	Strep, rapid	86403	
	Strep culture	87081	
	Strep A	87880	
	TB	86580	
	UA, complete, non-automated	81000	
	UA, w/o micro, non-automated	81002	
	UA, w/ micro, non-automated	81003	
	Urine colony count	87086	
	Urine culture, presumptive	87088	
	Wet mount/KOH	87210	
	Vaccines		
	DT, <7 y		90702
	DTP		90701
	DtaP, <7 y		90700
	Flu, 6-35 months		90657
	Flu, 3 y +		90658
	Hep A, adult		90632
	Hep A, ped/adol, 2 dose		90633
	Hep B, adult		90746
	Hep B, ped/adol 3 dose		90744
	Hep B-Hib		90748
	Hib, 4 dose		90645
	HPV		90649
	IPV		90713
	MMR		90707
	Pneumonia, >2 y		90732
	Pneumonia conjugate, <5 y		90669
	Td, >7 y		90718
	Varicella		90716
	Tetanus toxoid adsorbed, IM		90703
	Immunizations & Injections		**Units**
	Allergen, one	95115	
	Allergen, multiple	95117	
	Imm admn <8 yo 1st Inj	90465	
	Imm admn <8 yo each add inj	90466	
	Imm <8 yo oral or intranasal	90467	
	Imm admn <8 yo each add	90468	
	Imm admin, one vacc	90471	
	Imm admin, each add'l	90472	
	Imm admin, intranasal, one	90473	
	Imm admin, intranasal, each add'l	90474	
	Injection, joint, small	20600	
	Injection, joint, intermediate	20605	
	Injection, ther/proph/diag	90772	
	Injection, trigger pt 1-2 musc	20552	

Today's charges:		
Today's payment:		
Balance due:		

Job 1 Router- Edward Gorman 2 of 6

Date of service: 10/28/09	Insurance: FLEXIHEALTH PPO				Router Number: 2473
Patient name: DIANE PARKER	Coinsurance:	Copay:			Physician Name: MURRAY
Account #: PAR001	Noncovered Waiver?	yes	no	n/a	

x	Office visit	New	x	Est
	Minimal (RN only)		✓	99211
	Problem focused	99201	✓	99212
	Exp problem focused	99202		99213
	Detailed	99203		99214
	Comp	99204		99215
	Comprhen/Complex	99205		
	Well visit	**New**	**x**	**Est**
	< 1 y	99381		99391
	1-4 y	99382		99392
	5-11 y	99383		99393
	12-17 y	99384		99394
	18-39 y	99385		99395
	40-64 y	99386		99396
	65 y +	99387		99397

x	Medicare preventive services	
	Pap	Q0091
	Pelvic & breast	G0101
	Prostate/PSA	G0103
	Tobacco couns/3-10 min	G0375
	Tobacco couns/>10 min	G0376
	Welcome to Medicare exam	G0344
	ECG w/Welcome to Medicare	G0366
	Hemoccult, guaiac	G0107
	Flu shot	G0008
	Pneumonia shot	G0009
	Consultation/preop clearance	
	Exp problem focused	99242
	Detailed	99243
	Comp/mod complex	99244
	Comp/high complex	99245
	Other services	
	After posted hours	99050
	Evening/weekend appointment	99051
	Home health certification	G0180
	Home health recertification	G0179
	Care Plan oversight	99374
	Care Plan Oversight >30 mins	99375
	Post-op follow-up	99024
	Prolonged/60min total	99354
	Prolonged/each add 30 mins	99355
	Special reports/forms	99080
	Disability/Workers comp	99455
	Smoking Cessation <10 mins	99406
	Smoking Cessation >10 mins	99407
	ETOH/SA screening <30 mins	99408
	Online E/M by MD	99444
	Phone E/M <10 mins	99441
	Phone E/M <20 mins	99442
	Phone E/M <30 mins	99443
	Anticoagulant Mgmt <90 days	99363
	Anticoagulant Mgmt >90 days	99364
	In office emergency serv	99058
	Other services	
	Supplies	
	Surgical Tray	99070

x	Office procedures		
	Cerumen removal	69210	
	ECG, w/interpretation	93000	
	ECG, rhythm strip	93040	
	Endometrial biopsy	58100	
	Fracture care, cast/splint Site: _______________	____	
	Nebulizer	94640	
	Nebulizer demo	94664	
	Spirometry	94010	
	Spirometry, pre and post	94060	
	Vasectomy	55250	
	Skin procedures		**Units**
	Foreign body, skin, simple	10120	
	Foreign body, skin, complex	10121	
	I&D, abscess	10060	
	I&D, hematoma/seroma	10140	
	Laceration repair, simple Site: _______ Size: _____	120__	
	Laceration repair, layered Site: _______ Size: _____	120__	
	Laser Light Tx	96597	
	Lesion, biopsy, one	11100	
	Lesion, biopsy, each add'l	11101	
	Lesion, excision, benign Site: _______ Size: _____	114__	
	Lesion, excision, malignant Site: _______ Size: _____	116__	
	Lesion, paring/cutting, one	11055	
	Lesion, paring/cutting, 2-4	11056	
	Lesion, shave Site: _______ Size: _____	113__	
	Nail removal, partial (+T mod)	11730	
	Nail rem, w/matrix (+T mod)	11750	
	Skin tag, 1-15	11200	
	Wart, flat, 1-14	17110	
	Destruction lesion, 1st	17000	
	Destruct lesion, each addl 2-14	17003	
	Medications		**Units**
	Ampicillin, up to 500mg	J0290	
	B-12, up to 1,000 mcg	J3420	
	Epinephrine, up to 1ml	J0170	
✓	Kenalog, 10mg	J3301	3
	Lidocaine, 10mg	J2001	
	Normal saline, 1000cc	J7030	
	Phenergan, up to 50mg	J2550	
	Progesterone, 150mg	J1055	
	Rocephin, 250mg	J0696	
	Testosterone, 200mg	J1080	
	Tigan, up to 200 mg	J3250	
	Toradol, 15mg	J1885	
	Albuterol	J7609	
	Depo-Provera 50 mg	J1055	
	Depo-Medrol 40 mg	J1030	

Diagnoses	Code
1 (R) heel pain	
2 Plantar fasciitis	
3	
4	

Next office visit:
Recheck • Preventative • (PRN) [circled]

Referral to:

x	Laboratory		-90
	Venipuncture	36415	
	Blood glucose, monitoring device	82962	
	Blood glucose, visual dipstick	82948	
	CBC, w/ auto differential	85025	
	CBC, w/o auto differential	85027	
	Cholesterol	82465	
	Hemoccult, guaiac	82270	
	Hemoccult, immunoassay	82274	
	Hemoglobin A1C	85018	
	Lipid panel	80061	
	Liver panel	80076	
	KOH prep (skin, hair, nails)	87220	
	Metabolic panel, basic	80048	
	Metabolic panel, comprehensive	80053	
	Mononucleosis	86308	
	Pregnancy, blood	84703	
	Pregnancy, urine	81025	
	Renal panel	80069	
	Sedimentation rate	85651	
	Strep, rapid	86403	
	Strep culture	87081	
	Strep A	87880	
	TB	86580	
	UA, complete, non-automated	81000	
	UA, w/o micro, non-automated	81002	
	UA, w/ micro, non-automated	81003	
	Urine colony count	87086	
	Urine culture, presumptive	87088	
	Wet mount/KOH	87210	

x	Vaccines	
	DT, <7 y	90702
	DTP	90701
	DtaP, <7 y	90700
	Flu, 6-35 months	90657
	Flu, 3 y +	90658
	Hep A, adult	90632
	Hep A, ped/adol, 2 dose	90633
	Hep B, adult	90746
	Hep B, ped/adol 3 dose	90744
	Hep B-Hib	90748
	Hib, 4 dose	90645
	HPV	90649
	IPV	90713
	MMR	90707
	Pneumonia, >2 y	90732
	Pneumonia conjugate, <5 y	90669
	Td, >7 y	90718
	Varicella	90716
	Tetanus toxoid adsorbed, IM	90703

x	Immunizations & Injections		Units
	Allergen, one	95115	
	Allergen, multiple	95117	
	Imm admn <8 yo 1st Inj	90465	
	Imm admn <8 yo each add inj	90466	
	Imm <8 yo oral or intranasal	90467	
	Imm admn <8 yo each add	90468	
	Imm admn, one vacc	90471	
	Imm admn, each add'l	90472	
	Imm admn, intranasal, one	90473	
	Imm admn, intranasal, each add'l	90474	
	Injection, joint, small	20600	
	Injection, joint, intermediate	20605	
	Injection, ther/proph/diag	90772	
	Injection, trigger pt 1-2 musc	20552	

Instructions:

-ice 15 min/day before bed -10 days
-Motrin 400mg bid

Physician signature

x Murray MD

Today's charges:		
Today's payment:		
Balance due:		

Job 1 Router- Diane Parker 3 of 6

Date of service: 10/28/09	Insurance: SIGNAL HMO				Router Number: 2469
Patient name: CAMILLE EMERY	Coinsurance:	Copay:	10.00		Physician Name: KEMPER
Account #: CAM001	Noncovered Waiver?	yes	no	n/a	

X	Office visit	New	X	Est
N/A	Minimal (RN only)	N/A		99211
	Problem focused	99201		99212
	Exp problem focused	99202		99213
	Detailed	99203	✓	99214
	Comp	99204		99215
	Comprhen/Complex	99205		
	Well visit	**New**	**X**	**Est**
	< 1 y	99381		99391
	1-4 y	99382		99392
	5-11 y	99383		99393
	12-17 y	99384		99394
	18-39 y	99385		99395
	40-64 y	99386		99396
	65 y +	99387		99397
	Medicare preventive services			
	Pap			Q0091
	Pelvic & breast			G0101
	Prostate/PSA			G0103
	Tobacco couns/3-10 min			G0375
	Tobacco couns/>10 min			G0376
	Welcome to Medicare exam			G0344
	ECG w/Welcome to Medicare			G0366
	Hemoccult, guaiac			G0107
	Flu shot			G0008
	Pneumonia shot			G0009
	Consultation/preop clearance			
	Exp problem focused			99242
	Detailed			99243
	Comp/mod complex			99244
	Comp/high complex			99245
	Other services			
	After posted hours			99050
	Evening/weekend appointment			99051
	Home health certification			G0180
	Home health recertification			G0179
	Care Plan oversight			99374
	Care Plan Oversight >30 mins			99375
	Post-op follow-up			99024
	Prolonged/60min total			99354
	Prolonged/each add 30 mins			99355
	Special reports/forms			99080
	Disability/Workers comp			99455
	Smoking Cessation <10 mins			99406
	Smoking Cessation >10 mins			99407
	ETOH/SA screening <30 mins			99408
	Online E/M by MD			99444
	Phone E/M <10 mins			99441
	Phone E/M <20 mins			99442
	Phone E/M <30 mins			99443
	Anticoagulant Mgmt <90 days			99363
	Anticoagulant Mgmt >90 days			99364
	In office emergency serv			99058
	Other services			
	Supplies			
	Surgical Tray			99070

Instructions:

X	Office procedures		
	Cerumen removal		69210
	ECG, w/interpretation		93000
	ECG, rhythm strip		93040
	Endometrial biopsy		58100
	Fracture care, cast/splint Site: ______________		
	Nebulizer		94640
	Nebulizer demo		94664
	Spirometry		94010
	Spirometry, pre and post		94060
	Vasectomy		55250
	Skin procedures		**Units**
	Foreign body, skin, simple	10120	
	Foreign body, skin, complex	10121	
	I&D, abscess	10060	
	I&D, hematoma/seroma	10140	
	Laceration repair, simple Site: ________ Size: _____	120__	
	Laceration repair, layered Site: ________ Size: _____	120__	
	Laser Light Tx	96597	
	Lesion, biopsy, one	11100	
	Lesion, biopsy, each add'l	11101	
	Lesion, excision, benign Site: ________ Size: _____	114__	
	Lesion, excision, malignant Site: ________ Size: _____	116__	
	Lesion, paring/cutting, one	11055	
	Lesion, paring/cutting, 2-4	11056	
	Lesion, shave Site: ________ Size: _____	113__	
	Nail removal, partial (+T mod)	11730	
	Nail rem, w/matrix (+T mod)	11750	
	Skin tag, 1-15	11200	
	Wart, flat, 1-14	17110	
	Destruction lesion, 1st	17000	
	Destruct lesion, each addl 2-14	17003	
	Medications		**Units**
	Ampicillin, up to 500mg	J0290	
	B-12, up to 1,000 mcg	J3420	
	Epinephrine, up to 1ml	J0170	
	Kenalog, 10mg	J3301	
	Lidocaine, 10mg	J2001	
	Normal saline, 1000cc	J7030	
	Phenergan, up to 50mg	J2550	
	Progesterone, 150mg	J1055	
	Rocephin, 250mg	J0696	
	Testosterone, 200mg	J1080	
	Tigan, up to 200 mg	J3250	
	Toradol, 15mg	J1885	
	Albuterol	J7609	
	Depo-Provera 50 mg	J1055	
	Depo-Medrol 40 mg	J1030	

Diagnoses	Code
1 Enuresis	
2 Fatigue	
3 adenoid Enlargement	
4 possible UTI	

Next office visit: 14 days

Recheck (circled) • Preventative • PRN

Referral to: Eric Nicks MD

Physician signature

X Sally Kemper MD

X	Laboratory		-90
	Venipuncture	36415	
	Blood glucose, monitoring device	82962	
	Blood glucose, visual dipstick	82948	
	CBC, w/ auto differential	85025	
	CBC, w/o auto differential	85027	
	Cholesterol	82465	
	Hemoccult, guaiac	82270	
	Hemoccult, immunoassay	82274	
	Hemoglobin A1C	85018	
	Lipid panel	80061	
	Liver panel	80076	
	KOH prep (skin, hair, nails)	87220	
	Metabolic panel, basic	80048	
	Metabolic panel, comprehensive	80053	
	Mononucleosis	86308	
	Pregnancy, blood	84703	
	Pregnancy, urine	81025	
	Renal panel	80069	
	Sedimentation rate	85651	
	Strep, rapid	86403	
	Strep culture	87081	
	Strep A	87880	
	TB	86580	
	UA, complete, non-automated	81000	
	UA, w/o micro, non-automated	81002	
✓	UA, w/ micro, non-automated	81003	
	Urine colony count	87086	
✓	Urine culture, presumptive	87088	
	Wet mount/KOH	87210	
	Vaccines		
	DT, <7 y		90702
	DTP		90701
	DtaP, <7 y		90700
	Flu, 6-35 months		90657
	Flu, 3 y +		90658
	Hep A, adult		90632
	Hep A, ped/adol, 2 dose		90633
	Hep B, adult		90746
	Hep B, ped/adol 3 dose		90744
	Hep B-Hib		90748
	Hib, 4 dose		90645
	HPV		90649
	IPV		90713
	MMR		90707
	Pneumonia, >2 y		90732
	Pneumonia conjugate, <5 y		90669
	Td, >7 y		90718
	Varicella		90716
	Tetanus toxoid adsorbed, IM		90703
	Immunizations & Injections		**Units**
	Allergen, one	95115	
	Allergen, multiple	95117	
	Imm admn <8 yo 1st Inj	90465	
	Imm admn <8 yo each add inj	90466	
	Imm <8 yo oral or intranasal	90467	
	Imm admn <8 yo each add	90468	
	Imm admin, one vacc	90471	
	Imm admin, each add'l	90472	
	Imm admin, intranasal, one	90473	
	Imm admin, intranasal, each add'l	90474	
	Injection, joint, small	20600	
	Injection, joint, intermediate	20605	
	Injection, ther/proph/diag	90772	
	Injection, trigger pt 1-2 musc	20552	

Today's charges:		
Today's payment:		
Balance due:		

Job 1 Router- Camille Emery 4 of 6

Date of service: 10/28/09	Insurance: FLEXIHEALTH PPO				Router Number: 2471
Patient name: ALAN SHUMAN	Coinsurance:	Copay:			Physician Name: LYNN
Account #: SHU001	Noncovered Waiver?	yes	no	n/a	

x	Office visit	New	x	Est
	Minimal (RN only)			99211
	Problem focused	99201		99212
	Exp problem focused	99202		99213
	Detailed	99203		99214
	Comp	99204		99215
	Comprhen/Complex	99205		
	Well visit	**New**	**x**	**Est**
	< 1 y	99381		99391
	1-4 y	99382		99392
	5-11 y	99383		99393
	12-17 y	99384		99394
	18-39 y	99385		99395
	40-64 y	99386		99396
✓	65 y +	99387		99397
	Medicare preventive services			
	Pap			Q0091
	Pelvic & breast			G0101
	Prostate/PSA			G0103
	Tobacco couns/3-10 min			G0375
	Tobacco couns/>10 min			G0376
	Welcome to Medicare exam			G0344
	ECG w/Welcome to Medicare			G0366
	Hemoccult, guaiac			G0107
✓	Flu shot			G0008
✓	Pneumonia shot			G0009
	Consultation/preop clearance			
	Exp problem focused			99242
	Detailed			99243
	Comp/mod complex			99244
	Comp/high complex			99245
	Other services			
	After posted hours			99050
	Evening/weekend appointment			99051
	Home health certification			G0180
	Home health recertification			G0179
	Care Plan oversight			99374
	Care Plan Oversight >30 mins			99375
	Post-op follow-up			99024
	Prolonged/60min total			99354
	Prolonged/each add 30 mins			99355
	Special reports/forms			99080
	Disability/Workers comp			99455
	Smoking Cessation <10 mins			99406
	Smoking Cessation >10 mins			99407
	ETOH/SA screening <30 mins			99408
	Online E/M by MD			99444
	Phone E/M <10 mins			99441
	Phone E/M <20 mins			99442
	Phone E/M <30 mins			99443
	Anticoagulant Mgmt <90 days			99363
	Anticoagulant Mgmt >90 days			99364
	In office emergency serv			99058
	Other services			
	Supplies			
	Surgical Tray			99070
	Instructions:			

x	Office procedures		
	Cerumen removal		69210
	ECG, w/interpretation		93000
	ECG, rhythm strip		93040
	Endometrial biopsy		58100
	Fracture care, cast/splint Site: ______		____
	Nebulizer		94640
	Nebulizer demo		94664
	Spirometry		94010
	Spirometry, pre and post		94060
	Vasectomy		55250
	Skin procedures		**Units**
	Foreign body, skin, simple	10120	
	Foreign body, skin, complex	10121	
	I&D, abscess	10060	
	I&D, hematoma/seroma	10140	
	Laceration repair, simple Site: ______ Size: ____	120__	
	Laceration repair, layered Site: ______ Size: ____	120__	
	Laser Light Tx	96597	
	Lesion, biopsy, one	11100	
	Lesion, biopsy, each add'l	11101	
	Lesion, excision, benign Site: ______ Size: ____	114__	
	Lesion, excision, malignant Site: ______ Size: ____	116__	
	Lesion, paring/cutting, one	11055	
	Lesion, paring/cutting, 2-4	11056	
	Lesion, shave Site: ______ Size: ____	113__	
	Nail removal, partial (+T mod)	11730	
	Nail rem, w/matrix (+T mod)	11750	
	Skin tag, 1-15	11200	
	Wart, flat, 1-14	17110	
	Destruction lesion, 1st	17000	
	Destruct lesion, each addl 2-14	17003	
	Medications		**Units**
	Ampicillin, up to 500mg	J0290	
	B-12, up to 1,000 mcg	J3420	
	Epinephrine, up to 1ml	J0170	
	Kenalog, 10mg	J3301	
	Lidocaine, 10mg	J2001	
	Normal saline, 1000cc	J7030	
	Phenergan, up to 50mg	J2550	
	Progesterone, 150mg	J1055	
	Rocephin, 250mg	J0696	
	Testosterone, 200mg	J1080	
	Tigan, up to 200 mg	J3250	
	Toradol, 15mg	J1885	
	Albuterol	J7609	
	Depo-Provera 50 mg	J1055	
	Depo-Medrol 40 mg	J1030	
	Diagnoses		**Code**
	1 Vaccinations		
	2		
	3		
	4		

Next office visit:
Recheck • Preventative • PRN
Referral to:

Physician signature

x Alberta Lynn

x	Laboratory		-90
	Venipuncture	36415	
	Blood glucose, monitoring device	82962	
	Blood glucose, visual dipstick	82948	
	CBC, w/ auto differential	85025	
	CBC, w/o auto differential	85027	
	Cholesterol	82465	
	Hemoccult, guaiac	82270	
	Hemoccult, immunoassay	82274	
	Hemoglobin A1C	85018	
	Lipid panel	80061	
	Liver panel	80076	
	KOH prep (skin, hair, nails)	87220	
	Metabolic panel, basic	80048	
	Metabolic panel, comprehensive	80053	
	Mononucleosis	86308	
	Pregnancy, blood	84703	
	Pregnancy, urine	81025	
	Renal panel	80069	
	Sedimentation rate	85651	
	Strep, rapid	86403	
	Strep culture	87081	
	Strep A	87880	
	TB	86580	
	UA, complete, non-automated	81000	
	UA, w/o micro, non-automated	81002	
	UA, w/ micro, non-automated	81003	
	Urine colony count	87086	
	Urine culture, presumptive	87088	
	Wet mount/KOH	87210	
	Vaccines		
	DT, <7 y		90702
	DTP		90701
	DtaP, <7 y		90700
	Flu, 6-35 months		90657
✓	Flu, 3 y +		90658
	Hep A, adult		90632
	Hep A, ped/adol, 2 dose		90633
	Hep B, adult		90746
	Hep B, ped/adol 3 dose		90744
	Hep B-Hib		90748
	Hib, 4 dose		90645
	HPV		90649
	IPV		90713
	MMR		90707
✓	Pneumonia, >2 y		90732
	Pneumonia conjugate, <5 y		90669
	Td, >7 y		90718
	Varicella		90716
	Tetanus toxoid adsorbed, IM		90703
	Immunizations & Injections		**Units**
	Allergen, one	95115	
	Allergen, multiple	95117	
	Imm admn <8 yo 1st Inj	90465	
	Imm admn <8 yo each add inj	90466	
	Imm <8 yo oral or intranasal	90467	
	Imm admn <8 yo each add	90468	
✓	Imm admin, one vacc	90471	
✓	Imm admin, each add'l	90472	
	Imm admin, intranasal, one	90473	
	Imm admin, intranasal, each add'l	90474	
	Injection, joint, small	20600	
	Injection, joint, intermediate	20605	
	Injection, ther/proph/diag	90772	
	Injection, trigger pt 1-2 musc	20552	

Today's charges:		
Today's payment:		
Balance due:		

Job 1 Router- Alan Shuman 5 of 6

Aetna
Paul Morgan
ID No: 4671921D
Group No: G2271
Subscriber: Paul Morgan
25% coinsurance

159 Metro Dr, Milwaukee, WI 52631 (800)666-5584

Job 1 Insurance Card 1 of 2

Signal HMO
Paul Morgan
ID No: 001245793

Group No: 442
Subscriber: Nancy Morgan
Copay: $10/$20

4500 Old Town Way, Lowville, NY 01453 (800)555-2121

Job 1 Insurance Card 2 of 2

Date of service: 10/28/09	Insurance: AETNA/SIGNAL HMO		Router Number: 2475
Patient name: PAUL MORGAN	Coinsurance:	Copay:	Physician Name: SCHWARTZ
Account #: MOR001	Noncovered Waiver?	yes / no / n/a	

x	Office visit	New	x	Est
	Minimal (RN only)			99211
	Problem focused	99201		99212
	Exp problem focused	99202		99213
	Detailed	99203		99214
	Comp	99204		99215
	Comprhen/Complex	99205		
	Well visit	**New**	**x**	**Est**
	< 1 y	99381		99391
	1-4 y	99382		99392
	5-11 y	99383		99393
	12-17 y	99384		99394
	18-39 y	99385		99395
	40-64 y	99386		99396
	65 y +	99387		99397

x	Medicare preventive services	
	Pap	Q0091
	Pelvic & breast	G0101
	Prostate/PSA	G0103
	Tobacco couns/3-10 min	G0375
	Tobacco couns/>10 min	G0376
	Welcome to Medicare exam	G0344
	ECG w/Welcome to Medicare	G0366
	Hemoccult, guaiac	G0107
	Flu shot	G0008
	Pneumonia shot	G0009
	Consultation/preop clearance	
	Exp problem focused	99242
	Detailed	99243
	Comp/mod complex	99244
	Comp/high complex	99245
	Other services	
	After posted hours	99050
	Evening/weekend appointment	99051
	Home health certification	G0180
	Home health recertification	G0179
	Care Plan oversight	99374
	Care Plan Oversight >30 mins	99375
	Post-op follow-up	99024
	Prolonged/60min total	99354
	Prolonged/each add 30 mins	99355
	Special reports/forms	99080
	Disability/Workers comp	99455
	Smoking Cessation <10 mins	99406
	Smoking Cessation >10 mins	99407
	ETOH/SA screening <30 mins	99408
	Online E/M by MD	99444
	Phone E/M <10 mins	99441
	Phone E/M <20 mins	99442
	Phone E/M <30 mins	99443
	Anticoagulant Mgmt <90 days	99363
	Anticoagulant Mgmt >90 days	99364
	In office emergency serv	99058
	Other services	
	Supplies	
✓	Surgical Tray	99070
	Valium PO 10 mg	
	Zofran 4mg PO	
	Instructions:	

x	Office procedures		
	Cerumen removal		69210
	ECG, w/interpretation		93000
	ECG, rhythm strip		93040
	Endometrial biopsy		58100
	Fracture care, cast/splint		____
	Site: ________________		
	Nebulizer		94640
	Nebulizer demo		94664
	Spirometry		94010
	Spirometry, pre and post		94060
✓	Vasectomy		55250
	Skin procedures		**Units**
	Foreign body, skin, simple	10120	
	Foreign body, skin, complex	10121	
	I&D, abscess	10060	
	I&D, hematoma/seroma	10140	
	Laceration repair, simple	120__	
	Site: _______ Size: _____		
	Laceration repair, layered	120__	
	Site: _______ Size: _____		
	Laser Light Tx	96597	
	Lesion, biopsy, one	11100	
	Lesion, biopsy, each add'l	11101	
	Lesion, excision, benign	114__	
	Site: _______ Size: _____		
	Lesion, excision, malignant	116__	
	Site: _______ Size: _____		
	Lesion, paring/cutting, one	11055	
	Lesion, paring/cutting, 2-4	11056	
	Lesion, shave	113__	
	Site: _______ Size: _____		
	Nail removal, partial (+T mod)	11730	
	Nail rem, w/matrix (+T mod)	11750	
	Skin tag, 1-15	11200	
	Wart, flat, 1-14	17110	
	Destruction lesion, 1st	17000	
	Destruct lesion, each addl 2-14	17003	
	Medications		**Units**
	Ampicillin, up to 500mg	J0290	
	B-12, up to 1,000 mcg	J3420	
	Epinephrine, up to 1ml	J0170	
	Kenalog, 10mg	J3301	
✓	Lidocaine, 10mg	J2001	
	Normal saline, 1000cc	J7030	
	Phenergan, up to 50mg	J2550	
	Progesterone, 150mg	J1055	
	Rocephin, 250mg	J0696	
	Testosterone, 200mg	J1080	
	Tigan, up to 200 mg	J3250	
	Toradol, 15mg	J1885	
	Albuterol	J7609	
	Depo-Provera 50 mg	J1055	
	Depo-Medrol 40 mg	J1030	

Diagnoses	Code
1 Elective Sterilization	
2	
3	
4	

Next office visit:

Recheck • Preventative • PRN

Referral to:

Physician signature

x Dr Schwartz MD

x	Laboratory		-90
	Venipuncture	36415	
	Blood glucose, monitoring device	82962	
	Blood glucose, visual dipstick	82948	
	CBC, w/ auto differential	85025	
	CBC, w/o auto differential	85027	
	Cholesterol	82465	
	Hemoccult, guaiac	82270	
	Hemoccult, immunoassay	82274	
	Hemoglobin A1C	85018	
	Lipid panel	80061	
	Liver panel	80076	
	KOH prep (skin, hair, nails)	87220	
	Metabolic panel, basic	80048	
	Metabolic panel, comprehensive	80053	
	Mononucleosis	86308	
	Pregnancy, blood	84703	
	Pregnancy, urine	81025	
	Renal panel	80069	
	Sedimentation rate	85651	
	Strep, rapid	86403	
	Strep culture	87081	
	Strep A	87880	
	TB	86580	
	UA, complete, non-automated	81000	
	UA, w/o micro, non-automated	81002	
	UA, w/ micro, non-automated	81003	
	Urine colony count	87086	
	Urine culture, presumptive	87088	
	Wet mount/KOH	87210	
	Vaccines		
	DT, <7 y		90702
	DTP		90701
	DtaP, <7 y		90700
	Flu, 6-35 months		90657
	Flu, 3 y +		90658
	Hep A, adult		90632
	Hep A, ped/adol, 2 dose		90633
	Hep B, adult		90746
	Hep B, ped/adol 3 dose		90744
	Hep B-Hib		90748
	Hib, 4 dose		90645
	HPV		90649
	IPV		90713
	MMR		90707
	Pneumonia, >2 y		90732
	Pneumonia conjugate, <5 y		90669
	Td, >7 y		90718
	Varicella		90716
	Tetanus toxoid adsorbed, IM		90703
	Immunizations & Injections		**Units**
	Allergen, one	95115	
	Allergen, multiple	95117	
	Imm admn <8 yo 1st Inj	90465	
	Imm admn <8 yo each add inj	90466	
	Imm <8 yo oral or intranasal	90467	
	Imm admn <8 yo each add	90468	
	Imm admin, one vacc	90471	
	Imm admin, each add'l	90472	
	Imm admin, intranasal, one	90473	
	Imm admin, intranasal, each add'l	90474	
	Injection, joint, small	20600	
	Injection, joint, intermediate	20605	
	Injection, ther/proph/diag	90772	
	Injection, trigger pt 1-2 musc	20552	

Today's charges:		
Today's payment:		
Balance due:		

Job 1 Router- Paul Morgan 6 of 6

Douglasville Medicine Associates
Patient Registration Form

Patients must complete all information prior to seeing the physician. A copy of your insurance card(s) and driver's license will be made for your file.

Patient Name: PAUL MORGAN Date of Birth: 8 / 18 / 68
Sex: (Male) or Female Social Security Number: 047-91-5571 Marital Status: M
Address Line 1: 47 BARRINGTON HIGHWAY
Address Line 2: ____
City: ROCHESTER
State: NY Zip Code: 14699
Home Telephone: (717) 555-4747 Work Telephone: (717) 555-9191
Cellular Telephone: (717) 555-0067 Email address: PMorgan@vonage.com

Patient's Work Status (Full-Time, Part-Time, Retired, Student): ____
Employer Name: ROCHESTER TIRE CO.
Address Line 1: R763 MAIN STREET
Address Line 2: ____
City: ROCHESTER State: NY Zip: 14691
Telephone: (717) 555-9191
If patient is a minor, who is the primary guardian? ____

Primary Insurance Company: AETNA
Subscriber ID Number 4671921D Policy Group #: G2271
Subscriber Name: PAUL MORGAN Birth date: 8/18/58
Subscriber Social Security Number: 047-91-5571 Relationship to patient: SELF

Secondary Insurance Company: Signal HMO
Subscriber ID Number 001245793 Policy Group #: 442
Subscriber Name: Nancy Morgan Birth date: 5/22/59
Subscriber Social Security Number: 062 99-3475 Relationship to patient: Wife

Complete this section if your treatment is for an injury or accident.
Were you injured at work? ____ Is this covered by Workers' Compensation? ____
If Yes, Contact person at your Employer ____
Were you involved in an auto accident? ____ Provide insurance company, contact information, and claim number: ____

Date & time of Accident ____ Place of Accident ____
How did injury happen? ____
Name of Physician who treated you at time of accident: ____

Financial Responsibility Statement/ Release of Information Authorization
"I authorize the release of any medical information necessary to my insurance company and the Payment of Benefits to the Physician for services provided.

X Paul Morgan ____ Date ____
Signature of Patient or Legal Guardian

Job 1 Registration Paper work- Paul Morgan 1 of 5

Douglasville Medicine Associates
Patient Registration Form

OUR FINANCIAL POLICY

By law, we must collect your carrier designated co-pay at the time of service. Please be prepared to pay that co-pay at each visit. We are also required to collect any portion of the deductible that has not been satisfied. If your plan requires a coinsurance instead of a co-pay and we participate with the plan, we will accept the designated payment and bill you accordingly for any deductible and coinsurance your plan indicates you are responsible for on their explanation of benefits.

Payment is expected at the time of service unless other financial arrangements have been made prior to your visit. If you are uninsured, you may qualify for a hardship discount. Ask one of our staff members for more information.

You are responsible for timely payment of your account. Douglasville Medicine Associates reserves the right to reschedule or deny a future appointment on delinquent accounts.

WE ACCEPT CASH, CHECKS, MASTERCARD AND VISA

THANK YOU for taking the time to review our policy.

Paul Morgan ____________________ 10/28/09 ____________

(Responsible Party Signature) (Date)

Job 1 Registration Paper work- Paul Morgan 2 of 5

Douglasville Medicine Associates
5076 Brand Blvd., Suite 401 ▪ Douglasville, NY 01234 (123)456-7890

Patient Name:______________________________

Record #:_____________

I acknowledge that I have received a written copy of Douglasville Medicine Associates Notice of Patient Privacy Practices. I also acknowledge that I have been allowed to ask questions concerning this notice and my rights under this notice. I understand that this form will be part of my record until such time as I may choose to revoke this acknowledgement. If I am not the patient, I am the authorized representative of a minor child or authorized by law to act for and on the patient's behalf.

Paul Morgan ______________________ 10/28/09 ______________

Signature of Patient or Authorized Agent Date

Patient (or authorized agent) refused to sign Notice of Privacy Practices.

Please describe events. ____

____

__________________________ ______________

Signature of DMA Employee Date

Job 1 Registration Paper work- Paul Morgan 3 of 5

Douglasville Medicine Associates
5076 Brand Blvd., Suite 401▪Douglasville, NY 01234

CONSENT TO TREATMENT

Patient Name: Paul Morgan Date: 10/28/09

I, Paul Morgan, hereby voluntarily consent to outpatient treatment and evaluation at Douglasville Medicine Associates for Myself. This includes routine diagnostic procedures, examination and medical treatment including, but not limited to, routine laboratory work (such as blood, urine and other studies), x-rays, heart tracing and administration of medications prescribed by the physician.

I further consent to the performance of those diagnostic procedures, examinations and rendering of medical treatment by the medical staff and their assistants.

I understand that this consent form will be valid and remain in effect as long as I receive medical care at Douglasville Medicine Associates.

This form has been explained to me and I fully understand this Consent To Treatment and agree to its contents.

Paul M [signature]
Signature of Patient or
Person Authorized to consent for patient

Self
Relationship to patient

____
Signature of Witness

Job 1 Registration paper work- Paul Morgan 4 of 5

Douglasville Medicine Associates
5076 Brand Blvd, Suite 401~ Douglasville, NY 01234

ASSIGNMENT OF BENEFITS AND PATIENT REPRESENTATION

Patient Name:______________________________ Chart # ____________

Insured Name:______________________________

Insurance Company Name ______________________________

Policy # ____________________ Group # ____________________

I hereby assign all medical and/or surgical benefits, to include major medical benefits to which I am entitled, to **Douglasville Medicine Associates**. This assignment will remain in effect until revoked by me in writing. A photocopy of this assignment is to be considered as valid as the original.

I understand that I am financially responsible for all charges whether or not paid by my insurance carrier. I understand that I will be responsible for any court costs or collection fees should it become necessary to take action to collect for services/supplies rendered.

I hereby authorize **Douglasville Medicine Associates** to release all medical information necessary to secure payment on my account.

I hereby authorize **Douglasville Medicine Associates** and medical billing staff members, to submit claims, on my behalf, to the insurance company listed on the copy of the current and valid insurance card I have provided to the Clinic in good faith. I fully agree and understand that the submission of a claim does not absolve me of my responsibility to ensure that the bill for medical services is paid in full.

I authorize **Douglasville Medicine Associates** and its medical billing representative, to be my personal representative, which allows the Clinic to: (1) submit any and all appeals when my insurance company performs an adverse benefit determination as defined in 29 CFR 2560-503-1, (2) submit any and all requests for benefit information from my employer and/or health insurance company, and (3) initiate formal complaints to any State or Federal agency that has jurisdiction over my benefits.

I fully understand and agree that I am responsible for full payment of the medical debt I owe the Clinic, if my insurance company has refused to pay 100% of my covered benefits, within ninety (90) days of any and all appeals or request for information. A photocopy of this document shall be considered as effective and valid as the original.

Patient Paul M ____________________ 10/28/09 ____________
(signature) (date)

Patient Representative ______________________________
(date)

Relationship to Patient ______________________________

Witness ______________________________
(signature) (date)

Job 1 Registration Paper work- Paul Morgan 5 of 5

Date of service: 10/28/09	Insurance: PRUDENTIAL			Router Number: 2466
Patient name: BARRY JURCH	Coinsurance:	Copay:		Physician Name: HEATH
Account #: JUR001	Noncovered Waiver?	yes	no	n/a	

x	Office visit	New	x	Est
	Minimal (RN only)			99211
	Problem focused	99201		99212
	Exp problem focused	99202	✓	99213
	Detailed	99203		99214
	Comp	99204		99215
	Comprhen/Complex	99205		
	Well visit	**New**	**x**	**Est**
	< 1 y	99381		99391
	1-4 y	99382		99392
	5-11 y	99383		99393
	12-17 y	99384		99394
	18-39 y	99385		99395
	40-64 y	99386		99396
	65 y +	99387		99397
	Medicare preventive services			
	Pap			Q0091
	Pelvic & breast			G0101
	Prostate/PSA			G0103
	Tobacco couns/3-10 min			G0375
	Tobacco couns/>10 min			G0376
	Welcome to Medicare exam			G0344
	ECG w/Welcome to Medicare			G0366
	Hemoccult, guaiac			G0107
	Flu shot			G0008
	Pneumonia shot			G0009
	Consultation/preop clearance			
	Exp problem focused			99242
	Detailed			99243
	Comp/mod complex			99244
	Comp/high complex			99245
	Other services			
	After posted hours			99050
	Evening/weekend appointment			99051
	Home health certification			G0180
	Home health recertification			G0179
	Care Plan oversight			99374
	Care Plan Oversight >30 mins			99375
	Post-op follow-up			99024
	Prolonged/60min total			99354
	Prolonged/each add 30 mins			99355
	Special reports/forms			99080
	Disability/Workers comp			99455
	Smoking Cessation <10 mins			99406
	Smoking Cessation >10 mins			99407
	ETOH/SA screening <30 mins			99408
	Online E/M by MD			99444
	Phone E/M <10 mins			99441
	Phone E/M <20 mins			99442
	Phone E/M <30 mins			99443
	Anticoagulant Mgmt <90 days			99363
	Anticoagulant Mgmt >90 days			99364
	In office emergency serv			99058
	Other services			
✓	Flu Screen			
	Supplies			
	Surgical Tray			99070

Instructions:

- Liquids
- Tamiflu
- Rest

x	Office procedures		
	Cerumen removal		69210
	ECG, w/interpretation		93000
	ECG, rhythm strip		93040
	Endometrial biopsy		58100
	Fracture care, cast/splint Site: ______		____
	Nebulizer		94640
	Nebulizer demo		94664
	Spirometry		94010
	Spirometry, pre and post		94060
	Vasectomy		55250
	Skin procedures		**Units**
	Foreign body, skin, simple	10120	
	Foreign body, skin, complex	10121	
	I&D, abscess	10060	
	I&D, hematoma/seroma	10140	
	Laceration repair, simple Site: ____ Size: ____	120__	
	Laceration repair, layered Site: ____ Size: ____	120__	
	Laser Light Tx	96597	
	Lesion, biopsy, one	11100	
	Lesion, biopsy, each add'l	11101	
	Lesion, excision, benign Site: ____ Size: ____	114__	
	Lesion, excision, malignant Site: ____ Size: ____	116__	
	Lesion, paring/cutting, one	11055	
	Lesion, paring/cutting, 2-4	11056	
	Lesion, shave Site: ____ Size: ____	113__	
	Nail removal, partial (+T mod)	11730	
	Nail rem, w/matrix (+T mod)	11750	
	Skin tag, 1-15	11200	
	Wart, flat, 1-14	17110	
	Destruction lesion, 1st	17000	
	Destruct lesion, each addl 2-14	17003	
	Medications		**Units**
	Ampicillin, up to 500mg	J0290	
	B-12, up to 1,000 mcg	J3420	
	Epinephrine, up to 1ml	J0170	
	Kenalog, 10mg	J3301	
	Lidocaine, 10mg	J2001	
	Normal saline, 1000cc	J7030	
	Phenergan, up to 50mg	J2550	
	Progesterone, 150mg	J1055	
	Rocephin, 250mg	J0696	
	Testosterone, 200mg	J1080	
	Tigan, up to 200 mg	J3250	
	Toradol, 15mg	J1885	
	Albuterol	J7609	
	Depo-Provera 50 mg	J1055	
	Depo-Medrol 40 mg	J1030	

Diagnoses	Code
1 Fatigue	
2 Sore throat	
3 H1N1 flu	
4	

Next office visit:

Recheck • Preventative • (PRN)

Referral to:

Physician signature

X LD Heath MD

x	Laboratory		-90
	Venipuncture	36415	
	Blood glucose, monitoring device	82962	
	Blood glucose, visual dipstick	82948	
	CBC, w/ auto differential	85025	
	CBC, w/o auto differential	85027	
	Cholesterol	82465	
	Hemoccult, guaiac	82270	
	Hemoccult, immunoassay	82274	
	Hemoglobin A1C	85018	
	Lipid panel	80061	
	Liver panel	80076	
	KOH prep (skin, hair, nails)	87220	
	Metabolic panel, basic	80048	
	Metabolic panel, comprehensive	80053	
	Mononucleosis	86308	
	Pregnancy, blood	84703	
	Pregnancy, urine	81025	
	Renal panel	80069	
	Sedimentation rate	85651	
✓	Strep, rapid	86403	— (−)
	Strep culture	87081	
	Strep A	87880	
	TB	86580	
	UA, complete, non-automated	81000	
	UA, w/o micro, non-automated	81002	
	UA, w/ micro, non-automated	81003	
	Urine colony count	87086	
	Urine culture, presumptive	87088	
	Wet mount/KOH	87210	
	Vaccines		
	DT, <7 y		90702
	DTP		90701
	DtaP, <7 y		90700
	Flu, 6-35 months		90657
	Flu, 3 y +		90658
	Hep A, adult		90632
	Hep A, ped/adol, 2 dose		90633
	Hep B, adult		90746
	Hep B, ped/adol 3 dose		90744
	Hep B-Hib		90748
	Hib, 4 dose		90645
	HPV		90649
	IPV		90713
	MMR		90707
	Pneumonia, >2 y		90732
	Pneumonia conjugate, <5 y		90669
	Td, >7 y		90718
	Varicella		90716
	Tetanus toxoid adsorbed, IM		90703
	Immunizations & Injections		**Units**
	Allergen, one	95115	
	Allergen, multiple	95117	
	Imm admn <8 yo 1st Inj	90465	
	Imm admn <8 yo each add inj	90466	
	Imm <8 yo oral or intranasal	90467	
	Imm admn <8 yo each add	90468	
	Imm admin, one vacc	90471	
	Imm admin, each add'l	90472	
	Imm admin, intranasal, one	90473	
	Imm admin, intranasal, each add'l	90474	
	Injection, joint, small	20600	
	Injection, joint, intermediate	20605	
	Injection, ther/proph/diag	90772	
	Injection, trigger pt 1-2 musc	20552	

Today's charges:		
Today's payment:		
Balance due:		

Job 1 Router- Barry Jurch

Douglasville Medicine Associates

HOSPITAL CHARGE SHEET

☐Sarah Mendenhall, M.D.
☐D.J. Schwartrz, M.D.
☐L.D. Heath, M.D.
☐Sally Kemper, M.D.
☐Alberta Lynn, P.A.C.
☐Lance Murray, M.D.

Patient's Name: Julia Richard **Date(s) of Service:** 10/26/09 - 10/28/09

Place of Service: ☐ New York County Hospital ☑ Community General Hospital

☐Beaufort Regional Hospital ☐County Memorial Hospital

Hospital Visit Type: ☐Observation ☑Inpatient ☑Subsequent Visit ☐Emergency Room

☐Consultation ☑Initial Admission ☑Discharge Planning ☐Critical Care

Insurance Carrier: Century Senior **Insurance ID#** ___

Diagnosis/ICD-9: HTN, Substernal chest pain, Episodic HA

Procedure/Service Performed/CPT:

Initial adm - 10/26/09

Sub. visit - 10/27/09

Disch - 10/28/09

Signature: Sarah Mendenhall MD **Date given to biller:** 10/29/09

All visits were low level

Notes: Discharge Summary attached

Job 2 Hospital Charge Sheet- Julia Richard 1 of 2

Douglasville Medicine Associates

HOSPITAL CHARGE SHEET

☑ Sarah Mendenhall, M.D. ☐ Sally Kemper, M.D.
☐ D.J. Schwartrz, M.D. ☐ Alberta Lynn, P.A.C.
☐ L.D. Heath, M.D. ☐ Lance Murray, M.D.

Patient's Name: Julius Washington **Date(s) of Service:** 10/27/09

Place of Service: ☐ New York County Hospital ☑ Community General Hospital

☐ Beaufort Regional Hospital ☐ County Memorial Hospital

Hospital Visit Type: ☐ Observation ☐ Inpatient ☐ Subsequent Visit ☑ Emergency Room

☐ Consultation ☐ Initial Admission ☐ Discharge Planning ☐ Critical Care

Insurance Carrier: Great West **Insurance ID#** ______

Diagnosis/ICD-9: Acute Exacerbation Asthma
Bronchitis
Sinusitis

Procedure/Service Performed/CPT:
IV Steroids, Chest X-Ray, O2, Nebulizer TR
Ex prob foc exam mod decision making
Brought to ER when nocturnal cough got to pt
where couldn't breathe

Signature: Sarah Mendenhall MD **Date given to biller:** 10/28/09

Notes:

Job 2 Hospital Charge Sheet- Julius Washington 2 of 2

Century Senior Gap
Hugh Williams
ID No: 61H763
Group No: 32661
Subscriber: Hugh Williams
Copay: none

4500 Old Town Way, Lowville, NY 01453 (800)555-2121

Job 3 Insurance Card 1 of 2

Health Insurance

1-800-MEDICARE

Name of Beneficiary
HUGH WILLIAMS

Medicare Claim Number	Sex
011-55-3261A	M

is Entitled To:	**Effective Date**
Hospital (Part A)	10-01-2009
Medical (Part B)	10-01-2009

Sign Here: Hugh Williams

Job 3 Insurance Card 2 of 2

Date of service: 10/28/09	Insurance: MEDICARE/CENTURY		Router Number: 2472
Patient name: HUGH WILLIAMS	Coinsurance: 20%	Copay:	Physician Name: MENDENHALL
Account #: WIL001	Noncovered Waiver?	yes / no / n/a	

X	Office visit	New	X	Est
	Minimal (RN only)			99211
	Problem focused	99201		99212
	Exp problem focused	99202	✓	99213
	Detailed	99203		99214
	Comp	99204		99215
	Comprhen/Complex	99205		
	Well visit	**New**	**X**	**Est**
	< 1 y	99381		99391
	1-4 y	99382		99392
	5-11 y	99383		99393
	12-17 y	99384		99394
	18-39 y	99385		99395
	40-64 y	99386		99396
	65 y +	99387		99397
	Medicare preventive services			
	Pap			Q0091
	Pelvic & breast			G0101
✓	Prostate/PSA			G0103
	Tobacco couns/3-10 min			G0375
	Tobacco couns/>10 min			G0376
	Welcome to Medicare exam			G0344
	ECG w/Welcome to Medicare			G0366
	Hemoccult, guaiac			G0107
	Flu shot			G0008
	Pneumonia shot			G0009
	Consultation/preop clearance			
	Exp problem focused			99242
	Detailed			99243
	Comp/mod complex			99244
	Comp/high complex			99245
	Other services			
	After posted hours			99050
	Evening/weekend appointment			99051
	Home health certification			G0180
	Home health recertification			G0179
	Care Plan oversight			99374
	Care Plan Oversight >30 mins			99375
	Post-op follow-up			99024
	Prolonged/60min total			99354
	Prolonged/each add 30 mins			99355
	Special reports/forms			99080
	Disability/Workers comp			99455
	Smoking Cessation <10 mins			99406
	Smoking Cessation >10 mins			99407
	ETOH/SA screening <30 mins			99408
	Online E/M by MD			99444
	Phone E/M <10 mins			99441
	Phone E/M <20 mins			99442
	Phone E/M <30 mins			99443
	Anticoagulant Mgmt <90 days			99363
	Anticoagulant Mgmt >90 days			99364
	In office emergency serv			99058
	Other services			
	DRE			
	Supplies			
	Surgical Tray			99070
	Instructions:			

X	Office procedures	Code	Units
	Cerumen removal	69210	
	ECG, w/interpretation	93000	
	ECG, rhythm strip	93040	
	Endometrial biopsy	58100	
	Fracture care, cast/splint Site: ______	____	
	Nebulizer	94640	
	Nebulizer demo	94664	
	Spirometry	94010	
	Spirometry, pre and post	94060	
	Vasectomy	55250	
	Skin procedures		**Units**
	Foreign body, skin, simple	10120	
	Foreign body, skin, complex	10121	
	I&D, abscess	10060	
	I&D, hematoma/seroma	10140	
	Laceration repair, simple Site: ____ Size: ____	120__	
	Laceration repair, layered Site: ____ Size: ____	120__	
	Laser Light Tx	96597	
	Lesion, biopsy, one	11100	
	Lesion, biopsy, each add'l	11101	
	Lesion, excision, benign Site: ____ Size: ____	114__	
	Lesion, excision, malignant Site: ____ Size: ____	116__	
	Lesion, paring/cutting, one	11055	
	Lesion, paring/cutting, 2-4	11056	
	Lesion, shave Site: ____ Size: ____	113__	
	Nail removal, partial (+T mod)	11730	
	Nail rem, w/matrix (+T mod)	11750	
	Skin tag, 1-15	11200	
	Wart, flat, 1-14	17110	
	Destruction lesion, 1st	17000	
	Destruct lesion, each addl 2-14	17003	
	Medications		**Units**
	Ampicillin, up to 500mg	J0290	
	B-12, up to 1,000 mcg	J3420	
	Epinephrine, up to 1ml	J0170	
	Kenalog, 10mg	J3301	
	Lidocaine, 10mg	J2001	
	Normal saline, 1000cc	J7030	
	Phenergan, up to 50mg	J2550	
	Progesterone, 150mg	J1055	
	Rocephin, 250mg	J0696	
	Testosterone, 200mg	J1080	
	Tigan, up to 200 mg	J3250	
	Toradol, 15mg	J1885	
	Albuterol	J7609	
	Depo-Provera 50 mg	J1055	
	Depo-Medrol 40 mg	J1030	

Diagnoses	Code
1 Rectal Bleeding	
2 Constipation	
3 Fx hx Rectal polyps	
4	

Next office visit:

Recheck • Preventative • PRN

Referral to: Dr. Jones - GI Colonoscopy

Physician signature

X Sarah Mendenhall

X	Laboratory	Code	-90
	Venipuncture	36415	
	Blood glucose, monitoring device	82962	
	Blood glucose, visual dipstick	82948	
	CBC, w/ auto differential	85025	
	CBC, w/o auto differential	85027	
	Cholesterol	82465	
	Hemoccult, guaiac	82270	
	Hemoccult, immunoassay	82274	
	Hemoglobin A1C	85018	
	Lipid panel	80061	
	Liver panel	80076	
	KOH prep (skin, hair, nails)	87220	
	Metabolic panel, basic	80048	
	Metabolic panel, comprehensive	80053	
	Mononucleosis	86308	
	Pregnancy, blood	84703	
	Pregnancy, urine	81025	
	Renal panel	80069	
	Sedimentation rate	85651	
	Strep, rapid	86403	
	Strep culture	87081	
	Strep A	87880	
	TB	86580	
	UA, complete, non-automated	81000	
	UA, w/o micro, non-automated	81002	
	UA, w/ micro, non-automated	81003	
	Urine colony count	87086	
	Urine culture, presumptive	87088	
	Wet mount/KOH	87210	
	Vaccines		
	DT, <7 y		90702
	DTP		90701
	DtaP, <7 y		90700
	Flu, 6-35 months		90657
	Flu, 3 y +		90658
	Hep A, adult		90632
	Hep A, ped/adol, 2 dose		90633
	Hep B, adult		90746
	Hep B, ped/adol 3 dose		90744
	Hep B-Hib		90748
	Hib, 4 dose		90645
	HPV		90649
	IPV		90713
	MMR		90707
	Pneumonia, >2 y		90732
	Pneumonia conjugate, <5 y		90669
	Td, >7 y		90718
	Varicella		90716
	Tetanus toxoid adsorbed, IM		90703
	Immunizations & Injections		**Units**
	Allergen, one	95115	
	Allergen, multiple	95117	
	Imm admn <8 yo 1st Inj	90465	
	Imm admn <8 yo each add inj	90466	
	Imm <8 yo oral or intranasal	90467	
	Imm admn <8 yo each add	90468	
	Imm admin, one vacc	90471	
	Imm admin, each add'l	90472	
	Imm admin, intranasal, one	90473	
	Imm admin, intranasal, each add'l	90474	
	Injection, joint, small	20600	
	Injection, joint, intermediate	20605	
	Injection, ther/proph/diag	90772	
	Injection, trigger pt 1-2 musc	20552	

Today's charges:		
Today's payment:		
Balance due:		

Job 3 Router- Hugh Williams

Douglasville Medicine Associates
Patient Registration Form

Patients must complete all information prior to seeing the physician. A copy of your insurance card(s) and driver's license will be made for your file.

Patient Name: Hugh Williams Date of Birth: 10 / 21 / 34
Sex: (Male) or Female Social Security Number: 011 - 55 - 3261 Marital Status: M
Address Line 1: 220 Volunteer Way
Address Line 2: ____
City: Auburn
State: NY Zip Code: 14667
Home Telephone: (717) 555-1122 Work Telephone: (—)
Cellular Telephone: (—) Email address: hwilliams@yahoo.com

Patient's Work Status (Full-Time, Part-Time, (Retired), Student): ____
Employer Name: ____
Address Line 1: ____
Address Line 2: ____
City: ____ State: ____ Zip: ____
Telephone: (____) ____
If patient is a minor, who is the primary guardian? ____

Primary Insurance Company: Medicare
Subscriber ID Number 011553261A Policy Group #: ____
Subscriber Name: Same Birth date: Same
Subscriber Social Security Number: ____-____-____ Relationship to patient: Same

Secondary Insurance Company: Century Senior Gap
Subscriber ID Number 61H763 Policy Group #: 32661
Subscriber Name: same Birth date: Same
Subscriber Social Security Number: ____-____-____ Relationship to patient: same

Complete this section if your treatment is for an injury or accident.
Were you injured at work? ____ Is this covered by Workers' Compensation? ____
If Yes, Contact person at your Employer ____
Were you involved in an auto accident? ____ Provide insurance company, contact information, and claim number: ____

Date & time of Accident ____ Place of Accident ____
How did injury happen? ____
Name of Physician who treated you at time of accident: ____

Financial Responsibility Statement/ Release of Information Authorization
"I authorize the release of any medical information necessary to my insurance company and the Payment of Benefits to the Physician for services provided.

X Hugh Williams Date 10/28/09
Signature of Patient or Legal Guardian

Job 3 Registration Paper work- Hugh Williams 1 of 5

Douglasville Medicine Associates
Patient Registration Form

OUR FINANCIAL POLICY

By law, we must collect your carrier designated co-pay at the time of service. Please be prepared to pay that co-pay at each visit. We are also required to collect any portion of the deductible that has not been satisfied. If your plan requires a coinsurance instead of a co-pay and we participate with the plan, we will accept the designated payment and bill you accordingly for any deductible and coinsurance your plan indicates you are responsible for on their explanation of benefits.

Payment is expected at the time of service unless other financial arrangements have been made prior to your visit. If you are uninsured, you may qualify for a hardship discount. Ask one of our staff members for more information.

You are responsible for timely payment of your account. Douglasville Medicine Associates reserves the right to reschedule or deny a future appointment on delinquent accounts.

WE ACCEPT CASH, CHECKS, MASTERCARD AND VISA

THANK YOU for taking the time to review our policy.

Hugh Williams — 10/28/09

(Responsible Party Signature) (Date)

Job 3 Registration Paper work- Hugh Williams 2 of 5

Douglasville Medicine Associates
5076 Brand Blvd., Suite 401 ▪ Douglasville, NY 01234 (123)456-7890

Patient Name:______________________________

Record #:_____________

I acknowledge that I have received a written copy of Douglasville Medicine Associates Notice of Patient Privacy Practices. I also acknowledge that I have been allowed to ask questions concerning this notice and my rights under this notice. I understand that this form will be part of my record until such time as I may choose to revoke this acknowledgement. If I am not the patient, I am the authorized representative of a minor child or authorized by law to act for and on the patient's behalf.

Hugh Willi________________________ 10/28/09__________

Signature of Patient or Authorized Agent   Date

Patient (or authorized agent) refused to sign Notice of Privacy Practices.

Please describe events. ____

____

__________________________   _____________

Signature of DMA Employee   Date

Job 3 Registration Paper work- Hugh Williams 3 of 5

Douglasville Medicine Associates
5076 Brand Blvd, Suite 401~ Douglasville, NY 01234

ASSIGNMENT OF BENEFITS AND PATIENT REPRESENTATION

Patient Name:______________________________ Chart # ______________

Insured Name:____

Insurance Company Name ____

Policy # ______________________ Group # ______________________

I hereby assign all medical and/or surgical benefits, to include major medical benefits to which I am entitled, to **Douglasville Medicine Associates**. This assignment will remain in effect until revoked by me in writing. A photocopy of this assignment is to be considered as valid as the original.

I understand that I am financially responsible for all charges whether or not paid by my insurance carrier. I understand that I will be responsible for any court costs or collection fees should it become necessary to take action to collect for services/supplies rendered.

I hereby authorize **Douglasville Medicine Associates** to release all medical information necessary to secure payment on my account.

I hereby authorize **Douglasville Medicine Associates** and medical billing staff members, to submit claims, on my behalf, to the insurance company listed on the copy of the current and valid insurance card I have provided to the Clinic in good faith. I fully agree and understand that the submission of a claim does not absolve me of my responsibility to ensure that the bill for medical services is paid in full.

I authorize **Douglasville Medicine Associates** and its medical billing representative, to be my personal representative, which allows the Clinic to: (1) submit any and all appeals when my insurance company performs an adverse benefit determination as defined in 29 CFR 2560-503-1, (2) submit any and all requests for benefit information from my employer and/or health insurance company, and (3) initiate formal complaints to any State or Federal agency that has jurisdiction over my benefits.

I fully understand and agree that I am responsible for full payment of the medical debt I owe the Clinic, if my insurance company has refused to pay 100% of my covered benefits, within ninety (90) days of any and all appeals or request for information. A photocopy of this document shall be considered as effective and valid as the original.

Patient [signature] 10/28/09
(signature) (date)

Patient Representative ____
(date)

Relationship to Patient ____

Witness ____
(signature) (date)

Job 3 Registration Paper work- Hugh Williams 4 of 5

Douglasville Medicine Associates
5076 Brand Blvd., Suite 401▪Douglasville, NY 01234

CONSENT TO TREATMENT

Patient Name: Hugh Williams Date: 10/28/09

I, Hugh Williams, hereby voluntarily consent to outpatient treatment and evaluation at Douglasville Medicine Associates for Myself. This includes routine diagnostic procedures, examination and medical treatment including, but not limited to, routine laboratory work (such as blood, urine and other studies), x-rays, heart tracing and administration of medications prescribed by the physician.

I further consent to the performance of those diagnostic procedures, examinations and rendering of medical treatment by the medical staff and their assistants.

I understand that this consent form will be valid and remain in effect as long as I receive medical care at Douglasville Medicine Associates.

This form has been explained to me and I fully understand this Consent To Treatment and agree to its contents.

Hugh Williams
Signature of Patient or
Person Authorized to consent for patient

Self
Relationship to patient

Signature of Witness

Job 3 Registration Paper work- Hugh Williams 5 of 5

Date of service: 10/28/09	Insurance: CONSUMER ONE HRA				Router Number: 2468
Patient name: JORDAN CONNELL	Coinsurance:	Copay: $15.00			Physician Name: MURRAY
Account #: CON001	Noncovered Waiver?	yes	no	n/a	

x	Office visit	New	x	Est
	Minimal (RN only)			99211
	Problem focused	99201		99212
	Exp problem focused	99202		99213
	Detailed	99203		99214
	Comp	99204		99215
	Comprhen/Complex	99205		
	Well visit	**New**	**x**	**Est**
	< 1 y	99381		99391
	1-4 y	99382		99392
	5-11 y	99383		99393
	12-17 y	99384		99394
	18-39 y	99385		99395
	40-64 y	99386	✓	99396
	65 y +	99387		99397
	Medicare preventive services			
	Pap			Q0091
	Pelvic & breast			G0101
	Prostate/PSA			G0103
	Tobacco couns/3-10 min			G0375
	Tobacco couns/>10 min			G0376
	Welcome to Medicare exam			G0344
	ECG w/Welcome to Medicare			G0366
	Hemoccult, guaiac			G0107
	Flu shot			G0008
	Pneumonia shot			G0009
	Consultation/preop clearance			
	Exp problem focused			99242
	Detailed			99243
	Comp/mod complex			99244
	Comp/high complex			99245
	Other services			
	After posted hours			99050
	Evening/weekend appointment			99051
	Home health certification			G0180
	Home health recertification			G0179
	Care Plan oversight			99374
	Care Plan Oversight >30 mins			99375
	Post-op follow-up			99024
	Prolonged/60min total			99354
	Prolonged/each add 30 mins			99355
	Special reports/forms			99080
	Disability/Workers comp			99455
	Smoking Cessation <10 mins			99406
	Smoking Cessation >10 mins			99407
	ETOH/SA screening <30 mins			99408
	Online E/M by MD			99444
	Phone E/M <10 mins			99441
	Phone E/M <20 mins			99442
	Phone E/M <30 mins			99443
	Anticoagulant Mgmt <90 days			99363
	Anticoagulant Mgmt >90 days			99364
	In office emergency serv			99058
	Other services			
	PSA			
	Supplies			
✓	Surgical Tray			99070

Instructions:

Return for PSA & path results

x	Office procedures		
	Cerumen removal		69210
	ECG, w/interpretation		93000
	ECG, rhythm strip		93040
	Endometrial biopsy		58100
	Fracture care, cast/splint		____
	Site: ________________		
	Nebulizer		94640
	Nebulizer demo		94664
	Spirometry		94010
	Spirometry, pre and post		94060
	Vasectomy		55250
	Skin procedures		**Units**
	Foreign body, skin, simple	10120	
	Foreign body, skin, complex	10121	
	I&D, abscess	10060	
	I&D, hematoma/seroma	10140	
	Laceration repair, simple	120__	
	Site: ______ Size: _____		
	Laceration repair, layered	120__	
	Site: ______ Size: _____		
	Laser Light Tx	96597	
✓	Lesion, biopsy, one	11100	
	Lesion, biopsy, each add'l	11101	
	Lesion, excision, benign	114__	
	Site: ______ Size: _____		
	Lesion, excision, malignant	116__	
	Site: ______ Size: _____		
	Lesion, paring/cutting, one	11055	
	Lesion, paring/cutting, 2-4	11056	
	Lesion, shave	113__	
	Site: ______ Size: _____		
	Nail removal, partial (+T mod)	11730	
	Nail rem, w/matrix (+T mod)	11750	
	Skin tag, 1-15	11200	
	Wart, flat, 1-14	17110	
	Destruction lesion, 1st	17000	
	Destruct lesion, each addl 2-14	17003	
	Medications		**Units**
	Ampicillin, up to 500mg	J0290	
	B-12, up to 1,000 mcg	J3420	
	Epinephrine, up to 1ml	J0170	
	Kenalog, 10mg	J3301	
	Lidocaine, 10mg	J2001	
	Normal saline, 1000cc	J7030	
	Phenergan, up to 50mg	J2550	
	Progesterone, 150mg	J1055	
	Rocephin, 250mg	J0696	
	Testosterone, 200mg	J1080	
	Tigan, up to 200 mg	J3250	
	Toradol, 15mg	J1885	
	Albuterol	J7609	
	Depo-Provera 50 mg	J1055	
	Depo-Medrol 40 mg	J1030	

Diagnoses	Code
1 Well check	
2 enlarged prostate	
3 suspicious mole	
4	

Next office visit: 1 wk

Recheck • Preventative • PRN

Referral to:

Physician signature

x [illegible signature]

x	Laboratory		-90
✓	Venipuncture	36415	
	Blood glucose, monitoring device	82962	
	Blood glucose, visual dipstick	82948	
	CBC, w/ auto differential	85025	
✓	CBC, w/o auto differential	85027	
✓	Cholesterol	82465	
	Hemoccult, guaiac	82270	
	Hemoccult, immunoassay	82274	
	Hemoglobin A1C	85018	
✓	Lipid panel	80061	
	Liver panel	80076	
	KOH prep (skin, hair, nails)	87220	
	Metabolic panel, basic	80048	
	Metabolic panel, comprehensive	80053	
	Mononucleosis	86308	
	Pregnancy, blood	84703	
	Pregnancy, urine	81025	
	Renal panel	80069	
	Sedimentation rate	85651	
	Strep, rapid	86403	
	Strep culture	87081	
	Strep A	87880	
	TB	86580	
	UA, complete, non-automated	81000	
	UA, w/o micro, non-automated	81002	
	UA, w/ micro, non-automated	81003	
	Urine colony count	87086	
	Urine culture, presumptive	87088	
	Wet mount/KOH	87210	
	Vaccines		
	DT, <7 y		90702
	DTP		90701
	DtaP, <7 y		90700
	Flu, 6-35 months		90657
	Flu, 3 y +		90658
	Hep A, adult		90632
	Hep A, ped/adol, 2 dose		90633
	Hep B, adult		90746
	Hep B, ped/adol 3 dose		90744
	Hep B-Hib		90748
	Hib, 4 dose		90645
	HPV		90649
	IPV		90713
	MMR		90707
	Pneumonia, >2 y		90732
	Pneumonia conjugate, <5 y		90669
	Td, >7 y		90718
	Varicella		90716
	Tetanus toxoid adsorbed, IM		90703
	Immunizations & Injections		**Units**
	Allergen, one	95115	
	Allergen, multiple	95117	
	Imm admn <8 yo 1st Inj	90465	
	Imm admn <8 yo each add inj	90466	
	Imm <8 yo oral or intranasal	90467	
	Imm admn <8 yo each add	90468	
	Imm admin, one vacc	90471	
	Imm admin, each add'l	90472	
	Imm admin, intranasal, one	90473	
	Imm admin, intranasal, each add'l	90474	
	Injection, joint, small	20600	
	Injection, joint, intermediate	20605	
	Injection, ther/proph/diag	90772	
	Injection, trigger pt 1-2 musc	20552	

Today's charges:		
Today's payment:		
Balance due:		

Job 4 Router- Jordan Connell

Date of service: 10/29/09	Insurance: SELF PAY				Router Number: 2481
Patient name: CHRISSY KROUSE	Coinsurance:	Copay:			Physician Name: MURRAY
Account #: KRO001	Noncovered Waiver?	yes	no	n/a	

x	Office visit	New	x	Est
	Minimal (RN only)			99211
	Problem focused	99201		99212
	Exp problem focused	99202		99213
	Detailed	99203	✓	99214
	Comp	99204		99215
	Comprhen/Complex	99205		
	Well visit	**New**	**x**	**Est**
	< 1 y	99381		99391
	1-4 y	99382		99392
	5-11 y	99383		99393
	12-17 y	99384		99394
	18-39 y	99385		99395
	40-64 y	99386		99396
	65 y +	99387		99397
	Medicare preventive services			
	Pap			Q0091
	Pelvic & breast			G0101
	Prostate/PSA			G0103
	Tobacco couns/3-10 min			G0375
	Tobacco couns/>10 min			G0376
	Welcome to Medicare exam			G0344
	ECG w/Welcome to Medicare			G0366
	Hemoccult, guaiac			G0107
	Flu shot			G0008
	Pneumonia shot			G0009
	Consultation/preop clearance			
	Exp problem focused			99242
	Detailed			99243
	Comp/mod complex			99244
	Comp/high complex			99245
	Other services			
	After posted hours			99050
	Evening/weekend appointment			99051
	Home health certification			G0180
	Home health recertification			G0179
	Care Plan oversight			99374
	Care Plan Oversight >30 mins			99375
	Post-op follow-up			99024
	Prolonged/60min total			99354
	Prolonged/each add 30 mins			99355
	Special reports/forms			99080
	Disability/Workers comp			99455
	Smoking Cessation <10 mins			99406
	Smoking Cessation >10 mins			99407
	ETOH/SA screening <30 mins			99408
	Online E/M by MD			99444
	Phone E/M <10 mins			99441
	Phone E/M <20 mins			99442
	Phone E/M <30 mins			99443
	Anticoagulant Mgmt <90 days			99363
	Anticoagulant Mgmt >90 days			99364
	In office emergency serv			99058
	Other services			
✓	LASIX 10MG IM			
	Supplies			
	Surgical Tray			99070
	Instructions:			

x	Office procedures		
	Cerumen removal		69210
	ECG, w/interpretation		93000
	ECG, rhythm strip		93040
	Endometrial biopsy		58100
	Fracture care, cast/splint Site: ____________		____
	Nebulizer		94640
	Nebulizer demo		94664
	Spirometry		94010
	Spirometry, pre and post		94060
	Vasectomy		55250
	Skin procedures		**Units**
	Foreign body, skin, simple	10120	
	Foreign body, skin, complex	10121	
	I&D, abscess	10060	
	I&D, hematoma/seroma	10140	
	Laceration repair, simple Site: _______ Size: _____	120__	
	Laceration repair, layered Site: _______ Size: _____	120__	
	Laser Light Tx	96597	
	Lesion, biopsy, one	11100	
	Lesion, biopsy, each add'l	11101	
	Lesion, excision, benign Site: _______ Size: _____	114__	
	Lesion, excision, malignant Site: _______ Size: _____	116__	
	Lesion, paring/cutting, one	11055	
	Lesion, paring/cutting, 2-4	11056	
	Lesion, shave Site: _______ Size: _____	113__	
	Nail removal, partial (+T mod)	11730	
	Nail rem, w/matrix (+T mod)	11750	
	Skin tag, 1-15	11200	
	Wart, flat, 1-14	17110	
	Destruction lesion, 1st	17000	
	Destruct lesion, each addl 2-14	17003	
	Medications		**Units**
	Ampicillin, up to 500mg	J0290	
	B-12, up to 1,000 mcg	J3420	
	Epinephrine, up to 1ml	J0170	
	Kenalog, 10mg	J3301	
	Lidocaine, 10mg	J2001	
	Normal saline, 1000cc	J7030	
	Phenergan, up to 50mg	J2550	
	Progesterone, 150mg	J1055	
	Rocephin, 250mg	J0696	
	Testosterone, 200mg	J1080	
	Tigan, up to 200 mg	J3250	
	Toradol, 15mg	J1885	
	Albuterol	J7609	
	Depo-Provera 50 mg	J1055	
	Depo-Medrol 40 mg	J1030	

Diagnoses	Code
1 DM	
2 HTN	
3 Fluid Retention	
4	

Next office visit: 2 Wks
Recheck • Preventative • PRN
Referral to:

Physician signature
x [signature]

x	Laboratory		-90
	Venipuncture	36415	
	Blood glucose, monitoring device	82962	
	Blood glucose, visual dipstick	82948	
	CBC, w/ auto differential	85025	
	CBC, w/o auto differential	85027	
	Cholesterol	82465	
	Hemoccult, guaiac	82270	
	Hemoccult, immunoassay	82274	
✓	Hemoglobin A1C	85018	
	Lipid panel	80061	
	Liver panel	80076	
	KOH prep (skin, hair, nails)	87220	
	Metabolic panel, basic	80048	
	Metabolic panel, comprehensive	80053	
	Mononucleosis	86308	
	Pregnancy, blood	84703	
	Pregnancy, urine	81025	
	Renal panel	80069	
	Sedimentation rate	85651	
	Strep, rapid	86403	
	Strep culture	87081	
	Strep A	87880	
	TB	86580	
	UA, complete, non-automated	81000	
	UA, w/o micro, non-automated	81002	
	UA, w/ micro, non-automated	81003	
	Urine colony count	87086	
	Urine culture, presumptive	87088	
	Wet mount/KOH	87210	
	Vaccines		
	DT, <7 y		90702
	DTP		90701
	DtaP, ≤7 y		90700
	Flu, 6-35 months		90657
	Flu, 3 y +		90658
	Hep A, adult		90632
	Hep A, ped/adol, 2 dose		90633
	Hep B, adult		90746
	Hep B, ped/adol 3 dose		90744
	Hep B-Hib		90748
	Hib, 4 dose		90645
	HPV		90649
	IPV		90713
	MMR		90707
	Pneumonia, >2 y		90732
	Pneumonia conjugate, <5 y		90669
	Td, >7 y		90718
	Varicella		90716
	Tetanus toxoid adsorbed, IM		90703
	Immunizations & Injections		**Units**
	Allergen, one	95115	
	Allergen, multiple	95117	
	Imm admn <8 yo 1st Inj	90465	
	Imm admn <8 yo each add inj	90466	
	Imm <8 yo oral or intranasal	90467	
	Imm admn <8 yo each add	90468	
	Imm admin, one vacc	90471	
	Imm admin, each add'l	90472	
	Imm admin, intranasal, one	90473	
	Imm admin, intranasal, each add'l	90474	
	Injection, joint, small	20600	
	Injection, joint, intermediate	20605	
✓	Injection, ther/proph/diag	90772	
	Injection, trigger pt 1-2 musc	20552	

Today's charges:		
Today's payment:		
Balance due:		

Job 5 Router- Chrissy Krouse

Date of service: 10/29/09	Insurance: MEDICARE				Router Number: 2482
Patient name: NORMAN JOHNSON	Coinsurance: 20%	Copay:			Physician Name: HEATH
Account #: JOH001	Noncovered Waiver?	yes	no	n/a	

X	Office visit	New	X	Est
N/A	Minimal (RN only)	N/A		99211
	Problem focused	99201	✓	99212
	Exp problem focused	99202		99213
	Detailed	99203		99214
	Comp	99204		99215
	Comprhen/Complex	99205		
	Well visit	**New**	**X**	**Est**
	< 1 y	99381		99391
	1-4 y	99382		99392
	5-11 y	99383		99393
	12-17 y	99384		99394
	18-39 y	99385		99395
	40-64 y	99386		99396
	65 y +	99387		99397

X	Medicare preventive services	
	Pap	Q0091
	Pelvic & breast	G0101
	Prostate/PSA	G0103
	Tobacco couns/3-10 min	G0375
	Tobacco couns/>10 min	G0376
	Welcome to Medicare exam	G0344
	ECG w/Welcome to Medicare	G0366
	Hemoccult, guaiac	G0107
	Flu shot	G0008
	Pneumonia shot	G0009
	Consultation/preop clearance	
	Exp problem focused	99242
	Detailed	99243
	Comp/mod complex	99244
	Comp/high complex	99245
	Other services	
	After posted hours	99050
	Evening/weekend appointment	99051
	Home health certification	G0180
	Home health recertification	G0179
	Care Plan oversight	99374
	Care Plan Oversight >30 mins	99375
	Post-op follow-up	99024
✓	Prolonged/60min total	99354
	Prolonged/each add 30 mins	99355
	Special reports/forms	99080
	Disability/Workers comp	99455
	Smoking Cessation <10 mins	99406
	Smoking Cessation >10 mins	99407
	ETOH/SA screening <30 mins	99408
	Online E/M by MD	99444
	Phone E/M <10 mins	99441
	Phone E/M <20 mins	99442
	Phone E/M <30 mins	99443
	Anticoagulant Mgmt <90 days	99363
	Anticoagulant Mgmt >90 days	99364
	In office emergency serv	99058
	Other services	
	Supplies	
	Surgical Tray	99070
	Instructions:	

X	Office procedures	
✓	Cerumen removal	69210
	ECG, w/interpretation	93000
	ECG, rhythm strip	93040
	Endometrial biopsy	58100
	Fracture care, cast/splint Site: ______________	
	Nebulizer	94640
	Nebulizer demo	94664
	Spirometry	94010
	Spirometry, pre and post	94060
	Vasectomy	55250

X	Skin procedures		Units
	Foreign body, skin, simple	10120	
	Foreign body, skin, complex	10121	
	I&D, abscess	10060	
	I&D, hematoma/seroma	10140	
	Laceration repair, simple Site: _______ Size: _____	120__	
	Laceration repair, layered Site: _______ Size: _____	120__	
	Laser Light Tx	96597	
	Lesion, biopsy, one	11100	
	Lesion, biopsy, each add'l	11101	
	Lesion, excision, benign Site: _______ Size: _____	114__	
	Lesion, excision, malignant Site: _______ Size: _____	116__	
	Lesion, paring/cutting, one	11055	
	Lesion, paring/cutting, 2-4	11056	
	Lesion, shave Site: _______ Size: _____	113__	
	Nail removal, partial (+T mod)	11730	
	Nail rem, w/matrix (+T mod)	11750	
	Skin tag, 1-15	11200	
	Wart, flat, 1-14	17110	
	Destruction lesion, 1st	17000	
	Destruct lesion, each addl 2-14	17003	

X	Medications		Units
	Ampicillin, up to 500mg	J0290	
	B-12, up to 1,000 mcg	J3420	
	Epinephrine, up to 1ml	J0170	
	Kenalog, 10mg	J3301	
	Lidocaine, 10mg	J2001	
	Normal saline, 1000cc	J7030	
	Phenergan, up to 50mg	J2550	
	Progesterone, 150mg	J1055	
	Rocephin, 250mg	J0696	
	Testosterone, 200mg	J1080	
	Tigan, up to 200 mg	J3250	
	Toradol, 15mg	J1885	
	Albuterol	J7609	
	Depo-Provera 50 mg	J1055	
	Depo-Medrol 40 mg	J1030	

Diagnoses	Code
1 Impacted Cerumen	
2 Mental Retardation	
3 Autism	
4	

Next office visit:

Recheck • Preventative • PRN

Referral to:

Physician signature

X RD Heath MD

X	Laboratory		-90
	Venipuncture	36415	
	Blood glucose, monitoring device	82962	
	Blood glucose, visual dipstick	82948	
	CBC, w/ auto differential	85025	
	CBC, w/o auto differential	85027	
	Cholesterol	82465	
	Hemoccult, guaiac	82270	
	Hemoccult, immunoassay	82274	
	Hemoglobin A1C	85018	
	Lipid panel	80061	
	Liver panel	80076	
	KOH prep (skin, hair, nails)	87220	
	Metabolic panel, basic	80048	
	Metabolic panel, comprehensive	80053	
	Mononucleosis	86308	
	Pregnancy, blood	84703	
	Pregnancy, urine	81025	
	Renal panel	80069	
	Sedimentation rate	85651	
	Strep, rapid	86403	
	Strep culture	87081	
	Strep A	87880	
	TB	86580	
	UA, complete, non-automated	81000	
	UA, w/o micro, non-automated	81002	
	UA, w/ micro, non-automated	81003	
	Urine colony count	87086	
	Urine culture, presumptive	87088	
	Wet mount/KOH	87210	

X	Vaccines	
	DT, <7 y	90702
	DTP	90701
	DtaP, <7 y	90700
	Flu, 6-35 months	90657
	Flu, 3 y +	90658
	Hep A, adult	90632
	Hep A, ped/adol, 2 dose	90633
	Hep B, adult	90746
	Hep B, ped/adol 3 dose	90744
	Hep B-Hib	90748
	Hib, 4 dose	90645
	HPV	90649
	IPV	90713
	MMR	90707
	Pneumonia, >2 y	90732
	Pneumonia conjugate, <5 y	90669
	Td, >7 y	90718
	Varicella	90716
	Tetanus toxoid adsorbed, IM	90703

X	Immunizations & Injections		Units
	Allergen, one	95115	
	Allergen, multiple	95117	
	Imm admn <8 yo 1st Inj	90465	
	Imm admn <8 yo each add inj	90466	
	Imm <8 yo oral or intranasal	90467	
	Imm admn <8 yo each add	90468	
	Imm admin, one vacc	90471	
	Imm admin, each add'l	90472	
	Imm admin, intranasal, one	90473	
	Imm admin, intranasal, each add'l	90474	
	Injection, joint, small	20600	
	Injection, joint, intermediate	20605	
	Injection, ther/proph/diag	90772	
	Injection, trigger pt 1-2 musc	20552	

Today's charges:		
Today's payment:		
Balance due:		

Job 6 Router- Norman Johnson

Date of service: 10/29/09	Insurance: CONSUMER ONE			Router Number: 2480
Patient name: AIMEE	Coinsurance:	Copay:		Physician Name: KEMPER
Account #: BRA001	Noncovered Waiver?	yes	no	n/a

x	Office visit	New	x	Est
N/A	Minimal (RN only)	N/A		99211
	Problem focused	99201		99212
	Exp problem focused	99202		99213
	Detailed	99203	✓	99214
	Comp	99204		99215
	Comprhen/Complex	99205		
	Well visit	**New**	**x**	**Est**
	< 1 y	99381		99391
	1-4 y	99382		99392
	5-11 y	99383		99393
	12-17 y	99384		99394
	18-39 y	99385		99395
	40-64 y	99386		99396
	65 y +	99387		99397

x	Medicare preventive services	
	Pap	Q0091
	Pelvic & breast	G0101
	Prostate/PSA	G0103
	Tobacco couns/3-10 min	G0375
	Tobacco couns/>10 min	G0376
	Welcome to Medicare exam	G0344
	ECG w/Welcome to Medicare	G0366
	Hemoccult, guaiac	G0107
	Flu shot	G0008
	Pneumonia shot	G0009
	Consultation/preop clearance	
	Exp problem focused	99242
	Detailed	99243
	Comp/mod complex	99244
	Comp/high complex	99245
	Other services	
	After posted hours	99050
	Evening/weekend appointment	99051
	Home health certification	G0180
	Home health recertification	G0179
	Care Plan oversight	99374
	Care Plan Oversight >30 mins	99375
	Post-op follow-up	99024
	Prolonged/60min total	99354
	Prolonged/each add 30 mins	99355
	Special reports/forms	99080
	Disability/Workers comp	99455
	Smoking Cessation <10 mins	99406
	Smoking Cessation >10 mins	99407
	ETOH/SA screening <30 mins	99408
	Online E/M by MD	99444
	Phone E/M <10 mins	99441
	Phone E/M <20 mins	99442
	Phone E/M <30 mins	99443
	Anticoagulant Mgmt <90 days	99363
	Anticoagulant Mgmt >90 days	99364
	In office emergency serv	99058
	Other services	
	Lyme serology + Confirmation	
	Supplies	
	Surgical Tray	99070

Instructions:

x	Office procedures		
	Cerumen removal		69210
	ECG, w/interpretation		93000
	ECG, rhythm strip		93040
	Endometrial biopsy		58100
	Fracture care, cast/splint Site: ______		
	Nebulizer		94640
	Nebulizer demo		94664
	Spirometry		94010
	Spirometry, pre and post		94060
	Vasectomy		55250
	Skin procedures		**Units**
	Foreign body, skin, simple	10120	
	Foreign body, skin, complex	10121	
	I&D, abscess	10060	
	I&D, hematoma/seroma	10140	
	Laceration repair, simple Site: ______ Size: ____	120__	
	Laceration repair, layered Site: ______ Size: ____	120__	
	Laser Light Tx	96597	
	Lesion, biopsy, one	11100	
	Lesion, biopsy, each add'l	11101	
	Lesion, excision, benign Site: ______ Size: ____	114__	
	Lesion, excision, malignant Site: ______ Size: ____	116__	
	Lesion, paring/cutting, one	11055	
	Lesion, paring/cutting, 2-4	11056	
	Lesion, shave Site: ______ Size: ____	113__	
	Nail removal, partial (+T mod)	11730	
	Nail rem, w/matrix (+T mod)	11750	
	Skin tag, 1-15	11200	
	Wart, flat, 1-14	17110	
	Destruction lesion, 1st	17000	
	Destruct lesion, each addl 2-14	17003	
	Medications		**Units**
	Ampicillin, up to 500mg	J0290	
	B-12, up to 1,000 mcg	J3420	
	Epinephrine, up to 1ml	J0170	
	Kenalog, 10mg	J3301	
	Lidocaine, 10mg	J2001	
	Normal saline, 1000cc	J7030	
	Phenergan, up to 50mg	J2550	
	Progesterone, 150mg	J1055	
	Rocephin, 250mg	J0696	
	Testosterone, 200mg	J1080	
	Tigan, up to 200 mg	J3250	
	Toradol, 15mg	J1885	
	Albuterol	J7609	
	Depo-Provera 50 mg	J1055	
	Depo-Medrol 40 mg	J1030	

Diagnoses	Code
1 Early Onset Lymes	
2	
3	
4	

Next office visit:

Recheck • Preventative • PRN

Referral to:

Physician signature

X Sally Kemper, MD

x	Laboratory		-90
✓	Venipuncture	36415	—
	Blood glucose, monitoring device	82962	
	Blood glucose, visual dipstick	82948	
	CBC, w/ auto differential	85025	
	CBC, w/o auto differential	85027	
	Cholesterol	82465	
	Hemoccult, guaiac	82270	
	Hemoccult, immunoassay	82274	
	Hemoglobin A1C	85018	
	Lipid panel	80061	
	Liver panel	80076	
	KOH prep (skin, hair, nails)	87220	
	Metabolic panel, basic	80048	
	Metabolic panel, comprehensive	80053	
	Mononucleosis	86308	
	Pregnancy, blood	84703	
	Pregnancy, urine	81025	
	Renal panel	80069	
	Sedimentation rate	85651	
	Strep, rapid	86403	
	Strep culture	87081	
	Strep A	87880	
	TB	86580	
	UA, complete, non-automated	81000	
	UA, w/o micro, non-automated	81002	
	UA, w/ micro, non-automated	81003	
	Urine colony count	87086	
	Urine culture, presumptive	87088	
	Wet mount/KOH	87210	

x	Vaccines	
	DT, <7 y	90702
	DTP	90701
	DtaP, <7 y	90700
	Flu, 6-35 months	90657
	Flu, 3 y +	90658
	Hep A, adult	90632
	Hep A, ped/adol, 2 dose	90633
	Hep B, adult	90746
	Hep B, ped/adol 3 dose	90744
	Hep B-Hib	90748
	Hib, 4 dose	90645
	HPV	90649
	IPV	90713
	MMR	90707
	Pneumonia, >2 y	90732
	Pneumonia conjugate, <5 y	90669
	Td, >7 y	90718
	Varicella	90716
	Tetanus toxoid adsorbed, IM	90703

x	Immunizations & Injections		Units
	Allergen, one	95115	
	Allergen, multiple	95117	
	Imm admn <8 yo 1st Inj	90465	
	Imm admn <8 yo each add inj	90466	
	Imm <8 yo oral or intranasal	90467	
	Imm admn <8 yo each add	90468	
	Imm admin, one vacc	90471	
	Imm admin, each add'l	90472	
	Imm admin, intranasal, one	90473	
	Imm admin, intranasal, each add'l	90474	
	Injection, joint, small	20600	
	Injection, joint, intermediate	20605	
	Injection, ther/proph/diag	90772	
	Injection, trigger pt 1-2 musc	20552	

Today's charges:		
Today's payment:		
Balance due:		

Job 7 Router- Aimee Bradley

Date of service: 10/29/09	Insurance: MEDICARE				Router Number: 2483
Patient name: NANCY HERBERT	Coinsurance: 20%	Copay:			Physician Name: HEATH
Account #: HER001	Noncovered Waiver?	yes	no	n/a	

X	Office visit	New	X	Est
N/A	Minimal (RN only)	N/A		99211
	Problem focused	99201		99212
	Exp problem focused	99202		99213
	Detailed	99203		99214
	Comp	99204		99215
	Comprhen/Complex	99205		
	Well visit	**New**	**X**	**Est**
	< 1 y	99381		99391
	1-4 y	99382		99392
	5-11 y	99383		99393
	12-17 y	99384		99394
	18-39 y	99385		99395
	40-64 y	99386		99396
✓	65 y +	99387		99397

X	Medicare preventive services	
	Pap	Q0091
	Pelvic & breast	G0101
	Prostate/PSA	G0103
	Tobacco couns/3-10 min	G0375
	Tobacco couns/>10 min	G0376
	Welcome to Medicare exam	G0344
	ECG w/Welcome to Medicare	G0366
	Hemoccult, guaiac	G0107
	Flu shot	G0008
	Pneumonia shot	G0009
	Consultation/preop clearance	
	Exp problem focused	99242
	Detailed	99243
	Comp/mod complex	99244
	Comp/high complex	99245
	Other services	
	After posted hours	99050
	Evening/weekend appointment	99051
	Home health certification	G0180
	Home health recertification	G0179
	Care Plan oversight	99374
	Care Plan Oversight >30 mins	99375
	Post-op follow-up	99024
	Prolonged/60min total	99354
	Prolonged/each add 30 mins	99355
	Special reports/forms	99080
	Disability/Workers comp	99455
	Smoking Cessation <10 mins	99406
	Smoking Cessation >10 mins	99407
	ETOH/SA screening <30 mins	99408
	Online E/M by MD	99444
	Phone E/M <10 mins	99441
	Phone E/M <20 mins	99442
	Phone E/M <30 mins	99443
	Anticoagulant Mgmt <90 days	99363
	Anticoagulant Mgmt >90 days	99364
	In office emergency serv	99058
	Other services	
✓	Bone Density	
	Supplies	
	Surgical Tray	99070

Instructions:

X	Office procedures		
	Cerumen removal		69210
	ECG, w/interpretation		93000
	ECG, rhythm strip		93040
	Endometrial biopsy		58100
	Fracture care, cast/splint Site: ______________		
	Nebulizer		94640
	Nebulizer demo		94664
	Spirometry		94010
	Spirometry, pre and post		94060
	Vasectomy		55250
	Skin procedures		**Units**
	Foreign body, skin, simple	10120	
	Foreign body, skin, complex	10121	
	I&D, abscess	10060	
	I&D, hematoma/seroma	10140	
	Laceration repair, simple Site: _______ Size: _____	120__	
	Laceration repair, layered Site: _______ Size: _____	120__	
	Laser Light Tx	96597	
	Lesion, biopsy, one	11100	
	Lesion, biopsy, each add'l	11101	
	Lesion, excision, benign Site: _______ Size: _____	114__	
	Lesion, excision, malignant Site: _______ Size: _____	116__	
	Lesion, paring/cutting, one	11055	
	Lesion, paring/cutting, 2-4	11056	
	Lesion, shave Site: _______ Size: _____	113__	
	Nail removal, partial (+T mod)	11730	
	Nail rem, w/matrix (+T mod)	11750	
	Skin tag, 1-15	11200	
	Wart, flat, 1-14	17110	
	Destruction lesion, 1st	17000	
	Destruct lesion, each addl 2-14	17003	
	Medications		**Units**
	Ampicillin, up to 500mg	J0290	
	B-12, up to 1,000 mcg	J3420	
	Epinephrine, up to 1ml	J0170	
	Kenalog, 10mg	J3301	
	Lidocaine, 10mg	J2001	
	Normal saline, 1000cc	J7030	
	Phenergan, up to 50mg	J2550	
	Progesterone, 150mg	J1055	
	Rocephin, 250mg	J0696	
	Testosterone, 200mg	J1080	
	Tigan, up to 200 mg	J3250	
	Toradol, 15mg	J1885	
	Albuterol	J7609	
	Depo-Provera 50 mg	J1055	
	Depo-Medrol 40 mg	J1030	

Diagnoses	Code
1 Well check	
2 post menopause	
3 arthritis	
4	

Next office visit:
Recheck • Preventative (circled) • PRN
Referral to:

Physician signature
X LD Heath MD

X	Laboratory		-90
	Venipuncture	36415	
	Blood glucose, monitoring device	82962	
	Blood glucose, visual dipstick	82948	
	CBC, w/ auto differential	85025	
	CBC, w/o auto differential	85027	
	Cholesterol	82465	
	Hemoccult, guaiac	82270	
	Hemoccult, immunoassay	82274	
	Hemoglobin A1C	85018	
	Lipid panel	80061	
	Liver panel	80076	
	KOH prep (skin, hair, nails)	87220	
	Metabolic panel, basic	80048	
	Metabolic panel, comprehensive	80053	
	Mononucleosis	86308	
	Pregnancy, blood	84703	
	Pregnancy, urine	81025	
	Renal panel	80069	
	Sedimentation rate	85651	
	Strep, rapid	86403	
	Strep culture	87081	
	Strep A	87880	
	TB	86580	
	UA, complete, non-automated	81000	
	UA, w/o micro, non-automated	81002	
	UA, w/ micro, non-automated	81003	
	Urine colony count	87086	
	Urine culture, presumptive	87088	
	Wet mount/KOH	87210	
	Vaccines		
	DT, <7 y		90702
	DTP		90701
	DtaP, <7 y		90700
	Flu, 6-35 months		90657
	Flu, 3 y +		90658
	Hep A, adult		90632
	Hep A, ped/adol, 2 dose		90633
	Hep B, adult		90746
	Hep B, ped/adol 3 dose		90744
	Hep B-Hib		90748
	Hib, 4 dose		90645
	HPV		90649
	IPV		90713
	MMR		90707
	Pneumonia, >2 y		90732
	Pneumonia conjugate, <5 y		90669
	Td, >7 y		90718
	Varicella		90716
	Tetanus toxoid adsorbed, IM		90703
	Immunizations & Injections		**Units**
	Allergen, one	95115	
	Allergen, multiple	95117	
	Imm admn <8 yo 1st Inj	90465	
	Imm admn <8 yo each add inj	90466	
	Imm <8 yo oral or intranasal	90467	
	Imm admn <8 yo each add	90468	
	Imm admin, one vacc	90471	
	Imm admin, each add'l	90472	
	Imm admin, intranasal, one	90473	
	Imm admin, intranasal, each add'l	90474	
	Injection, joint, small	20600	
	Injection, joint, intermediate	20605	
	Injection, ther/proph/diag	90772	
	Injection, trigger pt 1-2 musc	20552	

Today's charges:		
Today's payment:		
Balance due:		

Job 9 Router- Nancy Herbert

Date of service: 10/28/09	Insurance: SELF PAY			Router Number: 2470
Patient name: RUSSELL LOGAN	Coinsurance:	Copay:		Physician Name: KEMPER
Account #: LOG001	Noncovered Waiver?	yes	no	n/a

X	Office visit	New	X	Est
N/A	Minimal (RN only)	N/A		99211
	Problem focused	99201		99212
	Exp problem focused	99202		99213
	Detailed	99203	✓	99214
	Comp	99204		99215
	Comprhen/Complex	99205		
	Well visit	**New**	**X**	**Est**
	< 1 y	99381		99391
	1-4 y	99382		99392
	5-11 y	99383		99393
	12-17 y	99384		99394
	18-39 y	99385		99395
	40-64 y	99386		99396
	65 y +	99387		99397
	Medicare preventive services			
	Pap			Q0091
	Pelvic & breast			G0101
	Prostate/PSA			G0103
	Tobacco couns/3-10 min			G0375
	Tobacco couns/>10 min			G0376
	Welcome to Medicare exam			G0344
	ECG w/Welcome to Medicare			G0366
	Hemoccult, guaiac			G0107
	Flu shot			G0008
	Pneumonia shot			G0009
	Consultation/preop clearance			
	Exp problem focused			99242
	Detailed			99243
	Comp/mod complex			99244
	Comp/high complex			99245
	Other services			
	After posted hours			99050
	Evening/weekend appointment			99051
	Home health certification			G0180
	Home health recertification			G0179
	Care Plan oversight			99374
	Care Plan Oversight >30 mins			99375
	Post-op follow-up			99024
	Prolonged/60min total			99354
	Prolonged/each add 30 mins			99355
	Special reports/forms			99080
	Disability/Workers comp			99455
	Smoking Cessation <10 mins			99406
	Smoking Cessation >10 mins			99407
	ETOH/SA screening <30 mins			99408
	Online E/M by MD			99444
	Phone E/M <10 mins			99441
	Phone E/M <20 mins			99442
	Phone E/M <30 mins			99443
	Anticoagulant Mgmt <90 days			99363
	Anticoagulant Mgmt >90 days			99364
	In office emergency serv			99058
	Other services			
✓	U/S (R) Leg			
	Supplies			
	Surgical Tray			99070
	Instructions:			

X	Office procedures		
	Cerumen removal		69210
	ECG, w/interpretation		93000
	ECG, rhythm strip		93040
	Endometrial biopsy		58100
	Fracture care, cast/splint Site: ________		
	Nebulizer		94640
	Nebulizer demo		94664
	Spirometry		94010
	Spirometry, pre and post		94060
	Vasectomy		55250
	Skin procedures		**Units**
	Foreign body, skin, simple	10120	
	Foreign body, skin, complex	10121	
	I&D, abscess	10060	
	I&D, hematoma/seroma	10140	
	Laceration repair, simple Site: ______ Size: ____	120__	
	Laceration repair, layered Site: ______ Size: ____	120__	
	Laser Light Tx	96597	
	Lesion, biopsy, one	11100	
	Lesion, biopsy, each add'l	11101	
	Lesion, excision, benign Site: ______ Size: ____	114__	
	Lesion, excision, malignant Site: ______ Size: ____	116__	
	Lesion, paring/cutting, one	11055	
	Lesion, paring/cutting, 2-4	11056	
	Lesion, shave Site: ______ Size: ____	113__	
	Nail removal, partial (+T mod)	11730	
	Nail rem, w/matrix (+T mod)	11750	
	Skin tag, 1-15	11200	
	Wart, flat, 1-14	17110	
	Destruction lesion, 1st	17000	
	Destruct lesion, each addl 2-14	17003	
	Medications		**Units**
	Ampicillin, up to 500mg	J0290	
	B-12, up to 1,000 mcg	J3420	
	Epinephrine, up to 1ml	J0170	
	Kenalog, 10mg	J3301	
	Lidocaine, 10mg	J2001	
	Normal saline, 1000cc	J7030	
	Phenergan, up to 50mg	J2550	
	Progesterone, 150mg	J1055	
	Rocephin, 250mg	J0696	
	Testosterone, 200mg	J1080	
	Tigan, up to 200 mg	J3250	
	Toradol, 15mg	J1885	
	Albuterol	J7609	
	Depo-Provera 50 mg	J1055	
	Depo-Medrol 40 mg	J1030	

Diagnoses	Code
1 (R) leg pain	
2 Lymphedema	
3 (+) Stemmer Sign	
4 Lipedema	
5. HTN	

Next office visit:

Recheck • Preventative • PRN

Referral to:

Physician signature

X S. Kemper MD

X	Laboratory		-90
	Venipuncture	36415	
	Blood glucose, monitoring device	82962	
	Blood glucose, visual dipstick	82948	
	CBC, w/ auto differential	85025	
	CBC, w/o auto differential	85027	
	Cholesterol	82465	
	Hemoccult, guaiac	82270	
	Hemoccult, immunoassay	82274	
	Hemoglobin A1C	85018	
	Lipid panel	80061	
	Liver panel	80076	
	KOH prep (skin, hair, nails)	87220	
	Metabolic panel, basic	80048	
	Metabolic panel, comprehensive	80053	
	Mononucleosis	86308	
	Pregnancy, blood	84703	
	Pregnancy, urine	81025	
	Renal panel	80069	
	Sedimentation rate	85651	
	Strep, rapid	86403	
	Strep culture	87081	
	Strep A	87880	
	TB	86580	
	UA, complete, non-automated	81000	
	UA, w/o micro, non-automated	81002	
	UA, w/ micro, non-automated	81003	
	Urine colony count	87086	
	Urine culture, presumptive	87088	
	Wet mount/KOH	87210	
	Vaccines		
	DT, <7 y		90702
	DTP		90701
	DtaP, <7 y		90700
	Flu, 6-35 months		90657
	Flu, 3 y +		90658
	Hep A, adult		90632
	Hep A, ped/adol, 2 dose		90633
	Hep B, adult		90746
	Hep B, ped/adol 3 dose		90744
	Hep B-Hib		90748
	Hib, 4 dose		90645
	HPV		90649
	IPV		90713
	MMR		90707
	Pneumonia, >2 y		90732
	Pneumonia conjugate, <5 y		90669
	Td, >7 y		90718
	Varicella		90716
	Tetanus toxoid adsorbed, IM		90703
	Immunizations & Injections		**Units**
	Allergen, one	95115	
	Allergen, multiple	95117	
	Imm admn <8 yo 1st Inj	90465	
	Imm admn <8 yo each add inj	90466	
	Imm <8 yo oral or intranasal	90467	
	Imm admn <8 yo each add	90468	
	Imm admin, one vacc	90471	
	Imm admin, each add'l	90472	
	Imm admin, intranasal, one	90473	
	Imm admin, intranasal, each add'l	90474	
	Injection, joint, small	20600	
	Injection, joint, intermediate	20605	
	Injection, ther/proph/diag	90772	
	Injection, trigger pt 1-2 musc	20552	

Today's charges:		
Today's payment:		
Balance due:		

Job 11 Router- Russell Logan

CHAPTER 8

Working in the Clinic: Payments, Collections, and Reporting

Background Basics

- Students must complete chapters 1–7 in their entirety.
- Students should have prior training in reading and interpreting EOBs because this is not discussed in this text.

Competency Checklist

- Office staff is responsible for accurately posting payments from carriers and patients, and for making proper adjustments.
- Staff is responsible for collecting monies due to the practice from insurance carriers and patients.
- Staff will run various daily and month-end reports to balance accounting and to determine payer trends.
- Staff must analyze EOBs and apply coding logic to appeal denied or partially reduced claims.
- Billing staff research delays in payments by troubleshooting various processes within the revenue cycle.
- Communicating with patients, insurance carriers, and physicians is a vital component of coding and billing functions.

The first two days of the simulation you worked at the front desk performing scheduling, registration, and insurance verification. Days three and four were spent coding, researching payment policies, and submitting claims. Today you will focus on posting payments from both patients and carriers, collections, and reporting. You will also assist Lindsay Morgan with researching payment policies, denials, and claims errors. When posting insurance payments pay close attention to the contracts we have with each carrier. Our job is to determine if we were paid correctly according to our contract. In chapter 6, one of your jobs was to update the office's fees in MOSS for each CPT code. In this chapter, we are interested in how much each carrier reimburses for a service. In lieu of having you enter each carrier's allowed amount for every CPT code, which is a laborious task, when posting insurance payments, you can enter these amounts at that time. Remember, the carrier fee schedules and allowances are located on the CD-ROM.

FRIDAY, October 30, 2009

Payment Posting

JOB 1: Add payment code *PATCC* for patient payment by credit card. Go to *File Maintenance* and click on *Lists.* Select #13 *Payment Codes.* Scroll down to the bottom to where you see the *. Enter the new code and description and *Close*.

JOB 2: Take the deposit slips you completed from Monday's and Tuesday's deposits and post these payments to each respective account.

JOB 3: The patient payments shown in Table 8-1 came in the mail. Post them to the appropriate date of service. Enter any credit card numbers, card type, and expiration date in the #14 *Notes* field. Check numbers go in the #5 *Reference* field.

JOB 4: An EOB from FlexiHealth PPO out-of-network needs to be posted. Post the payments. Then figure and apply the appropriate adjustments. The EOB is located at the end of the chapter. *(See Job 4, FlexiHealth PPO Out-of-Network EOB)*

JOB 5: An EOB from Flexihealth in-network is ready to post. Post the payments. Then figure and apply the appropriate adjustments. The EOB is located at the end of this chapter. *(See Job 5, FlexiHealth PPO EOB)*

JOB 6: An EOB from Consumer One HRA for Josephine Albertson needs to be posted. Post the payments. Then figure and apply applicable adjustments. The EOB is located at the end of this chapter. What is the contractual adjustment for this patient's service on 7/10/09? ______________________ *(See Job 6, Consumer One HRA EOB)*

JOB 7: Post the EOB for Aetna. Why was there no payment awarded? What needs to be corrected before the claim is resubmitted? What other research should be conducted before resubmitting to Aetna? ____
(See Job 7, Aetna EOB)

JOB 8: The following is an excerpt of an EOB received. Why did 81002 get denied? What does this mean? Was the denial appropriate? What action should you take?

PHYSICIAN NUMBER OR EIN	DATE OF SERVICE (MON DAY YR)	PROCEDURE CODE	MOD	MOD	MOD	DAYS/ UNITS	CHARGE SUBMITTED	COVERED CHARGE	AMOUNT ALLOWED	PATIENT LIABILITY DEDUCT.	COPAY	COIN.	OTHER	PAYMENT	MESSAGE
ACCT#		ID/CARD# 22953042						NAME: NELSON, MARK				CLAIM#: 6F386S170000			
20144	113006	99212				1	85.00	85.00	36.00	.00	10.00	5.20	.00	20.80	760
	113006	81002				1	.00	.00	.00	.00	.00	.00	.00	.00	025
		CLAIM TOTAL					85.00	85.00	36.00	.00	10.00	5.20	.00	20.80	

MED	MEDICARE ASSIGNMENT WAS ACCEPTED AND IS REFLECTED IN THE AMOUNT ALLOWED
PGB	THIS CLAIM/CHARGE WAS AUTOMATICALLY TRANSFERRED FROM MEDICARE
025	SEPARATE PROCEDURE COMBINED INTO SINGLE COMPLETE PROCEDURE
106	THIS BENEFIT PLAN DOES NOT COVER THIS
122	SERVICES WERE RENDERED AFTER THE PATIENT'S CANCELLATION DATE
169	WE REQUESTED OTHER HEALTH INSURANCE INFORMATION FROM THE MEMBER. WE WILL REVIEW THE CLAIM FOR BENEFITS WHEN WE RECEIVE THIS INFORMATION
367	AMOUNT EXCEEDS MAXIMUM ALLOWANCE
760	MAXIMUM BENEFITS HAVE BEEN ALLOWED

FRIDAY, October 30, 2009 (continued)

Secondary billing

JOB 9: Some of the patients you posted primary insurance payments for may have secondary insurance policies. Secondary insurance billing is often a cumbersome process because many secondary carriers still require hard copy claims along with a copy of the EOB from the primary carrier. To determine if secondary claims are pending, go to *Insurance Billing* and select *Secondary* as the *Billing Option. Sort Order* is *Patient Name.* Set *Provider* to *All. Service Dates* would be 1/1/09-10/15/09. *Patient and Account Number* is set to *All. Payer* can be set to *All* to capture all secondary claims. [Note: Because MOSS is a program written for educational purposes only, it does not have the sophistication that most practice management systems have with respect to insurance carrier set-up and claims submission. It cannot designate which carrier claims are set to go electronically versus via paper. In life, many secondary claims cross over to the secondary carrier when Medicare is primary. Keep in mind that any secondary claims generated here for Century Senior Gap would have automatically crossed over and would not necessitate printing a secondary claim. Disregard these claims.] Click on *Prebilling Worksheet,* print and compare to records be sure all claims have been prepped. When satisfied all are entered correctly, select *generate claims.* If you are satisfied with the claims and do not detect any errors, click on *Print Forms.* [NOTE: In life, the claim is generated with box 31 filled in with the provider's name and does not require a handwritten signature.]

JOB 10: Before the secondary claims can be mailed to the carriers, EOBs from the primary payer must be attached. Match up the EOBs where the patient's primary insurance made payment. You must deidentify this EOB by blacking out names, insurance ID numbers, and claim numbers of other patients located on the same EOB. Once this is accomplished, staple the EOB to the claim form by placing a single staple in the top left corner. Turn these in to your instructor.

Insurance denials

JOB 11: You received a denial from Galaxy Health stating that they are not the primary insurance for William Kostner. Take a look at his registration paperwork and see what insurance should be primary. Who is his primary insurance for this service? Refile his claim to the correct insurance carrier. Print this claim and turn it in to your instructor.

JOB 12: You have discovered that many claims are rejecting and carriers cannot identify the physicians as part of this group practice. It turns out MOSS was not set up correctly. Go into *File Maintenance, Practice Information,* and *Practice Settings.* Correct the practice NPI number and enter 7189396878. Delete all the legacy numbers for Medicare. The UPIN and Medicare numbers are no longer required. Make the *Medical Group Number* and the *NPI* number the same. The only identifying number used as of May 2008 is the practice's tax ID number and group and individual physician NPI numbers. Now go to the *Lists* tab and click on *Practice Physicians.* Correct the profile by doing the same thing—deleting the old legacy numbers. Do not change the physician's NPI number; leave it as it is. The physician's NPI number should print in block 24J of the claim form, and the practice NPI number in box 33a.

JOB 13: Rusty Potter's claim was denied. The EOB is located at the end of this chapter. Carefully examine the charges and codes submitted. What is wrong with this claim? What corrective action should be taken? A query should be initiated to the doctor for more information about the visit. Create a query and turn this in to your instructor. Visit Metastar.com and read the information on physician query form guidance or search the Internet to find criteria for generating physician queries before compiling yours. *(See Job 13, Rusty Potter EOB)*

JOB 14: Claims are rejecting from the clearinghouse. You have determined that the addresses for Drs. Murray, Kemper, and Mendenhall and for Alberta Lynn are wrong in the system. Go to *File Maintenance* and click on *Lists*. Update their addresses to the office address in *Practice Physicians.*

JOB 15: We received an EOB today from Medicare. The claim for Wilma Stearn DOS 10/15/09 is not paid correctly. The codes were bundled and only $7 was paid for 85014. Research the codes and charges submitted for this date and write an appeal letter explaining why the claim was not processed correctly. Visit the Empire State website and learn how to request an appeal through this Medicare carrier. Complete this process and turn in your appeal to your instructor. What documentation should you send, according to this website, with your appeal?

JOB 16: You received payment for a hospital visit for Alice Maxwell for DOS 9/15/09 -9/16/09. EOB states Dr. Heath is the provider, but you notice that Alberta Lynn (our PA) was the one who actually saw the patient in the hospital for subsequent daily visits on 9/15/09 and 9/16/09. Is this appropriate under the incident-to rule? Why or why not? Is the payment any different if Alberta Lynn is listed as the rendering provider instead of Dr. Heath?

JOB 17: This claim keeps rejecting and must be corrected before it will transmit correctly. Audit the claim form located at the end of this chapter and highlight the errors. Explain what the errors are by writing in the margin. Note any information that is missing or conflicting. Turn this in to your instructor. *(See Job 17, John Conway Claim Form)*

Collections

JOB 18: Cynthia Worthington's check for $20 on 10/19/09 was returned by the bank for insufficient funds. Assess the NSF charge to her account, enter the dummy diagnosis, and send her a letter explaining our policy for bounced checks. Tell her payment must be made in cash or cashier's check within seven days. Use the letterhead located on the CD-ROM.

FRIDAY, October 30, 2009 (continued)

JOB 19: The front desk calls you for assistance up front. Harold Prosser is checking out and he refuses to pay anything. He is a work-in patient today to get medication to treat a skin fungus. He has Century Senior Gap and Medicare Part A but it turns out that he does not have Medicare Part B. The employee has already tried to explain why he owes but he keeps saying, "Bill my insurance company," and will not cooperate. They have asked you to speak to the patient and see if you can get through to him. What will you say? What happened and how could this have been handled differently?

____

____

JOB 20: At the end of each month we print patient statements. Print statements for patients who have an outstanding patient balance. Turn these statements in to your instructor.

JOB 21: Megan Murray's account is delinquent. According to MOSS, her account balance is $518. Research her account to determine what is delaying payment. Look closely at the services provided, place of service, and so on. What do you find? When you view her patient ledger, has insurance paid anything on this account? What should be done to gather the information necessary to get this account paid? Compose a letter to be sent to the appropriate entity to obtain the information necessary or to obtain payment for these outstanding charges. Submit this letter to your instructor.

____

Reporting

JOB 22: Print the Monthly Summary and turn in to your instructor. Which insurance carrier had the most payments? Which carrier had the most adjustments? Are patient payments included in this report? ____

____

JOB 23: A patient called very upset and wanted to speak to someone about a claim and the diagnosis reported to the insurance company she had at that time. She proceeds to inform you that two years ago, one of the physicians in the group performed a skin biopsy/skin lesion excision of her left axilla. She has changed jobs and is trying to enroll in her company's medical plan and was subsequently turned down for coverage because she was told she has cancer, which is a preexisting condition. She is crying on the phone and says, "The doctor never told me I had cancer." The insurance company told her that a claim was filed with a diagnosis of skin cancer but she says she never had cancer. You told her you were going to pull her chart and research the notes and pathology report for that service and get back to her as quickly as possible. You pulled up her account in MOSS and see that the diagnosis code 173.5 was reported. You located her chart and reviewed the pathology report for this lesion removal. The diagnosis reads: *serous papillary tumor of borderline malignancy, left axilla*. What problem have you identified? What is the diagnosis code for this service? What needs to be done to rectify this situation?

____

____

____

JOB 24: A patient was seen in the office and treated by Dr. Heath for onychomycosis and prescribed Lamisil. The patient is upset because Cigna denied the pharmacy claim. According to Cigna's coverage policy, they will not authorize and allow Lamisil to be prescribed for onychomycosis alone. The letter the patient received stated that they will allow Lamisil treatment only if the patient also has debilitating pain in the feet and/or peripheral neuropathy. The patient is requesting that the diagnosis of pain be added to her preauthorization so that she does not have to pay for this medication out of pocket. The patient is frustrated because she and the physician have done everything Cigna has asked for during the preauthorization process—fungal stain with positive diagnosis for onychomycosis and trial of topical antifungal, which failed to treat this condition. The patient actually spoke to Dr. Heath and he is also frustrated by the red tape and feels this treatment is justified. He agreed to amend the authorization and refile it to Cigna. You discover this when you are filing the preauthorization into the patient's file. What is the problem here? What would this be classified as? What action should you take?

____

____

JOB 25: You've noticed an increase in claims denials and the error rate for appending the 25 modifier. You feel this is significant enough to warrant staff education on this topic and have asked April to speak at the next staff meeting. Prepare a document describing the proper use of this modifier in the office, rules of thumb to use when determining if the modifier is required, documentation requirements, significance of the global period, and so on. Provide some examples of when it is and is not appropriate to use this modifier. Provide this typewritten document to April (your instructor) prior to the meeting for her to review.

Auditing

Evaluation and Management (E/M) services are the foundation of physician services encompassing approximately one-third of all charges reported to third-party payers. E/M codes represent the provider's *evaluation* of the patient's condition and *management* of the patient's care. In the fight to control healthcare costs, today employers and insurance companies are now monitoring physician performance. Using computer software to analyze health claims and billing data, doctors are being profiled and compared to their peers. As discussed previously, both private and governmental carriers are compiling physician report cards using claims history data to assemble statistics and profiles (scorecards) that consist of ICD-9 and CPT codes reported as well as age of the patient, place of service, dates of service, and charges.

Physician profiles are rated and used to direct patients to effective and reasonably priced healthcare. Providers of a same specialty are compared based on several factors such as infection rate, mortality and morbidity rates, patient satisfaction, cost of services, education, and practice billing patterns. A caveat to this trending and benchmarking concept is that it relies on complete and accurate coding for services. The data used to formulate these scorecards, which often contain errors, is difficult for providers to correct once submitted and may not only damage a provider's reputation but also have a significant financial impact on a practice.

Detailed and quality documentation is necessary for appropriate reporting of services rendered as well as the patient diagnoses to adequately demonstrate the severity of the patient's overall condition. Medicare Advantage (MA) plans are reimbursed based upon the beneficiaries' chronic conditions. CMS conducts medical record reviews to validate and ensure the accuracy and integrity of claims data submitted to Medicare Advantage (MA) plans. Medicare Advantage plans are

FRIDAY, October 30, 2009 (continued)

randomly chosen by CMS to audit medical records and corresponding claims processed by that plan. MA plans are reimbursed by CMS based on a calculation of each patient's health status (called a risk adjustment factor [RAF]) and are compensated with a per-member premium that factors in the patient's disease management, case management, preventative services and other services that are not typically covered benefits to Medicare beneficiaries. The RAF resets each January 1 so it is vitally important to MA plans that providers document and submit chronic conditions that are monitored and treated each year. What does that mean to the provider? How does this impact you as a coder? The MA plan that processed claims for your practice or facility will be required to present medical records to substantiate claims or members that have been selected for audit. One thing is for certain, providers will be required to submit medical records for select dates of service being audited upon request of the MA plan. Part of our job at DMA is to perform prospective or pre-bill audits to reduce the likelihood of submitting an invalid or non-specific diagnosis and to confirm that the documentation substantiates the level of services provided to the patient. In order to report a diagnosis, the documentation should indicate that a disease or condition is being monitored, evaluated, assesed, and treated (MEAT).

Accurate coding has always been the key to prompt and accurate payment to providers and facilities. Reporting chronic conditions and diagnoses to the highest level of specificity is important to show resource utilization and will impact provider profiling and integrity of statistical data collected across the country tracking severity of illnesses, treatment protocols, and morbidity and mortality data. Its impact is felt both financially and in regulatory compliance when demonstrating medical necessity and justifying treatment option and level of E/M service reported. The goal should be to always report services at the highest level of specificity and accuracy. This is where we come in.

Our job is to review or audit the documentation and confirm the CPT and ICD-9 codes being reported and the accuracy of the claim forms prior to submission. When reviewing records, we are also looking for discrepancies in the diagnosis codes being billed versus the written documentation in the record and looking for lack of specificity. When we identify these areas, we then provide education to our providers about the need to be more explicit in their documentation practices, helping them develop ways of doing so and explaining why it is necessary (the financial impact is usually the driver that gets their attention!). Is it practical to audit every patient's charges and associated claims? Of course not! The goal is to pre-bill audit enough charges to get a cross-section of providers' documentation and coding patterns as well as various services provided on different days to encompass all staff members who enter data or perform billing services.

JOB 26: Job 26 is a two-part job. Your job in part I is to audit the cases located at the end of this chapter. Review the documentation and determine if it is adequate to report the level of service reported. Look for inconsistencies in the documentation, typos, transposed numbers, incorrect codes based on supporting documentation, and incorrect dates or place of service. When auditing and assigning E/M codes, use the tool located in Appendix C to assist you in determining the correct level. Part II entails correcting the errors and indicating what the correct code(s) and modifiers should be directly on the document. In addition to making the corrections, write a summary of the findings to the office manager along with any supporting documentation to be used in educating the providers about proper code assignment, reporting of services, and documentation. Turn these in to your instructor. *(See Job 26, Office Notes 1–4)*

Table 8-1 Patient Payments by Mail

Name	Payment Amount	Payment Method	Date of Service
Josephine Albertson	$30	check #847	7/10/09
Francois Blanc	$60	Credit card 15975365284 Visa Exp 01/10	10/23/09
Andrew Jefferson	$50	Check #6352	7/1/09
Megan Caldwell	$45	Check #7896	12/15/08
Alice Maxwell	$10	Check #1234	7/2/09
Evan Lagasse	$75	Credit card 9638451247 MC Exp 02/10	
Stanley Kramer	$100	Check #5943	10/23/09
Vito Mangano	$70	Credit Card 8745961235 Visa Exp 10/10	10/23/09
Justin McNamara	$80	Check #3214	12/18/08
Anna Pinkston	$78	Check #7536	10/16/09
Manuel Ramirez	$13.83	Cashier check	10/15/09
Wilma Stearn	$14.49	Check #8523	10/19/09

Class Discussion

You have concluded the first week of your simulation with DMA. Talk with your peers about what you found the most challenging. What during this simulation came as a surprise to you? Do you feel more confident about seeking employment in an office setting now that you have had this exposure? What job duties did you like best? Where do you need to sharpen your skills? Did you learn anything new? If so, describe this new knowledge. Were most of the exercises and jobs a review of material previously learned? Were the jobs and exercises challenging?

Day 5			Day 5		
Job No.	Patient Name	Documents	Job No.	Patient Name	Documents
Job 4	N/A	Router	Job 26	Jeremy Maxwell, Lilly Rose, Isiah Fulton, Isabelle Wright	Office Notes
Job 6	N/A	Router			
Job 7	N/A	Router			
Job 17	N/A	Claim form			

FLEXIHEALTH PPO OUT-OF-NETWORK
30 W. Fifth Ave
New York, NY 10002

Claim No. 1-99-12345678-00-zmm
Group Name: Douglasville Medicine Associates

Patient Name/ Account Number/Type of Service	Service Dates	Charge Submitted	Allowed Amount	Non-covered Amount	Patient Deductible	Patient Copay	Patient Coinsurance	Total Benefit	Remark Codes
Lagasse, Evan LAG001	11212008	$235.00	$56.25	$0.00	$56.25	$0.00	$0.00	$0.00	1
99395								$0.00	
	1 Patient has met $300.00 of the $400.00 deductible								
McNamara, Justin MCN00	12182008	$80.00	$34.00	$0.00	$0.00	$0.00	$6.80	$27.20	45
99212								$27.20	
	45 Charge exceeds fee schedule/maxiumum allowable or contracted/legislated fee arrangement								
Ybarra, Elane YBA001	10162009	$180.00	$85.00	$0.00	$85.00	$0.00	$0.00	$0.00	1
99212									
	10162009	$16.00	$15.00	$0.00	$0.00	$12.00	$3.00	$0.00	45
87081								$0.00	
	1 Patient has met $300.00 of the $400.00 deductible								
	45 Charge exceeds fee schedule/maxiumum allowable or contracted/legislated fee arrangement								

FLEXIHEALTH PPO OUT-OF-NETWORK
30 W. Fifth Ave
New York, NY 10002

124567986623

Douglasville Medicine Associates
5076 Brand Blvd, Suite 401
Douglasville, NY 01234

$27.20

VOID

Job 4 FlexiHealth PPO Out-of-Network EOB

FLEXIHEALTH PPO IN-NETWORK
30 W. Fifth Ave, Suite 100
New York, NY 10002

Claim No. 1-99-126325678-00-zmr
Group Name: Douglasville Medicine Associates

Patient Name/ Account Number/Type of Service	Service Dates	Charge Submitted	Allowed Amount	Non-covered Amount	Patient Deductible	Patient Copay	Patient Coinsurance	Total Benefit	Remark Codes
Alvarez, Francisco ALV001	11012008	$370.00	$130.50	$239.50	$0.00	$20.00	$0.00	$110.50	N14
10600								$110.50	
N14	Payment based on a contractual amount or agreement, fee schedule, or maximum allowable amoun								
	11012008	$67.00	$13.00	$54.00	$0.00	$0.00	$0.00	$13.00	N45
80053								$13.00	
N45	Charge exceeds fee schedule/maximum allowable or contracted/legislated fee arrangement								
	11012008	$38.00	$12.00	$26.00	$0.00	$0.00	$0.00	$12.00	N14 45
36415								$12.00	
N14	Payment based on a contractual amount or agreement, fee schedule, or maximum allowable amoun								
N45	Charge exceeds fee schedule/maximum allowable or contracted/legislated fee arrangement								

FLEXIHEALTH PPO IN-NETWORK
30 W. Fifth Ave, Suite 100
New York, NY 10002

126325678

Douglasville Medicine Associates
5076 Brand Blvd. Suite 401
Douglasville, NY 01234

$135.50

VOID

Job 5 FlexiHealth PPO EOB

CONSUMER ONE HRA
1230 Main St.
Missoula, MT 08896

Claim No. 2-55-126390014-00
Group Name: Douglasville Medicine Associates

Patient Name/ Account Number/Type of Service	Service Dates	Charge Submitted	Allowed Amount	Non-covered Amount	Patient Deductible	Patient Copay	Patient Coinsurance	Total Benefit	Remark Codes
Gordon, Eric GOR003	10/22/09	$180.00	$123.25	$56.75	$0.00	$0.00	$0.00	$123.25	N14 45
99214								$123.25	

N14 Payment based on a contractual amount or agreement, fee schedule, or maximum allowable amount
N45 Charge exceeds fee schedule/maximum allowable or contracted/legislated fee arrangement

CONSUMER ONE HRA
1230 Main St.
Missoula, MT 08896

126390014

Douglasville Medicine Associates
5076 Brand Blvd, Suite 401
Douglasville, NY 01234

$123.25

VOID

Job 6 Consumer One HRA EOB

Aetna
159 Metro Dr.
Milwaukee, WI 52631

Claim No. 100-7-9852333237
Group Name: Douglasville Medicine Associates

Patient Name/ Account Number/Type of Service	Service Dates	Charge Submitted	Allowed Amount	Non-covered Amount	Patient Deductible	Patient Copay	Patient Coinsurance	Total Benefit	Remark Codes
Blair, Donald BLA002	06122009 99281	$130.00	$30.00	$100.00	$0.00	$50.00	$0.00	$0.00	22 47
	6122009 26645	$1,702.00	$499.50	$1,202.50	$0.00	$0.00	$0.00	$0.00	22 47
								$0.00	

47 This (these) diagnosis(es) is (are) not covered, missing, or are invalid
22 This care may be covered by another payer per coordination of benefits

Aetna
159 Metro Dr.
Milwaukee, WI 52631

1358429610

Douglasville Medicine Associates
5076 Brand Blvd, Suite 401
Douglasville, NY 01234

$0.00

VOID

Job 7 Aetna EOB

United Health Care
1818 United Dr
Atlanta, GA 74569

Claim No. 100-5-9852641237
Group Name: Douglasville Medicine Associates

Patient Name/ Account Number/Type of Service	Service Dates	Charge Submitted	Allowed Amount	Non-covered Amount	Patient Deductible	Patient Copay	Patient Coinsurance	Total Benefit	Remark Codes
Potter, Rusty POT001 G0344	04302008	$205.00	$0.00	$0.00	$0.00	$0.00	$0.00	$0.00	129

129 Payment denied - Prior processing information appears incorrect.

United Health Care
1818 United Drive
Atlanta, GA 74569

1358429610

Pay to the order of

Douglasville Medicine Associates
5076 Brand Blvd. Suite 401
Douglasville, NY 01234

$0.00

VOID

Job 13 Rusty Potter EOB

1500

HEALTH INSURANCE CLAIM FORM

APPROVED BY NATIONAL UNIFORM CLAIM COMMITTEE 08/05

PICA | PICA | CARRIER

1. MEDICARE (Medicare #) [ ] MEDICAID (Medicaid #) [ ] TRICARE CHAMPUS (Sponsor's SSN) [ ] CHAMPVA (Member ID#) [ ] GROUP HEALTH PLAN (SSN or ID) [✓] FECA BLK LUNG (SSN) [ ] OTHER (ID) [ ]

1a. INSURED'S I.D. NUMBER (For Program in Item 1): 999385562

2. PATIENT'S NAME (Last Name, First Name, Middle Initial): Conway, John, W

3. PATIENT'S BIRTH DATE MM DD YY: 06 30 1969 — SEX M [✓] F [ ]

4. INSURED'S NAME (Last Name, First Name, Middle Initial): Conway, John W

5. PATIENT'S ADDRESS (No., Street): 803 Slate Dr, Apt 103

6. PATIENT RELATIONSHIP TO INSURED: Self [ ] Spouse [ ] Child [ ] Other [ ]

7. INSURED'S ADDRESS (No., Street): Same

CITY: Douglasville — STATE: NY

8. PATIENT STATUS: Single [ ] Married [✓] Other [ ]; Employed [✓] Full-Time Student [ ] Part-Time Student [ ]

CITY: — STATE:

ZIP CODE: 01234 — TELEPHONE (Include Area Code): ( )

ZIP CODE: — TELEPHONE (Include Area Code): ( )

9. OTHER INSURED'S NAME (Last Name, First Name, Middle Initial):

10. IS PATIENT'S CONDITION RELATED TO:

11. INSURED'S POLICY GROUP OR FECA NUMBER: M1S015

a. OTHER INSURED'S POLICY OR GROUP NUMBER:

a. EMPLOYMENT? (Current or Previous) YES [ ] NO [✓]

a. INSURED'S DATE OF BIRTH MM DD YY: 06 30 1969 — SEX M [✓] F [ ]

b. OTHER INSURED'S DATE OF BIRTH MM DD YY — SEX M [ ] F [ ]

b. AUTO ACCIDENT? YES [ ] NO [✓] PLACE (State)

b. EMPLOYER'S NAME OR SCHOOL NAME: Midway Investments

c. EMPLOYER'S NAME OR SCHOOL NAME:

c. OTHER ACCIDENT? YES [✓] NO [ ]

c. INSURANCE PLAN NAME OR PROGRAM NAME:

d. INSURANCE PLAN NAME OR PROGRAM NAME:

10d. RESERVED FOR LOCAL USE

d. IS THERE ANOTHER HEALTH BENEFIT PLAN? YES [ ] NO [✓] *If yes, return to and complete item 9 a-d.*

READ BACK OF FORM BEFORE COMPLETING & SIGNING THIS FORM.

12. PATIENT'S OR AUTHORIZED PERSON'S SIGNATURE I authorize the release of any medical or other information necessary to process this claim. I also request payment of government benefits either to myself or to the party who accepts assignment below.

SIGNED signature on file DATE 10012009

13. INSURED'S OR AUTHORIZED PERSON'S SIGNATURE I authorize payment of medical benefits to the undersigned physician or supplier for services described below.

SIGNED signature on file

PATIENT AND INSURED INFORMATION

14. DATE OF CURRENT: ◄ ILLNESS (First symptom) OR INJURY (Accident) OR PREGNANCY(LMP) MM DD YY: 09 29 2009

15. IF PATIENT HAS HAD SAME OR SIMILAR ILLNESS. GIVE FIRST DATE MM DD YY

16. DATES PATIENT UNABLE TO WORK IN CURRENT OCCUPATION FROM MM DD YY TO MM DD YY

17. NAME OF REFERRING PROVIDER OR OTHER SOURCE: Joshua Parker, MD — 17a. — 17b. NPI 56143

18. HOSPITALIZATION DATES RELATED TO CURRENT SERVICES FROM MM DD YY TO MM DD YY

19. RESERVED FOR LOCAL USE

20. OUTSIDE LAB? YES [ ] NO [✓] $ CHARGES

21. DIAGNOSIS OR NATURE OF ILLNESS OR INJURY (Relate Items 1, 2, 3 or 4 to Item 24E by Line)

1. 592.9
2. 599.0
3. ___ . ___
4. ___ . ___

22. MEDICAID RESUBMISSION CODE — ORIGINAL REF. NO.

23. PRIOR AUTHORIZATION NUMBER

	24. A. DATE(S) OF SERVICE From MM	DD	YY	To MM	DD	YY	B. PLACE OF SERVICE	C. EMG	D. PROCEDURES, SERVICES, OR SUPPLIES (Explain Unusual Circumstances) CPT/HCPCS	MODIFIER	E. DIAGNOSIS POINTER	F. $ CHARGES	G. DAYS OR UNITS	H. EPSDT Family Plan	I. ID. QUAL.	J. RENDERING PROVIDER ID. #
1	12	10	xx	12	10	xx	11		99215			201.00	1		NPI	7189396878
2	12	10	xx	12	11	xx	21		99220			241.00	1		NPI	7189396878
3	12	11	xx	12	12	xx	21		99217			109.00	1		NPI	7189396878
4															NPI	7189396878
5															NPI	7189396878
6															NPI	7189396878

25. FEDERAL TAX I.D. NUMBER SSN [ ] EIN [✓]

26. PATIENT'S ACCOUNT NO.: CON001

27. ACCEPT ASSIGNMENT? (For govt. claims, see back) YES [✓] NO [ ]

28. TOTAL CHARGE: $ 55100 00

29. AMOUNT PAID: $

30. BALANCE DUE: $ 55100 00

31. SIGNATURE OF PHYSICIAN OR SUPPLIER INCLUDING DEGREES OR CREDENTIALS (I certify that the statements on the reverse apply to this bill and are made a part thereof.)

L.D. Heath, MD — 100109

SIGNED — DATE

32. SERVICE FACILITY LOCATION INFORMATION

ouglasville Medicine Associate
5076 Brand Blvd, Suite 401
Douglasville, NY 01234

a. 9995010111 b.

33. BILLING PROVIDER INFO & PH # (123) 456-7890

L.D Heath, M.D.
5076 Brand Blvd, Suite 401
Douglasville, NY 01234

a. 7189396878 b.

PHYSICIAN OR SUPPLIER INFORMATION

Help

NUCC Instruction Manual available at: www.nucc.org — APPROVED OMB-0938-0999 FORM CMS-1500 (08-05)

Job 17 John Conway Claim Form

Isabelle Wright

5/7/xx

Ms. Wright is a 51-year old new patient. She had been seeing Dr. Willow for the past 5 years but was unhappy with that office and is seeking a new primary care doctor.

Patient gives history of:

1. Drinking 2 bottles of hard liquor per week. Not interested in quitting yet, wants to work on smoking cessation first.
2. Smoker-2 packs per day; wants to quit.
3. Anxiety/depression-is on paxil
4. Mitral valve prolapse
5. Hypothryroidism
6. GERD
7. S/P TAH and BSO
8. S/P cholecystectomy
9. Sinusitis
10. Urinary incontinence
11. Low back pain/degenerative disc disease

Denies: chest pain or shortness of breath

Current Medications:

1. Calcium 250mg/vitamin d 125 u tab 2 × a day as a mineral supplement
2. Synthroid 0.025mg 1 p.o. q day for thyroid replacement
3. Claritin 10mg tab 1 q. day for allergies
4. Paxil 40mg tab 1 p.o. q. day for depression
5. Xanax
6. Vioxx 50
7. Vicoden extra strength 750

PE: 140/80 Wt: 142

No distress. Husky smoker's voice. Fundi poorly visualized. PERRLA. CNS intact. Thyroid normal, no nodules. No LAD. Chest clear to auscultation. Coronary regular. Abdomen soft, non tender. No lower extremity edema. Mammogram within last 6 months.

AP:

1. Alcoholism-drinks 2 bottles of hard liquor per week. Discussed substance abuse treatment. Patient is interested in mental health clinic referral
2. Smoker-2 packs per day, wants to quit. Will recommend nicotine patches 14mg/24hr. Apply 1 patch topically every morning for 7 days. Do not smoke while using nicotine patch.
3. Anxiety/depression. Told patient will not prescribe Xanax with ETOH use. Will consult mental health clinic
4. Hypothryroidism-will check TSH levels today

5. GERD-lifestyle modifications for now
6. Sinusitis, chronic. Wrote new Rx for Claritin.
7. Low back pain/degenerative disc disease-patient will continue Vioxx from outside provider
8. Skin lesions-refer to dermatologist

Return to office in 3 months. I asked patient to have her records sent to my office for review.

The following codes were reported:

ICD-9: 244.9, 300.4, 477.9, 303.91, 305.1 Your Codes:____________________

CPT-4: 99204 Your Codes:____________________

Job 26 Isabelle Wright Office Note

Isiah Fulton

4/2/xx

70 yo patient well known to me with history of coronary artery disease, renal stones, arthritis. Skin cancer status post resection. Came for follow-up, no complaints, denied any chest pain or SOB. No problem with urination, regular bowel movements.

Current Medication:

1. Diltiazem
2. Lovastatin 20 mg qd

PE:

Vitals: Temp: 97.9 F; Pulse: 74, Respirations: 20, BP: 112/60, Weight: 181 lb BMI: 32.0

Pain: 0

Patient in no acute distress

Chest clear to A/P; normal inspiration efforts

Heart: S1S2 heard; neck- no bruit;

Abdomen, liver and spleen not palpable bowel sounds+, no hernias.

Digital rectal exam reveals no abnormality occult blood sent

Extremities: pedal pulses+ bilateral

LABS: PSA 6.0; BS 109; CR 0.8; CHOL 157; TG 107; LDL102

A/P:

Coronary artery disease- stable. Will increase Lovastatin to 40mg, and perform liver function test in 2 months. Continue ASA and Diltizam

BPH-PSA high followed by Urologist

Arthritis- stable

Return 2–3 months. STAT liver function test on return

ICD-9: 414.9, 716.90 Your Codes:____________________

CPT-4: 99212 Your Codes:____________________

Job 26 Isiah Fulton Office Note

Jeremy Maxwell

6/2/20XX

Patient is a 78-year-old man referred to me by Dr. Mack for ataxia, increasing over the last 2 mths, short term memory loss, and difficulty swallowing. He is here today with his son and wife who are helpful in providing much of his history. Old records were reviewed form Dr. Mack's office. He has an unsteady gait which is evident to me. He states since he had back surgery 6 yrs ago at L5-S1 for disintegration of his disk requiring fusion, he has weakness in his right leg and loss of sensation in bilateral feet. He has fallen many times in the last few years- all typically backwards. One fall down the steps in his drive way required Life Flighting him to a local trauma center and admission to ICU for 4 days. He has a cane that he uses in his home and a scooter to use when out shopping. He loses his balance easily such as when tilting his head backwards to put eyedrops in his eyes or standing up suddenly. He had a bout of vertigo several months ago with unexplained etiology. He does not complain of dizziness at this time. He has recently been treated for thyroid cancer with a thyroidectomy 2 mths ago. Since then, he has difficulty swallowing and can only eat soft foods and liquids. He and his wife both state that he has always had 'shaky hands' and attribute it to his nerves. His energy is poor.

PMH: Atrial fibrillation requiring cardioversion several times. Thyroid cancer diagnosed and treated 2 mths ago. Status post spinal surgery L5-S1 spinal stenosis. Colon polyps. Hiatal hernia. Hypercholesterolemia. Smoker for 30+ years. Drinks 1 scotch at night. Early stages of glaucoma. PCTA in 1993. IVC filter placed 5 yrs ago.

FH: Father died of heart disease with mitral valve prolapse. Mother died of heart disease. Brother died of complications from a fall while taking Coumadin for mitral valve disease.

Current Meds: Vitorin; aspirin, Lanoxin, Paxil, ocular drops, multivitamin.

PE: Wt 175; BP 132/80. Today he walked with a cane with support from his son. Pupils are irregular due to previous surgery for glaucoma. Right pupil is nonreactive, left pupil is 4mm and reactive to light. Facial expression and sensation is symmetric. He has poor dentition and has lost many teeth in the last 2 yrs. Tongue was midline. Oropharynx appears open. He states that he can't swallow his medicines and feels the sensation as something is caught in his throat and begins to cough. Many minutes later, he will cough up a pill from time to time. He has no carotid bruits. He was able to stand and sit on demand however, the second time I had him stand he lost his balance and fell back in his seat. He has no weakness to direct testing. He had some mild clumsiness with fine motor movements such as getting money out of his wallet or tying his shoes. Sensory examination reeveals no asymmetry to pinprick or light touch. Reflexes are absent. Plantar response is flexor. His hands are notably shaking at rest. Mini mental status exam performed and he struggled from time-to-time with short-term recall and putting things in order.

A: Cerebral ataxia. Marked idiopathic peripheral neuropathy. Possible TIA.

P: MRI of brain to rule out vascular accident and hydrocephalus. Sed rate, B12, thyroid panel, serum protein electrophoresis, Calcium, and liver functions. Return to the office in one week to review test results.

After the exam, I discussed the treatment options and prognosis with the patient, his wife, and son. Mrs. Maxwell is concerned about caring for him at home should he deteriorate further. We discussed options. We discussed the tests ordered and potential treatment options based on the test findings. Total face-to-face time was 70 minutes of which 35 mins was spent counseling the patient and his family.

ICD-9: 331.89, 356.8 Your Codes:________________

CPT-4:99205_____ Your Codes:________________

Job 26 Jeremy Maxwell Office Note

Lilly Rose

7/2/20XX

This is my first visit with this very pleasant 42-year-old African-American, here after recent asthma exacerbation. Dr. Miller asked me to evaluate her allergy and pulmonary status.

She had childhood asthma and has been off medication for many years. For the past two or three weeks, she has had sinus congestion that she thought was allergy-related, but the nocturnal cough became worse and worse to the point where she could no longer breathe. She was taken to the ER on Monday, three days ago. She received breathing treatment x2, was given steroids, and sent home.

Since then, she is better on the prednisone, but still having nocturnal coughing. The dyspnea appears improved. She is not on any antibiotics. She does not recall a flu-like illness preceding all this.

ALLERGIES: Latex. Milk.

PAST MEDICAL HISTORY: Childhood asthma.

SOCIAL HISTORY: She is married. Recently changed jobs. She is a nonsmoker, nondrinker. She has three children.

FAMILY HISTORY: Father has borderline diabetes and many siblings who are diabetic. Mother is alive and well, has depression and bipolar.

REVIEW OF SYSTEMS: Positive for allergies. No chest pain. She does have cough. No shortness of breath when she walks or is outdoors. Complete review of systems is otherwise negative. She also has a history of eczema. She has experienced lack of energy and

CURRENT MEDICATIONS:

1.Depo-Provera shots.

2.Prednisone 40 mg for 5-day course.

3.Albuterol inhaler as needed.

PHYSICAL EXAMINATION: She is in no acute distress, sounds a little bit congested. Weight is 169 lb, height is 5'5". Blood pressure 110/64, pulse is 72, temperature 98.9. PERRLA. Extraocular movements are intact. Oropharynx is benign. Good dentition. Nares: The septum appears deviated to the right somewhat. Neck is supple. No lymphadenopathy. Carotids 2+, no bruits. Lungs: Faint expiratory wheezes, otherwise clear. Cardiovascular: Regular rate and rhythm. Breast exam: Deferred. Abdomen: Soft, nontender. No organomegaly. Extremities: No clubbing, cyanosis, or edema. Neurologic: Nonfocal. Skin: Very dry.

IMPRESSION & PLAN:

1. **Asthma exacerbation** – Question origin as extrinsic versus other irritant such as viral URI. Plan: Start Advair today since she will be stopping prednisone after tomorrow. Monitor symptoms carefully. She may or may not need a controller. In six weeks I want to check her pulmonary function tests.
2. **Allergic rhinitis** - I gave her some Zyrtec 10 mg as needed. She may prefer Flonase in the future.
3. **Family history of diabetes** - We are going to check a fasting blood sugar as well as cholesterol. She is to return tomorrow for labs.
4. **Health maintenance** - She is going to get some old records sent here. Encourage regular physical activity.
5. **Check Thyroid functions** - draw blood today and send to lab.

ICD-9: 493.92, 477.9 Your Codes:__________________

CPT-4:99243 Your Codes:__________________

Job 26 Lilly Rose Office Note

PART IV

BILLING INTERNSHIP

CHAPTER

9 Remote Coding

Learning Objectives

When finished with this chapter, the student will be able to:

1. Explain the concept of outsourced coding.
2. Discuss how work is received by the coding company and returned to the client.
3. Assign ICD-9, CPT, and HCPCS codes for surgical procedures and supplies.
4. Sequence procedures according to ambulatory surgery center payment methodology.
5. Compile a portfolio of cases submitted with rationale for correct code assignment to use for future reference.

Key Terms

Ambulatory Surgery Center Covered Procedures
Ear, Nose, and Throat (ENT)
General Surgeon
Gynecology
Healthcare Billing and Management Association (HBMA)
Ophthalmology
Orthopedics
Outsource
Plastic Surgeon
Remote Coding
Urology

Background Basics

- Students should have completed a course in ICD-9-CM, CPT-4, and HCPCS coding methodologies.
- Students need a strong background in anatomy and medical terminology to decipher operative reports.
- Students must be able to read an operative report and must have had prior instruction on identifying significant procedures.
- Students need to load Encoder Pro on their computers to use in this chapter.

Competency Checklist

- Coders must have a strong foundation in coding guidelines to properly assign codes for diagnoses and procedures.
- Coders are responsible for reading and interpreting medical information to justify medical necessity and assign codes to the highest specificity.
- Coding staff have to be fluent in Medicare carrier coding requirements for reporting and the use of Correct Coding Edits.
- Many organizations provide coding software as a tool to enhance coder efficiency and skill.
- Coders who are able to code surgical procedures for multiple specialties are in high demand.
- Facility coding requires using facility-specific modifiers and sequencing rules that are different from professional coding.

Introduction

Historically, coding in surgical practices was typically performed by the surgeon. The surgeon would then record the CPT codes on his charge sheet and the biller would input the charges and file the claims. Over the last 15 years, there has been a paradigm shift with this duty back to a trained certified coder who is knowledgeable in coding guidelines, payer rules, global packaging, modifier usage, payment methodologies, and bundling edits. The adoption of the Correct Coding Initiative in 1996, implementation of HIPAA-mandated code sets, increased medical necessity scrutiny, and payer reporting rules have all played a role in this shift.

Part IV of this simulation shifts gears and allows you to experience working for a coding company called Surgery Coding Solutions (SCS). Their clients are free standing ambulatory surgery centers. You are a contracted coder for this clinic and are working off site. You are assigned to an ambulatory surgery center named Meadway MedSurg Clinic. Your job is to code their ambulatory surgeries. You will not be doing the billing for this facility, or entering codes or charges into MOSS. You will assign any applicable ICD-9, CPT-4, and HCPCS codes and record them on a Coding Capture Form. This form is faxed or emailed back to the clinic each day with the correct code assignment. This form also is used to query the surgeon and identify missing information needed to complete the code assignment. This form is located in Appendix H. Be sure to sequence the codes from highest paid procedure to lowest, based on the Ambulatory Surgery Center fee schedule. ICD-9 codes are listed with the appropriate CPT code for linkage on the claim form and any necessary modifiers.

Ambulatory Surgery Center Covered Procedures is a list produced by CMS depicting what surgical services may be rendered in an ASC (place of service [POS] 24) with the respective reimbursement for each of these services. To find this list of approved services, go to CMS's website at http://www.cms.hhs.gov to obtain this fee schedule. Click on *Medicare*. Under *Medicare Fee-for-Service Payment*, scroll down and select *Ambulatory Surgery Center Payment*. This screen will list several ZIP files. Select the most recent *ASC Approved HCPCS Codes and Payment Rates*. On the left side of the screen, select *Addenda Updates*. Select the most current version of the *ASC Approved HCPCS Codes and Payment Rates*. You will be asked to accept the AMA terms for CPT licensure by clicking *Accept*. Within this .zip file, open *Addendum AA ASC Covered Surgical Procedures*. This is an Excel spreadsheet. Do not print this file! Download it to your computer or flash drive to use throughout this chapter.

Discussion:

Research the ASC Surgery Center Covered Procedures or Approved HCPCS Codes list as well as the payment methodology for ASCs. What happens if a procedure is performed in the ASC that is not on this list? Who would be responsible for the fees incurred? Talk about ways that facilities can ensure that procedures that are not covered are not scheduled.

Outsourcing Coding Companies

Coders with a strong background in surgery are in demand. The healthcare industry has seen a shortfall of certified candidates for the past 10 years, and the trend is expected to continue for the next 10 years. Due to this widespread shortage of coders, facilities and physicians have opted to **outsource** this service. Outsourcing is contracting an outside company, commonly referred to as a *third party*, to provide this service at a negotiated rate. It may be a set fee per month, an hourly rate, or a charge per record coded. Coders may be physically located onsite at a hospital or practice performing this function, but they are not employees of that organization. Outsourcing is also accomplished by providing connection to the organization's computer system, which allows contracted coders to access the data and work remotely. **Remote coding** in contrast is not conducted onsite. Remote coding is coding performed offsite. This option has allowed staff to perform this function offsite with no interruption of work flow and has increased coder retention. Introduced in 2000, remote coding quickly became the hottest trend in the market. Coders working offsite may be located within a business establishment nearby or in another state or even out of the country, for example, in India. Most remote coders work out of their own homes and are networked into an organization's computer system. Remote coders can be either employees of the organization or contracted with an outside agency.

In some situations, the coding and the billing are both contracted out to a third party. The **Healthcare Billing and Management Association** is a good resource for third-party billers. It is a professional trade association comprised of third-party billing companies, both large and small. It provides education to members and monitors changes to the billing industry. It also is a great resource for billing compliance and pressing issues. AHIMA has some suggested remote coding policies, directives, and tools for implementation located on their website. Coders working remotely must have proven knowledge and experience and be organized, focused, and wise time-managers. The individual has to be resourceful, computer literate, and experienced enough to work independently. This job is not intended for the coding novice.

Surgery Coding Solutions (SCS)

Surgery Coding Solutions (SCS) is a third-party coding company that employs certified coders to abstract and code ambulatory surgery operative reports. Our company abides by the same coding rules and principals outlined in DMA's P&P manual. Coders must adhere to all coding guidelines. If the coder has any questions for the doctor or needs additional information, the patient's account is placed on hold until this information is received. CAUTION: We are contracted to code for the facility services, not the professional services. This impacts the modifiers available to use and how codes are sequenced on the claim form. If x-ray is used during the surgery, a –TC modifier is required to designate the technical component of that service from the professional component. Modifiers available for use by ASCs are located in the front cover of your *CPT Professional Edition* under *Modifiers Approved for Hospital Outpatient Use*.

Conditions of Employment

To reduce employer risk and to be compliant with HIPAA and DHEC, SCS requires that certain environmental and regulatory conditions be attained before authorizing work to a remote employee.

Home Environment

Prior to establishing a home office, the coder's home workplace must be inspected and approved by the supervisor. Factors to evaluate during the inspection include, but are not limited to, ergonomic requirements, technical equipment, safety, and confidentiality. The employee must have a private work area that can be locked. The area must be equipped with a working fire detector and nearby fire extinguisher.

Insurance

All employees of SCS must provide proof of homeowners or renters insurance.

Equipment

The remote coder provides his own desk, chair, and any office supplies necessary for remote coding work. A properly grounded duplex outlet and surge protector are required at the employee's expense. SCS provides the computer and necessary software. Only SCS software may be loaded on the PC. Use by anyone other than the SCS employee is strictly prohibited. This computer is to be used for SCS business only. It must have a user password and a screen saver, and it must be backed up daily. No major appliances may be on the same outlet as the computer. Extension cords are prohibited. Equipment or Internet problems must be promptly reported to the supervisor. The supervisor will determine if the employee must go to another reasonable site to finish the shift, make up the time on another workday, or take PTO.

There must be a dedicated telephone line with voice mail available for work-related contact with sites. The computer must have a high-speed Internet connection. Coders are required to have a shredder on site and destroy any printed material at the end of each week.

Security and Confidentiality

Staff can only access SCS servers by logging in through a password-equipped VPN. To ensure security and confidentiality, only the printers supplied by SCS may be connected to the computer. The coder must maintain confidentiality of information and not disclose or permit other persons to view, observe, examine, or copy any information, reports, or documents that concern patients or clients of SCS. The remote coder is required to sign a Confidentiality Agreement, assuring that all information will be maintained in the strictest confidence. Any breach of the Confidentiality Agreement may result in disciplinary action up to and including termination, per hospital or surgery center policy.

Work Flow

Facilities email OP notes daily from their secure websites to the coders assigned to their sites. With a coder-specific user name and password, the coder downloads the reports to his/her computer. The coder can then either choose to print these reports or view them on the screen. ICD-9, CPT, HCPCS codes, and any applicable modifiers are assigned for each surgery. Attention must be focused on the patient's insurance and age. If the patient has Medicare, watch for procedures that should be reported with a G code instead of the CPT-4 code. When listing more than one modifier, list the HCPCS Level II modifier or the one that affects payment first, followed by any others. For example, a -59 modifier is sequenced before an –LT modifier because this modifier affects payment.

The codes are recorded on the Coding Capture Form and sequenced in the proper order according to the ASC fee schedule. Keep this fee schedule with you where you will be doing your coding work so that you can refer to it quickly. Once the work is completed, it is returned to the facility via secure email. The Excel sheet is password-protected and opened by designated employees at the facility. If a path report is needed, indicate this in the last column under *Missing Information*. Path reports are faxed to the coder upon request, particularly those for colon biopsies, polypectomies, breast biopsies, and lesion removals. See Figure 9.1 to illustrate the proper completion of this form. For easier reading, leave one or two lines between patients on the sheet.

Date: 12/2/xx			Coder Name: Mary Howard, CPC				SURGERY CODING SOLUTIONS	
	MEADWAY MEDSURG CLINIC							
Patient Name	**Patient ID Number**	**Date of Service**	**CPT Code**	**Modifier(s)**	**ICD-9 Diagnosis Codes**	**HCPCS Level II**	**Physician Question-Addendum necessary to medical record**	**Missing Information/ Implant Description**
Morgan, Leonard	MOR 123	12/2/xx	45378	SG	211.3			
					562.10			
Wilson, Polly	WIL001	12/2/xx	28286	LT	735.0	L8699		K-wire
Poe, Hunter	POE234	12/2/xx						need path report

Figure 9.1 Coding Capture Form

Because you are a new employee, all of your work must be audited for accuracy for the first 30 days of employment. At the end of each day's work, submit this form to your instructor to check your work and provide feedback.

Meadway MedSurg Clinic (MMC)

The Meadway MedSurg Clinic (MMC) is a busy surgery center that averages 30 cases per day. They accept patients with private, commercial, managed care, and government-sponsored insurance. They are a multi-specialty clinic offering the following surgical specialties:

- ENT
- Orthopedics
- Urology
- Plastic Surgery
- Gynecology
- Ophthalmology
- General Surgery

Meadway MedSurg Providers

Dr. Gregory Wallace, a urologist, is board certified by the American Board of Urology. **Urology** is a specialty that focuses training and treatment on the urinary system—kidney, ureter, bladder, urethra, and prostate. Likewise, a urologist specializes in treatment of patients of all ages with urinary tract diseases or disorders. Dr. Raymond Ross, our general surgeon, is board certified by the American Board of Surgery. **General surgeons** are trained to operate on the abdomen and all abdominal organs, including treating hernias. Most general surgeons are also trained to surgically treat the thyroid, breasts, and vasculature of the extremities. Dr. Robyn Houser, our **plastic surgeon**, is board certified by the American Board of Plastic and Reconstructive Surgery. Plastic surgeons specialize in the medical and surgical treatment of traumatic injuries and congenital abnormalities that cause disfigurement of the face and skin. The field encompasses cosmetic enhancements as well as functionally reconstructive operations. We have one orthopedic surgeon, Dr. Thaddeus Morency, who is board certified by the American Board of Orthopedic Surgery. **Orthopedists** are orthopedic surgeons who specialize in the treatment of skeletal diseases and injuries including bones, ligaments, tendons, and cartilage. Dr. Abbey Murphy, who is in the field of **gynecology**, specializes in women's gynecological health and is board certified by the American Board of Obstetrics and Gynecology. She is a gynecologist who medically and surgically treats diseases and disorders of the female genital tract. Dr. Jeremy Moser is an ophthalmologist. **Ophthalmology** is a surgical subspecialty that treats and diagnoses diseases and trauma to the eye and surrounding areas, including the eyelid and lacrimal system. Dr. Lee Hackney is our **ear, nose, and throat (ENT)** surgeon. ENT is an acronym widely used to describe otolaryngologists, that is, physicians who specialize in diagnosing and treating diseases and disorders of the ears, nose, and throat.

Encoder Pro.com—Expert

Access to Encoder Pro.com software is included with this textbook. This software enables you to have access to Encoder Pro.com–Expert for a 59-ay trial period (Figure 9.2). You can use the software to complete these jobs or as a way to compare your work to see if you arrive at the same code selection using your books. At the end of the day, coders must be experts at using the three HIPAA code sets and finding the codes in the code books. Software only enhances your ability to find codes more quickly. This software does not assign codes for you. You still must interpret the documentation and logically follow coding rules. As discussed in chapter 2, this software is not a true encoder. It is an electronic code book

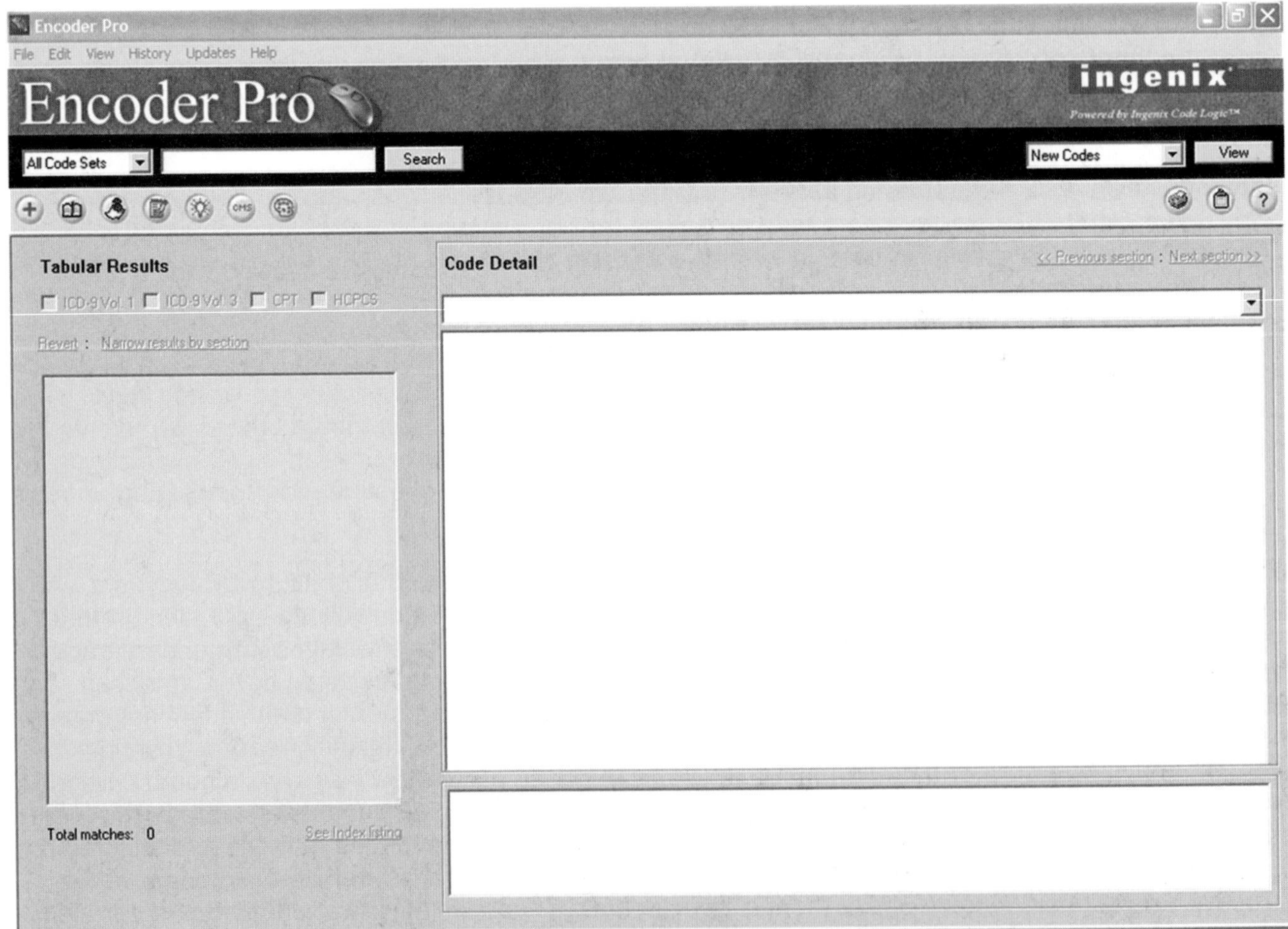

Figure 9.2 Encoder Pro Menu and screen

allowing you to search for ICD-9, CPT, and HCPCS II codes by entering either a key word (i.e., a diagnosis or a procedure) or by entering an actual code number. It does not walk you through the logic of assigning the code. There is a *Help* option located on the tool bar. It provides instructions on how to navigate the software and describes all the features.

This software allows users to search for codes by choosing one of the code sets or by searching all the codes sets simultaneously. Search can also be done by code book section lookup. Searches can be narrowed by choosing *Narrow Results by Section*. Doing so will break down the options by section of the book (e.g., radiology, surgery). You can use this feature as often as necessary to pare down the results to specific code sections. All the information you can access in the traditional code books is here with a few additional features. The software includes:

- ICD-9-CM Volume 1 and 3 codes and instructional notes
- AHA *Coding Clinic* references
- Access to the new, revised, and deleted Codes
- Ability to create user sticky notes and book marks
- Invalid codes, unspecified codes, and CC exclusions are all indicated
- CPT lay descriptions
- CPT section notes
- CPT Assistant references
- Special coverage instructions
- CPT color codes identify add-on, modifier −51 exempt, age- and sex-specific codes
- HCPCS color codes identify codes carrying quantity, special coverage instructions, and policy flags
- HCPCS Notes, Medicare coverage instructions

After conducting a search, codes are displayed so that the most likely codes are listed first (by rank) in the *Tabular Results* on the left of the screen. By clicking on any code listed here, a full description for the code and all neighboring codes will appear on the right of the screen under *Code Detail*. For ICD-9-CM codes, the *Code Detail* also shows excludes and includes notes, as well as *code first* and *code also* references. By highlighting a code under *Code Detail* additional information will appear in the dialog box on the bottom right with code-specific notes such as: ICD-9-CM instructional notes; *AHA Coding Clinic* references and annotations; lay descriptions of CPT; CPT *Assistant* references; AMA guidelines, and modifiers for the selected CPT code. See Figure 9.3 for an illustration of these details.

The dialog box will also display primary procedure codes for add-on codes, surgical and anesthesia cross walk codes, Medicare Physician Fee Schedule information, and unbundling edits from Medicare's Correct Coding Initiative. See Figure 9.4.

Load this software on your computer now.

Assigned Work

Work received is coded within 24 hours of receipt. It is expected that an outpatient surgery coder complete 5–10 OP notes per hour. Because you are an entry-level coder, you will be phased in to this production goal and are required to complete only 2 OP notes per hour. You are provided with 16 OP notes per day for a full week. The OP notes needed to complete your assignment are located at the end of this chapter. Part IV. Work is grouped by day. Read the OP notes and any accompanying path reports carefully and completely. If anything is missing, indicate this on the Charge Capture Form. Record the patient ID number, name, CPT codes, ICD-9 codes, HCPCS codes, and modifiers for each patient. You will need to make additional copies of Meadway Coding Capture form located on the CD-ROM. Turn in a form at the end of each day.

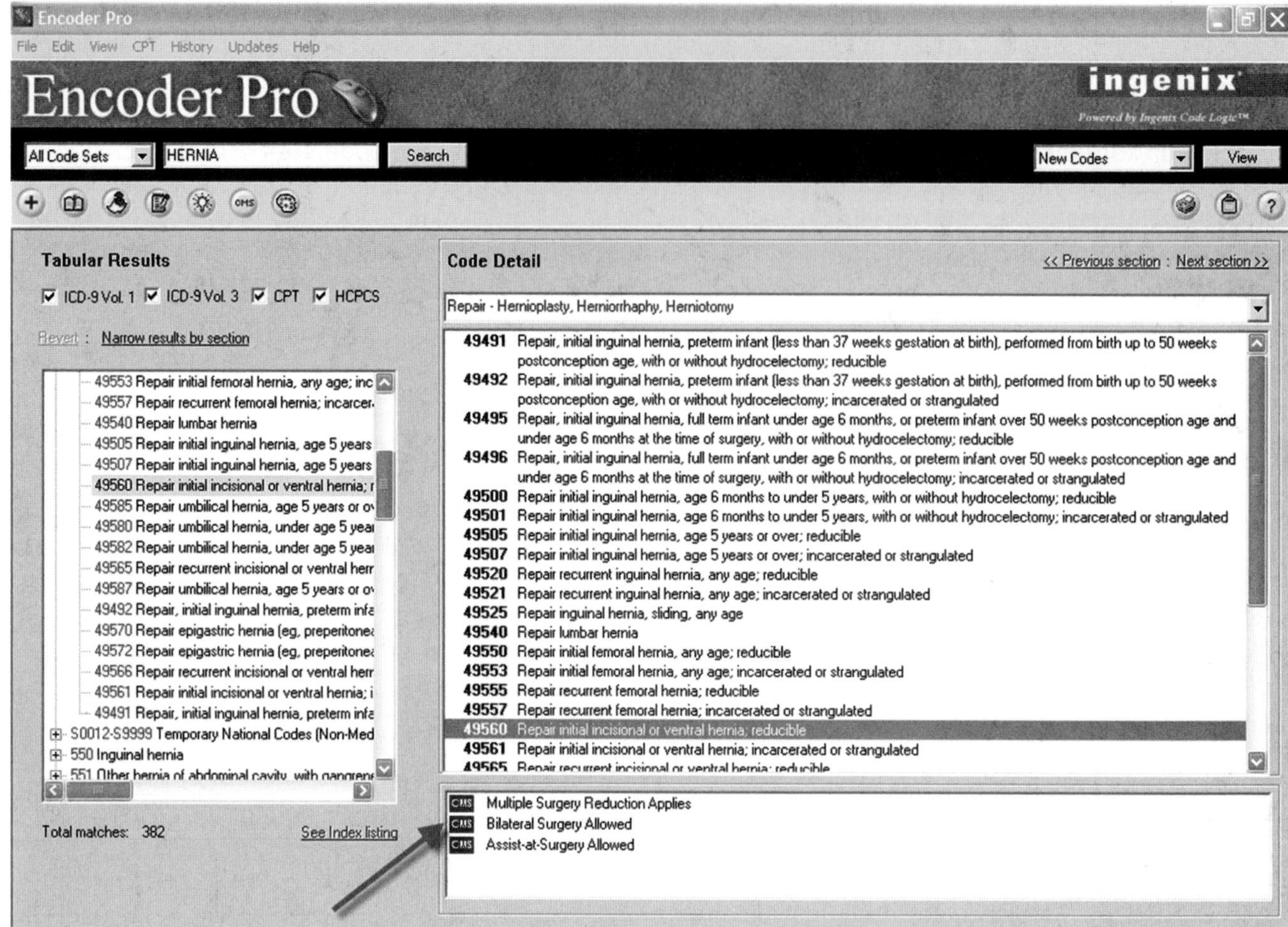

Figure 9.3 Code Specific Notes

Remember, facility coding is slightly different from how you coded for DMA. At MMC, you are coding for the facility, not the physician. The following list provides a few tips to apply when coding for ASCs:

- Append the –TC modifier for fluoroscopy codes.
- Append only those modifiers that are designated for facilities.
- Do not assign codes for drugs or routine supplies unless they are implants.
- Sequence all codes according to the ASC fee schedule with the highest paying procedure first.
- Do not assign codes that are included in the surgical package.
- Check CCI edits for all government payers and assign only the most comprehensive code.
- Do not assign an HCPCS supply code for intraocular lenses implanted in Medicare patients that have a cataract extraction unless the model number is listed in *CMS Recognized P-C IOLS and A-C IOLs*. If it is a special lens listed in this table, assign Q1003. Otherwise, it is considered part of the payment for the surgery. This list is located on the CMS website at http://www.cms.hhs.gov. Click on *Medicare*. Under *Medicare Fee-for-Service Payment*, scroll down and select *Ambulatory Surgery Center Payment*. Scroll to the bottom of the screen and click on *CMS Recognized P-C IOLS and A-C IOLs*. Print this out now for reference in coding ophthalmology cases.

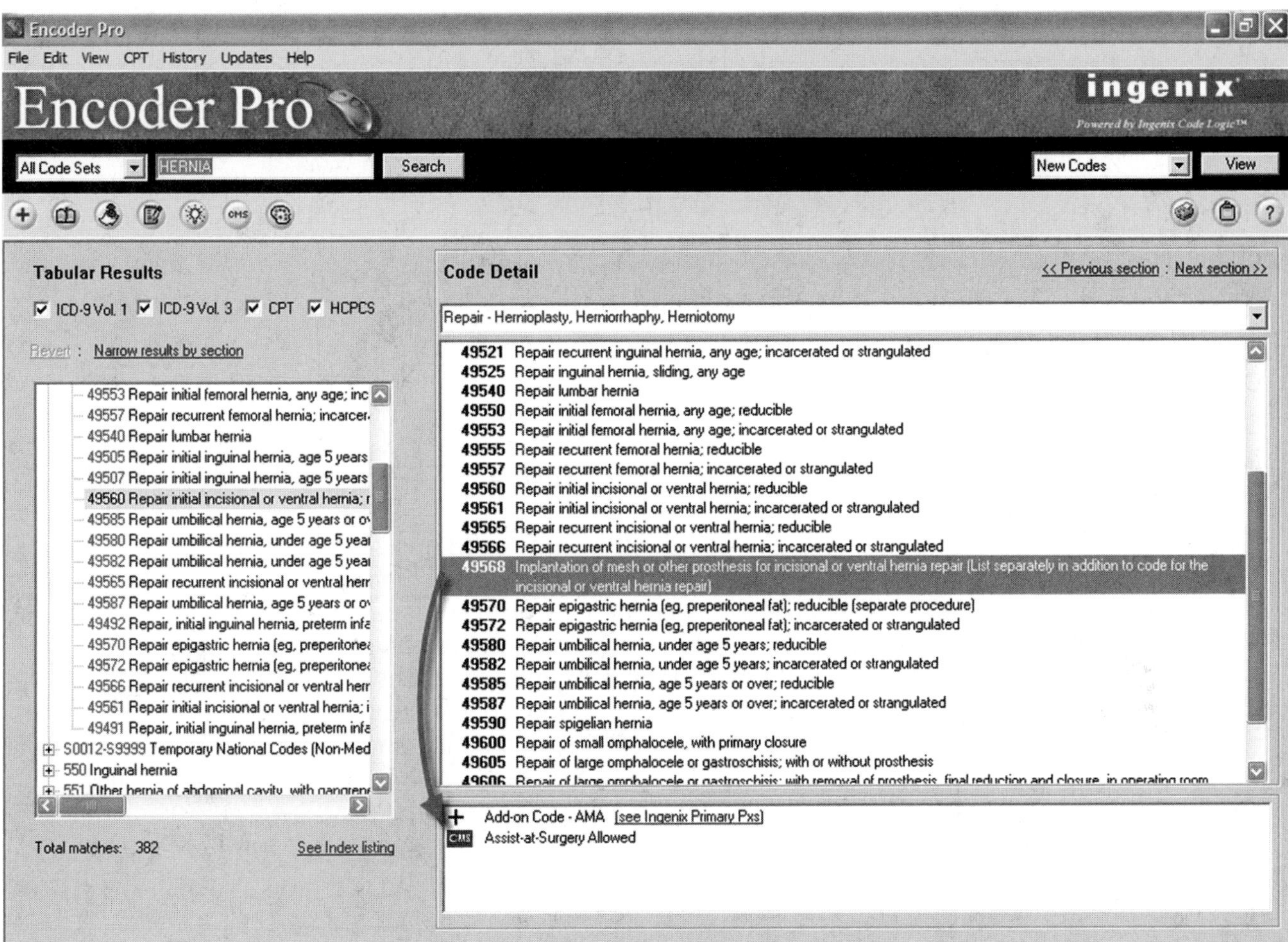

Figure 9.4 Encoder Pro screen shot with Code Detail

END OF CHAPTER QUESTIONS

1. What modifiers are appended for assistant surgeons? Which modifier is required by Medicare for assistant surgeons who are not MDs, such as RNPs or PACs? Would these modifiers be used by facilities?__________
2. What is the HCPCS level II code required for reporting knee arthroscopies on Medicare patients when procedures are performed in two different compartments of the knee? __________
3. Check the Medicare website and find out how often a Medicare patient who is at high risk for colon cancer can have a colonoscopy. __________
4. Search the Medicare website for colonoscopy LCDs for NY Empire Medicare Services or NCDs. What modifiers should the facility report for an incomplete colonoscopy? __________
5. A patient is seen in the ASC for a facet joint injection. The doctor lists degeneration of the lumbarsacral disc. Is this a covered diagnosis for a Medicare patient in South Carolina? Search http://www.palmettogba.com for an LCD. __________

DAY ONE

MEADWAY MEDSURG CLINIC

Name: Jordan, Bianca Date: 10/30/xx

Patient ID: JOR523 Insurance: Medicare

PREOPERATIVE DIAGNOSIS: Right ulnar neuropathy

POSTOPERATIVE DIAGNOSIS: Right ulnar neuropathy

OPERATIVE PROCEDURE: Right ulnar nerve neurolysis and transposition

SURGEON: Thaddeus Morency, M.D.

INDICATIONS: She had been experiencing signs and symptoms of ulnar neuropathy and was offered surgical treatment.

PROCEDURE: The patient was taken to the operating room, placed upon the operating table in a supine position. The right arm was prepped and draped in the usual manner. Local anesthesia was infiltrated to both sides of the incision and curvilinear incision was made on the right elbow. With sharp and blunt dissection, the ulnar nerve was identified. It was released from the surrounding cartilage, which was abundant and all the branches were preserved. The loop was placed around the nerve and enough length was released and was transposed without difficulty in front of the medial epicondyle. A sling was created from the subcutaneous tissue and the nerve was transposed without difficulty and without tension. A sling was anchored with 3-0 Vicryl. Subcuticular stitch was placed with 3-0 Vicryl after thorough and copious irrigation, and hemostasis. The skin was closed with 4-0 running nylon. The appropriate dressings were applied. The patient tolerated the procedure well and was taken back to the recovery room in satisfactory condition.

MEADWAY MEDSURG CLINIC

Name: Lime, Sylvia Date: 10/07/xx

Patient ID: LIM456 Insurance: Aetna

PREOPERATIVE DIAGNOSIS: Fibroepithelial vaginal polyp

POSTOPERATIVE DIAGNOSIS: Fibroepithelial vaginal polyp

OPERATION: Excision of fibroepithelial polyp

SURGEON: Abbey Murphy, M.D.

INDICATIONS: She is 40-years-old PARA-2022. LMP: 11/01/xx. She has a 2- to 3-cm prolapsing polyp from the anterior aspect of her vagina, which is troublesome and in the way. She is requesting excision.

OPERATIVE FINDINGS: Examination under anesthesia revealed a 3-cm vaginal polyp, prolapsing out the vagina, attached at 3:00. Using cautery set at 70/30 and a large loop attachment, the polyp was excised. Cautery was performed of the base and a few sutures were used.

OPERATIVE SUMMARY AND TECHNIQUES: The patient was brought to the operating room and after adequate IV sedation, the patient was prepped and draped in the usual manner for vaginal surgery. 1 cc of Marcaine without epi was injected around the base of the polyp. Using a large flat loop attached to cautery set at 70/30 cut/coag. The polyp was removed in one fell swoop. The base of the polyp was then cauterized with a ball cautery set at 50/50. Three sutures of 2.0 chromic were then placed to re-approximate the edges for further hemostasis. The specimen was sent to pathology.

MEADWAY MEDSURG CLINIC

Name: Schwartz, Marc — Date: 10/06/xx

Patient ID: SCH387 — Insurance: BCBS

PREOPERATIVE DIAGNOSIS: Symptomatic internal hemorrhoids

POSTOPERATIVE DIAGNOSIS: Symptomatic internal hemorrhoids

OPERATIVE PROCEDURE: Procedure for prolapse and hemorrhoids (stapled hemorrhoidipexy)

Surgeon: Raymond Ross, M.D.

INDICATIONS: This patient is a 46-year-old gentleman who has had problems with intermittent rectal bleeding and hemorrhoids. He has tried suppositories and fiber, but this has not improved his symptoms.

PROCEDURE: After informed written consent was obtained from the patient, he was taken to the operating room and placed in the prone-jackknife position. Appropriate monitors were fixed by anesthesia and then an appropriate time-out was performed. The buttocks were taped laterally and the perianal region was painted with Betadine. After adequate sedation, a perianal block was performed using .50% Marcaine with epinephrine. Approximately 20 cc were used. Next, a digital rectal exam was performed, which was normal. Next, a Fansler retractor was placed within the anal canal, exposing the anal canal. Using a 2.0 Prolene pursestring stitch, a pursestring was placed at the top of the hemorrhoid complex approximately 4-cm from the anal verge. This was done circumferentially. The Fansler retractor was removed and the stitch was pulled tight around my index finger within the anal canal. It seems that I had a good pursestring stitch. Next, the stapler head was placed past the pursestring and tied down. The stapler was then closed and fired in standard fashion. I waited one minute and opened the stapler and removed the stapler. I then packed the anal canal with gauze and evaluated the specimen. The rectal mucosa seemed to be intact with a complete donut. No significant abnormalities were noted.

Next, the Fansler retractor was placed back within the anal canal after the gauze was removed. The staple line was evaluated for bleeding, and there was no evidence of active bleeding. The anal canal was paced with Gelfoam. The patient tolerated the procedure well and there were no apparent complications.

MEADWAY MEDSURG CLINIC

Name: Ryan, Mike — Date: 10/15/xx

Patient ID: RYA907 — Insurance: Cigna

PREOPERATIVE DIAGNOSIS: Torn medial meniscus

POSTOPERATIVE DIAGNOSIS:

1. Grade 3 tear posterior horn medial meniscus
2. Medial plica
3. Grade 1 articular cartilage defect medial femoral condylar region

OPERATION:

1. Examination under anesthesia with diagnostic arthroscopy
2. Resection of plica and posterior horn meniscal tear

(Continued)

SURGEON: Thaddeus Morency, M.D.

PROCEDURE: The patient was brought to the surgery suite and after adequate anesthesia was positioned on the table and secured. The leg was then prepared for surgery by placing a tourniquet high on the thigh. The leg was then examined and noted to have a full range of motion with a mild clicking to the medial compartment with ranging, otherwise, stable in all planes. At this time the leg was prepared by placing the leg in a leg holding device and the leg was scrubbed from the tourniquet to the toes with a 10-minute Betadine scrub followed by Betadine prep and then draped in a sterile fashion. The leg was elevated and exsanguinated and the tourniquet inflated. Medial and lateral parapatellar work portals were created with a #11 stab blade. The arthroscope was introduced, and the knee was distended and examined. The suprapatellar pouch region was normal. There was a thickened medial plica which extended well over the medial femoral condylar area. This was resected back with a full-radius cutting blade. This allowed for exposure to the medial compartment easily. The medial gutter was otherwise clean. The articular surface of the medial femoral condyle had a laceration type tear into the cartilage itself. The underlying cartilage was completely intact. There was no evidence of eburnation of bone. This was not a flap tear and could not be displaced. The posterior horn meniscus had a small, grade 3, through and through extension in the white/white zone. This was resected back with a combination of the handheld upbiters, small cautery unit and small curved shaver. A smooth stable posterior horn meniscal rim was left in place.

The ACL (anterior cruciate ligament) and PCL (posterior cruciate ligament) were noted to be intact. The lateral compartment was completely normal with normal articular surfaces and normal menisci.

At this time the arthroscope was removed. The knee was drained. The wounds were closed with 4-0 nylon stitches. The knee was then injected with 10-mg Duramorph and 20-mg 0.25% Marcaine and sterile bandage was applied and the patient was taken to the recovery room. There were no intra-operative complications.

MEADWAY MEDSURG CLINIC

Name: Mavis, Stacey | Date: 10/25/xx

Patient ID: MAV249 | Insurance: Medicare

PREOPERATIVE and POSTOPERATIVE DIAGNOSIS: Cataract left eye

SURGEON: Jeremy Moser, M.D.

OPERATION: Extracapsular cataract extraction by phacoemulsification with posterior chamber intraocular lens implantation.

PROCEDURE: Following pupillary dilatation and preoperative sedation, the patient was brought to the operating room where retrobulbar anesthesia and lid akinesia were obtained with local infiltration of 2% Xylocaine with Epinephrine, Wydase and sodium bicarbonate. The eye was then prepped and draped in the usual sterile manner. The operating microscope was brought into position and used throughout the balance of the procedure. A half thickness, arcuate limbal incision with a 3-mm arc length was created at the temporal limbus. Beginning at this point, a crescent knife was used to develop a lamellar intracorneal incision that extended well into clear cornea but did not enter the anterior chamber. Limbal paracenteses were placed above and below the corneal tunnel. A 22 gauge sharp disposable needle with a bent tip was placed on the irrigation handpiece. This was introduced into the anterior chamber through the paracentesis to the right of the corneal tunnel and used to create a continuous circular capsulorrhexis.

(Continued)

Hydrodissection was performed with balanced salt solution. Amvisc plus was instilled in the anterior chamber. A 2.75-mm keratome was then used to enter the anterior chamber at the inner limit of the corneal tunnel. Through this opening, the phacoemulsification handpiece was introduced and the lens nucleus was removed by grooving and cracking the nucleus into quadrants, which were then phacoemulsified sequentially. The residual cortex was aspirated with the irrigation/aspiration handpiece. The posterior capsule was vacuumed. The capsular bag was inflated with intracameral Amvisc Plus. The inner opening of the corneal tunnel was extended to a full 3.5-mm with a short cut knife. An Alcon Acrysof model MA30AC, posterior chamber intraocular lens with a power of 20.0 diopters was inspected, irrigated, folded in half, and introduced through the corneal incision. The leading haptic was placed in the capsular bag nasally and as the lens unfolded in the anterior chamber and the trailing haptic was introduced, the lens was placed in the capsular bag and the trailing haptic in the bag as well. The lens was rotated a full 90° and noted to be well centered in the capsular bag. The irrigation handpiece was reintroduced and used to remove the residual Amvisc plus. The anterior chamber was then reformed and the pupil constricted with intracameral Miochol. The wound was checked and noted to be watertight. The previously placed lid speculum was removed. Ciloxan ointment was instilled. The lid was closed, covered with an eye pad, moderate pressure dressing and Fox shield. Having tolerated the procedure well, the patient was returned to the recovery room in good condition.

MEADWAY MEDSURG CLINIC

Name: Traci, Nick — Date: 10/12/xx

Patient ID: TRA249 — Insurance: Signal HMO

PREOPERATIVE and POSTOPERATIVE DIAGNOSIS: Menorrhagia unresponsive to medical therapy

SURGEON: Abbey Murphy, M.D.

INDICATIONS: Ms. Allen is to have hysteroscopy and D&C followed by endometrial ablation for menorrhagia unresponsive to medical therapy.

OPERATION:

1. Hysteroscopy
2. D&C (dilation and curettage)
3. Endometrial ablation

FINDINGS: Shaggy endometrium, no polyps or submucous fibroids noted

PROCEDURE: After induction of general anesthesia, Ms. Allen was placed in modified dorsal lithotomy position using Allen stirrups. Pelvic examination was done and the uterus was anterior, normal sized. There were no adnexal masses. The vagina and perineum were prepped and draped. A posterior weighted speculum was placed. The anterior lip of the cervix was grasped with a tenaculum.

The uterus sounded midplane to 8-cm. The os was dilated to accept the diagnostic hysteroscope. Hysteroscopy was performed. There was shaggy endometrium with areas of thinning endometrium. No polyps or submucous fibroids were noted. Fractional D&C was performed. Balloon endometrial ablation was then performed without difficulty.

MEADWAY MEDSURG CLINIC

Name: Bell, Mildred
Patient ID: BEL493

Date: 10/11/xx
Insurance: Medicare

PREOPERATIVE DIAGNOSIS:

1. Left lower quadrant abdominal pain, resolved
2. Without prior colon evaluation
3. Family history of colon cancer

POSTOPERATIVE DIAGNOSIS:

1. Sigmoid diverticulosis
2. Internal and external hemorrhoids
3. Colon polyps at the splenic flexure at 70-cm, rectosigmoid at 25-cm and 20-cm

OPERATION: Complete colonoscopy

SURGEON: Raymond Ross, M.D.

PROCEDURE: The patient was taken to the endoscopy suite after administration of I.V sedation by the anesthesia department. The patient was positioned in the left lateral decubitus position. The flexible colonoscope was navigated through the anus to 150-cm, at which time the ileocecal valve was identified and verified by light verification and palpation of the right lower quadrant. No tumors or masses or proximal colon polyps were identified. There was noted sigmoid diverticulosis and a scattering of diverticuli throughout the transverse and right colon. 3 polypoid lesions were identified, one at 70-cm near the splenic flexure and one at 25-cm and one at 20-cm. These were hot biopsied and electrodesiccated. The scope was withdrawn and the colon desufflated. Internal and external hemorrhoids were visualized at the outlet. The patient tolerated the procedure well and was sent to post procedure area for further monitoring.

NEW AGE PATHOLOGY

Name: Bell, Mildred
Patient ID: BEL493
SURGEON: Ross, Raymond M.D.

Date: 10/16/xx

DIAGNOSIS:

1. **Splenic Flexure: Hyperplastic polyp**

   Gross Description: Received in formalin labeled with patient's name and "splenic flexure" is one fragment of tan tissue measuring .4 × .2 × .2 cm.

2. **Rectosigmoid: Tubular adenoma.**

   Gross Description: Received in formalin labeled with patient's name and "rectosigmoid" is one fragment of tan tissue measuring .3 × .2 × .2 cm.

MEADWAY MEDSURG CLINIC

Name: Kendall, Joann Date: 10/25/xx
Patient ID: KEN498 Insurance: Aetna

PREOPERATIVE and POSTOPERATIVE DIAGNOSIS: Mass of dorsum of right foot

FINDINGS AND INDICATIONS: This 41-year-old white female had a right foot progressively painful over the dorsum of the foot. It was at the Lisfranc area of the joint. She had had progressively enlarging mass. X-rays revealed an osteophyte. It was elected to proceed with excision.

At the time of surgery, there was a fairly large old ganglion cyst and underneath hypertrophic bone. The cyst was removed and hypertrophic bone shaved.

OPERATION: Excision of mass right foot (ganglion on top of osteophyte)

SURGEON: Thaddeus Morency, M.D.

PROCEDURE: The patient was taken to the operating room and after satisfactory ankle block anesthesia, the right leg was prepped and draped in sterile manner. It was wrapped up to the ankle in Esmarch and then Esmarch was wrapped around and tied for tourniquet. The left foot was then exposed and the toes covered with a glove and then a dorsal incision was made over the mass. The skin and subcutaneous tissue were carefully divided down looking for the neurovascular bundles. It appeared to be on the lateral side. This was dissected free and retracted lateral.

A fairly large ganglion cyst was circumferentially resected. It was then freed. A small stalk went down to an osteophyte. The ganglion was excised and then a rongeur used to remove the stalk. A fairly large osteophyte was also present centrally and then 1 more on the lateral side. This was removed with a rongeur.

Final inspection revealed no further prominence. Closure was effected with 4-0 nylon and a pressure dressing was applied. The patient had the tourniquet let down and was transported to recovery room in stable condition having tolerated the procedure well.

MEADWAY MEDSURG CLINIC

Name: Cabler, Mia Date: 10/10/xx
Patient ID: CAB973 Insurance: Flexi-Health PPO

PREOPERATIVE and POSTOPERATIVE DIAGNOSIS: Closed displaced right 2nd metacarpal neck fracture

OPERATION: Open reduction internal fixation right metacarpal neck fracture

SURGEON: Thaddeous Morency, M.D.

PROCEDURE: After informed consent was obtained, the patient was brought to the operating room via stretcher and placed supine on the operating table and underwent uneventful general anesthesia with endotracheal intubation. A gram of Ancef was given intravenously. A well padded tourniquet was placed on the right upper arm and the right upper extremity was prepped and draped in sterile orthopedic fashion. Attempts were initially made for closed reduction and pinning of the fracture. This was attempted multiple times from a retrograde and anagrade fashion without success. A 3-cm incision was then made directly over the metacarpal head and fracture. Sharp dissection was carried out through the skin and subcutaneous tissue. The extensor tendon was then identified and slid ulnarly. A rent was made in the capsule. The fracture was identified and reduced.

(Continued)

From a proximal to distal fashion, a 0.062 K-wire was introduced into the metacarpal shaft, across the fracture and into the metacarpal head. It was found to be stable. Under AP, lateral, and oblique image intensification, the hardware was in good position and not penetrating the joint. It was then cut beneath the skin. All open wounds were then irrigated. The 2 stab wounds that had been made prior were closed with interrupted 4-0 nylon. The rent in the capsule was closed with figure-of-eight -0-Vicryl and then the skin was closed with 4-0 nylon.

The patient was placed in a sterile dressing and a dorsal blocking splint. She was awakened, extubated and transported to recovery room in satisfactory condition. There were no operative or anesthetic complications. Sponge and needle counts were correct × 2.

MEADWAY MEDSURG CLINIC

Name: Frankie, Russell　　Date: 10/30/xx

Patient ID: FRA492　　Insurance: Medicare

PREOPERATIVE and POSTOPERATIVE DIAGNOSIS: Nuclear sclerotic cataract left eye

OPERATION: Extracapsular cataract extraction by phacoemulsification with posterior chamber intraocular lens implantation

SURGEON: Jeremy Moser, M.D.

PROCEDURE: Following pupillary dilatation and preoperative sedation, the patient was brought to the operating room where retrobulbar anesthesia and lid akinesia were obtained with local infiltration of 2% Xylocaine with Epinephrine, Wydase and sodium bicarbonate. The eye was then prepped and draped in the usual sterile manner. The operating microscope was brought into position and used throughout the balance of the procedure. A half thickness, arcuate limbal incision with a 3-mm arc length was created at the temporal limbus. Beginning at this point, a crescent knife was used to develop a lamellar intracorneal incision that extended well into clear cornea but did not enter the anterior chamber. Limbal paracenteses were placed above and below the corneal tunnel. A 22 gauge sharp disposable needle with a bent tip was placed on the irrigation handpiece. This was introduced into the anterior chamber through the paracentesis to the right of the corneal tunnel and used to create a continuous circular capsulorrhexis.

Hydrodissection was performed with balanced salt solution. Amvisc plus was instilled in the anterior chamber. A 2.75-mm keratome was then used to enter the anterior chamber at the inner limit of the corneal tunnel. Through this opening, the phacoemulsification handpiece was introduced and the lens nucleus was removed by grooving and cracking the nucleus into quadrants, which were then phacoemulsified sequentially.

The residual cortex was aspirated with the irrigation/aspiration handpiece. The posterior capsule was vacuumed. The capsular bag was inflated with intracameral Amvisc Plus. The inner opening of the corneal tunnel was extended to a full 3.5-mm with a short cut knife. An Alcon Acrysof model MA30BA, posterior chamber intraocular lens with a power of 22.0 diopters was inspected, irrigated, folded in half, introduced through the corneal incision. The leading haptic was placed in the capsular bag nasally and as the lens unfolded in the anterior chamber and the trailing haptic was introduced, the lens was placed in the capsular bag and the trailing haptic in the bag as well. The lens was rotated a full 90° and noted to be well centered in the capsular bag. The irrigation handpiece was reintroduced and used to remove the residual Amvisc plus. The anterior chamber was then reformed and the pupil constricted with intracameral Miochol. The wound was checked and noted to be watertight. The previously placed lid speculum was removed. Ciloxan ointment was instilled. The lid was closed, covered with an eye pad, moderate pressure dressing and Fox shield. Having tolerated the procedure well, the patient was returned to the recovery room in good condition.

MEADWAY MEDSURG CLINIC

Name: Farris, Emily
Date: 10/11/xx

Patient ID: FAR491
Insurance: Medicaid

PREOPERATIVE and POSTOPERATIVE DIAGNOSIS: Mild dysplasia with positive high risk HPV (human papilloma virus)

OPERATION: Loop electrosurgical excision procedure (LEEP)

SURGEON: Abbey Murphy, M.D.

PROCEDURE: After adequate general anesthesia the patient was placed in the dorsal lithotomy position, using candy cane stirrups. It was obvious when we put her up that she was having menstrual bleeding. I usually schedule these cases for a week after the period but the patient's mother was not even aware that Emily was on her period, so I put the speculum in and cleaned the cervix with vinegar. She had a small amount of central white epithelium. I injected the cervix with 4-cc of lidocaine with epinephrine and took the small, 1-cm loop and made one central pass which removed the transformation zone to a depth of 1-cm. The cone bed was then cauterized and then Monsel solution was applied. The procedure was terminated at this point. The plastic, coated speculum that had been placed at the beginning was removed. The patient went to the recovery room in good condition. Sponge, needle and instrument counts were correct × 2.

She was discharged home on Motrin 800 mg and Wygesic for pain and is to call for heavy bleeding. It will be a little more difficult to determine whether she is having postoperative bleeding because she is on her period but I told her mother to call for anything unusual, fever or pain out of the ordinary.

MEADWAY MEDSURG CLINIC

Name: Erickson, Nola
Date: 10/11/xx

Patient ID: ERI957
Insurance: Prudential

PREOPERATIVE DIAGNOSIS:

1. Chronic constipation
2. Change in bowel habits
3. Personal history of blood in stool

POSTOPERATIVE DIAGNOSIS:

1. Melanosis coli
2. Internal and external hemorrhoids

OPERATION: Complete colonoscopy with biopsy of right colon.

SURGEON: Raymond Ross, M.D.

PROCEDURE: The patient was taken to the endoscopy suite after administration of I.V sedation by the anesthesia department. The patient was positioned in the left lateral decubitus position. The flexible colonoscope was navigated through the anus, navigated to 155-cm, at which time the ileocecal valve was identified and verified by light verification and palpation of the right lower quadrant. Melanosis coli was noted throughout the colon with staining noted evident throughout from the rectum to the proximal right colon. A representative area was biopsied in the proximal right colon. No tumors, masses or polyps were seen. No diverticuli were seen. Small internal and external hemorrhoids were visualized at the outlet. The patient tolerated the procedure well and was sent to the post procedure area for further monitoring.

MEADWAY MEDSURG CLINIC

Name: Flannagan, Teagan | Date: 10/9/xx
Patient ID: FLA494 | Insurance: Cigna

PREOPERATIVE and POSTOPERATIVE DIAGNOSIS:

1. Visual field impairment
2. Blepharochalasia upper lid

OPERATION: Upper lid blepharoplasty

SURGEON: Jeremy Moser, M.D.

PROCEDURE: With the patient under suitable IV sedation, in the supine position on the operating table, a pattern with French curl was drawn on the patient's eyelids with lateral to medial distances from the lid-lash margin of 4-mm and 8-mm in the central portion on each side. Thereafter, local anesthetic was injected, a 50/50 solution of 1% Xylocaine plus 0.25% Marcaine, 1:200,000 Epinephrine. He was prepped with Shur-Clens solution and draped aseptically. Thereafter, excision of the excess skin on the right upper eyelid and left upper eyelid were undertaken. Removal of the medial and lateral fat pads of the upper lids was undertaken with cauterization of all vessels and bases of fat pads. His vision was not affected by this during the operation except to improve the visual fields from drooping lids. Repair was undertaken with 6-0 nylon. The patient tolerated the procedure well. He will be seen in 4 days for suture removal.

MEADWAY MEDSURG CLINIC

Name: Fisher, Miles | Date: 10/5/xx
Patient ID: FIS741 | Insurance: Medicaid

PREOPERATIVE DIAGNOSIS: Secretory otitis media/recurrent otitis media

POSTOPERATIVE DIAGNOSIS: Secretory otitis media/recurrent otitis media

PROCEDURE PERFORMED: Bilateral tympanostomies with insertion of ventilating tubes

SURGEON: Lee Hackney, M.D.

ANESTHESIA: General inhalation

PROCEDURE: Upon induction of satisfactory inhalational anesthesia, his left ear was examined microscopically. Examination revealed a wax impaction, which was removed without difficulty. Further examination revealed an otitis media. A posterior-inferior myringotomy incision was performed and his middle ear was aspirated until dry. A Soileau ventilating tube was inserted without difficulty. Examination of his right ear revealed a subtotal wax impaction, which was removed without difficulty. A posterior-inferior myringotomy incision was performed and his middle ear was aspirated until dry. A Soileau ventilating tube was inserted without difficulty. TobraDex drops were inserted in each of his ear canals and a plug of cotton applied to each meatus. He was then allowed to react and taken to the recovery room in satisfactory condition.

MEADWAY MEDSURG CLINIC

Name: Murray, Kyle
Date: 10/5/xx

Patient ID: MUR753
Insurance: Signal HMO

PREOPERATIVE DIAGNOSIS: Phimosis, Balanitis

POSTOPERATIVE DIAGNOSIS: Same

PROCEDURE: Circumcision

SURGEON: Gregory Wallace

PROCEDURE: After the induction of general anesthesia, this 25-year-old patient was prepped and draped in the supine position.

A straight hemostat was placed on the dorsal surface of the foreskin and left in place for fifteen seconds. This was removed and scissors were used to cut along this line. A straight hemostat was placed on the ventral surface of the foreskin and left in place for fifteen seconds. Scissors were used to cut along this line. The excess foreskin was excised in freehand fashion using curved scissors. Bleeding points were coagulated with electrocautery. The foreskin was reapproximated using interrupted sutures of 3-0 chromic. 0.5% Marcaine was then injected for postop local anesthesia. Vaseline and 4 × 4 dressings were applied.

The patient tolerated the procedure well and left the OR in satisfactory condition.

MEADWAY MEDSURG CLINIC

Name: Lloyd, Evan
Date: 10/7/xx

Patient ID: LLO951
Insurance: Great West

PREOPERATIVE DIAGNOSIS: Left spermatocele

POSTOPERATIVE DIAGNOSIS: Same

OPERATIVE PROCEDURE: Left spermatocelectomy

SURGEON: Gregory Wallace, M.D.

PROCEDURE: The patient was taken to the operating suite and positioned in the supine position with the shaved scrotum exposed. A mid-line incision was made and taken down to the dartos layer. The large multiloculated spermatocele was identified. It was approximately 7 cm in greatest diameter. We got down to the avascular layer, dissected free, and circumferentially down to its base arising from the upper end of the epididymis. At this point it was cross-clamped and dissected, thus removing the structure. We oversewed the stump with #3-0 Vicryl. Hemostasis was meticulously secured. The testicle was replaced within the right hemiscrotum. The dartos layer was closed with #3-0 Vicryl. The skin was closed with #4-0 chromic in a horizontal interrupted fashion. Spray Op-Site dressing was applied. Scrotal support was placed over a fluffed gauze dressing. He tolerated the procedure well.

DAY TWO

MEADWAY MEDSURG CLINIC

Name: Kirby, Logan
Date: 10/2/xx
Patient ID: KIR952
Insurance: BCBS

PREOPERATIVE and POSTOPERATIVE DIAGNOSIS: Carpal tunnel syndrome bilateral

SURGEON: Thaddeus Morency, M.D.

FINDINGS AND INDICATIONS: This is a 39-year-old white male with progressive numbness and pain, night pain, and difficulty sleeping. He had had a work up that showed carpal tunnel syndrome. He had enough symptoms that he wishes to proceed with release and it was elected to do so. At the time of surgery he was noted to have hyperemia of the nerve, narrowing of the carpal tunnel, but no boss or ganglion.

OPERATION: Left carpal tunnel release

PROCEDURE: The patient was taken into the operating room and after satisfactory double tourniquet block the left arm was prepped and draped in a sterile manner. The left arm was then positioned and carpal tunnel incision was made based on 4th ray and thenar crease. Skin and subcutaneous tissues were divided down. Hemostasis was obtained with electrocautery. The transverse carpal ligament was then divided under direct vision with a knife and a freer in the carpal tunnel to protect the nerve. Palpation revealed no ganglion or boss. Inspection revealed the motor branch to be intact. The nerve was noted to be a little hyperemic and narrow consistent with irritation.

Following this, the wound was irrigated and closed. 4-0 nylon was used for closure. A sterile splint was applied after infiltrating the wound with Marcaine. The patient was transported to recovery room in stable condition, having tolerated the procedure well.

MEADWAY MEDSURG CLINIC

Name: Fossell, Catrina
Date: 10/2/xx
Patient ID: FOS863
Insurance: Flexi-Health PPO

PREOPERATIVE and POSTOPERATIVE DIAGNOSIS:

1. Chronic pelvic pain
2. Severe dyspareunia
3. Severe dysmenorrhea
4. Menorrhagia

SURGEON: Abbey Murphy, M.D.

FINDINGS: 10 weeks size uterus with 8-cm simple appearing left ovarian cyst, completely obliterating the entire left ovary. Surgically ligated fallopian tubes bilaterally. The right ovary was grossly normal appearing as well as the appendix, gallbladder and liver. There were multiple endometrial implants along the left ovarian fossa and left pelvic sidewall and posterior cul-de-sac. There was a hypertrophic appearing endometrial lining with a uterine septum noted.

(Continued)

OPERATION:

1. Diagnostic laparoscopy with ablation of endometriosis
2. Left salpingo-oophorectomy
3. Hysteroscopy D&C (dilation and curettage)

PROCEDURE: The patient was brought to the operating room with I.V. fluids running and placed on the operating table in the supine position. After general anesthesia was assured, the patient was then placed in dorsal lithotomy position. Examination under anesthesia was performed determining size, position and mobility of the uterus, found to be freely mobile, anteflexed and 10 weeks size. The patient was then prepped and draped in the usual sterile fashion and a bivalve speculum was the placed in vaginal vault until the cervix was eased into view. The anterior lip of the cervix was grasped with a single toothed tenaculum and an acorn uterine manipulator was then placed. The bivalve speculum was removed. The Foley catheter was placed with yellow clear urine noted.

The inferior umbilical area was infiltrated with 0.25% Marcaine with epinephrine and an inferior vertical umbilical incision was made followed by the Veress needle with placement verified using both the hanging drop saline technique and aspiration. The abdomen was then insufflated with approximately 3 liters of CO_2 and once adequate pneumoperitoneum was assured, a 5-mm blunt tip step trocar was then placed followed by the laparoscope. A second and third 5-mm blunt tipped trocars were placed suprapubically and in the left lateral abdominal wall in a similar fashion except under direct laparoscopic visualization. The pelvic cavity was thoroughly explored with the above findings noted. Because there was no discernible, healthy, left ovarian tissue noted, the decision was made to proceed with a left salpingo-oophorectomy as the left fallopian tube had already been surgically ligated. Therefore using 2-0 PDS endoloops, the infundibulopelvic ligament was isolated, ligated with 2-0 PDS endoloops and the specimen was then freed and sent to pathology using an endocatch, through a 12-mm blunt tipped step trocar which had now been placed in the umbilical area. The remaining pedicle stump was noted to be hemostatic. Using the harmonic scalpel ball, the multiple endometrial implants were ablated with the implants along the left ovarian fossa excised and sent to pathology for further evaluation.

With no further pathology noted, this concluded the operation. The laparoscope, probe and trocars were removed after the abdomen was emptied of CO_2. Excellent hemostasis was noted prior to this. The incisions were closed using 4-0 Vicryl suture in a subcuticular fashion. Sterile dressings were applied.

Attention was taken to performing the hysteroscopic portion of the procedure in which the bivalve speculum was placed and the acorn uterine manipulator was then removed. The cervix was gently dilated with Hegar dilators and a 5-mm hysteroscope was introduced with the above findings noted. There was no evidence of intercavitary polyp or fibroid noted. Therefore, the hysteroscope was removed and the endometrial cavity was then gently curetted with a moderate amount of tissue obtained and sent to pathology for further evaluation.

MEADWAY MEDSURG CLINIC

Name: Foster, Lily — Date: 10/2/xx

Patient ID: FOS524 — Insurance: BCBS

PREOPERATIVE DIAGNOSIS: Left axillary abscess

POSTOPERATIVE DIAGNOSIS: Left axillary abscess

PROCEDURE: Incision and drainage of left axillary abscess

SURGEON: Raymond Ross, M.D.

DESCRIPTION OF PROCEDURE: The patient was placed supine on the operating table, with both arms abducted to 90 degrees. General anesthesia was induced. A laryngeal airway was introduced. The left breast and axilla were prepped and draped into the operative field. An incision was made overlying the area of fluctuation of the left axilla. An abscess cavity was entered which measured about 20 cc in size. This was evacuated. A Penrose drain was inserted which was sewn in place with silk. The wound was closed with interrupted silk. The wound was dressed with dry gauze. The patient was sent in stable condition to the recovery room.

MEADWAY MEDSURG CLINIC

Name: Hughes, Pamela — Date: 10/9/xx

Patient ID: HUG329 — Insurance: Great West

PREOPERATIVE and POSTOPERATIVE DIAGNOSIS: Symptomatic cholelithiasis

OPERATION: Laparoscopic cholecystectomy with intraoperative cholangiogram

SURGEON: Raymond Ross, M.D.

PROCEDURE: The patient was taken to the operating room and after adequate induction of general endotracheal anesthesia, the patient was prepped and draped in the usual sterile manner. Then using a supraumbilical skin incision carried down through the dermis and subcutaneous tissue, linea alba was identified and opened sharply with care not to injure underlying organs. At this time the Hasson cannula was placed and secured u sing -1- Vicryl suture followed by insufflation of the abdomen to 12–17mmHg using carbon dioxide. At this point the abdominal cavity was scanned and no evidence of any obvious tumors or masses were seen. No obvious hernias were seen. At this point the trocars were placed under direct visualization to assure no injury to underlying organs. The gallbladder was grasped and positioned such that the cystic duct and cystic artery could be dissected free. The cystic duct was endoclipped twice well upon the neck of the gallbladder. The cystic artery was endoclipped twice proximally and once distally. A small opening was made in the cystic duct and the cholangiogram was fed through a 14 gauge angiocath into the right upper quadrant and into the cystic duct. Cholangiogram was obtained, which revealed the following: free flow in the duodenum, no intraluminal filling defect, normal size common bile duct, normal intrahepatic radicle. At this point the cystic duct catheter was removed, the cystic duct was endoclipped twice proximally and once distally and then divided. The cystic artery which had been previously endoclipped, was divided. The gallbladder was dissected free from the gallbladder bed and removed intact through the supraumbilical fascial defect.

The abdominal cavity was reinsufflated and irrigated with copious amounts of saline solution and one gram of Ancef and 8,000 units of heparin per liter and suctioned dry. There was no evidence of any bleeding or bile leakage. The clips were in good position.

Trocars were then removed under direct visualization to assure adequate hemostasis at the trocar sites. The supraumbilical fascia defects were approximated using a –1- Vicryl suture followed by approximation of the skin edges using skin clips. The patient tolerated the procedure well and was sent to the recovery room in satisfactory condition. All counts were correct.

MEADWAY MEDSURG CLINIC

Name: Holladay, Brad
Date: 10/2/xx
Patient ID: HOL624
Insurance: Medicare, BCBS

PREOPERATIVE DIAGNOSIS: Urinary frequency, abnormal PSA

POSTOPERATIVE DIAGNOSIS: Same

PROCEDURE: Transrectal ultrasound of the prostate and ultrasound guided prostate biopsies

SURGEON: Gregory Wallace, M.D.

ANESTHESIA: Local

INDICATIONS: This is a 67-year-old man with an abnormal PSA of 6.4. His prostate gland is enlarged but smooth.

PROCEDURE: Prostate ultrasound images were obtained in the transverse and longitudinal planes. Total gland volume was 108 cc with a gland length of 65.7 mm. The prostate capsule appears intact. The seminal vesicles are enlarged but symmetric. In the central gland, a large amount of hypertrophy is noted. In the peripheral zone, several small hypoechoic areas are seen. After injection of 10 cc of 1% Lidocaine through a spinal needle to the angle of seminal vesicles, seven biopsies were taken from each lobe of the prostate. The patient tolerated the procedure well and was returned to the dressing area in stable condition.

PATHOLOGY REPORT:

All biopsies consistent with benign prostatic hyperplasia.

MEADWAY MEDSURG CLINIC

Name: Roberts, Michael
Date: 10/9/xx
Patient ID: ROB664
Insurance: Medicare

PREOPERATIVE DIAGNOSIS: Right knee medial meniscal tear

POSTOPERATIVE DIAGNOSIS: Right knee grade III chondral defect in the medial femoral condyle

PROCEDURE:

1. Right knee arthroscopy and limited synovectomy.
2. Abrasion chondroplasty of medial femoral condyle defect. Defect size is 4-mm in diameter and 8-mm in length.
3. Grade II chondrosis of the medial patellar facet.

SURGEON: Thaddeus Morency, M.D.

ARTHROSCOPIC FINDINGS: He has a grade III chondral fissure that is about 3–4 mm in diameter and 6–10 mm in overall length. It is in the extension zone of the medial aspect of the medial femoral condyle. He also has grade II chondrosis of the medial patellar facet. The remaining aspects of the knee are normal.

(Continued)

PROCEDURE: Patient was brought to the operative suite after the right lower extremity was properly marked in the preoperative holding area. He was provided with IV antibiotics for prophylactic antibiotic coverage. After being brought to the operative suite where adequate anesthesia was performed, the right lower extremity was prepped using DuraPrep and Hibiclens and then draped in the usual sterile manner. Standard inferior medial and inferior lateral portals into the knee were made. A 30-degree arthroscope was introduced into the knee. The knee was filled with sterile saline. Systematic evaluation of the knee was performed with the findings as mentioned above.

I used a motorized shaver to perform a limited synovectomy and then I used the shaver to debride some of the periphery of the grade III lesion. There was no grade IV damage, and therefore no microfracture was performed. The arthroscope was then removed. Each portal was closed and the knee was then sterilely dressed and the patient was awakened and taken to the recovery room having tolerated the procedure without episode.

MEADWAY MEDSURG CLINIC

Name: Howard, Bruce — Date: 10/2/xx

Patient ID: HOW486 — Insurance: Great West

PREOPERATIVE DIAGNOSIS: Right ureteral calculus

POSTOPERATIVE DIAGNOSIS: Right ureteral calculus

OPERATION: ESWL

SURGEON: Gregory Wallace, M.D.

INDICATIONS FOR OPERATION: The patient has had continuous right renal colic. X-rays revealed a 9-mm calculus which was in the proximal ureter two weeks ago. The patient has continued to have colic and recent x-rays show no progression of the stone. He was scheduled for ESWL.

DESCRIPTION OF OPERATION:

After fluoroscopy was performed and the stone was identified over the sacrum, the patient was induced and maintained on anesthesia and LMA. The stone was visualized in two planes and then subjected to 1900 shocks. The intensity was raised to a maximum of 6 within the first 120 shocks and the patient tolerated this very well. No EKG changes. Frequency was left at 100 shocks per minute. At the end of 1800 shocks, there was no calcific density remaining so the procedure was terminated. The patient was then awakened, extubated and sent to the recovery room in good condition.

MEADWAY MEDSURG CLINIC

Name: Edwards, Dana Date: 10/2/xx

Patient ID: EDW753 Insurance: Self pay

PREOPERATIVE DIAGNOSIS: Bilateral hypomastia

POSTOPERATIVE DIAGNOSIS: Bilateral hypomastia

PROCEDURE PERFORMED: Bilateral breast augmentation

SURGEON: Robyn Houser, M.D.

INDICATIONS FOR PROCEDURE: The patient is a pleasant 34-year-old white female who presents with breast hypoplasia. The patient is seeking to increase her breast size to a size and shape that she feels is appropriate for her body frame. The patient and I discussed breast augmentation, the risks and complications at length and at the completion of discussion she has elected to proceed at this time.

PROCEDURE: After obtaining properly informed consent, the patient was marked in the holding area in the sitting position and then transported the operative suite and positioned upon the OR table in the supine position. After satisfactory attainment of general endotracheal anesthesia, the patient was prepped and draped in the usual manner. I proceeded at this time to make an incision on the right breast from 3 o'clock to 9 o'clock along the inferior border of the nipple areolar complex, dissected through the subcutaneous tissues and identified the lateral border of the pectoralis major muscle. I elevated the pectoralis major muscle and then proceeded to divide its insertions from the third intercostal space inferiorly and then laterally. I then proceeded at this time to irrigate the pocket copiously with saline and placed into the pocket a sizer. The sizer was inflated to 375 cc of volume. I then turned my attention toward the opposite left breast and a mirror image procedure was performed. I removed the sizers and irrigated the pocket with normal saline and bacitracin containing solutions. I then proceeded to place the Mentor style 68 implants into position inflated to 375 cc. The patient was brought to the sitting position. Corrections were made for the patient's breast asymmetries and another 20 cc was inflated in the right breast and correction for the higher inframammary crease on the right side, which was lowered. I then proceeded at this time to identify excellent symmetry. The patient was returned to the supine position. The fill valves were removed and sealed. 3-0 Vicryl was used deep suture, 4-0 Monocryl and 5-0 Monocryl sutures. One half-inch steri-strips were applied.

MEADWAY MEDSURG CLINIC

Name: Radcliff, Leslie
Date: 10/2/xx
Patient ID: RAD365
Insurance: Signal HMO

PREOPERATIVE DIAGNOSIS: Desired sterilization

POSTOPERATIVE DIAGNOSIS: Desired sterilization

PROCEDURE PERFORMED: Laparoscopic bilateral tubal ligation with Falope-Rings

SURGEON: Abbey Murphy, M.D.

PROCEDURE: The patient was transferred to the operating room with IV fluids infusing and placed on the operating room table in the dorsal supine position. After induction of general anesthesia she was placed in the dorsal lithotomy position with the Allen stirrups. At this time she was prepped and draped in the usual sterile fashion. A bivalve speculum was used and the cervix was visualized. A tenaculum was placed on the posterior aspect of the cervix and a Hulka uterine manipulator was placed in the uterus through the cervical canal to further manipulate the uterus. The bladder was drained of approximately 10 cc of clear yellow urine. Next attention was turned toward the abdominal portion of the procedure. An infraumbilical incision was made with a scalpel and a Veress needle was placed through this port without difficulty. Aspiration and saline drop technique were all appropriately normal and after the abdomen was insufflated with approximately 4 liters of CO_2 gas the Veress needle was removed with an opening pressure of 2 mmHg and a final pressure of 15 mmHg. The Veress needle was removed and a 5 mm disposable trocar was placed without incident. The camera was placed through this port and visualization of the anatomy below showed no evidence of bleeding or injury. The patient was placed in Trendelenburg and a 7–8 mm trocar was placed after a skin incision was made in the suprapubic region. This was done under direct laparoscopic visualization. With this in mind the Falope-ring applicator was loaded and visualization of the pelvic contents was made. The right fallopian tube was grasped with the Falope-ring applicator. The tube was followed out from its proximal origin from the uterus to its fimbriated end to make sure we had appropriate anatomical structure and a Falope-ring was applied to the right tube. On the left, the tube was flimsy and degenerated not amenable to clipping. The tube was removed in toto. There was no evidence of other pelvic abnormalities. The pneumoperitoneum was reduced, the trocars were removed and the incisions were closed using 4-0 Vicryl placing a deep stitch subcutaneously and closing the skin edges subcuticularly with 4-0 Vicryl.

MEADWAY MEDSURG CLINIC

Name: Houston, Grayson
Date: 10/8/xx
Patient ID: HOU123
Insurance: Manage Med

PREOPERATIVE DIAGNOSIS: Soft tissue mass left upper back

POSTOPERATIVE DIAGNOSIS: Sebaceous cyst

OPERATION: Excision of the sebaceous cyst with local tissue rearrangement

SURGEON: Robyn Houser, M.D.

PROCEDURE: After intravenous antibiotics and sedation, the patient was prepped and draped in the dorsal supine position. General anesthesia with an endotracheal tube was administered. An incision was made over the cyst retaining some skin attached to it. Dissection was carried around the cyst staying very carefully on the wall of the cyst. I removed the entire cyst in one piece creating an 8 cm defect. This was sent for permanent pathology. Electrocautery was then used for hemostasis. Site was irrigated with antibiotic solution It was closed in layers with #4-0 Monocryl and #6-0 nylon. The patient tolerated the procedure well. A bulky dressing and Bacitracin were applied to the wound.

MEADWAY MEDSURG CLINIC

Name: Miler, Shelby — Date: 10/30/xx

Patient ID: MIL483 — Insurance: Medicare

PREOPERATIVE DIAGNOSIS: Right inguinal hernia, recurrent

POSTOPERATIVE DIAGNOSIS: Right inguinal hernia, recurrent

PROCEDURE PERFORMED: Right inguinal hernia repair

ANESTHESIA: Local with IV sedation

SURGEON: Raymond Ross, M.D.

FINDINGS: The patient had a small right indirect inguinal hernia. The patient also had diffuse bulging of the muscular tissues superior to the inguinal canal.

PROCEDURE: With the patient in the supine position he was sedated. A sterile preparation of his abdomen and genitalia was done with Betadine. Drapes were applied in the usual manner. Local infiltration with Lidocaine and 0.50% Marcaine containing epinephrine was carried out as in the right inguinal area. Skin crease incision was deepened through the subcutaneous tissues until the external oblique aponeurosis of the external oblique muscle was reached. This was opened in the direction of its fibers down to and through the superficial inguinal ring identifying, exposing and protecting the ilioinguinal nerve.

The spermatic cord was then dissected off its bed at the level of the pubic tubercle and suspended on a Penrose drain. The cord was explored and a large direct inguinal hernia found. This was separated from the vital elements of the cord and reduced. A highly modified small PerFix plug was inverted into the field and inserted through the deep inguinal ring and fixed to the floor of the inguinal canal with vicryl. He was asked to cough and strain and he did so cooperatively. He demonstrated a competent hernia repair. The spermatic cord was then reduced onto its new bed in the external oblique aponeurosis, closed there over with interrupted 3-0 PDS. Scarpa's fascia was closed the same way and the skin closed with a continuous transcuticular 4-0 Prolene. Steri-Strips and a sterile dressing were applied.

MEADWAY MEDSURG CLINIC

Name: Mueller, Tony — Date: 11/2/xx

Patient ID: MUE931 — Insurance: Manage Med

PREOPERATIVE DIAGNOSIS: Bladder cancer

POSTOPERATIVE DIAGNOSIS: Same

SURGEON: Gregory Wallace, M.D.

PROCEDURE: Cystoscopy with bladder biopsies and fulguration

INDICATIONS: The patient is a 53-year-old male with a past history of superficial bladder cancer. Cystoscopy at annual follow up recently has revealed irregular mucosa at the dome of his bladder. He now presents for bladder biopsies and fulguration.

FINDINGS: On rectal examination, the prostate gland is 35 grams, smooth and firm and there are no rectal masses. At cystoscopy, the urethra appears normal. The prostatic fossa has some moderate obstruction. The bladder itself contains no foreign bodies or stones. The ureteral orifices are normal in size, shape and position. At the left dome of the bladder, and along the left bladder wall, two separate areas were identified with irregular mucosa each measuring 0.4 cm. Bladder biopsies

(Continued)

were taken and these areas were fulgurated. The patient will return to see me with within one to three weeks in the office to discuss the pathology results.

DESCRIPTION OF PROCEDURE: The patient was brought to the Operating Room where he was given general anesthetic. Next, he was prepped and draped in the sterile fashion in the lithotomy position. Rectal examination had been performed. A #21 French panendoscope was then introduced into the bladder and the findings as above. A thorough examination was made and then bladder biopsies performed. The Bugbee electrode was used to cauterize the biopsy areas. Finally, the bladder was emptied and the scope removed.

PATHOLOGY REPORT:

Transitional cell carcinoma of the bladder

MEADWAY MEDSURG CLINIC

Name: Martin, Tony — Date: 11/2/xx

Patient ID: MAR445 — Insurance: BCBS

PREOPERATIVE DIAGNOSIS: Right neck mass, rule out Hodgkin's disease

POSTOP DIAGNOSIS: Same

PROCEDURE: Excisional biopsy right cervical nodes

SURGEON: Raymond Ross, M.D.

ANESTHESIA: General

INDICATIONS: He is a 55-year-old who has a cluster of nodes on the right side of his neck. They appeared after a long bout with the flu. Fine needle aspiration is suggestive of Hodgkin's disease.

PROCEDURE: Following intubation and orotracheal anesthesia, the table was turned. A shoulder roll was placed into the right shoulder the area was prepped with pHisoHex drapes and 1% Xylocaine with epinephrine was infiltrated into the subcutaneous tissue. A 3 cm incision was carried out along the favorable skin tension line on the right lateral neck. This was 1–2 finger breadths below the inferior angle of the mandible. Dissection was carried down in to the subcutaneous fat. This was in the area of the spinal accessory nerve. Care was taken to watch for any adverse motion and to gently dissect in the area primarily bluntly. The mass was actually behind and deep to the sternocleidomastoid muscle posteriorly. There was a cluster of nodes. A 1.5 cm noted was removed piecemeal through the incision. This was sent for lymphoma protocol fresh to pathology. The wound was inspected and one small vessel was cauterized. The wound was closed in multiple layers using 4-0 Vicryl deep and then interrupted 5-0 Prolene was used to approximate the skin. The area was dressed with Bacitracin and a Band-Aid.

NEW AGE PATHOLOGY

Name: Martin, Tony — Date: 11/2/xx

Patient ID: MAR445

SURGEON: Ross, Raymond M.D.

DIAGNOSIS:

Lymph node, right neck: Hodgkin's lymphoma, mixed cellularity subtype

Mark Pavlov, M.D.
Pathologist

MEADWAY MEDSURG CLINIC

Name: Marshall, Toby | Date: 11/2/xx

Patient ID: MAR656 | Insurance: Flexi-Health PPO

PRE-OP DIAGNOSIS: Abdominal left testis

POST-OP DIAGNOSIS: Same

OPERATION: Second stage laparoscopic assisted left orchidopexy on vas

SURGEON: Gregory Wallace, M.D.

INDICATIONS: He was noted to have unpalpable left undescended testis at age 1½. He had a laparoscopy on 5/31/xx where he was found to have an abdominal testis. A first stage left orchidopexy on vas deferen was performed. He now returns for the second stage.

PROCEDURE: The patient was placed in the supine position. The three previous puncture sites were utilized. The abdomen was filled with CO_2 using the Veress needle. 5 mm step trocars were introduced. A 4-cm lens was utilized. The testis was located just inside the internal ring. The spermatic vessels were first freed by sharp scissor dissection. Hemostatis was secured throughout by means of electrocoagulation using the surgical diathermy at 15 for coagulation. The vas was freed medially. A small transverse incision was made in the mid portion of the scrotum. A subdartos pouch was created by blunt dissection. A Schnidt clamp was passed into the abdomen and the testicle was grasped and pulled down to the scrotum and anchored in place with two sutures. The scrotum was then closed with running suture of 5-0 Monocryl. The CO_2 was removed and the abdominal punctures were closed with one suture of Monocryl each.

MEADWAY MEDSURG CLINIC

Name: Murphy, Tamara | Date: 11/2/xx

Patient ID: MUR774 | Insurance: BCBS

PREOP DIAGNOSIS: Recurring acute adenotonsillitis

POSTOP DIAGNOSIS: Same

SURGEON: Lee Hackney, M.D.

OPERATION: Tonsillectomy

INDICATIONS: 12-year-old Tamara has had intermittent episodes of adenotonsillitis over the last 18 months. She has missed several days of school and her parents want to proceed with the surgery.

PROCEDURE: Under general anesthesia, the tongue depressor was inserted into the mouth. The tonsils were 3+ size. The nasopharyngeal area was examined and the adenoids were not enlarged at this time. The left tonsil was grasped with a tonsil forceps. Incision was made with a knifeblade through the anterior posterior tonsillar pillar. The superior portion of the tonsil was resected by blunt dissection. The wire snare was placed over the tonsil and tugged down. The same exact procedure was carried out on the right side. Once both tonsils were removed, the areas were carefully examined and no bleeding was noted.

MEADWAY MEDSURG CLINIC

Name: Spenser, Ruth Date: 11/2/xx

Patient ID: SPE336 Insurance: Manage Med

PREOP DIAGNOSIS: Right nasal polyp

POSTOP DIAGNOSIS: Probable nasal fibrogranuloma

OPERATION: Excision right nasal polyp with cautery

SURGEON: Lee Hackney, M.D.

INDICATIONS: She has a large friable polyp in the right nasal cavity causing some bleeding and obstruction.

PROCEDURE: The nose was cleansed and draped. IV conscious sedation was administered. The nose was anesthetized with 1.5 cc 4% cocaine and 1% Xylocaine with epinephrine. There was a large lesion with a very small pedicle attached to the medial surface of the anterior inferior turbinate. The lesion was removed with cutting forceps. The base was cauterized and the nose was patent at the end of the case. Specimen was sent to pathology for analysis.

NEW AGE PATHOLOGY

Name: Spenser, Ruth Date: 11/2/xx

Patient ID: SPE336

SURGEON: Lee Hackney, M.D.

DIAGNOSIS: Benign Polypoid granulation tissue

Nasal polyp is 1.5 × 1 × .5 cm somewhat fleshy appearing polypoid portion of whitish tissue having a more hemorrhagic cross section.

Mark Pavlov, M.D.
Pathologist

DAY THREE

MEADWAY MEDSURG CLINIC

Name: Williams, Roger Date: 10/30/xx

Patient ID: WIL789 Insurance: Manage Med

PREOP DIAGNOSIS: Axillary mass. History of lymphocytic nodular lymphoma of neck. Excised five years ago and in remission.

POST OP DIAGNOSIS: Rule out lymphoma.

OPERATION: Excision axillary mass.

SURGEON: Raymond Ross, M.D.

PROCEDURE: The patient was prepped and draped in sterile fashion. An incision was made through the skin overlying the axillary lymph node. Dissection is carried out and bleeding controlled with electrocautery. The deep axillary node is located and excised and sent to pathology. Layered closure is accomplished.

NEW AGE PATHOLOGY

Name: Williams, Roger Date: 10/30/xx

Patient ID: WIL789

SURGEON: Raymond Ross, M.D.

DIAGNOSIS: Well-differentiated nodular lymphocytic lymphoma

Node is 2.5 × 1 × 1 .5 cm somewhat fleshy appearing portion of whitish/necrotic tissue.

Mark Pavlov, M.D.
Pathologist

MEADWAY MEDSURG CLINIC

Name: Watkins, Mary — Date: 11/2/xx

Patient ID: WAT558 — Insurance: Great West

PREOP DIAGNOSIS: Umbilical hernia

POSTOP DIAGNOSIS: Same

OPERATION: Repair umbilical hernia

SURGEON: Raymond Ross, M.D.

PROCEDURE: Patient is taken to the operating room and placed in the supine position. MAC anesthesia was initiated. Abdomen is prepped and draped in the usual fashion. Local anesthetic was injected around the umbilicus. A linear incision was made across the base of the umbilicus and blunt dissection was carried down through the subcutaneous fat. The borders of the hernia were sharply and bluntly dissected. The fascia was then re-approximated with 0-Vicryl. The skin was closed with 4-0 Vicryl.

MEADWAY MEDSURG CLINIC

Name: Sheldon, Zachary — Date: 11/2/xx

Patient ID: SHE 902 — Insurance: Medicare

PREOPERATIVE DIAGNOSIS: Family history of colon cancer and colon polyps

POSTOPERATIVE DIAGNOSIS: Rectal polyp

PROCEDURE: Complete colonoscopy with intubation of terminal ileum and hot biopsy cautery polypectomy technique of rectal polyp

SURGEON: Raymond Ross, M.D.

INDICATIONS: Zachary is a 64-year-old man whose grandfather, in his late sixties, had colon cancer. He has had no change in bowel habits, rectal bleeding, abdominal pain, weight loss or anemia. The signs and symptoms of colorectal cancer as well as the various screening guidelines and tests were explained to the patient. It was recommended that he undergo a screening colonoscopy. After a thorough explanation of the procedure, alternatives, outcomes, associated risks and possible complications, he consented to proceed. He underwent an Osma prep tablet bowel preparation.

PROCEDURE: He was taken to the endoscopy suite and placed in the left lateral decubitus position and with supplemental oxygen and appropriate monitoring was slowly titrated with the intravenous sedation. Digital rectal examination was performed. The anal sphincter tone was normal. No masses were palpable. The prostate was of normal size and without nodularity. The Olympus video colonoscope was inserted into the rectum and passed through the entire colon to the base of the cecum as evidenced by visualization of the ileocecal valve, appendiceal orifice and triangulation of the colonic haustra. Photo documentation was obtained. The bowel preparation

(Continued)

was excellent. The scope was then advanced through the ileocecal valve into the terminal ileum where it was slowly withdrawn and the findings were as follows:

FINDINGS:

1. Terminal ileum–normal. No evidence of inflammatory bowel disease.
2. Cecum–normal.
3. Ascending colon–normal.
4. Transverse colon–normal.
5. Descending colon–normal.
6. Sigmoid colon–normal.
7. Rectum–Including the retroflexed view of the anal canal–a 5 to 6-mm sessile polyp was present in the mid-to-distal rectum. This was completely removed by hot biopsy cautery polypectomy technique. The tissue was retrieved and sent to pathology. Internal hemorrhoids were moderate in size.

Final Diagnosis:

1. Mid-to-distal rectal polyp—removed by hot biopsy cautery polypectomy technique.
2. Family history of colon cancer and colon polyps, with no evidence of blood, cancer, inflammation of diverticular disease.
3. Moderate size internal hemorrhoids.
4. Normal prostate.

MEADWAY MEDSURG CLINIC

Name: Wilson, Tammy — Date: 11/1/xx

Patient ID: WIL902 — Insurance: Humana

PREOP DIAGNOSIS: Breast masses

POSTOP DIAGNOSIS: Fibrocystic cyst, right; intraductal carcinoma, left

OPERATION: Excisional breast biopsies, bilateral

SURGEON: Raymond Ross, M.D.

This is a 64-year-old patient who was seen in mammography two weeks ago and was noted to have an abnormality. Patient has had a lump in the upper outer quadrant of the right breast but the abnormality was noted on the left breast. Radiologist referred this patient to me for biopsy.

Patient was prepped and draped for bilateral breast biopsy. Excisional biopsy is performed on the right without difficulty. Lesion appeared benign but was sent to pathology for analysis. Wound was closed with running chromic suture. A previously placed radiologic marker was identified in the left breast. Excision was carried out. Specimen was sent to pathology for frozen section. Frozen section confirmed the lesion to be intraductal carcinoma. Decision was made to proceed with lumpectomy. A second frozen section was submitted and margins were clean. No further dissection was required. The wound was closed with 4-0 Vicryl.

MEADWAY MEDSURG CLINIC

Name: Walker, Rick
Date: 11/2/xx
Patient ID: WAL964
Insurance: Aetna
PREOP DIAGNOSIS: Lung mass
POSTOP DIAGNOSIS: Lung mass, left upper lung
OPERATION: Bronchoscopy with biopsy
SURGEON: Raymond Ross, M.D.

Patient is a 59-year-old male with lung mass noted on prior x-ray. Patient is a long-time smoker of 30 years. He is here today for outpatient diagnostic bronchoscopy. After adequate MAC anesthesia, a fiberoptic bronchoscope was introduced into the bronchial tree. A needle is advanced through a channel in the scope under fluoroscopic guidance and tissue is aspirated from the upper lobe mass for pathologic evaluation. There were no complications and the patient was transferred to the recovery area.

NEW AGE PATHOLOGY

Name: Walker, Rick
Date: 11/2/xx
Patient ID: WAL964
SURGEON: Raymond Ross, M.D.
DIAGNOSIS: Oat cell carcinoma

Mark Pavlov, M.D.
Pathologist

MEADWAY MEDSURG CLINIC

Name: Barth, Joyce
Date: 11/3/xx
Patient ID: BAR252
Insurance: Medicare
PREOPERATIVE DIAGNOSIS: Cataract, right eye
POSTOPERATIVE DIAGNOSIS: Cataract, right eye
OPERATIVE PROCEDURE: Right eye phacoemulsification and cataract extraction with intraocular lens implant, model SN60WF power of 20.0 diopters
SURGEON: Jeremy Moser, M.D.

PROCEDURE DESCRIPTION: The patient was brought into the operating room. A 2% lidocaine gel was instilled into the conjunctival sac. Tetracaine drops were instilled into the conjunctival sac. The patient was then prepped and draped in the sterile fashion. A lid speculum was placed in the eye. The anesthesiologist was monitoring the patient and sedating her as necessary for relaxation. A peritomy was performed with Westcott scissors. Wet-field cautery was used for hemostasis on the scleral bed. A partial-thickness scleral groove was created 3 mm in length and 1 mm from the limbus. Through the scleral groove, the scleral tunnel was dissected into clear cornea. The anterior chamber was entered with a 3.0 mm keratome. Viscoelastic was used to fill the anterior chamber.

(Continued)

A capsulorrhexis was then performed with a cystotome. Balanced salt solution was used to hydrodissect the nucleus. A 15-degree blade was used to create a side-port paracentesis in the 2 o'clock meridian. The phacoemulsification unit was then used to emulsify the nucleus in a circular fashion. The remaining cortical material was aspirated with the I&A handpiece. Viscoelastic was used to fill the anterior chamber. A posterior chamber lens model SN60WF power of 20.0 diopters was then inserted into the capsular bag, centered into place with a Sinskey hook. The I&A handpiece was used to remove any remaining viscoelastic from the anterior chamber. Miochol solution was used to fill the anterior chamber. Scleral tunnel incision was found to be intact without leaking. Wet-field cautery was used to reapproximate the conjunctiva at the limbus and a subconjunctival injection of Decadron and Ancef was given in the inferior fornix. A patch and shield was placed in the eye and the patient left the operating room in good condition.

MEADWAY MEDSURG CLINIC

Name: Marlow, Jake — Date: 11/3/xx

Patient ID: MAR761 — Insurance: Cigna

PREOPERATIVE DIAGNOSIS: Right hand, radial volar ganglion cyst

POSTOPERATIVE DIAGNOSIS: Right hand, radial volar ganglion cyst specimen sent

OPERATIVE PROCEDURE: Excision of right volar ganglion cyst, radial side

ANESTHESIA: General, LMA, and 1 g Ancef given IV piggyback preoperatively

SURGEON: Tad Morency, M.D.

COMPLICATIONS: None

TOURNIQUET TIME: 40 minutes

INDICATIONS: He is a 29-year-old gentleman with a work-related injury to the right wrist. He had a painful right volar ganglion cyst, which continued to increase in size, giving him pain and some numbness and tingling in the thumb and index finger. The patient would like to have surgical treatment and understands the risks and benefits of the procedure including the possibility of death associated with general endotracheal anesthesia. Damaged nerves and vessels, specifically nerve about the radial superficial versus median branch, especially damaged nerves and vessels, radial artery and vein. The patient would like to go with the operative procedure.

PROCEDURE DESCRIPTION: He was cleared preoperatively and brought to the operating room on 01/15/2008. Following adequate general anesthesia LMA, the right upper extremity was prepped and draped in the usual fashion. Preoperatively, the Ancef 1 g IV piggyback was administered. The right upper extremity was prepped and draped in the usual fashion with placement of tourniquet well-padded in the right proximal arm. The right upper extremity was exsanguinated. The tourniquet was insufflated to 250 mmHg for a total of 40 minutes. Longitudinal incision centered over the ganglion cyst over the area of the radial artery was performed. Care was taken to dissect the ganglion cyst just radial to it, where the sensory nerve as well as artery and vein, which were enveloped around and care was taken to not injure these and to non-traumatically retract them radially. The sac of the 2 cm × 2 cm ganglion cyst went all the way down through the volar radiocarpal ligament to the radioscaphoid joint. No bony spicule was appreciated on palpation. Thorough irrigation was performed. The sac and its clear contents were sent for pathology evaluation.

The subcutaneous tissue was closed with #4-0 Vicryl suture subcutaneously, closed by alternating simple and vertical mattress sutures with #3-0 monofilament nylon suture. Nonadherent gauze followed by sterile 4 × 4s, fluffs between each fingers with an Ace wrap was placed. The patient was extubated and brought to the recovery room in stable condition.

MEADWAY MEDSURG CLINIC

Name: Balog, Lily
Date: 11/3/xx

Patient ID: BAL339
Insurance: Aetna

PREOPERATIVE DIAGNOSIS:
1. Lumbar spondylosis
2. Cervical spondylosis

POSTOPERATIVE DIAGNOSIS:
1. Lumbar spondylosis
2. Cervical spondylosis

OPERATIVE PROCEDURE:
1. Bilateral L4-L5, L5-S1 facet joint injection under fluoroscopy
2. Bilateral C5-C6 medial branch block under fluoroscopy

ANESTHESIA: MAC

SURGEON: Thaddeus Morency, M.D.

INDICATIONS: Ms. Balog has chronic neck and back pain, facet loading is positive at both levels, so we decided to do this procedure. The procedure was explained to the patient with advantages, disadvantages, complications, and alternatives. She accepted to undergo the procedure. An informed consent was obtained.

PROCEDURE DESCRIPTION: The patient was taken to the procedure room. She was put in prone position on the table. Skin was prepped with Betadine × 3. She was draped in sterile fashion. Under fluoroscopy left oblique view of lumbar spine, left L4-L5 and L5-S1 facet joints were identified. Corresponding skin incision sites were marked. A 0.5 inch long 22-gauge spinal needle was inserted and under standard fluoroscopy guidance to enter the lower part of the facet joint. After negative aspiration, 1 cc of solution was injected in each joint, which was made by 40 mg of Depo-Medrol and 8 cc of 0.5% Marcaine. Similar procedure was carried out on the right side at similar two levels under right oblique view without any difficulty. The fluoroscope was then put to AP on the neck at C5-C6 levels on both sides. The lateral masses with her necks were identified. Corresponding skin incision sites were marked to reach 5 mm medial to the neck. Then, 3.5 inch long 22-gauge spinal needle was inserted and under standard fluoroscopy guidance to reach the periosteum 5 mm medial to the neck. After negative aspiration, 0.5 cc of solution was injected at each level. Similar procedure was done on both sides. Then skin was cleaned. Band-Aids were applied.

The patient tolerated the procedure well. She did not complain of any paresthesia after the procedure. She was kept in the recovery area in stable condition.

MEADWAY MEDSURG CLINIC

Name: Butler, Mark | Date: 11/3/xx

Patient ID: BUT554 | Insurance: United Health Care

PREOPERATIVE DIAGNOSIS: Heel spur, left foot

POSTOPERATIVE DIAGNOSIS: Heel spur, left foot

PROCEDURE: Endoscopic plantar fasciotomy, left foot

SURGEON: Thaddeus Morency, M.D.

CHIEF COMPLAINT AND HISTORY OF PRESENT ILLNESS: The patient presents with a painful heel spur of the left foot that has been symptomatic for approximately six months duration. She relates pain in the morning with initial weight bearing or after rest. The pain does diminish with ambulation. Previous conservative treatment has consisted of cortisone injections, orthotics, physical therapy and NSAID, which have yielded unsatisfactory results. The patient desires surgical correction of the deformity at this time. The patient does have medical history of asthma, varicose veins and chronic anemia.

PROCEDURE: The patient was brought to the operative suite and placed on the operating room table in the supine position. An IV was started and anesthesia was administered. The patient was given 1 gram of Ancef one-half hour prior to surgery. The left foot was elevated, exsanguinated with an Esmarch bandage. An ankle cuff was inflated to 250 mmHg and the operative procedure was begun: Endoscopic plantar fasciotomy, left foot. A 1-cm transverse skin incision was made on the medial aspect of the left heel just at the level of the plantar fascia. The incision was deepened through subcutaneous tissue with a straight hemostat. The straight hemostat was then inserted superiorly and inferiorly over and under the plantar fascia. An elevator was then inserted and the obturator was inserted and exited out the lateral side of the foot. A small horizontal incision was made to accommodate the exit of the obturator. The plantar fascia was then visualized with a probe approximately. 4.5 cm of the plantar fascia was isolated. With the use of a hook knife, the 4.5 mm or approximately two-thirds of the plantar fascia was then resected in toto. The hook knife was then inserted to remove any additional fibers. There was found to be complete resection of the medial plantar fascia. The surgical site was then irrigated with sterile saline solution and suctioned. The incisions were closed with 4-0 nylon suture medially and laterally on the heel. The patient was given 2.5 cc of .50% Marcaine plain, and 1 cc of Dexamethasone sodium phosphate postoperatively. The surgical sites were then dressed with silks and sterile gauze and sterile cling Ace bandage. The patient left the operating room for the recovery room in good condition. Vital signs were stable.

MEADWAY MEDSURG CLINIC

Patient: Davis, Sloan Date: 11/3/xx

Patient ID: DAV121 Insurance: Medicare

PROCEDURE PERFORMED: Colonoscopy with biopsy

SURGEON: Raymond Ross, M.D.

INDICATIONS: Longstanding history of ulcerative colitis

The bowel prep was with Fleet Phospho-Soda with excellent results

FINDINGS:

1. There were no polyps or neoplastic lesions.
2. There was some mild periinflammation in the rectum and sigmoid colon.
3. Random biopsies were taken throughout the colon and the terminal ileum to gauge the extent of disease.

DESCRIPTION OF PROCEDURE: Informed consent was obtained from the patient. The patient was brought into the Minor Procedure Room and placed in the left lateral decubitus position. Moderate sedation was then administered. Digital rectal exam was performed with no masses palpated. The scope was advanced into the rectum through the anus and inflammation was noted with loss of vascular markings. This continued through the sigmoid colon up to about 50 cm, whereupon the inflammation resolved and normal-appearing mucosa appeared proximally to the cecum and including the terminal ileum, which was intubated. Biopsies were then taken mainly of the colon, terminal ileum, right colon, transverse colon, descending colon, sigmoid colon, and rectum for extent of disease as well as to rule out dysplasia. No polyps or tumors were noted. The patient's bowel prep was excellent with very good visualization of the mucosa. Air was suctioned out. The scope was withdrawn. The patient tolerated the procedure well and was sent to the PACU for recovery.

RECOMMENDATIONS:

1. Await pathology results.
2. Continue Cortenema daily or twice a day until symptoms resolve.
3. Repeat colonoscopy in one to three years depending on pathology.

NEW AGE PATHOLOGY

Name: Davis, Sloan Date: 11/3/xx

Patient ID: DAV121

SURGEON: Raymond Ross, M.D.

DIAGNOSIS: Small intestinal mucosa without significant changes. No active inflammation.

Microscopic: Small intestinal mucosa demonstrating a preserved villous architecture without an increase in the lamina propria inflammatory cells.

Gross: Received in formalin labeled with patient's name and "Terminal ileum" measuring .2 × .2 × .1 and .4 × .2 × .1 cm.

Diagnosis: Ccolonic mucosa without significant changes. No active colitis, granulomata or dysplasia present.

Microscopic: Colonic mucosa with preserved architecture and without significant inflammatory infiltrates.

Gross: Received in formalin labeled with patient's name and "Transverse colon" measuring .6 × .6 × .1 cm.

Mark Pavlov, M.D.
Pathologist

MEADWAY MEDSURG CLINIC

Name: Lynn, Meredith — Date: 11/3/xx
Patient ID: LYN779 — Insurance: BCBS

PREOPERATIVE DIAGNOSIS: Cholecystitis

POSTOPERATIVE DIAGNOSIS: Difficult airway

OPERATIVE PROCEDURE: None

SURGEON: Raymond Ross, M.D.

NOTE: Ms. Lynn presented for a cholecystectomy. She was taken to the operating room after being sedated in the holding area. An attempt was made at administration of general anesthesia. The anesthesiologist was unable to intubate the patient due to difficult anatomy. It was felt for the best interest of the patient to cancel the procedure. The patient was transported to the recovery room in stable condition. The surgery is to be rescheduled at the hospital.

MEADWAY MEDSURG CLINIC

Name: Nagy, Helen — Date: 11/3/xx
Patient ID: NAG662 — Insurance: Galaxy Health

PREOPERATIVE DIAGNOSIS: Menorrhagia and benign endometrial polyp on endometrial biopsy

POSTOPERATIVE DIAGNOSIS: Menorrhagia and benign endometrial polyp on endometrial biopsy

OPERATIVE PROCEDURE: Dilatation and curettage Hysteroscopy

SURGEON: Abbey Murphy, M.D.

COMPLICATIONS: None

INDICATIONS: This is a 39-year-old black female with history of menorrhagia. Routine evaluation revealed benign endometrial polyp on endometrial biopsy, therefore she was consented for D&C hysteroscopy for more thorough evaluation of her endometrial lining.

PROCEDURE: The patient was identified and brought to the operating room with IV running. She was placed into the dorsal lithotomy position and given general anesthesia. She was prepped and draped in the usual sterile fashion. Her bladder was straight catheterized for small amount of clear yellow urine. Her Nuvo-Ring was removed and discarded. The sidearm speculum was placed into the vagina. The cervix was visualized. The anterior lip was grasped with the single-tooth tenaculum. The cervix was serially dilated until the hysteroscope could pass. Hysteroscopy was performed, which revealed a thickened endometrial lining and questionable polypoid tissue. The hysteroscope was removed and then a sharp curet was then performed in all quadrants until a uniformly gritty texture was appreciated throughout. The curet was removed and a hysteroscopy was repeated, which revealed absence of the aforementioned thickened tissue. Therefore all instruments were removed from the patient's vagina. She was awakened and returned to the recovery room having tolerated the procedure well. Hemostasis was excellent.

MEADWAY MEDSURG CLINIC

Name: Lopez, Marcus — Date: 11/3/xx

Patient ID: LOP524 — Insurance: Select Health

PREOPERATIVE DIAGNOSIS: Low back pain and lumbar radiculitis

POSTOPERATIVE DIAGNOSIS: Low back pain and lumbar radiculitis

PROCEDURE PERFORMED: Caudal epidural steroid injection

ANESTHESIA: 4 cc of 2% lidocaine

INJECTATE: 40 mg of Kenalog and 2 cc of Omnipaque 240 and 7 cc of preservative free sterile 0.9% saline

COMPLICATIONS: None

PHYSICIAN: Thaddeus Morency, M.D.

DESCRIPTION OF PROCEDURE: After discussion of the risks, benefits, and alternative to the procedure, the patient consented and brought to the procedure room and assumed a prone position on the fluoroscopic imaging table. Following this, a wide area of the patient's low back was prepped sterilely with Betadine solution × 3 and allowed to dry thoroughly. L5-S1 interspace was identified fluoroscopically. The overlying tissues were infiltrated with 2 cc of 2% lidocaine. Under fluoroscopic guidance, a 20-gauge 3.5 inch sterile Tuohy needle was then directed towards the L5-S1 interspace. However, the needle did not gain access through the epidural space. The needle was then withdrawn. Hemostasis was achieved immediately at that spot and caudal approach was then performed. The midline in the upper buttock was prepped sterilely with Betadine solution × 3 and allowed to dry thoroughly. The sacral hiatus was identified digitally. The overlying tissues were then infiltrated with 2 cc of 2% lidocaine under fluoroscopic guidance. A #20-gauge 1.5 inch sterile hypodermic needle was introduced into and through the sacral hiatus with a loss of resistance noted. Following this, injectate as above was instilled slowly and easily and fluoroscopic imaging revealed an epidural pattern to the flow of the injectate. The needle was then withdrawn. Hemostasis was achieved immediately. The patient was washed off and bandaged and accompanied back to the recovery room from where he was discharged without any complaints or complications. Please note, at no time during the injection the patient ever complained of any lancinating pain or paresthesias.

MEADWAY MEDSURG CLINIC

Name: Rogers, Megan Date: 11/3/xx

Patient ID: ROG773 Insurance: Medicaid

PREOPERATIVE DIAGNOSIS: Recurrent acute otitis media

POSTOPERATIVE DIAGNOSIS: Recurrent acute otitis media

SURGEON: Lee Hackney, M.D.

ANESTHESIA: General

PROCEDURE: Bilateral tympanostomy tube insertion

ESTIMATED BLOOD LOSS: Minimal

COMPLICATIONS: None

INDICATION: This is a 2-year-old with recurrent history of acute otitis media status post bilateral tympanostomy tube insertion approximately 6–8 months ago. She presented with a right otitis media followed by a second suppurative otitis media due to displaced ear tubes. The risks, benefits and alternatives of replacement of right tympanostomy tube with examination under anesthesia of the left ear were discussed with the parents who agreed to proceed with surgical management. Discussions regarding adenoidectomy were initiated; however the parents did not wish to proceed.

PROCEDURE: The patient was brought to the operating suite and maintained in supine position. General anesthesia was administered via mask ventilation without complications. I then proceeded to evaluate the right ear. A displaced tympanostomy tube was noted to be in the lateral ear canal, which was removed used alligator forceps. Cerumen was removed from the ear canal using cerumen loop. An incision was made into the anterior/inferior aspect of the tympanic membrane a myringotomy knife. Amber colored fluid was suctioned followed by placement of the Armstrong grommet beveled tympanostomy tube followed by Floxin drops. I then proceeded to evaluate the left ear in a similar fashion. The tube was noted to be displaced and was removed from the ear canal. The previously made myringotomy site was noted to still be patent with some minor thickening around the incision site. I did one of the myringotomies using a myringotomy knife, followed by insertion of a tympanostomy tube. There was some mucoid secretions around the myringotomy site, however none was suctioned from the middle ear. Floxin drops were applied. The completed the procedure. The patient tolerated the procedure well and was taken back to the recovery room in satisfactory condition. All counts were declared correct at the end of the procedure and the patient was transferred to the recovery room in a stable condition.

MEADWAY MEDSURG CLINIC

Name: Opolin, Rachel Date: 11/3/xx
Patient ID: OPO443 Insurance: Cigna
PREOPERATIVE DIAGNOSIS: Prolapsing bleeding internal hemorrhoids
POSTOPERATIVE DIAGNOSIS: Prolapsing bleeding internal hemorrhoids
PROCEDURE: PPH (procedure for prolapse and hemorrhoids—stapled hemorrhoidipexy)
SURGEON: Raymond Ross, M.D.
ANESTHESIA: Intravenous sedation with local (30-ml .50% Marcaine with epinephrine)

INDICATIONS: Ms. Opolin is a 69-year-old woman with anemia who was recently admitted to New York General Hospital with rectal bleeding and profound anemia. She received four units of packed red blood cells. She also underwent an upper endoscopy and colonoscopy. She was found to have very mild duodenitis, two small polyps, moderate diverticulosis and very large hemorrhoids with visible blood. The nature and management of hemorrhoidal disease, as well as the medical and surgical treatment alternatives was discussed at length with Rachel. It was recommended that she undergo PPH (Procedure for prolapse and hemorrhoids) for treatment of her bleeding internal hemorrhoids, which resulted in anemia.

PATHOLOGICAL FINDINGS: Anorectal inspection revealed moderate sized, mildly edematous external hemorrhoids with no perianal erythema, fissures or fistula. There were multiple groups of very large erythematous internal hemorrhoids. The distal rectal mucosa was otherwise normal. There was no evidence of inflammatory bowel disease.

PROCEDURE: Rachel was taken to the operating room and placed in the prone jackknife position and administered intravenous sedation. The buttocks were taped apart and the perianal area was prepped and painted with Betadine and sterilely draped. Local anesthesia was infiltrated circumanally and in the deep periphery for bilateral rectal block. The anus was gently digitally dilated two fingerbreadths and examination under anesthesia was performed with the findings as noted above.

The Fansler retractor was placed to expose the field of operation. Beginning posteriorly a 2-0 Prolene suture was placed circumferentially in a pursestring fashion approximately 4 to 5 cm above the dentate line along the submucosal plane. Care was taken not to incorporate the underlying rectal wall or rectovaginal septum. When this was completed, the Fansler retractor was removed and the PPH anal canal dilator and obturator were then placed over the pursestring suture and carefully positioned to protect the anal sphincter complex and keep the anoderm out of the field of operation. The PPH 0-3 stapler was then fully opened and the anvil was placed proximal to the pursestring suture. The pursestring suture was secured around the shaft of the anvil and retrieved through the barrel of the stapler with the suture threader. The suture was secured upon itself and retracted as the stapler was then fully closed. The 4-cm mark on the barrel of the stapler was just up within the anal verge indicating proper positioning. The stapler was kept closed for 30 seconds during which time digital examination of the posterior vaginal wall revealed no dimpling or umbilication to suggest incorporation of the vaginal wall. The head of the stapler could be felt to move cephalad, caudad and laterally free and clear of the posterior vaginal wall. The stapler was fired, released, removed, opened and inspected. There was a circumferentially complete donut of tissue comprised of only mucosa and submucosa, with no evidence of muscle or fat. This was sent to pathology. The staple line was inspected. It was circumferentially intact. There was a small amount of bleeding coming from the anterior aspect, which was controlled with a figure-of-eight suture of 3-0 chromic. The anal canal and rectum were copiously irrigated and the staple line inspected for several minutes. There was no evidence of any bleeding. Additional local anesthesia was infiltrated above and below the staple line. Digital examination revealed the staple line to be well positioned. The perianal skin was covered with Bacitracin ointment, sterile gauze and taped securely.

MEADWAY MEDSURG CLINIC

Name: Suggs, Ruby
Date: 11/3/xx

Patient ID: SUG335
Insurance: Medicare

PREOPERATIVE DIAGNOSIS: Cataract, left eye

POSTOPERATIVE DIAGNOSIS: Nuclear sclerotic cataract, left eye

SURGEON: Jeremy Moser, M.D.

ANESTHESIA: Local with sedation

PROCEDURE: Left eye phacoemulsification and cataract extraction with intraocular lens implant, model SN60WF power 19.0 diopters

PROCEDURE: The patient was brought to the operating room and sedated by the anesthesiologist. The left periorbital area was prepped with alcohol swabs. A parabulbar block was administered consisting of 4% Xylocaine and 0.75% Marcaine and Wydase in a mixture. 4 cc was given parabulbar. Lidocaine 2% gel was instilled into the conjunctival sac. The patient was then prepped and draped in a sterile fashion.

A lid speculum was placed in the eye. A peritomy from 10 to 11 o'clock was performed. Wet-field cautery was used for hemostasis on the scleral bed. A partial thickness scleral groove was created 3-mm in length and 1-mm from the limbus. Through this scleral groove, a scleral tunnel was dissected into clear cornea. The anterior chamber was then entered with a 3.0- mm keratome through the scleral tunnel incision. Viscoelastic was used to fill the anterior chamber. A capsulorrhexis was performed with the cystotome. Balanced salt solution was used to hydrodissect the nucleus. The phacoemulsification unit was used to emulsify the nucleus in a quadrant cracking fashion. The remaining cortical material was aspirated with the I&A handpiece. Viscoelastic was used to fill the capsular bag and anterior chamber. A posterior chamber lens model SN60WF power 19.0 diopters was inserted into the capsular bag and centered into place with a Sinskey hook. The I&A handpiece was used to remove any remaining viscoelastic from the capsular bag and anterior chamber. Miochol solution was then placed into the eye. The scleral tunnel incision was found to be intact without leakage. Wet-field cautery was used to re-approximate the conjunctiva at the limbus. A subconjunctival injection of Ancef and Decadron was given in the inferior fornix. A patch and shield was placed on the eye. The patient left the operating room in good condition.

MEADWAY MEDSURG CLINIC

Name: Chase, Ella
Date: 11/3/xx

Patient ID: CHA116
Insurance: Flexi-Health

PREOPERATIVE DIAGNOSIS: Dysfunctional uterine bleeding, failed medical management

POSTOPERATIVE DIAGNOSIS: Dysfunctional uterine bleeding, failed medical management

OPERATIVE PROCEDURE: Fractional dilation and curettage

SURGEON: Abbey Murphy, M.D.

CLINICAL NOTE: The patient is a 53-year-old perimenopausal, para 3, 0, 0, 3, LMP October 2, prolonged and heavy with passage of clots, contraception tubal. She has been evaluated in the past for dysfunctional bleeding with a negative saline sonogram and a benign endometrial biopsy.

(Continued)

In the past, she has been managed with Prometrium and Nor-QD; however, this medical management did not seem to help her bleeding at this point in time and we are proceeding to a dilation and curettage.

OPERATIVE FINDINGS: Exam under anesthesia revealed an anteverted, firm, normal-sized uterus with normal adnexa on D&C, the os was patulous to a small-to-medial size sharp and serrated curette. Scant endometrial tissue was recovered. Scant endocervical tissue was recovered as well.

OPERATIVE SUMMARY AND TECHNIQUE: The patient was brought to the operating room and after adequate IV sedation; she was prepped and draped in the usual manner for vaginal surgery. An exam prior to the procedure revealed the above findings. The patient was then cathed for 100 cc of clear urine. A sidearm speculum was placed in the vagina and the anterior lip of the cervix was grasped with a double-tooth tenaculum. The cervix was pulled forward and the os was found to be patulous and easily admitted a small sharp curette. Curettage was then performed and immediately, the endometrium sounded gritty. The uterus was then explored with ureteral stone forceps. Curettage proceeded with a small serrated curette followed by a medium sharp curette. Scant tissue was recovered. Prior to curetting the endometrium, a small serrated curette was placed within the endocervical canal and endocervical sample was obtained as well. After completely curetting the endometrium, the surgeon deemed the procedure complete. The tenaculum was removed from the cervix and the tenaculum site was hemostatic. Speculum was removed from the vagina. Estimated blood loss was 20 cc. Sponge and instrument counts were correct × 2. The patient was taken to the recovery room in good condition. Two specimens were sent from the operating room and labeled endometrial curettings and endocervical curettings.

MEADWAY MEDSURG CLINIC

Name: Harris, Anna — Date: 11/3/xx

Patient ID: HAR339 — Insurance: Aetna

PREOPERATIVE DIAGNOSIS: Painful hammertoe deformity, 2nd, 3rd digits, left foot

POSTOPERATIVE DIAGNOSIS: Painful hammertoe deformity, 2nd, 3rd digits, left foot

PROCEDURE: Arthroplasty 2nd and 3rd digit left foot with K-wire fixation

SURGEON: Thaddeus Morency, M.D.

ANESTHESIA: IV sedation; local using a 50/50 mix of 1% Xylocaine plain, and 0.5% plain Marcaine in a 50/50 mix

INDICATIONS: The patient was brought to the operating room, alert and awake in the supine position, and transferred to the operating table. Once IV sedation was achieved, local anesthesia, using approximately 10 cc of the 50/50 mixture was then performed. The patient was prepped and draped in the usual sterile manner for surgery. Attention was directed to the left foot. The limb was exsanguinated and the tourniquet inflated to 250 mmHg. Attention was then directed to the 2nd digit at the level of the PIPJ, where two converging semi-elliptical incisions were performed centered over the joint. The skin incision was deepened and the skin wedge removed in toto. The extensor tendon was transected and reflected proximally and distally. Collateral ligaments were severed, delivering the head of the proximal phalanx to the operative site. Using a power sagittal saw, the hypertrophied head of the proximal phalanx was excised in toto. The area was inspected and irrigated with copious amounts of normal saline. Next, .045 K-wire was placed from proximal to distal exiting the distal end

(Continued)

of the toe. Next, the K-wire was retrograded into the proximal phalanx stabilizing the toe in a rectus position. The K-wire at the distal end was bent, cut and capped. The tendon was re-approximated using 4-0 Vicryl suture. The skin incision was re-approximated using 5-0 nylon suture. Attention was directed to the third digit on the left, where the same exact procedure was performed without variation. One-half cc of Dexamethasone was infiltrated into each operative site. Betadine soaked Owens silk was placed upon the skin incisions and a dry, sterile compression dressing was placed upon the foot. The patient was brought from the operating room, alert and awake in the supine position. The patient tolerated all procedures and anesthesia well and left with the OR with vital signs stable.

MEADWAY MEDSURG CLINIC

Name: Shenk, Lolly — Date: 11/3/xx

Patient ID: SHE446 — Insurance: United Healthcare

PREOPERATIVE DIAGNOSIS: Left anterior fistula in ano

POSTOPERATIVE DIAGNOSIS: Left anterior intersphincteric (submuscular) fistula in ano

PROCEDURE: Submuscular anal fistulotomy

SURGEON: Raymond Ross, M.D.

INDICATIONS: Ms. Shenk is a 31-year-old woman who developed a left anterior perianal abscess. This was incised and drained. Cultures revealed the presence of E-coli. She was treated with antibiotics. On follow-up examination, she was found to have a left anterior 1- to 2-mm external fistulous opening with a small amount of mucopurulent drainage. When probed, it extended 1.5 cm inward toward the anal canal. The nature and management of a perianal abscess and anal fistula was discussed at length. It was recommended that she undergo an anal fistulotomy. After a thorough explanation of the procedure, alternatives, outcomes, associated risks and possible complications, she consented to proceed.

PATHOLOGICAL FINDINGS: Anorectal inspection revealed small external and internal hemorrhoids. The distal rectal mucosa was normal with no evidence of inflammatory bowel disease. Scarring was present over the left anterior aspect of the anal verge. A 1- to 2-mm opening was present, which tracked directly inward along the anal canal. At the level of the dentate line was a deep anal crypt with a 1-mm pinpoint opening. The fistula tracked subcutaneously then intersphincterically at the distal edge of the internal sphincter muscle. There were no other fistulae. Anteriorly, a shallow fissure was present.

PROCEDURE: The patient was taken to the operating room and placed in the prone jackknife position and administered intravenous sedation. The buttocks were taped apart and the perianal area was prepped and painted with Betadine and sterilely draped. Local anesthesia was infiltrated circumanally and in the deep periphery for bilateral rectal block. The anus was gently digitally dilated to two fingerbreadths and examination under anesthesia was performed with the findings as noted above. A fistula probe was gently used to exam the external opening. It tracked directly inward. Hydrogen peroxide was injected and the internal opening was identified. The fistula probe was then placed along the fistula tract. The overlying skin was incised to reveal subcutaneous tissue and the distal fibers of the internal sphincter muscle. A primary fistulotomy was then performed. Granulation tissue was present along the fistula tract. This was removed by curettage. The tract was inspected. There was no evidence of any side branches. The edges of the wound were then marsupialized to the fibrous base of the tract with two continuous 3-0 Vicryl sutures. The wound was irrigated and inspected. There was no evidence of any bleeding.

MEADWAY MEDSURG CLINIC

Name: Duval, Lisa Date: 11/3/xx

Patient ID: DUV225 Insurance: Aetna

PREOPERATIVE DIAGNOSIS: Symptomatic large endometrial polyp

POSTOPERATIVE DIAGNOSIS: Symptomatic large endometrial polyp

OPERATION: Hysteroscopy, dilation and curettage; examination under anesthesia

SURGEON: Abbey Murphy, M.D.

CLIICAL NOTE: Lisa is a 49-year-old peri-menopausa woman, PARA-3033, with a large endometrial polyp, which was quite symptomatic causing dysfunctional bleeding. The endometrial polyp was diagnosed by saline sonogram and measured approximately 5 cm.

OPERATIVE FINDINGS: Examination prior to the procedure revealed gauze and one laminaria in the vagina and cervix. The uterus was anteverted and of top-normal size. On hysteroscopy, a very large endometrial polyp was encountered. The polyp was removed with a curettage and the ureteral stone forceps. Curettage revealed a moderate amount of tissue, as well. Ostia were normal. 1200 cc of 1.5% Glycine was utilized and recovered.

OPERATIVE SUMMARY AND TECHNIQUES: The patient was brought to the operating room and after adequate general anesthesia with LMA with protection was prepped and draped in the usual manner for vaginal surgery. Examination prior to procedure revealed the above findings. A speculum was placed in the vagina and the anterior lip of the cervix was grasped with a double-tooth tenaculum. The cervix was pulled forward and was found to be patulous and easily admitted a 3-mm 30-degree hysteroscope attached to 1.5% Glycine. The hysteroscope was threaded through the endocervical canal into the uterine cavity under direct visualization. An enormous polyp was encountered immediately and photographed. The base of the polyp was found to be fundal. The polyp was located fundally between the ostia. The ostia were identified, photographed, and were normal. The hysteroscope was then removed and the ureteral stone forceps were then placed into the uterine cavity and the base of the polyp was grasped and using a twisting, circular motion, the polyp was removed. Several other passes with the ureteral stone forceps removed fragments of polyp. Endometrial curetting was then performed with a small, sharp serrated curet and a large sharp curet. Moderate tissue was obtained. Several passes with the stone forceps also revealed a clean cavity. The hysteroscope was then replaced within the uterine cavity under direct visualization to verify the complete removal of the enormous polyp. Complete removal was verified, as the cavity was clear. Photographs were taken. The surgeon deemed the procedure to be complete. The hysteroscope was removed. The tenaculum was removed from the cervix. An exam post-procedure revealed a firm, anteverted uterus. The tenaculum site was hemostatic. The patient was taken to the recovery room in good condition. All sponge and instruments counts were correct × 2. There were no complications.

DAY FOUR

MEADWAY MEDSURG CLINIC

Name: Milligan, Tori — Date: 11/3/xx

Patient ID: MIL123 — Insurance: BCBS

PREOPERATIVE and POSTOPERATIVE DIAGNOSIS: Mass of dorsum of right foot

OPERATION: Excision of mass right foot (ganglion on top of osteophyte)

SURGEON: Thaddeus Morency, M.D.

FINDINGS AND INDICATIONS: This 41-year-old white female had a right foot progressively painful growth over the dorsum of the foot. It was at the Lisfranc area of the joint. She had had progressively enlarging mass. X-rays revealed an osteophyte. It was elected to proceed with excision. At the time of surgery, there was a fairly large old ganglion cyst and underneath hypertrophic bone. The cyst was removed and hypertrophic bone shaved.

PROCEDURE: The patient was taken to the operating room and after satisfactory ankle block anesthesia the right leg was prepped and draped in sterile manner. It was wrapped up to the ankle in Esmarch and then Esmarch was wrapped around and tied for tourniquet. The left foot was then exposed and the toes covered with a glove and then a dorsal incision was made over the mass. The skin and subcutaneous tissue were carefully divided down looking for the neurovascular bundles. It appeared to be on the lateral side. This was dissected free and retracted lateral.

A fairly large ganglion cyst was circumferentially resected. It was then freed. A small stalk went down to an osteophyte. The ganglion was excised and then a rongeur used to remove the stalk. A fairly large osteophyte was also present centrally and then one more on the lateral side. This was removed with a rongeur.

Final inspection revealed no further prominence. Closure was effected with 4-0 nylon and a pressure dressing was applied. The patient had the tourniquet let down and was transported to recovery room in stable condition having tolerated the procedure well.

MEADWAY MEDSURG CLINIC

Name: Huss, Nora — Date: 11/3/xx

Patient ID: HUS898 — Insurance: Aetna

PREOPERATIVE and POSTOPERATIVE DIAGNOSIS: Carpal tunnel syndrome bilateral

OPERATION: Left carpal tunnel release

SURGEON: Thaddeus Morency, M.D.

FINDINGS AND INDICATIONS: this is a 39-year-old white female with progressive numbness and pain, night pain and difficulty sleeping. She had had a work up which showed carpal tunnel syndrome. She had enough symptoms that she wishes to proceed with release and it was elected to do so. At the time of surgery she was noted to have hyperemia of the nerve, narrowing of the carpal tunnel, but no boss or ganglion.

(Continued)

PROCEDURE: The patient was taken into the operating room and after satisfactory double tourniquet block the left arm was prepped and draped in a sterile manner. The left arm was then positioned and carpal tunnel incision was made based on 4th ray and thenar crease. Skin and subcutaneous tissues were divided down. Hemostasis was obtained with electrocautery. The transverse carpal ligament was then divided under direct vision with a knife and a freer in the carpal tunnel to protect the nerve. Palpation revealed no ganglion or boss. Inspection revealed the motor branch to be intact. The nerve was noted to be a little hyperemic and narrow consistent with irritation.

Following this, the wound was irrigated and closed. 4-0 nylon was used for closure. A sterile splint was applied after infiltrating the wound with Marcaine. The patient was transported to recovery room in stable condition, having tolerated the procedure well.

MEADWAY MEDSURG CLINIC

Name: Gray, Diana — Date: 11/3/xx

Patient ID: GRA449 — Insurance: BCBS

PREOPERATIVE and POSTOPERATIVE DIAGNOSIS: Left breast mass

OPERATION: Left breast biopsy with frozen section

SURGEON: Raymond Ross, M.D.

INDICATIONS: the patient is a 64-year-old white female who had bloody drainage from the left nipple with a small mass at 3 o'clock at the nipple. Therefore she is scheduled for a breast biopsy. Mammogram did not notice any abnormalities.

PROCEDURE: The patient was brought to the operating room and placed supine on the operating room table. MAC sedation was started and the left breast was sterilely prepped and draped. 1% lidocaine with 0.5% Marcaine with epinephrine was injected in the left nipple and a marking pen was used to make a circumferential incision just to the left of the nipple. A 2.5-cm incision was made and sharp dissection was carried down along the skin to include about ½ of the nipple complex. As transection was carried across the nipple complex, there was old blood coming up. There was also some dirty yellow fluid that looked like it could be abscess. This was cultured and sensitivity was sent for this. There was some firm lipomatous tissue around the hard mass that was about 1 × 1 cm. This was completely excised out for total mass of about 2 cm. The specimen was sent for pathology and came back as intraductal papillomatosis with no sign of malignancy. Bovie cautery was used to hemostasis. The wound was closed with 3-0 Vicryl. The 4-0 Vicryl was used to close subcuticularly and dressing applied. The patient tolerated the procedure well.

PLAN: We will give her a prescription for pain medication and have her come back in 1 weeks time.

MEADWAY MEDSURG CLINIC

Name: Wilson, Dale — Date: 11/3/xx

Patient ID: WIL331 — Insurance: Cigna

PREOPERATIVE DIAGNOSIS: Torn medial meniscus

POSTOPERATIVE DIAGNOSIS:

1. Grade 3 tear posterior horn medial meniscus
2. Medial plica
3. Grade 1 articular cartilage defect medial femoral condylar region

OPERATION:

1. Examination under anesthesia with diagnostic arthroscopy
2. Resection of plica and posterior horn meniscal tear.

SURGEON: Thaddeus Morency, M.D.

PROCEDURE: The patient was brought to the surgery suite and after adequate anesthesia was positioned on the table and secured. The leg was then prepared for surgery by placing a tourniquet high on the thigh. The leg was then examined and noted to have a full range of motion with a mild clicking to the medial compartment with ranging, otherwise, stable in all planes. At this time the leg was prepared by placing the leg in a leg holding device and the leg was scrubbed from the tourniquet to the toes with a 10-minute Betadine scrub followed by Betadine prep and then draped in a sterile fashion. The leg was elevated and exsanguinated and the tourniquet inflated. Medial and lateral parapatellar work portals were created with a #11 stab blade. The arthroscope was introduced, and the knee was distended and examined.

The suprapatellar pouch region was normal. There was a thickened medial plica which extended well over the medial femoral condylar area. This was resected back with a full-radius cutting blade. This allowed for exposure to the medial compartment easily. The medial gutter was otherwise clean. The articular surface of the medial femoral condyle had a laceration type tear into the cartilage itself. The underlying cartilage was completely intact. There was no evidence of eburnation of bone. This was not a flap tear and could not be displaced. The posterior horn meniscus had a small, grade 3, through and through extension in the white/white zone. This was resected back with a combination of the handheld upbiters, small cautery unit and small curved shaver. A smooth stable posterior horn meniscal rim was left in place.

At this time the arthroscope was removed. The knee was drained. The wounds were closed with 4-0 nylon stitches. The knee was then injected with 10-mg Duramorph and 20-mg 0.25% Marcaine and sterile bandage was applied and the patient was taken to the recovery room. There were no intra-operative complications.

MEADWAY MEDSURG CLINIC

Name: Kelly, Emma | Date: 11/2/xx

Patient ID: KEL774 | Insurance: United Health Care

PREOPERATIVE and POSTOPERATIVE DIAGNOSIS: Desired sterilization

OPERATION: Laparoscopic assisted bilateral tubal ligation with Filshie clips

SURGEON: Abbey Murphy, M.D.

PROCEDURE: The patient was brought back to the operating room with IV fluids running and placed in the supine position on the operating table. After induction with general endotracheal anesthesia was performed the patient was then placed in the dorsal lithotomy position.

Examination under anesthesia was performed determining size, position and mobility of the uterus. It was found to be freely mobile anteflexed and 6 weeks sized. The patient was then prepped and draped in the usual sterile fashion and a bivalve speculum was placed in the vaginal vault until the cervix was eased into view. The anterior lip of the cervix was then grasped with a single toothed tenaculum and an acorn uterine manipulator was then placed. The bivalve speculum was then removed and a Foley catheter was also placed with yellow clear urine noted.

The inferior umbilical area was infiltrated with 0.25 % Marcaine with Epinephrine and an inferior vertical umbilical incision was then made followed by the Veress needle with placement verified using both the hanging drop saline technique and aspiration. The abdomen was then insufflated with approximately 3 liters of CO_2 and once adequate pneumoperitoneum was assured a 12-mm blunt tipped step trocar was then placed followed by the laparoscope. The pelvic cavity was thoroughly explored with the above findings noted.

The fallopian tubes were identified bilaterally from the cornu of the tube down through the fimbriated ends. In the isthmic ampullated portion of the tube, a Filshie clip was placed perpendicularly, transecting the tube and this was performed bilaterally. Excellent hemostasis was noted. Photographic evidence was taken of the ligation.

This concluded the operation. The laparoscope, probe and trocar were removed after the abdomen was emptied of CO_2.

The incision was then closed using 4-0 Vicryl suture in a subcuticular fashion. Sterile dressing was applied. The acorn uterine manipulator and tenaculum were also removed with excellent hemostasis noted. The Foley catheter was removed with yellow, clear urine noted. Sponge, needle and instrument counts were recorded correct. The patient tolerated the procedure well and was taken to post anesthesia recovery in excellent condition.

MEADWAY MEDSURG CLINIC

Name: Cruthers, Tami — Date: 11/3/xx

Patient ID: CRU334 — Insurance: BCBS

PREOPERATIVE and POSTOPERATIVE DIAGNOSIS: Failed intrauterine pregnancy

OPERATION: D&C

SURGEON: Abbey Murphy, M.D.

FINDINGS: Significant amount of tissue required to be suctioned and curettaged

PROCEDURE: The patient was taken to the operating room in supine position. Anesthesia was instituted and the patient was prepped and draped in the dorsal lithotomy position. The bladder was drained and the cervix isolated. The uterus was sounded and the cervix was dilated to accommodate an 8-mm suction curette. Tissue and blood were removed. Sharp curettage was performed and the suction curette used once again to remove remaining clots of blood. Sharp curette was once again performed to ensure adequacy of procedure. Good hemostasis was noted. The procedure was terminated. The patient was taken to recovery room in stable condition.

MEADWAY MEDSURG CLINIC

Name: Kaplan, Doris — Date: 11/3/xx

Patient ID: KAP552 — Insurance: Medicare

PREOPERATIVE DIAGNOSIS: Dislocated intraocular lens

POSTOPERATIVE DIAGNOSIS: Anterior dislocation of intraocular lens

PROCEDURE PERFORMED: Removal and replacement of intraocular lens left eye

SURGEON: Jeremy Moser, M.D.

PROCEDURE: Under MAC anesthesia, the patient received retrobulbar injection and Van Lint block for akinesia and anesthesia of the globe. She had 20 minutes of a pinky ball, followed by prep and drape in the usual sterile fashion. An eyelid speculum was placed. A fornix-based conjunctival flap was made, hemostasis was obtained with wet field cautery. A previous corneal suture was removed from the 7 o'clock position. The chamber was entered at the 1 o'clock position with a 15 degree Superblade. The previous scleral tunnel was opened with the keratome, in looking at the position of the lens and knowing that it could not be relocated, the scleral tunnel was extended to 6 mm. An attempt to rotate the lens out of the bag was unsuccessful. An attempt to try to make notches or to cut the bag with a retinal scissors was unsuccessful so the entire lens with the inferior zonule still attached was removed without difficulty. It should be noted that a significant amount of Healon was instilled beneath the implant before any manipulation of the procedure had started. Miochol was instilled into the anterior chamber. A lens Schiøtz glide was placed and then the implant was slid into position, the glide was removed and superior pole were placed using the Lister manipulator. Two peripheral iridotomies were performed by making self sealing stab incisions with a 15 degree Superblade going through the cornea and then going through the iris. The scleral tunnel was sewn and watertight. Before the last suture was placed, the I&A apparatus was used to remove the Healon from the chamber and from the vitreous cavity. There was no vitreous to the wound. The last suture was placed, tied and cut. The wound was watertight. The pressure in the eye was adjusted using a 27 gauge needle through the self sealing stab incision. The wound again was tested and found to be watertight. The conjunctiva was tacked closed with wet field cautery. A subconjunctival injection of gentamicin and Ancef were given. Topical Maxitrol ointment was applied. The eyelid was closed, patched and a Fox shield was applied.

MEADWAY MEDSURG CLINIC

Name: Gentili, Nick
Date: 11/2/xx

Patient ID: GEN775
Insurance: Medicare

PREOPERATIVE and POSTOPERATIVE DIAGNOSIS:

1. Visual field impairment
2. Blepharochalasia upper lid

OPERATION: Upper lid blepharoplasty

SURGEON: Robyn Houser, M.D.

PROCEDURE: With the patient under suitable IV sedation, in the supine position on the operating table, a pattern with French curl was drawn on the patient's eyelids with lateral to medial distances from the lid-lash margin of 4-mm and 8-mm in the central portion on each side. Thereafter, local anesthetic was injected, a 50/50 solution of 1% Xylocaine plus 0.25% Marcaine, 1:200,000 Epinephrine. He was prepped with Shur-Clens solution and draped aseptically. Thereafter, excision of the excess skin on the right upper eyelid and left upper eyelid were undertaken. Removal of the medial and lateral fat pads of the upper lids was undertaken with cauterization of all vessels and bases of fat pads. His vision was not affected by this during the operation except to improve the visual fields from drooping lids.

Repair was undertaken with 6-0 nylon. The patient tolerated the procedure well.

MEADWAY MEDSURG CLINIC

Name: Altman, Mike
Date: 11/2/xx

Patient ID: ALT226
Insurance: Prudential

PREOPERATIVE and POSTOPERATIVE DIAGNOSIS: Meatal stenosis

OPERATION: Meatotomy

SURGEON: Gregory Wallace, M.D.

PROCEDURE: After informed consent was obtained from the patient's mother, the patient was taken to the operating room and prepped and draped in the usual sterile manner in the supine position. The meatus was visualized and a straight hemostat used to crimp the urethral meatus at the 6 o'clock position. Metzenbaum scissors were then used to incise the crimped area. Redundant tissue was excised. 4-0 chromic was placed in an interrupted manner. Good hemostasis was noted. The urethral meatus was noted to be approximately an 8 French diameter at the conclusion of the meatotomy. He was stable to recovery room.

MEADWAY MEDSURG CLINIC

Name: Cadman, Luke | Date: 11/3/xx

Patient ID: CAD116 | Insurance: Signal HMO

PREOPERATIVE and POSTOPERATIVE DIAGNOSIS: Closed displaced right 2nd metacarpal neck fracture

OPERATION: Open reduction internal fixation right metacarpal neck fracture

PROCEDURE: After informed consent was obtained, the patient was brought to the operating room via stretcher and placed supine on the operating table and underwent uneventful general anesthesia with endotracheal intubation. A gram of Ancef was given intravenously. A well padded tourniquet was placed on the right upper arm and the right upper extremity was prepped and draped in sterile orthopedic fashion. Attempts were initially made for closed reduction and pinning of the fracture. This was attempted multiple times from a retrograde and anagrade fashion without success. A 3-cm incision was then made directly over the metacarpal head and fracture. Sharp dissection was carried out through the skin and subcutaneous tissue. The extensor tendon was then identified and slid ulnarly. A rent was made in the capsule. The fracture was identified and reduced. From a proximal to distal fashion, a 0.062 K-wire was introduced into the metacarpal shaft, across the fracture and into the metacarpal head. It was found to be stable. Under AP, lateral, and oblique image intensification, the hardware was in good position and not penetrating the joint. It was then cut beneath the skin. All open wounds were then irrigated. The 2 stab wounds that had been made prior were closed with interrupted 4-0 nylon. The rent in the capsule was closed with figure-of-eight -0- Vicryl and then the skin was closed with 4-0 nylon.

The patient was placed in a sterile dressing and a dorsal blocking splint. He was awakened, extubated and transported to recovery room in satisfactory condition. There were no operative or anesthetic complications. Sponge and needle counts were correct × 2.

MEADWAY MEDSURG CLINIC

Name: Williams, Christine | Date: 11/3/xx

Patient ID: WIL883 | Insurance: Signal HMO

PREOPERATIVE DIAGNOSIS: Residual consecutive exotropia

POSTOPERATIVE DIAGNOSIS: Same

OPERATION: Left medial rectus advancement (5.0 mm)
Left lateral rectus re-recession (4.0 mm)

This is a healthy 6-year-old girl with a history of strabismus for which she has had two previous surgeries. She initially had esotropia for which she had a bimedial recession. She then had a re-op of her left eye one year later. She still has residual exotropia and presents for further surgery for residual consecutive exotropia.

The patient was taken to the OR and placed under general anesthesia. The eyes were prepped and draped in a routine manner. Attention was turned to the left eye. A limbal incision was made over the medial rectus. A blunt and sharp dissection was used to lyse overlying Tenon's detachment as

(Continued)

well as intramuscular septum for a distance of 6 mm back. Two Vicryl sutures were placed in the belly of the muscle with a square knot centrally and a single locking bite at each pole. Attention was turned to the lateral rectus. Tenon's capsule was cleaned from the surface of the lateral rectus and the intramuscular membranes were cut on either side of the lateral rectus. A double-armed 6-0 Vicryl suture was laced in the insertion of the lateral rectus. The muscle was reattached to the globe 3.0 mm posterior to the original insertion. Conjunctiva was closed with interrupted sutures.

MEADWAY MEDSURG CLINIC

Name: Cook, Larry
Date: 11/3/xx
Patient ID: C00991
Insurance: Signal HMO

PREOPERATIVE DIAGNOSIS: Basal cell carcinoma of nose, recurrent

POST OPERATIVE DIAGNOSIS: Same

SURGEON: Robyn Houser, M.D.

PROCEDURE:

1. Excision basal cell carcinoma with frozen section
2. Full-thickness skin graft from right ear to nose

OPERATION: The patient was taken to the OR and placed in the supine position where IV sedation was administered. The patient's nose was marked around the lesion in question. The previous skin graft was taken off and sent in its entirety. The lesion was circumscribed and removed in a discoid fashion. The lesion was sent for frozen section where analysis revealed clear margins—peripheral and deep. A crescentic skin graft was taken in full-thickness. Hemostasis was achieved using electrocautery. Small medial and lateral flaps were elevated and this layer was closed with a running horizontal mattress suture of 4-0 nylon. The graft was thinned appropriately and inset to the nasal defect using 5-0 chromic. A bolster dressing was placed of Xeroform gauze and was sutured using 5-0 nylon. Antibiotic ointment was applied behind the right ear.

MEADWAY MEDSURG CLINIC

Name: Reynolds, Sharon
Date: 11/3/xx
Patient ID: REY235
Insurance: Signal HMO

PREOPERATIVE DIAGNOSIS: Atypical nevus of the back

POST OPERATIVE DIAGNOSIS: Same

SURGEON: Robyn Houser, M.D.

INDICATIONS: The patient has a .8 × 1.1 cm lesion on her back that was biopsied last week. Pathology was consistent with atypical nevus.

PROCEDURE: The patient was placed in the prone position. Initial infiltration was carried out widely around the nevus. Following this the lesion was excised using a 15-blade in an elliptical fashion. Meticulous hemostasis was checked. The wound was undermined to facilitate primary tension free closure. Defect size was 1.8 cm and wound closure was accomplished in layers using deep and subQ sutures of 4-0 clear nylon and the skin closed with interrupted sutures of 5-0 black nylon. Standard dressing was applied.

MEADWAY MEDSURG CLINIC

Name: Christy, Joel
Date: 11/2/xx
Patient ID: CHR774
Insurance: Flexi Health
PREOPERATIVE DIAGNOSIS: Foreign bodies, right face
Traumatic scars, right face, 2 cm and 1 cm
POSTOPERATIVE DIAGNOSIS: Same
SURGEON: Robyn Houser, M.D.
PROCEDURES: Removal of foreign bodies × 3, right face
Complex wound revision 2 cm, 1 cm right face
Laser resurfacing of traumatic scars less than 20 sq cm, right face

OPERATION: The patient was taken to the OR and placed in the supine position. Patient was prepped and draped. The first foreign body was identified by palpation and a small stab incision was made with a 15-blade. Three small pieces of glass were removed after incusing the capsule. No further foreign bodies were palpable. The 2 cm scar was then excised in elliptical fashion and closed in layers using 5-0 Monocryl and 6-0 nylon mattress sutures. The same was used to close the small stab incision. Another small incision was made on the right cheek where he had some scar adhesions causing an abnormal dimple when he smiled. The scar was created in a Z-pattern and was closed in the same way using 6-0 nylon. Finally all laser resurfacing was performed with one pass at 100 microns over the scarred areas which were previously marked in the holding area. This was 100 microns of ablation only and no coagulation. Aquaphor was applied to the lasered areas and Steri-Strips were applied to the two wound revisions.

MEADWAY MEDSURG CLINIC

Name: Lowell, Neil
Date: 11/3/xx
Patient ID: LOW337
Insurance: Signal HMO
PREOPERATIVE DIAGNOSIS: Nevus sebaceous, right scalp
POST OPERATIVE DIAGNOSIS: Same
SURGEON: Robyn Houser, M.D.
PROCEDURE: Excision of nevus, right scalp, 2 cm
Complex wound closure, 6 cm

OPERATION: The patient was previously marked in the preop area. He was prepped and draped. The lesion was excised elliptically and brought together. It was apparent that the defect would be closed under a fair amount of tension. Wide undermining was performed both bluntly and sharply using cautery. Galeal scoring was performed as well. During the scoring process, the bleeder was divided at the superior aspect. This was cauterized. The defect was closed in layers using 2-0 Monocryl and 4-0 Prolene. The patient was awakened and taken to recovery.

MEADWAY MEDSURG CLINIC

Name: West, Jacob
Date: 11/3/xx
Patient ID: WES665
Insurance: Cigna

PREOPERATIVE DIAGNOSIS: Status post flip-flap closure of the urethral fistula

POST OPERATIVE DIAGNOSIS: Same

PROCEDURE: Urethral calibration and removal of suprapubic tube

SURGEON: Gregory Wallace

OPERATION: This boy underwent hypospadias repair and closure of the urethral fistula on September 4th. Since his suprapubic tube was clamped off he has had painful urination. A urine culture was obtained and he was started on Cipro. The voiding seems to be getting better with each void. He is now here for calibration. If the urethra is wide open, the suprapubic tube will be removed. In view of all his past difficulties, this step was deemed essential to avoid recurrence of the fistula.

Under general anesthesia the patient was placed in the supine position and washed with Betadine paint. The urethra was calibrated with bougie à boule to greater than 12 Fr. Accordingly, the suprapubic tube was removed after cutting the stitches. A Band-Aid was applied. Neosporin ointment was applied to the urethral meatus.

MEADWAY MEDSURG CLINIC

Name: Jacobs, Austin
Date: 11/3/xx
Patient ID: JAC456
Insurance: United Healthcare

PREOPERATIVE DIAGNOSIS: Status post hypospadias repair
Excess skin
Epidermoid cyst

POSTOPERATIVE DIAGNOSIS: Same

SURGEON: Gregory Wallace, M.D.

PROCEDURE: Revision circumcision

INDICATIONS: This child underwent hypospadias surgery at 18 months. He now has excess skin and an epidermoid cyst.

OPERATION: The patient was prepped and draped. A holding stitch os #5-0 silk was placed in the glans penis. The cyst on the left dorsal side was first excised using a scalpel. The excess skin was then excised transversely on each side on the ventral surface. A transverse closure was accomplished distally and then on the ventral surface of the penis in order to make the skin sit comfortably. Z-plasty was performed using subcutaneous sutures of #6-0 Vicryl and the skin was reapproximated with interrupted sutures of #6-0 Vicryl in a horizontal mattress fashion. The urethra was calibrated easily to a #8 French. A mild compression dressing of Telfa and Tegaderm was applied circumferentially along with a 2 × 2 which was taped in place.

MEADWAY MEDSURG CLINIC

Name: Walters, Clay
Date: 11/2/xx
Patient ID: WAL121
Insurance: Signal HMO

PREOPERATIVE DIAGNOSIS: Ventral chordee

POSTOPERATIVE DIAGNOSIS: Same

OPERATION: Ventral chordee repair

SURGEON: Gregory Wallace, M.D.

INDICATIONS: This boy was known to have a ventral chordee without hypospadias.

PROCEDURE: Adhesions between the glans penis and the foreskin were freed by sharp dissection. A holding stitch of 5-0 silk was placed in the glans penis to be removed at the termination of the procedure. Using 3.5x magnification throughout the procedure, a circumcising incision was made. The incision was carried down ventrally to the penoscrotal junction. The penis was freed dorsally down to the pubis and eventually down to the penoscrotal junction. The artificial erection now revealed that there was ventral chordee. Two parallel incisions were made on the distal shaft of the penis and these parallel transverse incisions were connected with two interrupted sutures of 4-0 Prolene. Artificial erection now revealed the penis to be fully straightened. The foreskin was then divided into Byres flaps, The Byers flaps were rotated around to the ventral surface of the penis to be vertically in the midline. The skin had been incised vertically in the midline down to the penoscrotal junction. The skin was then reapproximated vertically in the midline using interrupted suture of 6-0 Vicryl for the subcutaneous tissue which is sutured to the Buck's fascia ventrally and interrupted horizontal mattress suture of 6-0 Vicryl for the skin on the ventral surface of the penis. Excess foreskin was enxised and the circumferential closure was completed with interrupted sutures of 6-0 Vicryl in a horizontal mattress fashion. A penile nerve block was then performed with .5% Marcaine with 1:200,000 epinephrine for post-op pain control. The holding suture of 5-0 silk was removed.

MEADWAY MEDSURG CLINIC

Name: Dalton, William
Date: 11/3/xx
Patient ID: DAL442
Insurance: Cigna

PREOPERATIVE DIAGNOSIS: Bilateral undescended testes

POSTOPERATIVE DIAGNOSIS: Same

OPERATION: Right orchidopexy

SURGEON: Gregory Wallace, M.D.

INDICATIONS: This boy was found to have irregular skin following circumcision. He is also found to have bilateral undescended testes, both of which are palpated in the groin.

(Continued)

FINDINGS: At surgery the child was found to be rather obese and there was a very large amount of subcutaneous fat which necessitated use of the Balfour retractor for exposure. Because of the child's large size, it was decided to stage the orchidopexy.

PROCEDURE: A transverse incision was made in the right groin. Subcutaneous fatty tissue was incised using the Bovie. The external oblique aponeurosis was opened in the direction of its fibers. The testicle was located outside the external ring in the groin and freed up to the level of the internal ring. The lateral spermatic ligaments of Denis Browne were then freed in the retro peritoneal spaces. The scrotum was digitally dilated. The floor of the inguinal canal was taken down by blunt dissection. The testicle was brought under the inferior epigastric vessels. A small transverse incision was made in the mid portion of the scrotum. A sub dartos pouch was then created by blunt dissection. The testicle was brought down to the bottom of the scrotum and anchored in place using two sutures of 3-0 Vicryl. The scrotum was closed with a running subcuticular suture of 5-0 Monocryl. The inguinal canal was reconstructed using a running suture of 3-0 Vicryl from the internal oblique aponeurosis to the shelving border of the inguinal ligament. The skin was closed with running subcuticular suture of 5-0 Monocryl. An ilioinguinal nerve block was performed for post op pain control.

MEADWAY MEDSURG CLINIC

Name: Deats, Wayne | Date: 11/3/xx

Patient ID: DEA646 | Insurance: Flexihealth PPO

PREOPERATIVE DIAGNOSIS: Meatal stenosis

POSTOPERATIVE DIAGNOSIS: Same

PROCEDURE: Meatotomy

SURGEON: Gregory Wallace, M.D.

OPERATION: The patient was taken to the OR and prepped and draped. The meatus was visualized and a straight hemostat was used crimp the urethral meatus at the 6 o'clock position. Metzenbaum scissors were then used to incise the crimped area. Redundant tissue was excised. 4-0 chromic was placed in an interrupted manner. Good hemostasis was noted. The urethral meatus was noted to be approximately an 8 French diameter at the conclusion of the meatotomy.

DAY FIVE

MEADWAY MEDSURG CLINIC

Name: Chase, Winston — Date: 11/4/xx

Patient ID: CHA979 — Insurance: Cigna

PREOPERATIVE DIAGNOSIS: Phimosis

POSTOPERATIVE DIAGNOSIS: Same

PROCEDURE: Circumcision

INDICATIONS: Mother wishes to have this 4½-year-old adopted boy circumcised. Upon examination, he was found to have physiological phimosis.

OPERATION: The patient was placed in the supine position prepped and draped. Adhesions were freed by sharp scissors dissection. A holding stitch of 5-0 silk was placed in the glans penis to be removed at the termination of the procedure. The foreskin was removed using a sleeve technique. Using 3.5X magnification throughout the procedure, the skin of the shaft of the penis was reapproximated to the skin of the coronal sulcus using interrupted sutures of 6-0 Vicryl in a horizontal mattress fashion. A mild compression dressing of Telfa and Tegaderm was applied. Neosporin was applied to the glans.

MEADWAY MEDSURG CLINIC

Name: Chavis, Sam — Date: 11/4/xx

Patient ID: CHA995 — Insurance: Signal HMO

PREOPERATIVE DIAGNOSIS:

1. Type I ventral chordee
2. Concealed penis

POSTOPERATIVE DIAGNOSIS: Same

SURGEON: Gregory Wallace, M.D.

PROCEDURE: Type I ventral chordee repair and concealed penis repair. Artificial erection. Penile nerve block.

INDICATIONS: This boy was noted to have Type I ventral chordee and concealed penis. He was not circumcised as an infant.

OPERATION: The boy was prepped and draped. A holding stitch of 5-0 silk was placed in the glans penis after separating all the adhesions. The skin of the shaft of the penis was ten circumscribed with a skin marking pencil and then a scalpel. The incision was carried vertically down the midline to the penoscrotal junction. The incision was carried transversely at the penoscrotal junction. The penis was freed dorsally down to the pubis and ventrally down to the penoscrotal junction. Artificial erection now revealed a straight penis. The foreskin was then transilluminated to create two Byars flaps. The Byars flaps were rotated around to the ventral surface of the penis for closure. Using 3.5X magnification throughout the procedure, three sutures of 30- PDS were placed around the

(Continued)

subcutaneous tissue of the lower abdominal wall to the prepubic fascia. The skin of the shaft of the penis was then reapproximated vertically in the midline at the penoscrotal junction. The subcutaneous tissue was sutures to the Buck's fascia of the ventral surface of the penis with interrupted sutures of 6-0 Vicryl. The scrotum was sutured to the skin with interrupted sutures of 6-0 Vicryl in a horizontal mattress fashion. The excess foreskin was excised and the circumferential closure was completed with interrupted sutures of 6-0 Vicryl. An 8 French Dover Foley urethral catheter was inserted into the bladder with 3 cc in the balloon. The catheter was allowed to sterile gravity drain using a double diaper technique.

MEADWAY MEDSURG CLINIC

Name: Sanders, Joan
Date: 11/4/xx

Patient ID: SAN754
Insurance: Medicare

PREOPERATIVE DIAGNOSIS: Recurrent ureteral malignancy

POSTOPERATIVE DIAGNOSIS: Carcinoma of the ureter

SURGEON: Gregory Wallace, M.D.

PROCEDURE: Cystourethroscopy

INDICATIONS: Patient is status post urothelial tumor removal of the right ureter and is presenting with hematuria and flank pain.

OPERATION: After satisfactory general anesthesia, the patient was placed in the dorsolithotomy position. Her genitalia were cleansed and prepped in sterile fashion. A #21 panendoscope was inserted. A cystourethroscopy was performed which revealed a normal urethra. The bladder neck and bladder appeared normal. Using a flexible ureteroscope retrograde ureteroscopy was performed all the way to the right renal pelvis. One tumor was found at the ureteropelvic junction measuring less than .5 cm in size. Using a rigid ureteroscope, a Bugbee electrode was used to fulgurate the tumor. Examination of the left ureter was normal.

MEADWAY MEDSURG CLINIC

Name: Ingles, Wilma
Date: 11/4/xx

Patient ID: ING743
Insurance: Medicare

PREOPERATIVE DIAGNOSIS: Urethral stenosis

POSTOPERATIVE DIAGNOSIS: Same

SURGEON: Gregory Wallace, M.D.

PROCEDURE: Cystoscopy and internal urethrotomy

OPERATION: Under general anesthesia, the patient was prepped and draped and placed in the lithotomy position. The cystoscope was introduced and the bladder was examined. No lesions or stones were noted. Ureteral orifices were in normal position. Urethra was noted to be tight to the passage of a 16 bougie. Urethrotome was inserted and inflated to 44 French size and a cut was made at the 11 o'clock. A 16 Foley was inserted and left in to be removed in recovery.

MEADWAY MEDSURG CLINIC

Name: Rawe, Philip
Date: 11/4/xx
Patient ID: RAW338
Insurance: Medicare
PREOPERATIVE DIAGNOSIS: Right groin hernia
POSTOPERATIVE DIAGNOSIS: Indirect right groin hernia
PROCEDURE: Hernia repair with Marlex mesh
SURGEON: Raymond Ross, M.D.
INDICATIONS: The patient is having symptomatic right groin pain.

OPERATION: The right groin was prepped and draped. Right groin crease line incision was made. External oblique was opened along the fibers. The inguinal nerve was identified and protected and cord structures were separated. There was medium size indirect hernia. The sac was opened. The hernial sac was transfixed twice with a 2-0 Vicryl tie of the neck. The distal part of the sac was excised. A medium size Marlex plug soaked in Ancef was placed in the internal ring anchored inferiorly to the inguinal ligament superiorly to the transversalis with 2-0 Prolene in an interrupted fashion and only a patch was placed on the floor anchored medially to the pubic tubercle and inferiorly to the inguinal ligament superior to transversalis. Medial cord structures and the inguinal nerve were transposed. The external oblique was closed with 2-0 Vicryl. The skin was closed subcuticularly with Monocryl.

MEADWAY MEDSURG CLINIC

Name: Hunter, Rosemary
Date: 11/4/xx
Patient ID: HUN654
Insurance: Aetna
PREOPERATIVE DIAGNOSIS: Right breast lump
POSTOPERATIVE DIAGNOSIS: Pending path
SURGEON: Raymond Ross, M.D.
PROCEDURE: Right breast lump excision

INDICATIONS: This 18-year-old girl has noted a lump in her breast since September. She thinks it has gotten larger. It is non-tender. She has no discharge or any other symptoms. Breast ultrasound showed non-specific nodules.

OPERATION: General anesthesia was induced. Her arms were positioned out to arm boards. Her right breast chest and neck were prepped and draped in sterile fashion. The lump was easily palpable at approximately 10 o'clock at the tail of the right breast. A curvilinear skin incision was made using a 15 blade, and subcutaneous tissues were divided using electrocautery. The lump was identified elevated into the wound and dissected free from the surrounding tissue using electrocautery. It was felt to be benign in nature, very rubbery without obvious calcifications or irregularities. The wound was irrigated and examined for hemostasis. The dermis was reapproximated with interrupted 4-0 Vicryl and the skin edges were closed with running subcuticular.

(Continued)

NEW AGE PATHOLOGY

Name: Hunter, Rosemary Date: 11/4/xx

Patient ID: HUN654

SURGEON: Raymond Ross, M.D.

DIAGNOSIS:

1. Fibroadenoma
2. Interlobular fibrosis
3. No evidence of malignancy

Received fresh for gross evaluation in a container labeled with the patient's name and right breast mass measuring 2.0 gm 2.0 × 1.7 × 1.2 cm tan to pink-tan tissue.

MEADWAY MEDSURG CLINIC

Name: Abrams, Mitchell Date: 11/4/xx

Patient ID: ABR012 Insurance: Medicare

PREOPERATIVE DIAGNOSIS: Incarcerated periumbilical ventral hernia

POSTOPERATIVE DIAGNOSIS: Same

SURGEON: Raymond Ross, M.D.

PROCEDURE: Repair of periumbilical ventral hernia incarcerated with Marlex mesh.

INDICATIONS: Patient is having symptomatic periumbilical ventral hernia about 4 cm and he wants to have it repaired because of its enlarging size.

OPERATION: Abdomen was prepped and draped. 0.25% Marcaine was infiltrated in the periumbilical area. A transverse incision was made infraumbilically. Incision was deepened and umbilical skin was separated. The preperitoneal fat and the omentum were incarcerated. It was separated from the defect. The defect was found 3 cm just below the umbilical defect and another 1 cm defect both are connected. 4 × 3 Marlex mesh soaked in Ancef was placed inlay anchored to the overlaying fascia with a 2-0 Prolene and an onlay patch was placed in addition. It was anchored to the edges of the fascia continuous to 2-0 Prolene. Subcutaneous tissue was approximated with 3-0 Vicryl. Skin was closed subcuticularly with Monocryl.

MEADWAY MEDSURG CLINIC

Name: Suarez, Ramona Date: 11/4/xx

Patient ID: SUA464 Insurance: Aetna

PREOPERATIVE DIAGNOSIS: Cholelithiasis

POSTOPERATIVE DIAGNOSIS: Cholecystitis with cholelithiasis

SURGEON: Raymond Ross, M.D.

PROCEDURE: Laparoscopic cholecystectomy with intraoperative cholangiogram

FINDINGS: The patient had dense adhesions around the gallbladder. No acute inflammation. No gangrene. Patient had a previous midline incision but there were very little adhesions and none located in the right upper quadrant.

OPERATION: Incision was made to the right side of the umbilicus and angled Veress needle toward the right side to avoid any possible midline adhesions. Needle was inserted easily. Abdomen was insufflated without incident and the trocar was then inserted. Three additional trocars were placed. The gallbladder was elevated and cholangiogram was attempted. Could not get any flow of contrast out of the gallbladder itself. In spite of maneuvering the gallbladder and manipulating it could still not get any dye to evacuate through the cystic duct. Therefore, changed plans to dissect out the gallbladder and then do a transcystic cholangiogram. Once the dense adhesions were taken down and the gallbladder freed the artery was identified and clipped and divided. The duct was then cleared of fatty tissue and some lymphatic channels. The duct was opened. Catheter inserted and a cholangiogram was performed. Saw a small size common duct with complete filling but could not demonstrate the ampullar area very clearly because of dye that had already dripped into the abdomen or possibly some that had gone ahead during the dissection of the gallbladder. At this point divided the duct after clipping it and then continued to dissect out the gallbladder and brought out through one of the trocar sites. Fluid and CO_2 were aspirated.

MEADWAY MEDSURG CLINIC

Name: Smith, Jared Date: 11/4/xx

Patient ID: SMI777 Insurance: Aetna

PREOPERATIVE DIAGNOSIS: Thyroglossal duct cyst

POSTOPERATIVE DIAGNOSIS: Same

SURGEON: Lee Hackney, M.D.

PROCEDURE: Excision thyroglossal duct cyst

OPERATION: An incision was made in the upper neck and a platysmal flap raised superiorly and inferiorly exposing the anterior neck over the hyoid bone. The firm cyst was noted just above and to the left of the midline just above the hyoid. This was dissected out cleanly down to the base of the hyoid bone. The hyoid bone was then split in the midline and carried forward down over the thyroid cartilage. The entire mass was then tied off and delivered with the midline of the hyoid bone. Bleeding was controlled with electrocautery and the skin closed with 3-0 chromic subcutaneous and 4-0 nylon suture.

MEADWAY MEDSURG CLINIC

Name: Casper, Nicholas Date: 11/4/xx
Patient ID: CAS373 Insurance: Aetna
PREOPERATIVE DIAGNOSIS: Desire for permanent sterilization
POSTOPERATIVE DIAGNOSIS: Same
SURGEON: Gregory Wallace, M.D.
OPERATION: Bilateral vasectomy

PROCEDURE: The patient was placed in the supine position. He was given 1 mg Versed IV. His scrotum was shaved and his genitals were prepped and draped. The median raphe was marked with a marking pencil. Buffered 1% Xylocaine without epinephrine was injected into the median raphe and the vas deferens was grasped on each side and the perivasal tissue was infiltrated with buffered Xylocaine. An incision was made in the median raphe in the upper part of the scrotum. On each side the vas was again palpated and additional Xylocaine was infiltrated around the vas. An Allis clamp was used to grasp the vas and using electrocautery the tissue within the clamp that was anterior to the vas was scored. The vas then elevated into the incision and a hemostat was placed partway across each end that had been elevated. The vas was divided and the segment submitted to pathology. The lumen of each cut end was then cauterized with the needle tip electrode. The distal end of the vas was upon itself and ligated again. With tension held on the distal end and the proximal sutures out, the perivasal tissue was sutured over the proximal end with #4-0 chromic catgut placed in a figure-of-eight fashion. This same procedure was repeated on the opposite side. The scrotal incision was closed with figure-of-eight suture of #3-0 chromic catgut. The skin was closed with interrupted 4-0 chromic mattress sutures.

MEADWAY MEDSURG CLINIC

Name: Jasquich, Helen Date: 11/4/xx
Patient ID: JAS161 Insurance: Cigna
PREOPERATIVE DIAGNOSIS: Macromastia
POSTOPERATIVE DIAGNOSIS: Same
SURGEON: Robyn Houser, M.D.
OPERATION: Bilateral reduction mammoplasty

PROCEDURE: The patient was previously marked in the preoperative holding area with Wise pattern incisions, planning for an inferior pedicle technique. The patient was prepped and draped in sterile fashion. Local anesthesia was used to infiltrate both pectoral pockets. A 42 mm areolar template was created and 10 cm pedicle based was used. Scoring incisions were made. The procedure was first performed on the left and then a mirror image procedure performed on the right. The anterior portion of the pedicle was deepithelialized. The medial and lateral columns were developed and dissection was performed in the fatty layer anterior to the pectoral fascia. The medial, lateral, and

(Continued)

central portions were excised en bloc. Hemostasis was achieved throughout the procedure with sharp bursts of electrocautery. The areolar template was used to create a neoareola. The areola was approximated to the neoareola skin using horizontal mattress sutures of 5-0 nylon. The dermis was approximated in the vertical limb in the inframammary crease using inverted 2-0 Monocryl. The skin was closed in the vertical limb using a running suture of 5-0 nylon. The skin was closed in the inframammary crease using a running subcuticular suture of 4-0 Monocryl.

MEADWAY MEDSURG CLINIC

Name: Carter, Deborah — Date: 11/4/xx

Patient ID: CAR882 — Insurance: Self pay

PREOPERATIVE DIAGNOSIS: Abdominal and thigh lipodystrophy

POSTOPERATIVE DIAGNOSIS: Same

PROCEDURE: Suction assisted lipectomy of the abdomen, hips, and thighs

SURGEON: Robyn Houser, M.D.

OPERATION: The patient was taken to the OR and placed under general anesthesia. Standard tumescent solution was injected in to the abdomen, hips, and thighs. 600 cc were injected into the abdomen, 100 cc into the hips, 200 cc into the outer thighs, and 100 into the inner thighs. 475 cc was removed from the abdomen, 225 cc from hips, 300 from thighs, 125 cc from inner thighs for a total of 1125 cc. The patient had very nice contours and good transitions from abdomen to hips and hips to thighs. The portal sites were closed using 5-0 nylon. Compression garment was applied to the upper body and lower extremities.

MEADWAY MEDSURG CLINIC

Name: Brand, Melissa — Date: 11/4/xx

Patient ID: BRA686 — Insurance: Prudential

PREOPERATIVE DIAGNOSIS: Desires permanent sterilization

POSTOPERATIVE DIAGNOSIS: Same

SURGEON: Abbey Murphy, M.D.

OPERATION: Laparoscopic tubal ligation by cautery and transection

PROCEDURE: She was placed in the lithotomy position and candy-cane stirrups with no pressure on the knees or ankles and bladder was catheterized of urine after sterile prep. A weighted speculum was placed into the vagina. A tenaculum was placed on the anterior lip of the cervix. The cervix was grasped gently and was attached to a suction cannula and then the tenaculum was removed. A vertical subumbilical incision was made with a knife and gently placing the Veress needle intraperitoneally. Opening pressure was 4 mm of Hg. The abdomen was insufflated

(Continued)

with approximately 2½ liters of carbon dioxide. The Ethicon disposable trocar was inserted with the first attempt. The suprapubic 5 mm port was placed in the standard fashion with the Ethicon disposable cannula without difficulty. The Kleppinger forceps were placed through the suprapubic incision and the right fallopian tube was grasped in its mid portion and carefully visualized and photographed. The fimbriae were visualized. It was cauterized four times with excellent blanching effect and then transected with the Bock scissors. The same procedure was carried out on the left side. There was no evidence of adhesions. The intestines appeared normal. The gas was allowed to egress and the instruments were removed under direct visualization. The incisions were closed with 4-0 Vicryl. The suction cannula was removed and the vagina inspected. There was no evidence of bleeding.

MEADWAY MEDSURG CLINIC

Name: Middleton, James — Date: 11/4/xx

Patient ID: MID551 — Insurance: BCBS

PREOPERATIVE DIAGNOSIS: Right nasal polyp

POSTOPERATIVE DIAGNOSIS: Right nasal polyp, probable nasal fibrogranuloma

SURGEON: Lee Hackney, M.D.

OPERATION: Excision right nasal polyp with cautery

INDICATIONS: James has a large friable polyp in the right nasal cavity causing some bleeding and obstruction. Procedure's risks, benefits and alternatives were discussed.

PROCEDURE: The patient was brought to the OR and was anesthetized topically with 1.5 cc 4% cocaine and 1% Xylocaine with epinephrine was used before and after the prep. A total of 4 cc was used. The patient's lesion was large with a very small pedicle attached to the medial surface of the anterior inferior turbinate. This lesion was removed with a cutting forceps. The base was cauterized and the nose was widely patent at the end of the procedure.

NEW AGE PATHOLOGY

Name: Middleton, James — Date: 11/4/xx

Patient ID: MID551

SURGEON: Lee Hackney, M.D.

DIAGNOSIS: Benign polypoid granulation tissue (nasal polyp)

Gross: Nasal polyp 1.5 × 1 × 0.5 cm somewhat fleshy appearing Polypoid portion of whitish tissue having a more hemorrhagic cross section.

MEADWAY MEDSURG CLINIC

Name: Ramsey, David
Patient ID: RAM454

Date: 11/4/xx
Insurance: BCBS

PREOPERATIVE DIAGNOSIS: Chronic paranasal sinusitis polyposis

POSTOPERATIVE DIAGNOSIS: Same

OPERATION:

1. Bilateral endoscopic frontal sinusotomy and polypectomy
2. Bilateral ethmoidectomy
3. Imaged guided surgery

SURGEON: Lee Hackney, M.D.

INDICATIONS: Mr. Ramsey is a 31-year-old with a history of chronic sinusitis and polyposis. He has CT evidence of prior sinus surgery. He has recurrent frontal sinus disease with ethmoid polyps. Because of his prior sinus surgery, image guided technique is used.

PROCEDURE: The headpiece was placed. The intranasal mucosa was vasoconstricted with Afrin 4 cc 0.25% cocaine and 1% Xylocaine with epinephrine. The system was calibrated using a straight shaver blade, straight suction tip and a 90-degree suction tip. Beginning on the left side, there was not much of an identifiable middle turbinate seen. The sphenoid was patent as was the maxillary sinus. Shaver was used to remove the polyps from the middle meatus opening up the nasal frontal area. Some of the polyps in this area were removed using a true cut forceps opening up this area. The sinus was irrigated out, work was done primarily anteriorly. On the right side there was a smaller frontal area. There was what appeared to be a small middle turbinate remnant. The sphenoid was patent. There were some polyps up in the superior aspect of the maxillary sinus on the right side. These were removed using true cut forceps. The shaver was use again using the Insta-trak system to open up the polyps in the ethmoid remnant. The nasofrontal area was much smaller than the left side. He tolerated the procedure well and was sent to recovery.

MEADWAY MEDSURG CLINIC

Name: Linker, Marilyn
Patient ID: LIN959

Date: 11/4/xx
Insurance: Medicare

PREOPERATIVE DIAGNOSIS: Subacute narrow angle glaucoma, right eye

POSTOPERATIVE DIAGNOSIS: Same

OPERATION: Peripheral iridotomy, right eye

SURGEON: Jeremy Moser, M.D.

PROCEDURE: The patient was brought to the laser room where 0.50% tetracaine drops and 0.50% Iopidine drops were instilled in the right eye. The patient's head was then fixated in the laser delivery system slit lamp apparatus and following parameters of treatment were delivered to the right eye in the superior nasal quadrant periphery. The power setting was 3 mJ. The pulse setting was one five applications were made to create penetration. The patient tolerated the procedure well and was sent to recovery.

MEADWAY MEDSURG CLINIC

Name: West, Shirley
Date: 11/4/xx
Patient ID: WES626
Insurance: BCBS

PREOPERATIVE DIAGNOSIS: Thyroid eye disease with lower lid retraction

POSTOPERATIVE DIAGNOSIS: Same

SURGEON: Jeremy Moser, M.D.

OPERATION: Correction of lower lid retraction with placement of an Alloderm graft

PROCEDURE: The right lower lid was infiltrated with 1% Lidocaine with epinephrine. An incision at the inferior edge of her previous auricular cartilage graft was made and the retractors of the lower lid cut. Its greater recipient bed approximately 5 mm in height. The bed was wider temporarily because the auricular cartilage graft did not completely go into position using interrupted and running 6-0 chromic and 7-0 chromic suture. Upon completion of the procedure a soft contact lens was placed over the cornea to protect it. The lid put on superior traction with a Frost suture 4-0 silk. It was taped to the forehead.

MEADWAY MEDSURG CLINIC

Name: Francis, Adrian
Date: 11/4/xx
Patient ID: FRA323
Insurance: Flexi-Health

PREOPERATIVE DIAGNOSIS: Mass posterior thoracic area, rule out epidermal cyst

POSTOPERATIVE DIAGNOSIS: Same

OPERATION: Excision of mass in the posterior part of the thoracic area

SURGEON: Raymond Ross, M.D.

INDICATIONS: The patient has a 5 cm mass suggestive of epidermal cyst.

PROCEDURE: The patient was placed in the prone position. The back was prepped and draped. 1% Xylocaine mixed with 0.25% Marcaine was infiltrated. A 6 cm elliptical incision was made. Incision was deepend to the underlying fascia. The mass was excised. Bleeding points were cauterized. Subcutaneous tissue was approximated with 3-0 Vicryl. Skin was closed with Monocryl.

NEW AGE PATHOLOGY

Name: Francis, Adrian
Date: 11/4/xx
Patient ID: FRA323

SURGEON: Raymond Ross, M.D.

DIAGNOSIS: Benign Epidermal Inclusion Cyst

Gross: Large unoriented skin excision measuring 4.2 × 1.0 × 1.5 cm in depth. The specimen is sectioned to reveal an oval cystic lesion filled with keratinous material.

MEADWAY MEDSURG CLINIC

Name: Isaac, Stephanie — Date: 11/4/xx

Patient ID: ISA484 — Insurance: BCBS

PREOPERATIVE DIAGNOSIS: Periprosthetic infection, chronic, left breast

POSTOPERATIVE DIAGNOSIS: Same

OPERATION: Removal of left breast prosthesis

SURGEON: Robyn Houser, M.D.

INDICATIONS: The patient is a 53-year-old with an acquired absence of her left breast having undergone a mastectomy as treatment for breast cancer. The breast mound has been reconstructed with a prosthesis. The procedure has been complicated by history of prior radiation. She has developed a chronic history of inflammation and drainage from the left breast. She was evaluated by an infectious disease specialist who has recommended removal of the prosthesis.

PROCEDURE: The anterior thorax was prepped and draped in the usual manner. The previous incision was identified and the scar was excised over a 4 cm distance. The dissection was continued with the Bovie to expose the pectoralis muscle which was divided in the direction of its fibers. A thin capsule was identified and incised to allow the removal of the prosthesis. Some thickness was present along the inferolateral aspect. This was incised with the Bovie and explored. A mild scarred capsule was present in this area but no other abnormalities were noted. The Jackson-Pratt drain was placed and brought out through the inferolateral stab incision. The pectoralis muscle was repaired with sutures of 4-0 Monocryl. The skin incision was repaired win layers with deep sutures of 4-0 Monocryl and skin closure using 4-0 Prolene.

MEADWAY MEDSURG CLINIC

Name: Ross, Everett — Date: 11/4/xx

Patient ID: ROS717 — Insurance: Medicare

PREOPERATIVE DIAGNOSIS: Hoarseness

POSTOPERATIVE DIAGNOSIS: Same

OPERATION: Microdirect laryngoscopy and biopsy of left vocal cord

SURGEON: Lee Hackney, M.D.

PROCEDURE: Following difficult intubation, the table was turned and maxillary tooth guard was inserted. An operating laryngoscope was introduced. He had a very difficult examination secondary to his weight and very short neck. I was able to examine the larynx. There were diffusely inflamed vocal cords but the only area in question was actually on the superior aspect of the left vocal cord anteriorly. The edges of the vocal cord while somewhat inflamed did not reveal any significant nodules or ulcerations that were seen previously. With the microscope in position the nodular swelling was biopsied on the superior aspect of the left vocal cord. The larynx was then sprayed with Xylocaine. Photos were taken pre and post.

(Continued)

NEW AGE PATHOLOGY

Name: Ross, Everett Date: 11/4/xx

Patient ID: ROS717

SURGEON: Lee Hackney, M.D.

DIAGNOSIS: Acutely and chronically inflamed squamous mucosa with nonspecific reactive epithelial atypia and stromal degenerative changes consistent with vocal cord nodule.

Gross: Received in Ultrum labeled "Nodule left vocal cord" are two strips of soft tan tissue in one cassette.

Appendix A: Policy and Procedure Manual

Table of Contents

Purpose

The purpose of these policies and procedures (P&P) is to promote consistent application of Douglasville Medicine Associates' (DMA) standards as they relate to accounts receivables, coding, and collection practices. The P&P in this manual are intended to provide guidelines to foster operational performance and ensure compliance with federal and state billing guidelines.

Standards

All patients are to be treated professionally and compassionately, regardless of race, color, sex, religion, age, national origin, or financial status.

All patient demographics and financial information are prequalified prior to the patient being seen. This information is maintained and updated on a regular basis.

Financial notification and payment arrangements are made with all patients and/or responsible parties.

All professional services and supplies are accounted for and accurately billed in a timely manner.

All billing and collection functions are performed in a manner that expedites payment, reduces days outstanding, and minimizes the risk of bad debts.

Overview of Business Functions

This manual divides the business functions within Douglasville Medicine Associates into two major groups called business office (back office) and patient access (front office). Each group maintains responsibility and accountability for the tasks they perform. Front office activities include "point of service" activities such as scheduling appointments, special tests, and surgeries; obtaining insurance information; collecting copays and coinsurance; and charge capture. Business or back office functions are behind the scenes and involve more communication with the insurance carriers after the patient was treated.

Most business office staff do not have face-to-face contact with patients but they do generally speak to them on the phone regarding statements received and information needed to get claims paid by the carrier.

Front Office (FO) Duties

- Scheduling
- Patient demographics
- Collection of copay
- Insurance eligibility and verification
- Preauthorization for special tests and surgery
- Patient financial counseling
- Charge capture

Business Office (BO) Duties

- Claims submission and billing
- Third-party payers (electronic or paper claims)
- Monthly statements
- Accounts receivable (payment posting)
- Adjustments
- Account follow-up
- Reports
- Tracking payer trends
- Analysis
- Month-end close

Front Office Pre-Visit Responsibilities

1. Obtain new patient information such as insurance carrier, responsible party, date of birth (DOB), Social Security Number (SSN), and medical records appropriate to patient visit
2. Obtain referrals, precertification, and authorizations
3. Review appointment schedule in advance of patient visit; note any copay and patient responsibility amounts for office collection
4. Complete insurance verification and confirm eligibility dates on all new patients and those scheduled for office procedures
5. Enter all acquired demographics and insurance information into computer system
6. Track limited authorizations and referral numbers
7. Provide financial counseling prior to any treatment
8. Track and update accounts information for special circumstances such as bankruptcy, estates, and research
9. Prepare all patient charts for the next day's appointments

Front Office Daily Duties

1. Maintain current and complete patient demographic and insurance information. Ask the patient if there are any changes to his address, phone number, or insurance. Obtain copy of insurance card(s), driver's license, and a patient demographic form on each new patient. Obtain copy of insurance cards and driver's license as well as a new patient demographic form at the beginning of each new year.
2. Ensure that any advance notification, Advanced Beneficiary Notices (ABN), and out-of-network and noncovered waivers have been reviewed with the patients and signed *prior* to the patient being seen in the back.
3. Complete charge entry in an accurate and timely manner.
4. Collect copays, coinsurance, and deductibles. Offer payment arrangements to patients who are unable to pay their balances in full at the time of service.
5. Provide each patient with a receipt for all payments made at the office.
6. Return patient telephone calls in a timely manner, using appropriate telephone etiquette.
7. Research and process all returned mail received by contacting the patient or searching online.
8. Place main phone lines on the automated service at lunch and after 5:00 p.m.
9. Process mail (i.e., sort by doctor and department) and distribute upon receipt. All insurance and patient checks are forwarded immediately to the BO for processing. The BO will date stamp, copy, and post to the appropriate accounts.
10. Process requests for medical records twice a week. Must verify patient's authorization

to release records, prepayment (when necessary), and the physician's approval.

11. Maintain medical records (i.e., preparing new charts, locating existing charts, purging old charts, filing loose material, requesting records from other offices, etc.).

Essential Front Office Post-Visit Functions

1. Prepare bank deposits.
2. Review the daily patient schedule and patient sign-in log to verify that all routers have been received (lest any no-shows and cancellations). Ensure add-ons have been accounted for at the end of the workday. If any routers are missing, check with the physicians or medical assistant.
3. Review each router form for complete and accurate information.
4. Track patient referral authorizations and request additional visits when appropriate.
5. Cancel out of the schedule any patient cancellations or no-shows.
6. Follow up on any outstanding balance greater then 45 days with the appropriate payer.
7. Combine multiple accounts for the same patient when they are discovered.

Business Office

This section of the manual describes positions and respective functions performed in the business office.

Coder/Biller Responsibilities

The following is a list of tasks and responsibilities of this position.

1. Account representatives review and file workers' compensation claims, handle documentation and claim requests, and follow up on outstanding claims.
2. Code services to the highest level of specificity with appropriate documentation.
3. Insurance claims are processed at the end of each day. Claim errors are corrected and refiled immediately. Paper claims are reviewed for accuracy before being sent and are processed daily. Denials or claim delay trends are monitored and reported to the office manager.
4. Patient statements are generated electronically 1–2 times a week along with a regular cycle of collection letters. The patient receives the first statement at checkout. The patient will receive another statement once the primary insurance carrier pays. Thirty days after this statement, another statement is generated. A past due letter is sent at 45 days. Following this is another statement at 60 days, a second past due letter at 75 days, another statement at 90 days, and a final past due letter at 105 days. From this point, the account should be referred to the physician for action (i.e., referral to outside collections or write-off).
5. The billers work EOBs, researching any denials or improper payments, comparing fee schedules to payments, and posting payments to MOSS.
6. The coder/biller maintains all fee schedules, contracts, and payer reimbursement information.
7. Physicians are responsible for ensuring the accuracy and timeliness of charge submissions (office and hospital). All documentation for procedures will be provided to the coder/biller daily. E/M level codes will be provided to the coder along with supportive documentation. Any coding discrepancies will be brought to the office manager's attention for a second opinion. Any coding discrepancies will be discussed with the appropriate physician.

Authorization and Precertification

Prior to a patient's initial visit, referral information is obtained from the patient's primary care physician. All applicable services and/or items are authorized in accordance with the payer's guidelines prior to initiation of the first visit or treatment.

Purpose

To ensure necessary authorizations have been secured prior to service being rendered so that payment can be obtained from third-party payers.

Procedure

1. At the time of referral, ask the primary care physician's office for authorization.
2. If the primary care physician does not have the authorization information, a clinic staff member must call and obtain the referral from the payer. All referrals and authorizations will be documented and maintained in the patient's file.
3. If an authorization cannot be obtained from the payer, the patient is notified of his/her financial responsibility prior to the service being rendered (i.e., provide financial counseling and obtain an out-of-network waiver).
4. All subsequent services must be recertified in accordance with the payer's guidelines and documented in the patient's file. To alert staff when a renewal is needed, notes must be placed in MOSS reflecting the number of visits or days of care authorized.

Registration

All patients must complete the required admission documentation upon their initial visit. Any information not obtained during the scheduling or referral process is obtained at the time of registration. All data collected during the registration process must be accurate and complete.

Purpose

To ensure that all patient demographic and financial information is current and accurate. To obtain necessary signatures, consents, and releases of information as required by law. To collect and complete all information necessary to establish a new patient in the billing system.

Procedure

1. Review the patient schedule 24 hours in advance to identify outstanding balances. Ask patients for any outstanding balances upon check-in.
2. Upon arrival at the practice, have the patient complete all of the necessary forms for registration. Make sure the forms are complete. Unanswered questions or scant information may signal that the patient cannot read or is uncooperative.
3. Obtain all necessary signatures from the patient.
4. Have all new patients fill out the patient history questionnaire.
5. Make copies of the following:
   - Driver's license
   - Insurance identification card
6. Obtain any other specific documentation or information, as needed, to establish a complete financial record on the patient.
7. Provide the patient with the clinic's HIPAA statement and patient's bill of rights.
8. If authorization from the primary care physician has not been obtained prior to the patient's arrival, the front office staff will attempt to contact the referring physician and insurance carrier. If an authorization is not obtained within 30 minutes of the patient's appointment time, the appointment will be canceled and rescheduled for a later date.

Scheduling

Each staff member must be trained in patient scheduling. Staff will screen patient calls and attempt to schedule each appointment based on the patient's condition and provider availability. A first available time is always offered. If no appointment is available, the call is forwarded to the physician's nurse to assess the severity of the patient's illness and discuss this with the doctor to work the patient into the schedule.

All scheduled appointments should be verified the day before the visit.

Always document no-shows and cancellations. A $20 no-show fee is assessed to the patient's account. In order to assess this fee, the diagnosis code 123.45 must also be entered.

Keep a copy of the schedule and the sign-in sheet.

Insurance Verification Policy

It is a policy of this practice that insurance coverage and eligibility benefits be verified for all new patients and hospital admissions regardless of insurance type. Coverage and benefits will also be verified for any patient who indicates a change to their coverage and for all high dollar procedures.

Procedure

1. All new patient appointments, inpatient admissions, high dollar procedures, and known insurance changes will be pulled from the appointment schedule three days prior to the patient's arrival.
2. Insurance coverage and benefits eligibility will be verified either by going to the insurance carrier website or by contacting the carrier via phone.
3. The insurance verification worksheet will be completed for each patient in question. It is important to indicate the date this information was verified and the contact person at the insurance company.
4. If insurance benefits cannot be verified within a day of the patient's scheduled appointment, the patient will be contacted. Coverage information will be requested from the patient. If information is unobtainable, the patients will be notified that they will be considered self-pay and will be responsible for fees incurred related to services rendered. The patient may opt to reschedule the appointment until such information can be acquired.
5. If the patient desires to keep said appointment and agrees to be self-pay, refer to the self-pay policy.

Insurance Verification

Date:____________________ Initials:_________________

Instructions: Call the insurance company or check eligibility online. Obtain the following information. Call the patient and inform them of their coverage and copayment/coinsurance responsibility. For all inpatient or outpatient surgery, benefits must be verified as well as surgical coverage. Ask if surgery must be preauthorized. If so, give the insurance company all requested information (i.e., diagnosis, date of scheduled surgery, where surgery is scheduled, and planned surgical procedure). Some carriers want the ICD-9 and CPT codes at this time. Fill out demographic information before calling the insurance carrier. Fill in the sheet and scan it into the electronic record if available.

Demographics:

Patient Name:________________________ DOB:_________________

Insurance Plan:________________________ Insurance ID #:___________________

Group # (if any):___________________

Subscriber Name:________________________ Subscriber DOB:_______________

Subscriber SSN:________________________

Benefits (office visits/surgery/hospitalization):

Coverage dates: Effective from:________________ to ______________

Deductible Met? Y/N Balance:_______ Copayment amt:______ Coverage:__________

Precertification/Preauthoriziation (surgery/hospitalization)

Coinsurance amount:________________ Preauthorization needed for surgery? Y/N

Facility Name:____

Patient Diagnosis:_____________________________ ICD-9:_____________________

Surgical Procedure:____________________________ CPT:______________________

Authorization Number:______________________________

Rep. Spoke With:______________________ Date Patient Informed:_____________

Coinsurance and Copayments (COPAYS)

Copayments will be collected in accordance with federal, state, and payer-specific contractual agreements. This includes, but is not limited to, collections of copayments at the time of service for all contracted nongovernmental payers. Copayments on government payers are billed monthly following receipt of reimbursement from the payer. Copayments will not be waived and will not exceed the amount contractually the provider of service is legally entitled to receive.

Purpose

To ensure compliance with all federal, state, and contracted agreements.

The term *coinsurance* or *copayment* is used to describe the amount remaining on the charge after the primary insurance has been paid. This amount is the responsibility of the patient or secondary insurance.

Procedure

The following steps should be taken when processing copayments or coinsurances.

Contracted, Nongovernment Payers, Self-Pay

1. The patient's specific copayment obligation is to be documented on the insurance verification form and keyed into MOSS. For self-pay patients, the fee for an office visit is disclosed to the patient upon scheduling.
2. The copayment responsibility is discussed with the patient, if possible, during the appointment reminder call and during registration.
3. A payment plan may be established for coinsurances but not for copays. Payment plans may also be established for self-pay patients.

Government Payers

1. Ask Medicare patients if they are a Medicare beneficiary or a member of a Medicare Senior Plan to ensure that current benefit information is always on file.
2. Document the patient's copayment in MOSS.
3. The copayment responsibility is discussed with the patient, if possible, during the appointment reminder call and during registration.
4. Explain that the outstanding copayment will be billed directly to the patient on a monthly basis and will be sent to collections at 60 days.

Payment Plans and Credit Terms

Purpose

Payment and credit terms are firmly established with the patient and/or responsible party for self-pay patients prior to the first visit. These arrangements should be documented, signed, dated, and approved by the office manager.

Procedure

Payment plans offered to patients are designed to be sensitive to each patient's financial situation and to establish the practice's minimum collection amount. Payment arrangements help to define the timeframe and terms for collecting an account and allow appropriate adjustments to be made to accounts receivable, thus minimizing or artificially inflating accounts receivable.

It is preferred that patients pay their out-of-pocket financial obligations within six months. The front office staff or office manager will need to meet with the patient prior to the procedure and estimate the cost of services.

If a patient misses two consecutive payments without contacting the business office, the payment arrangement terms are void and the patient's account will be placed into collection activity.

Payment Agreement

Date: ______________

I am provided with fees for services for which I am responsible. The fees are for either proposed services or for services previously rendered by a physician at Douglasville Medicine Associates. I have been encouraged to pay this balance in full; however, I have elected to make monthly installments. I either do not have health insurance or I have a coinsurance or deductible due. The installments I have agreed to are outlined below:

Date(s) of Service	Account #	Beginning Balance	Today's Payment	Number of Installments	Amount of Each Installment	Future Payment Dates

I understand that my account will be considered delinquent if my scheduled payment is more than four business days late. I understand that I may be legally responsible for all collections costs involved with the collection of this account, including all court costs, reasonable attorney's fees, and all other expense incurred with collection if I default on this agreement. I further understand that failure to meet the prescribed payment schedule can result in listing of this debt with local, regional, and national credit reporting agencies, and it may have a negative effect on the granting of future credit. **If at any time during the duration of this payment plan I move or change my phone number, I will notify Douglasville Medicine Associates of this change.**

This office does not assess interest or finance charges on balances even though this is considered a loan. I acknowledge that I will receive a monthly statement with a return addressed envelope for mailing my payment. Payments are mailed to:

5076 Brand Blvd, Suite 401, Douglasville, NY 01234

I had an opportunity to ask questions regarding charges and my balance, and I received adequate answers from a staff member. I have read the above description of this payment plan and agree to all its terms.

______________________________ ______________________________

Patient Name Patient Signature

Clinic Employee:______________________________ Date:______________________

Prompt Pay Discount

If approved by the office manager, the business office may offer private pay patients with private indemnity insurance and self-pay patients a prompt pay discount. The arrangement should apply only to balances over $500 and applies only if the balance is paid the day of service. A discount of 20% is offered for patients who pay in full the day of service.

Indigent Patients

At DMA, patients who are deemed indigent according to federal poverty standards qualify for discounts.

Purpose

The intent of the indigent care process is to provide DMA and its physicians with a systematic financial evaluation of patients who indicate they are unable to meet their financial obligations. This process permits the physician to be better informed, to evaluate treatment options, and to direct the patient toward community or state assistance programs.

Procedure

An indigent patient is a patient (1) who is financially impoverished, (2) who has no medical insurance coverage, (3) who has been denied Medicaid benefits, and (4) whose income does not exceed 150% of the federal poverty income limits as published by the Department of Health and Human Services. If these patients are seen, the practice will not expect payment and will adjust the balance off to charity.

Complete the following financial worksheet to determine if the patient is indigent. Once you have verified all supportive documentation and established the patient as indigent, the physician will need to determine the medical approach and the duration of care. The office manager, along with the board, will discuss terms and the number of charitable patients the practice can accommodate.

Financial Hardship Eligibility Form

Name ______________________ SS# ____________

Address ____ DOB ____________

City, State, Zip ______________________________ Acct. # ____________

For us to make a determination as to whether you meet our practice criteria for establishing financial hardship status, please answer the following questions and submit substantiating documents (if applicable).

Number of persons living in household: ____________

Their ages: ____________

Monthly household income: ____________ (all sources; submit proof, stubs, etc.)

Other factors to be considered: ____

____

____

Employment status: ____________________Employed (salary: $____________ week/month)

____________________Unemployed

____________________Retired (monthly income: $____________)

Housing status: ____________Rent

____________Own

Monthly payment: $____________

If you qualify, we will waive all charges not paid by your insurance carrier(s) for a period of ____________. This agreement can be revoked at our discretion.

____________________ ____________ ____________________

Patient Signature Date Approved by

FEDERAL POVERTY INCOME LIMITS			
Family Size	**100%**	**133%**	**150%**
1	$658	$875	$987
2	$885	$1176	$1316
3	$1111	$1478	$1645
4	$1338	$1779	$1974
5	$1565	$2081	$2303
6	$1791	$2382	$2632
7	$2018	$2684	$2961
8	$2245	$2985	$3290
9	$2471	$3287	$3619
10	$2698	$3588	$3948
11	$2925	$3890	$4277
12	$3151	$4191	$4606
13	$3378	$4493	$4935
14	$3605	$4794	$5264
15	$3831	$5095	$5593
For each additional family member	$227	$302	$329

Encounter Form/Router

All patients seen in the office have a corresponding charge ticket or router. All services and billable supplies are documented here. This is done to ensure that all patients and their respective insurance carriers are charged for services and/or supplies uniformly and accurately.

Procedure

1. Every patient that comes to the practice for service is issued a router.
2. The patient's name, account number, physician name, and codes are clearly documented on the router.
3. All service items are documented on the router either by checking the appropriate box or by writing the service in the comments section of the router.
4. Each router must be accounted for the next business day.
5. Discrepancies of any kind—dates, duplicate services, missing routers, conflicting information—must be researched and resolved immediately.

Charge Tracking

The coder/biller will enter charges each day for all services provided, whether in the office or offsite. All charges must be accounted for and tracked in such a manner that ensures all routers and charge tickets are accounted for by the next business day. Charge entry should be done within 24 hours of services rendered to ensure timely capture of charges to expedite billing and receivables.

Procedure

1. All routers are accounted for at the end of the day by reconciling them to the patient schedule and sign-in sheet.
2. All charges are reviewed for accuracy, completeness, and compliant coding.

3. Any discrepancies in either of the two previous steps should be reconciled immediately. If any compliance issues are identified, notify the office manager.

Claims Errors and Rejections

The business office will track all payers' request for information, as well as returned, rejected, and unbillable claims daily.

Purpose

To prevent delays in claims processing caused by incomplete patient demographics, data entry errors, or incomplete clinical information.

Procedure

1. Review upon receipt all daily correspondence from insurance carriers via electronic remittance advice (ERA), hard copy EOB, or claims acknowledgement or rejection reports.
2. Respond immediately to all requests for additional information.
3. Appeal denials when necessary.
4. Track all claims errors to include initial scrubbing of claims in MOSS, clearinghouse rejections, and carrier rejections. Review for trends and communicate your findings to the office manager to coordinate training with staff.

Daily Deposit

The business office personnel are responsible for daily posting of all mail payments and making respective adjustments. Front office staff is responsible for over the counter collections and payment posting during check-in and/or checkout. An employee who posts money in MOSS for a given day's deposit is not permitted to take the deposit to the bank.

Purpose

To ensure accurate accounting and aging of the accounts receivable system.

Procedure

1. All checks, money orders, cash, and credit card payments received in the mail are forwarded to the business office. Any copayments collected over the counter are posted in MOSS at the time of check-in or checkout. Patients are provided a receipt for all payments. A receipt can be a copy of the router with the amount collected indicated at the bottom of the page.
2. The coder/biller is responsible for preparing the deposit slip. The office manager takes the deposit to the bank.
3. Bank deposit receipts are kept with the respective deposit slip along with copies of checks and EOBs for that day's deposit.

Payment Posting

Business office personnel post all payments received via mail daily. Front office staff post all money collected from office visits daily. During the insurance payment posting, the account balance is adjusted according to payer contracts.

Purpose

To ensure consistent and efficient posting of payments and adjustments to patient accounts.

Procedure

1. Payments are posted to an account based on account number. Patient payments should be posted to the oldest unpaid account first. Insurance payments are posted based on date of service indicated on the explanation of benefits (EOB).
2. Enter the check number into the computer. Checks can be posted as a "batch" check meaning the same check number may apply to several patient accounts.
3. Information required to appropriately post an insurance payment and process a contractual write-off is obtained from the EOB.
4. Notes must be placed in the system for all denials or inaccurate payments for use in claims follow-up. At the time of payment posting, line items that are not paid in accordance with payer contract guidelines are flagged for review and follow-up. If the payment is less than 100% of the expected or contracted amount, the EOB must be reviewed for reason codes. Action must be taken to appeal a line item or an entire claim

if it is determined that the services and codes were reported correctly by calling the payer customer service department. This action includes, but is not limited to, filing an appeal, submitting documentation, and requesting a fair hearing.

5. After contractual adjustments, transfer any remaining balance to the secondary and/or tertiary insurance, if applicable, and finally to the patient or responsible party.

Returned Checks

To establish a standardized procedure for processing and reporting returned patient checks for nonsufficient funds (NSF) and returned by the bank.

Procedure

1. Notify the office manager that a check has been returned.
2. Add an entry into the account in MOSS indicating the reason for the returned check.
3. Make an adjustment to debit the patient's account for the amount of the check.
4. Assess a $25 fee for the returned check. Enter the diagnosis code 123.45. This is a dummy code created for the purpose of allowing MOSS to accept miscellaneous fees such as this NSF fee or no show fees since all fees require a diagnosis code.
5. Send the check back to the bank for deposit a second time.
6. Send the patient an NSF letter and request payment in a cashiers check or cash.
7. If the patient does not respond in 7 days, contact the patient to request they make good on the check and to collect a return check fee.
8. If payment is not received in 14 days, place the account into collections.

Refund Request

Patients and insurance companies will contact the office requesting refunds on overpayments. Patient accounts with credit balances should be monitored for timely refunding.

Purpose

To ensure that refund requests and credit balances are handled in a timely manner and that appropriate support documentation accompanies all refund requests. To ensure that corresponding debit adjustments are accurately input to resolve credit balances.

Procedure

All requests for refunds must be researched and resolved in a timely manner. A patient's request for a refund should be investigated thoroughly. All EOBs for dates of service in question and receipts of payment must be researched. A response must be provided to the patient within 3 business days of request. If a refund is appropriate, submit this information to the office manager to process the request. A payer's request for refunds must be researched within 14 working days of receiving the request to avoid recoupment. Insurance requests are processed just as patient requests are. If a refund is necessary, notify the office manager to cut a check. Make a note in the system explaining the circumstances along with a debit adjustment to MOSS to avoid inappropriate credits.

Business office staff must run reports from MOSS monthly and assess if refunds are required by researching any outstanding balance on prior accounts. Accounts with a credit balance will be reflected in parentheses ( ). Any account with a prepay will not be issued a refund until all insurance payments are received.

Collections Protocol

The business office staff must pursue collection of outstanding patient account balances and perform all subsequent write-offs in a timely manner. Douglasville Medicine Associates personnel will adhere to the Fair Debt Collection Act and New York State law during the pursuit of payment on outstanding patient account balances.

Purpose

To define practice guidelines and parameters to be employed during the collection of patient account balances.

Procedure

1. Personnel *do not* engage in any conduct that may be construed as harassment, oppression, or abuse of any person(s) in connection with collection of debt. This includes, but is not limited to:
   - Verbal abuse
   - Threats to inform debtor's employer of debt
   - Invasion of individual privacy
2. Telephone collections may occur Monday through Friday, 8:00 a.m.–9:00 p.m., Saturday, 8:00a.m.–5:00 p.m., unless instructed otherwise by the patient.
3. Patients may be contacted at their place of employment, unless otherwise instructed by the patient.
4. All accounts must be approved by the office manager prior to referring the account to a collection agency.
5. Threats of legal action may not be used *unless* such action is likely.
6. Bad debt write-offs should occur as soon as an account is determined to be uncollectible.

Account Follow-Up

Accounts to be worked are assigned by the office manager based on age of account and dollar value. The oldest accounts and the highest dollar accounts are worked first.

Purpose

To ensure all patient accounts receive timely follow-up and revenue streams are consistent.

Procedure

- All accounts over 30 days old are reviewed and pursued for prompt payment. This is accomplished by following up with the insurance companies on these accounts.
- The MOSS system should be used to run aging reports by age bracket (0–30, 31–60, 61–90, 91–120, 120+) to systematically follow up on accounts.
- Accounts over 30 days will be worked every 14 days until payment is received by the insurance carrier.
- All follow-up calls and Internet inquires should be noted in MOSS with the following details:
  - Name of contact person at insurance company
  - Brief summary of discussion
  - Actions taken
  - Date payment is expected

Medical Abbreviations

Common Medical Abbreviations

This list is a quick reference for students and employees to use when reading handwritten or typed medical record documentation. This is not an inclusive list but rather a condensed version of common acronyms and symbols used at our practice.

Purpose

To promote consistency and uniformity in medical record documentation. This list of abbreviations is the only set of abbreviations permitted in Douglasville Medicine Associates records.

ABBREVIATION	MEANING
@	at
AAA	Abdominal aortic aneurysm
Ab, Ab	Antibody
AB	Abortion
Abd, ABD	Abdomen
ABG	Arterial blood gas
ABN	Abnormal; Advanced Beneficiary Notice (Medicare)
ABO	A system of classifying blood groups
a.c.	Before meals
ACE	Angiotensin converting enzyme
ACL	Anterior cruciate liagment
ACTH	Adrenocorticotr opic hormone, corticotropin
AD	Right ear; Alzheimer's disease
ADH	Antidiuretic hormone
ADL	Activities of daily living
ad lib	As desired
Afib	Atrial fibrillation
AFL	Atrial flutter
AFP	Alpha-fetoprotein
AID	Artificial insemination donor
AIDS	Acquired immunodeficiency syndrome
AKA	Above the knee amputation; also known as
aka	Alcoholic ketoacidosis
ALT	Alanine aminotransferase (formerly SGPT)
ALS	Amyotrophic lateral sclerosis
AMA	Against medical advice
AMI	Acute myocardial infarction
AML	Acute myelogenous leukemia
ANA	Antinuclear antibody
A/O	Alert and oriented
AODM	Adult onset diabetes mellitus
AP	Anteroposterior
A&P	Anterior and posterior; auscultation & percussion
AQ, aq.	Water
ARDS	Adult respiratory distress syndrome
ARF	Acute renal failure
AS	Left ear; aortic stenosis
*as	Without
ASHD	Atherosclerotic heart disease

(continued)

ABBREVIATION	MEANING
ASA	Aspirin, acetylsalicylic acid
ASAP	As soon as possible
ASCVD	Arteriosclerotic cardiovascular disease
ASHD	Arteriosclerotic heart disease
ASO	Antistreptolysin-O
AST	Aspartate aminotransferase (formerly SGOT)
AU	Both ears
AV	Arteriovenous, atrioventricular
bact	Bacteriology
BBB	Bundle branch block
b.i.d.	Twice a day
BIH	Bilateral inguinal hernia
BKA	Below the knee amputation
BLS	Basic life support
BM	Black male; bone marrow; bowel movement
BMR	Basal metabolic rate
BP	Blood pressure
BPH	Benign prostatic hypertrophy
bpm	Beats per minute
BR	Bedrest; bathroom
BS	Blood sugar; bowel sounds; breath sounds
BSA	Body surface area
BTL	Bilateral tubal ligation
BUN	Blood urea nitrogen
BX, Bx	Biopsy
C	Celsius, centigrade; complement
*c	With
Ca	Calcium
CA, Ca, ca	Cancer, carcinoma
CABG	Coronary artery bypass graft
CAD	Coronary artery disease
caps	Capsules
CAV	Cytoxan, adrimycin, and vincristine
CBC	Complete blood count
CC, C.C.	Chief complaint; comorbid condition
cc	Cubic centimeter
CCU	Coronary care unit
CEA	Carcinoembryonic antigen
cg	Centigram
CHF	Congestive heart failure
CK	Creatine kinase

ABBREVIATION	MEANING
Cl	Chloride, chlorine
CLL	Chronic lymphocytic leukemia
cm	Centimeter
CN	Cranial nerve
CNS	Central nervous system
c/o	Complains of
CO	Carbon monoxide; cardiac output
CO_2	Carbon dioxide
COMP	Compound
COPD	Chronic obstructive pulmonary disease
CPK	Creatine phosphokinase
CPR	Cardiopulmonary resuscitation; C-reactive protein
CRF	Chronic renal failure
C&S	Culture and sensitivity
CSF	Cerebrospinal fluid
CT	Computed tomography
CTS	Carpal tunnel syndrome
cu	Cubic
CVA	Cerebrovascular accident
c/w	Consistent with
Cx	Cervix; canceled
CxR	Chest x-ray
Cysto	Cystoscopy
D&C	Dilatation and curettage
d/c	Discontinue; discharge
DIC	Disseminated intravascular coagulation
DIFF, diff	Differential blood count
dl	Decliter (100 ml)
DIP	Distal interphalangeal joint
DJD	Degenerative joint disease
DM	Diabetes mellitus
DNA	Deoxyribonucleic acid
DO	Doctor of osteopathy
DOA	Dead on arrival
DOB	Date of birth
DP	Dorsalis pedis
DPT	Diphtheria, pertussis, and tetanus (toxoids/vaccine)
d/s	Discharge summary
DSA	Digital subtraction angiography

(*continued*)

ABBREVIATION	MEANING
DTR	Deep tendon reflexes
DUB	Dysfunctional uterine bleeding
DUI	Driving under the influence
D/W	Dextrose in water
DX, Dx, dx	Diagnosis; disease
Dz	Disease
ECF	Extracellular fluid
ECG	Electrocardiogram
ED	Emergency department
EDC	Estimated date of conception
EEG	Electroencephalogram
EKG	Electrocardiogram
EMG	Electromyogram
ENT	Ear, nose, and throat
EOM	Extraocular movement
ERA	Estroadiol receptor assay
ERCP	Endoscopic retrograde cholangiopancreatography
ESR	Erythrocyte sedimentation rate
ETOH	Alcohol
EUA	Evaluation under anesthesia
exc	Excision
Ext	Extremities; external
F	Fahrenheit
F.B.	Foreign body
FBS	Fasting blood sugar
FDA	Food and Drug Administration
FDP	Flexor digitorum profundus
FH	Family history
FSH	Follicle-stimulating hormone
ft	Foot, feet (measure)
F/u	Follow up
FUO	Fever of undetermined origin
Fx	fracture
g, gm	Gram
gastroc	Gastrocnemius
GERD	Gastroesophageal reflux disease
GFR	Glomerular filtration rate
GI	Gastrointestinal
GP	General practitioner
G6PD	Glucose-6-phosphate dehydrogenase
gr	Grain

ABBREVIATION	MEANING
Grav	Gravida (pregnancy)
gt, gtt	Drop, drops
GTT	Glucose tolerance test
GU	Genitourinary
GYN, gyn	Gynecology
H/A	Headache
Hb	Hemoglobin
HCG	Human chorionic gonadotropin
HCl	Hydrochloric acid, hydrochloride
HCO_3	Bicarbonate
HCT	Hematocrit
HCTZ	Hydrochlorothiazide
HDL	High-density lipoprotein
HDN	Hemolytic disease of the newborn
HEENT	Head, eyes, ears, nose, throat
Hep	Heparin
Hg	Mercury
Hgb	Hemoglobin
HGH	Human growth hormone
HI	Hemagglutination inhibition
HLA	Human leukocyte antigen
HNP	Herniated nucleus pulposus
H/O	History of
H_2O	Water
HOB	Head above bed
HPI	History of present illness
HR	Heart rate
Hr	Hour
HRT	Hormone replacement therapy
h.s.	At bedtime, hour of sleep
Hx	History
Hz	Hertz (cycles per second)
IABP	Intra-aortic balloon pump
ICF	Intracellular fluid
ICS	Intercostal space
ICU	Intensive care unit
I&D	Incision and drainage
IDDM	Insulin dependent diabetes mellitus
IgA	Immunoglobulin A

(continued)

ABBREVIATION	MEANING
IgD	Immunoglobulin D
IgE	Immunoglobulin E
IgG	Immunoglobulin G
IgM	Immunoglobulin M
IHSS	Idiopathic hypertrophic subaortic stenosis
I.M.	Intramuscular
inf	Inferior
inj	Inject
I&O	Intake and output
IPPB	Intermittent positive-pressure breathing
IU	International unit
IUD	Intrauterine device
IUI	Intrauterine insemination
IVF	In vitro fertilization
I.V.	Intravenous
IVP	Intravenous pyelogram
IVDU	Intravenous drug user
IVU	Intravenous urography
Jt., j.t.	Joint
JRA	Juvenile rheumatoid arthritis
K	Potassium
kcal	Kilocalorie (food calorie)
kg	kilogram
KO	Keep open; knocked out
KUB	Kidneys, ureters, and bladder
l	Liter
LAD	Left anterior descending (coronary artery)
LAMA	Left against medical advice
lat	Lateral
lb	Pound
LBBB	Left bundle branch block
LBP	Lower back pain
LCA	Left coronary artery
LDH	Lactate dehydrogenase
LDL	Low-density lipoprotein
LE	Lupus erythematosus
LEEP	Loop electrosurgical excision procedure
LIH	Left inguinal hernia
LH	Luteinizing hormone
LLQ	Left lower quadrant
lt	Left

ABBREVIATION	MEANING
LP	Lumbar puncture
LR	Lactated ringers; labor room; light reflex; lateral rectus
LUQ	Left upper quadrant
LWOT	Left without treatment
LV	Left ventricle
M	Molar
m	Meter; minim
MCH	Mean corpuscular hemoglobin
MCHC	Mean corpuscular hemoglobin concentration
MCV	Mean corpuscular volume
MD	Medical doctor, muscular dystrophy
mm	Millimicron (nanometer)
mEq	Millequivalent
Mg	Magnesium
mg	Milligram
M g	Microgram
MI	Myocardial infarction
ml	Milliliter
m	Micron
m l	Microliter
mm	Millimeter
mM	Millimole
m m	Micrometer, micron
m mol	Micromole
mo	Month
MOM	Milk of Magnesia
MR	Medial rectus; mental retardation; mitral regurgitation; medical record
MRI	Magnetic resonance imaging
MS	Multiple sclerosis; morphine sulfate
MSH	Melanocyte-stimulating hormone
MUGA	Multigated acquisition (scanning)
MVA	Motor vehicle accident
MVR	Mitral valve replacement
N	Nitrogen; normal (strength of solution)
Na	Sodium
NaCl	Sodium chloride
NAD	No acute distress
NB	newborn
ng	Nanogram (millimmicron)

(*continued*)

ABBREVIATION	MEANING
NGT	Nasogastric tube
NKA	No known allergies
NOS	Not otherwise specified
NPO	Nothing by mouth
NSAID	Nonsteroidal anti-inflammatory drug
N&V	Nausea and vomiting
NWb	Non-weight bearing
Ob-GYN	Obstetrics and gynecology
Obs	observation
OCD	Obsessive compulsive disorder
OD	Right eye
OM	Otitis media
o.s.	Left eye
OTC	Over the counter (a drug that can be obtained without a prescription)
Ou	Both eyes
oz	Ounce
P	Phosphorus; pressure; pulse
PA	Physician assistant
$PaCO_2$	Partial pressure of carbon dioxide in arterial blood
PaO_2	Partial pressure of oxygen in arterial blood
Pap	Papanicolaou smear
Para	Prior births
p.c.	After meals
PCO_2	Partial pressure of carbon dioxide
PO_2	Partial pressure of oxygen
peds	Pediatrics
PEG	Percutaneous endoscopic gastrostomy tube
PERRLA	Puplis equal, round, react to light, and accommodation
pg	Picogram (micromicrogram)
pH	Hydrogen ion concentration
PID	Pelvic inflammatory disease
PIP	Proximal interphalangeal joint
PKU	Phenylketonuria
PMH	Past medical history
PMS	Premenstrual syndrome
P.O., p.o.	By mouth
POC	Products of conception
PPD	Purified protein derivative (of tuberculin)
ppm	Parts per million

ABBREVIATION	MEANING
p.r.n., PRN	As needed, whenever necessary
Pro time	Prothrombin time
PSA	Prostate-specific antigen
PSH	Past surgical history
psi	Pounds per square inch
PT	Physical therapy
PTA	Prior to admission; percutaneous transvenous coronary angioplasty
PTCA	percutaneous transluminal coronary angioplasty
PTH	Parathyroid hormone
PUD	Peptic ulcer disease
PVC	Premature ventricular contraction
PVD	Peripheral vascular disease
PX	Physical exam
q	Every
q.d.	Every day
q.h.	Every hour
q2h	Every 2 hours
q4h	Every 4 hours
q.i.d.	Four times a day
R	Respirations; roentgen
RA	Rheumatoid arthritis; room air
RAIU	Radioactive iodine uptake
RBBB	Right bundle branch block
RBC	Red blood cell
RCA	Right coronary artery
RDS	Respiratory distress syndrome
RF	Rheumatic fever; rheumatoid factor
Rh	Rhesus blood factor
Rh neg. (Rh−)	Rhesus factor negative
Rh pos. (Rh+)	Rhesus factor positive
RIA	Radioimmunoassay
RLQ	Right lower quadrant
RN	Registered nurse
RNA	Ribonucleic acid
R/O	Rule out
ROM	Range of motion (of joint); rupture of membranes; right otitis media
ROS	Review of systems
RR	Recovery room; regular rate; regular rhythm

(*continued*)

ABBREVIATION	MEANING
R/S	Rescheduled
RSD	Reflex sympathetic dystrophy
Rt, RT, ®	Right
RUE	Right upper extremity
RUQ	Right upper quadrant
Rx	Prescription; therapy; treatment
s*	Without
SaO_2	Systemic arterial oxygen saturation (%)
SBE	Subacute bacterial endocarditis
S.C., SQ, subq	Subcutaneous
SCC	Sickle cell crisis
sec	Second
sed rate	Sedimentation rate
SGOT	Serum glutamic-oxalacetic transaminase (see AST)
SGPT	Serum glutamic-pyruvic transaminase (see ALT)
SH	Social history
SI	International System of Units; sacroiliac; stroke index
SIADH	Syndrome of inappropriate antidiuretic hormone
SIDS	Sudden infant death syndrome
SLE	Systemic lupus erythmatosus
SOB	Short of breath
s/p	Status post
spec	Specimen
sp gr	Specific gravity
S&S	Signs and symptoms
ss*	One-half
Staph	staphylococcus
stat	Immediately
STD	Sexually transmitted disease
sx	Symptoms; surgery
T	Temperature; thoracic, to be followed by number designating specific thoracic vertebra
T&A	Tonsillectomy and adenoidectomy
TAB	Therapeutic abortion
Tabs	Tablets
TAH	Total abdominal hysterectomy
TB	Tuberculosis
T&C	Type and crossmatch
temp.	Temperature
T of F	Tetralogy of Fallot

ABBREVIATION	MEANING
TIA	Transient ischemic attach
TIBS	Total iron-binding capacity
t.i.d.	Three times a day
TKO	To keep open
TM	Tympanic membrane
TMJ	Temporomandibular joint
TNM	Tumor, node, metastasis (tumor staging)
TO, T.o.	Telephone order
TPA	Tissue plasminogen activator
TPN	Total parenteral nutrition
TPR	Temperature, pulse, respirations
TSH	Thyroid-stimulating hormone
tsp	Teaspoon
TSS	Toxic shock syndrome
TURP	Transurethral resection of prostate
Tx	Treatment
UA, u/a	Urinalysis
UGI	Upper gastrointestinal
ULQ	Upper left quadrant
ung	Ointment
URI	Upper respiratory infection
URQ	Upper right quadrant
US, u/s	Ultrasound
USI	Urinary stress incontinence
UTI	Urinary tract infection
UVL	Ultraviolet light
VA	Visual acuity
VD	Venereal disease
VDRL	Venereal Disease Research Laboratory (test for syphilis)
Vent.	Ventilator
VF	Visual fields
Vfib	Ventricular fibrillation
V.O., v/o	Verbal order
VS	Vital signs
VSD	Ventricular septal defect
VSS	Vital signs stable
VST	Ventricular septal defect
VT	Ventricular tachycardia
UTI	Urinary tract infection

(continued)

ABBREVIATION	MEANING
WBC	White blood cell
w/	With
WBT	Weight bearing to tolerance
w/c, W/C	Wheel chair; Workers' compensation
WD	Well-developed
WDLL	Well differentiated lymphocytic lymphoma
WF	White female
WHO	World Health Organization
WM	White male
w/n	Within
WN	Well nourished
WNL	Within normal limits
WNV	West Nile Virus
w/u	Work up
y.o., y/o	Years old

Small Balance Adjustments

To reflect a realized account receivable balance, any balance of $5 and under is written off if the account meets criteria below.

Purpose

To adjust small uncollectible balances whereby the effort to collect monies would cost more than the balance itself. Judgment is being made that there is little likelihood that this money will be collected in the near future. Reasonable collection efforts have taken place over the course of the 120-day period leading up to the adjustment.

Procedure

Any balance of $5 or less is written off when the following conditions are met:

1. The balance is not a Medicaid copay that was not collected at the time of service.
2. The balance is greater than 120 days old.
3. There is no insurance balance due. The balance should be strictly patient responsibility.
4. Each month the business office will run a report from MOSS and carry out the small balance write-off.

Missed Appointments

Purpose

To encourage patients to keep their appointments and remain compliant with their treatment follow-up. To maintain consistency in scheduling and patient flow. To reduce the number of last minute canceled appointments.

DMA calls patients the day before their appointment to remind them. At checkout, appointment cards are also provided when the patient schedules their next appointment. It is a policy of DMA to charge a $20 missed appointment fee to patients who do not show for their scheduled appointment and do not call to cancel within a reasonable timeframe. According to the *CMS Claims Processing Manual*, Medicare patients can also be charged this fee if they miss their appointment as long as they are charged the same fee that non-Medicare patients are charged. A letter is sent to the patient explaining the policy along with an invoice for the missed appointment fee. Indicate in the schedule that the appointment is missed.

Coding Policy

Purpose

To ensure compliance with official ICD-9 and CPT-4 coding guidelines for reporting diagnoses and procedures. To reduce incidences of reporting false claims due to incomplete medical documentation. To reduce medical necessity claims denials.

1. Medical record documentation will be available for review for proper assignment of codes. When coding from a medical record, the following reports are used (source documents). Ancillary reports and nursing documentation can be used to support code assignment or to generate a physician query, but cannot be used solely to code from unless a physician's documentation corroborates the same information located in these reports.
2. Codes are assigned only from the following source documents: H&P, progress notes, consultation, discharge summary, operative or procedure reports, router, hospital charge ticket, and physician orders. Only codes for services provided and documented will be reported. Billing for services not provided is fraudulent and will not be permitted. Physicians will be queried for any services indicated on the router that are not documented in the chart.
3. Coders will adhere to official coding guidelines at all times as stated in the *CPT Assistant* and *Official Guidelines for Coding and Reporting ICD-9 Codes*.
4. Codes will be properly linked on the claim form pointing the appropriate ICD-9 diagnosis codes to the respective CPT code to demonstrate medical necessity.
5. Coders are required to check CCI edits for bundling of codes for all government payers. Only comprehensive codes will be submitted for payment unless a modifier is appropriate. They are also required to check monthly with the AMA and CMS websites for updates in new codes.
6. HCPCS codes are applied when coding and billing for supplies other than syringes, gauze, suture, and Marcaine. Surgical tray for Medicare patients is coded to A4550.
7. Coders are required to reference official coding sources for guidance. Coding staff will have access to *CPT Assistant*, *Coding Clinic for HCPCS*, and *Coding Clinic*.
8. Noncovered services will not be billed to any payer without a signed waiver on file. Medicare patients are required to sign an ABN if the claim is likely to be denied, with an estimate of the patient's out of pocket expense for this service.
9. Modifiers for physician services will be appended when applicable.
10. Coders must achieve and sustain an accuracy level of 95%. Charts will be randomly audited by Lindsay Morgan for proper assignment of ICD-9, CPT, and HCPCS codes and modifiers. If coders fall below this level, they will be 100% reviewed and provided additional education until their accuracy rate is achieved. If after a reasonable amount of time the 95% accuracy rate is not achieved or sustained, the employee will be moved to a noncoding position or terminated.
11. Physicians must be queried when there is a discrepancy in documentation or lack of documentation to assign the most specific code. All queries are handled in writing. Discussions can be held with the provider, but the official process is carried out by generating a query document and putting the chart on the physician's desk. When a primary code results in an unspecified code, the coder is to query the provider for a more specific diagnosis if possible. If the provider is able to provide such information, he/she is asked to document this in the record as an addendum.
12. Coders will not up code to generate more revenue for the practice. Only services that are documented will be coded and submitted. Codes also will not be assigned for a service where an NCD or LCD is published for the sake of meeting medical necessity unless the diagnosis is valid and documented.

Coding Procedure

Purpose

To provide a consistent and ethical process for assigning diagnosis and procedure codes. Codes for surgical procedures are checked against the global days to determine global period and possible modifier need. Visits for post-op follow-up within the global are reported with 99024.

How to Code a Diagnosis from a Record

1. Identify all main terms included in the diagnostic statement or report.
2. Locate each main term in the alphabetic index.
3. Refer to any subterms indented under the main term. The subterms form individual line entries and describe the essential differences by site, etiology, or clinical type.
4. Follow cross-reference instructions if needed, especially if the code needed is not located under the first main entry that is looked up. Must follow all directions for *see also*, *code also*, and so on.
5. Verify the code chosen in the tabular.
6. Read and be guided by any instructions here.
7. Choose the most specific code. Assign 3-digit codes only when no 4-digit codes appear in that entry. Assign a fifth digit for any subcategory where a fifth digit is provided. Not all codes have 4 or 5 digits.
8. Continue coding until all independent diagnoses and procedures are captured and the reason for service is fully identified.

How to Code from an OP Note

1. Read through the entire report.
2. Review the diagnoses and procedures and see if they match the body of the report.
3. Locate any potential diagnoses or procedures that are not mentioned at the top of the report.
4. Identify any complications that occurred.
5. If pre- and post-op diagnoses are different, use the post-op diagnosis because this was determined after surgery.
6. If specimens were removed, review the pathology report to verify the diagnosis and size of lesion. If there is a discrepancy between the pathological and surgical diagnoses, query the surgeon.
7. Sequence the codes from the highest RVU to lowest.

Appendix B: Employee Privacy Acknowledgement

I understand that while performing my official duties I will have access to protected health information. I understand that:

- Protected health information is individually identifiable health information that is created, maintained, or used within the office.
- Protected health information is not available to the public.
- Special precautions are necessary to protect this type of information from unlawful or unauthorized access, use, modification, disclosure, or destruction.

I agree to:

- Access, use, or modify protected health information only for the purposes of performing my official duties.
- Never access or use protected health information out of curiosity, or for personal interest or advantage. Records of immediate family members of staff will be stored separately and processed only by supervisory staff.
- Never show, discuss, or disclose protected health information to or with anyone who does not have the legal authority. Staff must verify identity and properly executed authorizations to disclose information before releasing any information not required by law.
- Never remove protected health information from the work area without authorization.
- Never share passwords with anyone or store passwords in a location accessible to unauthorized persons.
- Always store protected health information in a place physically secure from access by unauthorized persons.
- Dispose of protected health information by using a shredder. I will not dispose of such information in wastebaskets or recycle bins.
- I understand that penalties for violating one of the above limitations may include disciplinary action, termination, and/or civil or criminal prosecution.

"I certify that I have read and understand the Privacy Acknowledgement Statement printed above."

_______________________ _________

Employee Signature Date

Employee Manual Acknowledgment

This employee manual is intended as a general guide to the rules, policies, and procedures of Douglasville Medicine Associates. Please read the handbook, as it has been prepared for your information and understanding of the policies, philosophies, and practices. This manual does not contain all the information you will need as an employee. We will provide any additional information orally and/or in writing. We reserve the right to make changes to the employee manual without prior notice. Upon completion of your review of this handbook, sign the statement below and return it to your supervisor.

I, ____________________, have received and read a copy of the Policy and Procedure Manual. I understand that it is up to me to read the manual and to familiarize myself with its contents.

I have familiarized myself with the contents of this manual. By my signature below, I acknowledge, understand, accept, and agree to comply with the information contained therein. I understand this handbook is not intended to cover every situation that may arise during my employment, but is simply a general guide to the goals, policies, and practices.

I understand that the Employee Policy and Procedure Manual is not a contract of employment and should not be deemed as such.

_______________________ _________

Employee Signature Date

Appendix C: E/M Coding Tool, Directions and Definitions

Instructions on How to Use Tool

To accurately assign a level E/M code, the coder must count elements (or bullets) in each of the three key components: history, exam, and medical decision making. By doing so, the E/M code is supported by documentation appropriate for the level of service provided. Most providers will assign their own E/M codes, and the coder will assign the ICD-9 codes and additional procedure codes for other services provided. Coders must be able to audit chart documentation and arrive at an E/M code. Total visit time and time spent on counseling is recorded to determine if time is a driver in level of code assignment; *only* if it is 50% of the visit time being spent on counseling and coordination of care.

Review the documentation and follow the steps recording your findings on the E/M Tool.

Step 1 Identify the place of service (POS), patient type, and patient status.

Step 2 Record the amount of time spent during the encounter. Mark time spent on counseling.

Step 3 Determine the amount or level of history by checking the applicable boxes and counting them.

Step 4 Determine the extent of the exam by checking the applicable boxes and counting them.

Step 5 Determine the level of medical decision making.

Step 6 Determine the overall level of service now that the three key components are established and time is recorded.

NOTE: You cannot count an element more than one time. If you count constitutional in HPI, you can't count it again in ROS. This is referred to as double dipping.

Definitions

History

Chief Complaint: Reason patient is seeking care today

History of Present Illness: Description of the patient's problem from the onset to the present time, including location, quality, severity, duration, timing, context, modifying factors, and associated signs and symptoms

Location: Where is the problem, pain, symptom (e.g., head, heel, arm)?

Quality: Description of problem, symptom, pain—what does it feel like? Sensation or pattern (e.g., itchy, sharp, sporadic)

Severity: Severity of symptom or pain, or patient feels well (e.g., mild, moderate, acute, scale of 1–10)

Duration: How long has the problem, symptom, pain been present (e.g., week, day, hours)?

Timing: When does this problem, symptom, pain occur (e.g., night, seldom, frequently, when walking, laying down)?

Context: Instances that can be associated with problem, symptom, pain (e.g., what they are doing when this occurs, how something happened, it happens when they eat certain foods, it happens only when laying on side)

Modifying Factors: What has the patient done to alleviate the problem, symptom, or pain? Did this make it better or worse (e.g., over the counter meds made it somewhat better, eating tomatoes makes it worse)?

Associated Signs and Symptoms: Other problems, symptoms, pain that occur when this problem occurs (e.g., headache causes nausea, fever and rash)

Past History: Current medications, prior surgeries or hospitalizations, prior illnesses, immunizations, allergies, diet

Social History: Illegal drug use, alcohol use, marital status, children, occupation, education, living arrangements, sexual history, hobbies, and employment

Family History: Hereditary high risk diseases, cause of parents' death, children, siblings, associated diseases related to CC

Review of Systems (ROS): Questions and answers or inventory of body systems and any problems or symptoms associated with each system

Constitutional: BP, height, weight, pulse, respirations, patient's general appearance, temperature, fatigue, chills, malaise, appetite, restrictions, weight loss

Integumentary: Any changes to skin—itching, rashes, lesions, changes in color, changes to moles, nail color

Neurological: Headaches, dizziness, weakness, loss of balance, loss of consciousness, head injures, seizures, changes in speech, concentration, sensory changes

Eyes: Blurry vision, glasses, contacts, double vision, any vision changes, last eye exam, itching, burning spots, floaters

ENT: Hearing loss or changes, pain, ringing, congestion, nose bleeds, discharge, hoarseness, sore throat, ulcers, gums problems, sneezing, last dental exam, cold sores

Gastrointestinal (GI): Heartburn, vomiting, diarrhea, constipation, indigestion, gas, change in bowel habits, blood in stool, nausea, use of digestive aids, gallbladder disease, hemorrhoids

Endocrine: Weight changes, hair changes, changes in shoe or glove size, heat/cold intolerance, sleep disturbances, increase/decrease appetite or thirst, weakness, previous hormone therapy

Genitourinary (GU): Last menstrual period (LMP), contraception, sex life, menses, pregnancies, births, abortions, erections, discharge, urgency, frequency, menopause, puberty, etc.

Respiratory: Cough, asthma, pneumonia, wheezing, shortness of breath (SOB), exposure to TB, sputum production, dyspnea on exertion

Cardiovascular (CV): Chest pain, pressure, palpitations, high BP, positional breathing, heart murmur, changes in color of extremities, coldness or numbness in extremities, leg pain or firmness

Hematology/Lymphatic: any anemia, bruise easy, previous blood transfusions, etc.

Musculoskeletal (MS): Joint pain or stiffness, swelling of extremities, fracture history, muscle cramping, twitches, limitations in activities, weakness

Psychiatric: Problems sleeping or concentrating, mood changes, depression, compulsions, lack of appetite, communication/socialization issues, memory, judgment

Allergic/Lymphatic: Sneezing, tenderness or swelling of lymph glands, chronic clear nasal drainage, hives, eczema, allergies to food, etc.

> Patient has abdominal pain with intermittent nausea and vomiting (GI), urinary urgency (GU), malaise (constitutional), headache (neuro), achy muscles (MS). No palpitations (CV), cough (resp), or known allergies (allergy).

E/M CODING TOOL
(Based on 1995 E/M Guidelines)

Patient Status: ☐New Patient ☐Established Patient Encounter Time: ________ Time spent counseling:______
(must be >50% total encounter time)

Patient Type: ☐Office Visit ☐Preventative ☐Consult ☐ER Visit ☐Hospital Visit

Step 3: HISTORY

CHIEF COMPLAINT (Required for all): ____

History of Present Illness (HPI) Review of Systems (ROS) **PFSH**

Elements: Elements:

☐Location ________________
☐Quality ________________
☐Severity ________________
☐Timing ________________
☐Duration ________________
☐Context ________________
☐Modifying Factors ________________
☐Associated signs & symptoms ________________

☐Constitutional ☐GU ☐MS
☐Eye ☐Integ (skin, breast) ☐Psych
☐ENT/mouth ☐Aller/Immuno ☐Endocrine
☐Neuro ☐Hemato/Lymph ☐GI
☐Resp ☐CV ☐All other Negative

Elements:
☐Past Medical
☐Family
☐Social

HPI **ROS** **PFSH**

**Can't count the same element in both HPI and ROS*

HPI:
1–3 = **Brief** (1–2 chronic)
4 + = **Extended**
Status of at least 3 chronic or inactive Conditions = **Detailed**
Status of at least 3 chronic or inactive Conditions = **Comprehensive**

ROS:
0 = **None**
1 = **Problem pertinent** (+ and – related to problem)
2–9 = **Extended**
10+ = **Complete** (Min of 10)

PFSH:
0 = None
1 = Pertinent/Detailed (Min 1 from PFS)
2 = Complete (Est. Pt & ER Pt min of 2)
3 = Complete (New Pt, Consults)

To select Level of Service: Circle the applicable level of each of the three—HPI, ROS, PFSH. All must be in the same column below. If not, select the lowest level met.

HISTORY	PROBLEM FOCUSED	EXPANDED PF	DETAILED	COMPREHENSIVE
HPI	Brief	Brief	Extended	Extended
ROS	None	Problem Pertinent	Extended	Complete
PFSH	None	None	Pertinent	Complete

Step 4: EXAM

Organ Systems
☐Constitutional
☐Cardiovascular
☐Eyes
☐ENT
☐GI
☐GU
☐Hematologic/Lymphatic/Immunologic
☐Musculoskeletal
☐Neurologic
☐Psychiatric
☐Respiratory
☐Skin

Body Areas
☐Head, face
☐Neck/Thyroid
☐Chest, including breasts and axillae
☐Abdomen
☐Genitalia, groin, buttocks
☐Back, including spine
☐Extremity (☐RUE ☐LUE ☐RLE ☐LLE)

LEVEL OF EXAM (circle the one based on how many systems/areas checked):

Problem Focused Exam ⇨1 body area or organ system (limited exam of the affected body area/organ system)
Expanded Problem Focused Exam ⇨2–4 body areas and/or organ systems (limited exam)
Detailed Exam ⇨5–7 body areas and/or organ systems (extended exam)
Comprehensive Exam ⇨8 or more organ systems

Step 5: MEDICAL DECISION MAKING (comes from the Assessment and Plan)

To determine level of MDM, answer the questions in A and B and risk determined from Table of Risk.

A. DIAGNOSIS OR MANAGEMENT OPTIONS (once you get to 4 stop; that's as high as you can go)

A. Number of Dx & Tx Options	Points	# of Problems	Total
Self-limited or minor (stable, improved or worsening)	1	Max #2	
Established problem (to examiner); stable, improved	1		
Established problem (to examiner); worsening	2		
New problem (to examiner) no additional workup planned	3	Max #1	
New problem (to examiner) additional workup planned (tests outside of this visit)	4		
TOTAL POINTS			

B. AMOUNT & COMPLEXITY OF DATA INVOLVED

B. Amount and/or Complexity of Data Involved	Points	Total
Review and/or order of clinical lab tests	1	
Review and/or order of tests in Radiology Section (except Echo)	1	
Review and/or order of tests in Medicine Section (EEG, EKG, etc.)	1	
Discussion of test results with the performing physician	1	
Decision to obtain old records and/or additional history from other than patient	1	
Review and summarization of old records and/or obtained history from someone other than patient	2	
Independent visualization of image, tracing or specimen itself (not simply a review of the report)	2	
TOTAL POINTS		

C. OVERALL RISK (Choose these based on the Table of Risk on next page. Circle the level for each of the three elements. Highest level of any of the categories determines overall risk.)

OVERALL RISK	MINIMAL	LOW	MODERATE	HIGH
Presenting Problem	Minimal	Low	Moderate	High
Diagnostic Procedures	Minimal	Low	Moderate	High
Management Options	Minimal	Low	Moderate	High

DETERMINE MEDICAL DECISION MAKING LEVEL

(Use points from A and B above & circle level for each of the three must have 2 in the same column if not level in center is chosen.)

FINAL MDM LEVEL	Straightforward	Low	Moderate	High
A. Number of Dx & Tx Options	1 Minimal	2 Limited	3 Multiple	4 Extensive
B. Amount and/or Complexity of Data Involved	0-1 Minimal	2 Limited	3 Moderate	4 Extensive
C. Risk of Complications/Morbidity/ Mortality	Minimal	Low	Moderate	High

TABLE OF RISK (1 bullet from any box supports level in 1st column)			
Level of Risk	**Presenting Problem(s)**	**Diagnostic Procedure(s) Ordered**	**Management Options Selected**
Minimal	• One self-limited or minor problem, e.g., cold, insect bite, tinea corporis These typically go away on their own	• Laboratory tests requiring venipuncture • Chest x-rays • EKG/EEG • Urinalysis • Ultrasound, e.g., echocardiography • KOH prep	• Rest • Gargles • Elastic bandages • Superficial dressings
Low	• Two or more self-limited or minor problems • One stable chronic illness, e.g., well controlled hypertension, non-insulin dependent diabetes, cataract, BPH • Acute uncomplicated illness or injury, e.g., cystitis, allergic rhinitis, simple sprain	• Physiologic tests not under stress, e.g., pulmonary function tests • Non-cardiovascular imaging studies with contrast, e.g., barium enema • Superficial needle biopsies • Clinical laboratory tests requiring arterial puncture • Skin biopsies	• Over-the-counter drugs • Minor surgery with no identified risk factors • Physical therapy • Occupational therapy • IV fluids without additives
Moderate	• One or more chronic illnesses with mild exacerbation, progression, or side effects of treatment • Two or more stable chronic illnesses • Undiagnosed new problem with uncertain prognosis, e.g., lump in breast • Acute illness with systemic symptoms, e.g., pyelonephritis, pneumonitis, colitis • Acute complicated injury, e.g., head injury with brief loss of consciousness	• Physiologic tests under stress, e.g., cardiac stress test, fetal contraction stress test • Diagnostic endoscopies with no identified risk factors • Deep needle or incisional biopsy • Cardiovascular imaging studies with contrast and no identified risk factors, e.g., arteriogram, cardiac catheterization • Obtain fluid from body cavity, e.g., lumbar puncture, thoracentesis, culdocentesis	• Minor surgery with identified risk factors • Elective major surgery (open, percutaneous, or endoscopic) with no identified risk factors • Prescription drug management (change dose, start/stop meds) • Therapeutic nuclear medicine • IV fluids with additives • Closed treatment of fracture or dislocation without manipulation
High	• One or more chronic illnesses with severe exacerbation, progression, or side effects of treatment • Acute or chronic illnesses or injuries that pose a threat to life or bodily function, e.g., multiple trauma, acute MI, pulmonary embolus, severe respiratory distress, progressive severe rheumatoid arthritis, psychiatric illness with potential threat to self or others, peritonitis, acute renal failure • An abrupt change in neurologic status, e.g., seizure, TIA, weakness, sensory loss	• Cardiovascular imaging studies with contrast with identified risk factors • Cardiac electrophysiological tests • Diagnostic endoscopies with identified risk factors • Discography	• Elective major surgery (open, percutaneous, or endoscopic) with identified risk factors • Emergency major surgery (open, percutaneous, or endoscopic) • Parenteral controlled substances • Drug therapy requiring intensive monitoring for toxicity • Decision not to resuscitate or to de-escalate care because of poor prognosis

Step 6: DETERMINE OVERALL LEVEL OF SERVICE

Find the patient type based on location of service. Circle the levels of History (H), Exam (E), and Medical Decision Making (MDM) derived from the worksheet. Assign the code based on the criteria that 2 of 3 or 3 of 3 must be met.

New Patient Office/Outpatient (3 of 3)			
H	E	MDM	CODE
PF	PF	SF	99201
EPF	EPF	SF	99202
D	D	L	99203
C	C	M	99204
C	C	H	99205

Estab Patient Office/Outpatient (2 of 3)			
H	E	MDM	CODE
PF	PF	SF	99212
EPF	EPF	L	99213
D	D	M	99214
C	C	H	99215

Initial Inpatient (3 of 3)			
H	E	MDM	CODE
D	D	SF/L	99221
C	C	M	99222
C	C	H	99223

Subsequent Inpatient (2 of 3)			
H	E	MDM	CODE
PF	PF	SF/L	99231
EPF	EPF	M	99232
D	D	H	99233

Outpatient Observation (3 of 3)			
H	E	MDM	CODE
D	D	SF/L	99218
C	C	MDM	99219
C	C	H	99220

Same Day Admit/Discharge (3 of 3)			
H	E	MDM	CODE
D	D	SF/L	99234
C	C	MDM	99235
C	C	H	99236

Appendix D: AHIMA Standards of Ethical Coding

In this era of payment based on diagnostic and procedural coding, the professional ethics of health information coding professionals continue to be challenged. A conscientious goal for coding and maintaining a quality database is accurate clinical and statistical data. The following standards of ethical coding, developed by AHIMA's Coding Policy and Strategy Committee and approved by AHIMA's Board of Directors, are offered to guide coding professionals in this process.

1. Coding professionals are expected to support the importance of accurate, complete, and consistent coding practices for the production of quality healthcare data.
2. Coding professionals in all healthcare settings should adhere to the ICD-9-CM (International Classification of Diseases, 9th revision, Clinical Modification) coding conventions, official coding guidelines approved by the Cooperating Parties, the CPT (Current Procedural Terminology) rules established by the American Medical Association, and any other official coding rules and guidelines established for use with mandated standard code sets. Selection and sequencing of diagnoses and procedures must meet the definitions of required data sets for applicable healthcare settings.
3. Coding professionals should use their skills, their knowledge of currently mandated coding and classification systems, and official resources to select the appropriate diagnostic and procedural codes.
4. Coding professionals should only assign and report codes that are clearly and consistently supported by physician documentation in the health record.
5. Coding professionals should consult physicians for clarification and additional documentation prior to code assignment when there is conflicting or ambiguous data in the health record.
6. Coding professionals should not change codes or the narratives of codes on the billing abstract so that meanings are misrepresented. Diagnoses or procedures should not be inappropriately included or excluded because payment or insurance policy coverage requirements will be affected. When individual payer policies conflict with official coding rules and guidelines, these policies should be obtained in writing whenever possible. Reasonable efforts should be made to educate the payer on proper coding practices in order to influence a change in the payer's policy.
7. Coding professionals, as members of the healthcare team, should assist and educate physicians and other clinicians by advocating proper documentation practices, further specificity, and resequencing or inclusion of diagnoses or procedures when needed to more accurately reflect the acuity, severity, and the occurrence of events.
8. Coding professionals should participate in the development of institutional coding policies and should ensure that coding policies complement, not conflict with, official coding rules and guidelines.
9. Coding professionals should maintain and continually enhance their coding skills, as they have a professional responsibility to stay abreast of changes in codes, coding guidelines, and regulations.
10. Coding professionals should strive for optimal payment to which the facility is legally entitled, remembering that it is unethical and illegal to maximize payment by means that contradict regulatory guidelines.

**Reprinted with permission from AHIMA Journal of American Medical Record Association, October 2000*

Appendix E: Getting Started With Medical Office Simulation Software (MOSS) Version 2.0

About Medical Office Simulation Software 2.0

In MOSS, the main menu screen orients you to the general functions of most practice management software programs. Basic components common to most practice management software include: Patient Registration; File Maintenance; Procedure Posting; Insurance Billing; Claims Tracking; Posting Payments; Patient Billing; Report Generation; Appointment Scheduling.

What's new in MOSS 2.0:

- Uses Microsoft Access 2007 and compatible with Windows Vista
- Claims Tracking is a new area of the program that simulates receiving an electronic explanation of benefits (EOB) or remittance advice (RA) from an insurance carrier
- CMS-1500 forms populate based on insurance type selected to meet the needs of medical billing programs
- Each insurance has a fee schedule
- Date parameters expanded to a five-year range
- Improved Search functionality
- Improved Reports functionality
- New reports added: Aging patient balance report, Individual patient balance report, patient ledger report, prebilling report
- Adjustment functionality corrected to type of adjustment; additional adjustment types added
- Patient ledger updated to track payment history
- Prebilling report added prior to generating claims
- Expanded seed data added to the program

MOSS 2.0 is a single-user program that is designed to be used with various Procedures in the Administrative section of this book. Procedures that utilize MOSS are clearly marked in the procedure title.

Installation and Setup Requirements

1. Take the MOSS 2.0 CD in the back of this book and place it into your CD-ROM drive.
2. Medical Office Simulation Software 2.0 should begin setup automatically. Follow the on-screen prompts to install MOSS and Access Runtime.
3. If MOSS does not begin setup automatically, follow these instructions:
   - Double-click on My Computer.
   - Double-click the Control Panel icon.
   - Double-click Add/Remove Programs.
   - Click the Install button, and follow the onscreen prompts.
4. When you finish installing MOSS, it will be accessible through the Start menu:

   Select Start > All Programs > Medical Office Simulation Software > MOSS (to open the software)
5. At the logon screen, click OK to enter MOSS. Your user name and password are already loaded for you. You may change your password after you have logged in, by going to the File Maintenance area of the software (see the next section).

Changing Your Password

1. Once in the program, select **File Maintenance** from the Main Menu screen.

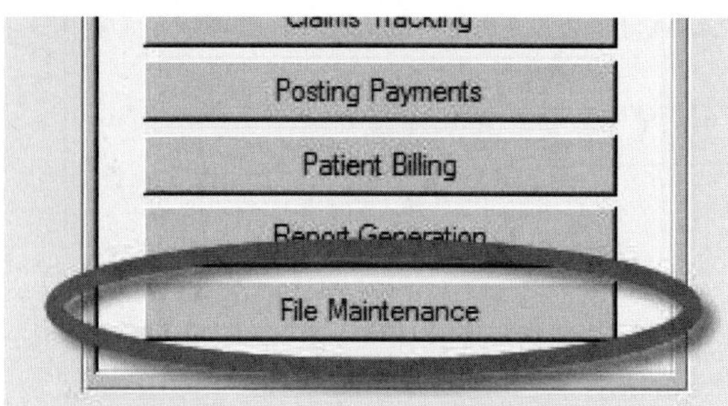

2. Select the button next to **1. Change Password**.

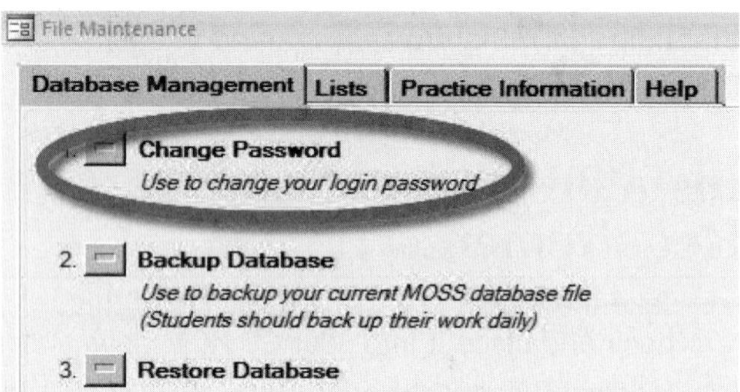

3. Enter the current password "Student1" and then your new password.

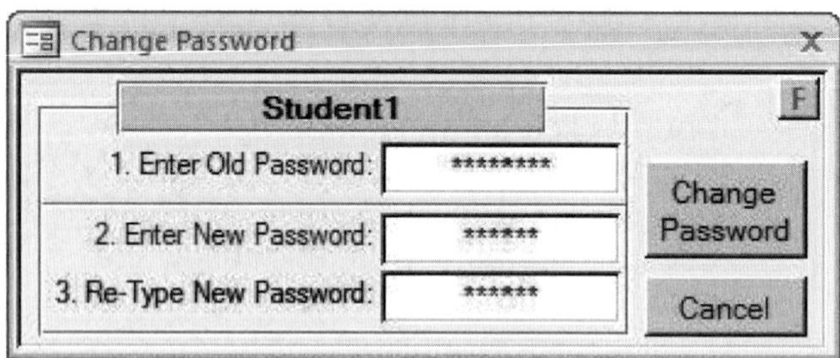

4. Click **Change Password** when you are finished. We recommend that if you change your password, you write your new password down and keep it in a secure place.

Sections of the Program

MOSS features a Main Menu screen consisting of buttons that provide access to specific areas.

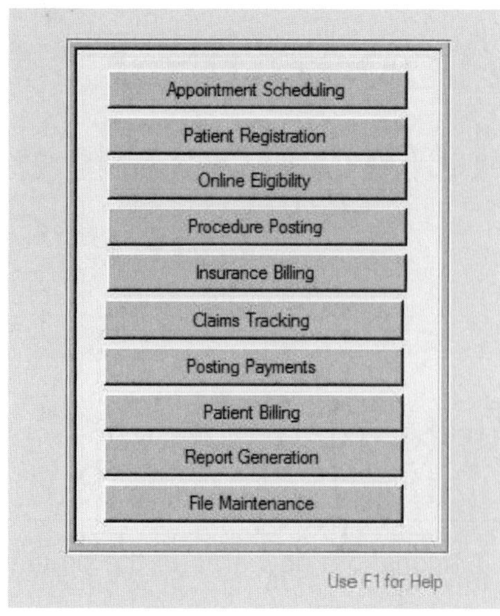

Alternatively, there is an icon bar along the top left to quickly access the areas of the software, or the user may choose to navigate the software by using the pull-down menus below the software title bar.

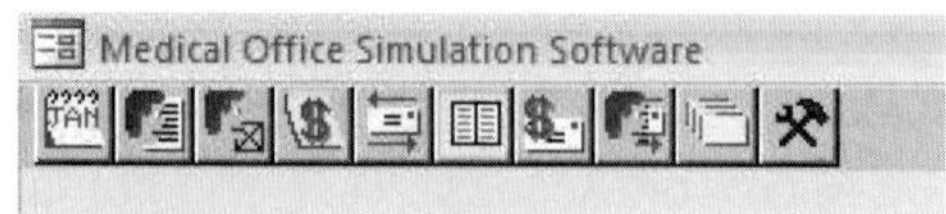

Patient Registration

The patient registration area allows the user to input information about each patient in the practice, including demographic, Health Insurance Portability and Accountability Act (HIPAA), and medical insurance information. From the Main Menu screen, click on the Patient Registration button to search for a patient, or to add a new patient, using the command buttons along the bottom of the patient selection dialog box.

Appointment Scheduling

The appointment scheduling system enables the user to make appointments and also cancel, reschedule, and search for appointments. MOSS allows for block scheduling, as well as several print features including appointment cards and daily schedules.

Procedure Posting

In the procedure posting system, patient fees for services are applied, in addition to relevant information such as service dates and place of service information. When procedures are input into the procedure posting system, the software assigns the fee to be charged according to the fee schedule for the patient's insurance.

Insurance Billing

The insurance billing system is designed to prepare claims to be sent to insurance companies for the medical office to receive payment for services provided. MOSS allows the user to generate and print a paper claim or simulate sending the claim electronically.

Claims Tracking

Claims Tracking is a new area of the program, which simulates receiving an electronic explanation of benefits (EOB) or remittance advice (RA) from an insurance carrier.

Posting Payments and Patient Billing

In the posting payments system, the user may input payments received by the practice from patients or insurance companies, as well as enter adjustments to the account. Once the payment from the primary insurance company has been posted, the software can generate a claim to a secondary insurance company, if applicable, or generate a bill to be sent directly to the patient to collect the outstanding balance.

File Maintenance

The File Maintenance System is a utility area of the program that contains common information used by various systems within the software. It is also an area where the setup of the software system can be adjusted or customized.

Feedback Mode and Balloon Help

Under the Help tab in File Maintenance, the user can turn Feedback Mode and Balloon Help on or off. Feedback Mode will alert the user when essential fields have not been completed before allowing data to be saved. Balloon Help offers explanations, clarification, or reminders for certain fields.

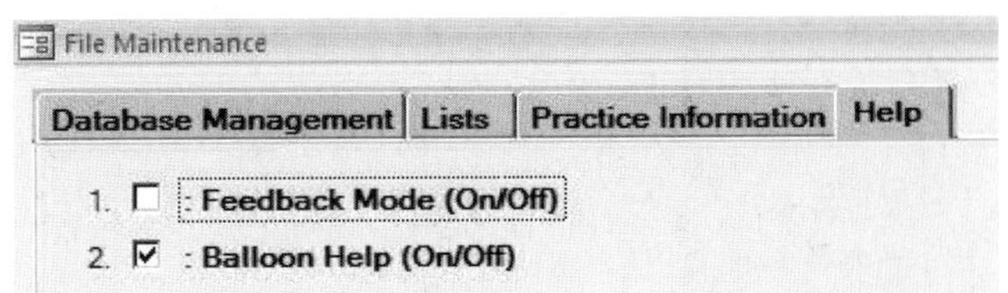

Creating Back Up Files

You may create a back up file of the work you've completed in the program at any time. We recommend that you do this frequently.

1. Click on File Maintenance, and then click the button next to **2. Backup Database**.

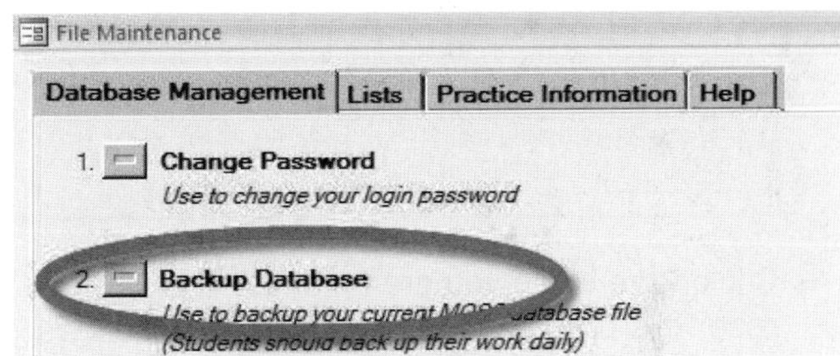

2. Click Yes at the prompt.

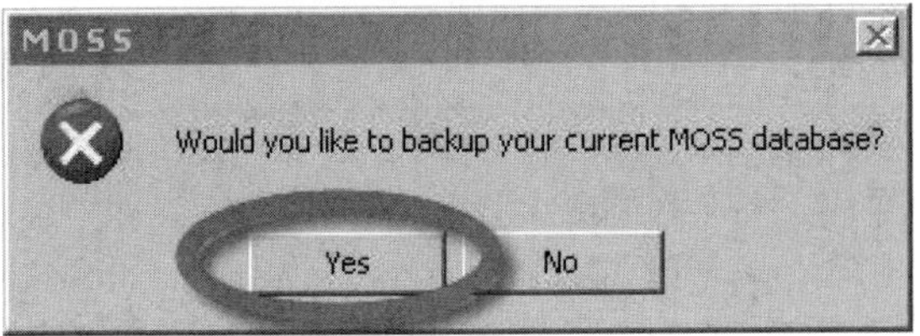

3. Now, select a location to save your backup file. We recommend that you save the database on a flash drive (in most computers, this is your E:/ or F:/ computer drive). When saving your file, you may also choose to rename the file. You may rename the file to anything you choose; **however, you must keep the file extension (.mde) in the file name.**

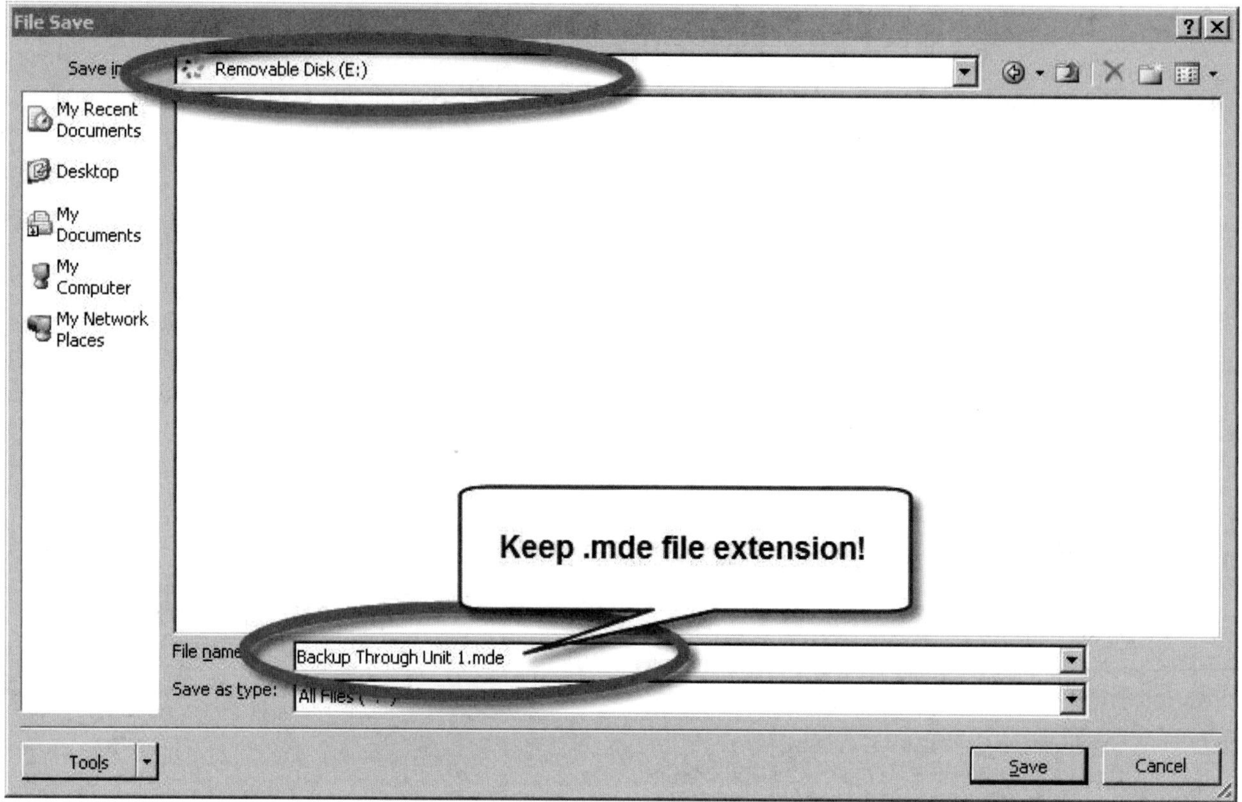

4. Click **Save** when you are finished. You will receive a prompt telling you that your file was completed successfully. Click **OK**.

Restoring Back Up Files

You may restore a back up file of the work you've saved in the program at any time.

1. Click on File Maintenance, and then click the button next to **3. Restore Database**. Note that restoring a back up file is an irreversible process.

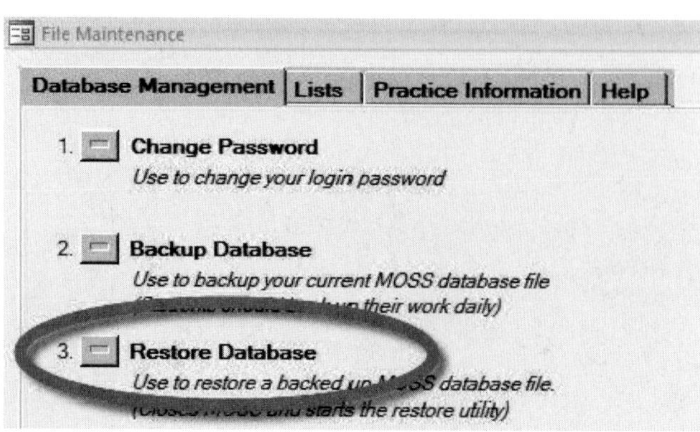

2. Click **Yes** at the prompt.
3. Click **Restore MOSS From Backup** at the next prompt.

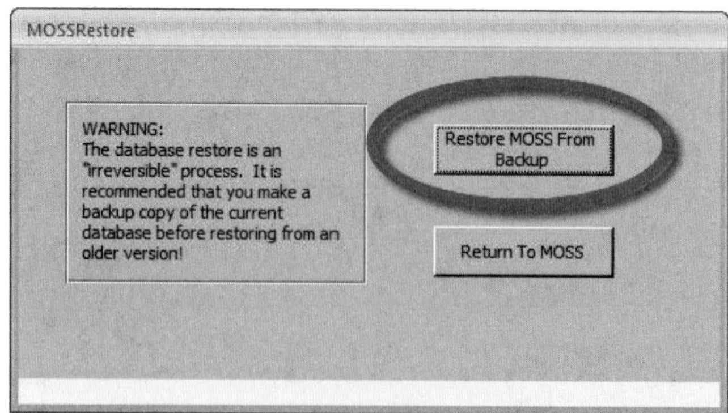

4. Click **Yes** at the following prompt. (Remember that restoring a back up file is an irreversible process.)

5. Find the back up file that you've created, click once to highlight it, and then click **OK**.

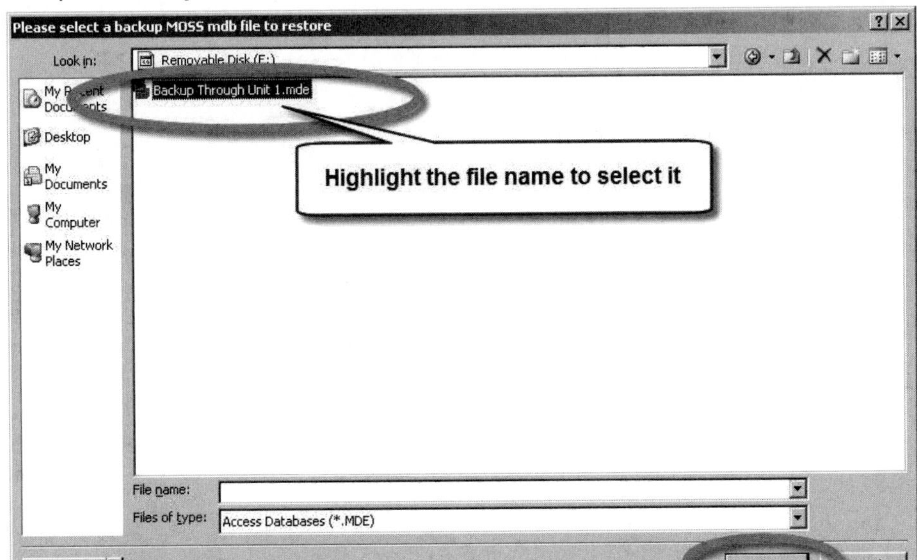

6. Click **Yes** at the following prompt.

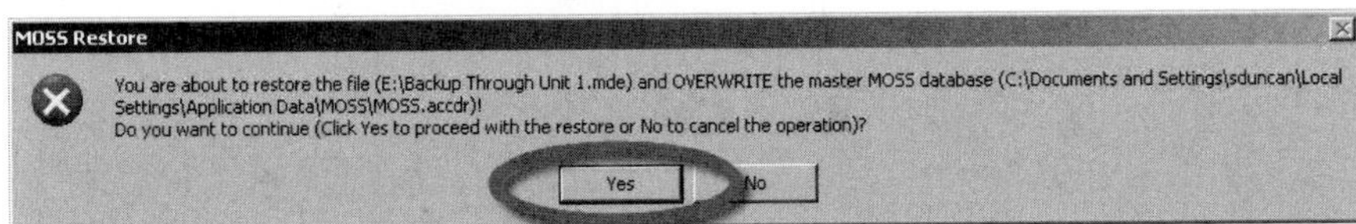

7. Click the button **Return To MOSS**.

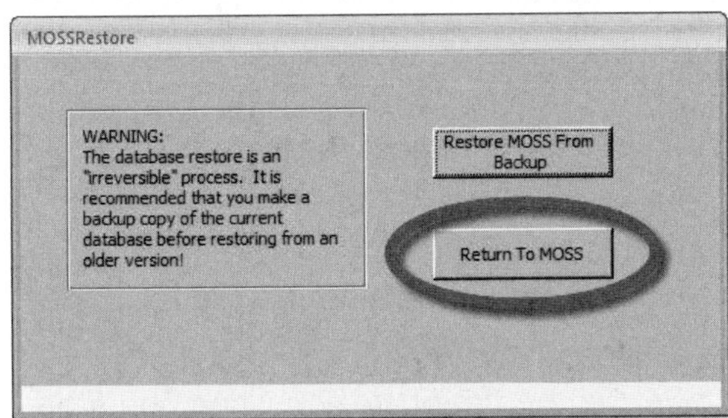

8. You have successfully restored your back up database. You will need to log in to the new database to start working.

MOSS Frequently Asked Questions

- If my program has adopted MOSS, can multiple students use the same computer in our school computer lab?

Your network administrator should install MOSS on each student's personalized space on a school's computer or network. Multiple students can use one computer—*as long as each student has MOSS installed on their own personalized space on a school's computer or network.*

For programs that do not have network privileges, students should use the backup/restore utility in MOSS, saving the MOSS.mde file to a flash drive.

- I have Microsoft Access on my computer. Do I need to install Access Runtime on my computer?

Yes, you should install Access Runtime on your computer to go along with the program. It will not cause any problems to your system, or otherwise interfere with the Microsoft Access program on your computer.

- Will MOSS run on a Citrix server?

Unfortunately, it will not. MOSS is designed for use in a Local Area Network, not a Wide Area Network like Citrix.

Technical Support Information

Technical Support at Delmar Cengage Learning is available from 8:30 a.m. to 6:30 p.m. Eastern Standard time.

- Telephone: 1-800-648-7450
- E-mail: delmarhelp@cengage.com

Glossary

A

A/B MAC The Medicare Modernization Act of 2003 mandated that CMS replace the numerous carriers administering the Medicare Part A and Part B fee-for-service programs with entities.

Abuse consists of practices that are inconsistent with sound fiscal, business, or medical practices, and result in unnecessary cost or in reimbursement for services that are not medically necessary or that fail to meet professionally recognized standards for health care.

Access controls that limit employees to what they can view or edit.

Accounts Receivable keep cash flowing into the practice and to receive appropriate payment, the claims must be submitted in a timely manner and without errors.

Adjudication a series of steps to validate the claim and determine payment.

Advance Beneficiary Notice serves as proof that the provider notified the Medicare beneficiary before treatment that the procedure will not be covered, and Medicare is expected to deny payment for certain services because they may not be deemed reasonable and necessary.

Adverse Benefit Determination an incorrectly paid or denied health benefit.

Ambulatory Surgery Center Covered Procedures is a list produced by CMS depicting what surgical services may be rendered in an ASC (place of service [POS] 24) with the respective reimbursement for each of these services.

American Recovery and Reinvestment Act (ARRA) was signed into law by President Bush in 2009. ARRA establishes the first federal requirements on health data breach reporting and notification. This act modifies the HIPAA privacy and security regulations and was designed to facilitate the widespread adoption of electronic technology used to exchange medical information.

Audit trails allow managers to monitor what and when staff members viewed.

Autoposting the ability of systems to import ERA data directly and bypass human data entry with advances in computer software development and EDI.

B

Back up refers to making a copy of every file on the server and storing it in a separate file for use in the event of a disaster, file corruption, or accidental deletion of data.

Balance Bill is a term used to describe billing a patient the difference between the amount the provider bills the carrier and the negotiated allowed amount (insurance paid amount). The provider accepts payment of this negotiated rate and contractually cannot balance bill the patient the difference. The difference is written off using a contractual adjustment.

Batch is made up of several claims released as a group and submitted as one file on a given day.

Beneficiary is an individual covered under an insurance policy. It may or may not be the subscriber of the policy.

Billing Cycle is the time between when one statement is sent and the next statement is sent.

Birthday Rule if both parents are insured and list their children as covered under both plans, staff must identify which of these plans is the child's primary insurance. The parent with the earliest birthday in the year is designated as having the primary insurance. In the event the parents are divorced and they do not share joint custody, the plan of the custodial parent is primary and the plan of the other parent is secondary.

Breach occurs when protected information is released, without consent, to unauthorized entities or if security of patient records is compromised and accessed by unauthorized entities.

Business associates perform functions on behalf of a covered entity such as a billing company, a transcription company, a copying service, an attorney, a consultant, or a marketing firm such as Gallop Poll that conducts patient satisfaction surveys.

C

Carrier Medical insurance can be attained by an individual or by a group. Individual medical insurance is a contract between the patient and insurance company.

Clearinghouse is a business associate that is contracted by a provider to receive electronic insurance claim files from the provider.

Co-insurance is a shared portion of payment allowed by an insurance company for outpatient or inpatient services.

Code Sets codes used to identify specific diagnosis and clinical procedures on claims and encounter forms.

Consent Form demonstrates proof of consent obtained from the patient for medical or surgical treatment. It should indicate that the patient was informed of the nature of the treatment, the risks, complications, alternatives to treatment, and consequences of the treatment or procedure.

Consult documents the services rendered by a specialist whose opinion or advice was requested by another physician in the treatment of a patient.

Content Reject generated because of missing data elements from the claim form. These can occur from the clearinghouse or from the payer.

Contractual Adjustment or an insurance adjustment, writing off any difference between what the provider charged for a service and what was actually allowed and paid per the insurance fee schedule.

Communication sharing of information and the manner in which we relate to others.

Compliance means of adhering to state and federal laws and requirements.

Component Code represents the lesser procedure or service when reported with another code.

Comprehensive Code represents the major procedure or service when reported with another code.

Consultation (consult) a specialist whose opinion or advice was requested by another physician in the treatment of a patient. The requesting physician should fill out an order requesting the consultation. The consultant must provide any information regarding any special treatment or further testing required. They must also tell the referring physician what treatment recommendations they have.

Coordination of Benefits (COB) Insurance policies have contract provisions built in to explain how the policies will be listed when the patient has two or more insurances.

co-pay/co-payment is a predetermined fixed amount that a patient must pay for an office visit each time they visit. It typically ranges from $2 to $50 depending on the insurance plan and benefits.

Coverage means that the carrier agrees to pay the cost of these items and services.

Covered Entity health plans, health care clearinghouses, and health care providers who conduct health care transactions such as billing, enrollment, and eligibility verification electronically.

Credentialing the process of collecting and validating data about a respective applicant for medical staff that includes examining the professional qualifications of a physician or licensed provider and comparing those qualifications against a facility's or carrier's requirements for medical staff.

D

Database is a collection of data or files stored in the computer.

Deductible is a designated amount of out-of-pocket money a patient must pay before the insurance company will begin paying for covered services.

Dunning Message specific messages to a patient or group of patients, or you can include a standard message such as "Your insurance has paid. The balance due is your responsibility." The message serves as a way of communicating with the patient, clarifying a situation, or explaining the reason for their balance and will print on all statements.

E

Ear, Nose, and Throat (ENT) ENT is an acronym widely used to describe otolaryngologists, that is, physicians who specialize in diagnosing and treating diseases and disorders of the ears, nose, and throat.

Edits describes to the provider what the error is so it can be corrected and resent.

Electronic claim insurance claims transmitted digitally over the Internet to a carrier or clearinghouse.

Electronic data interchange (EDI) The exchange of health care and financial information electronically over the Internet or phone lines between insurance carriers, providers, and their financial institutions.

Electronic Funds Transfer (EFT) claims that can be submitted and payments received electronically.

Electronic medical records increase the efficiency of health care delivery, which usually means saving/making money and improving patient care through enhanced communication of medical information between health care workers, facilities, patients, and third-party payers.

Electronic Remittance Advice (ERA) these documents house the payment information from the carrier to the provider.

Employee Retirement Income Security Act (ERISA) is a federal law. It was enacted in 1974 to protect employees' pension plans. But as employers started to add health insurance as a benefit of employment, health benefit plans were placed under the protection of this law.

Encoder tools that assist the coder in assigning the most accurate and specific codes possible, grouping hospital inpatient services into (DRGs) and outpatient services into APCs.

Encounter Form also known as superbill, charge ticket, and router. Checklist form that is filled out by the provider that reflects the diagnoses and procedures/services provided for a patient encounter.

Encryption is a method of converting plain text into cipher text, which is similar to a secret code.

Exclusions are noncovered or uncovered and if received must be paid for by the patient

F

False Claims any claim that is incorrectly reported to the government for services or supplies provided. The False Claims Act allows parties to sue submitters of incorrect claims.

Family practice (FP) strives to provide comprehensive health care for individuals and families.

Fee Schedule means that the provider agrees to treat patients with that insurance coverage at a negotiated rate.

Format Reject are technical rejects that occur at the batch level and not at the claim level. Format rejects are comprised of claim form formatting errors where information must be populated in certain fields and loops of the electronic claim and relate to the initial practice management system setup.

Fraud purposely billing Medicare for services that were never provided or received and/or the intentional deception or misrepresentation that could result in unauthorized benefit.

G

General Practitioner (GP) referred to as family physicians that treat acute and chronic illnesses, provide preventive care, perform minor office surgeries, and conduct health education for all ages.

General Surgeon trained to operate on the abdomen and all abdominal organs, including treating hernias. Most general surgeons are also trained to surgically treat the thyroid, breasts, and vasculature of the extremities.

Government Plans/Programs are state or federally funded plans such as Medicare, Medicaid, Tricare, and BlueCross Federal.

Group Plan group policies offered by employers as part of their fringe benefit packages for employees.

Gynecology specializes in women's gynecological health and is board certifi ed by the American Board of Obstetrics and Gynecology. Gynecologist who medically and surgically treats diseases and disorders of the female genital tract.

H

Healthcare Billing and Management Association (HBMA) is a good resource for third-party billers. It is a professional trade association comprised of third-party billing companies, both large and small. It provides education to members and monitors changes to the billing industry.

Health Information Technology for Economic and Clinical Health Act (HITECH) is considered to be a framework or a health information technology

(HIT) infrastructure to protect electronic medical records.

Health Insurance Portability and Accountability Act of 1996 (HIPAA) enacted to protect health information, enforce security of health records, provide standards for electronic transmission of health information, and provide continuous coverage of health insurance to departed employees.

HIPAA Privacy Rule federal privacy standard to protect patients' health information and physical medical record.

HIPAA Transaction and Code Sets Standards were meant to streamline and improve the efficiency of health care electronic transactions.

History and Physical (H&P) includes detailed information about a patient's health history and physical examination performed by the physician.

Hypertext markup language (HTML) content written in a special computer language that uses custom codes called tags.

I

Incident To Billing services rendered by physician extenders under the physician's ID number. The PA is the rendering provider, and the MD is the billable provider.

Independent Practice Association (IPA) an organization of physicians who have joined together for purposes of contracting with insurance companies and to share in administrative expenses.

Individual Plan health care plan purchased directly from the insurance carrier by the subscriber (versus an employer).

Information technology (IT) is a term used to describe an assortment of mechanical and electronic devices that automate the way we store, retrieve, communicate, and manage information.

L

Laboratory Report show results of laboratory tests performed per physician order. These could range from sputum cultures to blood work or urinalysis. These are typically computer-generated by the lab that is analyzing the specimen.

Limitations on policies they cap the benefit at some level by placing limits either on the number of paid visits for a particular service or the dollar amount they will reimburse up to.

LISTSERV is a mailing list system that allows individuals to subscribe to an electronic mailing list.

Local area network (LAN) is also called an intranet, which is private internet that is accessible by staff only.

Local Coverage Determination (LCD) state specific CMS carrier policies regarding services provided to Medicare beneficiaries.

M

Medical Necessity procedures or services deemed necessary based on the patient's documented condition.

Medicare Physician Fee Schedule (MPFS) is the physicians' official source of payment and coverage information for Medicare beneficiaries.

Medicare Secondary Payer a term used by Medicare to indicate that Medicare is not responsible for paying primary benefits.

Medication List to compile and maintain a complete list of current medications the patient is consuming. This list is updated at each visit and changes are noted as needed.

Medigap a federally regulated plan sold to individuals, is common secondary insurance to Medicare. It is designed to supplement Medicare coverage. Medigap, like much other supplemental insurance, will pick up or pay the patient's deductible and coinsurance for covered services, eliminating the need to bill or collect from the patient.

Minimum Necessary Standard reasonable efforts to limit PHI to the least amount of information necessary to accomplish the intended purpose of the use, disclosure, or request.

Mutually Exclusive services that cannot be reasonably performed at the same session either by CPT definition or the medical impossibility or improbability that they could be performed at the same session.

N

National Correct Coding Initiative (NCCI) is a system of coding edits used nationally by Medicare. It is also known as the *National Correct Coding Policy* *for Part B Medicare Carriers.* The purpose of the initiative is to control improper coding that can lead to overpayments and to ensure uniform payment policies and procedures were followed.

National Provider Identification (NPI) is a unique number assigned to each provider by the National Provider System. This 10-digit number replaces the former UPIN and Medicare PIN numbers effective 2007.

National Provider Identifier is a ten-digit number assigned to each health care provider and is the standard for identifying them to payers when fi ling claims.

Nonparticipating the provider has no agreement with the payer. Depending on the plan, patients may still seek treatment from a nonparticipating provider and have coverage, although the coverage will be less and the patient's out-of-pocket expense will be greater.

O

Operative Report describes the surgical procedure itself and individuals who participated. These are referred to as procedure notes when surgical procedures are performed in the office.

Ophthalmology is a surgical subspecialty that treats and diagnoses diseases and trauma to the eye and surrounding areas, including the eyelid and lacrimal system.

Orthopedists orthopedic surgeons who specialize in the treatment of skeletal diseases and injuries including bones, ligaments, tendons, and cartilage.

Outsource is contracting an outside company, commonly referred to as a *third party,* to provide this service at a negotiated rate.

P

Pathology Report describes the microscopic and macroscopic details of tissue removed surgically. A final diagnosis will be present once examination of the specimen is completed.

Participating Most insurance carriers require the provider to have a signed contract or agreement on file demonstrating that they are participating with that plan. Participating with a plan means that the provider agrees to treat patients with that insurance coverage at a negotiated rate.

Patient Assessment a nursing form used to document discussions and initial interview with the patient about their health status.

Patient Information Sheet is referred to by many names: admission/discharge sheet, summary sheet, demographic sheet, face sheet, or identification sheet. This sheet is usually computerized and generated upon registration in a facility.

Personal digital assistants (PDAs) are small portable computers that utilize internet wireless access, Microsoft desktop applications, phone directory, and calendar.

Personal health record (PHR) is an electronic health record that is initiated and maintained by an individual—the patient.

Pay-for-Performance programs and the requirements for reporting. CMS has launched a series of quality initiatives to encourage improved quality of care for patients in various healthcare settings. The intent of pay-for-performance programs is to reward the delivery of high-quality care with financial incentives.

Plastic Surgeon is board certified by the American Board of Plastic and Reconstructive Surgery. Plastic surgeons specialize in the medical and surgical treatment of traumatic injuries and congenital abnormalities that cause disfigurement of the face and skin. The field encompasses cosmetic enhancements as well as functionally reconstructive operations.

Physician Assistant (PA-C) health care professionals licensed to practice medicine with physician supervision.

Physician Orders represent the physician's plan for direction of the patient's therapeutic and diagnostic course.

Physician Quality Reporting Initiative (PQRI) a voluntary quality reporting program established by CMS in which physicians or other eligible professionals collect and report their practice data in relation to a set of patient care performance measures that are established annually.

Physician self-referral is the practice of a physician referring a patient to a medical facility in which he/she or a member of the immediate family has a financial interest, be it ownership, investment, or a structured compensation arrangement.

Portal is an access point or gateway to a network that requires a user name and password.

Premium Each month, either the employer or patient pays a premium to secure insurance coverage for the following month. The premium can be compared to dues for a membership to a health club. The cost of the premium is determined by the carrier, cost saving provisions, types of coverage purchased, health factors, risk involved, and the law of averages.

Progress Notes notes from any clinical discipline but in the physician offi ce typically only the physician and the nurses will document these. They are a means of communication between health care providers about the patient's course of treatment, changes in condition, responses to treatment, observations made, conversations with family members and patient, and so on.

Protected Health Information (PHI) individually identifiable health information that is collected, transmitted, or housed in paper form or electronically such as on CD-ROM, over the Internet, or via modem.

Provider medical professional providing the care or service to the patient. Physicians, physician assistants (PA-C), nurse practitioners (RN-P), nurses, therapists, chiropractors, nutritionists, laboratories, and facilities.

Provider report cards help uninsured patients to shop for the lowest health care treatment available online.

R

Radiology Report or x-ray reports document the radiologist's interpretation of radiologic and fluoroscopic diagnostic tests performed per physician order.

Real-time is a computer term that describes the time an application receives information and how quickly it responds.

Real-time Claims Submission If a vendor has the capability to communicate in real-time with a payer, the provider will know instantaneously if a claim is rejected by the payer, not just by a clearinghouse.

Recovery Audit Contractor Program (RAC) are companies that contract with Medicare to find and correct improper payments made to Medicare providers and suppliers.

Remote Coding is coding performed offsite. This option has allowed staff to perform this function offsite with no interruption of work flow and has increased coder retention.

Review of Systems an inventory of a patient's body systems obtained during the history whereby the patient indicates positive or negative responses to medical questions about that body system.

S

Scrubbing the process of checking or auditing the claim against predefined items is called.

Significant Procedure procedures that are surgical in nature, carry a procedural risk, carry an anesthetic risk, and require specialized training.

SOAP Notes the acronym is used to remind the provider to document a specific patient's subjective complaint, record observations and exams, declare an opinion or a diagnosis, and provide the plan for treating or further diagnosing the existing problem.

Source Documents documents completed by or signed off by a physician to include H&P, Progress Notes (physician), Physician Orders, Consults, OP Reports (handwritten or typed), Pathology Reports.

Statement a bill that itemizes a patient's account to include all charges, payments, and remaining balance.

Subscriber the holder or the guarantor of the policy. The subscriber is never a child, with the exception of Medicaid and Medicare (if they are disabled). The subscriber and the other members covered under the plan are also referred to as insured members. They are responsible for paying the premiums for the policy and any balance remaining on a claim after insurance has paid and contractual adjustments are made.

Summary Plan Description (SPD) The summary plan description is an important document that tells participants what the plan provides and how it operates. It provides information on when an employee can begin to participate in the plan, how services and benefits are calculated, when benefits become vested, when and in what form benefits are paid, and how to file a claim for benefits.

Swipe Cards are plastic cards representative of an insurance card that has a small processor and memory system with a magnetic stripe similar to a credit card.

T

Telemedicine is essentially the delivery of some form of health care information or service via telecommunication via phone or Internet.

U

Unbundling charging and reporting services individually to Medicare when they should have been reported under the most comprehensive e code available from the AMA.

Urologist is a medical doctor that subspecializes in urology which is the focused study and treatment of patients of all ages with urinary tract diseases or disorders.

Urology specialty that focuses training and treatment on the urinary system—kidney, ureter, bladder, urethra, and prostate. Likewise, a urologist specializes in treatment of patients of all ages with urinary tract diseases or disorders.

V

Virtual private networks (VPNs) allow external users to log into an organization's intranet and work as if they were onsite.

W

Wide area networks (WANs) link together computers across a large geographical area.

Index

T

IMPORTANT! READ CAREFULLY: This End User License Agreement ("Agreement") sets forth the conditions by which Cengage Learning will make electronic access to the Cengage Learning-owned licensed content and associated media, software, documentation, printed materials, and electronic documentation contained in this package and/or made available to you via this product (the "Licensed Content"), available to you (the "End User"). BY CLICKING THE "I ACCEPT" BUTTON AND/OR OPENING THIS PACKAGE, YOU ACKNOWLEDGE THAT YOU HAVE READ ALL OF THE TERMS AND CONDITIONS, AND THAT YOU AGREE TO BE BOUND BY ITS TERMS, CONDITIONS, AND ALL APPLICABLE LAWS AND REGULATIONS GOVERNING THE USE OF THE LICENSED CONTENT.

1.0 SCOPE OF LICENSE

1.1 Licensed Content. The Licensed Content may contain portions of modifiable content ("Modifiable Content") and content which may not be modified or otherwise altered by the End User ("Non-Modifiable Content"). For purposes of this Agreement, Modifiable Content and Non-Modifiable Content may be collectively referred to herein as the "Licensed Content." All Licensed Content shall be considered Non-Modifiable Content, unless such Licensed Content is presented to the End User in a modifiable format and it is clearly indicated that modification of the Licensed Content is permitted.

1.2 Subject to the End User's compliance with the terms and conditions of this Agreement, Cengage Learning hereby grants the End User, a nontransferable, nonexclusive, limited right to access and view a single copy of the Licensed Content on a single personal computer system for noncommercial, internal, personal use only. The End User shall not (i) reproduce, copy, modify (except in the case of Modifiable Content), distribute, display, transfer, sublicense, prepare derivative work(s) based on, sell, exchange, barter or transfer, rent, lease, loan, resell, or in any other manner exploit the Licensed Content; (ii) remove, obscure, or alter any notice of Cengage Learning's intellectual property rights present on or in the Licensed Content, including, but not limited to, copyright, trademark, and/or patent notices; or (iii) disassemble, decompile, translate, reverse engineer, or otherwise reduce the Licensed Content.

2.0 TERMINATION

2.1 Cengage Learning may at any time (without prejudice to its other rights or remedies) immediately terminate this Agreement and/or suspend access to some or all of the Licensed Content, in the event that the End User does not comply with any of the terms and conditions of this Agreement. In the event of such termination by Cengage Learning, the End User shall immediately return any and all copies of the Licensed Content to Cengage Learning.

3.0 PROPRIETARY RIGHTS

3.1 The End User acknowledges that Cengage Learning owns all rights, title and interest, including, but not limited to all copyright rights therein, in and to the Licensed Content, and that the End User shall not take any action inconsistent with such ownership. The Licensed Content is protected by U.S., Canadian and other applicable copyright laws and by international treaties, including the Berne Convention and the Universal Copyright Convention. Nothing contained in this Agreement shall be construed as granting the End User any ownership rights in or to the Licensed Content.

3.2 Cengage Learning reserves the right at any time to withdraw from the Licensed Content any item or part of an item for which it no longer retains the right to publish, or which it has reasonable grounds to believe infringes copyright or is defamatory, unlawful, or otherwise objectionable.

4.0 PROTECTION AND SECURITY

4.1 The End User shall use its best efforts and take all reasonable steps to safeguard its copy of the Licensed Content to ensure that no unauthorized reproduction, publication, disclosure, modification, or distribution of the Licensed Content, in whole or in part, is made. To the extent that the End User becomes aware of any such unauthorized use of the Licensed Content, the End User shall immediately notify Cengage Learning. Notification of such violations may be made by sending an e-mail to infringement@cengage.com.

5.0 MISUSE OF THE LICENSED PRODUCT

5.1 In the event that the End User uses the Licensed Content in violation of this Agreement, Cengage Learning shall have the option of electing liquidated damages, which shall include all profits generated by the End User's use of the Licensed Content plus interest computed at the maximum rate permitted by law and all legal fees and other expenses incurred by Cengage Learning in enforcing its rights, plus penalties.

6.0 FEDERAL GOVERNMENT CLIENTS

6.1 Except as expressly authorized by Cengage Learning, Federal Government clients obtain only the rights specified in this Agreement and no other rights. The Government acknowledges that (i) all software and related documentation incorporated in the Licensed Content is existing commercial computer software within the meaning of FAR 27.405(b)(2); and (2) all other data delivered in whatever form, is limited rights data within the meaning of FAR 27.401. The restrictions in this section are acceptable as consistent with the Government's need for software and other data under this Agreement.

7.0 DISCLAIMER OF WARRANTIES AND LIABILITIES

7.1 Although Cengage Learning believes the Licensed Content to be reliable, Cengage Learning does not guarantee or warrant (i) any information or materials contained in or produced by the Licensed Content, (ii) the accuracy, completeness or reliability of the Licensed Content, or (iii) that the Licensed Content is free from errors or other material defects. THE LICENSED PRODUCT IS PROVIDED "AS IS," WITHOUT ANY WARRANTY OF ANY KIND AND CENGAGE LEARNING DISCLAIMS ANY AND ALL WARRANTIES, EXPRESSED OR IMPLIED, INCLUDING, WITHOUT LIMITATION, WARRANTIES OF MERCHANTABILITY OR FITNESS FOR A PARTICULAR PURPOSE. IN NO EVENT SHALL CENGAGE LEARNING BE LIABLE FOR: INDIRECT, SPECIAL, PUNITIVE OR CONSEQUENTIAL DAMAGES INCLUDING FOR LOST PROFITS, LOST DATA, OR OTHERWISE. IN NO EVENT SHALL CENGAGE LEARNING'S AGGREGATE LIABILITY HEREUNDER, WHETHER ARISING IN CONTRACT, TORT, STRICT LIABILITY OR OTHERWISE, EXCEED THE AMOUNT OF FEES PAID BY THE END USER HEREUNDER FOR THE LICENSE OF THE LICENSED CONTENT.

8.0 GENERAL

8.1 Entire Agreement. This Agreement shall constitute the entire Agreement between the Parties and supercedes all prior Agreements and understandings oral or written relating to the subject matter hereof.

8.2 Enhancements/Modifications of Licensed Content. From time to time, and in Cengage Learning's sole discretion, Cengage Learning may advise the End User of updates, upgrades, enhancements and/or improvements to the Licensed Content, and may permit the End User to access and use, subject to the terms and conditions of this Agreement, such modifications, upon payment of prices as may be established by Cengage Learning.

8.3 No Export. The End User shall use the Licensed Content solely in the United States and shall not transfer or export, directly or indirectly, the Licensed Content outside the United States.

8.4 Severability. If any provision of this Agreement is invalid, illegal, or unenforceable under any applicable statute or rule of law, the provision shall be deemed omitted to the extent that it is invalid, illegal, or unenforceable. In such a case, the remainder of the Agreement shall be construed in a manner as to give greatest effect to the original intention of the parties hereto.

8.5 Waiver. The waiver of any right or failure of either party to exercise in any respect any right provided in this Agreement in any instance shall not be deemed to be a waiver of such right in the future or a waiver of any other right under this Agreement.

8.6 Choice of Law/Venue. This Agreement shall be interpreted, construed, and governed by and in accordance with the laws of the State of New York, applicable to contracts executed and to be wholly preformed therein, without regard to its principles governing conflicts of law. Each party agrees that any proceeding arising out of or relating to this Agreement or the breach or threatened breach of this Agreement may be commenced and prosecuted in a court in the State and County of New York. Each party consents and submits to the nonexclusive personal jurisdiction of any court in the State and County of New York in respect of any such proceeding.

8.7 Acknowledgment. By opening this package and/or by accessing the Licensed Content on this Web site, THE END USER ACKNOWLEDGES THAT IT HAS READ THIS AGREEMENT, UNDERSTANDS IT, AND AGREES TO BE BOUND BY ITS TERMS AND CONDITIONS. IF YOU DO NOT ACCEPT THESE TERMS AND CONDITIONS, YOU MUST NOT ACCESS THE LICENSED CONTENT AND RETURN THE LICENSED PRODUCT TO CENGAGE LEARNING (WITHIN 30 CALENDAR DAYS OF THE END USER'S PURCHASE) WITH PROOF OF PAYMENT ACCEPTABLE TO CENGAGE LEARNING, FOR A CREDIT OR A REFUND. Should the End User have any questions/comments regarding this Agreement, please contact Cengage Learning at Delmar.help@cengage.com.

Capstone Simulation for Coding

Minimum System Requirements

- Microsoft Windows XP w/SP 2, Windows Vista w/ SP 1, Windows 7
- Mac OS X 10.5, or 10.6
- Processor: Minimum required by Operating System
- Memory: Minimum required by Operating System
- CD-ROM drive
- Adobe Reader 8.2 or higher. Adobe Reader is free and is available for free download here: http://get.adobe.com/reader/
- Microsoft Word 97 or higher
- Microsoft Excel 97 or higher

Windows Instructions

1. Insert disc into CD-ROM drive.
2. From My Computer, double-click the icon for the CD drive.
3. Double-click on any of the files to open them in their associated programs.

Mac Instructions

1. Insert disc into CD-ROM drive.
2. Once the disc icon appears on your desktop, double click on it to open it.
3. Double-click on any of the files to open them in their associated programs.

Technical Support

Telephone: 1-800-648-7450

8:30 A.M.-6:30 P.M. Eastern Time

E-mail: delmar.help@cengage.com